JUnit Recipes

JUnit Recipes

Practical Methods for Programmer Testing

J.B. RAINSBERGER
with contributions by SCOTT STIRLING

Greenwich
(74° w. long.)

To my mother, Joan.

I wish I had finished this in time.

For online information and ordering of this and other Manning books, please visit www.manning.com. The publisher offers discounts on this book when ordered in quantity. For more information, please contact:

Special Sales Department
Manning Publications Co.
209 Bruce Park Avenue Fax: (203) 661-9018
Greenwich, CT 06830 email: manning@manning.com

Manning Publications Co.
209 Bruce Park Avenue
Greenwich, CT 06830

Copyeditor: Mark Goodin
Typesetter: Martine Maguire-Weltecke
Cover designer: Leslie Haimes

ISBN 1932394230

Printed in the United States of America
1 2 3 4 5 6 7 8 9 10 – VHG – 07 06 05 04

brief contents

PART 1 THE BUILDING BLOCKS 1

1 ■ Fundamentals 3
2 ■ Elementary tests 22
3 ■ Organizing and building JUnit tests 71
4 ■ Managing test suites 102
5 ■ Working with test data 136
6 ■ Running JUnit tests 173
7 ■ Reporting JUnit results 188
8 ■ Troubleshooting JUnit 233

PART 2 TESTING J2EE 257

9 ■ Testing and XML 265
10 ■ Testing and JDBC 308
11 ■ Testing Enterprise JavaBeans 370
12 ■ Testing web components 443
13 ■ Testing J2EE applications 508

PART 3 MORE JUNIT TECHNIQUES 541

14 ■ Testing design patterns 543
15 ■ GSBase 572
16 ■ JUnit-addons 585
17 ■ Odds and ends 603

APPENDICES 629

A ■ Complete solutions 629
B ■ Essays on testing 673
C ■ Reading List 696

contents

foreword *xv*
preface *xvii*
acknowledgments *xix*
about this book *xxii*
about the cover illustration *xxx*

PART 1 THE BUILDING BLOCKS 1

1 ***Fundamentals 3***

1.1 What is Programmer Testing? 4
1.2 Getting started with JUnit 10
1.3 A few good practices 17
1.4 Summary 20

2 ***Elementary tests 22***

2.1 Test your equals method 26
2.2 Test a method that returns nothing 33
2.3 Test a constructor 37
2.4 Test a getter 41
2.5 Test a setter 44
2.6 Test an interface 48

2.7 Test a JavaBean 54
2.8 Test throwing the right exception 56
2.9 Let collections compare themselves 61
2.10 Test a big object for equality 63
2.11 Test an object that instantiates other objects 66

3 *Organizing and building JUnit tests* ***71***
3.1 Place test classes in the same package as production code 74
3.2 Create a separate source tree for test code 77
3.3 Separate test packages from production code packages 79
3.4 Factor out a test fixture 83
3.5 Factor out a test fixture hierarchy 87
3.6 Introduce a Base Test Case 90
3.7 Move special case tests to a separate test fixture 92
3.8 Build tests from the command line 94
3.9 Build tests using Ant 96
3.10 Build tests using Eclipse 99

4 *Managing test suites* ***102***
4.1 Let JUnit build your test suite 103
4.2 Collect a specific set of tests 107
4.3 Collect all the tests in a package 111
4.4 Collect all the tests for your entire system 114
4.5 Scan the file system for tests 116
4.6 Separate the different kinds of test suites 120
4.7 Control the order of some of your tests 123
4.8 Build a data-driven test suite 127
4.9 Define a test suite in XML 133

5 *Working with test data* *136*

5.1 Use Java system properties 138
5.2 Use environment variables 142
5.3 Use an inline data file 145
5.4 Use a properties file 147
5.5 Use ResourceBundles 152
5.6 Use a file-based test data repository 154
5.7 Use XML to describe test data 156
5.8 Use Ant's <sql> task to work with a database 157
5.9 Use JUnitPP 159
5.10 Set up your fixture once for the entire suite 161
5.11 Perform environment setup once for multiple test runs 164
5.12 Use DbUnit 170

6 *Running JUnit tests* *173*

6.1 See the name of each test as it executes 177
6.2 See the name of each test as it executes with a text-based test runner 178
6.3 Execute a single test 180
6.4 Execute each test in its own JVM 181
6.5 Reload classes before each test 182
6.6 Ignore a test 185

7 *Reporting JUnit results* *188*

7.1 Using a Base Test Case with a logger 190
7.2 Using Log4Unit 194
7.3 Getting plain text results with Ant 198
7.4 Reporting results in HTML with Ant's <junitreport> task 202
7.5 Customizing <junit> XML reports with XSLT 205

7.6 Extending Ant's JUnit results format 208
7.7 Implementing TestListener and extending TestRunner 215
7.8 Reporting a count of assertions 224

8 *Troubleshooting JUnit* **233**
8.1 JUnit cannot find your tests 235
8.2 JUnit does not execute your custom test suite 237
8.3 JUnit does not set up your test fixture 239
8.4 Test setup fails after overriding runTest() 241
8.5 Your test stops after the first assertion fails 244
8.6 The graphical test runner does not load your classes properly 250
8.7 JUnit fails when your test case uses JAXP 252
8.8 JUnit fails when narrowing an EJB reference 253

PART 2 TESTING J2EE 257

Introduction
Designing J2EE applications for testability 259
The Coffee Shop application 263

9 *Testing and XML* **265**
9.1 Verify the order of elements in a document 273
9.2 Ignore the order of elements in an XML document 277
9.3 Ignore certain differences in XML documents 281
9.4 Get a more detailed failure message from XMLUnit 288
9.5 Test the content of a static web page 290
9.6 Test an XSL stylesheet in isolation 297
9.7 Validate XML documents in your tests 302

10 *Testing and JDBC 308*

10.1 Test making domain objects from a ResultSet 317
10.2 Verify your SQL commands 322
10.3 Test your database schema 327
10.4 Verify your tests clean up JDBC resources 335
10.5 Verify your production code cleans up JDBC resources 343
10.6 Manage external data in your test fixture 346
10.7 Manage test data in a shared database 349
10.8 Test permissions when deploying schema objects 352
10.9 Test legacy JDBC code without the database 357
10.10 Test legacy JDBC code with the database 360
10.11 Use schema-qualified tables with DbUnit 363
10.12 Test stored procedures 366

11 *Testing Enterprise JavaBeans 370*

11.1 Test a session bean method outside the container 378
11.2 Test a legacy session bean 387
11.3 Test a session bean method in a real container 394
11.4 Test a CMP entity bean 397
11.5 Test CMP meta data outside the container 400
11.6 Test a BMP entity bean 408
11.7 Test a message-driven bean inside the container 414
11.8 Test a message-driven bean outside the container 420
11.9 Test a legacy message-driven bean 422
11.10 Test a JMS message consumer without the messaging server 426
11.11 Test JMS message-processing logic 430
11.12 Test a JMS message producer 433
11.13 Test the content of your JNDI directory 439

12 *Testing web components 443*

12.1 Test updating session data without a container 446
12.2 Test updating the HTTP session object 452
12.3 Test rendering a JavaServer Page 456
12.4 Test rendering a Velocity template 465
12.5 Test a JSP tag handler 468
12.6 Test your JSP tag library deployment 474
12.7 Test servlet initialization 477
12.8 Test the ServletContext 480
12.9 Test processing a request 483
12.10 Verify web page content without a web server 491
12.11 Verify web form attributes 494
12.12 Verify the data passed to a page template 495
12.13 Test a web resource filter 500

13 *Testing J2EE applications 508*

13.1 Test page flow 510
13.2 Test navigation rules in a Struts application 519
13.3 Test your site for broken links 522
13.4 Test web resource security 525
13.5 Test EJB resource security 530
13.6 Test container-managed transactions 536

PART 3 MORE JUNIT TECHNIQUES 541

14 *Testing design patterns 543*

14.1 Test an Observer (Event Listener) 545
14.2 Test an Observable (Event Source) 550
14.3 Test a Singleton 556
14.4 Test a Singleton's client 559

14.5 Test an object factory 562
14.6 Test a template method's implementation 566

15 *GSBase 572*

15.1 Verify events with EventCatcher 574
15.2 Test serialization 577
15.3 Test object cloning 579
15.4 Compare JavaBeans using "appears equal" 581

16 *JUnit-addons 585*

16.1 Test your class for compareTo() 587
16.2 Collect tests automatically from an archive 590
16.3 Organize test data using PropertyManager 591
16.4 Manage shared test resources 593
16.5 Ensure your shared test fixture tears itself down 597
16.6 Report the name of each test as it executes 599

17 *Odds and ends 603*

17.1 Clean up the file system between tests 605
17.2 Test your file-based application without the file system 608
17.3 Verify your test case class syntax 614
17.4 Extract a custom assertion 617
17.5 Test a legacy method with no return value 620
17.6 Test a private method if you must 625

A *Complete solutions 629*

A.1 Define a test suite in XML 630
A.2 Parameterized Test Case overriding runTest() 634
A.3 Ignore the order of elements in an XML document 637
A.4 Test an XSL stylesheet in isolation 639

A.5 Validate XML documents in your tests 645
A.6 Aspect-based universal Spy 649
A.7 Test a BMP entity bean 653

B ***Essays on testing 673***
B.1 Too simple to break 674
B.2 Strangeness and transitivity 677
B.3 Isolate expensive tests 681
B.4 The mock objects landscape 689

C ***Reading List 696***

references 700
index 705

foreword

Bones: I doubt that this combination of things was ever used to make a tranquilizer before.

Kirk: How soon will it be ready?

Bones: Right now.

Kirk: Good. How long will it take for the tranquilizer to have an effect?

Bones: Three or four seconds.

Kirk: How did you manage to test it?

Bones: It has not been tested.

Spock: It's not necessary, Captain.

Bones: It's simple. Nothing can go wrong.

Kirk: Up to now, everything's gone wrong. I want it tested ... and now.

Scotty: Would a volunteer solve the problem?

Bones: It would.

Scotty: Then I volunteer. *(He takes a long pull on a bottle of whiskey.)* It's to kill the pain.

Spock: But this is painless.

Scotty: *(Smirking.)* Well, you should've warned me sooner, Mr. Spock. Fire away. *(Scotty breathes deeply of the tranquilizing fumes, but there is no effect.)*

Kirk: It doesn't work.

Spock: Indeed. Fascinating.

Kirk: It was our last chance.

Spock: Captain, you don't seem to understand. It did not function, but it must function. Nothing could go wrong, Captain. It should work.

Kirk: A scientific fact ...

Spock: But if the tranquilizer does not function, which is clearly impossible, then a radical alteration of our thought patterns must be in order.

Adapted from "Spectre of the Gun", *Star Trek* original series
Episode No: 056, Air Date: 10.25.1968, Stardate: 4385.3

The book you are currently holding is a remarkable compendium of recipes written for those of us who use JUnit in our daily work. This is not another book on TDD, nor is it a basic tutorial on JUnit. Instead, this book is a suite of techniques—both simple and advanced—for using JUnit in a real, professional, environment.

Have you ever wondered how to test a servlet, or an XSLT script, or an entity bean? Are you concerned about how to name and organize your test case classes? Have you ever had trouble testing databases, or organizing large amounts of test data? This book has recipes for these, and many other, testing conundrums. The recipes are well written, easy to understand, and very pragmatic. Each is written in pattern form, spelling out the problem to be solved, the context of that problem, and the various recipes that solve that problem.

I first met J.B. in New Orleans at *XP Agile Universe*, 2003. He was an enthusiastic participant in the *FitFest* exercise. He was in the *FitFest* lab, writing tests and code, at every opportunity. He was also an outspoken participant in many of the impromptu discussions and conversations that dominate those conferences. I was very impressed by his knowledge and skill, and made a note to investigate more of his writings. I was not disappointed. It became clear to me that J.B. knows his stuff. Or, as one of my close associates said to me: "J.B. sure knows a lot of tricks."

When I first learned that J.B. was writing this book, my expectations for it were high; yet he managed to exceed them. No other book manages to cram as much wisdom, knowledge, and practical advice about JUnit and unit testing into a single volume. Reading it convinces me that J.B. knows JUnit, and all the surrounding add-ons and environments, cold. I am quite certain that it will be one of those books that rests on my bookshelf in easy reach so I can look something up in a hurry.

ROBERT C. MARTIN
Founder, Object Mentor Inc.

preface

If you have ever met me, either online or in person, then perhaps you have heard me tell this story.

I was working on a large project at the IBM labs in Toronto. It was in the middle of the year 2000, long after the Y2K craze had ended, and I had spent nearly three months working on a component scheduled for delivery in about one month. The defects were coming in steadily from our testing department, and each fix was just another patch on top of an increasingly disgusting Big Ball of Mud. It was around that time that I read a draft of *Extreme Programming Installed,* by Ron Jeffries, Ann Anderson, and Chet Hendrickson. With the help of the Internet, this draft led me to www.junit.org, where I learned about this great new tool for testing Java code, called JUnit. Within minutes I knew this would help my cause.

Soon after this, I marched into my manager's office and announced that there was no way I would be able to patch the existing code to fix the remaining defects in time to deliver. The code had become too complicated to understand. I could not predict how many new defects I would inject while fixing the ones we knew about. We simply were not getting feedback quickly enough. "Send me home," I told him, "and let me write it all again from scratch. I'll use JUnit to test it as I go. It will work." He did. When it came down to it, what choice did he have?

Even before I knew how to use JUnit effectively, I rewrote three months' worth of code in nine long days, with JUnit by my side. What had originally taken well over 500 hours of effort and didn't work had been rebuilt in about 100 hours, including a suite of over 125 tests. That was enough for me—I was hooked on JUnit.

Since that time I have involved myself in the JUnit community, not only as a practitioner of Test-Driven Development, but also by answering questions at the JUnit Yahoo! group. Over the years I have refined my JUnit technique to the point where I am certain I could write that same component in closer to 25 hours of work. The ability to eliminate 95% of the time needed for any task is significant; and while there's no way to prove it, I attribute the majority of that savings to JUnit.

In 2001 I read a number of complaints about the JUnit documentation. Apparently there were no suitable tutorials. I decided to write "JUnit: A Starter Guide," a tutorial which still draws over 1000 readers monthly. That tutorial was the genesis of this book, even though I didn't know it at the time. Much of this book's content has been refined from the answers I have provided to questions on the JUnit mailing lists. Still more came from hard-won personal experience using JUnit on various projects. I wanted this book to describe how I use JUnit; I did *not* want it to present some idealized view of how one *ought* to use it. There's already too much opinion and waving of hands out there—but not in here. This book contains JUnit techniques that work, because they have made my projects successful. For that reason it is worth noting two things: much of what I present here is my opinion, backed up by my experience; and this is not the only way to do it. This book contains recommendations—not rules.

By the time this book is printed and in your hands, things will have changed. Some of these recipes might be obsolete. There is not much I can do about that—people are discovering great new ways to use JUnit every day. Even if a few of these recipes become dated, the concepts—the motivations behind the recipes—never change. Test isolation is important. Smaller tests are more powerful. Separating the implementation from the interface makes testing easier. Decoupling your code from the framework makes testing *possible*. Watch for these recurring themes throughout. They are the most valuable part of the book, because they will help you long after all of us stop writing software in Java, whenever *that* happens. If you find them useful, then I have done my job as an author and as a member of the JUnit community.

acknowledgments

Sometime in late 2002 I identified two main goals for 2003: become more involved in the XP/Agile Universe conference and write a book. Although this book is about six months late in arriving on the shelf, I am happy to report that I achieved both goals. One typically does not achieve one's goals without help, so I would like to take this opportunity to thank those who helped me write this book.

First, I would like to thank the people at Manning Publications, who contacted me in March 2003 and asked me to write a book about one of my favorite topics, JUnit. Vincent Massol, author of *JUnit in Action*, was kind enough to recommend me, and everyone I dealt with at Manning was very supportive of the work. Jackie Carter did an excellent job not only as reviewer and editor, but she also held my hand throughout the entire process. A first-time author would do well to have someone like Jackie as part of the team! I would also like to thank publisher Marjan Bace, not only for helping make this a quality book, but for his patience with my impatience in arriving at the book's title. Marjan is relentless in achieving his desired result, and while working with him can be tiring, it is a satisfying kind of fatigue that comes from doing good, hard work. In addition to Jackie and Marjan, I would like to thank Susan Capparelle, Clay Andres, Lianna Wlasiuk, Leslie Haimes, and Mary Piergies for providing extra source material, reviewing the manuscript, designing the cover, and producing the final copy. Alistair Cockburn measures a successful project, in part, by whether the team would be happy to run another project the same way; in that sense, this project has been a resounding success!

An entire community of people helped make this book what it is—membership in the book's Yahoo! group reached 100 just before going to press. I am constantly amazed at the Internet's ability to bring people together and encourage them to collaborate with one another. It is impossible to make this an exhaustive list, but here are my hearty thanks to the following contributors: Vladimir Bossicard, Simon Chappell, Roger Cornejo, Ward Cunningham, Mark Eames, Sven Gorts, Paul Holser, Dave Hoover, Ramnivas Laddad, Jason Menard, Rick Mugridge, Jonathan Oddy, Kay Pentecost, Paolo Perrotta, Bret Pettichord, Ilja Preuß, Michael Rabbior,

Neil Swingler, Edmund Schweppe, and Chad Woolley. They helped me work through examples, reviewed the manuscript, suggested recipes, argued the ideas, and hunted down references. What more could one ask?

A few contributors stand out from the group, so I wanted to thank them especially. The first of these is Scott Stirling, who contributed the chapters "Working with Test Data" and "Reporting JUnit Results." In addition to providing recipes, Scott was heavily involved in the early draft of the book's table of contents, ensuring that we covered a wide selection of fundamental concepts. I only wish that Scott had had more time to contribute!

Eric Armstrong contributed more to the improvement of early copies of this manuscript than any other reviewer. If you decide to write a book, figure out a way to make Eric excited about it and it will be much better than it might have been without him. When Eric ran out of time, Robert Wenner stepped in and filled his shoes. Without their in-depth and detailed comments, this book would not be nearly as polished as it is. After Eric and Robert had finished, George Latkiewicz gave the entire book another once-over, shining a bright light on the kinds of minor inconsistencies and out-of-date statements that make readers angry and authors looks bad. George has done an excellent job of making us look good.

Mike Bowler not only answered all my questions about HtmlUnit and GSBase, but also provided me with a much-needed sounding board. He helped me identify common problem areas in J2EE testing and advised me on which recipes were particularly important to include. I have never had a bad experience working with Mike and recommend it to everyone who gets the opportunity.

The Extreme Programming and Agile Software Development communities have been instrumental in providing me with the opportunity to write this book. Not only is Kent Beck responsible for the xUnit framework itself, but those communities have welcomed me into their discussions and given me the chance to learn and grow as a programmer. I am grateful for both their patience with me and their advice for me. With this book I hope to give something back in exchange for all the help and support they have provided.

In particular, I would like to thank Uncle Bob—or Robert C. Martin, if you prefer—for agreeing to write the foreword to this book. I don't like to throw around terms like "role model," but Bob is certainly one for me. I can only dream of having the credibility necessary to get away with the brutally honest criticism he gives. Like many people in the Agile community, Bob's focus is on solving the problem rather than assessing blame; but when you're wrong, you're wrong, and he has no problem pointing out when it's *his* mistake. Bob makes it easy to respect him, and when he talks, I listen—*hard.* Thank you, Bob!

As a young student I despised writing of any kind until I met teachers like Bruce Adlam and Caroline Schaillee. For the parts of this book that are well written, they deserve much of the credit; and for the rest, I take all the blame. Nick Nolfi also deserves credit for giving me interesting programming problems to solve and cultivating in me the joy of writing code. I should apologize to the poor ICON computers in the school's computing lab that had to put up with my continual physical abuse. It was nothing personal.

My wife, Sarah, made this book possible by not blinking an eye when I announced that I was going to leave the relative security of full-time employment to write it. Without her continuing support and encouragement, I never would have gotten through it. I promise to do my part when it comes time for her to write *her* first book.

Finally I would like to thank my mother, Joan Skillen, not just for doing the tremendous amount of work it took to raise me, but specifically for giving up so much so that I could pursue my passion.

about this book

Beyond unit tests

As Test-Driven Development practitioners, we have a tendency to write about JUnit exclusively as a tool for writing Object Tests. Because much of the JUnit community intersects with the TDD community, this seems like a reasonable thing to do; however, you may not be a TDD practitioner. Your current project may use JUnit, but only to write tests for existing code or to write tests at a higher-level view of the system than its objects. We would hate to leave you out of the conversation, as JUnit is certainly suitable for writing other kinds of tests.

There are Integration Tests, which are still Programmer Tests, that focus more on the collaboration of a number of objects, rather than the behavior of a single object at a time. These tests are important to provide confidence that your classes "talk to each other" the way they should. Integration Tests come with a different set of problems than Object Tests. Integration Tests are often more brittle than Object Tests because they have more complex fixtures: you need to set up a number of objects in just the right state before invoking the behavior you want to test. You may even want to test the integration between your system and external resources, such as a database, a network-based service, or the file system. We explore how to write effective tests at all levels (Object, Integration, End-to-End) when slower or less-available external resources such as these are involved. Because this tends to come up in the context of J2EE applications, part 2 of this book, "Testing J2EE," provides numerous recipes for writing tests around these kinds of resources and you can adapt them to virtually any situation.

There are Customer Tests, whose purpose is to provide the customer or end user some evidence that the features they need are present in the system. These tests tend to execute slowly and involve almost the entire system. The greatest challenge to Customer Tests, besides getting customers to write them, is writing them in such a way that trivial changes in the system's user interface do not break them. Solving these problems is beyond the scope of this book, but we've tried to provide some recommendations.

There are End-to-End Tests which thoroughly test the entire system from end to end, and therefore these tests are the most difficult to manage. These are usually the most difficult to automate effectively, and for that reason many projects prefer to focus their energy on automating Object Tests and leave End-to-End Tests for a manual testing process. JUnit can help you here, especially when combined with proven techniques and feature-rich extensions. In these cases we are predominantly talking about user interface-level testing. If you are writing web applications, then HtmlUnit (http://htmlunit.sourceforge.net) may be the most important tool in your toolkit. It provides both an HTTP client to simulate a web browser, and a layer of customized assertions that allow you to analyze the web pages with which your application responds. We provide recipes for putting HtmlUnit to good use in chapter 13, "Testing J2EE Applications," along with other specialized JUnit testing packages in part 3, "More Testing Techniques."

Finally, no single volume can cover every conceivable way to use JUnit, so there is more you can do with JUnit than what is included here. Kent Beck once said of JUnit that his goal was to create a framework that did what *everyone* would need it to do without piling on features that only *some people* would need. He wanted us to think, "JUnit is good, but once I added *this little feature right here*, it became perfect." Open source projects have sprung up everywhere with custom extensions to JUnit, and we provide some recipes that may help you start on your way to your own custom JUnit project. The more, the merrier.

How this book is organized

The first part of this book contains recipes devoted to the *building blocks* of writing tests with JUnit. If we have done our job well as authors, then every test you write with JUnit will be reducible to some collection of these building block recipes. Chapter 1 presents a general introduction to JUnit, including why to use it, what to use it for, how to install it, and how to write the code for your test. This is also where we introduce the concept of Object Testing. Writing effective object tests is the main theme of this book, and we believe this consists mainly of figuring out how to write any test in terms of the recipes in chapter 2, "Elementary Tests." Now if this were easy, then there would be no need for the other 15 chapters in this book; but real life intercedes pretty quickly into all but the simplest projects, so in the remaining chapters of part 1 we have provided recipes for dealing with the complexities of writing tests for your project.

Chapter 3, "Organizing and Building JUnit Tests," describes how to organize your test source code and how to build your tests. Not only do we provide recipes for where your test source code should sit on the file system, but we also provide recipes that guide the correspondence between test classes and production classes. In addition, we provide some examples of building your tests, either from within your IDE, or as part of an automated build process.

Chapter 4, "Managing Test Suites," provides advice on collecting your tests into "test suites." A test suite is a collection of tests that execute as a group. Our typical goal is to execute all the tests all the time, but you may not be able to do this on your project just yet. We have provided some recipes describing a number of different ways to collect tests into custom suites.

Chapter 5, "Working with Test Data," contains recipes for managing data within your tests. All things being equal, we prefer to keep test data hard coded and within the test. We prefer this approach because it supports the notion of tests as documentation—when the logic and the data for a test are separated from one another, the test is more difficult to read. On the other hand, if you need 100 pieces of information for a test, then hard coding it all directly into the test renders it difficult to read. We need a variety of strategies for expressing the data we need in our tests, and we have shared many of these strategies with you as recipes in this chapter.

Chapter 6, "Running JUnit Tests," discusses a number of strategies for executing your tests. Usually we like to execute all the tests all the time; but if you need to execute just one test, or ignore some tests, or even execute each test in a separate virtual machine, then our recipes will help.

Chapter 7, "Reporting JUnit Results," contains techniques for customizing the way JUnit reports test results. If you need more information than "370 run, 2 failed, 1 error," then this chapter will help you get the extra information you need, and in the format you need it. The chapter provides techniques for reporting test results from Ant, as well as hooking into the JUnit framework itself.

We conclude part 1 with chapter 8, "Troubleshooting JUnit." This chapter contains recipes for solving problems you may have using JUnit itself. Many of these problems are common to first-time JUnit users, including configuration errors and typos. Some are problems you encounter for the first time as you begin to use JUnit to test more complex systems, such as those based on J2EE.

Part 2 begins with chapter 9, "Testing and XML." You cannot swing a dead cat in a J2EE application without hitting XML documents, so we thought it logical to start with XML testing techniques, centered around XMLUnit and XPath.

Next is chapter 10, "Testing and JDBC," with recipes for testing the database, the first expensive, external resource that most JUnit novices encounter when they start writing tests. This chapter motivates the mock objects discussion that runs intermittently throughout the rest of the book. In this chapter we discuss separating persistence services from JDBC and testing each separately. We also explore ways to minimize the amount of JDBC client code you need to write, so that you can write and execute a small number of tests against a live database. We also highlight DbUnit, a tool that helps maintain test data for those times when you *do* need to test against the database.

Chapter 11, "Testing Enterprise JavaBeans," is by far the most complex chapter of this book. The complexity of EJBs is matched by the complexity of how to test them effectively. Once again, we treat both refactoring towards a testable design, and testing legacy EJBs inside the container. We look at MockEJB, a package that provides some mock objects support, especially for EJB, but mostly for its MockContext, a mock implementation of a JNDI directory. Given the pervasiveness of JNDI in J2EE applications, MockContext proves extremely handy when testing your integration with the J2EE framework. Finally, we include some JMS recipes in this chapter, as the most common use of JMS is in message-driven beans.

With the back end complete, we turn our attention to the front end. Chapter 12, "Testing Web Components," describes how to test servlets, JSPs, Velocity templates, and web resource filters. As with our EJB chapter, we discuss ways to separate application logic from the servlet framework, as well as how ServletUnit provides a mock container environment for testing legacy web front ends. Our recipes include how to use HtmlUnit to verify the content of dynamic web pages *in isolation from the rest of the application*, which we believe is a woefully underestimated testing practice. This is the reason we prefer the Velocity web page template package over JSP: it is easy to use the Velocity engine in standalone mode, whereas as we write these words, no standalone JSP engine is available for use in testing.

Chapter 13, "Testing J2EE Applications," discusses more end-to-end concerns. We describe using HtmlUnit to test your web application from end to end. The bulk of the recipes in this chapter focus on treating what seem to be end-to-end concerns as component concerns so that we can test them in isolation. The more you can test in isolation, the easier the tests are and the more benefit you gain from writing and executing them.

Part 3 begins with chapter 14, a brief look at testing and Design Patterns. We could easily fill an entire book with a discussion of how to test *all* the class Design Patterns, but because this is not that book, we have chosen a sample of patterns that we encounter on almost every project: Singleton, Observer/Observable, Factory and Template method. We think you will find that once you have employed the techniques in this book several times and understood the general principles, then you will have little trouble deciding how to test a flyweight design, or an adapter, or a composite.

We spend the next two chapters discussing two popular extensions to JUnit. Chapter 15 provides recipes related to the open source project GSBase (http://gsbase.sourceforge.net). This product includes some utilities to make it easier to write JUnit tests, as well as some test fixtures you can use directly in your projects. Chapter 16 discusses another open source project, JUnit-addons (http://junit-addons.sourceforge.net), which includes not only testing utilities, but an alternative to the standard JUnit test runners that features a more open extension architecture. This architecture makes it easy to monitor and analyze your test runs, something that the JUnit test runners themselves do not directly support. We highlighted both of these projects, not only because we have used them extensively in our work, but also because there are rumors of a merger between the two. The resulting project would certainly become a de facto standard JUnit extension.

There are some recipes that simply did not seem to fit into other chapters, so we collected them into chapter 17, "Odds and Ends." Here we have a handful of recipes covering a number of testing techniques, including file-based applications, test case syntax, and testing private methods. Had we thought longer and harder about it, we could have placed those recipes elsewhere in this book, but we had to stop *sometime.*

We collected some complete solutions to earlier recipes and placed them in appendix A, "Complete Solutions." In cases where a full solution requires hundreds of lines of code, and we did not want to distract you from reading the rest of the recipe, we moved those solutions nearer the back of the book. This way you could read the complete solutions—even use them in your projects—when you are ready for *all* the details.

In appendix B we present a small collection of essays on Programmer Testing that go a few steps beyond JUnit, but help to set the context for our advice throughout the rest of the book. This appendix, too, could easily have expanded into an entire book, but we have chosen only a few key topics on which to expand beyond the recipes.

Finally we provide a Reading List—a collection of books, articles, and web sites that we have considered important in our own work. We highly recommend them to you for further study on Java testing, Java programming, and more.

Coding conventions

Because this is a book about programming, we ought to spend some time describing our coding conventions. What follows is a quick list of decisions we have made about our code examples.

We generally do not use abbreviations. Among the rare exceptions to this rule are `e` for an exception object in a `catch` block and the class name suffix `Impl` for "implementation." In general, abbreviations serve only to make the typist's job easier and everyone else's job more difficult. We decided to spend more time typing so that you would more easily understand our code. As far as we are concerned, that is just doing our job, as authors and as programmers.

We do not mark identifiers as global, class-level, or instance-level with any special prefix or suffix. Some projects want to use a leading underscore character; others use a trailing underscore character; yet others prefer the pseudo-Hungarian notation of prefixing instance-scoped identifiers with "m_" meaning "member." We feel that such markings interfere with refactoring and therefore do not use them. We want to be able to refactor this code as much as we need.

We use deprecated code as little as possible. The point of deprecating methods is to discourage their use. Accordingly, because this book will be read—one hopes—by many people, we do not wish to encourage others to use methods that are no longer meant to be used. If we use a deprecated method in an example, it is because by press time we were unable to find a suitable alternative. We want this code to last as long as it can.

We sometimes use "on demand" import statements. These are import statements such as `import java.sql.*`. Some people believe that the on-demand import is evil and should be abolished, but we believe that a sign of good design is dependency on few packages, meaning little coupling and few import statements.

If you need to import many classes from a given package—motivating you to import on demand—that is a sign of a cohesive package.

We sometimes use `public` fields. Please do not faint. Long considered the worst coding offence known to Java programmers—and for a time before Java—Ward Cunningham has challenged this notion and suggested that `public` fields are not only sufficient, but preferred. There is less code to maintain, which reduces the potential for defects. We restrict our use of `public` fields to Value Objects, including the Presentation Objects we plan to place on web page templates such as JSPs or Velocity macros.

NOTE *Ward on public fields*—When we asked Ward about using public fields, he said, "One reason we tell our compilers so much about our programs is so that they can reason about what we've written on our behalf. But we always have to ask, is the reasoning helping us get our work done? If no, then it is time to do something different. We've learned enough about automatic testing in the last decade to change the return on investment in declarations forever."

We prefer to use and extend existing software. That means that if we need to add a feature and we know that someone has already built it, we incorporate it, rather than reinvent the wheel, as it were. Notable among the projects our sample code depends on is the Jakarta Commons Collections project. We started writing our own utilities, but decided instead to use existing material and augment it when necessary. We want to discourage others from giving in to the *not invented here* syndrome that is an epidemic among programmers.

In certain instances, a line of code or a command must be typed as one line, with no returns, or it will not work. Sometimes those lines are too long to fit within the width of a page; in those instances we use an arrow (⇛) to indicate that you are to keep typing on the same line.

Common references

We refer to two key works through this book, both by Martin Fowler—*Refactoring: Improving the Design of Existing Code* and *Patterns of Enterprise Application Architecture.* Most of our citations are given as footnotes or with an inline description of the work we are citing, but because we refer to these two books so frequently, we have adopted a shorthand notation. When you see references such as [Refactoring, 230], you know we mean p. 230 of *Refactoring*; and when you see such references as

[PEAA, 412], you know we mean p. 412 of *Patterns*. See our Reading List in the back of the text for a list of books and articles we recommend as additional reading.

The example code comes to life!

In the course of writing this book—in particular in the course of refactoring the example code—we extracted a number of small engines and utilities that we intend to use in future projects. We have released the project under the name "Diasparsoft Toolkit," freely available online at www.diasparsoftware.com/toolkit. The code for the examples used in this book is available for download from the publisher's website, www.manning.com/rainsberger.

Author Online

Purchase of *JUnit Recipes* includes free access to a private web forum run by Manning Publications where you can make comments about the book, ask technical questions, and receive help from the author and from other users. To access the forum and subscribe to it, point your web browser to www.manning.com/rainsberger. This page provides information on how to get on the forum once you are registered, what kind of help is available, and the rules of conduct on the forum.

Manning's commitment to our readers is to provide a venue where a meaningful dialog between individual readers and between readers and the author can take place. It is not a commitment to any specific amount of participation on the part of the author, whose contribution to the AO remains voluntary (and unpaid). We suggest you try asking the author some challenging questions lest his interest stray!

The Author Online forum and the archives of previous discussions will be accessible from the publisher's website as long as the book is in print.

about the cover illustration

The figure on the cover of *JUnit Recipes* is a "Kabobiques," an inhabitant of the Kabobi area of Niger in Central Africa. The illustration is taken from a Spanish compendium of regional dress customs first published in Madrid in 1799. The book's title page states:

> *Coleccion general de los Trages que usan actualmente todas las Nacionas del Mundo desubierto, dibujados y grabados con la mayor exactitud por R.M.V.A.R. Obra muy util y en special para los que tienen la del viajero universal*

which we translate, as literally as possible, thus:

> *General collection of costumes currently used in the nations of the known world, designed and printed with great exactitude by R.M.V.A.R. This work is very useful especially for those who hold themselves to be universal travelers*

Although nothing is known of the designers, engravers, and workers who colored this illustration by hand, the "exactitude" of their execution is evident in this drawing. The "Kabobiques" is just one of many figures in this colorful collection. Their diversity speaks vividly of the uniqueness and individuality of the world's towns and regions just 200 years ago. This was a time when the dress codes of two regions separated by a few dozen miles identified people uniquely as belonging to one or the other. The collection brings to life a sense of isolation and distance of that period and of every other historic period except our own hyperkinetic present. Dress codes have changed since then and the diversity by region, so rich at the time, has faded away. It is now often hard to tell the inhabitant of one continent from another. Perhaps, trying to view it optimistically, we have traded a cultural and visual diversity for a more varied personal life. Or a more varied and interesting intellectual and technical life. We at Manning celebrate the inventiveness, the initiative, and, yes, the fun of the computer business with book covers based on the rich diversity of regional life of two centuries ago brought back to life by the pictures from this collection.

Part 1

The building blocks

So you want to write tests with JUnit. Where do you begin?

This part of the book lays the groundwork for effectively using JUnit to design and test Java code. Once you understand and can apply these recipes to your work, you will have the foundation you need to write JUnit tests for any behavior you will ever need to implement—all such tests reduce to one or more of the recipes in the next several chapters. The challenge is to recognize these smaller, simpler patterns within the larger code and class structures you find in a typical, industrial-grade Java application. Before we tackle those larger problems, we first handle some smaller ones.

By the end of part 1 you will have seen over 60 essential JUnit techniques covering every aspect of testing: writing, organizing, building, and executing tests, plus managing their data and reporting their results. The recipes in parts 2 and 3 refer often to the recipes in part 1, so be prepared to return to this material often. Before long, the techniques they teach you will become very familiar to you.

1 Fundamentals

This chapter covers

- An introduction to Programmer Testing
- Getting started with JUnit
- A few good practices for JUnit
- Why testing replaces debugging

We hate debugging.

You look up at the clock to see how late it is because you *still* have a handful of defects that need to be fixed *tonight.* Welcome to the "fix" phase of "code and fix," which is now entering its third month. In that time, you have begun to forget what your home looks like. The four walls of your office—assuming you even *have* four walls to look at—are more familiar than you ever wanted them to be. You look at the "hot defects" list and see one problem that keeps coming back. You thought you fixed that last week! These testers...when will they leave you alone?!

Fire up the debugger, start the application server—grab a coffee because you have five minutes to kill—set a breakpoint or two, enter data in 10 text fields and then press the Go button. As the debugger halts at your first breakpoint, your goal is to figure out which object *insists* on sending you bad data. As you step through the code, an involuntary muscle spasm—no doubt from lack of sleep—causes you to accidentally step over the line of code that you *think* causes the problem. Now you have to stop the application server, fire up the debugger again, start the application server again, then grab a stale doughnut to go with your bitter coffee. (It was fresh six hours ago.) Is this really as good as it gets?

Well, no. As a bumper sticker might read, "We'd rather be Programmer Testing."

1.1 What is Programmer Testing?

Programmer Testing is not about testing programmers, but rather about programmers performing tests. In recent years some programmers have rediscovered the benefits of writing their own tests, something we as a community lost when we decided some time ago that "the testing department will take care of it." Fixing defects is expensive, mostly because of the time it takes: it takes time for testers to uncover the defect and describe it in enough detail for the programmers to be able to re-create it. It takes time for programmers to determine the causes of the defects, looking through code they have not seen for months. It takes time for everyone to argue whether something is really a defect, to wonder how the programmers could be so stupid, and to demand that the testers leave the programmers alone to do their job. We could avoid much of this wasted time if the programmers simply tested their own code.

The testing that programmers do is generally called *unit testing,* but we prefer not to use this term. It is overloaded and overused, and it causes more confusion than it provides clarity. As a community, we cannot agree on what a *unit* is—is it a method, a class, or a code path? If we cannot agree on what *unit* means, then there is little chance that we will agree on what *unit testing* means. This is why we use the term *Programmer Testing* to describe testing done by programmers. It is also why we use the term *Object Tests* to mean tests on individual objects. Testing individual objects in isolation is the kind of testing that concerns us for the majority of this book. It is possible that this is different from what you might think of as testing.

Some programmers test their code by setting breakpoints at specific lines, running the application in debug mode, stepping through code line by line, and examining the values of certain variables. Strictly speaking, this is Programmer Testing, because a programmer is testing her own code. There are several drawbacks to this kind of testing, including:

- It requires a debugging tool, which not everyone has installed (or wants to install).
- It requires someone to set a breakpoint before executing a test and then remove the breakpoint after the test has been completed, adding to the effort needed to execute the test multiple times.
- It requires knowing and remembering the expected values of the variables, making it difficult for others to execute the same tests unless they know and remember those same values.
- It requires executing the entire application in something resembling a real environment, which takes time and knowledge to set up or configure.
- To test any particular code path requires knowing how the entire application works and involves a long, tedious sequence of inputs and mouse clicks, which makes executing a particular test prone to error.

This kind of manual Programmer Testing, while common, is costly. There is a better way.

1.1.1 The goal of Object Testing

We defined the term *Object Testing* as testing objects in isolation. It is the "in isolation" part that makes it different from the manual testing with which you are already familiar. The idea of Object Testing is to take a single object and test it by itself, without worrying about the role it plays in the surrounding system. If you build each object to behave correctly according to a defined specification (or contract), then when you piece those objects together into a larger system, there is a much greater chance that the system will behave the way you want. Writing Object Tests involves writing code to exercise individual objects by invoking their methods directly, rather than testing the entire application "from the outside." So what does an Object Test look like?

1.1.2 *The rhythm of an Object Test*

When writing an Object Test, a programmer is usually thinking, "If I invoke *this* method on *that* object, it should respond *so*." This gives rise to a certain rhythm—a common, recurring structure, consisting of the following sequence:

1. Create an object.
2. Invoke a method.
3. Check the result.

Bill Wake, author of *Refactoring Workbook*, coined the term the three "A"s to describe this rhythm: "arrange, act, assert." Remembering the three "A"s keeps you focused on writing an effective Object Test with JUnit. This pattern is effective because the resulting tests are repeatable to the extent that they verify *predictable* behavior: if the object is in *this* state and I do *that*, then *this* will happen. Part of the challenge of Object Testing is to reduce all system behavior down to these focused, predictable cases. You could say that this entire book is about finding ways to extract simple, predictable tests from complex software, then writing those tests with JUnit.

So how *do* you write Object Tests?

1.1.3 *A framework for unit testing*

In a paper called "Simple Smalltalk Testing: With Patterns,"[1] Kent Beck described how to write Object Tests using Smalltalk. This paper presented the evolution of a simple testing framework that became known as *SUnit*. Kent teamed up with Erich Gamma to port the framework to Java and called the result *JUnit*. Since 1999, JUnit has evolved into an industry standard testing and design tool for Java, gaining wide acceptance not only on open source (www.opensource.org) projects, but also in commercial software companies.

Kent Beck's testing framework has been ported to over 30 different programming languages and environments. The concepts behind the framework, known in the abstract as xUnit,[2] grew out of a few simple rules for writing tests.

---

1 www.xprogramming.com/testfram.htm.

2 Framework implementations replace *x* with a letter or two denoting the implementation language or platform, so there is SUnit for Smalltalk, JUnit for Java, PyUnit for Python, and others. You can find a more or less complete list of implementations at www.xprogramming.com/software.htm.

Tests must be automated

It is commonplace in the programming community to think of testing as entering text, pushing a button, and watching what happens. Although this *is* testing, it is merely one approach and is best suited for End-to-End Testing through an end-user interface. It is *not* the most effective way to test down at the object level. Manual code-level testing generally consists of setting a breakpoint, running code in a debugger, and then analyzing the value of variables. This process is time consuming, and it interrupts the programmer's flow, taking time away from writing working production code. If you could get the computer to run those tests, it would boost your effectiveness considerably. You *can* get the computer to run those tests if you write them as Java code. Because you're already a Java programmer and the code you want to test is written in Java, it makes sense to write Java code to invoke methods on your objects rather than invoking them by hand.

NOTE *Exploratory testing*—There is a common perception that automated testing and exploratory testing are opposing techniques, but if we examine the definition that James Bach gives in his article "What is Exploratory Testing?"[3] we can see that this is not necessarily the case. Exploratory testing is centered on deciding which test to write, writing it, then using that feedback to decide what to do next. This is similar to Test-Driven Development, a programming technique centered on writing tests to help drive the design of a class. An exploratory tester might perform some manual tests, learn something about the system being tested, keep the knowledge, and discard the tests. He values the knowledge gained more than the tests performed. In Test-Driven Development, a *test driver*[4] uses his tests as a safety net for further changes to the code, so it is important to develop and retain a rich suite of tests. In spite of these differences, the two approaches share a key trait: testing is focused on learning about the software. Exploratory testers learn how the software works, and test drivers learn how the software ought to be designed. We recommend using the exploratory testing approach in general, then automating the results when possible to provide continuous protection against regression. If you are trying to add tests to code that has no tests, you will find the exploratory testing techniques useful to reverse engineer the automated tests you need.

In addition to being automated, tests also need to be repeatable. Executing the same test several times under the same conditions must yield the same results. If a

---

[3] www.satisfice.com/articles/what_is_et.htm.

[4] This is a bit of slang from the Test-Driven Development community: when you are writing code using the techniques of Test-Driven Development, you are said to be *test driving* the code.

test is not repeatable, then you will find yourself spending a considerable amount of time trying to explain why today's test results are different from yesterday's test results, even if there is no defect to fix. You want tests to help you uncover and prevent defects. If running a test costs you time and effort and does a poor job of uncovering or preventing defects, then why use the test?

Tests must verify themselves

Many programmers have already embraced automating their tests. They recognize the value in pressing a button to execute a stable, repeatable test. Because the programmer needs to analyze the value of variables, he often writes code to print the value of key variables to the screen, then looks at those values and judges whether they are correct. This process, while simple and direct, interrupts the programmer's flow; and worse, it relies on the programmer knowing (and remembering) which values to expect. When he is first working on a part of a system, this poses no problem, but four months from now he might not remember whether the value should be 37 or 39—he won't know whether the test passes or fails. To solve this problem, the test itself must know the expected result and tell us whether it passes or fails. This is easy to do: add a line of code to the end of the test that says, "This variable's value should be 39: print OK if it is and Oops if it is not."

Tests must be easy to run simultaneously

As soon as you have automated, self-verifying tests in place, you'll find yourself wanting to run those tests often. You will come to rely on them to give you immediate feedback as to whether the production code you are writing behaves according to your expectations. You will build up sizable collections of tests that verify the simple cases, the boundary conditions, and the exceptional cases that concern you. You will want to run all these tests in a row and let them tell you whether any of them failed. You could run each test one by one—you could even write little scripts to run many of them in succession, but eventually you want to concentrate on writing the tests without worrying about how to execute them. You can do this by grouping tests together into a common place, such as the same Java class, then providing some automatic mechanism for extracting the tests from the class and executing them as a group. You can write this "test extraction" engine once and then use it over and over again.

1.1.4 Enter JUnit

JUnit was created as a framework for writing automated, self-verifying tests in Java, which in JUnit are called *test cases.* JUnit provides a natural grouping mechanism for related tests, which it calls a *test suite.* JUnit also provides *test runners* that you can use to execute a test suite. The test runner reports on the tests that fail, and if none fail, it simply says "OK." When you write JUnit tests, you put all your knowledge into the tests themselves so that they become entirely programmer independent. This means that anyone can run your tests without knowing what they do, and if they are curious, they only need to read the test code. JUnit tests are written in a familiar language—Java—and in a style that is easy to read, even for someone new to this style of testing.

1.1.5 Understanding Test-Driven Development

Many of the recommendations we make in this book come from our experience with Test-Driven Development. This is a style of programming based on the fundamental idea that if you write a test *before* you write the production code to pass that test, you derive several benefits free of charge:

- Your system is entirely covered by tests.
- You build your system from loosely coupled, highly cohesive objects.
- You make steady progress, improving the system incrementally by making one test pass, then another, then another, and so on.
- A passing test is never more than a few minutes away, giving you confidence and continual positive feedback.

In addition to writing the test first, you *refactor* code as you write; that is, you identify ways to improve the design of your system as you build it with the goal of reducing the cost of building new features. A *well-factored* design is one that is free of duplication, has only the classes it needs, and is self-documenting in the sense that classes and methods have names that make it clear what they are or do. Such a system is easy to change, easy to extend, and easy to understand, all of which make for happy programmers, happy project managers, happy end users, and ultimately, happy CEOs.[5]

There is a large and growing community of Test-Driven Development (TDD) practitioners (or test drivers), including the authors of this book. In spite of our enthusiasm for this style of programming, this is *not* a book on TDD, but a book on using JUnit effectively. We highly recommend Kent Beck's *Test-Driven Development: By Example*[6] for a more thorough treatment of TDD. We hope that this book will serve as a companion to Beck's work, at least for Java programmers.

---

[5] We would also hope it makes for happy stockholders, but that is generally beyond our control.

[6] Kent Beck, *Test-Driven Development: By Example.* Addison-Wesley, 2002.

1.2 Getting started with JUnit

To this point we have decided that there is more to testing than setting breakpoints and looking at the values of variables. We have introduced JUnit, a framework for repeatable, self-verifying Object Tests. The next step is to start writing some JUnit tests, so let us look at downloading and installing JUnit as well as writing and executing tests.

1.2.1 Downloading and installing JUnit

JUnit is easy to install and use. To get JUnit up and running, you must:

1. Download the JUnit package.
2. Unpack JUnit to your file system.
3. Include the JUnit *.jar file on the class path when you want to build or run tests.

Downloading JUnit

At press time, the best place to find JUnit is at www.junit.org. You will find a download link to the latest version of the product. Click the Download link to download the software to your file system.

Unpacking JUnit

You can unpack JUnit to any directory on your file system using your favorite *.zip file utility. Table 1.1 describes the key files and folders in the JUnit distribution.

Table 1.1 What's inside the JUnit distribution

File/Folder	Description
junit.jar	A binary distribution of the JUnit framework, extensions, and test runners
src.jar	The JUnit source, including an Ant buildfile
junit	Samples and JUnit's own tests, written in JUnit
javadoc	Complete API documentation for JUnit
doc	Documentation and articles, including "Test Infected: Programmers Love Writing Tests" and some material to help you get started

To verify your installation, execute the JUnit test suite. That's right: JUnit is distributed with its own tests written using JUnit! To execute these tests, follow these steps:

1. Open a command prompt.
2. Change to the directory that contains JUnit (D:\junit3.8.1 or /opt/junit3.8.1 or whatever you called it).
3. Issue the following command:

```
> java -classpath junit.jar;. junit.textui.TestRunner
⇒  junit.tests.AllTests
```

You should see a result similar to the following:

```
.........................................
.........................................
.........
Time: 2.003

OK (91 tests)
```

For each test, the test runner prints a dot to let you know that it is making progress. After it finishes executing the tests, the test runner says "OK" and tells you how many tests it executed and how long it took.

*Including the *.jar file on your class path*

Look at the command you used to run the tests:

```
> java -classpath junit.jar;. junit.textui.TestRunner junit.tests.AllTests
```

The class path includes junit.jar and the current directory. This file must be in the class path both when you compile your tests and when you run your tests. This is also the *only* file you need to add to your class path. This is a simple procedure because the current directory—the one where you unpacked JUnit—happens to be the location of the *.class files for the JUnit tests.

The next parameter, `junit.textui.TestRunner`, is the class name of a text-based JUnit test runner. This class executes JUnit tests and reports the results to the console. If you want to save the test results for later review, redirect its output to a file. If the tests do not run properly, see chapter 8, "Troubleshooting JUnit," for details. If you have trouble executing your tests, or you need to execute them a special way, see chapter 6, "Running JUnit Tests," for some solutions.

The last parameter, `junit.tests.AllTests`, is the name of the test suite to run. The JUnit tests include a class `AllTests` that builds a complete test suite containing about 100 tests. Read more about organizing tests in chapter 3, "Organizing and Building JUnit Tests."

1.2.2 Writing a simple test

Now that you can execute tests, you'll want to write one of your own. Let us start with the example in listing 1.1.

Listing 1.1 Your first test

```
package junit.cookbook.gettingstarted.test;

import junit.cookbook.util.Money;
import junit.framework.TestCase;

public class MoneyTest extends TestCase {      // Create a subclass of TestCase
    public void testAdd() {                    // Each test is a method
        Money addend = new Money(30, 0);       // 30 dollars, 0 cents
        Money augend = new Money(20, 0);

        Money sum = addend.add(augend);
        assertEquals(5000, sum.inCents());     // The parameters should be equal
    }
}
```

This test follows the basic Object Test rhythm:

- It creates an object, called `addend`.
- It invokes a method, called `add()`.[7]
- It checks the result by comparing the return value of `inCents()` against the expected value of 5,000.

Without all the jargon, this test says, "If I add $30.00 to $20.00, I should get $50.00, which happens to be 5,000 cents."

This example demonstrates several aspects of JUnit, including:

- To create a test, you write a method that expresses the test. We have named this method `testAdd()`, using a JUnit naming convention that allows JUnit to find and execute your test automatically. This convention states that the name of a method implementing a test must start with "test."
- The test needs a home. You place the method in a class that extends the JUnit framework class `TestCase`. We will describe `TestCase` in detail in a moment.

---

[7] If you are confused as to what an *augend* is, blame Kent Beck (who, we're sure, will just blame Chet Hendrickson, but that's not our fault). We are simply repeating his discovery that this is the proper term for the second argument in addition: you add the *augend* to the *addend*. We can be an obscure bunch, we programmers.

- To express how you expect the object to behave, you make assertions. An assertion is simply a statement of your expectation. JUnit provides a number of methods for making assertions. Here, you use `assertEquals()`, which tells JUnit, "If these two values are not the same, the test should fail."
- When JUnit executes a test, if the assertion fails—in our case, if `inCents()` does not return 5,000—then the test fails; but if no assertion fails, then the test passes.[8]

These are the highlights, but as always, the devil is in the details.

1.2.3 Understanding the TestCase class

The `TestCase` class is the center of the JUnit framework. You will find `TestCase` in the package `junit.framework`. There is some confusion among JUnit practitioners—even among experienced ones—about the term *test case* and its relation to the `TestCase` class. This is an unfortunate name collision. The term *test case* generally refers to a single test, verifying a specific path through code. It can sound strange, then, to collect *multiple* test cases into a single class, itself a subclass of `TestCase`, with each test case implemented as a method on `TestCase`. If the class contains multiple test cases, then why call it `TestCase` and not something more indicative of a *collection* of tests?

Here is the best answer we can give you: to write a test case, you create a subclass of `TestCase` and implement the test case as a method on the new class; but at runtime, each test case executes as an instance of your subclass of `TestCase`. As a result, each test case is an instance of `TestCase`. Using common object-oriented programming terminology, each test case is a `TestCase` object, so the name fits. Still, a `TestCase` class contains many tests, which causes the confusion of terms. This is why we take great care to differentiate between a test case and a test case *class*: the former is a single test, whereas the latter is the class that contains multiple tests, each implemented as a different method. To make the distinction clearer, we will never (or at least almost never) use the term *test case*, but rather either *test* or *test case class*. As you will see later in this book, we also refer to the test case class as a *fixture*. Rather than cram more information into this short description, we will talk about fixtures later. For now, think of a fixture as a natural way to group tests together so that JUnit can execute them at once. The `TestCase` class provides a default mechanism for identifying which methods are tests, but you can collect the

---

[8] Exceptions might get in the way, but we'll discuss this in due time.

tests yourself in customized suites. Chapter 4, "Managing Test Suites," describes the various ways to build test suites from your tests.

The class `TestCase` extends a utility class named `Assert` in the JUnit framework. The `Assert` class provides the methods you will use to make assertions about the state of your objects. `TestCase` extends `Assert` so that you can write your assertions without having to refer to an outside class. The basic assertion methods in JUnit are described in table 1.2.

Table 1.2 The JUnit class `Assert` provides several methods for making assertions.

Method	What it does
`assertTrue(boolean condition)`	Fails if `condition` is false; passes otherwise.
`assertEquals(Object expected, Object actual)`	Fails if `expected` and `actual` are not equal, according to the `equals()` method; passes otherwise.
`assertEquals(int expected, int actual)`	Fails if `expected` and `actual` are not equal according to the == operator; passes otherwise. There is an overloaded version of this method for each primitive type: `int, float, double, char, byte, long, short,` and `boolean`. (See Note about `assertEquals()`.)
`assertSame(Object expected, Object actual)`	Fails if `expected` and `actual` refer to different objects in memory; passes if they refer to the same object in memory. Objects that are not the same might still be equal according to the `equals()` method.
`assertNull(Object object)`	Passes if object is `null`; fails otherwise.

JUnit provides additional assertion methods for the logical opposites of the ones listed in the table: `assertFalse()`, `assertNotSame()`, and `assertNotNull()`; but for `assertNotEquals()` you need to explore the various customizations of JUnit, which we describe in part 3, "More Testing Techniques."

NOTE Two of the overloaded versions of `assertEquals()` are slightly different. The versions that compare `double` and `float` values require a third parameter: a *tolerance level*. This tolerance level specifies how close floating-point values need to be before you consider them equal. Because floating-point arithmetic is imprecise at best,[9] you might specify "these two values can be within 0.0001 and that's close enough" by coding `assertEquals(expectedDouble, actualDouble, 0.0001d)`.

---

[9] See "What Every Computer Scientist Should Know About Floating-Point Arithmetic" (http://docs.sun.com/source/806-3568/ncg_goldberg.html).

1.2.4 Failure messages

When an assertion fails, it is worth including a short message that indicates the nature of the failure, even a reason for it. Each of the assertion methods accepts as an optional first parameter a `String` containing a message to display when the assertion fails. It is a matter of some debate whether the programmer should include a failure message *as a general rule* when writing an assertion. Those in favor claim that it only adds to the self-documenting nature of the code, while others feel that in many situations the context makes clear the nature of the failure. We leave it to you to try both and compare the results.[10]

We will add that `assertEquals()` has its own customized failure message, so that if an equality assertion fails you see this message:

```
junit.framework.AssertionFailedError: expected:<4999> but was:<5000>
```

Here, a custom failure message might not make the cause of the problem any clearer.

1.2.5 How JUnit signals a failed assertion

The key to understanding how JUnit decides when a test passes or fails lies in knowing how these assertion methods signal that an assertion has failed.

In order for JUnit tests to be self-verifying, *you* must make assertions about the state of your objects and *JUnit* must raise a red flag when your production code does not behave according to your assertions. In Java, as in C++ and Smalltalk, the way to raise a red flag is with an exception. When a JUnit assertion fails, the assertion method throws an exception to indicate that the assertion has failed.

To be more precise, when an assertion fails, the assertion method throws an error: an `AssertionFailedError`. The following is the source for `assertTrue()`:[11]

```
static public void assertTrue(boolean condition) {
    if (!condition)
        throw new AssertionFailedError();
}
```

When you assert that a condition is true but it is *not*, then the method throws an `AssertionFailedError` to indicate the failed assertion. The JUnit framework then catches that error, marks the test as failed, remembers that it failed, and moves on to the next test. At the end of the test run, JUnit lists all the tests that failed; the rest are considered as having passed.

---

[10] As Ron Jeffries asks, "Speculation or experimentation—which is more likely to give you the correct answer?"

[11] Well, not exactly, because the code is highly factored. Rather than show you three methods, we have translated them into one that does the same thing.

1.2.6 The difference between failures and errors

You normally don't want the Java code that you write to throw errors, but rather only exceptions. General practice leaves the throwing of errors to the Java Virtual Machine itself, because an error indicates a low-level, unrecoverable problem, such as not being able to load a class. This is the kind of stuff from which we mortals cannot be expected to recover. For that reason, it might seem strange for JUnit to throw an error to indicate an assertion failure.

JUnit throws an error rather than an exception because in Java, errors are unchecked; therefore, not every test method needs to declare that it might throw an error.[12] You might suppose that a `RuntimeException` would have done the same job, but if JUnit threw the kinds of exceptions your production code might throw, then JUnit tests might interfere with your production. Such interference would diminish JUnit's value.

When your test contains a failed assertion, JUnit counts that as a failed test; but when your test throws an exception (and does not catch it), JUnit counts that as an error. The difference is subtle, but useful: a failed assertion usually indicates that the production code is wrong, but an error indicates that there is a problem either with the test itself or in the surrounding environment. Perhaps your test expects the wrong exception object or incorrectly tries to invoke a method on a `null` reference. Perhaps a disk is full, or a network connection is unavailable, or a file is not found. JUnit cannot conclude that your production code is at fault, so it throws up its hands and says, "Something went wrong. I can't tell whether the test would pass or fail. Fix the problem and run this test again." That is the difference between a failure and an error.

JUnit's test runners report the results of a test run in this format: "78 run, 2 failures, 1 error."[13] From this you can conclude that 75 tests passed, 2 failed, and 1 was inconclusive. Our recommendation is to investigate the error first, fix the problem, and then run the tests again. It might be that with the error out of the way, all the tests pass!

---

[12] It is entirely possible that checked exceptions in Java are a waste of time. As we write these words, "checked exceptions are evil" returns 18,500 results from Google. Join the debate!

[13] Looks like you have some work to do!

1.3 A few good practices

The recipes in this book reflect a collection of good practices that we have gathered through hard-won experience. We did not learn them all in one day and neither will you, but we think that the following *good practices* give you a suitable place to start.

1.3.1 Naming conventions for tests and test classes

Names are important. The names of your objects, methods, parameters, and packages all play a significant role in communicating what your system is and does. A programmer ought to be able to sit down at a computer, browse your code, and form an accurate mental model of your system just by reading the names. If not, then the names are wrong. We understand that this is a strong statement. We also understand that finding the right name is not always easy—far from it. We understand that naming the parts of your system is at times difficult, but we believe that finding the right name is always worth the effort.

So it is with your tests: name your tests precisely. The name of a test should summarize the test in a few words, because if it can't, then you need to write additional documentation explaining the test. How much better can you explain what a test does than by pointing to the code that implements it? Your goal is to make that code as easy to read as this book—or easier.

Naming tests

Start with the test itself: the name of a test should describe the behavior you are testing, rather than how the test is implemented. In other words, a test name should *reveal intent.* If you are writing an object in a banking system, then you will write a test for the special case where someone attempts to withdraw too much money. You might name this test `testWithdrawWhenOverdrawn()`, or `testWithdrawWithInsufficientFunds()`. Perhaps even `testWithdrawTooMuch()` suffices. But `testWithdraw200Dollars()` is a doubtful choice: it might describe what the test *does*, but not *why*. Confronted with seeing this test name for the first time, a programmer would ask, "Why is withdrawing $200 so special?" We recommend making that obvious in the name of the test. For the *happy path* cases (the straight-ahead scenario in which nothing goes wrong), we recommend simply naming your test after the behavior you are testing. For the test that withdraws money successfully from an account, the name `testWithdraw()` is perfect. If you do not say otherwise, the reader can assume that you are testing a happy path.

One common convention is to use the underscore character between the name of the behavior and the particular special case. Some programmers prefer names such as `testWithdraw_Overdrawn()` or `testWithdraw_Zero()`. This makes the test methods easier to read: it separates the behavior under test from the special conditions being tested. We endorse this convention, although after three or four special cases for a given behavior, you should consider moving these special case tests to a separate *test fixture*—a class that defines both tests and the objects on which those tests operate. See recipe 3.7, "Move special case tests to a separate test fixture," for a full discussion of this technique.

Naming test case classes

When naming your test case classes, the simplest guideline is to name the test case class after the class under test. In other words, your tests for `Account` go into the class `AccountTest`, your tests for `FileSystem` go into the class `FileSystemTest`, and so on. The principal benefit of this naming convention is that it is easy to find a test, as long as you know the class being tested. While we recommend starting out with this naming convention, it is important to understand that this is *only* a naming convention, and not a requirement of JUnit. We are surprised by the number of programmers who ask us what to do about test case classes that grow unusually large or become difficult to navigate. Any class that becomes too large should be split into smaller classes, JUnit or otherwise. We recommend identifying the tests that share a common fixture and factoring them into a separate test case class, to which the questioner responds, "But don't they all have to be in the same `TestCase` class?" The answer to that is no!

We mentioned earlier that each test is an instance of your subclass of `TestCase`. What we did not mention at the time is that your test case class is simply a container for related tests. How to distribute your tests into the various test case classes is up to you. There are some useful guidelines, which we describe in chapter 3. If you find that three tests belong together and should be separated from the rest of the tests for that class, then move them. We recommend naming the new test fixture after what those tests have in common. If there are six special cases for withdrawing money from an account, then move them into a test case class called `AccountWithdrawalTest` or `WithdrawFromAccountTest`, depending on whether you prefer noun phrases or verb phrases. We prefer verb phrases and would likely choose `WithdrawFromAccountTest`.

1.3.2 Test behavior, not methods

This brings us to another recommendation when writing tests: your tests should focus on the behavior they are testing without worrying about which class is under test. This is why our test names tend to be verbs rather than nouns: we test behavior (verbs) and not classes (nouns). Still, the difference between behavior and methods might not be clear: we implement behavior as methods, so testing behavior *must* be about test methods. But that's not entirely true. We *do* implement behavior as methods, but the way we choose to implement a certain behavior depends on a variety of factors, some of which boil down to personal preference. We make a number of decisions when implementing behavior as methods: their names, their parameter lists, which methods are public and which are private, the classes on which we place the methods, and so on—these are *some* of the ways in which methods might differ, even though the underlying behavior might be the same. The implementation can vary in ways that the tests do not need to determine.

Sometimes a single method implements all the required behavior, and in that case, testing that method directly is all you need. More complex behaviors require the collaboration of several methods or even objects to implement. If you let your tests depend too much on the particulars of the implementation, then you create work for yourself as you try to refactor (improve the design). Furthermore, some methods merely participate in a particular feature, rather than implement it. Testing those methods in isolation might be more trouble than it is worth. Doing so drives up the complexity of your test suite (by using more tests) and makes refactoring more difficult—and all for perhaps not much gain over testing the behavior at a slightly higher level. By focusing on testing behavior rather than each individual method, you can better strike a balance between test coverage and the freedom you need to support refactoring.

To illustrate the point, consider testing a stack. Recall that a stack provides a few basic operations: push (add to the top of the stack), pop (remove from the top of the stack), and peek (look at the top of the stack). When deciding how to test a stack implementation, the following tests spring to mind:

- Popping an empty stack fails somehow.
- Peeking at an empty stack shows nothing.
- Push an object onto the stack, then peek at it, expecting the same object you pushed.

- Push an object onto the stack, then pop it, expecting the same object you pushed.
- Push two different objects onto the stack, then pop twice, expecting the objects in reverse order from the order in which you pushed them.

Notice that these tests focus on *fixture*—the state of the stack when the operation is performed—rather than on the operation itself. Notice also how the methods combine to provide the desired behavior. If `push()` does not work, then there is no good way to verify `pop()` and `peek()`. We can say the same for the other methods. Moreover, when using a stack, you use all three operations, so it does not make sense to test them in isolation, but rather to test that the stack generally behaves correctly, depending on its contents. Does this point to a poor design where methods are overly coupled? No. Instead it reinforces the fact that an object is a cohesive collection of related operations on the same set of data. The object's *overall* behavior—a composite of the behaviors of its methods in a given state—is what is important, so we recommend focusing your test effort on the object as a whole, rather than its parts.

1.4 Summary

We all have the experience of having to track down a defect, whether in our code or someone else's. This horrible act that we call *debugging* generally consists of two different, concomitant activities: reasoning about what *might* have gone wrong and groping in the dark for the slightest clue as to what *actually* went wrong. When we are debugging, we start with the former; but when it becomes clear that the problem is worse than we feared, we end up doing the latter, and at that point there is no way to know when (or if) we will solve the problem.

The most elementary debugging technique has become known as `printf`, after the C library function to print text to the screen. Even Java programmers will say, "Throw some `printf`s in there and see what's going on" (although it might be the fashion to say `println` because that's what Java calls it). The idea is to narrow down the location of the defect to some reasonably small area of the code and then litter it with temporary code that prints the value of variables to the screen. You then run the system, reproduce the defect, and analyze the values of the variables.

Does this sound familiar yet?

What you are doing is exploratory testing, as James Bach described it. The only difference is that you might not have access to a debugger to make the process smoother: you only have a log file or the console to look at, and you had better look quickly, because the `println` statements whiz past you before you know it!

Why not write a test instead? You have already identified the area of the code that seems to exhibit the problem by narrowing it down to someplace that invokes a method on an object. Write a test that exercises that method. Rather than grope around looking at the value of every variable you can find, determine the input to the method where the defect occurs and then use that input in your test. Make an assertion with the result you expect, and then run the test. Keep adding tests until you find the source of the problem; then when you change the offending code, run your test to verify that the problem is solved. Doing this increases the frequency (and effectiveness!) of the feedback you get each time you think you've solved the problem. After you have solved the problem—and this is the most important part—*keep the test!*

That's right: rather than walking away from this debugging session with only another war story to tell your programmer buddies, walk away with tests that provide insurance against reinjecting the defect into the system at a later date. *You* might forget the cause of the problem or how you solved the problem, but the *tests* will never forget. Save your hard work for posterity and avoid having to go through this again at a customer site or two days before release or during your next product demo to the CEO.

Stop debugging. Write a test instead.

2 Elementary tests

This chapter covers

- General techniques for testing individual methods
- Specific techniques for testing JavaBeans
- Specific techniques for testing interfaces
- Comparing objects for equality in tests

The simplest kind of Programmer Test you will write verifies the return value of a method. This technique is *the* building block for all the testing you will ever do with JUnit. In the rest of this book we try to reduce every complex testing problem down to this, the simplest of scenarios. We begin by describing this scenario in detail; then the remaining recipes in this chapter will build gradually from there. These recipes provide not only the solutions to common problems, but also a rudimentary vocabulary that we can use to describe the solutions to larger, more complex testing problems. If verifying a method's return value is the atom of unit testing, then these recipes are the lightest molecules: the ones that come first and the ones from which complex organic compounds are built. By the end of this book you will have strategies for handling most of, if not all, the testing problems you encounter.

Here is how to test a method that returns a value: invoke the method and compare its return value against the value you expect:

```
public void testNewListIsEmpty() {
    List list = new ArrayList();
    assertEquals(0, list.size());
}
```

The method `size()` returns the number of elements in a list. If we were testing "by hand" we would print this value to the screen and verify it with our own eyes: "Zero? Yep. Passes." With JUnit you go one step further, capturing this expectation by *making an assertion*: writing a line of code that describes what you expect, and then letting JUnit compare your expectation against the actual result. JUnit provides methods with names that start with the word *assert* so that you can make assertions in your tests. A test passes, then, if all its assertions hold true.

Recall Bill Wake's three "A"s: arrange, act, assert. Our previous example follows this pattern as simply as possible: start with an empty list (arrange), ask for its size (act), and verify that the size is zero (assert). This is about as simple as a JUnit test can get.

The method `assertEquals()` allows you to compare either primitive values or objects. Recall that a primitive value is a value of type `int`, `float`, `boolean`, `double`, `long`, `char`, or `byte`.[1] You can open the source for the JUnit class `junit.framework.Assert` to see how the assert methods are implemented. The framework compares primitives as values, so that `assertEquals(3, value)` passes as long as `value` is a numeric primitive variable with the value 3. If the method you wish to test

---

1 Strictly speaking, this list includes `short`; but frankly, we have never used it, and so we tend to forget that it exists.

returns an `Object`, rather than a primitive, then you need to do more work to compare its return value against an expected value.

There are two techniques for comparing the expected value to the actual return value from the method you have invoked. The first technique is to compare each readable property of the method's return value with the values you expect. The second is to create an object representing the value you expect and then compare it to the actual value with a single line of code. This second technique is the one we favor. To illustrate the difference, consider the following example:

```
public void testSynchronizedListHasSameContents() {
    List list = new ArrayList();
    list.add("Albert");
    list.add("Henry");
    list.add("Catherine");

    List synchronizedList = Collections.synchronizedList(list);
    assertEquals("Albert", synchronizedList.get(0));
    assertEquals("Henry", synchronizedList.get(1));
    assertEquals("Catherine", synchronizedList.get(2));
}
```

Here we are testing `Collections.synchronizedList()`. This method is supposed to add thread-safety features to a `List` without affecting the contents of the list. Our test verifies that making a `List` thread safe in this way does not disturb the contents. The method `synchronizedList()` is simple in that it directly returns a value which we can inspect for correctness. We do this by treating each element of the list as a readable property of the list and comparing each one to the corresponding elements in the original list. This is the first technique we described. It works fine, but it has its shortcomings.

The most notable shortcoming of this technique is that it involves a great deal of typing—too much typing, it seems, for something so simple. Certainly, it is possible to replace the checks with a loop that compares the elements at the corresponding index of the two lists:

```
public void testSynchronizedListHasSameContents() {
    List list = new ArrayList();
    list.add("Albert");
    list.add("Henry");
    list.add("Catherine");

    List synchronizedList = Collections.synchronizedList(list);
    for (int i = 0; i < list.size(); i++) {
        assertEquals(list.get(i), synchronizedList.get(i));
    }
}
```

Here we have removed duplication by creating a loop. This is better, but there still seems to be too much to read—or type—compared to our mental model of this test. If we were to describe the test in words, we might say, "We put some items in a `List` and wrap it in a `synchronizedList`, and the new `List` should be the same as the old `List`." Admittedly the use of the word "same" is a little sloppy here, since Java programmers tend to say "the same object" when referring to two references to the same object in memory. Perhaps more accurate is "The new `List` should equal the old `List` in terms of comparing elements." Even better, "The two lists' corresponding elements should be equal." It seems that the code we want to type just says "`list` should be equal to `synchronizedList`," as long as we define "equal" to mean "having the same elements." Fortunately Java has such a method: `Object.equals()`. Even better, it turns out that the contract of `List.equals()` says that lists are equal if they have the same elements at the same indices. Perfect! Not only do we get to write the test we want to write, but we can push the responsibility of determining equality into the objects that are best equipped to do it: the lists themselves.

```
public void testSynchronizedListHasSameContents() {
    List list = new ArrayList();
    list.add("Albert");
    list.add("Henry");
    list.add("Catherine");

    List synchronizedList = Collections.synchronizedList(list);
    assertEquals(list, synchronizedList);
}
```

This simplifies the test considerably. We can even simplify the test further by taking advantage of the method `Arrays.asList()`:

```
public void testSynchronizedListHasSameContents() {
    List list = Arrays.asList(
        new String[] { "Albert", "Henry", "Catherine" });
    assertEquals(list, Collections.synchronizedList(list));
}
```

We could write this test in one statement, but it seems to be most readable in its current form. Not bad considering where we started.

The general form of the simplest test you can write, then, is as follows:

1. Create an object and put it in a known state.
2. Invoke a method, which returns the "actual result."
3. Create the "expected result," which may be a primitive value or a more complex `Object`.
4. Invoke `assertEquals(expectedResult, actualResult)`.

Writing tests like this will drive you to implement the `equals()` method for your Value Objects. See recipe 2.1, "Test your equals method," for details on how your `equals()` method ought to behave. Once you have this technique under your belt, almost everything else you do with JUnit reduces to this one case.

When testing *get* and *set* methods, you apply this technique directly (see recipe 2.4, "Test a getter," and recipe 2.5, "Test a setter"). In order to use this technique effectively, you need to implement `equals()` correctly (see recipe 2.1, "Test your equals method"), and in cases where you cannot apply this technique directly, you need to find another way to expose a return value so that you can compare it to your expectations (see recipe 2.2, "Test a method that returns nothing"). The other recipes in this chapter discuss various elementary tests that form the basis for the rest of the recipes in this book. These early recipes address the most common and simplest testing issues.

2.1 Test your equals method

◆ Problem

You want to test your implementation of `equals()`.

◆ Background

Surprisingly enough, even though a strong object-oriented design depends on implementing the `equals()` method correctly, many programmers implement this method incorrectly. If you want to take advantage of the rest of this book, you need to implement `equals()` correctly for a certain number of your classes: in particular your Value Objects. Although you generally will not have occasion to compare instances of action- or processing-oriented classes, you will need to compare instances of Value Objects, which these processing-oriented classes use to receive input and provide output. To store these Value Objects in collections (`List`, `Set`, `Map`) requires implementing `equals()` and `hashCode()` appropriately.[2] Doing so becomes all the more important when you want to write Object Tests, because in those tests you assert the equality of Value Objects and primitive values a great deal of the time.

---

[2] See chapter 3 of Joshua Bloch, *Effective Java: Programming Language Guide*, Addison-Wesley, 2001; or Peter Haggar, *Practical Java: Programming Language Guide*, Addison-Wesley, 2000, the section entitled "Objects and Equality."

NOTE *Value Objects*—A Value Object represents a value, such as an `Integer`, `Money`, or a `Timestamp`. What makes a Value Object different from other objects is that even if you have 20 different objects that all represent the same value, you can use those objects interchangeably—that is, you can treat them *equally*. It does not matter whether they are different objects in memory: 5 is 5 is 5, so if you have three objects each representing the number 5, you can use one of them in place of another without changing the meaning of your program. You need to implement `equals()` to reflect the fact that, in spite of being different objects in memory, my $20 is the same as your $20.

The wrapper classes for the primitive types behave as Value Objects (`Integer`, `Double`, and so on). `String` also behaves this way. Many examples in this book use a class called `Money`, and `Money` objects are certainly Value Objects.

Note that if your object is not a Value Object, then there is likely no need to test for equals at all, so stop here. This is true of most objects outside your application's domain model.

NOTE *A quick review of* `equals()`—The contract of the method `equals()` is not complex, but it may be unfamiliar to programmers who did not study equivalence relations during their time in mathematics class, so a quick review is in order. The method `equals()` must satisfy three well-known properties: the reflexive, symmetric, and transitive properties, also known as *RST* by mathematics students trying to memorize the names.

- The reflexive property says that an object is equal to itself.
- The symmetric property says that if I am equal to you, then you are equal to me and the other way around.
- The transitive property says that if I am equal to you and you are equal to that guy over there, then I am equal to that guy over there. To use the ancient saying: "Equals of equals are equal."

Beyond these mathematical properties, the `equals()` method must be consistent: no matter how many times you call it on an object, `equals()` answers the same way as long as neither object being compared changes. Finally, no object equals `null`.

With this in mind, you are ready to test your Value Objects for their implementation of `equals()`.

◆ Recipe

If you were to try to write the various tests on your own, you would quickly find out that it is a considerable amount of work. If you want to see that work first before taking a shortcut, skip to the Discussion section of this recipe and then come back here. If you just want to get to the point, we simplify this recipe considerably by taking advantage of the good work of Mike Bowler. His open source package GSBase (http://gsbase.sourceforge.net) provides a number of utilities for writing JUnit tests, including something called the `EqualsTester`. This class runs a complete suite of tests on your Value Object to determine whether your implementation of `equals()` satisfies all the necessary properties.

Listing 2.1 shows an example of using `EqualsTester` to test `equals()` for the `Money` class.

Listing 2.1 Testing `Money.equals()` with `EqualsTester`

```
package junit.cookbook.common.test;

import junit.cookbook.util.Money;
import junit.framework.TestCase;
import com.gargoylesoftware.base.testing.EqualsTester;

public class MoneyTest extends TestCase {
    public void testEquals() {
        Money a = new Money(100, 0);
        Money b = new Money(100, 0);
        Money c = new Money(50, 0);
        Object d = null;

        new EqualsTester(a, b, c, d);
    }
}
```

Let us explain a little more fully the parameters you need to pass to `EqualsTester`:

- `a` is a control object against which the other three objects are to be compared.
- `b` is a different object in memory than `a` but equal to `a` according to its value.
- `c` is expected not to be equal to `a`.
- If the class you are testing is `final`—cannot be subclassed—then `d` ought to be `null`; otherwise, `d` represents an object that looks equal to `a` but is not. By "looks equal," we mean (for example) that `d` has the same properties as `a`, but because `d` has additional properties through subclassing, it is not equal to `a`.

Returning to our example, the test will fail if we set `d` to `null` while allowing subclasses of `Money`. We must decide whether to declare the class `Money` to be `final` or change the test to the following:

```
public class MoneyTest extends TestCase {
    public void testEquals() {
        Money a = new Money(100, 0);
        Money b = new Money(100, 0);
        Money c = new Money(50, 0);
        Money d = new Money(100, 0) {
            // Trivial subclass
        };

        new EqualsTester(a, b, c, d);
    }
}
```

`EqualsTester` provides a quick way to test Value Objects for equality, defined as "having properties with the same respective values," which is sufficient for the vast majority of business applications.

◆ *Discussion*

To understand why we recommend using `EqualsTester`, let us develop the tests ourselves.

We start with the reflexive property and write this test:

```
public class MoneyEqualsTest extends TestCase {
    private Money a;

    protected void setUp() {
        a = new Money(100, 0);
    }

    public void testReflexive() {
        assertEquals(a, a);
    }
}
```

The next property is the symmetric one. We need another `Money` object for that:

```
package junit.cookbook.common.test;

import junit.cookbook.util.Money;
import junit.framework.TestCase;

public class MoneyEqualsTest extends TestCase {
    private Money a;
    private Money b;

    protected void setUp() {
        a = new Money(100, 0);
        b = new Money(100, 0);
    }

    public void testReflexive() {
        assertEquals(a, a);
```

```
        assertEquals(b, b);
    }

    public void testSymmetric() {
        assertEquals(a, b);
        assertEquals(b, a);
    }
}
```

You may be tempted to write `testSymmetric()` as a logical implication, doing something like this:

```
public void testSymmetric() {
    assertTrue(!a.equals(b) || b.equals(a));
}
```

This assumes that you remember how to convert an implication into a logic statement involving only AND, OR, and NOT. Maybe you do, maybe you do not. The good news is it does not matter, because by writing the test as we did previously, the test fails *only if* either assertion fails. In other words, there is an implicit AND between those assertions, so that both the forward and reverse equalities are verified. The direct approach works, so we are content with that. In the process, we added `b` to the reflexivity test, just to have another data point to help us be more confident in the code that passes these tests.

The next property to test is transitivity. This normally would require three objects, but it turns out that in the vast majority of cases, the reflexive and symmetric properties together are enough to guarantee transitivity. The exceptional case is pretty unusual, so rather than describe it here, we leave it to a separate chapter. See essay B.2, "Strangeness and transitivity," for details.

Now that we have verified that objects are equal when we expect them to be, we need to verify that objects are *not* equal when we expect them *not* to be. This requires introducing a third object different from the first two. We add a declaration for this new object as a field in our test case class, as well as the corresponding tests:

```
public class MoneyEqualsTest extends TestCase {
    private Money a;
    private Money b;
    private Money c;

    protected void setUp() {
        a = new Money(100, 0);
        b = new Money(100, 0);
        c = new Money(200, 0);
    }
```

```
    public void testReflexive() {
        assertEquals(a, a);
        assertEquals(b, b);
        assertEquals(c, c);
    }

    public void testSymmetric() {
        assertEquals(a, b);
        assertEquals(b, a);

        assertFalse(a.equals(c));
        assertFalse(c.equals(a));
    }
}
```

These tests say that `c` should equal itself (as should every object), but `a` should not equal `c` and the other way around. You may notice the use of `assertFalse (a.equals(c))`. There is no `assertNotEquals()` method in JUnit, although you can find it in some of the extension projects, such as JUnit-addons. Some members of the community have asked for it, but it is still not part of JUnit. It is easy enough to write, so if you find you prefer to have it, then we recommend implementing it yourself.

At this point we have checked the three main properties. For consistency, we need to check equality on a pair of objects a number of times. Because we can't use an infinite loop here, we choose a nice high number of comparisons that gives us some confidence without making the tests needlessly slow:

```
public class MoneyEqualsTest extends TestCase {
    // No changes to the other tests

    public void testConsistent() {
        for (int i = 0; i < 1000; i++) {
            assertEquals(a, b);
            assertFalse(a.equals(c));
        }
    }
}
```

Even at 1,000 iterations, the test only lasted 0.05 seconds on a midrange laptop, so the test should be fast enough. The last thing to do is compare the objects to `null`:

```
public class MoneyEqualsTest extends TestCase {
    // No changes to the other tests

    public void testNotEqualToNull() {
        assertFalse(a.equals(null));
        assertFalse(c.equals(null));
    }
}
```

We choose not to compare `b` with `null` because the other tests show that `a` and `b` are already equal. If you want to add the extra test, it does no harm, but we do not think it provides any value.

This covers all the basic properties of `equals()`. Although it is not an exhaustive test, it should detect defects in an implementation of `equals()` in any classes you might find in business applications programming. Examine the source of `EqualsTester` to see what additional tests Mike Bowler decided were worth implementing.

NOTE In addition to testing `equals()`, the `EqualsTester` verifies that `hashCode()` is consistent with `equals()`. This means that if two objects are equal, then their hash codes are also equal, but not necessarily the other way around. Without these extra tests, it is possible to put an object into a `Map` with one key object and not be able to retrieve it with another key object, even if the two key objects are equal. We say this from experience. If you do not want to or need to write a suitable hashing algorithm, we recommend implementing `hashCode()` to throw an `UnsupportedOperationException`, which adheres to the basic contract of `Object` but fails loudly if you later try to use this object as a key in a `Map`.[3] An alternative is to return a constant value, such as 0, but that reduces hashing to a linear search, which may cause a performance problem if done often enough.

Alternative

JUnit-addons also provides an equals tester, which it calls `EqualsHashCodeTestCase`. The intent is the same, but the code is different. You subclass this test case class and override methods to return instances of your Value Objects. One method, `createInstance()`, returns the control object; the other method, `createNotEqualInstance()`, returns objects that you expect not to be equal to the control objects. You need to implement these methods to return new objects on each invocation, rather than create one instance and keep returning it. The test will, for example, invoke `createInstance()` twice and then compare the two objects using `equals()`. If you return the same object twice, the test fails, so you do not necessarily have to remember to do this correctly. Listing 2.2 shows how we tested `Money` using this technique.

---

[3] Thanks go to Ilja Preuß for recommending this technique. It is consistent with the practice of adding a `fail()` statement to a new test until it has been fully implemented. Until then, it can only fail, rather than pass silently.

Listing 2.2 Testing `Money.equals()` with `EqualsHashCodeTestCase`

```
package junit.cookbook.common.test;

import junit.cookbook.util.Money;
import junitx.extensions.EqualsHashCodeTestCase;

public class MoneyEqualsTestWithJUnitAddons
    extends EqualsHashCodeTestCase {

    public MoneyEqualsTestWithJUnitAddons(String name) {
        super(name);
    }

    protected Object createInstance() throws Exception {
        return Money.dollars(100);
    }

    protected Object createNotEqualInstance() throws Exception {
        return Money.dollars(200);
    }
}
```

To summarize the main differences between the two utilities, you use `EqualsTester` within a single test, whereas you use `EqualsHashCodeTestCase` by subclassing. Also, `EqualsTester` tests for the "subclass equals" issue, whereas `EqualsHashCodeTestCase` does not. Otherwise, use whichever technique you prefer.

◆ Related

- B.2—Strangeness and transitivity
- GSBase (http://gsbase.sourceforge.net)
- JUnit-addons (http://junit-addons.sourceforge.net)

2.2 Test a method that returns nothing

◆ Problem

You want to test a method that has no return value.

◆ Background

One of the most common questions for people new to JUnit is, "How do I test a method that returns *void*?" The primary reason for this question is that there is no direct way to determine what such a method does. Because you cannot compare an expected value against an actual, returned value, you need some other way to describe the expected behavior and compare it to the actual behavior.

◆ *Recipe*

If a method returns no value, it must have some observable side effect, such as changing the state of an object; otherwise it does nothing. If it does nothing, then there is no need to test it and likely no need to use it, so get rid of it. If it has an observable side effect, you need to identify it and then make the appropriate assertions based on that side effect.

Let us test adding an object to a collection. The method `Collection.add(Object)` returns no value. In spite of this, there is an intuitive way to verify whether the object was successfully added to the collection:

1. Create an empty collection.
2. The collection should not contain the item in question.
3. Add the item in question.
4. *Now* the collection should contain the item in question.

Translating that into code, we test `ArrayList.add()`:

```
public class AddToArrayListTest extends TestCase {
    public void testListAdd() {
        List list = new ArrayList();
        assertFalse(list.contains("hello"));
        list.add("hello");
        assertTrue(list.contains("hello"));
    }
}
```

We saw that `List.contains(Object)` allows us to confirm a side effect of the correct behavior of `add()`. Even though `add()` returns no value, we were able to identify a change in `list`'s state that implies that `add()` behaves correctly.

We can apply the same technique to a method that loads data from some source but does not explicitly signal that that data was successfully loaded.[4] This test loads data from a properties file and then makes some assertions about the properties we expect to find:

---

[4] Perhaps it should signal that information through a return value, because that would be useful to client objects other than the tests.

```
public void testLoadProperties() throws Exception {
    Properties properties = new Properties();
    properties.load(new FileInputStream("application.properties"));
    assertEquals("jbrains", properties.getProperty("username"));
    assertEquals("jbra1ns", properties.getProperty("password"));
}
```

Notice that this test is somewhat brittle because it duplicates expected values with data found outside the test, namely in a file on the file system. We address this problem in recipe 5.3, "Use an inline data file." Still, the test uses the `load()` method's key side effect to verify its behavior: that the expected data is correctly loaded from the specified properties file. (And, no, I don't really use that password for anything, so don't bother trying it.)

◆ *Discussion*

The effectiveness of this technique relies on the existence of an observable side effect. Any method—any block of code, for that matter—must either return a value or have a side effect; otherwise, by definition it has no behavior. The only remaining question is whether the current design allows you to see the side effect. A cache generally does not provide a way to view its contents, since caching is usually an implementation detail. Without adding diagnostic methods to query whether the cache has been hit, there is no way to observe the behavior of a caching mechanism. Of course, if your cache does not provide some means of verifying cache hits, how do you know that it is caching anything?[5]

Even with an observable side effect, you may question the value of using one method to test another. Returning to the `List` example, we used `contains()` to test `add()`, but typically, `add()` is used to test `contains()`. The test in question is generally the exact test we wrote previously to verify `add()`! There appears to be a chicken-and-egg problem here: we cannot guarantee the correctness of `add()` without having already demonstrated the correctness of `contains()`, and the other way around. Does this mean that our tests mean nothing?

The answer is no. We are testing behavior, and not methods. When we say "We will test adding objects to a collection," that leads to testing a number of different operations: add, clear, remove, contains, find, and so on. All these operations on a collection pertain to testing the ability to add objects. Taken together, the methods

---

[5] Imagine a programmer codes his intention to cache an object by naming a method `getObjectFromCache()`. In his haste to complete his programming task, he defers implementing the cache until later. Three months later, in a formal code walkthrough, someone finally notices that there is no cache in this class. A test would have prevented this.

implement certain behaviors, such as the ability to have many objects in a collection or eliminate duplicate elements (for a set, in particular). We recommend you worry about the bigger picture—testing behavior—rather than testing individual methods. Certainly some behavior is straightforward and best implemented by a single method, but it is the object that we care about, and not just the method. If we need to invoke `add()`, `contains()`, and `clear()` to verify that our collection properly sorts elements as they are added to the list, then we invoke them. We will have more to say on this issue throughout the book.

NOTE *The tests are the specification!*—If `add()` and `contains()` contain defects that cancel one another out, then the test passes and we can argue that the behavior is correct. We hope that future tests will uncover the defects, but if that never happens then we have incorrect code that exhibits correct behavior. *If code does the wrong thing but no test fails, does it have a defect?* More and more JUnit users say, "No." They say that "The tests are the specification," which means that we describe what our code does by providing the tests our code passes. A feature is not present unless there are tests to verify it. Each test is a claim that the code behaves a certain way, so if no test exists to verify that we can add an object twice to the same `List`, then we cannot assume that that would work. This certainly puts pressure on the programmer to write enough tests!

If there is no way to observe a method's side effect, then in order to test it you must expose one.[6] Although you may cringe at the notion of adding behavior "just for testing," we argue that the return on investment far outweighs the cost of adding a simple query method, so long as it is, indeed, simple. In most cases, converting an invisible side effect into an observable one provides additional design benefits beyond "mere" testability. One example is allowing a reusable class to emerge from a larger class in which it is currently trapped. As you gain more experience with JUnit, you will discover this for yourself. We will also return to this point as needed throughout the book.

◆ *Related*

- 5.3—Use an inline data file
- 14.2—Test an Observable (Event Source)
- B.4—The mock objects landscape

[6] Jason Menard points out that you can use reflection to create an observable side effect by gaining access to otherwise invisible data or methods. We prefer not to do this, because it is often more work than just adding a method. But it is a viable alternative. We describe using JUnitX for this purpose in chapter 17.

2.3 Test a constructor

◆ Problem

You want to test a constructor.

◆ Background

Testing a constructor can seem like chasing your own tail.

The straightforward approach would be to use the constructor to instantiate an object and then compare that object to an expected value using `assertEquals()`. That test would be very simple—you could even write it on one line if you wanted to. There is only one problem: to create the expected value requires—that's right—using the constructor you want to test. Such a test is not very satisfying. It says, "If the constructor works, then it works." Great.

So how *do* you test a constructor?

◆ Recipe

If your class exposes readable properties, then the solution is straightforward: you can compare their values against the values you had passed into the constructor. Here, a readable property may be exposed either directly as a field or through a *get* method.

NOTE *Just for testing*—It is most common to test classes entirely through their `public` interface. If you adopt this approach as a rule, then you will encounter some cases where you need to add a `public` method to your class's interface—often a *getter*—in order to gain access to the data you need to verify a given behavior. This is a controversial issue among programmers: adding the method seems to break encapsulation "just for testing," which introduces a trade-off that different people evaluate differently. As with any such situation, it is up to you to try both options and measure the difference.

The simplest kind of constructor test uses exposed internal state to verify that parameters passed to the constructor reached the appropriate properties. Here is a simple example:

```
public void testInitializationParameters() {
    assertEquals(762, new Integer(762).intValue());
}
```

You can use the method `intValue()`, which returns the underlying value of the `Integer` object, to verify that the constructor correctly stores the value you passed in through the constructor. Even though it does not have *get* in the name, `intValue()` is a *get* method.

If your class does not expose readable properties, then you must build some other observable side effect that you can use to verify the correctness of the constructor. It is possible to write a method named `isValid()` to help verify the sanity of your object without violating the data-hiding principle. Such a test would look like this:

```
public void testInitializationParameters() {
    BankDepositCommand command = new BankDepositCommand(
        "123", Money.dollars(125, 50), today());
    assertTrue(command.isValid());
}
```

This technique also applies well to testing JavaBeans. See recipe 2.7, "Test a JavaBean," for details.

◆ *Discussion*

Most of these tests seem too simple to be worth writing, which is why many programmers do not write them. This is the reason that *we* often do not write them. On occasion we will be bitten (you know where) by a defect we introduced precisely because we did not write such a test. It is up to you to determine, based on experience and your defect rate, whether writing such tests provides sufficient return on investment to continue doing so. The saying goes, "Test until fear turns to boredom."

If you would like a more immediately useful heuristic, use the following technique to effectively verify any default values you might assign to properties during object initialization. Consider a `Money` class whose objects default to zero dollars when no parameters are passed to the constructor. The test would resemble the following:

```
public void testDefaultInitializationParameters() {
    assertEquals(0L, new Money().inCents());
}
```

Here we use the method `inCents()` to answer the underlying value of the `Money` object, represented in cents (which simply avoids using floating-point numbers), to verify that the default amount of a `Money` object is zero dollars, which is also zero cents.

In general, though, a constructor *on its own* does not do enough to warrant its own set of tests. Most constructors accept no parameters, store parameters in instance variables, or pass their parameters to other, more interesting methods. If you're worried that storing parameters in instance variables might break, then see the essay "Too simple to break" in appendix B. If your constructor delegates to more interesting methods, then test those methods rather than this constructor. If your constructor validates its parameters, then see recipe 2.8, "Test throwing the right exception," for examples of tests that expect a method to throw a particular exception.

Alternatives

You may not wish to expose your object's data through readable properties because you have no other need to do so. In this case, how do you verify that the parameters you passed into the constructor were correctly stored? Your first thought may be, "Because the test cannot extract the actual values to compare to the expected values, it should give the expected values to the object and let it make the comparison." Here is an example of such a test, again using the class `Money`:

```
public void testValueInCents() {
    assertTrue(new Money(0, 50).valueInCentsIs(50));
}
```

This test uses a new method `valueInCentsIs()`, which compares the parameter with the internal state of the `Money` object and then returns `true` if the two are equal and `false` otherwise. Although this works, it is our opinion that this code is less clear than simply introducing the `inCents()` method and comparing the results within the test. This is a matter of personal taste, and you may decide differently. Try them both; then compare the results.

More to the point, however, `valueInCentsIs()` does not hide data any better than `inCents()` does. The former method tries to act like `equals()` but falls short. If you want that behavior, then you need to use `equals()`, but as we said, that leads to using the constructor to test the constructor. Because we cannot use the solution we want to use, we should choose the simplest alternative available and add `inCents()`. It may look like the method directly exposes the value of a field, but that is only an accident of the way the data is stored. If the implementation of `Money` changes to store its value in two fields (dollars and cents) rather than one (cents), then by making the corresponding change to `inCents()`, clients of `Money` need not know the difference. Even if you change the method name to `getCents()`, which looks even more like it is directly exposing a field, remember that the method is merely a read-only property and that properties can be calculated on the fly, rather than simply representing the value of a field. The data remains hidden.

Pitfalls

Before leaving this topic, we would like to share examples of the kinds of tests we often see novice programmers write for constructors, which are either entirely unnecessary or testing the wrong thing, depending on your perspective.

Here is a common constructor "test":

```
public void testConstructorDoesNotAnswerNull() {
    assertNotNull(new Integer(762));
}
```

According to the Java language specification, a constructor always either creates an object in memory or throws an exception, so there is no way for a constructor to answer `null` except for the Java interpreter or compiler to fail. Other creation methods may choose to answer `null` to indicate that an object was not created, but we consider that to be unnecessarily confusing.

Here is another common constructor "test":

```
public void testConstructorAnswersRightType() {
    assertTrue(new Integer(762) instanceof Integer);
}
```

Also according to the Java language specification, if a constructor returns an object, it can only return an object of the class's type and nothing else. The only way in Java to achieve polymorphic construction of objects is through a factory method. For this reason, there is no need to verify the type of object answered by a constructor: the language guarantees its correctness.

The two preceding tests are examples of what is called *testing the platform.* The only way that those tests could fail would be if there were an error in the Java language itself. Unless you are writing tests for the Java language itself, you are wasting effort verifying behavior over which you have no control.[7] You have enough code to test, so *don't test the platform.*

◆ *Related*

- 2.4—Test a getter
- 2.5—Test a setter
- 2.7—Test a JavaBean
- 14.2—Test an Observable (Event Source)
- B.1—Too simple to break

---

[7] The only exception that comes to mind is a Learning Test, which helps you learn how third-party code works. See Kent Beck, *Test-Driven Development: By Example,* p. 136.

2.4 Test a getter

◆ Problem

You want to test an object's *get* methods, but many of the tests seem overly simple. You want to know which tests are needed and which are not.

◆ Background

People new to JUnit are often also new to Programmer Testing. Wide-eyed and enthusiastic, these people want to test *everything*. Because they are still learning how to write tests, they zoom in on the simplest parts of their applications to test, and few things are simpler than the vast majority of methods whose name starts with "get." This combination of enthusiasm and lack of experience leads the programmer to write many, many tests for these methods. This leads to an empty feeling: the feeling that not much is to be gained by all this testing. Perhaps this recipe can help.

The heuristic we describe for deciding whether to write a test for a *get* method follows a more general rule: do not test methods that are *too simple to break* (see the essay by the same name in appendix B). A method that only answers the value of a field can only break if the underlying Java compiler or interpreter does not work properly. No coding error (excluding typos) can cause a method such as the following not to work correctly:

```
public class Money {
    private int cents;

    // Code omitted for brevity

    public long inCents() {
        return cents;
    }
}
```

The method `inCents()` truly cannot break on its own. For this reason, we do not recommend going out of your way to write a test for it. Further, since this type of *get* method is *too simple to break*, it is commonly assumed to work and used to test constructors. See recipe 2.3, "Test a constructor," for details.

◆ Recipe

The rule of thumb is this: if the *get* method simply answers the value of a field, then consider not writing a test for it; however, if the method does anything more complex than that, consider writing the test. If you decide that the test is worth writing, then the test is simple: because a *get* method returns a value, compare that result with an expected result. We described how to write this kind of test in the introduction to this chapter.

If the *get* method in question does *any* kind of real work, then it certainly warrants a test. This kind of test uses the techniques described in the introduction to this chapter. Typically, you pass a parameter into the constructor and then verify that the get method calculates the appropriate value. We take this example from Dave Thomas and Andrew Hunt's *Programming Ruby* and adapt it to the Java language. The following constructor for the `Song` class accepts a song title, the name of the recording artist, and the duration of the song, measured in seconds:

```
package junit.cookbook.common.test;

import junit.cookbook.common.Song;
import junit.framework.TestCase;

public class SongTest extends TestCase {
    public void testDurationInMinutes() {
        Song song = new Song("Bicyclops", "Fleck", 260);
        assertEquals(4.333333d, song.getDurationInMinutes(),
            0.000001d);
    }
}
```

As we mentioned in chapter 1, "Fundamentals," when comparing floating-point numbers, you need to specify a tolerance level. In this case, we decided that a difference of one one-millionth of a minute is acceptable.

In this case, a song's duration (in seconds) is stored in a field and the duration in minutes is calculated. The parameter `260` passed in to the constructor represents the duration in seconds, and the method `getDurationInMinutes` calculates the duration in minutes. The authors recommend writing this test because the duration in minutes is calculated, based on the duration in seconds. Consider two different implementations of `Song` that could pass this test. The first is straightforward: the method `getDurationInMinutes()` performs the calculation on demand, as shown in listing 2.3.

Listing 2.3 `Song.getDurationInMinutes()`

```
package junit.cookbook.common;

public class Song {
    private String name;
    private String artistName;
    private int duration;
```

```
    public Song(String name, String artistName, int duration) {
        this.name = name;
        this.artistName = artistName;
        this.duration = duration;
    }

    public double getDurationInMinutes() {
        return (double) duration / 60.0d;
    }
}
```

Listing 2.4 shows an alternate implementation that passes the test.

Listing 2.4 An alternate implementation of `Song.getDurationInMinutes()`

```
package junit.cookbook.common;

public class Song {
    private String name;
    private String artistName;
    private int duration;
    private double durationInSeconds;

    public Song(String name, String artistName, int duration) {
        this.name = name;
        this.artistName = artistName;
        this.duration = duration;
        this.durationInSeconds = (double) duration / 60.0d;
    }

    public double getDurationInMinutes() {
        return durationInSeconds;
    }
}
```

This implementation calculates the duration in seconds within the constructor and stores that value for future use. This can be done as a performance optimization. In this case, although the *get* method is now *too simple to break*, you ought to keep the test, because now it verifies that the constructor performs the proper calculation. The test assumes that the *get* method works—and how could it not?—for testing the constructor. Either way, the test is useful.

◆ *Discussion*

In spite of the JUnit community's attempts to determine how simple something has to be before it is considered *too simple to break*, there continues to be a considerable difference of opinion as to which methods are complex enough to be tested. If you do not yet have an opinion on the matter, we suggest that you *write many tests.* Read all you want—including the rest of this book and a few other good ones, but if you do not write the tests, then you will not accumulate the observations you need to make an informed choice. If, at that point, you think we are crazy, then please let us know!

◆ ***Related***

- 2.3—Test a constructor
- B.1—Too simple to break

2.5 Test a setter

◆ ***Problem***

You want to test your *set* methods, but the tests you write look too simple to be valuable.

◆ ***Background***

A common question for novice JUnit users is, "Should I test my *set* methods?" This is also an unexpected source of disagreement within the JUnit users community. We strongly believe that basic *set* methods are *too simple to break*; however, if you are determined to test them, then it is important to understand effective ways to test them.

◆ ***Recipe***

The most common use of a *set* method is in a simple JavaBean. In this case, the bean is little more than a bag of data, wrapping a collection of fields exposed as read/write properties. In this case, there is a *get* method for each *set* method you want to test, making the implementation pattern as simple as this:

```
public void testSetProperty() {
    Bean bean = new Bean();
    bean.setProperty(newPropertyValue);
    assertEquals(newPropertyValue, bean.getProperty());
}
```

The code in italics changes from test to test: `Bean` is the class name of your JavaBean, and `Property` is the name of the property you want to test. Here is a description of this implementation pattern:

1 Name the test method appropriately: change `Property` to the name of the bean property whose `set` methods you are testing.
2 Create an instance of your bean class.
3 If `newPropertyValue` is a complex property, such as an indexed property or another JavaBean itself, then initialize `newPropertyValue` accordingly.
4 If `property` is a more complex object than a `String`, then you need to ensure that `equals()` is appropriately implemented for that property's class. See recipe 2.1, "Test your equals method," for details.

◆ Discussion

If you do not have the corresponding *get* method and prefer not to build it for the lone purpose of verifying the *set* method, then you need to identify an observable side effect of calling the *set* method and verify that side effect.

Another common use of *set* methods is the Command design pattern. If the command is submitted to a command interpreter for execution, then likely the command has a corresponding *get* method for each *set* method: otherwise, how can the command interpreter use the command's input parameters? If, on the other hand, the command follows the "action" pattern—providing its own `execute()` method—then the command can fully encapsulate its input parameters, leaving no direct way to verify that the *set* method behaves as expected. In this case, it is necessary to execute the command (or action, if you prefer the stricter terminology) and analyze the side effects of the execution to verify that the input parameter was set as expected.

Look at this example of a simple action class that performs a bank transfer. You can see the difficulties that arise when you try to test the *set* method of a well-encapsulated field:

```
package junit.cookbook.common;

import junit.cookbook.util.Bank;
import junit.cookbook.util.Money;

public class BankTransferAction {
    private String sourceAccountId;
    private String targetAccountId;
    private Money amount;

    public void setAmount(Money amount) {
        this.amount = amount;
    }
```

```
    public void setSourceAccountId(String sourceAccountId) {
        this.sourceAccountId = sourceAccountId;
    }

    public void setTargetAccountId(String targetAccountId) {
        this.targetAccountId = targetAccountId;
    }

    public void execute() {
        Bank bank = Bank.getInstance();
        bank.transfer(sourceAccountId, targetAccountId, amount);
    }
}
```

Although the implementation of this action is quite simple, we are forced to use the `execute()` method to test the behavior of the various `set` methods, because there is no other observable side effect at our disposal.

Notice that this action follows the strict implementation pattern of an `execute()` method that takes no parameters. Ordinarily, programmers follow this rule to allow for an `Action` superclass or interface that enforces the existence of the `execute()` method. Because the action is self-encapsulating and self-executing, it is not clear what design advantage is gained from enforcing this particular implementation pattern, but we prefer not to pass judgment on the people who think it's a good idea.[8] In order to write a test for this class, we would like to substitute our own `Bank` object and verify the parameters used to invoke its `transfer` method. The lone challenge to this approach is substituting a "spy" bank object in place of the one that the production code uses. Our choices include exposing a new `execute()` method that accepts a bank object as a parameter and exposing a `setInstance()` method on `Bank` allowing us to substitute bank objects at will. Neither option is particularly palatable. These unfortunate trade-offs tend to arise when using global data.[9] We show the results of the first option here, and leave implementing the second as an exercise for you.

First, listing 2.5 shows a more open action class.

---

[8] If you have not heard of "Grandma's Ham," read the book *Code Complete* by Steve McConnell, Microsoft Press, 1993, p. 43.

[9] A more thorough discussion of the testing difficulties that global data presents can be found in the online article "Use Your Singletons Wisely" (www-106.ibm.com/developerworks/webservices/library/co-single.html).

Listing 2.5 An easier-to-test BankTransferAction

```
package junit.cookbook.common;

import junit.cookbook.util.Bank;
import junit.cookbook.util.Money;

public class BankTransferAction {
    private String sourceAccountId;
    private String targetAccountId;
    private Money amount;

    public void setAmount(Money amount) {
        this.amount = amount;
    }

    public void setSourceAccountId(String sourceAccountId) {
        this.sourceAccountId = sourceAccountId;
    }

    public void setTargetAccountId(String targetAccountId) {
        this.targetAccountId = targetAccountId;
    }

    public void execute() {
        execute(Bank.getInstance());
    }

    public void execute(Bank bank) {
        bank.transfer(sourceAccountId, targetAccountId, amount);
    }
}
```

Next, listing 2.6 shows a test to verify the input parameters.

Listing 2.6 BankTransferActionTest

```
package junit.cookbook.common.test;

import junit.cookbook.common.BankTransferAction;
import junit.cookbook.util.Bank;
import junit.cookbook.util.Money;
import junit.framework.TestCase;

public class BankTransferActionTest extends TestCase {
    public void testSettingInputParameters() {
        BankTransferAction action = new BankTransferAction();
        action.setSourceAccountId("source");
        action.setTargetAccountId("target");
```

```
            action.setAmount(Money.dollars(100));
            action.execute(new Bank() {
                public void transfer(String sourceAccountId,
                                     String targetAccountId,
                                     Money amount) {
                    assertEquals("source", sourceAccountId);
                    assertEquals("target", targetAccountId);
                    assertEquals(Money.dollars(100), amount);
                }
            });
        }
    }
```

Suddenly the extra typing that writing the `get` methods requires is not so bad.

We have observed over time that the number of failing *set* methods and the resulting time spent trying to diagnose those failures is not nearly significant enough to warrant expending this amount of effort on testing them. Our recommendation is that you concentrate on testing those parts of your code that are much more likely to break. If failing *set* methods is the problem that hurts you the most, then relax, because your code is in far superior shape compared to the vast majority of other projects out there!

◆ *Related*

- 2.1—Test your equals method
- 2.4—Test a getter
- B.1—Too simple to break

2.6 *Test an interface*

◆ *Problem*

You want to test an interface, but there is no way to instantiate an interface. You want to test more than just all the current implementations; you want to test *all possible* implementations.

◆ *Background*

When publishing an interface, the intent is usually to enforce a certain common behavior among all implementations of that interface. This behavior must be common not only for all existing implementations, but also for any implementation that any programmer might ever write. You then need to write tests that capture the requirements of the common behavior (the interface) but allow future implementations to be tested against those same requirements without duplicating the underlying test code.

◆ *Recipe*

You should introduce an *abstract test case* whose methods test the intended common behavior and that uses factory methods to defer creating the object under test to the implementation's test case. Follow these steps:

1. Select one of the implementation's test cases.
2. Create a new `abstract` test case class that stores the tests for the intended behavior. Change the implementation's test case so that it extends the new abstract test case.
3. For each implementation test that verifies only interface-scope behavior, identify each place where an instance of the implementation is created.[10]
4. Inside the test, find the code that creates the object under test. Move this code into a separate creation method, but store the instantiated object in a reference to the *interface*, and not the *implementation*. Repeat until the test has no more direct references to the implementation by its class name.
5. Create an `abstract` method in the abstract test case for each creation method you extracted.
6. Now that the test refers only to the interface and other methods in the abstract test case, move the test up into the abstract test case.
7. Repeat until all such tests have been moved up into the abstract test case.
8. Repeat all the steps for each implementation test case until the only tests remaining in the implementation test cases verify implementation-specific behavior.

Next we'll illustrate this technique by testing the interface `java.util.Iterator`. We start with listing 2.7, which shows a concrete test for the `java.util.List` iterator.

---

[10] Interface-scope behavior only invokes methods on the interface and does not invoke any implementation-specific methods.

Listing 2.7 ListIteratorTest

```
package junit.cookbook.test;

import java.util.ArrayList;
import java.util.Iterator;
import java.util.List;
import java.util.NoSuchElementException;
import junit.framework.TestCase;

public class ListIteratorTest extends TestCase {
    private Iterator noMoreElementsIterator;

    protected void setUp() {
        List empty = new ArrayList();
        noMoreElementsIterator = empty.iterator();
    }

    public void testHasNextNoMoreElements() {
        assertFalse(noMoreElementsIterator.hasNext());
    }

    public void testNextNoMoreElements() {
        try {
            noMoreElementsIterator.next();
            fail("No exception with no elements remaining!");
        }
        catch (NoSuchElementException expected) {
        }
    }

    public void testRemoveNoMoreElements() {
        try {
            noMoreElementsIterator.remove();
            fail("No exception with no elements remaining!");
        }
          catch (IllegalStateException expected) {
        }
    }
}
```

See recipe 2.8, "Test throwing the right exception"

Next we introduce the abstract test case `IteratorTest` and move most of the concrete test case `ListIteratorTest` up into `IteratorTest`. The end result is the following new `IteratorTest`:

```
package junit.cookbook.test;

import java.util.Iterator;
import java.util.NoSuchElementException;
import junit.framework.TestCase;
```

```
public abstract class IteratorTest extends TestCase {
    private Iterator noMoreElementsIterator;

    protected abstract Iterator makeNoMoreElementsIterator();

    protected void setUp() {
        noMoreElementsIterator = makeNoMoreElementsIterator();
    }

    public void testHasNextNoMoreElements() {
        assertFalse(noMoreElementsIterator.hasNext());
    }

    public void testNextNoMoreElements() {
        try {
            noMoreElementsIterator.next();
            fail("No exception with no elements remaining!");
        }
        catch (NoSuchElementException expected) {
        }
    }

    public void testRemoveNoMoreElements() {
        try {
            noMoreElementsIterator.remove();
            fail("No exception with no elements remaining!");
        }
        catch (IllegalStateException expected) {
        }
    }
}
```

It turns out that we were able to move all the tests up into `IteratorTest` once we extracted the method `makeNoMoreElementsIterator()`. This method is the only thing we needed to leave behind in `ListIteratorTest`:

```
package junit.cookbook.test;

import java.util.ArrayList;
import java.util.Iterator;
import java.util.List;

public class ListIteratorTest extends IteratorTest {      <-- 1
    protected Iterator makeNoMoreElementsIterator() {     <-- 2
        List empty = new ArrayList();
        return empty.iterator();
    }
}
```

1 IteratorTest instead of TestCase

2 Return the appropriate type of iterator

❶ Rather than extend `junit.framework.TestCase` directly, `ListIteratorTest` now extends our abstract test case `IteratorTest`.

❷ The `ListIteratorTest` implementation of this creation method returns an iterator over an empty `List`. Similarly, if you were testing a `Set`-based iterator, you would create a `SetIteratorTest` (extending `IteratorTest`) whose `makeNoMoreElementsIterator()` would return an iterator over an empty `Set`.

◆ *Discussion*

The abstract test case works because of the way that test hierarchies behave in JUnit. A `TestCase` class inherits all tests from any `TestCase` subclass above it in the class hierarchy. In our case, `ListIteratorTest` inherits the tests from `IteratorTest`, so that the tests in `IteratorTest` are executed when we run `ListIteratorTest` in a test runner.

It is worth mentioning an observation by Eric Armstrong, a regular contributor to the JUnit Yahoo! group: "An interface defines syntax, but does not actually specify semantics, even though they are frequently implied. An accompanying test suite, on the other hand, *can* specify the semantics. We should require *every* public interface to be accompanied by a test suite!"[11] When publishing an interface or abstract class as part of a framework, it is a good idea to provide an Abstract Test Case to codify the essential expectations the framework puts on any client extension.

To that end, return to the Javadoc for the method `Iterator.remove()`, which you can find online. This method may throw two different exceptions: `IllegalStateException` to indicate that you are using the method incorrectly, and `UnsupportedOperationException` to indicate that this implementation of `Iterator` does not support removing elements. If you were implementing such an iterator, your tests for `remove()` would all expect an `UnsupportedOperationException`, rather than possibly an `IllegalStateException`. You could do even better. You could also add the method `supportsRemove()` to the Abstract Test Case, which returns `true` if the iterator implementation under test supports `remove()`, and `false` otherwise. (The concrete test implements the method, not the abstract test.) The expected behavior for `remove()` now depends on the return value of `supportsRemove()`, as shown in listing 2.8.

---

[11] Personal communication by e-mail.

Listing 2.8 A more complete IteratorTest

```
public abstract class MoreCompleteIteratorTest extends TestCase {
    // Other tests as in IteratorTest

    protected abstract boolean supportsRemove();    <-- Should the iterator under test support remove?

    public void testRemoveNoMoreElements() {
        try {
            noMoreElementsIterator.remove();
            if (supportsRemove()) {
                fail("No exception with no elements remaining!");
            } else {
                fail("No exception when attempting to remove!");
            }
        }
        catch (IllegalStateException expected1) {
            if (!supportsRemove()) {    <-- Not supposed to support remove!
                fail("Expecting UnsupportedOperationException on "
                        + "attempt to remove!");
            }
        }
        catch (UnsupportedOperationException expected2) {
            if (supportsRemove()) {    <-- Supposed to support remove!
                fail("Expecting IllegalStateException on attempt "
                        + "to remove!");
            }
        }
    }
}
```

This test more completely captures the contract of `Iterator`, as the Javadoc defines it.

Finally, you will have classes that implement multiple interfaces. We recommend testing each interface's contract separately, rather than sticking to the rule of "one test case class per production class."

◆ Related

- Design by Contract, as described by Bertrand Meyer and implemented in the Eiffel programming language (http://archive.eiffel.com/doc/manuals/technology/contract/page.html)
- Ward Cunningham's Wiki (http://c2.com/cgi/wiki?AbstractTestCases)

2.7 Test a JavaBean

◆ *Problem*

You want to test a JavaBean, but the tests you write seem to be both repetitive and brittle.

◆ *Background*

Because a JavaBean is little more than a collection of *get* and *set* methods, the tests that you write for your bean look like nothing more than a repetition of the code under test. This is decidedly not satisfying. If you feel this way about testing JavaBeans, then you're not alone.

◆ *Recipe*

In many ways, there is nothing special about testing a JavaBean:

- For a bean property that interacts directly with a field and performs no calculations, there is little to gain from testing the corresponding *get* and *set* methods. Don't waste your time testing them.
- For a calculated bean property, write simple tests to verify that the property is correctly calculated.
- For bean methods, there is typically nothing special to do; therefore, test each method as you would any other simple method.
- For bean event methods such as property change events, use the techniques found in recipe 14.2, "Test an Observable (Event Source)," treating the bean as an event source—because that is exactly what it is!

The one testing technique that applies well to JavaBeans is the *sanity check*. The JavaBean specification requires a no-argument constructor, whereas most beans have properties that require non-`null` values. This means that instances of your bean are virtually guaranteed *not* to be properly initialized just after the constructor finishes. We call such an object *insane*, because if you call any of its methods at this point, you have no idea what you're going to get.

To implement a sanity check for your JavaBean, introduce a method called `isValid()` whose responsibility is to verify that all required properties indeed have non-`null` values. Your tests use `isValid()` to communicate which properties are required and which are optional. As one reviewer pointed out, it would be nice if `java.util.Calendar` provided such a method!

In a simple JavaBean where writable properties map directly to fields on the class, it may seem unnecessary to write tests for the *set* methods, because they are *too simple to break.* Still, it is worthwhile to write tests such as the following for your JavaBeans. In this example, we test a Command object:

```
public void testBankTransferCommandIsValid() {
    BankTransferCommand command = new BankTransferCommand();

    command.setSourceAccountId("123-456A");
    command.setTargetAccountId("987-654B");
    command.setAmount(Money.dollars(1000));

    assertTrue(command.isReadyToExecute());
}
```

This test communicates something important to the programmer reading it: that if the programmer sets the source account ID, target account ID, and amount to transfer, then the command will be ready to execute. In this case, we have renamed `isValid()` to the more intention-revealing name of `isReadyToExecute()`. This test shows sufficient conditions for the bank transfer command to be ready to execute, or valid. For completeness, it is recommended to add tests such as the following:

```
public void testNeedsAmount() {
    BankTransferCommand command = new BankTransferCommand();

    command.setSourceAccountId("123-456A");
    command.setTargetAccountId("987-654B");
    // Do not set amount

    assertFalse(command.isReadyToExecute());
}
```

This test says that without providing the amount to transfer, the command will not be ready to execute. Although the comment is not strictly required, it clarifies which of the writable properties has not been set. Rarely are comments needed, because the code can almost always be written clearly enough to stand on its own; however, to indicate the *absence* of code requires something other than code.

◆ Discussion

When using this technique, you should provide one test per required property. Each verifies that without setting that property, the object is invalid. Because here all three properties are required, we would have four tests in total (one "positive" one and three "negative" ones).

This recipe describes what *not* to test as much as what to test. Whenever you encounter this kind of advice, keep in mind that you should test anything in which you do not already have confidence. We are only trying to save you some effort by recommending which tests you can skip, but if you feel you need them, then write them. Do not let our recommendations become rules, because they are only guidelines. Remember the underlying reason for these guidelines: test until fear turns to boredom. If you are worried about your JavaBean working, test everything until you are confident enough to test less. Eventually you will let your guard down, and a defect will creep in that your tests do not find. In this case, write more tests until your confidence returns. This cycle generally continues without end.

◆ Related

- 2.4—Test a getter
- 2.5—Test a setter
- 14.2—Test an Observable (Event Source)
- B.1—Too simple to break

2.8 Test throwing the right exception

◆ Problem

You want to verify that a method throws an expected exception under the appropriate circumstances. You may also be looking for "the simplest way" to write such a test.

◆ Background

To understand how to implement this kind of test, you need to know how JUnit decides whether a test passes or fails. A test fails (with either a failure or an error) if an assertion fails or it throws an exception; otherwise, the test passes. In other words, if a test *falls through*—meaning it executes from beginning to end without exiting from the middle—then it passes. This is enough to infer the way you ought to write this kind of test: it should fail if the offending line of code does not throw an exception; it should catch only the expected exception type; and it should throw any other exceptions up into the JUnit framework.

◆ *Recipe*

The following code demonstrates the implementation pattern for writing tests for throwing an exception:

```
public void testConstructorDiesWithNull() throws Exception {
    try {
        Fraction oneOverZero = new Fraction(1, 0);
        fail("Created fraction 1/0! That's undefined!");
    }
    catch (IllegalArgumentException expected) {
        assertEquals("denominator", expected.getMessage());
    }
}
```

Now that you have seen the pattern, we'll describe it here in more detail:

1. Identify the code that might throw the exception and place it in a `try` block.
2. After invoking the method that might throw an exception, place a `fail()` statement to indicate "If we got here, then the exception we expected was not thrown."
3. Add a `catch` block for the expected exception.
4. Inside the `catch` block for the expected exception, verify that the exception object's properties are the ones you expect, if desired.
5. Declare that the test method `throws Exception`. This makes the code more resistant to change. Someone may change the method under test so that it declares it might throw additional checked exceptions. That change likely does not affect your test, so it ought not to cause your test to stop compiling.

◆ *Discussion*

If the method under test throws an unexpected exception—something other than the exception for which you are testing—then JUnit reports an error, rather than a failure, because the test method throws that exception up into the JUnit framework. Recall that an error generally indicates a problem in the environment or with the test itself, rather than a problem in the production code. If the production code throws an unexpected exception, then indeed, perhaps there is some underlying problem that hinders the test's normal execution.

Returning to the example, note the name we use for the exception identifier: `expected`. This is important, as it is a clear message to the programmer that throwing this exception—or catching it, depending on your perspective—is a good thing. Because exceptions are used to model aberrant code execution paths, we're accustomed to seeing exceptions as a bad thing. This kind of test is an exception—pun intended.

In many cases, it is not necessary to make assertions about the expected (caught) exception. If asserting the correctness of the type of exception caught is sufficient to give you confidence in the correctness of the production code, then leave the exception handler empty. In this case, some programmers like to add a comment reading "Expected path." We feel that naming the exception object `expected` communicates that fact effectively without the need for a comment. This is a matter of personal taste, so do whatever works for you.

An alternative is to catch all exceptions that the method could possibly throw, adding a failure statement for each exception you do not expect. Often, when a programmer wants to do this, it is to report unexpected exceptions as failures, rather than as errors. We recommend against doing this for two simple reasons:

- Doing so requires extra code compared to simply throwing the unexpected exceptions up into the JUnit framework, and all things being equal, less code is easier to maintain.
- There is little to gain by reporting the unexpected exception as a failure. In many cases, you handle the two the same way. Some unexpected exceptions are production code problems and some are environment problems, and it is usually difficult to distinguish them without depending strongly on the underlying object's implementation details.

A more object-oriented approach

Just when it looked like there was no more to write on this subject, an esteemed member of the JUnit community, Ilja Preuß (IL-ya PROYSS), presented a more object-oriented option for this code:

```
public void testForException() {
    assertThrows(MyException.class, new ExceptionalClosure() {
        public Object execute(Object input) throws Exception {
            return doSomethingThatShouldThrowMyException();
        }
    });
}
```

Although some find Java's anonymous inner class syntax a little difficult to read, the method's intent could not be more clear: "Assert that this block of code throws that kind of exception." Implement the method `assertThrows()` as follows:

```
public static void assertThrows(
    Class expectedExceptionClass,
    ExceptionalClosure closure) {

    String expectedExceptionClassName
        = expectedExceptionClass.getName();

    try {
        closure.execute(null);
        fail(
            "Block did not throw an exception of type "
                + expectedExceptionClassName);
    }
    catch (Exception e) {     <-- Forced to do this
        assertTrue(
            "Caught exception of type <"
                + e.getClass().getName()
                + ">, expected one of type <"
                + expectedExceptionClassName
                + ">",     <-- Detailed failure message
            expectedExceptionClass.isInstance(e));     <-- Verify the caught exception class
    }
}
```

Rather than catching only the exception we expect, we need to catch them all, because we cannot know at compile time which exception class to expect. When making an assertion generic like this one, a good failure message is important, because you are removing control of the failure message from the invoker. The alternative is to add another parameter to `assertThrows()` that accepts a custom failure message. Finally, because we must catch all exceptions, we are forced to test the caught exception class against our expectation. The method `Class.isInstance(Object)` answers whether the parameter is an instance of the class. It is the same as using `instanceof`.

In addition to revealing intent, this approach avoids duplicating the exception-checking algorithm in hundreds of tests. That's quite an improvement!

You will notice the use of `ExceptionalClosure`, which requires some introduction. A *closure* is simply a wrapper for a block of code, as is directly supported in languages like Smalltalk and Ruby. Rather than reinvent the wheel, we usually use the `Closure` interface from the Jakarta Commons project (http://jakarta. apache. org) as often as we can. Unfortunately for this recipe, we cannot use it because its `execute()` method does not declare that it might throw a checked exception, so it can only throw an unchecked one—that is, a descendant of `RuntimeException`. To compensate for this deficiency, we added the interface `ExceptionalClosure` to Diasparsoft Toolkit, which does what `Closure` does, but whose `execute()` method might throw an exception.

Once you have implemented `assertThrows()` once, you can move it up into your own customized assertion superclass and use it whenever you want. See recipe 17.4, "Extract a custom assertion," for a discussion of customized assertions.

Watch your assertions

Be careful with your assertions about the exception you expect to throw: if you verify the exception object too closely, you may introduce overly strong coupling between the tests and the production code. The resulting test is more brittle than it needs to be.[12] Consider what happens if the exception message is meant to be displayed to an end user, and you write an assertion that checks that message directly. Typically, you will write a test that resembles the following:

```
public void testNameNotEntered() {
    try {
        login("", "password");
        fail("User logged in without a user name!");
    }
    catch (MissingEntryException expected) {
        assertEquals("userName", expected.getEntryName());
        assertEquals(
            "Please enter a user name and try again.",
            expected.getMessage());
    }
}
```

This test is clear: if a user attempts to log in without providing a user name, then login throws a `MissingEntryException` including both a name for the missing entry and a message suitable to present to the end user. This appears to be good cohesion: the exception object contains simplified exception data for you to use as well as a user-readable message. This looks like everything that the object could need.

While the first assertion in the `catch` block is a good idea, we have reservations about the second. Although the name `userName` is internal to the program and part of its behavior, the user-readable message could change at any time without affecting the way the login feature is implemented. In short, if `userName` changes, then the test likely needs to change; however, the test likely does *not* need to change in response to a change in the user-readable message. As the test is written now, a change to either requires a change in the test.

In this case, we recommend removing the second assertion and keeping the first. It is a general design goal to keep user-readable messages separate from the

---

[12] For example, you may rewrite `assertThrows()`, changing the "expected exception class" parameter to an "expected exception object" parameter, which is a stronger assertion—perhaps too strong.

internals of an object's behavior. You can always test an exception message by simply instantiating the exception and checking the return value of `toString()` or `getMessage()`. There is no need to actually *throw* the exception to test this aspect of the exception class's behavior.

◆ ***Related***

- 17.4—Extract a custom assertion
- Jeff Langr, *Essential Java Style: Patterns for Implementation*, Prentice Hall PTR, 1999
- Jakarta Commons project (http://jakarta.apache.org)

2.9 Let collections compare themselves

◆ ***Problem***

You want to verify the contents of a collection. Your first instinct is to check for the items you expect, one by one. You are wondering if there is an easier way.

◆ ***Background***

If you are new to JUnit, then it's also possible that you are also new to Java. We have seen this more recently, particularly as high schools, colleges, and universities begin using JUnit in their Introduction to Java courses. We think this is a positive development, as we firmly believe in learning a programming language by writing tests. In particular, some of the most elementary aspects of a new language can be strange: printing output to a console or executing the entry point of an application. Doing these things in Smalltalk or using the Microsoft Foundation Classes application framework is not straightforward at all, but the xUnit test runners are the same, whatever language you use.[13] If you are new to Java, then you may not be familiar with how to ask objects to compare themselves with one another, and so you may have concluded that item-by-item comparison is the only way to verify the contents of a collection. There is a simpler way.

◆ ***Recipe***

Build a collection from the items you expect—possibly in the order in which you expect them—and then compare that collection to the collection you get (from a method, most frequently) using `assertEquals()`. Let the corresponding implementation

[13] See www.xprogramming.com/software.htm for a list of languages and environments that have an implementation of the xUnit testing framework.

of `equals()` determine whether the collections are equal. We provide an example of this technique in the introduction to this chapter, so now to help you use this approach in your tests, we summarize the behavior of the `equals()` method for the various collection classes. See table 2.1.

Table 2.1 The behavior of `equals()` for each type of `Collection`

Kind of collection	Behavior of `equals()`
`List`	Two lists are "equal" if they contain the same elements, each at the corresponding index in the list. It does not matter whether the implementations of the `List` interface are the same. An `ArrayList` and a `LinkedList` that have these properties are equal.
`Set`	Two sets are "equal" if they contain the same elements. It does not matter whether the implementations of the `Set` interface are the same. A `HashSet` and `TreeSet` having this property are equal.
`Map`	Two maps are "equal" if their "key sets" are equal and each key maps to the same value in both maps. It does not matter whether the implementations of the `Map` interface are the same. A `HashMap` and a `TreeMap` having these properties are equal.
`Collection`	Two collections are "equal" if they are the same kind of collection (`List`, `Set`, `Map`) and are equal when treated as the corresponding kind of collection. A `List` is not equal to a `Set`, even if they contain the same elements.

It is a simple matter to compare collections then, as long as you compare collections "of the same kind." For sample code, refer to the introduction to this chapter, which includes examples of comparing `List` objects for equality using `assertEquals()`.

◆ *Discussion*

If you have two collections stored as `Lists`, but you'd like to compare them without regard to the order of their elements, then you have several options, depending on the nature of the `Lists`. If you know the `Lists` do not contain multiple copies of the same element, then simply convert the `Lists` to `Sets` and compare the resulting `Sets`. This is as simple as `assertEquals(new HashSet (expectedList), new HashSet(actualList))`.

If, however, the `Lists` might contain multiple copies of the same element, you need to be sure that the corresponding number of copies is the same for each element. You could build a custom assertion method yourself or use GSBase's `BaseTestCase`, which includes the method `assertCollectionsEqual()`. This method compares the two collections as though they were "unindexed" `Lists`: two collections are equal if they contain the same number of copies of the same elements, even if in a different order. GSBase effectively compares unordered views of the two collections. This method is invaluable, but if you prefer a more object-oriented approach, then you need a new collection that encapsulates an unordered view of a `List`.

We usually call this kind of collection a `Bag`. A `Bag` is a collection of elements that is unindexed but allows multiple copies of the same element. Some call this collection a `Multiset`. Two `Bags` are equal if they contain the same number of copies of the same elements, so the `equals()` method should be implemented to reflect this desired behavior. You could implement this collection class yourself or search for implementations of it on the Web. You can think of GSBase's `assertCollectionsEqual()` as the `equals()` method for an emerging `Bag` class or interface. Likely the only reason GSBase does not provide a full-on implementation of `Bag` is that its creator, Mike Bowler, has not yet needed one. If you do, then consider submitting a patch to GSBase—but be sure your patch is fully tested with JUnit!

◆ Related

- GSBase (http://gsbase.sourceforge.net)

2.10 Test a big object for equality

◆ Problem

You have a Value Object with many (say more than six) key properties.[14] You have tried writing a test with `EqualsTester` or `EqualsHashCodeTestCase`, but that test seems inadequate.

◆ Background

GSBase's `EqualsTester` (see recipe 2.1, "Test your equals method") takes four parameters: two objects that ought to be different (not the same object) but equal, a third object that ought not to be equal to the first, and a fourth object—a subclass of the first object's class—that also ought not to be equal to the first. While this is effective for most business purposes, you may need a more thorough test, with $n+3$ objects: two that are equal, n that are different from those two and the last one which is a subclass. Here, n is the number of key properties in your

[14] By *key properties* we mean those properties of a Value Object for which different values mean the objects are no longer equal. The concept is analogous to the object's primary key if it were a row in a database.

Value Object class. The `EqualsHashCodeTestCase` found in JUnit-addons suffers the same problem, because it only operates on two unequal instances of your Value Object class.

◆ *Recipe*

It sounds like we need to generalize the equals testing concept to operate on an arbitrary collection of objects that ought not to be equal from the "control object." To that end we have added this testing utility to Diasparsoft Toolkit under the name `ValueObjectEqualsTest`. The central algorithm has been shamelessly taken from JUnit-addons, with permission of course, and generalized to check each different way that a Value Object can be different from another. First, let us look at how to use `ValueObjectEqualsTest`. You can find an example—albeit a stultifyingly abstract and meaningless one[15]—in listing 2.9. After you subclass `ValueObjectEqualsTest`, you implement three methods.

Listing 2.9 Using `ValueObjectEqualsTest` with five key properties

```
package com.diasparsoftware.java.lang.test;

import java.util.*;

import com.diasparsoftware.util.junit.ValueObjectEqualsTest;

public class ValueObjectEqualsTestFivePropertiesTest
    extends ValueObjectEqualsTest {

    protected List keyPropertyNames() {      <-- The names of the key properties
        return Arrays.asList(
            new String[] { "key1", "key2", "key3", "key4", "key5" });
    }

    protected Object createControlInstance() throws Exception {
        return new FiveKeys(1, 2, 3, 4, 5);
    }

    protected Object createInstanceDiffersIn(String keyPropertyName)
        throws Exception {      <-- Each object is different from the control in the value of that key property

        if ("key1".equals(keyPropertyName))
            return new FiveKeys(6, 2, 3, 4, 5);
        else if ("key2".equals(keyPropertyName))
            return new FiveKeys(1, 6, 3, 4, 5);
        else if ("key3".equals(keyPropertyName))
            return new FiveKeys(1, 2, 6, 4, 5);
```

---

15 Sorry about that.

```
        else if ("key4".equals(keyPropertyName))
            return new FiveKeys(1, 2, 3, 6, 5);
        else if ("key5".equals(keyPropertyName))
            return new FiveKeys(1, 2, 3, 4, 6);

        return null;
    }
}
```

Each value object is defined by a set of *key properties*, the properties that make two instances of the value object unequal. It is common for all the properties of a value object to be its key properties, but it is not necessary. To provide the equals test with the names of those properties, implement `keyPropertyNames()`, to return a list of the key property names. The order in which you return them is not important. We arbitrarily decided to return them in alphabetical order.

Just like `EqualsHashCodeTestCase`, you need to define a "control" instance: the object against which the others will be compared for equality. Implement `createControlInstance()` to return a new object each time. Which object you decide to return is arbitrary, but that choice dictates how you implement the remaining required method. We chose the sample values 1, 2, 3, 4, and 5 for our control object.

Just like `EqualsHashCodeTestCase`, you need to implement the last method to return objects that are different from the control object. When you implement `createInstanceDiffersBy(String keyPropertyName)`, you must return an object that differs from the control object *in the specified key property*. In our example, when the test asks for an instance that differs in the `key1` property, we return the values 6, 2, 3, 4, 5, where the first key (`key1`, get it?) is different from the first key of the control object. From there, we imagine you see the pattern.

◆ Discussion

If you want your equals test to verify more than just a few simple cases, you can build a Parameterized Test Case (see recipe 4.8, "Build a data-driven test suite") from scratch, in which each test accepts three parameters: two objects and a `boolean` flag to indicate whether the parameters ought to be equal. The resulting test defines `equals()` using the technique known as *specification by example*. You specify how `equals()` ought to behave purely through examples: each saying, "This object and that object should be equal, but *this* object and *that* object over there should *not* be equal." If you provide enough examples, you eventually arrive at a point where only a few sensible implementations of `equals()` work, of which any one is likely suitable. Any time the `equals()` method returns the wrong value, you can determine which objects uncovered the defect and add them to the test to prevent those problems from recurring.

◆ Related

- 2.1—Test your equals method
- 4.8—Build a data-driven test suite

2.11 Test an object that instantiates other objects

◆ Problem

You want to test an object in isolation, but it instantiates other objects that make testing difficult or expensive.

◆ Background

There are opposing forces in object-oriented design. We use *aggregation* to express the notion that an object *owns* another object to which it refers, much the way a car owns its wheels. On the other hand, to test an object in isolation, we need to be able to piece objects together like a jigsaw puzzle. This means that tests prefer objects that use composition more than aggregation. If the object you want to test instantiates other objects, then it is difficult to test the larger object without relying on the correctness of the smaller object, and that violates the principle of testing objects in isolation.

We find it unfortunate that a majority of programmers remain in the dark about the power of extensive Programmer Testing. One side effect of this trend is an overuse of aggregation. Designs are replete with objects that instantiate other objects or retrieve objects from globally accessible locations. These programming practices, when left unchecked, lead to highly coupled designs that are difficult to test. We know: we have inherited them and even built some of them ourselves. This recipe introduces one of the fundamental testing techniques leading to a small design improvement, making it possible to test an object in isolation.

◆ Recipe

To deal with this problem, you need to pass the object under test an alternate implementation of the object it plans to instantiate. This creates two small problems that you need to solve:

- How do you create an alternate implementation of this object's collaborator?
- How do you pass it in to the object?

To simplify the discussion, we will use the term *Test Object* (not to be confused with Object Test—sorry about that) to refer to an alternate implementation of a class or interface that you use for testing. There are a number of different kinds of Test Objects: fakes, stubs, and mocks, and we discuss the differences in the essay "The mock objects landscape" in appendix B.

Creating a Test Object out of an *interface* is simple: just create a new class and implement the interface the simplest way you can, and you have finished. This is the simplest kind of Test Object. We use EasyMock (www.easymock.org/) throughout this book to generate Test Objects for interfaces.[16] We use this package both because it eliminates some repetitive work and because it adds some consistency and uniformity to the way we *fake out* interfaces. This makes our tests easier to understand—at least to programmers familiar with EasyMock! You can find numerous examples of using EasyMock to create Test Objects out of the J2EE interfaces in part 2.

Creating a Test Object out of a *class* can be as simple as creating a subclass and then either faking out or stubbing out all its methods.[17] A fake method returns some predictable, meaningful, hard-coded value, whereas a stub method does nothing meaningful—only what is required to compile. You may find it advantageous to extract an interface [Refactoring, 341] and change the class under test so that it refers to its collaborator through an interface, rather than the class. This allows you to use EasyMock as we described previously. Beyond that, the more your classes collaborate with one another through interfaces, the more flexible (and testable!) your design.

As for the second part of the problem, there are essentially two ways to pass your Test Object into the object under test: either augment the constructor or add a setter method. We recommend passing Test Objects into the constructor simply to avoid the extra complexity of having to invoke the setter method in the test. To illustrate this technique, take the example from J. B.'s article "Use Your Singletons Wisely."[18] In it, a `Deployment` uses a `Deployer` to deploy something to a file. In the

[16] Had we written this chapter a few months later, we would have been using jMock (http://jmock.codehaus.org/), but that is the risk you take when writing a book.

[17] Again, jMock makes this easier using CGLib (http://cglib.sourceforge.net/). Through bytecode manipulation, you can fake concrete classes as easily as interfaces.

[18] www-106.ibm.com/developerworks/webservices/library/co-single.html.

example, there only needs to be one Deployer, so it is easily designed as a Singleton. (See recipe 14.3, "Test a Singleton," for more on testing and Singletons.) The method Deployment.deploy(), then, looks as follows:

```
public class Deployment {
    public void deploy(File targetFile) throws FileNotFoundException {
        Deployer.getInstance().deploy(this, targetFile);
    }
}
```

Notice that Deployment uses the class-level method Deployer.getInstance() to obtain its Deployer. If you want to fake out the Deployer, you need to pass a Deployer into Deployment somehow. We recommend passing it in through a constructor, so we add a constructor and instance variable to store the Deployer:

```
public class Deployment {
    private Deployer deployer;

    public Deployment(Deployer deployer) {
        this.deployer = deployer;
    }

    public void deploy(File targetFile) throws FileNotFoundException {
        deployer.deploy(this, targetFile);
    }
}
```

But wait! Where did Deployer.getInstance() go? We cannot just lose this bit of code: now that we have removed the no-argument constructor, we need to add a new one and have it supply the Singleton Deployer by default:

```
public class Deployment {
    private Deployer deployer;

    public Deployment() {
        this(Deployer.getInstance());
    }

    public Deployment(Deployer deployer) {
        this.deployer = deployer;
    }

    public void deploy(File targetFile) {
        deployer.deploy(this, targetFile);
    }
}
```

Now when the production code creates a Deployment using the no-argument constructor, it will see the behavior it has come to expect: the Deployment will use the Singleton Deployer. Our tests, however, can substitute a fake Deployer in order to do things such as simulate what happens if the target deployment file does not exist. Here is the code for a "crash test dummy" `Deployer`—one that always signals that the target file does not exist:

```
public class FileNotFoundDeployer extends Deployer {
    public void deploy(Deployment deployment, File targetFile)
        throws FileNotFoundException {

        throw new FileNotFoundException(targetFile.getPath());
    }
}
```

Now we can test how our `Deployment` class behaves when the `Deployer` fails to deploy because the target file was not found. We use the technique in recipe 2.8, "Test throwing the right exception":

```
public void testTargetFileNotFound() throws Exception {
    Deployer fileNotFoundDeployer = new FileNotFoundDeployer();
    Deployment deployment = new Deployment(fileNotFoundDeployer);

    try {
        deployment.deploy(new File("hello"));
        fail("Found target file?!");
    }
    catch (FileNotFoundException expected) {
        assertEquals("hello", expected.getMessage());
    }
}
```

This test shows how to substitute a Test Object in place of an object's collaborator, as well as how to create a Test Object by subclassing the production class. We effectively make the collaborator an optional parameter to the constructor: if we do not provide one, then the class provides a sensible default implementation. We use this technique and variations of it throughout the book and indeed throughout our work.

◆ Discussion

We have used a Test Object to *simulate* not being able to find the target file, rather than *re-creating* that scenario, which would involve trying to deploy to a real nonexistent file on the file system. We strongly recommend simulating these conditions, because re-creating them can be prone to error. What happens if you specify a Windows filename for your nonexistent file, and then someone executes the test on a UNIX machine? On the UNIX file system, your Windows filename may not even be a valid filename. Worse, what if you happen to choose a "nonexistent" filename that matches a file residing on someone's machine? You *could* use JVM properties to look for the machine's temporary directory, but all in all it is simpler to simulate the error condition than re-create it.

Faking out class-level and global data and methods is difficult, because you cannot override a class-level method by subclassing; *and* even if you could, code that uses a class-level method hard-codes the name of the class, defeating your attempt to substitute behavior through subclassing. There is considerable discussion in the JUnit and Test-Driven Development communities regarding the use of class-level methods and how to overcome their use in creating testable designs. The consensus is that it is best to minimize the use of class-level methods by moving them into new classes and making them instance level, at least when it makes sense. There are several coping strategies, including hiding class-level methods behind a facade that makes these methods look like they are instance level. These all require considerable and mechanical refactoring, generally done without the safety net of tests! Fortunately, Chad Woolley has begun building a toolkit that uses aspects to make it possible to fake out even class-level methods.[19]

His toolkit, named Virtual Mock (www.virtualmock.org/), promises to provide an easier way to build the refactoring safety net that you need to repair highly coupled designs—particularly those that make heavy use of class-level methods and data. Although still in the alpha stage as we write these words, Chad's work is exciting, and we recommend that you add Virtual Mock to your arsenal for the next time you inherit such a design. That said, we strongly recommend using Virtual Mock objects to install a safety net for refactoring; do not use it to cover up the bad *smells* in your design, but rather let it enable you to start cleaning it up.[20]

◆ Related

- 2.8—Test throwing the right exception
- 14.3—Test a Singleton
- B.4—The mock objects landscape
- The Virtual Mock project (www.virtualmock.org)

---

[19] www.parc.xerox.com/aop.

[20] Martin Fowler popularized the use of the term *smell* for something about a program that we don't like. We now commonly say that code smells, or design smells, or the process smells, to indicate that something is not quite right.

3 Organizing and building JUnit tests

This chapter covers

- Deciding where to place production code and test code
- Dealing with duplicate test code
- Organizing special case tests
- Building tests in various development environments

Once you understand the fundamentals of writing JUnit tests, the next step is to begin writing them. Once you open your favorite Java editor and begin writing test code, you need to decide into which package you should place the test code. Although this decision seems simple enough, there is a considerable difference between placing your test code in the same package as your production code[1] or in a different package. For that reason, we offer a few recipes to help you decide which to do.

After deciding on a package for your tests, you can only type two words (`public class`) before you come to the class name of your new test. At this point you need to decide how to organize your tests into test case classes. Many tutorials on JUnit suggest writing one `TestCase` class per production class; however, those authors generally mean that to be a simple guideline for programmers just starting out. As you write your tests, the names you choose can tell you when it may be time to move tests into a new fixture. We provide a few recipes that describe when to reorganize your test code.

In order to execute your new test, you need to save your new source file. You need to decide whether to separate your test source code from your production source code. Some programming environments support multiple source trees quite easily, others do not. We offer some recipes that suggest how to keep from mixing up your tests and your production code.

Before you can execute your test, you need to build the new test class, which brings into question how to organize your build tree. You may need or want to keep your tests entirely separated from your production code, or you may decide to distribute your tests. To help you decide, we offer some recipes that describe each, including when each choice might be particularly desirable.

A place to start

Before diving into the recipes in this chapter, let us review the simplest and most straightforward way to organize your tests. When you are ready to start writing tests, begin by creating a new test case class that corresponds to the class you plan to test. This guideline applies both to existing production classes and to production classes you are "test driving." Following our previous advice for naming test case classes (see chapter 1, "Fundamentals"), add `Test` to the end of the production class name to get your test case class name. Continuing with our example,

---

[1] We will use the terms *production code* and *test code* to differentiate the code that implements your system from the code that tests your system.

you place your first tests for the `Money` class in a new test case class named `MoneyTest`. To simplify things further, place this test alongside class `Money`, in the same package and in the same source code directory.

The simplest way to start is to write each test for `Money` as a method in `MoneyTest`. If your first test verifies that the default constructor sets the underlying `Money` value to $0.00, then you should have something that resembles listing 3.1.

Listing 3.1 Simple `Money` test

```
package junit.cookbook.organizing;

import junit.framework.TestCase;

public class MoneyTest extends TestCase {
    public void testDefaultAmount() {
        Money defaultMoney = new Money();
        assertEquals(0, defaultMoney.inCents());
    }
}
```

As you think of more tests for `Money`, write each one as a new method in `MoneyTest`. Remember to name your methods starting with "test" so that the JUnit test runners automatically execute them. Eventually you will find that a number of tests use the same objects—that is, objects initialized to the same state. When you see this begin to happen, you may end up with duplicated code within your tests. We recommend removing that duplication by creating a *test fixture* (see recipe 3.4, "Factor out a test fixture"). As you build up fixtures inside your `TestCase` class, you may find that certain tests use one part of the fixture and other tests use another part of the fixture. This may signal the need to separate your tests into different `TestCase` classes. Over time, the new test fixtures begin to arrange themselves—as if by magic—into a `TestCase` hierarchy. See recipe 3.5, "Factor out a test fixture hierarchy," for details on how to factor out the common parts of existing test fixtures into a kind of "superfixture." At some point, you may decide that you need to separate the test source code from the production source code, either to simplify distributing your application or even just to keep the tests from "muddling up" your production code. See recipe 3.2, "Create a separate source tree for test code," for details.

The recipes in this chapter help you organize and build your tests effectively, using best practices acquired over the years through hard experience. We cannot cover all possible—or even feasible—approaches, but we have shared what has worked well for us.

3.1 Place test classes in the same package as production code

◆ Problem

You either do not wish to, or cannot, place test classes in a separate package from the production code under test.

◆ Background

Many Test-Driven Development practitioners prefer to place their test classes in a separate package from their production code, as this practice tends to improve the production system's design over time. We like this practice, and this is our default mode of operation. This is easy enough to do when writing tests for code not yet written, but less so when writing tests for existing code.

We are not often fortunate enough to work on *greenfield* projects where we are building new components or systems from the ground up. For the most part, we are called in to either add features to or fix systems already in production, and in spite of JUnit's increasing popularity, it remains less common to join a project that uses JUnit than it is to join a project *not* using JUnit.[2] If you have inherited code with inadequate tests and your job is to add those tests, then you may not be able to place your test classes where you like.

The majority of systems in production are not designed to be easy to test. We don't mean that the programmers intentionally made testing difficult—although in some cases that wouldn't surprise us—but that most programmers are not aware of the need to design testable systems. There are a number of reasons why this is so, and contrary to what some might believe, programmer incompetence is low on the list.[3] A programmer can easily execute "tests" by hand using breakpoints, the debugger, and her eyes. If you are reading this book, then you obviously want to go beyond this primitive form of testing and are beginning to write tests for your inherited code using JUnit. Pretty soon, if you haven't done so already, you will attempt to write an assertion and realize that you have no way to talk to the object that knows whether your assertion passes or fails. Something has to give.

---

[2] When the day comes that this statement is no longer true, we hope someone lets us know, in case we miss it. We may well have lost some of our mental faculties by then, but we hold out hope.

[3] Although we prefer not to offend anyone, we tactfully point out that lack of focus on testing is the number one reason why programmers build difficult-to-test systems. That focus generally needs to come "from above."

◆ *Recipe*

When you write a test class, simply place it in the same package as the production code you plan to test. Your test will have access to all but the private parts of the production class's interface, allowing you to write tests for behavior that would otherwise remain hidden from you.

◆ *Discussion*

We prefer not to place test classes in the same package as the code they test, because the resulting tests tend to be brittle. That is, small changes in the production code affect an unexpectedly large number of tests. In particular, *purely structural* changes to the production code can lead to changes in the tests, even though the simplest tests to write are the ones that depend only on the observable behavior of the code under test! Purely structural changes include the following:

- Renaming a method that client classes use indirectly by calling other methods (the method being renamed has protected or package-level visibility)
- Changing the method signature (parameters, return type) of such an indirectly called method
- Extracting a number of indirectly called methods into a new "helper" class

In many cases, we choose to perform these refactorings to improve the code. Renaming the method may better reveal its intent or, at a minimum, replace a nonsensical or abbreviated name with a name programmers can more easily understand. Changing the method signature may remove unnecessary parameters or replace difficult-to-understand parameters—such as `boolean` flags[4]—with more easily understood parameters (such as symbolic constants). Extracting a number of methods into a new class generally simplifies any design by reducing the number of responsibilities per class, a technique we use to simplify naming certain tests, as you will see in recipe 3.4. Tests that impede refactoring increase costs in a number of ways:

- You waste time performing the current refactoring.
- Your annoyance at the current refactoring discourages you from performing future refactorings.
- "Ugly" code leads to "ugly" tests.

---

[4] In Java, C, or Ruby, where parameters are matched by their position in the parameter list, it is impossible to understand from the call site what `getTreeCellRendererComponent(myJTree, aValue, true, false, true, 0, false)` means!

Although the first problem is evident, the second is subtler and potentially more damaging. The goal of refactoring is to improve the system's design incrementally over time to reduce future costs. Refactoring does this by adding features, fixing defects, and training others to navigate the code. Refactoring the design incrementally on an ongoing basis tends to go against human nature. This slow, methodical refactoring requires a certain level of discipline that not all of us have (or, at the very least, not all of us can maintain over time), so you need to avoid any situation that encourages you to abandon your discipline. Brittle, overly dependent tests are an excellent way to discourage ongoing refactoring, so any practice that naturally leads to brittle tests is to be used with caution. This is why we strongly recommend placing tests in a separate package from the production code (see recipe 3.3 for details). If you decide to place your test code in the same package as your production code, then consider whether to move the test source code into a separate directory structure, as this provides some of the benefits of a separate test package. We cover this technique in recipe 3.2.

The last problem is perhaps the worst, as it is a positive feedback loop of negative feelings. Poorly factored code is difficult to test. The tests we *do* write for such code are usually poorly factored themselves. Both the production code and the test code are brittle, difficult to read, and costly to maintain. If you just keep adding production code and test code without refactoring any of it, then both become progressively worse, taking more and more time and effort to develop. Eventually, usually sooner than you realize, the most cost-effective strategy is to stop trying, rip it all out, and start over. It is better to deal with the problem now, while it is fresh in your mind, than later when you are under more pressure and have forgotten what to do. Any small technique that can help you avoid this situation is worth trying.

Although we recommend against it, we recognize the reasons why you may need to place tests in the same package as the production code. One particular situation involves wanting to test a `protected` method before making it `public`. In this case, we recommend that you use this as a starting point from which you slowly refactor the production code to allow *all* your tests to compile using only the production code's collective `public` interface. If you undertake this task, get some coffee, grab your copy of *Refactoring*, and, above all, *take your time*. It's not easy, but it's usually worth it, even if you only refactor a little at a time.

◆ *Related*

- 3.2—Create a separate source tree for test code
- 3.3—Separate test packages from production code packages
- 3.4—Factor out a test fixture

3.2 Create a separate source tree for test code

◆ Problem

You want to be able to easily distribute your production code separately from your test code. You would also prefer not to confuse yourself or others by mixing up test code with production code.

◆ Background

Although we wish that programmers would ship their test code, it is still the norm to distribute production code without the corresponding tests. For good or for ill, more projects operate this way, either by choice or by corporate decree. You have decided that you need your test classes to be built to a separate part of the file system from your production classes. If you have tried targeting two build trees from the same source tree, then you know that it is at best confusing and at worst impossible to comprehend. If you have not tried to do it, then save yourself some brain cells: read this recipe rather than trying it yourself.

◆ Recipe

Choose two different parts of your file system: one for your production source code and another for your test source code. Also choose two different parts of the file system as build targets for each source tree. One common way to do this is to have two different directories inside your *workspace* (the part of the file system to which you check out the project on which you're working).[5] Although the names vary from project to project, here are the basic steps:

1. Create directories called source/production for the production source code and source/test for the test source code.
2. Configure your build mechanism (Ant, simple script, whatever you have) to build the directory source/production into a directory called classes/production and the directory source/test into a directory called classes/test.
3. When running your tests, you need both classes/production and classes/test in your test runner's class path; however, when running the system itself, ignore the test classes directory.
4. When distributing your production code, simply package the directory classes/production, along with whatever accompanying documentation you might provide.

---

[5] You are using a version control system such as CVS, right?

Organizing your source code this way makes it very easy to ignore the tests—both source and classes—whenever you need to distribute the production code. Even so, to bundle the tests along with the production code, simply package an extra directory structure. You have the flexibility of choosing either one without incurring much cost at all. Although you may make your project build slightly more complex, it is still quite manageable. See the rest of this chapter for other recommendations when building your tests.

◆ *Discussion*

You may wonder what *tangible* benefits there are to gain from adding a layer of complexity to your development environment. We can think of two, although there are others. Project managers may be interested in monitoring the ratio of test code to production code to identify whether the team is roughly writing the proper amount of programmer test code. The "sweet spot" tends to be in the neighborhood of 1:1, although in some cases 5:4 (five lines of test code for four lines of production code) is appropriate. Less test code means the team has a false sense of security about the degree to which the tests provide a refactoring safety net. More test code may indicate that the team is spending too much effort writing tests, although this is often a good problem to have.[6] In addition to making it easier for project managers to count test code separately from production code, it is easier for those installing the product to decide whether to remove the tests from their installation. Imagine that you could install the product with its tests, execute those tests on the target platform to verify the installation, and then remove or archive the tests to save disk space. That would be nice for your customers. You gain these benefits and more, just from separating test source code from production source code during development. It sounds like a good trade-off to us!

It is increasingly common to see projects using full-featured Java IDEs rather than the command line and a trusty text editor such as jEdit (www.jedit.org). Since the open source Eclipse project became established, it is now possible to obtain an excellent Java IDE without paying for licenses, making it easier for programmers to manage their project resources. The majority of these IDEs organize resources into *projects* consisting of a directory containing source files, built classes, documents—whatever resources you need to write, build, and distribute code. It is natural, then, to place tests in their own projects to keep them separate from their production

[6] The more experienced the team is with programmer testing, the more you ought to pay attention to writing "too much" test code—it could be a sign that the team is stalling, unsure which features to implement. They might need extra direction, including more customer tests.

code. (But not *too* far away. The further away the tests are, the more easily people will forget they are there!)

If you are (or plan to become) a practitioner of Test-Driven Development, you will write a number of different kinds of tests for your production code: Object Tests, Integration Tests, Customer Tests, End-to-End Tests, Database Tests, and so on. Create a different project in your IDE for each kind of test you plan to write. Name each test project after both the name of the project containing the code under test and the kind of test you plan to put into the project. For an online banking application, you might have Online Banking Model Programmer Tests and Online Banking Customer Tests, among others. This further separation makes it easier to run certain subsets of your tests, particularly for the End-to-End Tests that tend to run more slowly than your Programmer Tests. Using the IDE to divide code into projects provides a natural and simple way to separate test code from production code. See recipe 4.6, "Separate the different kinds of test suites."

◆ *Related*

- 3.1—Place test classes in the same package as production code
- 3.3—Separate test packages from production code packages
- 4.6—Separate the different kinds of test suites

3.3 *Separate test packages from production code packages*

◆ *Problem*

You do not want your tests to have intimate knowledge of the classes under test. You find it difficult to navigate your source tree because the production classes are interspersed with test classes.

◆ *Background*

The easiest way to organize your tests is to place them directly alongside your production code, in the same package and source tree. If you do this, all the code you need to compile is in one directory structure, simplifying your build process. Taking this approach also ensures that you build your tests at the same time that you build your production code, avoiding an entire set of problems. This seems fine until you begin (or someone else working on the same project begins) to write tests that "know too much" about the implementation of the code they are meant to test. This trap is easy to fall into, because the compiler does not complain when you do this. You have this problem if, as you refactor the production code, you find yourself continually changing these tests, even in response to purely internal changes upon which no other class should depend. This is not only a waste of time but also a source of frustration, and it flies in the face of the object-oriented principle of encapsulation. You need a way to improve the situation so that the tests do not have too much access to the production code.

◆ *Recipe*

We recommend placing your tests in a different package than the production code under test. This way, the compiler detects any attempt by the tests to use the non-`public` parts of the classes under test, forcing the tests to use only those parts of the production code intended to be exposed to the outside world.

Placing your tests in a separate package from the production code creates a *test package hierarchy*. This hierarchy should mimic your production code package hierarchy: create one test package for each production code package so that the test package tree has the same shape as the production code package tree.

Assuming you apply this technique, the last details to consider are how to name your test packages and where to place them. There are two prevailing conventions:

- For each production code package, add the subpackage `test` to the end of the production code package name to get the name of the corresponding test package. To test the Java collections framework, you create a test package named `java.util.test`.
- Create a top-level package named `test`, and then place all test packages inside this top-level package, with each test package otherwise named the same as the corresponding production code package. To test the Java I/O libraries, you create a test package named `test.java.io`.

As with most naming conventions, it matters little which you choose, so long as everyone on the project applies it consistently.

◆ *Discussion*

It is interesting to see what happens when you place your tests in a different package than your production code. As a result, your tests are forced to use the code under test through its `public` methods. The jury is still out whether using “outsider” tests leads to better or worse designs—there are arguments to support each point of view—but there is one simple argument in its favor. When you test code only through `public` methods, the tests better reflect the way that clients use that code, which helps identify significant design problems—ones that will actually affect the way others use the code.[7]

As you begin testing behavior, rather than methods, your design will tend to show certain characteristics. In particular, there will be a `public` method for each operation, representing an "entry point" for exercising the behavior. For a collection, these operations include `add()` and `remove()`. Behind this `public` method there may be non-`public` methods that the former invokes to help do its work. For a collection, these "helpers" may include resizing a dynamically sized collection when the underlying data structure runs out of space. This is part of the `add()` behavior but not necessarily a method you expect the outside world to invoke. Typically, you extract blocks of code and place them in `private` methods. There will come a time during the testing of a complex bit of behavior that you will want to test one of those `private` methods on its own.

If you want to write a test for that `private` method, the design may be telling you that the method does something more interesting than merely helping out the rest of that class's `public` interface. Whatever that helper method does, it is complex enough to warrant its own test, so perhaps what you really have is a method that belongs on another class—a collaborator of the first. If you extract the smaller class from the larger one, the helper method you want to test becomes part of the newly extracted class's `public` interface, so it is now "out in the open" and visible to the test you are trying to write. Moreover, by applying this refactoring, you have taken a class that had (at least) two independent responsibilities and split it into two classes, each with its own responsibility. This supports the Single Responsibility Principle of object-oriented programming, as Bob Martin describes it.[8] You can conclude that having tests in a separate package helps separate responsibilities effectively, improving the production system's design.

On the other hand, it may be necessary to add methods to a class's `public` interface just for testing. Consider a class that acts as an event source. The typical Java event/listener design implies that an event source has methods for registering and deregistering listeners, usually called `addBlahListener()` and `removeBlahListener()`, where `Blah` is the kind of event this event source generates. Typically there is no way to query the event source for its event listeners, because only the event source needs to know who might be listening for its events. In spite of this, you may want to write a test that verifies that `addBlahListener()` correctly adds the `BlahListener`.

---

7 Thanks to Roger Cornejo for reminding us of this simple but salient point.

8 Robert C. Martin, *Agile Software Development, Principles, Patterns, and Practices*. Prentice-Hall, 2002.

At this point you have two options:

- Your test adds the listener and then asks the event source, "Do you have the listener I just added?"
- Your test adds a Spy listener, asks the event source to generate an event, and then verifies that your Spy listener "heard" the event.

Certainly the second option is much more complex than the first, a design trade-off we discuss in recipe 14.5, "Test an Object Factory." The first option, however, requires adding a method such as `containsBlahListener()` that answers the question, "Do you have this listener?" If your test were in the same package as the event source, you could make the event source's internal collection of listeners `protected` or give them package-level visibility, allowing the test to query the collection without polluting the `public` interface with a method that only the tests need. You can conclude that having tests in a separate package weakens the production system's design.

Which is the right answer? As usual, there is no definitive right answer to this question. Test-Driven Development practitioners typically argue that there is no such thing as "just for testing," but rather that having comprehensive tests is important enough to warrant adding whatever methods are necessary to a class's `public` interface to make the class more testable. A testable design is usually a good design. Still, if half a class's `public` interface consists of methods that *only* the tests use, then it is possible that another design problem is crying out to be solved. Deciding whether this is the case requires judgment that typically comes only from experience. In programming, as in life, practice makes perfect.

NOTE If you use IBM's VisualAge for Java (VAJ), it may be *necessary* to place your tests in a different package than your production code. If you want your test code in a different project than your production code, then you must place your tests in a different package, because VAJ does not support multiple projects containing packages with the same name. Unless you want to place your tests and production code in the same VAJ project, write a script to "strip out" the tests during packaging; you have no choice but to move tests to a separate package.[9]

[9] See http://c2.com/cgi/wiki?OrganizeJavaUnitTests.

◆ Related

- 3.1—Place test classes in the same package as production code
- 14.5—Test an Object Factory
- Robert C. Martin, *Agile Software Development, Principles, Patterns, and Practices.* Prentice-Hall, 2002.

3.4 Factor out a test fixture

◆ Problem

You have written several tests for the same production class, and they contain duplicate code. Knowing that duplication is the root of all evil in software, you want to remove it.

◆ Background

One of the earliest patterns you see when writing tests for the same production class is that the first few lines of each test look the same. Remember that each test has three basic parts: create some objects, invoke some methods, check the results. The second of these three is usually different for each test; deciding which method to invoke usually identifies the test: "If I call the constructor with *these* parameters, I expect *that* result; but if I pass `null`, then the constructor should throw *that* kind of exception." This is the kind of internal dialog—or external, if you're talking to a Pair Programming partner—that leads to the list of tests you intend to write for a class. Duplication is possible here, but relatively uncommon.

The third part of the test, checking the result, depends entirely on the method you invoke. If the tests invoke different methods, the expected results will also be different. You normally only see duplication here if there is duplication in invoking the method.

Creating the object, however, leads to the most duplication from test to test. It is common to have many more methods on a class than constructors, so once you write even a *second* test for your class, you run the risk of duplicating the "create some objects" part of the first test, because you may well be calling the same constructor with the same parameters. Because this kind of duplication is so common, it would be nice if JUnit had a built-in mechanism for eliminating it.

Kent Beck calls the objects under test a *test fixture*: a "configuration" of objects whose behavior is easy to predict.[10] Using Kent's terms, the first part of a test—the

[10] Kent Beck, "Simple Smalltalk Testing: With Patterns" (www.xprogramming.com/testfram.htm). This is the original paper in which Kent describes SUnit, a Smalltalk-based predecessor to JUnit.

"create some objects" part—can be called "create a fixture." The goal is to create some objects and then initialize them to some known state so that you can predict their responses to invoking methods on them.

◆ *Recipe*

Identify the duplicated test fixture code in your tests. Move that code into a new method called `setUp()`. The resulting code may no longer compile because you are now declaring variables in `setUp()` and then using them in your tests. Change those variables into instance-level fields so that both `setUp()` and your tests can refer to them. Because each test executes in its own instance of your test case class, there is no need to worry about instance-level fields being set incorrectly from test to test. When you execute your tests, the test runner invokes `setUp()` before each test. Every other test you write in this test case class can use this common test setup.

To illustrate this technique, listing 3.2 shows three `Money` tests that use the same `Money` object.

Listing 3.2 `MoneyTest` before moving code into `setUp()`

```
package junit.cookbook.organizing.test;

import junit.cookbook.util.Money;
import junit.framework.TestCase;

public class MoneyTest extends TestCase {
    public void testAdd() {
        Money addend = new Money(12, 50);
        Money augend = new Money(12, 50);
        Money sum = addend.add(augend);
        assertEquals(2500, sum.inCents());
    }

    public void testNegate() {
        Money money = new Money(12, 50);
        Money opposite = money.negate();
        assertEquals(-1250, opposite.inCents());
    }

    public void testRound() {
        Money money = new Money(12, 50);
        Money rounded = money.roundToNearestDollar();
        assertEquals(1300, rounded.inCents());
    }
}
```

Notice that the first line of each of these three tests is almost identical. Each test uses a `Money` object representing $12.50, so this object appears to be a candidate to move into `setUp()`. Because `testAdd()` calls its object `addend` and the others call it `money`, you first need to rename `addend` to `money` to make the first line in all three tests identical. Then you can move that line into `setUp()`. Finally, change `money` from a local variable to an instance-level field so that `setUp()` and the test methods can all use it. When you've finished, the code looks like listing 3.3, with the new fixture code highlighted in bold print.

Listing 3.3 MoneyTest after moving code into setUp()

```
package junit.cookbook.organizing.test;

import junit.cookbook.util.Money;
import junit.framework.TestCase;

public class MoneyTest extends TestCase {
    private Money money;

    protected void setUp() throws Exception {
        money = new Money(12, 50);
    }

    public void testAdd() {
        Money augend = new Money(12, 50);
        Money sum = money.add(augend);
        assertEquals(2500, sum.inCents());
    }

    public void testNegate() {
        Money opposite = money.negate();
        assertEquals(-1250, opposite.inCents());
    }

    public void testRound() {
        Money rounded = money.roundToNearestDollar();
        assertEquals(1300, rounded.inCents());
    }
}
```

Each test now assumes that there is already a `Money` object called `money` with the value $12.50. The test duplication has been removed.

◆ Discussion

JUnit provides direct support for test fixtures through two methods, `setUp()` and `tearDown()`, found in `junit.framework.TestCase`. When you subclass `TestCase`, you can override these methods to set up and tear down (clean up) the fixture for each test. To see how JUnit uses these fixture methods, examine the source for runBare(), another TestCase method:

```
public void runBare() throws Throwable {
    setUp();
    try {
        runTest();
    }
    finally {
        tearDown();
    }
}
```

When it is time to execute your test, the framework invokes runBare(), which sets up your fixture, runs the test, and then tears down your fixture. Notice that by placing tearDown() in a finally block, this method is guaranteed to be called even if the test fails. This is particularly important to avoid the situation where your test initializes some expensive, external resource and then is left unable to clean up after itself. It may leave an open database connection, files on the file system, or something on a network. Executing these tests repeatedly in a short time period may exhaust system resources—yours or someone else's. It is very important for a test to tear down any fixture that it sets up. In our example, there was nothing in our fixture to clean up: when the test finishes executing, the underlying TestCase object simply goes out of scope and is ready to be garbage collected. This is why we did not override tearDown(). By default—that is, in TestCase itself—setUp() and tearDown() do nothing.

We would be remiss if we failed to mention one disadvantage to extracting common setup code into a test fixture. The resulting tests use instance-level fields that are initialized in another method, and this level of indirection introduces extra steps for someone trying to read the tests. Rather than reading each test method as a complete "story," the programmer has to look at setUp(), the field declarations, and the test. One of the benefits of implementing tests as methods is that they are easy to read; however, extracting part of a test's code into a different method *without* leaving behind an explicit call to that method can bewilder the programmer trying to read the test. We want to avoid hearing, "Where did these objects come from?!" If you name the fields appropriately, then the test will communicate effectively. As always, names are important.

To counter this disadvantage, we feel that removing duplication ultimately does more good than the harm that might be done by making the tests slightly less easy to read. We argue that before long, the JUnit practitioner is trained to remember that the framework invokes setUp() before each test and therefore automatically looks for that method when reading a test for the first time. Also, if the tests are sufficiently focused on a single behavior, then they tend to be short. If the entire test case class fits on one screen, then perhaps it is not so much more difficult to read than the alternative. As always, we recommend that you try both techniques and decide which works better for you, your team, or your project.

◆ Related

- 3.5—Factor out a test fixture hierarchy
- 3.7—Move special case tests to a separate test fixture
- 5.10—Set up your fixture once for the entire suite

3.5 Factor out a test fixture hierarchy

◆ Problem

You have multiple test fixtures that share some common objects. These objects are duplicated in the various `TestCase` classes that implement your fixture. You would like to reuse these objects, rather than duplicate them.

◆ Background

This problem arises most frequently when writing Customer Tests or End-to-End Tests—that is, tests that target the entire system, rather than a single class. On occasion, JUnit users—the ones who focus almost entirely on JUnit as a Test-Driven Development tool—forget the programmers out there who are *not* Test-Driven Development practitioners who nonetheless use JUnit because it provides an easy-to-use Java framework for writing tests.[11] We mention this because a Test-Driven Development practitioner would say, "If you have such large fixtures, then your tests are too large. Change your tests so that they focus on a smaller piece of the system. If you do that, then your problem will go away." They are right, but that answer is like a typical mathematician's answer: focused, accurate, and useless.[12]

If you can make your fixtures smaller or if you can identify parts of your fixture that not all your tests actually share, then so much the better: we prefer a simpler test case hierarchy to a more complex one. If you cannot make things any simpler—or at least cannot see how to do it *yet*—then you should at least try to move

[11] On occasion the authors themselves are guilty of this, although we are starting to catch on. There is hope.

[12] It's an old joke, and possibly not a good one, but the tradition must live on.

the common fixture to one place; and because you're reading this recipe, that must be what you want to do.

◆ *Recipe*

The secret to solving this problem is simple: even though you are writing tests, those tests are still implemented by methods and objects, so treat them as methods and objects. One way to extract duplicate behavior in a group of classes is to create a class hierarchy by applying the refactoring Extract Superclass [Refactoring, 336]. In case you do not have Martin's book handy, here is a step-by-step approach:

1. Select two test case classes that have fixture code in common.
2. Create a new subclass of `TestCase`. This becomes the superclass for the test case classes with overlapping test fixtures. In this recipe, we call this new class `BaseFixture`, but you should name it something more meaningful.
3. Declare `BaseFixture` as an `abstract` class. There's no reason to create instances of this class.
4. Change your test case classes so that they inherit from `BaseFixture` rather than directly from `TestCase`.
5. Copy the overlapping fixture into `BaseFixture`—that is, copy the fields and the code in `setUp()` that initializes those fields. You likely need to change the fields, declaring them as `protected` rather than `private`; otherwise, the test case classes cannot use them. You could encapsulate the fields in `protected` *get* methods, but in this case we think that's extra code for no reason.
6. From each test case class, remove the fixture fields and the code from `setUp()` that you moved into `BaseFixture`.
7. Add `super.setUp()` at the *beginning* of each test case class's `setUp()` method.

Now you can rebuild and rerun your tests to verify that their behavior has not changed. You can repeat these steps for as many test case classes as you have that share common fixture objects.

After you verify that you have not introduced any errors during these steps, look at the `setUp()` methods and see whether any could be eliminated because of being empty or containing only `super.setUp()`.

◆ *Discussion*

We can summarize this recipe by saying, "Extract a superclass of your test case classes, declaring it `abstract` because there is no reason to instantiate it." If we could be certain that everyone had read Martin's excellent work, we could certainly have done that. Extracting a Super Fixture, to give this recipe a snappier title, embodies the spirit of this recipe by combining these two key points:

- It is a good idea to eliminate duplicate test fixture code by moving it up into a superclass.
- We often do not see the duplication until it happens.

This second point is the reason that this recipe's title mentions *factoring out* a test fixture hierarchy rather than *building it in*. If we knew exactly where all the duplication would be, then we would avoid it; however, we have observed that such clairvoyance is out of our grasp. Instead, we content ourselves to eliminate duplication as soon as we find it. This recipe is just another tool in the toolbox for managing design complexity.

When deciding whether to use this recipe, consider the *amount* of duplication in your test fixtures. While your test fixtures need not be identical to use this recipe effectively, there needs to be enough duplication to warrant the complexities of introducing a new class and moving fields around. Sometimes it is the tests, and not the fixture code, that are duplicated, as in recipe 2.6, "Test an interface." Although the compiler is unaffected by the complexity of your test class hierarchy, humans are: other programmers need to be able to read your test code. You may even find it difficult to navigate your own complex test case hierarchies after a few months away from the code. While some people feel that eliminating *all* duplication is the One True Path, remember that eliminating duplication is only a rule. If, after thoughtful reasoning, you have decided to break the rule, then by all means go ahead. If breaking the rule lands you in trouble, try to remember which rule you broke so that you can learn from your mistake.

One more thing: remember to call `super.setUp()` and `super.tearDown()`, as necessary. When you subclass `TestCase` directly, you do not need to worry about this, because the superclass implementations do nothing; but now you may have superclass implementations of each method that do something very important! This is a common mistake—one we will all continue to make until the end of our programming days—so don't feel bad about it. Instead, see chapter 8, "Troubleshooting JUnit," for other common mistakes when writing JUnit tests.

◆ ***Related***

- 3.4—Factor out a test fixture
- 3.6—Introduce a Base Test Case
- 8.3—JUnit does not set up your test fixture

3.6 Introduce a Base Test Case

◆ ***Problem***

You have a common set of methods that you would like to use throughout your tests. It would be nice to refer to these methods as though they were part of the test case class, rather than as class-level methods on some utility class.

◆ ***Background***

It is very common over time to build up a sizable library of reusable utility methods for JUnit tests. Perhaps the most common type of reusable method is the custom assertion. As we explain in recipe 17.4, "Extract a custom assertion," if you make the same kind of assertion often enough, and if you want the same failure message every time you make that assertion, then we recommend wrapping the underlying condition and failure message into a new assertion method. This new method's name should start with `assert` to help classify it as an assertion. Whoever uses this method will know immediately that it might cause an assertion failure.

You may want to use this custom assertion in other test cases, and not just the one that "gave birth" to it. In this case, you need to make it available to other test case classes somehow. This recipe describes a simple way to do it.

◆ ***Recipe***

If you treat these commonly used utility methods the same way you would treat fixture objects, then you can apply recipe 3.5 and move the utility methods into the new superclass. This recipe is essentially a special case of that one, although we have some additional recommendations to make.

Introduce a *base test case*—that is, a class to act as the superclass for all your test case classes. If you have already written some tests, then simply change them all to inherit from your new base test case class, which we often call `BaseTestCase`. (We have tried to come up with more meaningful names, but failed. If you have any suggestions, then please let us know.) Even if `BaseTestCase` has no methods to begin with, starting your project with a base test case provides a natural place for programmers to put any utility methods that they believe other tests will need to use.

If a method ends up in `BaseTestCase` that does not need to be there, it is a simple matter to "push it down" into the specific test case class (or subhierarchy) that uses it. It is also easy to pull any commonly used method up into `BaseTestCase` as needed, because all test case classes in your project already inherit from `BaseTestCase`.

◆ Discussion

The Test-Driven Development purist may read this recipe and say, "You aren't gonna need it."[13] In short, they argue that a `BaseTestCase` should evolve naturally from the needs of the design, rather than being forced onto a project from the beginning. We wholeheartedly agree with the YAGNI principle and believe that this is *not* a violation of it. Our experience on several projects has told us that, sooner or later, a `BaseTestCase` pops up out of the design.

In the course of refactoring test code—especially in Customer Tests or End-to-End Tests—we routinely add two basic kinds of commonly used methods: custom assertions and extensions to the testing framework. This is true whether we use JUnit, HttpUnit, HtmlUnit, DbUnit, or any of the other frameworks out there. Invariably, we end up with a collection of methods that all our tests ought to be using, and because we cannot change `TestCase`, we need a bridge between JUnit and our extensions to it. That is the central function of `BaseTestCase`: to provide a home for these extensions.

Some advanced JUnit practitioners have even taken to extracting some of their JUnit extensions—the ones that apply to any problem domain—and packaging them into a `BaseTestCase` that they take with them from project to project. The open source project GSBase (http://gsbase.sourceforge.net) includes one such `BaseTestCase` implementation that includes a number of useful JUnit extensions, such as comparing unordered collections, asserting that an object is an `instanceof` a specific class, even a reimplementation of `assertSame` with a more useful failure message than the one that JUnit provides by default.

Introducing a `BaseTestCase`, then, is a rare example of speculative design that always seems to work, which is why we recommend it for any project using JUnit.

◆ Related

- 3.5—Factor out a test fixture hierarchy
- 17.4—Extract a custom assertion
- GSBase (http://gsbase.sourceforge.net)

---

[13] Read http://c2.com/cgi/wiki?YouArentGonnaNeedIt to find out more about this catch-phrase.

3.7 Move special case tests to a separate test fixture

◆ ***Problem***

You have written several tests for special cases of the same system behavior. You have noticed duplication both in the test code and in the test names.

◆ ***Background***

There are a few forces that lead you to the realization that some of your tests are slightly out of their element. The first thing you notice is that you have seven different tests for the same behavior, while others have only one or two. The next thing you notice is that the names of your tests all look the same:

```
testConnect()
testConnect_ConnectionRefused()
testConnect_WrongAddress()
testConnect_NullAddress()
testConnect_TemporarilyUnavailable()
```

You next look at the rest of the tests and notice that they use *these* fixture objects while your other tests use *those* fixture objects, and they don't seem to overlap. Clearly, these tests don't belong with the rest. This happens most often when there is an unusually large number of special cases for a single behavior, but these warning signs can emerge for any reason.

◆ ***Recipe***

You should move the special case tests into their own fixture, naming the fixture after the behavior under test. Follow these instructions:

1. Create a new test case class and name it after the behavior under test. In our example, we might name the test case class `ConnectToWebServiceTest`.[14]
2. Copy the test methods and corresponding fixture objects from the old test case class into the new test case class.
3. Rename the test methods, removing the name of the behavior under test and leaving the name of the special case. In our example, the tests would be renamed to `testHappyPath()`, `testConnectionRefused()`, `testWrongAddress()`, `testNullAddress()`, and `testTemporarilyUnavailable()`.[15]

---

[14] We didn't really say what it was we were trying to connect to, so arbitrarily we choose "web service."

[15] We like the phrase *happy path*. If you don't, then try `testSuccessful()` or something boring like that.

4 Run your tests, verifying that they still behave as they did before.

5 Remove the tests from the other test case class. Remove any test fixture objects that the remaining tests are not using.

6 Add the new test case class to any manually built customized test suites that include the other test case class.

You end up with two test case classes where there was previously one. The old one contains the remaining tests, and the new one contains all the special cases for that specific behavior. Because you have taken care to use good names, it should still be easy to find the tests when you need them. If your development environment does not provide an easy way to find all references to a method, leave a comment in the old test case class indicating where the tests are located.

◆ *Discussion*

If you never thought of doing this, you might be a novice JUnit practitioner.[16] When we started out with JUnit, they told us to write one test case class per production code class, keeping all the tests for that class together in one place. This makes sense as a starting point, but there is no need to cram dozens of tests into one class, especially once it becomes clear that that is difficult to navigate and maintain. These guidelines have a way of developing into rules and even *laws* if the people following the guidelines do so without an understanding of why. If you believed that your tests *have to* stay in the same test case class, then we're here to tell you, "It's all right. Move the tests to another test case class. Nothing bad will happen." We're here to take the magic away and leave you with a better understanding.

The one-test-case-per-class guideline is there to give you a place to start organizing your tests. It would be silly for you to obsess over exactly where to place your first test, so we tell you, "If you're testing the class `Chicken`, then put your test in a class called `ChickenTest`." It's a simple rule to follow and a sound place to start. It allows you to get past worrying about what to do and on to *doing* it. If you think of something better later, then starting doing *that.*

"I'll take a good plan violently executed now over a perfect plan tomorrow."—General George Patton.[17]

---

[16] Our apologies to comedian Jeff Foxworthy.

[17] Of course, on the other hand, "As long as I hold on to the ball, nothing bad can happen."—Mediocre major-league baseball pitcher Brian Horton.

- ***Related***
  - 3.4—Factor out a test fixture
  - 3.5—Factor out a test fixture hierarchy

3.8 Build tests from the command line

- ***Problem***

You would like to build your tests using the command line, rather than relying on a full-featured IDE.

- ***Background***

We love all the great Java IDEs available these days. There are even times when we wonder if we could possibly live without them. Unfortunately, there are a number of occasions where using an IDE is not an option.

The unattended build is an example of such an occasion. If you are running nightly builds using scheduled Ant scripts or using Cruise Control, then you need to run your tests from a command-line interface suitable for scripting. There are less fortunate situations in which you need to rely on building tests from the command line.

You may be forced to work—we hope temporarily—in an operating system that does not support your favorite IDE or, indeed, *any* IDE.[18] You may be forced to work in a windowless environment, such as a remote `telnet` session over a slow network connection or into a server on which you do not have permission to run a windowing environment. We have seen programmers forced into debug sessions over dial-up from North America to Australia, so don't think it will never happen to you. Eventually it will.

In this situation—especially when diagnosing defects—you may want to make a small change to your tests and then rebuild them and execute them in this kind of hostile environment. You want to know exactly which libraries you need to build your tests and which of those fancy automatic class path IDE features you can live without.

[18] We know that this is rare nowadays, but the moment we start to believe that we'll always have access to an IDE is the moment someone will tell us to work on some crazy platform no one has ever heard of. It could happen.

◆ Recipe

Fortunately, JUnit is about as simple as it gets. To build your tests in a plain-vanilla, command-line environment, simply put junit.jar on the class path when you run the Java compiler. You will find junit.jar in the root directory of the JUnit package you download from the JUnit web site. See chapter 1 for details on downloading, installing, and looking through the JUnit package.

If you follow our recommendations in recipe 3.2, "Create a separate source tree for test code," then your Java compile command will look something like this, at least on flavors of UNIX:

```
$ javac -classpath $JUNIT_HOME/junit.jar:$PROJECT_HOME/classes/production
⇒  -d $PROJECT_HOME/classes/test $PROJECT_HOME/source/test/*.java
```

This command makes some assumptions: that you have set the environment variable `JUNIT_HOME` to point to the location on the file system where you have unpacked JUnit; that you have set the environment variable `PROJECT_HOME` to point to the root of your project's directory structure; and that you only need to compile the tests in the root of your test source code directory structure. If you run the command from the root of your project, then omit the references to `PROJECT_HOME`, because that would be the current working directory. As a general rule, it is better to use environment variables than to refer to hard-coded, fully qualified path names. Environment variables are easier to change than the (eventually) large number of scripts that refer to those paths.

◆ Discussion

With the plain-vanilla Java compiler you cannot recursively compile all the Java classes in a given directory structure, something that we view as a restriction so severe that we would never use the compiler on its own for large projects. That is one reason to use tools such as Ant or your favorite IDE to build both your production code and your tests. The automated, repeatable build process is such an important project management practice that we typically assume that all projects do it, and Ant is the standard Java project build tool, so we recommend it highly. See recipe 3.9, "Build tests using Ant," to automate (among other things) compiling all the test classes in your test source code tree. It is possible to write a shell script to do the work, but Ant provides a platform-independent way to do it. The solution is portable and relatively easy to set up in a foreign environment. It is certainly easier than learning how to write shell scripts for some crazy platform that no one has ever heard of.

◆ ***Related***

- 3.9—Build tests using Ant

3.9 Build tests using Ant

◆ ***Problem***

You need to build your tests in an environment where you cannot use your usual IDE. You can build the tests from the command line, but you would like to automate this task in a portable way.

◆ ***Background***

In recipe 3.8, we describe the conditions under which it may be necessary to build your tests without your trusty IDE. We also describe the most serious limitation in using the Java compiler to build your tests: there is no direct support for building all the tests in your test source tree. If you need to work in this strange environment for a prolonged period of time—that is, you need to build all your tests more than once or twice—you'll want to automate the build so that you can concentrate on higher-level thinking, such as solving the problem before you. We like to remind ourselves that the computer is supposed to do work for *us* and not the other way around. We should not waste our time satisfying some operating system or Java compiler.

◆ ***Recipe***

Ant to the rescue! If you're unfamiliar with Ant, then run (don't walk) to http://ant.apache.org and read about this automated build tool that has become an industry standard among Java programmers. Ant is simple to install and integrates well with JUnit.

Building your tests with Ant is straightforward: use the `<javac>` task to build your test classes, specifying a source directory, a target directory, and a few elements on the class path, notably JUnit itself. If you already know how to build your tests from the command line, then transcribing that command into an Ant target is easy. Start with the simplest example: the test source, production source, and all the classes are in the same directory on the file system. Just add junit.jar to the build-time class path and everything works. Listing 3.4 shows a simple Ant buildfile that builds the tests.

Listing 3.4 A minimal Ant buildfile for JUnit tests

```
<project name="Simplified Project Structure" default="compile">
    <property name="junit.home" value="d:/junit3.8.1" />
    <target name="compile">
        <javac fork="yes" srcdir="." includes="**/*.java">
            <classpath>
                <pathelement path="${junit.home}/junit.jar" />
            </classpath>
        </javac>
    </target>
</project>
```

Here we have the simplest Ant buildfile we can think of that includes building JUnit tests. Because the test source code and production source code is all in one place—at the root of the project's directory structure—it's enough simply to build every Java class we find. The only item we need in the build-time class path is JUnit itself. It is a best practice in Ant not to hard code the location of tools such as JUnit into your Ant tasks, but rather to factor them out into properties. Although this book is not meant to be a primer on Ant, we have used a property to refer to junit.jar, as we would on a real project.[19] This covers the simplest case.

If you follow our recommendations on separating the test source code and test classes from the production code, then your buildfile will look like the one in listing 3.5.

Listing 3.5 A more useful Ant buildfile for JUnit tests

```
<project name="Simplified Project Structure" default="compileTest">
    <property name="junit.home" value="d:/junit3.8.1" />

    <target name="compileTest" depends="compileProduction">
        <javac fork="yes"
               srcdir="source/test" includes="**/*.java"
               destdir="classes/test">
            <classpath>
                <pathelement path="${junit.home}/junit.jar" />
                <pathelement path="classes/production" />
            </classpath>
        </javac>
    </target>
```

[19] Actually, we would move this property into a properties file because we expect the person using this buildfile to need to change that property to suit her environment. We decided that a separate properties file would be too much of a distraction for this example, so we left the property inside the buildfile.

```
    <target name="compileProduction">
        <javac fork="yes"
               srcdir="source/production" includes="**/*.java"
               destdir="classes/production" />
    </target>
</project>
```

The biggest difference between this buildfile and the one in listing 3.4 is that there are two targets: one to build the production code and one to build the tests. Because we have placed the tests and production source in different source trees, we need a different target for each source tree: Ant does not support specifying multiple "source tree to destination tree" mappings in a single task.

Next, notice that the `compileTest` target depends on the `compileProduction` target. This ensures that the tests are always built with the most up-to-date production code. Failure to include this dependency can lead to difficult-to-diagnose class incompatibility problems when running your tests: the Java interpreter generates `ClassCastException`, `VerifyError`, or one of a host of odd-sounding and confusing errors, when what you *really* need is the message "Your classes are out of date. Build again."

Finally notice that we must add classes/production to the build-time class path of the test classes, as the tests depend on classes in the production code *but not the other way around.* If your production classes need your test classes in the build-time class path, then you have a serious dependency problem: specifically, you have test classes in your production code. If moving the class into the test source tree doesn't work, then the situation is much worse: your class has some production features and some test-only features. You'll have to split that class in two and put the corresponding part in the right place for your project to build. Although not ideal, doing so ensures that test-only features do not gum up the works of your production-quality system. The increased discipline is worth it.

◆ Discussion

Using Ant to build your project, even if you *always* have access to your favorite IDE, can help point out dependency problems in your code. As you saw in the previous example, it is easy to create a class that is part production and part test utility but not realize that the class lives this double life, because the IDE manages class paths and the like, freeing you from having to figure it out for yourself. We all want our IDE to simplify our lives (at least as programmers), but you should be concerned when a feature of your IDE allows you to be *too* lazy. The IDE is a tool, and not a crutch; you should be able to build your system without the IDE, just in case you ever need to. This is the reason we recommend managing your build with Ant.

◆ ***Related***

- 3.8—Build tests from the command line

3.10 Build tests using Eclipse

◆ ***Problem***

You've been using Eclipse to write code for a while, but you haven't built JUnit tests yet. You'd like to know if there is anything specific to know about building JUnit tests with Eclipse.

◆ ***Background***

Eclipse, the powerful open source IDE of choice these days, is interesting in that, on its own, it does virtually nothing. All the real power behind Eclipse comes in the form of high-powered plug-ins. After downloading Eclipse, trying it out, and using it on a daily basis, you begin to wonder whether you'll ever know everything there is to know about using Eclipse effectively. While there are definite limits to the power of the Eclipse plug-ins, it can seem as though they provide limitless benefit. It can be easy to believe that integrating something like JUnit into Eclipse is fraught with complexity.

◆ ***Recipe***

Eclipse makes building your tests simple, whether you decide to put everything in one project and one source tree or use multiple projects and multiple source trees. Your task consists of little more than setting a few Java project properties. As with building your tests using any other tool set, you must have junit.jar on your build-time class path, and your test code must have the production code in its build-time class path. If you already know how to do these things with Eclipse, then go to it; but if you don't, then read on.

Adding JUnit to your project's build-time class path is the same whether you have one "kitchen drawer" Eclipse project[20] or have separated each kind of test

[20] That is, a project into which you throw everything. It's a wonder we ever find anything in there.

code into its own project. The steps in table 3.1 describe how to add JUnit to a project's Java Build Path.

NOTE If you don't have a Classpath Variable for JUnit, then follow these steps first:

1. From the workbench menu bar, select Window > Preferences.
2. In the left pane of the Preferences dialog, expand Java and then select Classpath Variables.
3. At the list of Classpath Variables, press New.
4. At the New Variable Entry dialog box, enter `JUNIT_JAR` for the Name and then browse to (or type) the location of `junit.jar` on your file system. Press OK.
5. Press OK at the Preferences dialog box to return to the workbench.

Your Classpath Variable is now ready to use in your project's Java Build Path.

Table 3.1 Adding JUnit to an Eclipse project's Java Build Path

	Action	Result
1	Right-click the project and then select Properties.	Eclipse opens the project properties dialog box.
2	In the left pane, select Java Build Path.	Eclipse displays the Source tab, showing the various source folders in your project. Here you can add, change, or remove source folders to manage multiple source trees. No matter how many source trees you have, all the classes will be built to the same folder, the output folder, which you can choose at the bottom of this pane.
3	Select the Libraries tab.	Eclipse lists the external *.jar files and class folders—that is, folders containing loose class files—where the Java compiler currently looks for classes during compilation.
4	Press Add Variable.	Eclipse lists all available Classpath Variables. These variables point to various locations on the local file system and allow you to install JUnit to any location you choose without having to change the build path of every project that depends on it.
5	Select `JUNIT_JAR`, and then press OK.	Eclipse adds `JUNIT_JAR` to the list of *.jar files on the project's build path.
6	Select the Order and Export tab.	Eclipse shows the order in which locations on the build path are evaluated. When searching for a class at build time, Eclipse starts at the top of the list, then works its way to the bottom, so that classes from libraries near the top of the list are used before classes from libraries near the bottom of the list.

Table 3.1 Adding JUnit to an Eclipse project's Java Build Path *(continued)*

	Action	Result
7	Select `JUNIT_JAR` from the list and then press Up repeatedly until `JUNIT_JAR` comes directly after `JRE_LIB`, the Java Runtime Environment.	This step is optional, but it's useful if your project includes extensions to JUnit that may conflict with classes in JUnit itself. Extensions to JUnit should not attempt to change the JUnit framework, but if you need to use such an extension, this is the way to cope with that unfortunate situation.
8	Press OK.	Eclipse rebuilds your project using the changes to the Java Build Path. You return to the workbench.

Now that you have added JUnit to your project's Java Build Path, simply configure your source trees and your build output folder as you need for your project. By default, Eclipse suggests naming your directories "source" and "classes" for each Java project. Much of the time, these settings suffice.

If you follow our recommendations in recipe 3.2, then you will have separate Eclipse projects for your production code and each kind of test. In that case, use the Projects tab in your project's Java Build Path properties to include your production code project in the build path of each test code project. You may need to select multiple production code projects for a test project containing End-to-End Tests that use classes from the entire system.

◆ *Discussion*

Eclipse simplifies managing the build-time class path (or Java Build Path, which is probably a better term to use, anyway) by providing intuitive dialogs for adding projects and external *.jar files through Classpath Variables. We are generally quite happy with the features that Eclipse's Java Development Toolkit (JDT) provides; however, there is one minor feature missing.

We have recommended you have separate source and build trees for your production code and each kind of test you intend to write. This implies multiple source folders *and* multiple build output folders, a configuration that the Eclipse JDT does not enable by default within a single Eclipse project. You need to change the properties for each Eclipse project to enable different output folders for each source folder. Consult the Eclipse documentation for details.

◆ *Related*

- 3.2—Create a separate source tree for test code
- 3.9—Build tests using Ant

4 Managing test suites

This chapter covers

- Manually collecting tests into custom test suites
- Automatically collecting tests into different kinds of test suites
- Ordering and filtering tests in test suites
- Using Parameterized Test Cases to build a data-driven test suite

In JUnit, the smallest unit of "test execution" is the test suite. JUnit doesn't actually execute individual tests, but only executes test suites, so in order to execute your tests, you need to collect them into a test suite. The recipes in this chapter describe different ways to create and manage test suites.

The simplest test suite to create consists of all the tests in a test case class. This is so simple that JUnit does it for you. See recipe 4.1, "Let JUnit build your test suite." If you need to create your test suites by hand, go to recipe 4.2, "Collect a specific set of tests." If you have data-driven tests and don't want to write by hand a bunch of test methods that simply use your test data, see recipe 4.8, "Build a data-driven test suite." After that you'll probably want to move your test data outside the code. For that, see recipe 4.9, "Define a test suite in XML."

Building a test suite from a single test case class is just the beginning. The real power of JUnit comes from its ability to build arbitrarily complex test suites. Start with recipe 4.3, "Collect all the tests in a package," and then move on to recipe 4.4, "Collect all the tests for your entire system" so that you can execute all your tests at once.

After a while, though, you'll want to build these large test suites automatically. See recipe 4.5, "Scan the file system for tests." You may even want to categorize your tests and run the tests in a given category as one suite. For that, see recipe 4.6, "Separate the different kinds of test suites."

Finally there are times when you need some control over the tests in your test suite, but you don't want the burden of keeping track of every single test. In that case, see recipe 4.7, "Control the order of some of your tests" to find out how to gain just the control that you need.

In this chapter we concentrate on building the test suites without discussing exactly how to run them. This topic is complex enough without test runners getting in the way. We will assume that the goal is to build a single test suite so that even the simplest test runners can execute it. We will talk more about how to execute your tests in Chapter 6, "Running JUnit Tests."

4.1 Let JUnit build your test suite

◆ Problem

You would like to stop maintaining the list of tests in a test suite. You would rather have JUnit build the test suite from the tests in your test case class.

◆ *Background*

You may have read one of the first articles ever written about JUnit, entitled "Test Infected: Programmers Love Writing Tests."[1] This article was written in 1999, a time when JUnit was still in its infancy. Some of the techniques in this article are outdated. In particular, the article shows the reader how to build a test suite from the tests in the current test case class. The article shows the reader the following example:

```
public static Test suite() {
    TestSuite suite= new TestSuite();
    suite.addTest(new MoneyTest("testEquals"));
    suite.addTest(new MoneyTest("testSimpleAdd"));
    return suite;
}
```

This builds a test suite containing two tests implemented by the methods `testEquals()` and `testSimpleAdd()`. We call this *manually* building a test suite, or doing it *by hand*, because the programmer must remember to update this list of tests every time he adds a new test method. Before JUnit 2.0 this was the only way to build test suites, and if you last used JUnit "a long time ago"—back before version 2.0—then this may be the only way you know how to build a test suite.

It also may be that you learned to write test suites from another programmer who did not understand or know about how to let JUnit build test suites automatically. If you have been using this manual test suite–building technique, you recognize how error prone it can be: every time you add a test, you need to remember to update this `suite()` method. Removing or renaming a test is easier; at least JUnit fails at runtime, indicating that it cannot find the test. But if you *add* a test to your test case and not to your `suite()` method, then you may not notice that JUnit is not executing your test. This can lead to a false sense of progress, as you *think* your test passes, when JUnit is not executing it at all!

This recipe will help you avoid this unfortunate situation.

◆ *Recipe*

Since the advent of JUnit 2.0, the framework provides a way to build a test suite out of the test methods in your test case class. As long as you follow a few simple rules, JUnit will find your tests and execute them:

[1] http://junit.sourceforge.net/doc/testinfected/testing.htm.

- Your test methods must be instance-level, take no parameters, and return nothing. That is, you must declare them as `public void testMethodName()`. This is a general requirement for test methods in JUnit, whether you build the test suite yourself or let the framework do it, but it bears repeating.
- The name of your test method must start with "`test`" (without the quotes), all lowercase.

Otherwise, there are no restrictions on how you declare your test methods. You may throw whatever exceptions you like, although you should understand how JUnit handles that (see recipe 2.8, "Test throwing the right exception," for details). The code in your test can do whatever you need it to do, although it should follow the typical rhythm of a test: create some objects, invoke some methods, check the results.

Returning to the example in the "Test Infected" article, the authors have already named their test methods according to the rules. Although the article describes implementing the `suite()` method as follows, JUnit does even *that* automatically for you. If you omit the `suite()` method altogether, JUnit will build the "default" suite as though you wrote this code. (It does the same work, but a little differently, which causes a minor difficulty that we describe in recipe 4.3.)

```
public static Test suite() {
    return new TestSuite(MoneyTest.class);
}
```

We hope it is clear by now that you should *always* let JUnit build your test suite automatically. As you will see in other recipes, there are times when you need to build a suite by hand, but that should be the exception, rather than the rule. Let the framework do the heavy lifting.

◆ Discussion

JUnit uses Java reflection[2] to build the default test suite at runtime. In particular, JUnit searches your test case class for declared methods that follow the rules we have outlined and then adds those tests to a test suite. You can think of it as generating the "manual test suite" code at runtime. JUnit implements this feature in the class `junit.framework.TestSuite`. We summarize what each method does in table 4.1.

---

[2] These are the classes in the standard Java package `java.lang.reflect`.

Table 4.1 How JUnit builds the default test suite

`TestSuite` method	What it does
Constructor `TestSuite(Class)`	• Verifies there is a `public` constructor • Verifies the class itself is `public` • Invokes `addTestMethod()` for each declared method in the class • Extracts test methods for all tests in this class's superclasses up to the top of the class hierarchy • Issues a warning if there are no tests
`addTestMethod()`	• Verifies that the method is a `public` test method by invoking `isPublicTestMethod()` • Issues a warning if the test method is correctly named but not `public` • Creates the `Test` object for the method and adds it to the suite, if the method is a valid test method
`isPublicTest-Method()`	• Determines whether the method is a test method by invoking `isTestMethod()` • Determines whether the method is `public` • Returns true only if the method is both `public` and a test method
`isTestMethod()`	• Verifies that the method has no parameters, no return type, and a name starting with `test`

The way that JUnit builds the default test suite promotes writing isolated tests, a generally accepted good Programmer Testing practice. You ought not to rely on your tests executing in a particular order, nor should the failure of one test affect the outcome of the remaining tests in the suite. Commonly, programmers want to run a set of tests in a particular order because they share a common test fixture: they set up some data, run multiple tests using that data, and then throw the data away. To do this, not only do you need to set up and tear down the test fixture at the right time, but you also need to ensure that the tests run in a prescribed order. If not, a future test will look for fixture data that is not there. Even if the tests execute in the proper order, a failing test using a shared fixture typically leaves the fixture in an unexpected state, rendering the remaining tests essentially useless. You can learn about Kent Beck's early experience with automated tests in his discussion about the Test-Driven Development pattern he calls Isolated Test.[3]

He tells the story of long-running, GUI-based automated tests that his project ran every night. In the morning, Kent would see paper on his chair: either a single page saying, "Everything works"; or a stack of pages detailing the failures, one per failing test. He writes, "I noticed after a while that a huge stack of paper didn't

[3] Kent Beck, *Test-Driven Development: By Example* (Addison-Wesley, 2002), page 125.

usually mean a huge list of problems. More often it meant that one test had broken early, leaving the system in an unpredictable state for the next test." His conclusion: "Tests should be able to ignore one another completely. If I had one test broken, I wanted one problem. If I had two tests broken, I wanted two problems." The goal is to make it easier to decide from the list of failing tests where the production code is broken. This is one philosophy that underlies JUnit's design, and one of the ways in which JUnit works—subtly, mind you—to help you improve your design: writing isolated tests leads to highly cohesive, loosely coupled classes, a hallmark of good object-oriented design.

The last key point to have in mind is that the default test suite for a test case class includes more than just the test methods you have declared on that class. JUnit also adds any valid test methods it finds on any superclass of your test case class—all the way up to the root of the class hierarchy.[4] Although many beginning JUnit practitioners are surprised by this design choice, it is deliberate and makes sense: this is the mechanism that enables you to enforce an interface's contract. In other words, it allows you to execute the same tests on all implementations of an interface, or on all subclasses of an `abstract` class, such as a framework extension point. For more information on building Abstract Test Cases, see recipe 2.6, "Test an interface."

◆ Related

- 2.6—Test an interface
- 2.8—Test throwing the right exception
- 4.2—Collect a specific set of tests
- 4.5—Scan the file system for tests

4.2 Collect a specific set of tests

◆ Problem

You cannot use (or do not wish to use) the default test suite that JUnit creates from your test case class. You want to ignore certain tests or have control over the order in which JUnit executes the test, if not both.

---

[4] Strictly speaking, that would be the class `Object`, but for our purposes, we mean the class `TestCase`.

◆ *Background*

There are a number of good reasons to want to manually choose which tests go into the test suite for your test case class. Unfortunately, there are also a number of not-so-good reasons to want to do this, which is why we highly recommend reading the Discussion section of recipe 4.1, "Let JUnit build your test suite," before you read any further. If you are reading on, then either you remain unconvinced by our recommendations or you really do need to build your test suite by hand.

JUnit practitioners—in particular, the ones who also do Test-Driven Development—have the tendency to be dogmatic in their approach to writing tests. Looking to Kent Beck as a leader, we are told repeatedly how important it is to write isolated tests, as doing so forces us to work that little bit harder to improve our design. This works wonders when we are able to practice Test-Driven Development—that is, when the production code under test has not yet been written. In a legacy code environment, though, you do not have the luxury of a testable design. It is hard enough to achieve 100% test isolation in a well-designed system; it is generally impossible to do so in a system designed entirely without testing in mind. You may well be one of the lucky people charged with testing such a system, and if you are, then you almost certainly need to read this recipe, in addition to most of the rest of the recipes in this chapter. They provide instructions on controlling the order of tests in a test suite so that you can build a safety net to help you move toward 100% test isolation.

◆ *Recipe*

To build your test suite by hand, do the following:

1. Create a method on your test case class called `suite()`. It must be declared as `public static Test suite()`, taking no parameters and returning a `Test` object.[5]
2. In the body of your *custom suite method*, create a `TestSuite` object, and then add `Test` objects to the suite: either individual tests or other test suites. Return this `TestSuite` object.

That is a sketch of how to build the test suite by hand. We offer an example from "Test Infected":

---

[5] It actually returns a `TestSuite` object, but remember that `TestSuite` implements `Test`.

```
public static Test suite() {
    TestSuite suite= new TestSuite();
    suite.addTest(new MoneyTest("testMoneyEquals"));
    suite.addTest(new MoneyTest("testBagEquals"));
    suite.addTest(new MoneyTest("testSimpleAdd"));
    suite.addTest(new MoneyTest("testMixedSimpleAdd"));
    suite.addTest(new MoneyTest("testBagSimpleAdd"));
    suite.addTest(new MoneyTest("testSimpleBagAdd"));
    suite.addTest(new MoneyTest("testBagBagAdd"));
    return suite;
}
```

The order in which you specify these tests is the order in which JUnit executes them, if test order is important to you.

◆ *Discussion*

To understand this code in more depth, first note (or remember, if you already know this) that each test runs in its own instance of your test case class. This is one of the fundamental aspects of JUnit's design: it is the way that JUnit encourages test isolation. This is also the reason that we implement test fixture objects as instance-level fields on the test case class: each test is an instance of the test case class, so it has its own copy of the fixture. The constructor `MoneyTest(String)` takes as its parameter the name of the method that JUnit should call to execute the test. This constructor creates an instance of the test fixture (an isolated copy of the fixture) that invokes the specified method to run the actual test. When the framework executes this test, it eventually invokes the method `TestCase.runTest()`, which uses reflection (yet again!) to invoke the method whose name you provided to the test case class's constructor.[6]

The method `TestSuite.addTest()` simply encapsulates an internal collection—a `List`, in particular—of `Test` objects. When the framework runs the test suite, it runs each `Test` object in that suite in the order in which they appear in the list. Most of those `Test` objects are single tests, but JUnit allows you to build bigger suites out of smaller suites, so you can add either a `TestCase` or a `TestSuite` when you call `addTest()`. For an example of building a suite of suites, see recipe 4.3, "Collect all the tests in a package."

There is one simple consequence of the way JUnit lets you build a test suite that not many practitioners take advantage of. We do not know whether this is a use-

[6] This method also verifies that the test is a valid test method. Open the source for `junit.framework.TestCase` for more detail. There is no better documentation than the source code.

less feature or simply a large, collective blind spot.[7] Look back at the `suite()` method and notice one kind of duplication: the class name `MoneyTest`. This test suite is a collection of tests coming from the same test case class. If we specify some other test case class than `MoneyTest`, we can collect tests from a diverse set of test case classes. You may now ask yourself, "Why tell us this? What good is it?" Frankly, we have not leveraged this fact in any meaningful way in our past work with JUnit, but there is a particular scenario that we feel puts this feature to good use. It's nothing obscure: you can use it in the course of investigating defect reports coming from outside the programming team.

One of the recommendations that the Test-Driven Development community makes concerns what to do when someone else finds a defect in your team's code.[8] TDD practitioners would say that because someone else has found a defect, you have either missed a test that you should have written or written a test incorrectly. Often you have decided on an expected result that is *unexpected* for your users, so although your code passes your tests, the end users see behavior they do not expect. In this case, TDD recommends that you do as follows:

1. Identify the Customer Test (or functional test, or acceptance test) that does not match the expectations of the end users.
2. Use the Customer Test to help you determine which objects are involved in making that Customer Test pass, and then identify the Programmer Test that you either got wrong or missed altogether.
3. Fix (or write) the Programmer Test, make it pass, and then fix the Customer Test in the corresponding way. It may already pass as a result of your code changes, but if it does not, tie up whatever loose ends you may have to make the Customer Test pass.

At this point you have zero failing tests and can rerelease your software complete with a fix for this defect.

Now, what does this have to do with building a suite of JUnit tests?[9]

As you identify the Programmer Tests that match the failing Customer Test, we recommend creating a temporary suite for those tests. This test suite is an object-level view of the behavior the Customer Test verifies. As you work on the problem, execute the Programmer Test suite repeatedly as you go. This keeps you focused

---

[7] We suspect the feature is quite useful, but we may forget to use it the next time we have the opportunity.

[8] We think it couldn't happen to us.

[9] We try to get to the point quickly; we really do.

on fixing the problem at hand, while giving you object-level feedback on the effects of your changes. This is an alternative to running all the system's tests after every change, which will cause more changes—changes that you may not be ready to make yet—to ripple out and thus distract you from the work at hand. This Programmer Test suite may include tests from a number of different test case classes throughout the system, and JUnit allows you to build a test suite from an arbitrary slice of the system's entire collection of tests. That is quite handy.

After reading this, you might think it a good idea to start building these Programmer Test suites as you write (or receive) each Customer Test. We recommend against it: the relationship between a Customer Test and its constituent Programmer Tests may change a great deal over time, and the cost of maintaining those relationships in code is more than the time you might save discovering those relationships when required. Either way, we have described a typical scenario in which you may want to build a test suite from an arbitrary collection of tests.

◆ *Related*

- 4.1—Let JUnit build your test suite
- 4.3—Collect all the tests in a package

4.3 *Collect all the tests in a package*

◆ *Problem*

You have a number of test case classes in a package and would like to run them all at the same time, but the test runners ask you to specify a single test case class name. You need a way to collect all the tests in a package into a single test suite.

◆ *Background*

JUnit makes it easy to run the tests in a single test case class: simply pass the name of a test case class as a command-line parameter to the test runner. Because JUnit automatically builds a test suite from your test case class, it is not obvious how to collect the tests from multiple test case classes together into a single suite. Because you didn't have to do anything special to run all the tests in a single test case, how could you possibly know how to collect multiple test case classes together into one big test suite?

You may be tempted to move all those test methods into a single test case class. Don't. It makes navigating your test source code much more difficult. Different tests operate on different fixtures and so should be separated into different test case classes (see recipe 3.7, "Move special case tests to a separate test fixture"). Some day you will want to run one test case class's tests on their own. When that happens, don't copy the test methods back into a separate test case class! Follow this recipe instead.

◆ *Recipe*

To collect all the tests in a package, you build a custom test suite just as we describe in recipe 4.2, "Collect a specific set of tests," but rather than adding individual tests to the suite, add the suites from each test case class in your package. There are essentially two different ways to add a test suite to a larger test suite. The following example, taken from the class `junit.tests.AllTests`, shows both:

```
public static Test suite() {
    TestSuite suite= new TestSuite("Framework Tests");
    suite.addTestSuite(TestCaseTest.class);   <-- Add the default TestSuite
    suite.addTest(SuiteTest.suite());   <-- Add a custom TestSuite
    suite.addTestSuite(TestListenerTest.class);
    suite.addTestSuite(AssertTest.class);
    suite.addTestSuite(TestImplementorTest.class);
    suite.addTestSuite(NoArgTestCaseTest.class);
    suite.addTestSuite(ComparisonFailureTest.class);
    suite.addTestSuite(DoublePrecisionAssertTest.class);
    return suite;
}
```

We call this the AllTests pattern. The two methods you can use to add one test suite to another are `addTestSuite()` and the familiar `addTest()`. The first automatically extracts a test suite from the test case class you specify. The second uses the test case class's custom test suite method. In what must be called an unfortunate flaw in JUnit's design, you need to know when you build a suite of suites whether to use a test case's custom suite method or JUnit's automatic test suite extraction feature.[10] The only way to know this is to know the source code of the other test case classes in your package. Fortunately, the odds are high that you already do.

There are a few common conventions related to this technique:

- Name the package-level test suite class `AllTests`.
- Create one `AllTests` class per package.

---

[10] The method `TestSuite.addTestSuite(Class testClass)`, for example, does not bother to look for a custom `suite()` method at all, even though the test runners do.

- Collect the test suite from each package's `AllTests` into a larger `AllTests` class one level up in the package hierarchy. This is the way to build a suite for the entire system. See recipe 4.4, "Collect all the tests for your entire system" for details.

◆ *Discussion*

The method `TestSuite.addTestSuite()` is simply shorthand for writing `suite.addTest(new TestSuite(MyTestCase.class))`, as you can see by its implementation. (Look at the source!) JUnit practitioners had been writing this code so often in their `AllTests` classes that it became apparent a refactoring was in order to remove this duplication. You can now simply call `addTestSuite()` to extract a test suite from a test case class automatically and then add that suite into a larger one.

We mentioned in recipe 4.2, "Collect a specific set of tests," that you can invoke `addTest()` to add any `Test` object to a test suite, whether a single test or another test suite. In this case, `AllTests` includes `SuiteTest`'s custom test suite: first it invokes `SuiteTest.suite()`, returning a `TestSuite` object; then it adds that `TestSuite` object to its own, larger test suite. Use this technique to build up suites of custom test suites. If you know that `MyTestCase` collects its tests using the `suite()` method, then you should collect its tests by invoking `addTest(MyTestCase.suite())`.

Finally, note that the class that declares a `suite()` method does not have to be a subclass of `TestCase`. Such a class is typically just a collector for other test suites and does not define any tests of its own. In particular, one look at the source of `junit.framework.AllTests` reveals that it is just a regular Java class—not a descendant of `junit.framework.TestCase`. Although it is common for a test case class to provide its own custom `suite()` method, *any* class can collect tests into a `suite()` method.[11] This is another of those subtle parts of JUnit that even many experienced practitioners do not realize. In JUnit, an amazingly small amount of code can have its own nuances.

◆ *Related*

- 4.1—Let JUnit build your test suite
- 4.2—Collect a specific set of tests
- 4.4—Collect all the tests for your entire system

---

[11] Refer back to the discussion of arbitrary suites of tests in recipe 4.2.

4.4 Collect all the tests for your entire system

◆ Problem

You want to run all the tests in your entire system, but the test runners only allow you to run the tests in one test case class at a time.

◆ Background

It is a good programming practice to run all the tests in your entire system as often as you can. It may be uncomfortable to do this frequently if it takes a long time to execute the tests or if an external resource (database, network connection, or web service) you need is not always available. Still, the more often you can run all your tests, the less time there is between injecting a defect into your system and finding it. Keeping that time interval short generally leads to a high-quality system. Unfortunately, it can seem like JUnit makes it difficult to run all your tests because the test runners only seem to run the tests from one test case class at a time.

Sure, you could write a script to automate running the tests from each test case class in your system, but you'd rather have all those tests in one big suite. This way you can take advantage of the way JUnit reports the results: the total number of tests, failures, and errors in the entire system. Seeing something like "4,192 tests, 0 failures, 0 errors" *really* gives you a sense of completion.[12] You believe that there should be a way to do this with JUnit.

◆ Recipe

Here we examine building a suite of suites following the instructions we have already described in recipe 4.2, "Collect a specific set of tests," and in recipe 4.3, "Collect all the tests in a package."

To collect all the tests for your entire system, do as follows:

1. For each test package in your system, create an `AllTests` class. This class builds a test suite from all the test case classes in the package. For detailed instructions, see recipe 4.3, "Collect all the tests in a package."
2. Most of your test packages will contain other packages, forming a package hierarchy. For each test package containing another test package, add

[12] See Ron Jeffries, Ann Anderson, and Chet Hendrickson, *Extreme Programming Installed* (Addison-Wesley, 2000), page 45, for a discussion about how an ongoing sense of completion makes a project go faster and better.

each child package's `AllTests` suite to the parent package's `AllTests` suite. This means that most of your `AllTests` classes will collect test suites from both the test case classes in the current package and all the `AllTests` classes in the packages below them.

3 At the top of your test package hierarchy you should now have the "granddaddy" `AllTests` suite. This suite collects all the test suites from the packages below it, and each of these collects from the packages below it, and so on down to the very bottom of the hierarchy. This granddaddy `AllTests` suite contains every test in the system.

Because the granddaddy `AllTests` class has a `suite()` method, you can pass it as the parameter to your test runner to run every single test in your system.

Following is an example of a granddaddy `AllTests` suite: JUnit's own, found in `junit.tests.AllTests`. The name of the test suite is only used for display purposes, so choose any name you like:

```
public static Test suite() {
    TestSuite suite= new TestSuite("Framework Tests");
    suite.addTest(junit.tests.framework.AllTests.suite());
    suite.addTest(junit.tests.runner.AllTests.suite());
    suite.addTest(junit.tests.extensions.AllTests.suite());
    return suite;
}
```

This `suite()` method adds the `AllTests` suite from each main test package in JUnit: the framework tests, the test runner tests, and the extensions tests. Each of these packages has its own `AllTests` suite, and so on down until you reach the "leaf" packages—the ones at the bottom of the test hierarchy. JUnit does not have a particularly deep test package hierarchy, but it still demonstrates the technique we have described here.

◆ Discussion

One other issue that JUnit's own `AllTests` hierarchy demonstrates is that building ever-larger suites of suites requires discipline and can be prone to error. You need discipline to maintain the relationships among the various `AllTests` classes. A relatively straightforward refactoring such as moving a package around can force you to make considerable changes to the `AllTests` suites. Although many modern IDEs automate moving packages around or moving classes from package to package, they do not update your `AllTests` hierarchy for you—that remains *your* job. You will begin to resent your `AllTests` classes because of the ongoing, mechanical changes you continually need to make. We understand these feelings;

we've been there. This is why we recommend seeking automated alternatives to maintaining an `AllTests` hierarchy by hand. Refer to recipe 4.5, "Scan the file system for tests," for some specific advice in this direction.

Even though maintaining these suites by hand can be time consuming and prone to error, for small systems the technique works well. If you are just starting out with JUnit and are on a smaller project—or at the genesis of a project—we recommend you concentrate on gaining experience in the other aspects of testing your system using JUnit. After you master those more important fundamentals, look for automated alternatives to the `AllTests` hierarchy. We find it simpler to start out using this technique on a small project and then change to an automated technique later, after our project has converged on a particular source code layout, package structure, and so on. Many of the automated alternatives involve scanning your source tree and discovering JUnit tests. If you haven't settled on a source tree structure yet, then you might need to make ongoing changes to your automatic suite builder as the project evolves. Why go through the pain? Start small, but be able to deal with the evolving complexity. The remainder of this chapter—indeed, this book—will help.

◆ *Related*

- 4.3—Collect all the tests in a package
- 4.5—Scan the file system for tests
- 16.2—Collect tests automatically from an archive

4.5 Scan the file system for tests

◆ *Problem*

You want like to build a test suite from all the tests in a certain part of your file system, without having to maintain `AllTests` classes by hand.

◆ *Background*

When a project grows to a certain size, maintaining test suites by hand becomes a real chore. You feel this pain the most when you need to make a structural change to your project, such as moving classes from package to package or even moving packages around in the hierarchy. These kinds of changes should not affect the overall behavior of your system, and many modern IDEs support these operations with the click of a mouse, so why are you forced to rewrite all these `AllTests` classes? There has to be a better way.

The better way is to scan the file system for tests. Let some object discover all the test case classes in a given directory structure and then present them to you as a test suite.

◆ *Recipe*

Although you could build a utility to do the work of scanning a part of your file system for anything that might be a test, Mike Bowler's GSBase (http://gsbase.sourceforge.net) already provides that feature with `RecursiveTestSuite`. This test suite builder is simple to use: point it at a directory containing built test classes (not source) on your file system and specify a `TestFilter`, an object that identifies whether or not to add a test case class to the test suite.[13] You are still building a custom test suite, but you are building it programmatically rather than by specifying individual test case classes. Listing 4.1 shows an example of using `RecursiveTestSuite` with a `TestFilter` that simply accepts all test case classes.

Listing 4.1 Collecting all the tests in one part of the file system

```
import junit.framework.Test;

import com.gargoylesoftware.base.testing.RecursiveTestSuite;
import com.gargoylesoftware.base.testing.TestFilter;

public class AllTests {                  <-- No need to extend TestCase
    public static Test suite() throws Exception {      <-- Custom suite method
        return new RecursiveTestSuite("classes", new TestFilter() {
            public boolean accept(Class eachTestClass) {
                return true;      <-- Always add the test case
            }
        });
    }
}
```

The first parameter to the constructor for `RecursiveTestSuite` is a location on the file system, either a path name (as a `String`) or a `File` object (representing a directory). This is where the test suite builder looks for Java class files that look like tests. Following a prevailing naming convention, any class whose name ends with `Test` is considered a test case class. So the first thing `RecursiveTestSuite` does is collect all the classes it believes are test case classes.

---

13 This concept of filters is explained in detail in Jeff Langr's *Essential Java Style* (Prentice Hall PTR, 2000). Pay particular attention to chapter 4, "Collections." The techniques he describes there are derived from Smalltalk, where filters like this are everywhere.

You can then use the `TestFilter` to include (or exclude) test case classes according to any criterion you can determine from a class object, including whether it implements any interfaces. Implement the `accept()` method to return `true` for all the test case classes you want to include in your test suite and `false` for the ones you want to exclude. In our example, we include them all. You can use this technique to separate the different kinds of tests you write into different test suites. See recipe 4.6, "Separate the different kinds of test suites," for details.

◆ *Discussion*

Although this works well, you may find a warning such as the following when you use `RecursiveTestSuite` to run your tests:

```
junit.framework.AssertionFailedError: Cannot instantiate test case
```

You will see this warning if you have Abstract Test Cases (see recipe 2.6, "Test an interface"), which generally look like test case classes but, being declared `abstract`, cannot be instantiated. You can use the `TestFilter` to eliminate those `abstract` classes from the suite, as listing 4.2 shows.

Listing 4.2 Eliminating abstract classes from a test suite using `TestFilter`

```
import java.lang.reflect.Modifier;

import junit.framework.Test;

import com.gargoylesoftware.base.testing.RecursiveTestSuite;
import com.gargoylesoftware.base.testing.TestFilter;

public class AllTests {
    public static Test suite() throws Exception {
        return new RecursiveTestSuite("classes", new TestFilter() {
            public boolean accept(Class eachTestClass) {
                boolean classIsConcrete =
                    ! Modifier.isAbstract(
                        eachTestClass.getModifiers());

                return classIsConcrete;
            }
        });
    }
}
```

This test filter asks each test case class whether it is concrete (not `abstract`), ensuring that the suite contains only test case classes that JUnit can actually instantiate.

Alternative

JUnit-addons (http://junit-addons.sourceforge.net) also provides a way to build a test suite from an entire directory structure with its utility class `junitx.util.DirectorySuiteBuilder`. It also supports filtering tests based on criteria you specify, but the code looks a little different. We can write the previous example "gather all concrete `TestCase` classes" as shown in listing 4.3.

Listing 4.3 Eliminating abstract classes from a test suite using `DirectorySuiteBuilder`

```
public class AllConcreteTestsSuite {
    public static Test suite() throws Exception {
        TestFilter filter = new TestFilter() {
            public boolean include(Class eachTestClass) {     <- Include only concrete classes
                boolean classIsConcrete =
                    !Modifier.isAbstract(eachTestClass.getModifiers());

                return classIsConcrete;
            }

            public boolean include(String eachTestClassName) {     <- Do not filter based on class name
                return true;
            }
        };

        DirectorySuiteBuilder builder =
            new DirectorySuiteBuilder(filter);     <- Use the filter we created
        return builder.suite(new File("test/classes"));     <- Look in the directory test/classes for tests
    }
}
```

We can think of only one strong difference between this code and the `RecursiveTestSuite` worth mentioning: `RecursiveTestSuite`'s filter has a single "accept" method, whereas `DirectorySuiteBuilder` tests the class object and the class name separately. You may prefer the former because it is simpler. Deciding which tool to use is largely a matter of preference and depends mostly on which tools you are already using. If you are already using GSBase or JUnit-addons for something else, then stick with that package. There is talk between Mike Bowler and Vladimir Bossicard of joining the projects, anyway.

◆ *Related*

- 2.6—Test an interface
- 4.4—Collect all the tests for your entire system
- 4.6—Separate the different kinds of test suites

- GSBase (http://gsbase.sourceforge.net)
- JUnit-addons (http://junit-addons.sourceforge.net)

4.6 Separate the different kinds of test suites

◆ Problem

You have different kinds of tests—Programmer Tests, Customer Tests, End-to-End Tests—and you want to collect all the tests of a particular type to run them as a single suite.

◆ Background

As your project increases in size and in scope, you will build many different kinds of tests. Most commonly, you will have Programmer Tests and Customer Tests. You will want to be able to build a test suite from just the Programmer Tests because they generally execute more quickly and tend not to rely much on external resources (such as a database) that may not always be available. You will want to be able to build a test suite from just the Customer Tests when you want to verify that your team is progressing in the direction that the customers or end users need. There are a number of ways to keep the two separate, and this recipe explores a few techniques that have worked well.

◆ Recipe

You have several options are your disposal, which we highlight here and then discuss in detail in the next section:

- Maintain separate IDE projects for each kind of test. This is supported very well by most Java IDEs, but if you're using CVS you have to work harder to coordinate changes across the CVS module boundary.
- Maintain a separate test source tree for each kind of test, but in the same CVS module. While Ant supports this complex project structure, Eclipse (for one) does not.
- Classify each individual test case class and then use `RecursiveTestSuite` and `TestFilter` (see recipe 4.5, "Scan the file system for tests") to collect the test case classes that fit each classification. An easy way to differentiate Customer Tests from the rest is have them implement a *tag* interface called `CustomerTest`.[14]

[14] A tag interface is a Java interface with no methods. You can use these tag interfaces and simple `instanceof` checks to classify your classes. The most commonly used tag interface is `java.io.Serializable`.

There are likely others, but one of these three will satisfy your needs.

◆ Discussion

Your first option is to maintain separate test source trees, just as we recommend in chapter 3. It is easy to use `RecursiveTestSuite` to collect all the tests in the Programmer Tests source tree without worrying about the tests in the Customer Tests source tree. If you are using a project-based IDE such as Eclipse, then keep the different kinds of tests in different projects. In such an environment, this is the source code layout that we recommend. This option's one downfall is that you may need to coordinate changes to multiple projects in your source control repository, particularly if you use CVS. Each project is stored in its own CVS module, and CVS does not directly support versioning multiple modules together. To simulate this, you need to tag the modules with the same tag name to signify that those versions of the various projects go together. If you are using Subversion, which supports global versioning, this is not an issue; but until Subversion releases version 1.0, CVS will likely continue its dominance in the source control arena.[15] What should you do, then, if you need to coordinate changes across all the different kinds of tests you write *and* you are using a system such as CVS?

You can have multiple source trees within the same CVS module: there is certainly nothing to stop you; however, some IDEs do not support building from multiple, different source trees into different destination directories. (Fortunately, Eclipse does support this feature, although you have to enable it on a project-by-project basis.) You could move to Subversion, which supports global versioning, but there is another, less drastic solution that may be right for your project.[16]

The last solution we recommend is one we have used with success: identify each test case class as a Programmer Test or a Customer Test or an Integration Test (or whatever kind of test) by implementing a tag interface. Specifically, we recommend that your Customer Test case class implement the interface `CustomerTest`, and the other test case classes follow suit. You can then build your test suite using GSBase's `RecursiveTestSuite` utility and its accompanying `TestFilter`. (See recipe 4.5, "Scan the file system for tests," for details on using `RecursiveTestSuite`.) In this case, the test filter you build accepts test classes that implement the desired tag interface. Listing 4.4 shows an example of collecting all the Customer Tests, assuming that you identify them with a tag interface called `CustomerTest`.

---

[15] Subversion was nearing version 1.0 as we wrote this and more than likely has been released by the time you read this.

[16] Nothing against Subversion, but old habits die hard.

Listing 4.4 Collecting tests that implement the `CustomerTest` interface

```
import junit.framework.Test;

import com.gargoylesoftware.base.testing.RecursiveTestSuite;
import com.gargoylesoftware.base.testing.TestFilter;

public class AllCustomerTests {
    public static Test suite() throws Exception {
        return new RecursiveTestSuite("classes", new TestFilter() {
            public boolean accept(Class eachTestClass) {
                return (
                    CustomerTest.class.isAssignableFrom(
                        eachTestClass));
            }
        });
    }
}
```

Does eachTestClass implement CustomerTest?

The standard Java class `Class` provides the method `isAssignableFrom()` to answer the question, "Can I refer to an instance of *that* class through a reference to *this* class?"[17] For example, `List` is assignable from `ArrayList`, because we can assign an `ArrayList` to a `List` reference.[18] The choice of method names is a little clunky, in our opinion. If we had an instance of the test case class, we could have asked the simpler question, "Is `testObject instanceof CustomerTest`?" Still, you cannot fault GSBase for wanting to filter out unwanted test case classes before any instances of them are created, so we're stuck with a slightly more unwieldy way of filtering out the test case classes that are not Customer Tests. If it annoys you more than it annoys us, then simply change `RecursiveTestSuite`. That's what open source is all about.[19]

◆ *Related*

- 4.5—Scan the file system for tests

---

[17] It's worth noting that `MyClass.class.isAssignableFrom(object.getClass())` is the same as `object instanceof MyClass`.

[18] In object-oriented shorthand, an `ArrayList` *is-a* `List`.

[19] That is, the freedom to change software that doesn't work as you need it to, not randomly throwing away other people's hard work.

4.7 Control the order of some of your tests

◆ Problem

You have a test case class with some tests that need to execute in a particular order and others that do not. You want to specify the order of the order-dependent tests without worrying about the order of the rest of the tests.

◆ Background

If you follow the instructions in recipe 4.2, "Collect a specific set of tests," then you are forced to specify the order of all the tests in your test case class; otherwise, you remain at the mercy of JUnit's arbitrary ordering of your tests.[20] This can be annoying if only 3 of your 22 tests need to execute in a certain order. What you would really like to do is identify the order of a few tests, and let JUnit do the rest. Because JUnit doesn't seem to handle this situation very well, it is worth asking, "How did we get into this mess in the first place?" Actually, it's not very unusual.

Let's say you have a suite of order-dependent tests. Maybe you're writing tests for a legacy system, perhaps you have some End-to-End or Integration Tests in which multiple tests use a fixed fixture,[21] or you might have inherited tests from an uninspired programmer—it could be anything. Your goal is to refactor the tests in the direction of total test isolation, considered a good practice among JUnit practitioners. If you build your test suite using the `suite()` method, you have no way to know whether your incremental changes are really moving you in the direction of test isolation, because the order of the tests in your `suite()` method determines the order in which JUnit executes the tests. You're not getting that warm, fuzzy feeling that you're headed in the right direction.

Even if you can't refactor this way, you'd like to have as much test isolation as you can have, given the current tests. JUnit doesn't seem to support what you're trying to do.

◆ Recipe

GSBase to the rescue! Mike Bowler ran into this problem on a project and decided to write a test suite builder that guarantees the order of some tests but

---

[20] If you think you "know" the order in which JUnit automatically extracts tests from a test case class, then throw that information away as quickly as possible. JUnit makes no test-order guarantee. If you rely on its current implementation, and then it changes, you'll wish you hadn't "known" quite so much!

[21] Try saying that five times in a row.

leaves the rest to the order in which JUnit decides to execute them. He calls this an `OrderedTestSuite`. Using the `OrderedTestSuite` class is simple:

1 If your test case class does not already have a `suite()` method, create one. Refer to recipe 4.2, "Collect a specific set of tests," if you need detailed instructions.
2 Code your `suite()` method to create an `OrderedTestSuite` from your test case class, specifying as a list the names of the tests you wish to execute in a particular order. Return this `OrderedTestSuite` object.

It sounds simple, as it should, because it is. Here is an example:

```
public static Test suite() {
    String[] orderDependentTests = new String[] {
        "testQueryWithNoAccounts",
        "testInsert",
        "testInsertAccountExists",
        "testQueryWithOneAccount",
        "testDelete"
    };
    return new OrderedTestSuite(
        AccountDataStoreTest.class, orderDependentTests);
}
```

Let us look at how we arrived at this solution. Consider a test case class from an online banking application that verifies some basic operations on a data store for bank accounts. The person writing these tests decided it would be best to have the tests execute in a particular order; that way, each test does not need to set up and tear down its own fixture each time.[22] After some trial and error, you have determined that there are only five tests that need to run in a certain order:

1 Querying the accounts when there are none should return an empty collection of accounts.
2 Inserting a new account should work.
3 Inserting the same account a second time should fail with a duplicate key exception.
4 Querying the accounts with some accounts in the data store ought to return those accounts.
5 Deleting an existing account should work.

[22] The performance benefit seems tempting, and the apparent simplicity of the tests seems tempting, but believe us, you will feel much more pain later on. See recipe 4.1, "Let JUnit build your test suite."

There are other tests, though, that could be run in any order:

- Querying a certain account that isn't in the data store should fail with "object not found."
- Deleting an account that doesn't exist should fail with "object not found."
- Inserting a number of accounts in a row and then performing a mass delete should work.
- Performing a mass delete on no accounts should do nothing.

There may be more, but this second list of tests has a common fixture: an empty account data store. JUnit could execute them before or after executing the tests you care about—either works. By using `OrderedTestSuite`, JUnit can execute the first set of tests in the order you specify them and then execute the second set of tests in whatever order it chooses. Our example shows specifying the first set of tests as order-dependent but makes no explicit mention of the second set. It simply lets JUnit do its job. This is exactly what we are looking for.

◆ Discussion

We have said before—and will say again—that you should strive for 100% test isolation. Every time we have decided that test isolation is not important, it eventually slapped us in the face and showed us who is boss. We also admit that it is not always easy to achieve total test isolation. In particular, we may not have it right now. Even if you are an avid Test-Driven Development practitioner, you may inherit some tests that are order dependent. You can use `OrderedTestSuite` as a tool to help you refactor in the direction of total test isolation. Here is the basic approach:

1. Create an `OrderedTestSuite` that specifies the order of all the tests in the test case class, just as they are specified in the current `suite()` method.
2. Select a test to fix, and remove its dependence on the behavior of the preceding tests.
3. Remove the test you have fixed from the list of order-dependent tests.
4. Repeat until the list of order-dependent tests is empty.
5. Remove the `suite()` method, and let JUnit build the default test suite for you.

This may be time consuming, but it certainly works. Without `OrderedTestSuite`, you would not be able to perform this delicate code surgery incrementally with the tests as a safety net. Until you experience how calm you are when you make big changes with tests as a safety net, you don't know how empowering it can feel.[23] Using `OrderedTestSuite` in this situation enables a gradual transition to total test isolation without the risk of breaking the system along the way. In this way, `OrderedTestSuite` is invaluable.

Remember that `OrderedTestSuite` executes the order-dependent tests first, then the rest. The rest of your tests may assume an empty test fixture—that is, one in which no data has been changed by a test. If the last of the order-dependent tests leaves your fixture in an unknown state, then the remaining tests just won't work. To overcome this problem, add a *fixture barrier* at the end of the list of order-dependent tests. It is a barrier in that it protects the "good tests" from whatever havoc the "bad tests" might wreak. This is a method that cleans up the fixture, placing it in the state that the remaining tests expect. We usually call this method `resetFixture()`. Add this method to your class and code it to reset the fixture, as in this example:

```
public static Test suite() {
    String[] orderDependentTests = new String[] {
        "testQueryWithNoAccounts",
        "testInsert",
        "testInsertAccountExists",
        "testQueryWithOneAccount",
        "testDelete",
        "resetFixture"
    };
    return new OrderedTestSuite(
        AccountDataStoreTest.class, orderDependentTests);
}
```

This change causes JUnit to call `resetFixture()` after executing the order-dependent tests you've specified, creating a sparkling clean environment for the rest of the tests to use. Once you have refactored the remaining tests to have total test isolation, remove `resetFixture()`. This solution is a hack, and JUnit will erroneously report `resetFixture()` as a passed test; but because it is a temporary solution you're working toward removing, we promise not to call the JUnit Police.

It seems strange to view such a useful piece of software as something that you hope never to use and as something you want out of your code as soon as possible, but it is still an important tool in your arsenal as a JUnit practitioner.

---

[23] J. B. once spent 9 days changing 60% of a system because of massive database schema restructuring. The only reason it could be done in 9 days was because the system had a comprehensive suite of JUnit tests. Otherwise, large sections would had to have been rewritten, and no one knows how long *that* would have taken.

◆ ***Related***

- 4.1—Let JUnit build your test suite
- 4.2—Collect a specific set of tests

4.8 Build a data-driven test suite

◆ ***Problem***

You want to build a suite that runs the same test many times with different data.

◆ ***Background***

The obvious way to do this with JUnit is simple, but tedious. Let us describe how we first experienced this tedium.

We had a method we wanted to test, so we wrote a test. This first test verified a simple case and was easy both to write and to make pass. The next test tried a slightly more complex case, but it too was simple to write and make pass. At that point we had two test methods that looked very similar. The next test tried a boundary condition, where the output was a little different. We wrote this test, made it pass, and then saw the amount of duplication in our tests. All three tests did essentially the same thing: they invoked the same methods on the same kinds of objects. The only differences were the method parameters and the expected results. The names of the methods even showed some duplication: each test method's name had both the name of the method we were testing and the particular condition we were testing. We wanted to do something about all this duplication.

Being good little programmers, we factored out the common parts of the tests into a method that performed the core of the test by accepting the input and expected result as parameters. We called this method `doTest()` to indicate that it was actually performing the test. We changed all the JUnit test methods to call `doTest()` with the various parameters. This solution pleased us, but every time we wanted to test a new boundary condition, we had to add a test method that did nothing more than invoke `doTest()` with a new set of parameters. If all we're doing is adding new test data, why are we writing code? We should just be adding data somewhere.

This recipe describes how to parameterize a test case so that adding new tests is as simple as adding the new test data. These kinds of tests are generally referred to as *data-driven tests.*

◆ *Recipe*

First, you need to build a Parameterized Test Case. This is a test case class that defines a single test method but includes a custom suite method that provides the data for each test. The suite method builds a suite of tests, each test executing the same test method but providing a different test fixture for each instance of the test. The fixture contains the input to the test and the expected results. The end result is a suite of test objects, each of whose test method is the same, but whose test fixture is different. JUnit can then execute the resulting test suite, executing each test on its own, different fixture. Here is a sketch of how to transform a garden variety test case class into a Parameterized Test Case:

1. If you have not done so already, factor out the common parts of your test—what we call the *engine* of the test—into its own method. Call the method `doTest()`. Its parameters will be the input to the method under test and the result you expect.
2. Change each test method to call `doTest()` with the appropriate parameters.
3. At this point, you have a test case class whose test methods all delegate to `doTest()` and otherwise only specify the input and expected result for each test. Factor that data out into a test fixture.
4. Create a constructor for your test case class whose parameter list matches the parameter list of `doTest()`. Your constructor should call `super("doTest")` and then store the parameters in instance-level fields. For simplicity, name the fields the same as the parameters to `doTest()`.
5. Create a `suite()` method to build a custom test suite.
6. For each test method in your test case class, take the parameters you pass to `doTest()` and use them to create an instance of your test case class. Add this test object to the test suite. Remove the test method.
7. Once all the test methods have been removed, remove the parameter list from the method `doTest()`. It should now resemble a test method in that it is `public`, it occurs at the instance-level, it has no parameters, and it has no return value. Because you have added fields with the same name as the parameters to `doTest()`, the method should still compile.
8. Consider renaming `doTest()` to something that better reveals the intent of the test. Remember to change the first line of the new constructor to match the new name of this method.

You end up with a test suite created from test objects that correspond to the test methods you had written by hand before. Your test data was formerly scattered among the various test methods, but now it is found in one place: your new `suite()` method. This makes it easier to see at a glance all the data you use in your test suite.

To illustrate this technique, let us return to our `Money` class and consider a problem that Martin Fowler raises in *Patterns of Enterprise Application Architecture*: allocating an amount of money evenly to multiple accounts. Although splitting money *n* ways seems like a simple problem, people tend to be very concerned about rounding problems when their money is involved, so it is important to get this algorithm right.[24] The essence of the problem is that blindly rounding off to the nearest penny either loses money or creates it out of thin air, neither of which makes everyone happy. Because concrete examples are always better, consider how $1,000 should be split 6 ways: 2 of every 3 accounts receives $166.67, the other $166.66. In total, 4 accounts should receive $166.67 each and 2 accounts $166.66 each. The total remains exactly $1,000. Blindly rounding would have created two cents where there were none.[25]

You will want to have a number of these tests, with different amounts to split and different ways to split them. Each test does essentially the same thing: take an amount of money, split it some number of ways, and then check that the accounts received a fair "cut" of the money. The engines of the tests are the same, but the input and expected output are different; so we push the data into our custom `suite()` method, as you can see in listing 4.5.

Listing 4.5 `AllocateMoneyTest`

```
public class AllocateMoneyTest extends TestCase {
    private Money amountToSplit;
    private int nWays;
    private Map expectedCuts;

    public AllocateMoneyTest(
        Money amountToSplit,
        int nWays,
        Map expectedCuts) {

        super("testAllocate");
```

The test parameters become the fixture (annotation on the three private fields)

Must match test method name (annotation on `super("testAllocate");`)

[24] There are a surprising number of ways to get it wrong.

[25] Printing money causes inflation, which leads to the overall collapse of the economy. Programmers can do real damage when they put their minds to it.

```
        this.amountToSplit = amountToSplit;
        this.nWays = nWays;
        this.expectedCuts = expectedCuts;
    }

    public static Test suite() throws Exception {
        TestSuite suite = new TestSuite();

        Map oneGSixWays = new HashMap();
        oneGSixWays.put(new Money(166, 66), new Integer(2));
        oneGSixWays.put(new Money(166, 67), new Integer(4));
        suite.addTest(                          <-- Creates the first test
            new AllocateMoneyTest(
                new Money(1000, 0),
                6,
                oneGSixWays));

        Map oneGTwoWays =
            Collections.singletonMap(
                new Money(500, 0),
                new Integer(2));
        suite.addTest(                          <-- Creates the second test
            new AllocateMoneyTest(
                new Money(1000, 0),
                2,
                oneGTwoWays));

        return suite;
    }

    public void testAllocate() {
        List allocatedAmounts = amountToSplit.split(nWays);
        Map actualCuts = organizeIntoBag(allocatedAmounts);
        assertEquals(expectedCuts, actualCuts);
    }

    // A bag is a collection of objects that counts the
    // number of copies it has of each object.
    // The map's keys are the objects and the values are
    // the number of copies of that object.
    private Map organizeIntoBag(List allocatedAmounts) {
        Map bagOfCuts = new HashMap();

        for (Iterator i = allocatedAmounts.iterator();
            i.hasNext();
            ) {

            Money eachAmount = (Money) i.next();
            incrementCountForCutAmount(bagOfCuts, eachAmount);
        }
        return bagOfCuts;
    }
```

```
    private void incrementCountForCutAmount(
        Map bagOfCuts,
        Money eachAmount) {

        Object cutsForAmountAsObject =
            bagOfCuts.get(eachAmount);

        int cutsForAmount;
        if (cutsForAmountAsObject == null) {
            cutsForAmount = 0;
        }
        else {
            cutsForAmount =
                ((Integer) cutsForAmountAsObject).intValue();
        }

        bagOfCuts.put(
            eachAmount,
            new Integer(cutsForAmount + 1));
    }
}
```

The key points here are that you have created a test fixture from the old test parameters, your constructor must specify the test method name when calling `super()`, and you create a test object for each group of data you'd like to use in your test. These are the features of a Parameterized Test Case.

◆ Discussion

Note that although we named our test method `testAllocate()`, following the JUnit naming rules, we did so as a matter of convention rather than out of necessity. Because we built the test suite ourselves, we could have named the method any way we like, as long as it was otherwise a valid test method (meaning it is `public`, occurs at the instance-level, has no parameters, and has no return value). What is important is that the name you pass into the test case class's constructor is the name of your test method. JUnit still uses reflection to execute your test method. Unless you have good reason to change the name, we recommend following the convention. It is simply easier for everyone that way.

One drawback to this approach is that although each test operates on different data, all the tests in your suite will have the same name. This can make it difficult to determine exactly which test is failing from JUnit's output alone. One simple solution is to add the test input into the failure messages for each assertion in the test. This would work, but it is better to have meaningful names. You can achieve this by overriding `runTest()` and placing your test code directly inside that method. This way you sidestep JUnit's default behavior, which is to invoke a method whose name matches the name of the test case.[26] If you override `runTest()`, you can pass a more meaningful name as a parameter to the constructor of your test case class. For a complete example, refer to solution A.2, "Parameterized Test Case overriding runTest()."

The method you want to test may have a few different ways to respond to its input, depending on whether the input is valid. It is common, for example, for a method to process valid input but throw an exception on invalid input. In this case, you need to change your Parameterized Test Case a little. Build one test method for each major kind of behavior: one test verifies that the object under test correctly processes valid input; the other test verifies that the object throws the correct exception when it receives invalid input (see recipe 2.8, "Test throwing the right exception"). When you build the test suite, remember to choose the appropriate test method based on the input you plan to pass in—valid or invalid. You may decide to implement these different behaviors in separate Parameterized Test Cases, but if there are only a few data sets, it may be simpler to combine the two into a single test case class. As always, experiment with each solution and compare the results.

It is common to move the test data to a file, a database, or some other location away from the test code. This makes adding new test cases simpler because it avoids rebuilding Java code. For an example of externalizing test data to an XML document, see recipe 4.9, "Define a test suite in XML."

NOTE *Don't try this with Cactus!*—If you are using Cactus for in-container J2EE testing (see chapter 11, "Testing Enterprise JavaBeans"), then you cannot employ this technique to build a data-driven test suite. Cactus instantiates `TestCase` objects when executing tests on the server, which means that although you may be passing in test fixture objects on the client side, Cactus does not pass those fixture objects into the server-side test, rendering that fixture data useless for in-container testing. Your only recourse is to extract a method containing the test logic, such as the `doTest()` method from this recipe, and then write a test method for each combination of parameters that invokes `doTest()`. The main drawback is that adding new test data requires changing Java code rather than just data. You can probably generate the Parameterized Test Case class source code using something like the Velocity template engine, but we recommend

---

[26] This is part of the machinery that performs automatic test suite extraction from your test case class.

doing so only after you have analyzed the trade-off between manually maintaining the test and building the code generator (and then integrating it into your build and test environment).

◆ Related

- 2.8—Test throwing the right exception
- 4.9—Define a test suite in XML
- A.2—Parameterized Test Case overriding runTest()

4.9 Define a test suite in XML

◆ Problem

You want to externalize a data-driven test suite's data in an XML document. To do so, you need to know how to create a `TestSuite` object that contains test objects corresponding to the "test" elements in your XML document.

◆ Background

JUnit's design assumes that different tests test essentially different things. When we wrote about extracting a test fixture (recipe 3.4, "Factor out a test fixture"), we mentioned that of the three main parts of a test, it is usually only the first part that we duplicate among many tests: creating the objects to test. The other two parts—invoking methods and checking the results—vary from test to test; if they didn't, we would have to question why we have five tests when one might do an equally good job. This is the reason that, by default, each test is defined as a separate test method inside a test case class. This is certainly not the only way to write tests.

If you're reading this recipe, then likely it is because you have a small suite of data-driven tests that you'd like to run. These tests all invoke the same methods on the same objects, but the input and output vary from test to test. You started writing a few test methods, factored out the common part of the test—the engine—and you now have a bunch of test methods, each invoking the one method that executes the engine. Although you need only one method to implement the logic behind your test, you have written a number of test methods that simply invoke the engine with different parameters for the input and expected result. All that duplication! You feel that there *must* be a better way.

Don't worry, because there is, and if you have chosen XML as the way to define your test case input and output, this recipe will show you how to integrate your XML document into a JUnit test.

◆ *Recipe*

The following is a sketch of the solution:

1. Create an XML document to store the data for your tests. The document structure includes one XML element for each test. Each test element includes an XML element for the input and another XML element for the expected result.
2. Create a Parameterized Test Case using the instructions in recipe 4.8, "Build a data-driven test suite." In the process, you will create a custom suite method.
3. Change your custom suite method so that it loads your XML document, reads the input and expected result for each test, and then calls your new constructor to create the corresponding test object. Your `suite()` method returns a `TestSuite` containing a test object for each test in your XML document.

In essence, you are going one step beyond the Parameterized Test Case by pushing the test data out into a file—in this case, an XML document. Listing 4.6 shows an example of an XML document describing a test for the "allocate money" problem we describe in recipe 4.8.

Listing 4.6 Test data for splitting money *n* ways

```
<tests name="Money Allocation Tests">
    <test>    <-- One test tag per test
        <input>    <-- The input for this test
            <amount-to-split>$1000.00</amount-to-split>
            <number-of-ways>6</number-of-ways>
        </input>
        <expected-result>    <-- The output for this test
            <cut>
                <amount>$166.67</amount>
                <number>4</number>
            </cut>
            <cut>
                <amount>$166.66</amount>
                <number>2</number>
            </cut>
        </expected-result>
    </test>
</tests>
```

This format should be simple enough to read, although the expected result may need some explanation. We expect $1,000 split 6 ways to result in 4 accounts with $166.67 each and 2 accounts with $166.66 each. Because we need to give these concepts names for our XML document, we say that we expect 4 *cuts* of $166.67 each and 2 *cuts* of $166.66 each.

Our task is now to follow the earlier steps and create a Parameterized Test Case whose data comes from our XML document. Because the entire solution requires about 200 lines of code—well-factored, of course—we refer you to solution A.1, "Define a test suite in XML," to see how we parsed the XML document into test objects. The result is a suite of data-driven tests whose data source is an XML document.

◆ Discussion

Although we used XML to define our test data, you don't need to use XML to employ this technique. Any text file or other external data format is equally good: flat file, comma-separated values, or database tables. Ron Jeffries often uses a very simple file format for his Customer Tests: a kind of rudimentary structured text, with a section for the input, a section for the actions to execute, and then a section for the expected result. To see an example, consult Ron's *Adventures in C#* series at www.xprogramming.com.[27] The article "The First Customer Test" provides an example of writing a Customer Test using NUnit, a C# cousin of JUnit. Although the sample code is C#, most Java programmers do not have problems reading it. The most important lesson about writing Customer Tests is this: *you don't need a framework; you need tests.* The framework will evolve if you just start writing tests.

◆ Postscript

Not long after we wrote this recipe, we had the opportunity to work with Ward Cunningham's Fit framework for the first time (http://fit.c2.com). It is a spreadsheet- or table-based way to write Customer Tests and may be the next big wave in testing. This is the framework we've been waiting for. Go check it out.

◆ Related

- 3.4—Factor out a test fixture
- 4.8—Build a data-driven test suite
- A.1—Define a test suite in XML

---

[27] Either that or his book *Extreme Programming Adventures in C#* (Microsoft Press, 2004).

5 Working with test data

This chapter covers

- Retrieving test data from system properties
- Retrieving test data from environment variables
- Retrieving test data from files on disk
- Retrieving test data from a database
- Managing test data using such tools as Ant, JUnitPP, and DbUnit

Object-oriented software deals with data and behavior. If you are going to test most software prior to releasing it to users or into a production environment, you need test data to simulate inputs that trigger behavior you expect to occur when the software works correctly. Software is commonly written for transforming input data into different output data. You cannot test whether the system outputs the correct output data, usually, without providing it with test input data. Software can also be designed to generate answers from digested input data or to manage data storage and retrieval. Obviously, testing these software behaviors require a lot of test data.

JUnit and its extensions are used to test software at a variety of scopes, not just the unit level. JUnit is great for traditional unit testing and Test-Driven Development at the unit scope. It is also good for Integration Testing, often up to the subsystem level. At higher integration levels and in testing complex subsystems, a JUnit extension such as Cactus or JUnitEE must be used. Often your organization has its own in-house test harness based on extensions of JUnit that can be used to test these higher integration levels. You need different amounts and types of test data, depending on whether you want to write Object Tests, Integration Tests, or End-to-End Tests. Keep in mind that the more of the system you test at once, the more you need to engage the real production system for both retrieving and restoring test data between runs. This adds complexity to both the tests and the test environment and makes the task of writing and executing tests more difficult.

Test data should be specialized and designed to force the code under test into branches and states that are only tested when fed specific inputs. Working with test data includes *parameterizing* data in test cases, which means identifying data that changes from test to test and providing it externally. A simple approach to parameterizing involves abstracting test data into parameters that can be passed in, or retrieved dynamically, at runtime rather than hard coded directly into the test case classes. Parameterization is a good thing because it decouples your tests and your test data into separate concerns with separate alternatives and solutions available. Parameterized tests should rely on good, portable Java conventions and good practices and idioms for dynamically passing data to test cases at runtime. By the same token, another good practice is to avoid creating test harness infrastructure until it is needed; at that point, making test data globally available—possibly even in the test case class itself—makes more sense. A range of gradations exists in between the two extremes of parameterization and global (class-level) definition. Generating data dynamically (possibly large amounts of data, as in volume testing) and restoring the state of shared data between test runs are important tasks for some types of testing, especially database-related tests.

If you have test data that does not need to be variable, you probably can hard code it in your tests. Otherwise, there are several good practices for parameterizing test data out of test cases. Some techniques use basic built-in Java features, such as system properties, command-line arguments to the JVM, the Java Properties API, or `ResourceBundle`s. While parameterizing data and configuring test cases and suites with data are the main activities in working with test data, another important activity is setting up and restoring data to its initial state between test cases or test runs, preferably with some degree of efficiency so that test run durations are kept to a minimum. This chapter offers techniques for resetting database data and other general kinds of data using DbUnit and the JUnit `TestSetup` Decorator.

Data can come in a variety of forms, from primitive Java data type variables and `String`s, to XML files, to records in database tables. The nature of the data needed for testing is determined by the responsibilities of the classes under test. Once, when working on a commercial J2EE application server, we needed a great deal of test data in the form of EJB JARs, WARs, and EARs because we had to test application server responsibilities, such as the ability to deploy, undeploy, and redeploy J2EE EARs, WARs, and JARs. On another project, which involved human resources middleware applications, we needed test data in the form of large hierarchical data sets of managers and employees in a relational database. At both companies we needed different, smaller amounts of file-based test data to test service and application configurations, security settings, and utility classes. We also used environment variables and system properties to glue it all together and make test harnesses and test suites portable and easy to run on different user environments, platforms, and operating systems. Setting up and maintaining different types of test data is an important and time-consuming investment for unit and integration testing large and complex systems. Using portable solutions for these concerns even at the level of individual test cases enforces best practices, which is especially important as you move up the scale from utility classes to small command-line applications, to middleware applications, application servers, and so on. This chapter covers working with data in a variety of formats including XML, properties files, text files, relational databases, and system and environment variables. And it covers some best practices and useful JUnit extensions, such as JUnitPP and DbUnit, for working with databases and homegrown test data repositories.

5.1 Use Java system properties

◆ Problem

You need a quick and easy way to set and retrieve variable data in your tests at runtime.

◆ *Background*

Sometimes you need a simple and quick way to pass a small amount of variable data to your test cases. Hard coding the data and recompiling the test case every time you want to change a value is more time consuming and less efficient than making the variable something that can be passed in on the command line. A database is too heavy duty to set up and use in many situations (or the database might not be designed or finished when you need to be coding and testing). Even reading in a properties file to retrieve variables can be time consuming and cause undesirable overhead if there are only a few variables.

You shouldn't have to go to great lengths just to parameterize some test data for a one-off test or a test that occurs early in the project that you've written to try out a new API or investigate a design issue. Yet it would be nice to always stay within the realm of portable Java solutions. You should never need to hard code a path to a file on your Windows C: drive in a test case when you might turn around and e-mail that test to your colleague who wants to run it quickly from the command line without editing the source and recompiling it.

◆ *Recipe*

Use Java system properties on the command line, in your IDE settings, or in Ant to pass parameterized data values into the system environment of the JVM where they can be retrieved using methods of the `java.lang.System` class.

There are several ways to set a system property, depending on the way you launch tests. How you set the property also depends on whether you want to set the property programmatically or outside your test. The simplest is to key it in at the command prompt using the standard command-line option `-Dpropertyname=value` syntax accepted by the java application launcher. The `propertyname` is the name of the system property you want to create, and `value` is what you want the property to be set to, both of which can be any valid Java string. You can choose any name you want, but if you choose a name of one of the standard Java system properties, you override its value (which you probably don't want to do). Most of the standard properties begin with "`java.`" but you can refer to a list of their names (also called *keys*) in the Javadoc for `java.lang.System.getProperties()`.[1]

[1] The Javadoc does not contain a complete list—the keys listed there are guaranteed to be available, but there may be more.

The following command-line snippet demonstrates setting two system properties. The first is given the uninteresting name `FOO` and the value `BAR` and the second is given the name `spaces.are.ok` and the value "string with spaces":

```
java -DFOO=BAR -Dspaces.are.ok="string with spaces" [class] [arguments]
```

ANT TIP In Ant, system properties can be passed directly to the `<junit>` task with one or more `<sysproperty>` subelements as shown here. In an Ant build file, this is how you set the same `FOO` and `spaces.are.ok` properties we set on the command line in the previous example.

```
<junit printsummary="yes" dir="${basedir}" fork="yes">
    <sysproperty key="FOO" value="BAR"/>
    <sysproperty key="spaces.are.ok" value="string with spaces"/>
    <test name="some.company.SomeTestCase"/>
</junit>
```

NOTE *Eclipse*—If you are running your tests inside the Eclipse IDE, you can set system properties for JUnit test runs by using the Run wizard for JUnit run configurations as shown in figure 5.1. Other IDEs (NetBeans, IntelliJ IDEA, and JBuilder) have similar capabilities for passing system properties to their built-in JUnit test runners.

Regardless of the execution mechanism (whether you use the command line, Ant, or Eclipse), you access these system property values from your test by using

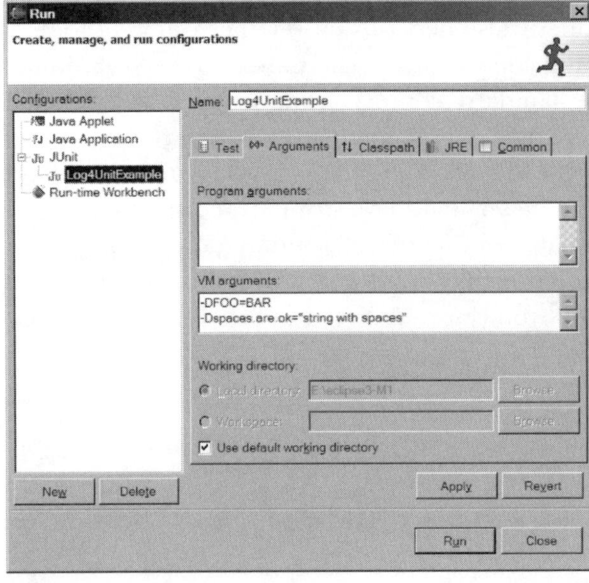

Figure 5.1
Setting system property arguments in Eclipse's JUnit Run wizard

java.lang.System.getProperty(String key). The name you give the property on the command line or in the key attribute of the <sysproperty> subelement determines the string you must pass to System.getProperty(String key) to retrieve its value. Listing 5.1 shows a complete example of getting two system properties and using them in an assertion.

Listing 5.1 SystemPropertyDemo

```
package junit.cookbook.testdata;

import junit.framework.TestCase;

public class SystemPropertyDemo extends TestCase {
    private String fooProperty = System.getProperty("FOO");
    private String spacesProperty = System.getProperty("spaces.are.ok");

    public void testSystemProperty() {
        if (fooProperty == null) {
            fail("Expected 'FOO' to be set as a system property.");
        } else {
            assertEquals("BAR", System.getProperty("FOO"));
        }
    }
}
```

You can run SystemPropertyDemo with any test runner, but here is the command line to run it with the text-based test runner:

```
java -DFOO=BAR -Dspaces.are.ok="string with spaces"  -cp .;junit.jar
➾ junit.textui.TestRunner junit.cookbook.testdata.SystemPropertyDemo
```

◆ Discussion

This recipe is most useful for String variables or primitive data type variables whose values can easily be converted from a String using the standard JDK conversion methods, such as Double.parseDouble(String s) or Boolean.getBoolean (String s).

In addition to being useful for dynamically setting a small number of variable values, this recipe is useful for setting configuration variables for your test framework. For example, a system property may be used to set a default global or package-level logging threshold (handy if you're using a logger for logging test results or test debug messages).

The overloaded System.getProperty(String key, String defaultValue) method returns a default value if a system property's value has not been set. For example, you may set a default value for the database server hostname to use when running a test locally on your desktop, which you know will be overridden with QA's test database hostname during the automated build. Here's an example of that usage:

```
String hostName = System.getProperty("database.hostname","localhost");
```

Two particular built-in Java system properties are worth special mention not only because they are always available from any Java runtime on any platform but also because they are relative to the current user's name and platform-specific temp directory. They are `user.home` and `java.io.tmpdir`. On Windows XP, these have the following values ("My User" would be replaced with your actual user name on your machine):

```
user.home       = C:\Documents and Settings\My User
java.io.tmpdir = C:\DOCUME~2\MYUSER~1\LOCALS~1\Temp\
```

On UNIX, `user.home` usually defaults to something similar to /home/myuser and `java.io.tmpdir` resolves to /tmp.

The `user.home` property can be useful for reading in user settings related to test data configuration, such as the local test data repository location. The `java.io.tmpdir` property can be useful for writing out temporary data files during testing, and it is the directory in which `java.io.File.createTempFile(String prefix, String suffix)` writes temporary files.

- ***Related***
  - 5.6—Use a file-based test data repository

5.2 Use environment variables

- ***Problem***

You need an easy way for users to set some global test data, such as the location of a test file, a data repository, or database connection parameters.

- ***Background***

We often distribute Java applications with a Windows *.bat file, a UNIX shell script, or an Ant build script as a convenience wrapper to enable end users to execute our apps. It is not uncommon to have several command-line options and arguments needing to be passed to the JVM when starting your application. But your users might not be savvy enough or don't need to be bothered with a lot of command-line parameters every time they have to execute your application. Your product may actually ship as a Weblogic domain instance, or an EAR file that has to be deployed on JBoss. Think of your product as a black box that users should be able to execute and run as easily as possible without knowing about implementation details such as whether they are even running a Java program. These are all reasons why you may want to provide a simplified wrapper script for your application, hiding the details of how to deploy and execute it. Such a script would depend on one or more system environment variables to configure some fundamental parameters of your tests, such as which database server to use or where to write out test results files.

Your first users are probably Release Engineering people or QA staff who will run your unit tests as part of qualifying builds. If a test breaks, someone in QA or development will probably need to execute the failing test on their desktop in order to debug the cause of the failure. Other users might be systems integrators or a professional services team completely outside your department or company, who use a set of unit tests shipped with your product as a regression test suite for their extensions, customizations, or configuration of your code. In cases such as these, there is an easy way to decouple your tests from their execution environment. Store information about the execution environment in environment variables and then pass those into your JUnit tests using Java system properties.

◆ *Recipe*

Require a system environment variable to be set prior to running your tests, and code your application wrapper script so that it passes the OS environment variable to your application as a Java system property (see recipe 5.1, "Use Java system properties"). Optionally, perform a check in the wrapper script to exit and warn the user if the variable has not been set.

For example, say that you want to access a critical operating system–specific variable, such as the APP_HOME environment variable in this UNIX bourne shell script:

```
#!/bin/sh
if [ -z "$APP_HOME" ]; then
    echo "Please set your APP_HOME environment variable"
    exit 1
fi
if [ ! -e "$APP_HOME" ]; then
    echo "Folder '$APP_HOME' does not exist."
    exit 1
fi
java -DAPP_HOME=$APP_HOME PrintSystemVar
```

Now the APP_HOME variable can be retrieved in a test class using System.getProperty(), as shown in listing 5.2.

Listing 5.2 PrintSystemVar

```
public class PrintSystemVar {

    public static final String APP_HOME = "APP_HOME";

    public static void main(String[] args) {
        System.out.println(PrintSystemVar.APP_HOME
                + " = " + getAppHome());
    }

    public static String getAppHome() {
        return System.getProperty(PrintSystemVar.APP_HOME, ".");
    }
}
```

Use "." if APP_HOME property not defined

This program declares a constant `APP_HOME String` variable and uses it to get the Java system property by that name and print it.

Discussion

Relying on a `HOME` environment variable is a good practice and a convention many professional software users are accustomed to using. Several popular applications that run in Java developer, testing, and production environments require their own environment variables. Here are a few common examples:

- Ant: `ANT_HOME`
- Java: `JAVA_HOME`, `CLASSPATH`
- Maven: `MAVEN_HOME`, `MAVEN_REPO`
- Weblogic: `BEA_HOME`, `WL_HOME`

Environment variables and Java system properties play the same role in decoupling your tests from the environment in which they execute. The principal difference between the two approaches is that environment variables are best used to hide operating system details, such as where third-party libraries are installed, whereas Java system properties are best used to hide test environment–specific details, such as the location of test data files or test suite descriptors (such as we described in recipe 4.9, "Define a test suite in XML").

Related

- 5.1—Use Java system properties

5.3 Use an inline data file

◆ Problem

You need a configuration file or input file for your test, and you don't want to worry about where the file should be stored in source control or bother writing special setup code in a test case to read it from the file system.

◆ Background

If you are testing a class that operates on small chunks of text or small input files and you just need to test a few different scenarios (say a dozen or less), it is probably easiest and fastest to code the file snippets in the test class.

Imagine that you have an application to test. A configuration system is planned but not yet implemented, so all you have in the meantime is a flat configuration file. Your test cases include configuration tests, and to cover a class fully with tests you need to use several different configuration files—maybe a different one for each test method. You could read the file in a `BaseTestCase` extension class from which all your other test cases could extend and inherit the retrieval mechanism. But this is already more infrastructure than you need for an elegant solution. The configuration files are just another type of input file, so consider coding them statically in the test classes. If at a later date you need less coupling between the tests and the test files (perhaps the tests are getting difficult to read and maintain with too many snippets of files statically coded into them), you can easily extract the files from the tests and save them as files on the file system.

◆ Recipe

Hard code or dynamically build the input file as a `String` or `StringBuffer` in your `TestCase` and "read" it using a `java.io.StringReader` instead of reading it from the file system.

Hard coding the input file is easy enough. Here is an imaginary XML configuration file coded as a `String`:

```
String configFile = "<?xml version='1.0'?>"
        + "<services>"
        +     "<service name='myService' version='1.0'>"
        +     "<service-param name='thread-pool-size'>8<service-param>"
        +     "<service-param name='session-timeout'>300<service-param>"
        +  "</service>"
        + "</services>";
```

Now the configuration file can be converted to a byte array using `String.getBytes()` and passed to a `Reader`, which is used to create a new `org.xml.sax.InputSource`:

```
Reader reader = new InputStreamReader(
        new ByteArrayInputStream(configFile.getBytes()));
InputSource inputSource = new InputSource(reader);
```

Here is a more flexible example of this technique from a test written for an `XMLUtils` class of a web services engine. This method takes a parameter that tells it what type of data you want the document returned as: a `String`, `StringReader`, or `ByteArrayInputStream`. The test data XML is hard coded into the `getInlineXml(String gimme)` method. An even more flexible approach is to overload the method to take more parameters, which are then used inside the method to customize the XML document before returning it:

```
/**
 * This is a utility method for creating XML document input sources
 * for this JUnit test class. The returned Object should be cast to
 * the type you request via the gimme (slang for "give me")
 * parameter.
 *
 * @param gimme is a String specifying the underlying type you want the
 * XML input source returned as; one of "string", "reader", or
 * "inputstream."
 */
public Object getInlineXml(String gimme) {
    String xmlString = "<?xml version='1.0'?>"
            + "<web-app>"
            + "<display-name>My App</display-name>"
            + "<servlet>"
            + "<servlet-name>MyServlet</servlet-name>"
            + "<servlet-class>"
            + "com.foo.bar.MyServlet"
            + "</servlet-class>"
            + "</servlet>"
            + "<servlet-mapping>"
            + "<servlet-name>MyServlet</servlet-name>"
            + "<url-pattern>servlet/MyServlet</url-pattern>"
            + "<url-pattern>*.select</url-pattern>"
            + "</servlet-mapping>"
            + "</web-app>";

    if (gimme.equals("string")) {
        return xmlString;
    } else if (gimme.equals("reader")) {
        return new StringReader(xmlString);
    } else if (gimme.equals("inputstream")) {
        return new ByteArrayInputStream(xmlString.getBytes());
    } else
        return null;
}
```

Build an XML document as a String

Choose how to return XML document

◆ Discussion

This recipe is a JUnit and Java variation of the UNIX shell-scripting concept of a *herefile* where an input data file or list of parameters is stored as text in the shell script file that calls it. The herefile is then read via standard input *as if* it were coming from a separate input source.

One of the main uses we have seen for this recipe is that of storing inline file snippets for XML parsing-related tests. We've also seen this recipe used to store inline XML configuration files in tests of a service management framework. Both scenarios are well served by this recipe. The question to ask yourself if you are considering this technique is, "Am I testing file I/O operations, or am I testing the processing of data that just happens to come from a file?" An inline data file separates these concerns and allows you to focus on processing the data rather than being concerned about where it came from.

There is a performance benefit of using this recipe if you have hundreds or thousands of tests. With inline file operations, no file is created on or read from the file system. In-memory file operations don't take up CPU or disk time or disk space. They are fast and efficient. Speed and efficiency are good attributes in an organization or project where you may wind up with anywhere from several hundred to thousands of JUnit tests, each with their own special needs for test data. It is important to trim the fat around tests to keep them fast and easy to run. Getting rid of input files for test data in certain circumstances lets your tests travel light.

◆ Related

- 5.4—Use a properties file
- 5.5—Use ResourceBundles

5.4 Use a properties file

◆ Problem

You need a quick and easy way to retrieve small amounts of simple, variable data in your tests at runtime, such as a few `String`s or numeric values. You have reached the point where an actual data file is more useful than any of the techniques covered so far.

◆ Background

As your suites of test cases grow, you will probably find that you need a more sophisticated and scalable technique than just environment variables and system properties to configure parameterized test data. Herefiles, as described in recipe 5.3, are useful for situations where the trade-off between hard coding test data and setting up build infrastructure to support test files is better on the side of hard coding the data inline. But when you have small, numerous miscellaneous `String` and numeric test data variables that you need or want to parameterize, you need a reusable, general-purpose way to externalize and retrieve test data. If you work on a team, you need an easy, low-tech yet elegant solution, because everyone on the team should be sharing good practices and establishing common ways to do things.

◆ Recipe

Store arbitrary, `String`-based test data in Java properties files. The Java runtime provides APIs for accessing data in properties files and specifies a standard, simple syntax for the properties files themselves.

Java properties files have been around for years and were overused for configuring Java applications, much as XML can be overused today for the same thing. They are handy little files, though, with a simple *key=value* data format and built-in APIs for reading and writing them and retrieving data from them. An octothorpe, also known as the pound sign (#), indicates a comment in a Java properties file. The API for loading and using properties files ignores anything on a line after an octothorpe. Comments provide an easy way to remove or add properties not by deleting them but by simply commenting them out with one octothorpe per line.

The `java.util.Properties` class provides several methods to load, list, save, and retrieve properties from Java properties files. As an example, assume we have a properties file called interest.properties with three properties that we parameterized out of our test case (please don't take our loan calculations seriously):

```
# properties for testing InterestCalculator
interest.rate = 5.5
principal.amount=150000.00
loan.duration.years=15
```

We pass the location of the interest.properties file to the JVM as a system property when executing the JUnit test runner:

```
java -Dtest.data.file=$TESTDATA_HOME/interest.properties
-cp .;junit.jar junit.textui.TestRunner
junit.cookbook.testdata.InterestCalculatorTest
```

We can easily retrieve the property values as `doubles` and `ints` from the properties file in our test's `setUp()` method, as shown in listing 5.3:

Listing 5.3 InterestCalculatorTest

```
package junit.cookbook.testdata;

import java.io.File;
import java.io.FileInputStream;
import java.io.IOException;
import java.util.Properties;

import junit.framework.TestCase;

public class InterestCalculatorTest extends TestCase {
    private double interestRate;
    private double loanAmount;
    private int loanDuration;
    String propertiesFile = System.getProperty("test.data.file");   <-- Get test.data.file system property

    public void setUp() throws IOException {
        FileInputStream fis = new FileInputStream(propertiesFile);
        Properties p = new Properties();
        p.load(fis);
            // Load fis into a java.util.Properties object via load(InputStream inStream)

        interestRate = Double.parseDouble(
            p.getProperty("interest.rate"));
        loanAmount = Double.parseDouble(
            p.getProperty("principal.amount"));
        loanDuration = Integer.parseInt(
            p.getProperty("loan.duration.years"));
            // Use getProperty(String key) and String parsing to retrieve properties
    }

    public void testInterestCalculation() {
        // fake interest calculation
    }
}
```

`InterestCalculatorTest`, listing 5.3, demonstrates how to read in a properties file, get property values from it, and assign them to instance variables in the test case. The `setUp()` method throws an `IOException` because we should let the test fail if the data file can't be found. The path to the file is provided by the `test.data.file` property.

You don't have to pull files from the file system. Files have the disadvantage of having to reside on the file system in a directory somewhere. File systems and path- and file-related conventions are platform specific and require test data directory and file location information to be externalized and set in a platform-specific way. Arguing about where to put test data files and how to name them is a common problem in team development environments, as is sharing code and testing conventions to eliminate duplication of effort. Instead, we pull files from the class path using `java.lang.Class.getResourceAsStream()`, as shown in the `setUp()` method in listing 5.4.

Listing 5.4 LoadPropsFromClasspathTest

```
package junit.cookbook.testdata;

import java.io.IOException;
import java.io.InputStream;
import java.util.Properties;

import junit.framework.TestCase;

public class LoadPropsFromClasspathTest extends TestCase {

    String name = "/" + System.getProperty("test.data.file",
                                          "test.properties");    ❶

    public void testLoadedProperties() throws IOException {
        InputStream is = this.getClass().getResourceAsStream(name);   ❷

        Properties p = new Properties();   ❸
        p.load(is);

        // We do not recommend using System.out and System.err in tests
        // as a general practice, but here we list the properties to
        // System.out just to demonstrate that they have been found and
        // loaded.
        p.list(System.out);   ❹
    }
}
```

❶ Prepend "/" to the resource name—see Javadoc for `java.lang.Class.getResourceAsStream()`.

❷ Get the `Class` instance for this object, and get an `InputStream` from the file in the classpath.

❸ Load the file into a `java.util.Properties` instance.

❹ List the properties to `System.out` to see their names and values.

Let us run `LoadPropsFromClasspathTest` with the following test.properties file, just to see what happens:

```
test.port=8080
test.hostname=localhost
test.jspfile=index.jsp
```

Next we add the directory containing test.properties to our runtime class path. This way we can retrieve the properties file by invoking `java.lang.Class.getResourceAsStream()`, listing them out to `System.out` to demonstrate that they were loaded:

```
java -cp .\bin;junit.jar;. junit.textui.TestRunner LoadPropsFromClasspathTest
-- listing properties --
test.jspfile=index.jsp
test.hostname=localhost
test.port=8080
```

◆ *Discussion*

When you find that you have enough test data to warrant breaking it up into a separate data file for each test class, you need to formalize where this data is placed and how it is accessed. One solution is to use `ResourceBundles`, as described in recipe 5.5, "Use ResourceBundles." However, because `ResourceBundles` are intended to be used for localization, you might resist the idea of twisting them into an API for retrieving test data from `String`-based files as demonstrated in the next recipe. We understand. All you need to emulate the functionality you want from `ResourceBundle` are Java properties files and some conventions to follow when adding a test data file for a test case.

The conventions to follow in order to emulate the basic functionality of the `ResourceBundle` API are as follows:

- Create one test data properties file for each of your JUnit test cases that need their own test data.
- Name the properties file with the same name or *basename* (basename is the test case's class name minus its packages) as its corresponding test case.
- Put the properties file in the same package and directory as its corresponding test case or in a separate but identical directory tree in your test data repository (see recipe 5.6, "Use a file-based test data repository").
- Create a method in a base `TestCase` extension, in a utility class, or in a code template that always looks up the data properties file the same way for all your tests. Use `File` and `FileInputStream` calls to read and load files from a separate test data repository. Use `java.lang.Class.getResource(String name)` or `java.lang.Class.getResourceAsStream(String name)` if you stored the properties files in the same package as the Java classes.

These requirements and more are supported by the `ResourceBundle` class, so we might just use that. (See recipe 5.5.)

Finally, do note that when you extract test data to files, you need to consider the corresponding drawbacks, which we describe in chapter 17, "Odds and Ends."

◆ Related

- 5.1—Use Java system properties
- 5.2—Use environment variables
- 5.5—Use ResourceBundles
- 5.6—Use a file-based test data repository
- 17.2—Test your file-based application without the file system

5.5 Use ResourceBundles

◆ Problem

You need an easy, accessible API for retrieving variable data in your tests at runtime, and you have enough tests to warrant breaking up test data into one data file per test class.

◆ Background

When you have numerous small `String` and numeric test variables to parameterize, you need a general-purpose way to externalize and retrieve test data. One solution is to use Java properties files and devise your own means for finding, reading, and processing them at runtime. A similar but more formalized and structured solution is to use properties files with the `java.util.ResourceBundle` API. `ResourceBundle` is a class that implements an algorithm for finding localized *.properties files and loading them.

◆ Recipe

Use the `ResourceBundle` API for its resource retrieval features, regardless of whether you use its localization support. Listing 5.5 shows a new version of `InterestCalculatorTest` from recipe 5.4, "Use a properties file," modified to use `ResourceBundle` to pick up a properties file from the class path.

Listing 5.5 `InterestCalculatorTest2`

```
package junit.cookbook.testdata;

import java.io.IOException;
import java.util.ResourceBundle;
```

```
import junit.framework.TestCase;

public class InterestCalculatorTest2 extends TestCase {

    private double interestRate;
    private double loanAmount;
    private int loanDuration;
    static final String BASE_NAME
            = "junit.cookbook.testdata.InterestCalculatorTest2";   ❶

    public void setUp() throws IOException {
       // let ResourceBundle search the classpath and automatically
       // load the corresponding properties file
       ResourceBundle rb = ResourceBundle.getBundle(BASE_NAME);   ❷

       // use ResourceBundle.getString(String key) instead of
       // Properties.getProperty(String key)
       interestRate = Double.parseDouble(
           rb.getString("interest.rate")));                ❸
       loanAmount = Double.parseDouble(
           rb.getString("principal.amount"));
       loanDuration =Integer.parseInt(
           rb.getString("loan.duration.years"));
    }

    public void testInterestCalculation() {
        // fake interest calculation stuff using interestRate,
        // loanAmount and loanDuration
    }
}
```

❶ `ResourceBundle`'s contract is that the `BASE_NAME` argument must be a fully qualified class name.

❷ Search the class path with `getBundle(String baseName)` to load a properties file matching `BASE_NAME`.

❸ Retrieve data variables with `ResourceBundle.getString(String s)`.

◆ Discussion

Note that using `ResourceBundles` doesn't require any file location to be passed as a system property. Instead it relies on the properties retrieval algorithm of the `ResourceBundle` class. The static `ResourceBundle.getBundle(String baseName)` method uses the `baseName` to look up a properties file in the class path by appending `.properties` to the `baseName` and looking for the resource in the class path of the current class loader at runtime. Because the name and the path to the test data file are now the same as that of the `TestCase` class itself (junit/cookbook/testdata), it is easy to find using `ResourceBundle.getBundle(String baseName)`. It is also easy to visually find in an IDE when you are editing a test and need to edit the test data that goes with it.

For this example to work according to the normal `ResourceBundle` conventions, you should rename the interest.properties file to InterestCalculatorTest2.properties and copy it to the directory in your class path (either on the file system or packaged inside a JAR file) that matches the package structure of the `InterestCalculatorTest2`. This is merely a convention, and although conventions exist to make it easier for each of us to understand what others have done, the Java police will not arrest you if you go against the grain.[2] You can put the file anywhere in the class path as long as the file name ends in .properties and the directory structure matches the path or package separators specified in the `baseName` (It makes no difference whether you use periods or forward slashes as path separators in the `baseName`). It is conventional to keep the name of the properties file the same as the name of the class that uses it, but you can always use the same file with multiple classes, in which case you may prefer to name the file by its functional area or by the name of a package of related tests that use it.

◆ Related

- 5.4—Use a properties file

5.6 Use a file-based test data repository

◆ Problem

You have a lot of file-based test data of different types located in different directories and files because you and your teammates never planned out where things should go. You need a shared repository for test data that all tests can use for their test data needs.

◆ Background

Some projects grow, and some projects are just large to begin with. The larger a project is in terms of people and lines of source code, the more important it becomes to establish and share conventions for things related to development and testing. Where to store test data for unit and integration tests is a good thing to establish so people don't reinvent the wheel or waste time looking for things they need when they join the project or transfer to work on a different part of the project.

---

[2] If you want to assert your individuality, then that is your right, but when part of team, work as a team.

◆ *Recipe*

Designate a directory as a shared test data repository in source control or on the company network that can be used for all test data for unit tests, as shown at bottom-left in figure 5.2. Alternatively, designate a data repository directory for each component, subsystem, or subproject. Pass in the location of the repository to your unit tests using one of the ways discussed earlier in this chapter: a system property on the command line, a system property pointing to a variable picked up from the environment or set by a script, a property in a properties file stored in `user.home`, and so forth. If all your tests extend a `BaseTestCase` of your own creation, encapsulate the retrieval of the data repository location in the `BaseTestCase` class and make it available to all subclasses through a `protected` variable or accessor method.

There are two main decisions to make in creating your test data repository: where to put it and what kind of structure it should have. Both decisions affect higher-level concerns such as how to configure development tools and build scripts to easily find the repository or repositories and locate resources. A shared network drive, an internal FTP site, or directories in source control are all good candidates. Keeping test data in source control makes it possible to version test data with the tests that use it.

Once you have decided where the repository should be located, consider its structure. How will tests locate their test data with the least amount of coding effort? Will tests share test data files or be required to maintain their own in a strict one-to-one mapping? Which format should you use: XML, properties, plain text, other consumables such as JARs and class files (imagine you are writing a

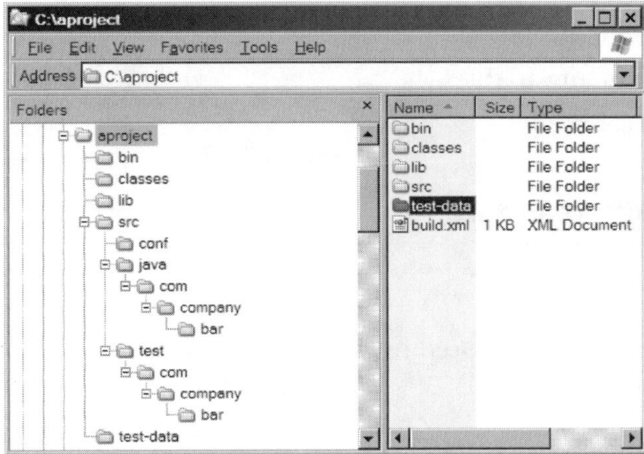

Figure 5.2
A top-level test-data directory in a project on Windows XP

WAR deployer or a class file parser)? Should test data be organized by its type or by the subsystem being tested or both? Should the data repository be shared across multiple subprojects, or should a separate repository be defined relative to each subproject? These are a few of the questions to consider.

For example, on a medium-sized commercial application server project having about a dozen major subsystems, we designated a single, top-level test data directory in source control. Test data files could be any format, and people were good about keeping the subdirectories clean and organized. The only structural mandate for its contents was that each subfolder under test-data had to be named the same name as a subsystem for which the test data was being checked. Beneath that level, there was little or no formal structure needed, because people writing unit tests were assigned and dedicated to testing a particular subsystem and used informal conventions to help maintain the subfolders and files pretty well. On a project in which people change responsibilities frequently or there are a large number of components to test, it may be useful to decide sooner how to organize the test data.

◆ Discussion

The main limitation of this recipe's approach is that it is file based. Many people need to retrieve test data from a relational database, in which case recipe 5.12, "Use DbUnit," will be helpful. A key advantage to a file-based approach is that your test data can easily be checked into source control in a repository structure and versioned along with the tests it supports. You can do the same thing with a database, but you have to write your own version-tracking and control system on top of the database.

◆ Related

- 5.1—Use Java system properties
- 5.2—Use environment variables
- 5.5—Use ResourceBundles

5.7 Use XML to describe test data

◆ Problem

You need to use test data already stored in XML documents, or your test data has evolved to the point where properties files no longer suffice.

◆ Background

Needing to read in and use XML in unit testing is common these days. Usually it is necessary because of service or component descriptors or document-based inter-process communication (such as Web services). But these aren't usually data files, per se.

◆ Recipe

There are two ways to approach this problem: either as a test data issue or as a way to define a test suite. We chose to place this recipe in chapter 4, "Managing Test Suites," but we thought you might also look for that recipe here. Consider this a forwarding address, then: please see recipe 4.9, "Define a test suite in XML."

◆ Discussion

In our experience, using XML for test data is more complicated than just creating the corresponding Java objects. It is not necessarily that XML is a poor choice, but rather that as a community we tend to choose more complex solutions than we need. For simple data sets, we recommend hard coding the data inside the test (see recipe 5.3, "Use an inline data file"). If you need to use files, we recommend simple properties files, as described in recipe 5.4. Only if you are *certain* that this is insufficient should you decide to store test data in XML format. Keep in mind that Object Tests tend to be simpler, smaller, and require less data, so it would be unusual indeed to store Object Test data as XML.

◆ Related

- 4.9—Define a test suite in XML

5.8 Use Ant's <sql> task to work with a database

◆ Problem

You need to test code that retrieves data from a database, so you need to populate the database with test data at the start of each test run.

◆ Background

At some point in your development and testing, you may want to start using a database as a repository for test data. Testing with databases can be problematic for several reasons, including:

- Database administrators or company policy may prevent you from accessing (even for reading only) live databases.

- Databases can grow to be large, complex, and time consuming.
- Restoring data to its initial state between test runs or even test methods can be time consuming, both in effort and in runtime performance.

◆ *Recipe*

Ant's `<sql>` task is a handy tool for eliminating JDBC code from your tests in an Ant-based build environment. It enables you to execute SQL and stored procedures from your buildfile, which can be used to set up test data during the build, prior to executing unit tests.

Here is an example of using the `<sql>` task to execute SQL in a file named `data.sql`:

```
<sql
    driver="org.database.jdbcDriver"
    url="jdbc:database-url"
    userid="sa"
    password="pass"
    src="data.sql"/>
```

In the next example, the SQL to execute is specified as the content of the `<sql>` element:

```
<sql
    driver="org.database.jdbcDriver"
    url="jdbc:database-url"
    userid="sa"
    password="pass">
insert into table some_table values(1,2,3,4);
truncate table some_other_table;
</sql>
```

Just make sure your JDBC driver is in the class path where Ant can find it.

◆ *Discussion*

The main recommendation here is to refer to some of the related recipes and use what works for you:

- Recipe 5.10, "Set up your fixture once for the entire suite"—A useful technique for avoiding the undesired and sometimes unnecessary overhead of executing `setUp()` and `tearDown()` before and after every test method.
- Recipe 5.12, "Use DbUnit"—A useful JUnit-based tool for facilitating test data `setUp()` and `tearDown()` with a database.

If you choose to separate test data from the test in this way, then it may make the test more difficult to read. At the same time, the technique in this recipe is easier to write than including the corresponding JDBC code to do it. This is one of those trade-offs that you just have to judge on a case-by-case basis, as it depends on all aspects of the project: the product, the tools, and the people. If you are able to avoid the trade-off entirely, then so much the better: we much prefer testing without live data, as we describe in detail in chapter 10, "Testing and JDBC."

◆ ***Discussion***

- 5.10—Set up your fixture once for the entire suite
- 5.12—Use DbUnit

5.9 Use JUnitPP

◆ ***Problem***

You want to provide a robust solution for Java properties-based test data files.

◆ ***Background***

Whether you are in QA or development, after you've dealt with the same set of unit tests for a while, you begin to wonder what you could do to refactor them. One thing that is hard to do up front because of the amount of planning involved, and just as hard later because of the rework involved, is establish a useful base class for all your tests. The cross-test problems that customized `BaseTestCases` are meant to solve are not obvious at the outset of the project. It would be great to avoid this test data management problem altogether by extending all `TestCases` from some well-planned, useful base class that took care of the data management somewhat transparently.

◆ ***Recipe***

Use JUnitPP's `junit.extensions.ConfigurableTestCase` as your base `TestCase`. JUnitPP is modeled after features found in a C++ test framework that its author had written a long time ago and become accustomed to using. JUnitPP popped up on the radar a couple of years ago in a *Doctor Dobbs Journal* article (see the "Related" section) where its author publicly unveiled it under the more C++ sounding "JUnit++." JUnitPP provides a JUnit extension called `ConfigurableTestCase` that provides a standard mechanism for retrieving test data from properties files. Download JUnitPP from http://junitpp.sourceforge.net. Listing 5.6 shows how to extend and use the features of JUnitPP's `ConfigurableTestCase`.

Listing 5.6 `InterestCalculatorConfigurableTest`

```
package junit.cookbook.testdata;

import junit.extensions.ConfigurableTestCase;

public class InterestCalculatorConfigurableTest
    extends ConfigurableTestCase {

    private static double interestRate;
    private static double loanAmount;
    private static int loanDuration;

    public InterestCalculatorConfigurableTest(String name) {
        super(name);
    }

    public void setUp() {
        interestRate = getDouble("interest.rate");
        loanAmount = getDouble("principal.amount");
        loanDuration = getInteger("loan.duration.years");
    }

    public void testInterestCalculation() {
        // fake interest calculation stuff using interestRate,
        // loanAmount and loanDuration
    }
}
```

Extend ConfigurableTestCase from JUnitPP

Use ConfigurableTestCase utility methods to get properties of different types

There is no file I/O, class path searching, or other silly stuff to load data files in the `TestCase` itself. So how does it work? JUnitPP automatically associates each `ConfigurableTestCase` with a property file that has the same name as the class but ends with .ini rather than .properties. So the property file for class `InterestCalculatorConfigurableTest` is named InterestCalculatorConfigurableTest.ini. By default, `ConfigurableTestCases` automatically find their data files in the same directory as the test case class's package name, relative to the directory from which the test runner was launched. In addition, `ConfigurableTestCases` look in a default list of relative directories: src, src/java, src/test, and src/test/java. The simplest thing to do is place the configuration file in the same directory as the built test case class's *.class file.

The default directory search that JUnitPP provides for properties files can be augmented in your tests by setting a system property named `junit.conf` to the name of a file or of a directory. The value of the `junit.conf` property is added to the list of default paths.

JUnitPP provides an analog to JUnit's `junit.extensions.TestSetup` (see recipe 5.10, "Set up your fixture once for the entire suite") in its `ConfigurableTestSetup` class.

◆ Discussion

JUnitPP also includes command-line options and support for running unit tests in load test or stress test mode, much like JUnitPerf (www.clarkware.com/software/JUnitPerf.html), but such options are not related to managing test data, so they are not covered in this chapter.

JUnitPP is a nice, simple, extensible framework for managing test data for tests that can use the Java properties file format for containing their data. Its only weakness may be that it is limited to supporting data having the Java properties file format.

◆ Related

- 5.4—Use a properties file
- 5.5—Use ResourceBundles
- 5.6—Use a file-based test data repository
- http://junitpp.sourceforge.net

5.10 Set up your fixture once for the entire suite

◆ Problem

You want the `setUp()` method to execute once for all methods in a `TestCase`, but the JUnit framework is designed to run `setUp()` before every single test method is run.

◆ Background

The `setUp()` method is JUnit's primary means for setting up test data fixtures in preparation for the execution of a test method (`tearDown()` is for cleaning up fixtures after a test method completes). Some users are surprised to realize that `setUp()` is called before every test method. Many users find that while they need `setUp()` and `tearDown()` before and after every test method, they also want a meta `setUp()` that can run once and only once for the whole suite of tests in their `TestCase` subclass. Most often this is because they need `setUp()` to establish a fixture that is expensive to initialize, such as a database connection, a J2EE or JDBC transaction, or an application deployment.

On one project, we were looking for ways to optimize one of our large JUnit-based test harnesses and make it run faster. After a code review in which we examined several test cases, we found a great deal of database initialization code in the `setUp()` and `tearDown()` methods of test cases that were contributing to overhead in terms of additional minutes spent negotiating with the database.

Some application servers provide a deployment API that you can call to have your application deployed programmatically. Many J2EE application servers support hot deployment and redeployment of applications just by copying deployable files to certain directories (which is easy enough to do programmatically from within a JUnit test). If your JUnit test is a kind of integration test where it needs to call out to an EJB or a servlet in a J2EE server automatically at test time, it is nice to control the deployment of the application containing the EJB or servlet from within your test. But deploying an application usually takes several seconds and isn't usually designed for high performance, so deploying and undeploying between every test method becomes slow and may uncover stress-related bugs in the application server's hot deployment feature. Database connections are relatively expensive to acquire, especially if you are not using a `DataSource` or connection pool but are reloading the database driver and getting a new connection between every single test method call.

To understand this recipe, you should first know what a Decorator is. A Decorator "wraps" itself around another object that implements the same interface it does. The Decorator effectively intercepts method invocations to the "wrappee," adding some extra behavior as desired. It is one of the structural patterns in the *Design Patterns* book, and is also known as Wrapper.

◆ *Recipe*

Use `junit.extensions.TestSetup` to do one-time `setUp()` in your `TestCase` so that `setUp()` and `tearDown()` in `TestSetup` get called once per test class rather than once before and after each test method.

The typical way to use this is as follows:

1. Implement a custom `suite()` method in your `TestCase`.
2. Create an anonymous class that extends `TestSetup`.
3. Implement `setUp()` and `tearDown()` inside the anonymous class.
4. Return an instance of your subclass of `TestSetup` at the end of the `suite()` method.

Listing 5.7 is a code example of our ongoing `InterestCalculatorTest` class, now modified to load its properties data file once by using a `TestSetup` Decorator in the `suite()` method.

Listing 5.7 InterestCalculatorTestWithTestSetup

```
package junit.cookbook.testdata;

import java.io.IOException;
import java.util.ResourceBundle;

import junit.extensions.TestSetup;
import junit.framework.Test;
import junit.framework.TestCase;
import junit.framework.TestSuite;

public class InterestCalculatorTestWithTestSetup extends TestCase {

    private static double interestRate;
    private static double loanAmount;
    private static int loanDuration;
    static final String baseName
            = "junit.cookbook.testdata.InterestCalculatorTestWithTestSetup";

    public static Test suite() {
        TestSuite testSuite = new TestSuite(
                InterestCalculatorTestWithTestSetup.class);

        TestSetup wrapper = new TestSetup(testSuite) {
            public void setUp() throws IOException {
                ResourceBundle rb =
                     ResourceBundle.getBundle(baseName);

                interestRate =
                     Double.parseDouble(rb.getString("interest.rate"));

                loanAmount = Double.parseDouble(
                     rb.getString("principal.amount"));

                loanDuration = Integer.parseInt(
                     rb.getString("loan.duration.years"));
            }
        };
      return wrapper;
    }

    public void testInterestCalculation() {
        // fake interest calculation
    }
}
```

Annotations: Create the TestSuite (at `suite()` / `new TestSuite(...)`); Wrap a TestSetup around the TestSuite (at `new TestSetup(testSuite)`); Invoked once for the entire suite (at `setUp()`)

Note that this code uses a `ResourceBundle` (see recipe 5.5) for the data that is to be loaded. You rename the properties file from that recipe's example to `InterestCalculatorTestWithTestSetup.properties` and then copy it to the directory in your class path that matches the package structure of the `InterestCalculatorTestWithTestSetup` (that is, junit/cookbook/testdata within your source tree).

◆ Discussion

One small disadvantage to this technique is that any variables you need to share between `TestSetup` in the `suite()` method and the rest of the `TestCase` have to be declared `static` because `suite()` is `static`.

Finally, we should mention one flaw in JUnit's implementation of `TestSetup`. When the wrapped test suite fails, `TestSetup.tearDown()` is not invoked, meaning that the shared fixture is not properly cleaned up. Much of the time this is not a grave concern; however, if you need *ensure* that the shared fixture is cleaned up properly at the end of the test suite, see recipe 16.5, "Ensure your shared test fixture tears itself down," which explains how to use an alternate implementation of `TestSetup`, found in JUnit-addons.

◆ Related

- 5.6—Use a file-based test data repository
- 16.5—Ensure your shared test fixture tears itself down

5.11 Perform environment setup once for multiple test runs

◆ Problem

Your testing environment is expensive and complex to set up. You need to do it once before you can run tests, but you do not need to (or cannot afford to) set it up before each test run. You would like to perform this environment setup only once.

◆ Background

Rakesh Madhwani provided the motivation for the recipe in the JUnit Yahoo! group. His problem was simple: he wanted to be able to execute a large test suite against a graphical user interface, but he did not want to start up and shut down the GUI for each test. He did not want to even start it up and shut it down for each test suite run. He wanted to launch the GUI once, execute the tests as many times as he liked, however he liked, and then shut the GUI down once when he had finished. His first try was using the `TestSetup` Decorator, but the `TestSetup` Decorator only provides support for one-time setup before and one-time teardown after each test suite run. What he wanted was one step further back: one-time setup before launching the test runner and one-time teardown when he finished using the test runner. This recipe provides various solutions to this problem, depending on which of the test runners you use and what kind of setup you need.

◆ Recipe

The approach you take to implement this one-time setup depends on any constraints you may have on how you execute tests, in general. Different tools admit different solutions to this problem. The solution also depends on the nature of your environment setup tasks. First, we present a summary of the various approaches in table 5.1, and then we describe each approach in turn.

Table 5.1 Summary of approaches to performing one-time environment setup

<table>
<tr><th>Setup tasks / Tool</th><th>Text-based test runner</th><th>Swing-based test runner</th></tr>
<tr><td>Initialize data or services outside the Java Virtual Machine.</td><td>Perform the one-time setup and teardown tasks manually as needed, or use a shell script.</td><td rowspan="2">Override the <code>terminate()</code> method to invoke your teardown code. Invoke your setup code before launching the test runner.</td></tr>
<tr><td>Initialize objects inside the Java Virtual Machine.</td><td>Nothing you can do: each test suite run occurs in a separate JVM.</td></tr>
</table>

Initializing data or services outside the Java Virtual Machine

You may need to start services outside your Java application, such as database servers, web servers, and so on. These kinds of tasks fall outside the purview of your tests, so it is best to configure your operating system, when possible, to start these services automatically. If you are unable to do this, then we recommend writing either shell scripts or an Ant target that starts all the various services you need before executing your tests. If you can configure the operating system to execute this script on startup, that would be great; otherwise, you really do have to simply depend on yourself to remember to perform these steps before executing your tests. The bad news is that you are not the only person who will ever need to run your tests, so what about educating others?

If you treat your test execution environment like a large tool (such as your IDE or a web browser), then it is logical to tell people, "Here is how you start the test environment. Make sure you do this before trying to execute any tests." It may be most effective to provide this information in the form of online or hard copy documentation. We hope your environment is not so complex that you need a user's guide just to execute tests, but we recognize that it happens, having seen it ourselves. It is generally impossible to remove the complexity altogether, but it is usually possible to reduce the complexity to "pushing a single button" with some clever automation.

NOTE *A one-button test environment*—If you think *your* test environment is too complex to automate, consider this story from our experience. J. B. worked in an organization that used VisualAge for Java as its development environment. The product we were building was made up of over 40 different projects on the workspace at once. Despite varying degrees of effort to reduce dependency among these projects, it was generally impossible to remove anything from the workspace and expect the overall product to work. In addition to this code complexity, the product required a database of some 200 tables and thousands of rows of startup data and test data. This was a complex environment.

After some time, a group decided to build a standard set of instructions to help a programmer install and set up this environment on her workstation. The instructions ran several pages and included close to 50 manual instructions. Although workable, it generally took over 30 minutes of attentive effort to set up the test environment, and it did not always work. Sometimes a programmer would go days without being able to write code. Finally, one programmer took matters into his own hands and used Microsoft's ScriptIt (which Microsoft has since retired) to automate VisualAge for Java. He crafted a series of scripts and worked with the organization's build team to automate the entire process of downloading code, importing it into VisualAge for Java, creating the database, and importing all the necessary data. The result was literally a single push of a button, resulting in a working test environment in approximately 25 minutes, every time. Although it was not much faster than the manual process, it could run unattended...*and it worked!*

Remember this story the next time someone complains that there is "no way" to automate your test environment.

Initializing Java objects within the Java Virtual Machine

You may need to set up some global data for your tests: data that is rather expensive to set up. So expensive, in fact, that you cannot afford to set it up per test—or even per test run! We highly recommend looking into changing this situation, because it appears to indicate some fairly serious design problems, but if you have to get something running *now*, then what you do depends on how you run your tests.

If you use the text-based test runner on its own, then we are sorry to say that you are out of luck. The text-based test runner executes each test suite in its own JVM, so you have to perform the one-time setup and teardown each time you execute a test suite. The good news is that you can automate this by creating your own simple custom test runner. The following code simply invokes its own `setUp()` before invoking the text-based test runner, and then invokes `tearDown()` afterward:

```
package junit.cookbook.running.test;

import junit.framework.*;
import junit.textui.TestRunner;

public class TextBasedOneTimeEnvironmentSetupTestRunner {
    public static Test suite() {
        TestSuite suite = new TestSuite();
        // Create your test suite...
        return suite;
    }

    private static void oneTimeEnvironmentSetUp() {
        System.out.println("Setup");
    }

    private static void oneTimeEnvironmentTearDown() {
        System.out.println("Teardown");
    }

    public static void main(String[] args) throws Exception {
        oneTimeEnvironmentSetUp();
        TestRunner.run(suite());
        oneTimeEnvironmentTearDown();
    }
}
```

In order to execute test suites many times in the same JVM, you need to use one of the graphical test runners, such as the Swing-based test runner. You *could* customize its behavior in a manner similar to how we added one-time setup and teardown to the text-based test runner, but as you will see, it is not quite so simple. If you try to copy the code from the previous example (changing `junit.textui.TestRunner` to `junit.swingui.TestRunner`), then your setup code executes as expected, but your teardown code executes before you close the test runner. In particular, this is what happens:

1. The JVM executes your setup code.
2. The JVM launches the test runner and executes the test suite.
3. The JVM executes your teardown code, leaving the test runner open and waiting for you to press Run again.

At this point, if you execute another test suite (possibly the same one), it may execute *while your custom teardown code is also executing*, which can only create a big mess.

You need a way for the test runner to wait until you press Exit before executing your teardown code. Fortunately, that is not difficult at all.

The Swing-based test runner declares the method `terminate()`, which it invokes when you press Exit or close the Test Runner window. This is the hook you need to execute your teardown code. Simply override `terminate()` and have it invoke your teardown code before invoking its superclass's implementation. Here is the complete code:

```
package junit.cookbook.running.test;

import junit.swingui.TestRunner;

public class SwingBasedOneTimeEnvironmentSetupTestRunner {
    private static void oneTimeEnvironmentTearDown() {
        System.out.println("Teardown");
    }

    private static void oneTimeEnvironmentSetUp() {
        System.out.println("Setup");
    }

    public static void main(String[] args) throws Exception {
        oneTimeEnvironmentSetUp();

        TestRunner testRunner = new TestRunner() {
            public void terminate() {
                oneTimeEnvironmentTearDown();
                super.terminate();
            }
        };

        testRunner.start(new String[] { "com.mycom.MyTestSuiteClass" });
    }
}
```

We bring one difference to your attention between this class and the one that uses the text-based test runner: the Swing-based test runner does not provide the same `run()` method that the text-based test runner provides, so it is necessary to pass in the fully qualified name of the test case class to execute. This is a minor annoyance, but not a serious roadblock.

◆ *Discussion*

One-time environment setup is a serious smell in any application, particularly if it is necessary to initialize data within the JVM before executing your first test. This is a sign that objects are relying on global data, which is not only bad for testing, but makes for a rigid, inflexible design. This is the kind of practice that drives up the cost of change. We strongly recommend that you take steps to reduce an object's dependence on global data, preferring instead to have that data provided to the object through its constructor. A particular case of this design problem deals with Singletons, which cause all manner of testing difficulties and which we discuss in more detail in chapter 14, "Testing Design Patterns."

Not long after we wrote this recipe, Rakesh grafted a solution onto the text-based test runner that addresses the more specific problem of running the same test multiple times with one-time setup. We include that solution here as a viable alternative for that problem. Create your own subclass of `junit.textui.TestRunner` and override this method:

```
protected TestResult start(String args[]) throws Exception {
    while(true) {
        result = doRun(getTest(testCase), wait);
    }
    return result;
}
```

This executes the test suite repeatedly until you stop the test runner by pressing the "break" button (CTRL+C, for example). Although this is one way to solve the problem, it has some drawbacks that we recommend you take into account before using it yourself:

- The tests run in an infinite loop, which means that you can never use this test runner as part of an automatic build-and-test process. Because that is not its purpose, there is little cause for concern.
- This solution duplicates some of the logic in the superclass, meaning that changes to the superclass (JUnit's text-based test runner) could affect the correctness of this solution. You need to remember this if you upgrade JUnit.

If none of these problems worry you, then this solution might just be simple enough to work!

◆ *Related*

- Chapter 6—Running JUnit Tests
- Chapter 14—Testing Design Patterns

5.12 Use DbUnit

◆ *Problem*

You need to reset your test database state between test runs, or you want utilities to help you manage test data coming from a database.

◆ *Background*

Anyone who has used JUnit to test code that accesses a database knows that JUnit's design to run `setUp()` before and `tearDown()` after every test method is suboptimal when setting up and tearing down heavy resources such as database connections. The `setUp()` method is the perfect place to obtain a database connection, if only it didn't get called before every single test method. Even if you work around the constant connection creation and destruction using a Singleton connection pool or a `TestSetup` Decorator (see recipe 5.10) to ensure one-time setup of connections and/or transactions, you still need a utility to facilitate refreshing the database state between test runs. DbUnit not only enables efficient connection management[3] but also comes with a standard API and set of utilities for resetting the state of the data in the database between test methods.

◆ *Recipe*

Extend `org.dbunit.DatabaseTestCase` or use DbUnit utility calls from a regular `TestCase` class to configure your test data. DbUnit includes an extension of `TestCase` for database testing, as well as a set of APIs and utilities for managing and restoring the state of test data in a database between test runs. It is maintained and developed by Manuel Laflamme and licensed under the Lesser GPL.

The main feature of DbUnit is that it does what it calls a `CLEAN_INSERT` operation before executing each test. `CLEAN_INSERT` performs a `DELETE_ALL` operation followed by an `INSERT` operation. The data to insert is provided by one of several implementations of `org.dbunit.dataset.IDataSet`, which may be XML-based, retrieved from another database call, or built programmatically in memory.

Here is an example from the DbUnit documentation, using it as a utility rather than extending `DatabaseTestCase`:

[3] DBUnit is not set this way "out of the box." See http://dbunit.sourceforge.net/bestpractices.html#connections.

```
public class SampleTest extends TestCase {
    public SampleTest(String name) {
        super(name);
    }

    protected void setUp() throws Exception {
        super.setUp();

        // initialize your database connection here
        IDatabaseConnection connection = null;
        // ...

        // initialize your dataset here
        IDataSet dataSet = null;
        // ...

        try {
            DatabaseOperation.CLEAN_INSERT.execute(connection, dataSet);
        }
        finally {
            connection.close();
        }
    }
    // . . .
}
```

◆ Discussion

Another technique for restoring the database's initial state between runs that we have used successfully with very large (30,000 to 100,000 employees' worth of data) databases is to back up the database instance files (such as the control files and data files in an Oracle instance) after you populate them with an initial set of data. Then you can shut down the database when you are done testing and do a cold copy restore of the database from the backup set of files. You can ask your local database administrator for help with this. Restoring databases from backup files is very useful in situations where you have a database that takes many minutes to an hour to restore or reload, but which only takes a few seconds to restore from a file system backup. If you compress the backup files with any zip utility on Windows or UNIX, you can often squeeze a multi-GB file down to a few dozen or hundred MB.

The principal alternative to managing test data for unit testing in a database is not to use one. This is not as silly as it might sound: are you testing code that uses a database or just code that needs data? Most of the time it is the latter—the code does not depend on how the data is stored. In that case, you can use mock objects instead to fake your tests into thinking they are getting data from a database. We use this technique extensively throughout part 2, "Testing J2EE." Of course, if you want to verify that your code uses the database properly, you need a database…or do you? See chapter 10, "Testing and JDBC," and decide for yourself.

◆ Related

- 5.10—Set up your fixture once for the entire suite
- http://dbunit.sourceforge.net/
- http://dbunit.sourceforge.net/bestpractices.html,
  Database testing best practices from the author of DbUnit
- www.agiledata.org/, Scott Ambler's excellent site for agile development and databases
- www.dallaway.com/acad/dbunit.html, Richard Dallaway's well-reasoned article on testing database code in Java

6 Running JUnit tests

This chapter covers

- Monitoring JUnit tests as they execute
- Executing individual tests
- Executing tests that need to reload classes
- Ignoring tests
- Using the JUnit-addons test runner

There are a number of ways to execute your tests, including a large variety of test runners, not all of which have the same set of features. JUnit provides three test runners: a text-based one, an AWT-based one, and a Swing-based one. We will describe each in turn. In addition to the ones that JUnit provides, a number of people have built their own test runners that include special features not found in the originals. The JUnit test runners were not built to be easily extended, and so whenever someone has wanted to add features, it has been shown to be easier to build a new test runner from the ground up. A person builds a custom test runner because he is either having a problem running tests in the current project or environment, or because a particular feature is needed that isn't available. You might find yourself in either of these same situations. The recipes in this chapter focus not only on solving such problems with your test runner, but also on finding the special features you might need in a test runner. For basic tutorials on the various test runners, refer to their web sites. Now, let's take a tour through the various test runners.

The basic test runners

JUnit provides one text-based and two graphical test runners. For most purposes, the AWT-based test runner has been entirely superseded by the Swing-based test runner; so we ignore the AWT-based test runner in this discussion, leaving us the text-based test runner and the Swing-based runner.

The text-based runner is implemented by the class `junit.textui.TestRunner`. It reports test progress and test results in text format to the console. In chapter 1 we used the text-based test runner to run JUnit's own tests as a way to verify the JUnit installation. The text-based runner is a candidate to be integrated with an automated build process such as Ant, Cruise Control,or Anthill.

The Swing-based runner is implemented by the class `junit.swingui.TestRunner`. It reports test progress graphically using a progress bar. The progress bar starts out green and turns red only when a test fails or an error occurs. This is the genesis of the slang "green bar" for "the tests pass 100%" and "red bar"for "some test fails." Figure 6.1 shows the Swing-based test runner with both success and failure.

When you launch either the text-based or Swing-based test runner, you pass the fully qualified name (package name and all) of the test suite you would like to execute as a command-line parameter. This can either be a test case class or any class that provides the `suite()` method. As an example, to launch the Swing-based runner in a Windows environment, issue the following command:

```
java -classpath <your classes>;%JUNIT_HOME%/junit.jar
⇛  junit.swingui.TestRunner <your test suite name>
```

Here we assume that you have an environment variable named `JUNIT_HOME` that points to the directory containing junit.jar. You do not need to use an environment variable—you could just hard code the path to JUnit in your command. If you plan to invoke JUnit test runners from a script you intend to use on multiple machines, we recommend referring to the location of JUnit through an environment variable; otherwise, you would either have to install JUnit to the same location on every machine or change the script on every machine to point to the location where JUnit is installed.

Using Ant

To execute your tests with Ant (http://ant.apache.org), you have two options: use the `<junit>` task or use the `<java>` task passing the class name of a test runner, such as `junit.textui.TestRunner`. Refer to the Ant manual (http://ant.apache.org/manual) for details on configuring and using the `<junit>` task.

The `<junit>` task allows you to use the `<batchtest>` task to create a test suite from tests on the file system. If you do not like the way Ant provides this feature, you can always launch the text-based test runner with `<java>` and use either GSBase's `RecursiveTestSuite` or JUnit-addons's `DirectorySuiteBuilder` to do the same thing, so neither approach can claim an advantage here. See chapter 4, "Managing Test Suites" for a discussion of these two test suite-building utilities.

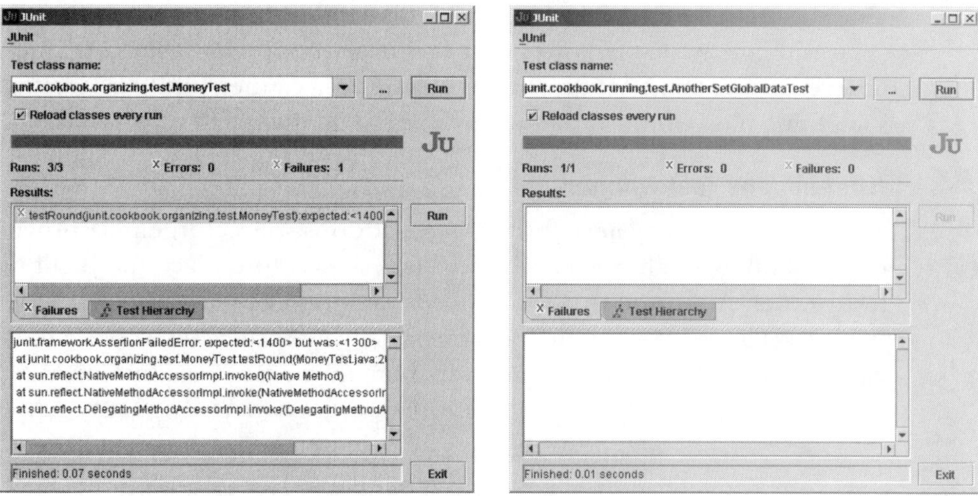

Figure 6.1 Swing-based test runner; left: one test error with a red bar; right: all tests pass with a green bar

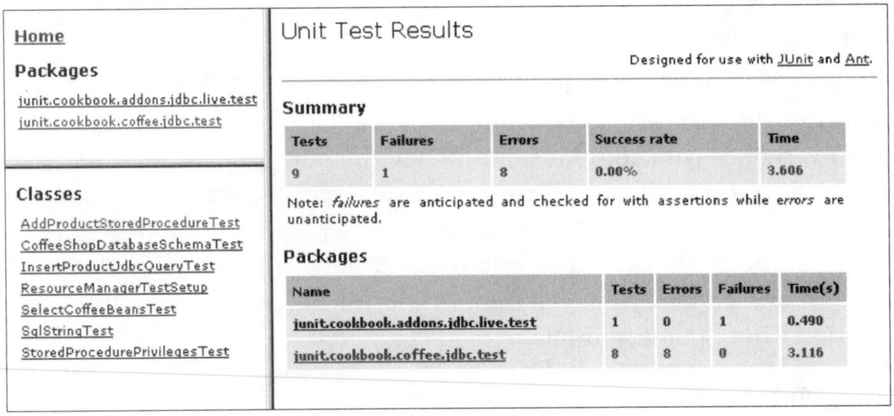

Home

Packages

junit.cookbook.addons.jdbc.live.test
junit.cookbook.coffee.jdbc.test

Classes

AddProductStoredProcedureTest
CoffeeShopDatabaseSchemaTest
InsertProductJdbcQueryTest
ResourceManagerTestSetup
SelectCoffeeBeansTest
SqlStringTest
StoredProcedurePrivilegesTest

Unit Test Results

Designed for use with JUnit and Ant.

Summary

Tests	Failures	Errors	Success rate	Time
9	1	8	0.00%	3.606

Note: *failures* are anticipated and checked for with assertions while *errors* are unanticipated.

Packages

Name	Tests	Errors	Failures	Time(s)
junit.cookbook.addons.jdbc.live.test	1	0	1	0.490
junit.cookbook.coffee.jdbc.test	8	8	0	3.116

Figure 6.2 A sample test execution report created by Ant's `<junitreport>` task.

The `<junit>` task does not report test progress to the console in the same manner that the JUnit text-based test runner does, and we feel that seeing that progress is very comforting, so we prefer it. This causes us to lean in the direction of using the `<java>` task to launch a text-based test runner.

If you want to publish build results to a web site, or if you simply like to see your test results in a format similar to Javadoc, then you want to use the `<junitreport>` task in conjunction with the `<junit>` task. JUnitReport takes XML output from the `<junit>` XML-based results formatter then applies an XSL stylesheet to it, yielding a summary much like Javadoc. You can see sample output in figure 6.2. Once again, refer to the Ant manual for details on using `<junitreport>`.

As with any trade-off, your best bet is to try both approaches and measure the difference. We tend to use the text-based test runner until we decide we want something more sophisticated, then we change.

JUnit-addons Test Runner

The JUnit-addons project (http://junit-addons.sourceforge.net) provides a test runner built with an open architecture designed to replace the JUnit text-based test runner. Although there are more command-line parameters than with the JUnit test runner, it is not necessary to specify them all when you use it. When you execute this test runner without any parameters you receive this message:

```
JUnit-addons Runner 1.0-alpha2 by Vladimir Ritz Bossicard
Usage: junitx.runner.TestRunner [-verbose]
                                 -runner.properties={filepath}
                                 -test.properties={filepath}
                                 -class classname
```

The `-class` option corresponds to the single parameter you pass to the JUnit test runner: the name of the test suite class to execute.

The "runner properties" direct the JUnit-addons test runner to configure itself with monitors (which can pause and resume the execution of tests) and listeners (which can obtain information about each test as it executes). You can use monitors and listeners to implement simple extensions such as custom test report formats. We describe the JUnit-addons test listener in detail in chapter 16, "JUnit-addons," but in the meantime, we describe a simple reporting extension in recipe 6.2. (In particular, see recipe 16.6, "Report the name of each test as it executes," which describes a minor defect in the JUnit-addons test runner documentation.)

The "test properties" help you specify test data paths, tool paths, and other environment settings on which your tests might depend. We do not discuss test properties in detail in this chapter, but do describe the general concept of using test properties in chapter 5, "Working with Test Data." The JUnit-addons test runner provides a small framework for organizing these files.

We provide recipes throughout this book that describe how to leverage the features in JUnit-addons. The JUnit-addons recipe in this chapter describes how to disable tests without removing test code (see recipe 6.6, "Ignore a test").

6.1 See the name of each test as it executes

◆ Problem

You would like to see the progress of the test run while it executes, including the name of the currently executing test.

◆ Background

If you introduce an infinite loop or deadlock into your code then the tests will eventually stop making progress. No failure message, nothing. If this happens you need to work "outside the system" to isolate the test (and therefore the production code) causing the problem. One easy way to get this information is to print out the name of each test as it starts. If there are no project or environmental constraints regarding the test runner you use to execute your tests, we have a simple solution for you.

◆ Recipe

If you need this feature, then we recommend simply executing the tests using a graphical test runner, such as the JUnit Swing-based test runner. The test runner's status bar displays the name of the currently executing test, so you can simply look at the point where the tests stop progressing and read the name of the offending test. Now you know where to look for the cause of the problem.

◆ Discussion

If, for some reason, you cannot or prefer not to use a Swing-based test runner, you can achieve the desired result with a little extra work. We describe our recommended technique in recipe 6.2.

◆ Related

- 6.2—See the name of each test as it executes with a text-based test runner
- 16.6—Report the name of each test as it executes

6.2 See the name of each test as it executes with a text-based test runner

◆ Problem

You would like to monitor the progress of your tests, including the name of the currently executing test, but you need or want to use a text-based test runner.

◆ Background

If you introduce an infinite loop or deadlock into your code then the tests will eventually stop making progress. No failure message, nothing. If this happens you need to work "outside the system" to isolate the test (and therefore the production code) causing the problem. One easy way to get this information is to print out the name of each test as it starts. This turns out to be easy to do if you can use a graphical test runner, but if your test environment assumes a text-based test runner then you have to solve this problem another way.

◆ Recipe

Because you're debugging, you probably have a short-term need for this feature. In this case, the easiest way to achieve this is to add a line of code to the `setUp()` method of your test case class that prints out the name of each test during execution.

```
public class MyNameIsTest extends TestCase {
    protected void setUp() {
        System.out.println(getName());
    }
    // ... your tests ...
}
```

If you would prefer to see the class name and the test name, then call `toString()`, rather than `getName()`. It depends on whether you need the additional context; `toString()` returns something like `MyNameIsTest(testNumberOne)`, whereas `getName()` returns just `testNumberOne`.

◆ *Discussion*

If you need a more permanent solution, the next step is to override the method `TestCase.runTest()` to print the name of the test just prior to executing the test. You could easily add "entry and exit" messages in this way.

```
public class MyNameIsTest extends TestCase {
    protected void runTest() throws Throwable {
        System.out.println("Starting test " + toString());
        super.runTest();
        System.out.println("Ending test " + toString());
    }
}
```

Remember to invoke `super.runTest()`; otherwise, your test will not execute! It is remarkably easy to forget to invoke the superclass's implementation when overriding a method, making this a slightly dangerous way to implement this feature. The good news is that you only need to do this once: push this method all the way up in your test case class hierarchy so that all your classes can use it (see recipe 3.6, "Introduce a Base Test Case"). The bad news is that by implementing this through inheritance, you constrain your design, as Java is a single-inheritance language. It would be nice to implement this either as a Decorator or as a runtime-configurable parameter—a feature you can easily add or remove as needed. The runtime-configurable parameter is likely the simpler solution and we describe how to add these to your tests in recipe 5.1, "Using Java system properties" as well as throughout chapter 5, "Working with Test Data."

If you do not mind changing test runners, you can use the JUnit-addons test runner as an alternative to this recipe. See recipe 16.6, "Report the name of each test as it executes."

◆ *Related*

- 3.6—Introduce a Base Test Case
- 5.1—Using Java system properties
- 6.1—See the name of each test as it executes
- 16.6—Report the name of each test as it executes

6.3 Execute a single test

◆ Problem

You would like to execute a single test, rather than all the tests in the current test case class.

◆ Background

You will most likely want to execute a single test right after it fails, especially if it is the only test in the suite that fails. Rather than extract the test into its own suite or build a Singleton suite with code, you would like your tools to handle the job.

◆ Recipe

As you might expect, the ability to execute a single test varies from IDE to IDE, but they all solve the problem the same way: they invoke their test runner's `run()` method with a single `TestCase` object. If your IDE does not support the ability to execute a single test then you might be able to add it, as with Eclipse or jEdit by changing either of their JUnit plug-ins.

One IDE that supports this "out of the box" is IDEA from IntelliJ. Place the insertion point inside a method definition *or* select a test from the Structure view, right-click, then select "Run *test name*." IDEA opens the test runner of your choice (text-based or Swing-based) and executes just the one test.

The Swing-based test runner also supports this feature (to a certain extent) through its Test Hierarchy tab. After executing the tests once, you can select individual tests and execute them again by switching to the Test Hierarchy tab, selecting a test and pressing the associated Run button. This solution has one major disadvantage: it requires executing the entire test suite at least once, which defeats in part the point of executing a single test.

◆ Discussion

Eclipse, the open source workbench for programmers, does not directly support executing a single test, but its open plug-in API makes it possible to add that feature, then assign it to a keystroke. JEdit, a well-known open source text editor, comes with a JUnit plug-in, but it does not yet support executing a single test. Given that it is at version 0.0.2 as we write these words, we can hardly expect such a relatively advanced feature to be there already.

One final note: executing a single test from a Parameterized Test Case (see recipe 4.8, "Build a data-driven test suite") is, in general, not possible. Given the way that JUnit creates a test suite, there is no way to select a test method *and* a single row of fixture data to be executed. From JUnit's point of view, a test is a test, even if it executes 100 times with 100 different fixture states. JUnit differentiates tests by their implementation (as different methods), rather than their runtime behavior (with different inputs).

◆ Related

- IntelliJ's web site (www.intellij.com)

6.4 Execute each test in its own JVM

◆ Problem

You have tests whose fixture includes global data such as caches and Singletons. You want to be able to set up each test separately without making Singletons writable or adding reset methods to the caches.

◆ Background

Robert DiFalco wanted to know how to do this, so he asked the JUnit Yahoo! group about it:

> "I have a lot of code that has to reset [global] state such as caches each time a test is run, code that is only needed for unit testing. If each test method ran in its own JVM, my testing code would not require me to make changes in the code I am testing."

If you need to test code that relies on global data, you might find it useful to execute tests in separate JVMs. The question you will have to consider after reading this recipe is the trade-off between applying this technique and performing the refactoring that we think such code needs.

◆ Recipe

You can execute each test in its own JVM if you run your tests from Ant. Use the `<junit>` and `<batchtest>` tasks to execute test suites in their own JVMs. This is what your buildfile should look like:

```
<target name="eachSuiteInSeparateJvm">
    <junit>
        <formatter type="plain" />
        <classpath>
            <pathelement location="test/classes" />
            <pathelement location="d:/junit3.8.1/junit.jar" />
        </classpath>
```

```
            <batchtest fork="yes" todir="logs">
                <fileset dir="test/source">
                    <include name="junit/cookbook/running/**/*.java" />
                    <exclude name="**/GlobalData.java" />
                </fileset>
            </batchtest>
        </junit>
    </target>
```

Pay particular attention to the use of the fork attribute in the <batchtest> task. By specifying fork="yes" you are telling the <batchtest> task to execute each test suite matching the include pattern in the <fileset> in a separate JVM. (See the Ant manual for details on the various attributes of the <batchtest> task.) Once you can execute each test suite in its own JVM, move each test method into its own test suite (in its own Java source file). Then each *test*, being in a separate file matching the include pattern, will execute in a separate JVM. Having each test in its own source file might not be a nice solution, but it *is* a solution.

◆ *Discussion*

This is another one of those techniques that is important to know when you need it, but that you wish you never had to use. Heavy use of global data signals a weakness in a system's design, as it leads to "come back" defects: you think you have fixed it, but eventually the defect comes back. If you have aspirations of refactoring the code away from heavy use of global data then this technique can help you establish the safety net you need to perform that refactoring. Implementing this recipe is *just annoying enough* that you will wish you did not have to do it, and feeling this pain just might motivate you not to rely so heavily on global data in the future.

◆ *Related*

- 6.5—Reload classes before each test

6.5 *Reload classes before each test*

◆ *Problem*

You want to execute each test with freshly loaded classes as a way to cope with production code that sets global data at startup.

◆ *Background*

In recipe 6.4, "Execute each test in its own JVM," we described the general problem: some of the classes involved in a test use global state and provide no direct way to reset that state. One approach is to expose that state so that we can reset it as needed; however, that involves changing the code before we begin to test it. We would rather install some tests before we change the code so that we have *some* confidence that we have not changed the code's behavior in some unexpected way. In the previous recipe we described using Ant to execute each test in its own JVM, but that is quite a heavyweight solution that can cause the tests to execute quite slowly. We would like a solution that has the benefits of executing each test in its own JVM (freshly loaded classes) without resorting to starting and stopping so many JVMs.

◆ *Recipe*

After involving himself in a mailing list discussion on the topic, Neil Swingler decided to build a simple solution to this problem: a `ReloadedTestCaseDecorator` that reloads classes before each test. You wrap each test in this decorator then execute the resulting test suite. Each test in the suite executes with freshly loaded classes. To illustrate this technique, let us try to test an object cache. Suppose you have an object directory that retrieves objects from a database or a network connection—each time you look up the same object, you incur unnecessary overhead, because the objects you retrieve never change. You want to add a cache onto the directory to avoid invoking the expensive object `lookup()` method more than once for each differently named object. Because you only need one cache, you decide to implement it as global methods and data. To be sure that your `ObjectCache` is actually caching the result, you want to verify whether cache hits occur when you expect them to. You start with the following tests:

```
package junit.cookbook.running.test;

import junit.cookbook.running.*;
import junit.framework.TestCase;

public class ObjectCacheHitTest extends TestCase implements Directory {
    protected void setUp() throws Exception {
        ObjectCache.directory = this;
    }

    public void testFirstLookup() throws Exception {
        assertEquals("there", ObjectCache.lookup("hello"));
        assertEquals(0, ObjectCache.countCacheHits());
    }

    public void testExpectingCacheHit() throws Exception {
        assertEquals("there", ObjectCache.lookup("hello"));
        assertEquals("there", ObjectCache.lookup("hello"));
        assertEquals(1, ObjectCache.countCacheHits());
    }
```

```
    // Self-Shunt method
    public Object get(String name) {
        return "there";
    }
}
```

Here we use the Self-Shunt pattern and let the test case class itself be the `Directory`. Even though its implementation of `get()` does *not* perform some expensive lookup operation, the production `Directory` will, but this particular implementation detail does not concern us right now. We have two tests, one that expects no cache hit on the first request to retrieve an object, and another test that retrieves the same object twice, expecting only one cache hit. The problem is that when you execute these tests, the second fails.

```
junit.framework.AssertionFailedError: expected:<1> but was:<2>
```

It seems that in the second test *both* invocations of `get()` resulted in cache hits, and not just the second one. This is the problem with Singletons: you need to reset the `ObjectCache`'s state before executing the second test; otherwise, it "inherits" whatever state the previous test left behind. Fortunately for us, `ReloadedTestCaseDecorator` comes to the rescue. To use this utility, you need to create a test suite "by hand" for your test case class (see recipe 4.2, "Collect a specific set of tests"), wrapping each test in the `ReloadedTestCaseDecorator`. We can approximate this well enough for most purposes by adding this `suite()` method to our test case class.[1]

```
public static TestSuite suite() {
    TestSuite suite = new TestSuite();

    Method[] methods = ObjectCacheHitTest.class.getMethods();
    for (int i = 0; i < methods.length; i++) {
        Method method = methods[i];
        String methodName = method.getName();
        if (methodName.startsWith("test")) {
            suite.addTest(
                new ReloadedTestCaseDecorator(
                    ObjectCacheHitTest.class,
                    methodName));
        }
    }

    return suite;
}
```

[1] Strictly speaking, this `suite()` method will include methods that may not be valid tests, but it is good enough for most purposes.

When we add this `suite()` method to our test case class, all the tests now pass! Each test executes against a freshly loaded `ObjectCache` with an empty cache. You can now add more tests without worrying about the state of the `ObjectCache` at the end of the previous test, just as if you instantiated a new one each time. This simplifies the tests considerably and does not require changing the class under test.

◆ ***Discussion***

Neil's solution uses a bytecode manipulation library called Javassist[2], part of the JBoss application server project. The `ReloadedTestCaseDecorator` instantiates each test after first reloading the test class. You can find a current version of Neil's code in the files section of the JUnit Yahoo! group.[3] The only real downside to this approach is that you need to decorate any test that needs to reload its fixture classes. We called this a downside only because it involves work; otherwise, we think it is a good thing: if your tests are going to do something as drastic as reload classes, then you want to *know* that it is happening—you want to intend to do it, and not just have it happen as a matter of course. The `suite()` method we provide in the example is essentially a universal one: simply put it in a utility class and use it wherever you need it.

◆ ***Related***

- 4.2—Collect a specific set of tests
- 6.4—Execute each test in its own JVM
- The Javassist project (www.jboss.org/developers/projects/javassist.html)

6.6 *Ignore a test*

◆ ***Problem***

You have a test that you would like to disable without removing its code. In other words, you would like to ignore it.

◆ ***Background***

Test-Driven Development purists argue that a test lives in only one of two states: passing or failing. There are times, though, when it is useful to have a third state: ignored. Vladimir Bossicard's weblog at artima.com contains an article in which he

---

2 www.csg.is.titech.ac.jp/~chiba/javassist/

3 http://groups.yahoo.com/group/junit/files/

describes the need to ignore tests. The most compelling need arises from two opposing forces: the desire to have all tests pass 100% and the desire to capture all your knowledge about how your objects should behave in the tests. In other words, you do not want to remove a test, even though you cannot make it pass right now.

Vladimir describes a few scenarios in which you would want to ignore a test. You might have identified a defect in an external library that you cannot fix. In this case, you would like to ignore the corresponding failing test until you deploy a new version of that library. You might also have identified a low-priority defect that you either do not know how to fix or do not have the time to fix. Although we would like to release defect-free code, there are times—especially times very close to an inflexible release date—when we are forced to let code go that we know is not defect free. It makes us feel bad when we do it, but sometimes we have little choice.[4]

Whether you want to ignore tests temporarily or for a longer period of time, we present an easy way to do each.

◆ *Recipe*

If you only need to ignore a test for a few seconds—that is, long enough to execute your tests once or twice—and you plan to reenable the test, then just add a few characters to the *beginning* of the test name. For example, to temporarily ignore a test named `testHappyPath()`, rename the method to `DISABLED_testHappyPath()`. JUnit will not identify the method as a test, because its name does not start with "test." We use `DISABLED` here, because it says what we're doing: disabling the test. While this approach works, it is not useful for ignoring tests for a longer period of time. You might want support for reporting how many tests are currently being ignored. In that case, you need something more than an arbitrary "disabled" marker.

JUnit-addons provides direct support for "ignoring" tests. To ignore a test, change its name so that it ends in `_ignored`. When you execute the tests with the JUnit-addons test runner, you receive the following report:

```
***

Elapsed time: 0 sec (3 tests + 1 ignored)

IGNORED

1) testDefaultInitializationParameters_ignored
   (junit.cookbook.common.test.ConstructorTest)
```

[4] We originally wrote "no choice," but we believe firmly that there is always a choice. It is generally a question of whether we have the courage to make the unpopular choice. We do not always have that courage.

To reenable the test, remove `_ignored` from the end of its name. That is all there is to it.

◆ *Discussion*

If you execute an ignored test using a plain-vanilla JUnit test runner, the test executes normally: the test runner does not recognize anything special about the test from its name. For this reason we recommend that when you mark a test as "ignored," make sure that the test *fails*. How could it pass? It could be empty, like this.

```
public void testDefectInThirdPartySoftware_ignored() {
}
```

The JUnit-addons test runner reports this test as "ignored," while the plain-vanilla JUnit test runner reports this test as *passed* because it does not contain a failing assertion! Executing this test with the plain-vanilla test runner gives you a false sense of security: your system *appears* to pass tests that you have not even implemented! You should only ignore tests that you have written but cannot make pass. If you have ideas for the next five tests you want to implement, write them on a list rather than in code. If you are not ready to code them, then code them later. You will save yourself some confusion.

If you find your collection of ignored tests growing then we recommend you move those tests into their own test suite (such as in a separate source tree). Execute them only when you think they have a chance of passing; that is, when you experience a change in the conditions that led you to ignore those tests in the first place. Many projects collect test metrics to indicate progress, so the more ignored tests your project carries, the more misleading your measurement of progress becomes. Also, if you are ignoring tests for a third-party library, you might find it useful to execute just those tests whenever you upgrade to a new version of the library. This would give you immediate feedback as to whether the new library is "any better" than the previous version, at least in terms of supporting your particular needs.

◆ *Related*

- Chapter 16—JUnit-addons
- The JUnit-addons web site (http://junit-addons.sourceforge.net)
- Vladimir Bossicard, "The Third State of your Binary JUnit Tests." (www.artima.com/weblogs/viewpost.jsp?thread=4603)
- Vladimir Bossicard's weblog (www.artima.com/weblogs/index.jsp?blogger=vladimir)

7 Reporting JUnit results

This chapter covers

- Logging from a Base Test Case
- Logging with Log4Unit
- Reporting results with Ant, including <junitreport>
- Customizing Ant's test run reports
- Using a custom TestListener
- Counting assertions

This chapter covers various tools and techniques available for reporting JUnit test results, including extending JUnit to write your own custom reporting mechanisms. JUnit by itself provides two simple mechanisms for reporting test results: simple text output to `System.out` and its famous Swing and AWT "green bar" GUIs (the AWT GUI being a vestige of JUnit's Java 1.1 support). The results reporting that JUnit provides out of the box is useful for developers at their desktops, but that is about it. You need to extend JUnit or use it with another tool if you want automated test reports in formats such as XML or HTML.

There are a slew of JUnit extensions out there, many of which revolve around subclassing `TestCase`. These extensions usually can be executed with the built-in JUnit test runners or with Ant's `<junit>` task with no extra work. Ideally you want reporting solutions that are reusable across any of these extensions; therefore, you should extend JUnit reporting by implementing or extending standard APIs in Ant or JUnit.

JUnit is most often executed in one of three contexts, each of which provides different reporting features and opportunities for extension:

- IDE
- Command line
- Ant build script (or, increasingly, Maven target)

NOTE Maven is a build tool that grew out of many people's collective experience using Ant to build, test, and manage Java-based projects. Maven promotes the concept of a *project object model*, which it creates through a standardized project deployment descriptor. Maven is firmly based on Ant and Jelly, an XML-based scripting language. For more information about Maven, visit maven.apache.org.

Some IDEs launch one of JUnit's built-in GUI test runners, while others have their own GUI test runner implementations with added features. Command-line test runners output results to a console, which can be redirected to a file. Ant's `<junit>` and `<junitreport>` suite of tasks together provide XML results files transformed to HTML reports.

Different report styles and formats serve different purposes and users. Managers like to see reports in their browsers or maybe on paper printouts in bug triage meetings. Developers and QA engineers like results displayed graphically in their IDEs so they don't have to "shell out" to the command line to run JUnit in a separate window.

7.1 Using a Base Test Case with a logger

◆ Problem

You want to perform logging from within your test cases.

◆ Background

JUnit automates evaluating assertions so that developers don't waste time routinely verifying the output of test methods. Logging from test cases should not be used as a way to verify that tests have passed. Let the JUnit framework handle that. But there are several situations where logging messages or even test results to a file, console, or other device is useful in JUnit testing. For example:

- Temporary debugging, which can be turned on or off by configuration
- Auditing and storage of test results
- Auditing of the test environment or data used during a test run
- Tracking the progress of tests that take a long time to run
- Trapping customized test results for import into a test management system

You can always configure and instantiate a logger from within any test case as you would from any other Java class. But if you are going to write many tests (especially if you are in a team environment, sharing common test infrastructure such as base test classes), it is practical to write a base test case class that provides the logging configuration and instantiation, and then subclass the log-providing class as desired. If you have a common base class that everyone uses for a particular subsystem or project, you can include the logging configuration as part of that class.

◆ Recipe

Create a base test case class that extends `junit.framework.TestCase` and provides a configured logger to its subclasses.

You have several options for finding and using a logger:

- Write your own logging mechanism
- Use a logger written by someone on your staff
- Use a logging library from a third party, such as Log4J, Avalon's LogKit, Jakarta Commons Logging
- Use the `java.util.logging` package in JDK 1.4

The pattern for setting up a logger in a base test class is the same, regardless of which logger you choose:

- Extend `TestCase` with a class named similarly to `BaseTestCase`, which might include other commonly used testing utilities (perhaps a JNDI `lookup()` utility, or some other custom logic about where to find, that finds test data).
- Set up a default configuration for the logger and initialize it in the `BaseTestCase`, and make the preconfigured logger accessible to subclasses through a protected variable, an accessor to retrieve the logger instance, or through inherited log methods.
- Make your test cases extend `BaseTestCase` so they can use the logger as needed.

Listing 7.1 shows a `BaseTestCase` class that configures two logger instances, one for static contexts, such as `static` initializer blocks and `suite()` methods, and one for non-`static` contexts, such as `setUp()`, `tearDown()`, and test methods. Two separate loggers for `static` and non-`static` might be overkill, but this allows the example to show two different approaches for setting up the logger. The example uses Apache Avalon's LogKit (any version of 1.*x* can compile and run with this example). In terms of features and ease of use, LogKit is a full-featured, flexible logging kit somewhere in between JDK 1.4's `java.util.logging` package and Jakarta's premier logger, Log4J. You can read more about LogKit and download the library at avalon.apache.org/logkit/.

NOTE Avalon is a Java platform for component-oriented programming including a core framework, utilities, tools, components, and containers hosted at Apache.

Listing 7.1 `BaseTestCase` configured with Avalon LogKit

```
package junit.cookbook.tests.reporting;

import junit.framework.TestCase;

import org.apache.log.Hierarchy;
import org.apache.log.LogTarget;
import org.apache.log.Logger;
import org.apache.log.Priority;
import org.apache.log.format.ExtendedPatternFormatter;
import org.apache.log.output.io.StreamTarget;

public class BaseTestCase extends TestCase {

    /**
     * Sets the default log level for both embedded loggers.
```

```
 * The default log level setting can be overridden via
 * -Dlog.level=... on the command line or with a
 * &lt;sysproperty key="log.level" value="${value}"/&gt;
 * in an Ant &lt;java/&gt; task running this test.
 * Valid values, in ascending order or severity, are
 * DEBUG, INFO, WARN, ERROR, FATAL_ERROR.
 */
protected static String logLevel = "INFO";

/**
 * Embedded <b>staticLogger</b>. This reference is static
 * and should be used for messages logged from static
 * code, such as static initializers and TestCase.suite()
 * methods.
 */
protected static Logger staticLogger =
    Hierarchy.getDefaultHierarchy().getLoggerFor("static.");

/**
 * <b>logger</b> is not static and should be used
 * everywhere except in places where a statically
 * configured logger is necessary.
 */
protected Logger logger =
    Hierarchy.getDefaultHierarchy().getLoggerFor("test.");

/** Logkit Logger output string format for
 * non-static <b>logger</b> */
protected String pattern =
    "%{priority}: %{message} in %{method}\n %{throwable}";

/** Logkit Logger output string format for <b>staticLogger</b> */
protected static String staticPattern =
    "%{priority}: %{message} in %{method}\n %{throwable}";

/**
 * Logkit extended formatter class, provides method
 * and thread info. This one is for the non-static
 * <b>logger</b>
 */
protected ExtendedPatternFormatter formatter =
    new ExtendedPatternFormatter(pattern);

/**
 * Logkit extended formatter class, provides method
 * and thread info. This one is for the <b>staticLogger</b>
 */
protected static ExtendedPatternFormatter staticFormatter =
    new ExtendedPatternFormatter(staticPattern);
```

```
    static {
        setLogLevelFromSystemProperty();
        // log everything to System.out target for now
        StreamTarget target =
            new StreamTarget(System.out, staticFormatter);
        staticLogger.setLogTargets(new LogTarget[] { target });
        Priority priority = Priority.getPriorityForName(logLevel);
        staticLogger.setPriority(priority);
    }

    public BaseTestCase() {
        setLogLevelFromSystemProperty();
        // log everything to System.out target for now
        StreamTarget target =
            new StreamTarget(System.out, formatter);
        logger.setLogTargets(new LogTarget[] { target });
        Priority priority = Priority.getPriorityForName(logLevel);
        logger.setPriority(priority);
    }

    private static final void setLogLevelFromSystemProperty() {
        String log_level = System.getProperty("log.level");
        if (null != log_level) {
            logLevel = log_level;
        }
    }
}
```

static initializer for configuring staticLogger

Constructor, where default log level is set and base logger is configured

The most important thing about the code example in listing 7.1 is the general technique of embedding a shared logger instance in a base test case class, not the specifics of using any particular logging implementation.

◆ *Discussion*

Loggers such as LogKit, Log4J, and the Java 1.4 logging API allow you to configure logging on a per-class or per-package basis, by log level or by named categories. Such configurability is useful for enabling logging for a particular subsystem or class hierarchy and helping isolate log messages from a particular set of tests or type of log message.

The advantage to extending a `BaseTestCase` (for logging and other utilities it might offer) is that subclasses can access the logger with no extra work. The drawback to any subclassing strategy is that it ties the subclasses to the parent class through inheritance. An alternative to subclassing is to write a logging utility class that configures and instantiates a shared logger, and then use that utility class from within your tests. This tack decouples your test case classes from a common base class added just for logging. But it is so common in practice to evolve a useful, in-house Base Test Case of some kind, that it is a good recipe to have in your personal cookbook.

◆ ***Related***

- 7.2—Using Log4Unit

7.2 Using Log4Unit

◆ ***Problem***

You want a ready-made solution for logging messages from within your test cases.

◆ ***Background***

Log4Unit is an extension of JUnit's `TestCase` class that gives you Log4J-based logging functionality with the least amount of effort. It provides the following features:

- Log4Unit derived test cases default to logging to `System.out` if the Log4J library is not present in the class path at runtime.
- Log4Unit configures and instantiates a Log4J logger instance and implements utility logging methods such as `info(Object message)` and `debug (Object message, Throwable t)` for you.
- Log4Unit comes with a customized Swing-based test runner that shows log statements and test summary information in a dialog box that pops up with the push of a button.

◆ ***Recipe***

Use Log4Unit (www.openfuture.de/Log4Unit/) to integrate your tests with the Log4J logger. Log4Unit is free, open source, and licensed under the Lesser GPL. The latest version as of this writing is v0.2.0. Download the .zip or .gzip file and unpack it into a new directory, such as log4unit-020.

You also need Log4J (http://logging.apache.org/log4j) to see the features of Log4Unit. The latest release of Log4J as of this writing is v1.2.8.

To use Log4Unit:

- Extend your `TestCases` from `junit.log4j.LoggedTestCase`.
- Write a Log4J configuration file (it can be in Java properties or XML format—see the Log4J documentation for details), or place the directory containing

Log4Unit's provided `log4j.properties` in your class path (probably the src/ directory where you unzipped Log4Unit).

- Add `log4j-1.2.8.jar` and `log4unit-0.2.0.jar` to your usual test class path.
- As another option, you can use `junit.logswingui.TestRunner` as your GUI test runner if you want to have access to the test summary: `java junit.logswingui.TestRunner [-noloading] [TestCase]`.

Listing 7.2 demonstrates some basic features of Log4Unit by showing you the simplest type of test you can write with Log4Unit. Note that we import and extend `junit.log4j.LoggedTestCase`. The `LoggedTestCase` superclass configures and instantiates a Log4J logger instance and implements utility logging methods such as `info(Object message)` and `debug(Object message`, Throwable t) for you. All we do in this example apart from extending the base class is call the inherited `info(Object message)` log method twice and `debug(Object message)` once to demonstrate the basic functionality and default logging configuration.

Listing 7.2 Log4UnitExample.java

```
package junit.cookbook.reporting.log4unit;

import junit.log4j.LoggedTestCase;

public class Log4UnitExample extends LoggedTestCase {   <-- Extending LoggedTestCase
    public void setUp() {
        debug("** SETUP ENTERED **");   <-- Example debug message
    }

    public void testConnection() {
        info("> entered " + this);   <-- Example info messages
        boolean connected = false;
        info("Initiating connection to server now");   <--
        // create Connection and set connected
        // to true if successful . . .
        connected = true;
        assertTrue(connected);
    }
}
```

First let's run `Log4UnitExample` from the command line using JUnit's built-in text-based test runner and see the resulting output.

NOTE The Log4J jar is needed to run, but not to compile this example; and some of these messages are generated at the DEBUG log level, so change your log4j.properties file from the INFO to DEBUG level to see them all.

```
java -cp lib\junit.jar;lib\log4j-1.2.8.jar;lib\log4unit-0.2.0.jar;classes
⇒  junit.textui.TestRunner junit.cookbook.reporting.log4unit.Log4UnitExample

30 Jun 2003 22:01:42,663 - Log4J successfully instantiated.
.30 Jun 2003 22:01:42,693 - ** SETUP ENTERED **
30 Jun 2003 22:01:42,713 - > entered
   testConnection(junit.cookbook.reporting.log4unit.Log4UnitExample)
30 Jun 2003 22:01:42,733 - Initiating connection to server now
30 Jun 2003 22:01:42,753 - Tear down finished.

Time: 0.08

OK (1 test)
```

You can see that the default logging configuration prints out date and time (to the millisecond) to the console, followed by a successful start-up message and default log messages for `setUp()` and `tearDown()`. We overrode `setUp()` with our own log message and let `tearDown()` print its default message. The two INFO messages we logged show up in the middle, displaying the test being executed and a message.

If you look in the directory from where you executed this command, you see a file named `bugbase-test.log`. Log4Unit produces this log and the console output because it uses Log4J to handle the calls to the various logging priorities (DEBUG, INFO, WARN, ERROR, and FATAL). In the default configuration the console and the log contain the same information, but you can configure Log4J to customize the output for each location.

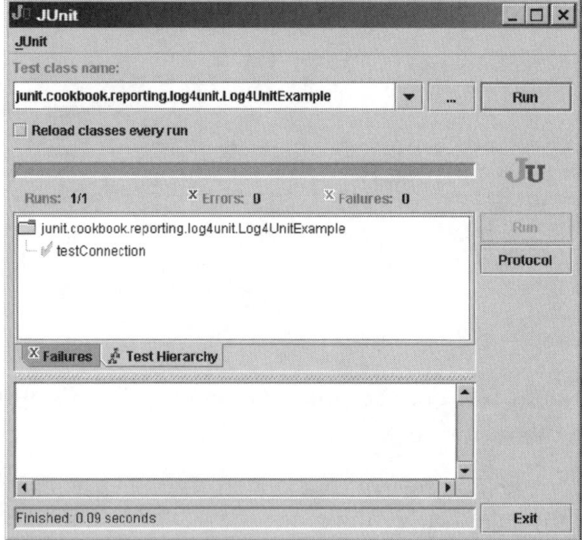

Figure 7.1
`junit.logswingui.TestRunner`
showing the Protocol button on the right

Log4J supports a plethora of possibilities for increasing log output and customizing the logging configuration. Some of it is useful for tests, such as source line numbers and elapsed time recording. But because these are features of Log4J and not Log4Unit, we won't delve into them here. Please refer to the Log4J web site for more information (http://logging.apache.org/log4j).

Another feature of Log4Unit is its customized Swing-based test runner with its test protocol feature. Running the same example with the `junit.logswingui.TestRunner`, we see a dialog box with a new Protocol button as shown in figure 7.1.

When you press the Protocol button a dialog box pops up with log statements and test summary information, as shown in figure 7.2.

◆ ***Discussion***

A helpful feature of Log4Unit is that test cases default to logging to `System.out` if the Log4J library is not present in the class path at runtime. If you are wondering how it does this, `LoggedTestCase`'s constructor discovers whether Log4J is available and sets a `boolean` flag accordingly. There is an `if` statement in each log method that passes the log message and level to `System.out` when the flag is `false`.

When running the `junit.logswingui.TestRunner`, you might see a large number of Log4J errors on the console display. These errors describe class loading problems caused by trying to reload Log4J classes that prefer not to be reloaded,[1] so if you see these messages the first time you use the Log4J test runner, you have two options:

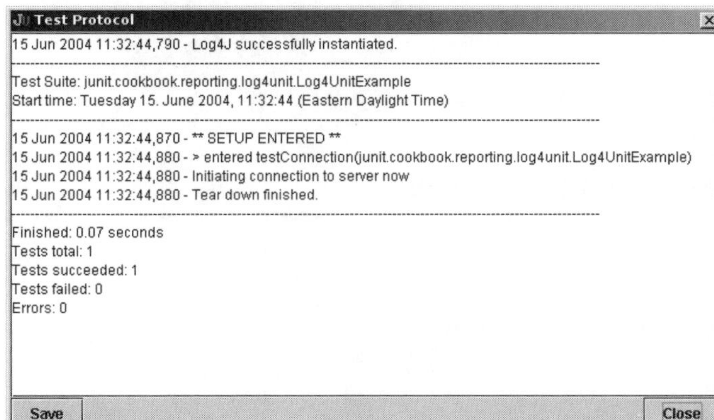

Figure 7.2
The Log4Unit Test Protocol dialog box, showing log statements and test summary information

---

[1] There are similar problems when trying to reload some JDBC driver classes within tests, an issue we deal with in more detail in chapter 10, "Testing and JDBC."

- Use the `-noloading` option, or
- Add the Log4J package (`org.apache.log4j.*`) to the "excluded classes" list as we describe in recipe 8.6, "The graphical test runner does not load your classes properly".[2]

You should be aware of the limitations to using Log4Unit:

- Log4Unit only supports Log4J. Log4J is a very flexible and powerful logging API, but sometimes you need to use another logging implementation. Log4Unit is open source and small, so you could pretty easily customize it to support the logging implementation of your choice, or abstract the logging implementation using a bridge such as Jakarta Commons Logging, found at http://jakarta.apache.org/commons/logging.html.
- Log4Unit *requires* your `TestCases` to extend `LoggedTestCase`. It is one thing to willingly extract a Base Test Case; it is another to be forced into it. That said, there's nothing about Log4Unit that prevents subclasses of `LoggedTestCase` from running in any other JUnit test runner. As we said, even if Log4J is not in the class path, the tests run as normal `TestCases` minus the logging features. Nevertheless, if you plan to write hundreds or thousands of tests, we recommend that you extend a base `TestCase` of your own from `LoggedTestCase` and extend all your other tests from your own base `TestCase`. That way, if you ever decide you need to remove or replace Log4Unit, you only have to change your base `TestCase` and not hundreds of `TestCases`.

◆ Related

- 7.1—Using a Base Test Case with a logger

7.3 Getting plain text results with Ant

◆ Problem

You want to output JUnit test reports in plain text.

---

[2] If you run your tests from Ant's `<junit>` tasks, then this option doesn't exist, but that is no problem because Ant uses its own test runner.

◆ Background

Plain text reports are useful in contexts such as Telnet terminals, UNIX and DOS command shells, and inline in email messages. Ant has the built-in capability to produce two types of plain text JUnit test reports: *brief* and *plain*, which are useful in these contexts.

◆ Recipe

Use the brief or plain formatter type to output plain text reports to a file or to the console. The `<junit>`, `<test>`, and `<batchtest>` tasks all support the use of the nested `<formatter>` element. Table 7.1 describes the attributes of the `<formatter>` element:

Table 7.1 Attributes of the `<formatter>` element of Ant's `<junit>`, `<test>`, and `<batchtest>` tasks for executing JUnit tests

Attribute	Description
`classname`	Lets you specify your own custom formatter implementation class instead of using *xml*, *plain*, or *brief* (see recipe 7.6, "Extending Ant's JUnit results format" for use of this extension feature).
`extension`	Extension to append to files output by the formatter. Required if using a custom formatter, but defaults to .txt for *plain* and *brief*, and .xml when using *xml*.
`type`	Choice of *xml*, *plain*, or *brief* (unless using your own formatter implementation with the `classname` attribute).
`usefile`	Whether to output formatted results to a file. Defaults to `true`.

The two formatting options we are concerned with in this recipe are the brief and plain types.

Listing 7.3 shows an Ant target for running a set of JUnit tests with the brief results formatter. You typically use this target in a complete Ant build script, of course. See recipe 7.4, "Reporting results in HTML with Ant's <junitreport> task" for a more complete build.xml example.

Listing 7.3 `junit-run` Ant target using brief results formatter

```
<!--property declarations, clean, compile and other build
targets omitted to save page space -->

<target name="junit-run"
        description="=> run JUnit tests">
    <junit haltonfailure="no" fork="yes" printsummary="no">   ❶
        <classpath>
```

```
                <pathelement location="${classes.dir}"/>
                <pathelement path="${java.class.path}"/>
            </classpath>
            <batchtest fork="yes">
                <formatter type="brief"        ❷
                           usefile="no"/>       ❸
                <fileset dir="${src.dir}">
                    <include name="${junit.includes}"/>
                    <exclude name="${junit.excludes}"/>
                </fileset>
            </batchtest>
        </junit>
    </target>
```

❶ *Eliminate duplicate summary information*—The brief text formatter already includes a summary at the end of a test run, so we set `printsummary` to `no` to avoid duplicating that information.

❷ *Use brief formatter*—This is how to specify the `brief` formatting type. As we have mentioned previously, the other available values are `plain` and `xml`.

❸ *Display results to console*—We have decided to display test results to the console, rather than to a file, so we set `usefile` to `no`.

The brief format type output looks like this on the console (we ran this Ant build target with the `-emacs` flag to reduce logging adornments):

```
junit-run:
Testsuite: junit.cookbook.tests.extensions.ReloadableTestClassLoaderTest
Tests run: 4, Failures: 0, Errors: 0, Time elapsed: 0.02 sec

Testsuite: junit.cookbook.tests.reporting.CookbookTestListenerTest
Tests run: 4, Failures: 0, Errors: 0, Time elapsed: 0.591 sec
```

Change the formatter to `type="plain"` and run it again. You can see the plain type output prints the name and elapsed time of each test method:

```
junit-run:
Testsuite: junit.cookbook.tests.extensions.ReloadableTestClassLoaderTest
Tests run: 4, Failures: 0, Errors: 0, Time elapsed: 0.03 sec

Testcase: testGetResourceString took 0.01 sec
Testcase: testGetResourceAsStreamString took 0 sec
Testcase: testLoadClassString took 0.02 sec
Testcase: testIsJar took 0 sec


Testsuite: junit.cookbook.tests.reporting.CookbookTestListenerTest
Tests run: 4, Failures: 0, Errors: 0, Time elapsed: 0.591 sec
```

```
Testcase: testStartTest took 0.561 sec
Testcase: testEndTest took 0.01 sec
Testcase: testAddError took 0.01 sec
Testcase: testAddFailure took 0 sec
```

We set `printsummary="no"` when using these formatters because the summary output just repeats some of the same information output by these formatters.

Both of these formatters will output one text file per test case class if you run your tests using the `<batchtest>` task, since the `<batchtest>` task dynamically picks up tests to run based on pattern matching for file names. We have our includes/excludes pattern match the source files here, but you could use classes (we use source file names because it saves time in pattern matching a mix of outer and inner class file names). If you want to automatically send the output of the results as text in the body of an e-mail message (since attaching dozens or hundreds of text files would be unusable to recipients of the e-mail), you can use the Ant `<concat>` and `<mail>` tasks to do so with a target like this:

```
<target name="mail-report">
    <property name="junit.report.file" value="junit-results.txt"/>
    <concat destfile="${junit.report.file}">
       <fileset dir="${junit.reports.dir}" includes="TEST-*.txt"/>
    </concat>
    <mail mailhost="mail.manning.net"
          mailport="25"
          subject="JUnit test results"
          tolist="jb@manning.com,ss@manning.com"
          messagefile="${junit.results.file}">
        <from address="autobuild@manning.com"/>
    </mail>
</target>
```

Each test result file is automatically named by the formatters as `TEST-classname.txt`, so it's easy to include them all in a `<fileset>`. The `<concat>` task concatenates all these files into one new file named by the `destfile` attribute, which is set by a property in our example to ensure that the same file is picked up and used below in the `<mail>` task. The `messagefile` attribute of the `<mail>` task will use the file specified by `${junit.results.file}` as the body of the email message that is sent. You could easily spruce up the target as shown to make it more dynamic, such as by using the `<tstamp>` task to create a time stamp property, which you could use to append to the email subject.

◆ *Discussion*

The easiest way to get off the ground with automated JUnit test results is by running JUnit tests in Ant, and running the outputs into automated emails or HTML reports. Test results can be output in XML by the `<junit>` task and transformed to HTML using the `<junitreport>` task.

◆ *Related*

- 7.4—Reporting results in HTML with Ant's <junitreport> task
- 7.5—Customizing <junit> XML reports with XSLT

7.4 Reporting results in HTML with Ant's <junitreport> task

◆ *Problem*

You need to easily and automatically report JUnit test results in a presentable HTML format.

◆ *Background*

You often need to make JUnit test results available as a report to a wider audience than the individual developer or QA engineer. The way to do this is with professional looking file-based reports, which can be emailed as attachments or posted online in HTML format. Tabular, cross-linked HTML reports are useful for their hyperlinked navigability, especially if you need to navigate around hundreds or thousands of test results.

◆ *Recipe*

Use Ant's `<formatter>` element to tell Ant to save the JUnit results in XML files. You can specify `<formatter>` under either `<junit>` or `<batchtest>`, depending on how you set up your target to run JUnit tests. In the same target you use to run the JUnit tests, or in a separate target if you prefer, use the `<junitreport>` task with a nested `<report>` element to transform the XML result files' output by the previous test run into a professional looking HTML report.

Listing 7.4 shows a simplified but functional Ant build script with one target for running a set of JUnit tests using `<batchtest>` and another for transforming the XML test results into HTML using the `<junitreport>` task.

Listing 7.4 build.xml using the `<junitreport>` task

```
<?xml version="1.0" encoding="UTF-8"?>
<project basedir="." default="junit-run" name="myproject">

    <property name="src.dir"     location="${basedir}/src"/>
    <property name="classes.dir" location="${basedir}/classes"/>
    <property name="junit.reports.dir" location="${basedir}/junit"/>
```

```
    <property name="junit.includes"
              value="junit/cookbook/tests/**/*Test.java"/>
    <property name="junit.excludes" value="**/AllTests.java"/>

    <!-- clean, compile and other build targets
         omitted for brevity -->

    <target name="junit-run"
            description="=> run JUnit tests">
        <mkdir dir="${junit.reports.dir}/xml"/>
        <junit haltonfailure="no" fork="yes"
               printsummary="withOutAndErr">
            <classpath>
                <pathelement location="${classes.dir}"/>
                <pathelement path="${java.class.path}"/>
            </classpath>
            <batchtest fork="yes" todir="${junit.reports.dir}/xml">  ❶
                <formatter type="xml"/>  ❷
                <fileset dir="${src.dir}">
                    <include name="${junit.includes}"/>
                    <exclude name="${junit.excludes}"/>
                </fileset>
            </batchtest>
        </junit>
    </target>

    <target name="junit-report" depends="junit-run"
            description="=> generate JUnit HTML report">
        <junitreport todir="${junit.reports.dir}/xml">
            <fileset dir="${junit.reports.dir}/xml">          ❸
                <include name="TEST-*.xml"/>
            </fileset>
            <report format="frames"  ❹
                    todir="${junit.reports.dir}"/>  ❺
        </junitreport>
    </target>
</project>
```

❶ The <batchtest> attribute `todir` specifies an output directory for individual test suite result files. For each test suite (test case class), `batchtest` generates a separate results file.

❷ Select the `xml` formatter.

❸ The <junitreport> attribute `todir` specifies an output directory for one merged XML file, containing the results of all the tests executed by <batchtest>. The <fileset> specifies which test result files to include in the final report.

❹ Choose the `frames` format to produce an HTML report that looks like Javadoc.

❺ Specify the output directly for the final HTML report.

Ant's `<junitreport>` task comes with two embedded XSL stylesheets for generating HTML reports: one with HTML frames and one without. The HTML frames report is organized similarly to standard Javadoc output with a three-paned, interlinked frameset that facilitates navigation.

The `noframes` report comes out as one long HTML page, which is definitely harder to navigate than the frames version if you have more than a few unit tests.

To choose which style of report to generate, you specify either `frames` or `noframes` to the `format` attribute of the `<report>` element. Internally, Ant maps these values to one of its two XSL stylesheets to produce the appropriate report format. For more discussion of the reporting options, including non-HTML options and ways to customize the default capabilities, see the remaining recipes in this chapter.

◆ *Discussion*

Other than some dependency checking for whether to run certain batches of tests and some extra system properties (such as `${test.data.dir}`) which one may want to declare, the targets shown in listing 7.4 are nearly identical to targets we have used on commercial projects to run and report JUnit tests in a team environment. We separate the running and reporting into two targets because this allows a developer to run just the tests without creating the HTML report. The `printsummary="withOutAndErr"` attribute setting of the `<junit>` task is used to output a summary of the test results to the console, so that a developer can see a summary of the test run without running the `junit-report` target to generate the HTML report. The report generation only takes a few seconds to execute, but it adds up over time if you are repeatedly running tests with Ant while working. We make the `junit-report` target depend on the `junit-run` target so that the release engineers can just call the `junit-report` target without having to call the `junit-run` target separately.

Using `<junitreport>` and its `<report>` element is the easiest way to produce professional looking JUnit HTML reports. If the default report formats provided by `<report>` are lacking or not to your taste, you can customize them or design your own reporting format, as discussed in recipe 7.5, "Customizing <junit> XML reports with XSLT" and recipe 7.6, "Extending Ant's JUnit results format."

◆ *Related*

- 7.5—Customizing <junit> XML reports with XSLT
- 7.6—Extending Ant's JUnit results format

7.5 Customizing <junit> XML reports with XSLT

◆ Problem

You are running JUnit with Ant and you need to customize the reports produced by the `<junitreport>` task.

◆ Background

If the two types of HTML reports that can be produced by Ant out of the box are not to your liking, you can define your own custom HTML output by customizing the existing XSL templates or by writing new ones from scratch.

Perhaps, instead of HTML output, you need a custom XML report format to facilitate importing test results into a test management system or a publishing engine (such as a PDF generator expecting a particular XML format). In these cases, you need a way to tell Ant to transform its default XML output into another XML format.

◆ Recipe

First, output test results in XML using the `<formatter type="xml">` (see recipe 7.3, "Getting plain text results with Ant"). Next, merge the results with the `<junitreport>` task. This creates one large XML results document. You have two main options for transforming this document using XSL stylesheets:

- Customize one of the `<junitreport>` XSL stylesheets that comes with Ant.
- Make `<junitreport>` use a custom XSL stylesheet of your own.

Customizing one of the existing XSL sheets is useful only if you want to mildly customize the format that Ant provides by default, such as embedding an image or changing the background color or fonts. This is because of some quirks and limitations of the `<report>` element (see the Discussion section for details).

For transforming XML formatted JUnit test results into HTML reports, Ant (since at least Ant 1.3) provides two XSL stylesheets in `$ANT_HOME/etc`: `junit-frames.xsl` and `junit-noframes.xsl`. Make a copy of either one for customization and keep your modified copy in a directory in your project. Then use your modified stylesheet to override the built-in default of the same name (either `junit-frames.xsl` or `junit-noframes.xsl`) by using the `styledir` attribute of the `<report>` element.

A simple but effective change to one of these stylesheets is to skip outputting into the HTML the listings of Java system property names and values recorded during the execution of each JUnit test. These properties listings are seldom useful, and they add many kilobytes of additional report file content, which can be an issue if trim, lightweight HTML reports are desired. Just comment out or delete the following elements (meaning everything between and including the opening and closing of the following named elements in the XSL) in `junit-noframes.xsl` (line numbers correspond to the line numbers in the actual `junit-noframes.xsl` file shipped with Ant 1.6.0):

1 Both `<script>` elements (lines 123–158)
2 The `<div class="Properties">` element (lines 271–276)
3 The `<xsl:template match="properties">` element (lines 334–340)

Then you can point Ant to your modified stylesheet's directory location (represented by the property variable `modified.xsl.dir` below) in a target utilizing the `<junitreport>` task and `<report>` element as shown in listing 7.5.

Listing 7.5 Ant script snippet using `<report>` element with custom stylesheet

```
<target name="junit-custom-report"
        description="=> generate XML and custom HTML reports">
    <junitreport todir="${junit.reports.dir}/xml">
        <fileset dir="${junit.reports.dir}/xml">
            <include name="TEST-*.xml"/>
        </fileset>
        <report format="noframes" styledir="${modified.xsl.dir}"/>
   </junitreport>
</target>
```

For more extreme transformations, we recommend using the `<style>/<xslt>` task (this task has two names, which can be used interchangeably in Ant scripts, but we prefer `<style>`) as you normally would, using the merged XML file output by the `<junitreport>` task as the input file to the transformation.

To use the `<style>` task with Ant's JUnit reporting, assume you have an XSL custom stylesheet written to transform `<junitreport>` XML results into another form of XML. Call it `custom-junitreport.xsl`. First, we usually want to merge together the individual XML results files output by the `<batchtest>` XML formatter during a test run. The `<junitreport>` task can merge all those files, and do nothing else, if you just leave out the `<report>` element, as shown in listing 7.6:

Listing 7.6 Ant script snippet using <junitreport> task to merge XML result files into one

```
<target name="junit-report"
        description="=> generate JUnit merged XML report">
    <junitreport todir="${junit.reports.dir}/xml">
        <fileset dir="${junit.reports.dir}/xml">
            <include name="TEST-*.xml"/>
        </fileset>
    </junitreport>
</target>
```

In the target shown in listing 7.6, the `<junitreport>` task merges together all the files matching the name pattern `TEST-*.xml` (which is the default output file naming pattern of the XML formatter) in the `${junit.reports.dir}`. By default, the resulting merged XML file is named TESTS-TestSuites.xml. The file TESTS-TestSuites.xml is then passed as input to the `<style>` task, where your custom stylesheet guides the transformation, as shown in listing 7.7:

Listing 7.7 Ant script snippet using <style> task just to transform XML results

```
<target name="transform" description="=> create custom JUnit report">
    <style in="${junit.reports.dir}/xml/TESTS-TestSuites.xml"      (1)
           out="TESTS-TestSuites.html"
           extension=".html"
           style="custom-junitreport.xsl"/>    (2)
</target>
```

(1) *Test results to transform*—The `in` attribute specifies the XML-based test results file to transform into a report. This file is a merged version of all the individual test suite result files.

(2) *XSL stylesheet for transformation*—The `style` attribute specifies your custom XSL stylesheet for transforming the XML-based test results. The stylesheet could transform XML into HTML, a PDF, plain text or any other format. In our example, the target is an HTML report.

◆ Discussion

When using the `<junitreport>` task with a custom stylesheet, you must place the custom stylesheet in the directory specified by the `styledir` attribute of the `<report>` element. You must name the stylesheet either `junit-frames.xsl` or `junit-noframes.xsl`. This is a quirk (arguably a defect) in the `<report>` element, which should be fixed so that it can take any file name for a stylesheet rather than demanding one of the two predefined file names to exist in a directory.

Another quirk is that the format attribute depends on the values frames or noframes (note that the default is frames, if format is left unspecified) even for custom stylesheets. Outside the context of HTML, specifying frames or noframes doesn't make much sense. What if your stylesheet outputs XML or PDF? A workaround is to always name your custom XSL sheet as junit-frames.xsl and leave format unspecified. Because the format attribute defaults to frames, you can leverage that fact and tolerate not having descriptive filenames. Of course, if you have multiple custom stylesheets, separate them by descriptive directory names.

Also note that the frames-based report includes test output captured from the System.out stream, whereas the noframes report does not.

It seems that the advantage of the <junitreport> task for this set of problems is primarily in its XML-merging capabilities. Once the XML results files have been merged into a single large XML file, it would seem to be as easy, if not easier, to use a custom XSL sheet with the regular Ant <style> task as it would be to configure the <report> element to use a custom stylesheet.

So the answer is probably this: if you need minor tweaks to the format, use the <report> task with one of the existing stylesheets and customize it. But if you need major changes to the output format, such as transforming the output to another XML structure, then use the <junitreport> task to merge the results into one file, and then use the <style> task to transform it with your custom stylesheet. The latter option gives you all the features and options of the <style> task without the quirky limitations of the <report> task (which requires Xalan 2 and doesn't support nearly as many options as style/xslt).[3]

◆ Related

- 7.4—Reporting results in HTML with Ant's <junitreport> task
- 7.6—Extending Ant's JUnit results format

7.6 Extending Ant's JUnit results format

◆ Problem

You are running JUnit with Ant and you need to customize the results format to add more information or adhere to a specialized format.

[3] In fact, why don't the Ant folks ditch the <report> task and just use the <style> task, at least under the covers?

◆ *Background*

We have seen a situation in which a legacy test results management system, originally developed without support for Ant or JUnit, needed to be outfitted with support for test results produced from JUnit, which was being run by Ant. One of the requirements was to make Ant's XML output of JUnit results conform to the input file format of the repository. The XML files could then be analyzed and reported on by the results management system without knowing their origin. The results repository took an XML input file that looked similar to the XML formatted results which Ant's `<junit>` task can output when using a nested `<formatter type="xml">` element. A good solution to the problem was to extend and customize the XML results format of Ant's XML formatter.

Another situation in which you might want to customize Ant's JUnit results format would be if you wanted your results to be in PostScript, PDF, or HTML format. You can output the desired format directly without producing intermediate XML results files that need to be processed by XSL.

◆ *Recipe*

1. Implement the interface `JunitResultFormatter` found in the package `org.apache.tools.ant.taskdefs.optional.junit`.
2. Specify the name of the custom formatter class in the `classname` attribute of the `<junitreport>` task in your build script.

Listing 7.8 shows one way to implement these steps in a custom results formatter that outputs reports in HTML format. Note that this class depends on Ant tools, so you need `ant.jar` and `ant-junit.jar`, which are both part of the Ant distribution, to compile it.

Listing 7.8 `HtmlJUnitResultFormatter`

```
package junit.cookbook.reporting.ant;

import java.io.*;
import java.text.NumberFormat;
import java.util.Hashtable;
import junit.framework.*;
import org.apache.tools.ant.BuildException;
import org.apache.tools.ant.taskdefs.optional.junit.*;

public class HtmlJUnitResultFormatter implements JUnitResultFormatter {

    /** Formatter for timings. */
    private NumberFormat nf = NumberFormat.getInstance();
```

```
/** Timing helper. */
private Hashtable testStarts = new Hashtable();

/** Where to write the log to. */
private OutputStream out;

/** Helper to store intermediate output. */
private StringWriter middle;

/** Convenience layer on top of {@link #middle middle}. */
private PrintWriter wri;

/** Suppress endTest if testcase failed. */
private Hashtable failed = new Hashtable();
private String systemOutput = null;
private String systemError = null;

public void setOutput(OutputStream out) {
    this.out = out;
}

public void setSystemOutput(String out) {
    systemOutput = out;
}

public void setSystemError(String err) {
    systemError = err;
}

public HtmlJUnitResultFormatter() {
    middle = new StringWriter();
    wri = new PrintWriter(middle);
}

/**
 * The whole testsuite ended.
 */
public void endTestSuite(JUnitTest suite) throws BuildException {
    String nl = System.getProperty("line.separator");
    StringBuffer header = new StringBuffer(
            "<html>"
                + nl
                + "<head><title>JUnit Results</title></head>"
                + nl
                + "<body>"
                + nl + "<table border=\"1\">" + nl);
        header.append(
                "<tr><th>Suite: "
                    + suite.getName()
                    + "</th><th>Time</th></tr>" + nl);

    StringBuffer footer = new StringBuffer();
        footer.append(nl + "<tr><td>");
        footer.append("Tests run:");
        footer.append("</td><td>");
```

```
    footer.append(suite.runCount());
    footer.append("</td></tr>" + nl + "<tr><td>");
    footer.append("Failures:");
    footer.append("</td><td>");
    footer.append(suite.failureCount());
    footer.append("</td></tr>" + nl + "<tr><td>");
    footer.append("Errors:");
    footer.append("</td><td>");
    footer.append(suite.errorCount());
    footer.append("</td></tr>" + nl + "<tr><td>");
    footer.append("Time elapsed:");
    footer.append("</td><td>");
    footer.append(nf.format(suite.getRunTime() / 1000.0));
    footer.append(" sec");
    footer.append("</td></tr>");
    footer.append(nl);

// append both the output and error streams to the log
if (systemOutput != null && systemOutput.length() > 0) {
    footer
        .append("<tr><td>Standard Output</td><td>")
        .append("<pre>")
        .append(systemOutput)
        .append("</pre></td></tr>");
}

if (systemError != null && systemError.length() > 0) {
    footer
        .append("<tr><td>Standard Error</td><td>")
        .append("<pre>")
        .append(systemError)
        .append("</pre></td></tr>");
}

footer.append("</table>" + nl + "</body>" + nl + "</html>");

if (out != null) {
    try {
        out.write(header.toString().getBytes());
        out.write(middle.toString().getBytes());
        out.write(footer.toString().getBytes());
        wri.close();
        out.flush();
    } catch (IOException ioe) {
        throw new BuildException("Unable to write output", ioe);
    } finally {
        if (out != System.out && out != System.err) {
            try {
                out.close();
            } catch (IOException e) {
            }
        }
```

```
            }
        }
    }

    /**
     * From interface TestListener.
     * <p>A new Test is started.
     */
    public void startTest(Test test) {
        testStarts.put(test, new Long(System.currentTimeMillis()));
        failed.put(test, Boolean.FALSE);
        wri.print("<tr><td>");
        wri.print(JUnitVersionHelper.getTestCaseName(test));
        wri.print("</td>");
    }

    /**
     * From interface TestListener.
     * <p>A Test is finished.
     */
    public void endTest(Test test) {
        synchronized (wri) {
            if (Boolean.TRUE.equals(failed.get(test))) {
                return;
            }
            Long secondsAsLong = (Long) testStarts.get(test);
            double seconds = 0;
            // can be null if an error occured in setUp
            if (secondsAsLong != null) {
                seconds = (System.currentTimeMillis()
                        - secondsAsLong.longValue()) / 1000.0;
            }

            wri.print("<td>");
            wri.print(nf.format(seconds));
            wri.print(" sec</td></tr>");
        }
    }

    /**
     * Interface TestListener for JUnit > 3.4.
     *
     * <p>A Test failed.
     */
    public void addFailure(Test test, AssertionFailedError t) {
        formatThrowable("failure", test, (Throwable) t);
    }

    /**
     * Interface TestListener.
     *
     * <p>An error occured while running the test.
     */
```

```
    public void addError(Test test, Throwable t) {
        formatThrowable("error", test, t);
    }

    private void formatThrowable(String type, Test test, Throwable t) {
        synchronized (wri) {
            if (test != null) {
                failed.put(test, Boolean.TRUE);
                endTest(test);
            }

            wri.println("<td><pre>");
            wri.println(t.getMessage());
            // filter the stack trace to squelch Ant and JUnit stack
            // frames in the report
            String strace = JUnitTestRunner.getFilteredTrace(t);
            wri.print(strace);
            wri.println("</pre></td></tr>");
        }
    }

    /**
     * From interface JUnitResultFormatter. We do nothing with this
     * method, but we have to implement all the interface's methods.
     */
    public void startTestSuite(JUnitTest suite) throws BuildException {
    }
}
```

Although this looks like an awful lot of code, the general idea is straightforward. At each stage of executing the test suite, Ant generates various events: one when the test suite starts executing, one when it ends, one for each test, and one for each test failure or error. For each of these events, we have provided an event handler that outputs HTML corresponding to each event.

For the "start test suite" event, there is nothing to do. If we wanted to add some kind of test suite header, we would have added that here. For the "start test" event, we start an HTML table row and write out the name of the test. What we write out next depends on how the test ends. If the test fails, we treat the assertion failure as a `Throwable` object (it is an `AssertionFailedError`, after all) and print the stack trace as preformatted text in a `<pre>` tag. This is the same behavior we use when the test ends with an error, due to throwing an unexpected exception. Finally, for the "end test suite" event, we write out a summary of the test run, with failure and error counts as well as any text written to the standard output and error streams. This is a pretty comprehensive report!

Here is an Ant target that can be used in an Ant build file for running tests and reporting results using our custom formatter:

```
<target name="ant-custom-formatter"
        description="-> demos custom Ant results formatter">
    <mkdir dir="${custom.reports.dir}"/>
    <junit printsummary="yes" haltonfailure="no">
        <classpath>
            <pathelement location="${classes.dir}"/>
            <pathelement path="${java.class.path}"/>
        </classpath>

        <batchtest fork="yes" todir="${custom.reports.dir}">
            <formatter classname=
              "junit.cookbook.reporting.ant.HtmlJUnitResultFormatter"
                extension=".html"
                usefile="true"/>
            <fileset dir="${src.dir}">
                <include name="**/tests/runner/AllTests.java"/>
            </fileset>
        </batchtest>
    </junit>
</target>
```

◆ *Discussion*

One limitation of our `HtmlJUnitResultFormatter` example is that it outputs one HTML file per test case class that executes. So while it is fine for reporting results for a few medium to large test suites, which will produce a few short- to medium-length HTML reports files, it becomes unusable when dealing with dozens or hundreds of test case classes.

This recipe could be enhanced to produce HTML frames documents to organize and link the individual HTML reports together. You should also be able to easily see how to write your own custom XML output formatter from this example—just use XML tags instead of HTML. Also, see Ant's own `XMLJUnitResultFormatter` for inspiration.

Generally, implementing custom reports formats comes down to a choice between writing Java extensions of Ant's JUnit APIs, as we do in this recipe, or writing new or customized XSL stylesheets for the `<junitreport>` task. The approach you choose often depends on which technology better suits your reporting requirements and the skill set of your team.

◆ *Related*

- 7.3—Getting plain text results with Ant
- 7.5—Customizing <junit> XML reports with XSLT

7.7 Implementing TestListener and extending TestRunner

◆ Problem

You want total control of the format of JUnit's test results reporting.

◆ Background

A common question on the JUnit Yahoo! group is how to customize JUnit's test results reporting. The default reporting of the text-based test runner is pretty bare bones ("." for pass, "E" for error, "F" for failure). The Swing-based and AWT-based runners display similar results in an interactive GUI.

For getting HTML or XML results files out of your JUnit test runs, the most common practice is to use Ant's `<junit>` and `<junitreport>` tasks to execute the tests and report the results. But we have come across cases where Ant is not or cannot be used or where Ant might be more of a hassle to work with than simply extending the JUnit framework. (If your only problem with Ant is that it does not support your target XML or HTML reporting format, first see recipe 7.6, and see if that's enough to solve your problem). In cases such as these, you can extend JUnit to format and output results any way you want by using APIs in the JUnit framework.

◆ Recipe

Implement `junit.framework.TestListener` to define the results format and output mechanism, and then extend `junit.runner.TestRunner` to "register" the listener with the test runner. We'll go through the process in steps.

NOTE *Observer/Observable*—In this context a `Listener`, as in `TestListener`, is one of the participants of an implementation of the Observer pattern as captured in the so-called "Gang of Four" (Erich Gamma, Richard Helm, Ralph Johnson, John Vlissides) book *Design Patterns.*

In short, a listener, also known as an observer or subscriber, is an object that attaches or registers itself with another object (the "observable") in order to receive updates or notifications when the observable changes state. The observable is also known as the "subject" or "publisher." Each publisher can have many subscribers. In our recipe here, the `CookbookTestRunner` is the publisher for the `CookbookTestListener`. But `TestRunners` can also be listeners (and implement the `TestListener` interface), registering themselves with test results in order to handle the display or routing of test events themselves. To see some source code examples of runners that are listeners, see `junit.awtui.TestRunner.runSuite()` and `junit.swingui.TestRunner.doRunTest(Test testSuite)`.

First, implement the `TestListener` interface to define the output format for results. Listing 7.9 shows the interface to implement in order to control results output for a test runner. Note that all the methods accept an object implementing `junit.framework.Test` (either a `TestCase` or a `TestSuite`) as a parameter.

Listing 7.9 `junit.framework.TestListener`

```
package junit.framework;

/**
 * A Listener for test progress
 */
public interface TestListener {

    /**
     * An error occurred.
     */
    public void addError(Test test, Throwable t);    <-- t is the unexpected Throwable causing the error

    /**
     * A failure occurred.
     */
    public void addFailure(Test test, AssertionFailedError t);    <-- t is the AssertionFailedError representing the failure

    /**
     * A test started.
     */
    public void startTest(Test test);    <-- Notification of a test starting

    /**
     * A test ended.
     */
    public void endTest(Test test);    <-- Notification of a test ending
}
```

Each test has the potential to produce one or more failures or errors as JUnit executes it. The `TestListener` is notified by a failure or error event if a test fails or has an error. The `TestListener` is not notified of successes so we can assume that any tests that start and end without an error or failure succeeded. Note that the listener also receives notification of start and end events. These events give us a good place to decorate and format each test and its results as it executes and notifies the test listener. Something that some people find strangely absent are `startSuite()` and `endSuite()` events and methods, since the API seems incomplete without them. But we can add these methods to our `TestListeners` and could even extend the `TestListener` interface with our own interface that required extra methods. In fact, this is what the Ant JUnit reporting tasks do, as we see elsewhere in this chapter.

For demonstration purposes we just need a simple test listener implementation that does something interesting. So we will write a listener that is capable of writing out test results in a simple XML format. The test listener is responsible for formatting the results of each test. The results are stored in XML as we build the document in memory using the `org.w3c.dom` API, and provide a `print()` method that serializes the XML to an output stream, and a `getXmlAsString()` method that returns the XML as a `String`. Listing 7.10 shows `CookbookTestListener`, our `TestListener` implementation.

Listing 7.10 `CookbookTestListener`

```
package junit.cookbook.reporting;

import java.io.PrintStream;
import java.io.StringWriter;
import java.text.NumberFormat;

import javax.xml.parsers.*;
import javax.xml.transform.*;
import javax.xml.transform.dom.DOMSource;
import javax.xml.transform.stream.StreamResult;

import junit.framework.*;
import junit.runner.BaseTestRunner;

import org.w3c.dom.*;

public class CookbookTestListener implements TestListener {

    PrintStream printStream;
    Document xmlOutput;
    Element xmlRoot;
    Element testCase;

    int errorCount = 0;
    int failureCount = 0;
    int testCaseCount = 0;

    /**
     * Default constructor creates a CookbookTestListener that streams
     * results to System.out.
     *
     * @throws ParserConfigurationException
     */
    public CookbookTestListener() throws ParserConfigurationException {
        this(System.out);
    }

    /**
```

```
 * Creates a new CookbookTestListener that captures results in an XML
   * Document and serializes the XML to the specified
   * <code>printStream</code>
 *
 * @param printStream to use for serializing XML results
 * @throws ParserConfigurationException
 */
public CookbookTestListener(PrintStream printStream)
    throws ParserConfigurationException {
  DocumentBuilderFactory factory = DocumentBuilderFactory.newInstance();
    DocumentBuilder builder = factory.newDocumentBuilder();
    xmlOutput = builder.newDocument();
    this.printStream = printStream;
}

public void startSuite(Test suite) {                                      ❶
    xmlRoot = (Element) xmlOutput.createElement("testsuite");
    xmlRoot.setAttribute("class",suite.toString());
    xmlOutput.appendChild(xmlRoot);
}

public void addError(Test test, Throwable t) {                            ❷
    errorCount++;
    Element error = (Element) xmlOutput.createElement("error");
    addThrowable(t, error);
}

public void addFailure(Test test, AssertionFailedError t) {               ❸
    failureCount++;
    Element failure = (Element) xmlOutput.createElement("failure");
    addThrowable(t, failure);
}

public void startTest(Test test) {                                        ❹
    testCase = (Element) xmlOutput.createElement("test");
    String methodStr = ((TestCase) test).getName();
    testCase.setAttribute("name", methodStr);
    xmlRoot.appendChild(testCase);
}

public void endTest(Test test) {                                          ❺
    testCaseCount = testCaseCount + test.countTestCases();
}

public void print() throws TransformerException {                         ❻
    Transformer transformer = getTransformer();
    DOMSource source = new DOMSource(xmlOutput);
    StreamResult streamResult = new StreamResult(printStream);
    transformer.transform(source, streamResult);
}

/**
 * @return output of the test results as a String
 */
```

```
    public String getXmlAsString() throws TransformerException {
        Transformer transformer = getTransformer();
        DOMSource source = new DOMSource(xmlOutput);
        StringWriter xmlString = new StringWriter();
        StreamResult streamResult = new StreamResult(xmlString);
        transformer.transform(source, streamResult);
        return xmlString.toString();
    }

    public void endSuite(TestResult testResult, long runTime) {
        Element summary  = (Element) xmlOutput.createElement("summary");
        Element tests    = (Element) xmlOutput.createElement("tests");
        Element errors   = (Element) xmlOutput.createElement("errors");
        Element failures = (Element) xmlOutput.createElement("failures");
        Element runtime  = (Element) xmlOutput.createElement("runtime");

        String testCount = String.valueOf(testResult.runCount());
        String errCount  = String.valueOf(testResult.errorCount());
        String failCount = String.valueOf(testResult.failureCount());
        String runTimeStr =
            NumberFormat.getInstance().format((double) runTime / 1000);

        tests.appendChild(xmlOutput.createTextNode(testCount));
        errors.appendChild(xmlOutput.createTextNode(errCount));
        failures.appendChild(xmlOutput.createTextNode(failCount));
        runtime.appendChild(xmlOutput.createTextNode(runTimeStr));

        xmlRoot.appendChild(summary);
        summary.appendChild(tests);
        summary.appendChild(errors);
        summary.appendChild(failures);
        summary.appendChild(runtime);
    }

    private void addThrowable(Throwable t, Element elem) {
        String trace = BaseTestRunner.getFilteredTrace(t);
        elem.setAttribute("message", t.getMessage());
        elem.appendChild(xmlOutput.createCDATASection(trace));
        testCase.appendChild(elem);
    }

    private Transformer getTransformer() throws TransformerException {
        TransformerFactory tFactory = TransformerFactory.newInstance();
        Transformer transformer = tFactory.newTransformer();
        transformer.setOutputProperty(
            javax.xml.transform.OutputKeys.INDENT, "yes");
        transformer.setOutputProperty(
            javax.xml.transform.OutputKeys.STANDALONE, "yes");
        return transformer;
    }
}
```

7

8

1. Report that a new test suite is executing. This creates an XML element that looks like `<testsuite class="com.mycom.test.MyTestSuite">`.

2. Report an error, complete with its message and a stack trace of the corresponding unexpected exception.

3. Report a failure, complete with its message and a stack trace of the corresponding `AssertionFailedError`.

4. Report that an individual test is starting to execute. This creates an XML element that looks like `<test name="testMyTestName">`.

5. Note that an individual test has completed, incrementing the running total of executed tests. For a `TestCase` object, `countTestCases()` always returns 1.

6. Write the XML document we are creating to the `TestListener`'s `PrintStream` using the *identity transform*.[4]

7. This method is useful during testing, or whenever you might want to see the XML document we are creating as a `String`.

8. Report the end of a test suite, including a summary of the test results.

Now we have implemented the listener methods that will receive callbacks from the test runner as tests are executed and test methods start, end, or have an error of failure. In each callback method we used DOM APIs to format the test class, test method names, failures, errors, and results as XML. The second thing we must do is to extend `TestRunner` so we can tell it to use our `TestListener` implementation for reporting results. To do that, we have to implement three methods: `main()` for executing the runner on the command line, `processArgs()` for handling command-line arguments, and `doRun()` to register our listener with the test runner. Then we can kick off the test run, and call the listener's `print()` method. Listing 7.11 shows our custom test runner.

Listing 7.11 `CookbookTestRunner`, an extension of `TestRunner`

```
package junit.cookbook.reporting;

import java.io.FileNotFoundException;
import java.io.FileOutputStream;
import java.io.PrintStream;

import javax.xml.parsers.ParserConfigurationException;
import javax.xml.transform.TransformerException;
```

[4] The identity transform is an XSL transformation that applies an identity template to each XML element. The result is output identical to the input: a copy of the input XML document.

```
import junit.framework.Test;
import junit.framework.TestResult;
import junit.textui.TestRunner;

public class CookbookTestRunner extends TestRunner {

    private static CookbookTestListener testListener;
    TestResult results = null;

    /**
     * Constructor for use with an output file.
     *
     * @param testCase name of Test to run
     * @param fileName
     */
    public CookbookTestRunner(String fileName, String testClassName)
        throws FileNotFoundException, ParserConfigurationException {

        if (fileName != null) {
            FileOutputStream fos = new FileOutputStream(fileName);
            PrintStream printStream = new PrintStream(fos);
            testListener = new CookbookTestListener(printStream);
        } else {
            testListener = new CookbookTestListener();
        }
        Test test = super.getTest(testClassName);
        results = this.doRun(test);
    }

    /**
     * Constructor for use without an output file.
     *
     * @param testCase name of Test to run
     * @throws ParserConfigurationException
     */
    public CookbookTestRunner(String testClassName)
        throws ParserConfigurationException {
        testListener = new CookbookTestListener();
        Test test = super.getTest(testClassName);
        results = this.doRun(test);
    }

    /**
     * The default implementation of TestRunner.start() calls this
     * method, so we need to override it or else we don't get a
     * chance to register the TestListener for the TestRunner.
     * Otherwise, override start(), which you might want to do if
     * extending the TestRunner's supported command-line arguments.
     *
     * @param test test case to execute, time and collect results from.
     */
    public TestResult doRun(Test test) {
        TestResult testEventDriver = createTestResult();
```

```
        testEventDriver.addListener(testListener);   <-- Register our custom TestListener

        testListener.startSuite(test);   <-- Signal the test is about to execute

        long startTime = System.currentTimeMillis();
        test.run(testEventDriver);   <-- Execute the Test
        long endTime = System.currentTimeMillis();
        long runTime = endTime - startTime;
        testListener.endSuite(testEventDriver, runTime);   <-- Signal the test has finished

        try {
            testListener.print();   <-- Write the test result
        } catch (TransformerException e) {
            e.printStackTrace();
        }
        return testEventDriver;
    }

    public static void main(String args[]) {

        TestResult results = null;
        CookbookTestRunner runner = null;

        if (args.length == 3 && args[0].equals("-o")) {
            try {
                runner = new CookbookTestRunner(args[1], args[2]);
            } catch (FileNotFoundException e) {
                e.printStackTrace();
            } catch (ParserConfigurationException e) {
                e.printStackTrace();
            }
        } else if (args.length == 1) {
            try {
                runner = new CookbookTestRunner(args[0]);
            } catch (ParserConfigurationException e) {
                e.printStackTrace();
            }
        } else {
            throw new RuntimeException(
                "Usage: java TestRunner [-o outputFile] Test "
                    + System.getProperty("line.separator")
                    + "where Test is the fully qualified name of "
                    + "a TestCase or TestSuite");
        }
    }

    /**
     * The CookbookTestRunner constructor runs a test class
     * and collects the results in a TestResult. This accessor
     * makes the TestResult accessible to clients.
     *
     * @return TestResult of test run executed by CookbookTestRunner
     */
```

```
    public TestResult getResults() {
        return this.results;
    }
}
```

That's it! Now we can run our test runner and see test results in XML. If we pass a filename with the -o flag we added, the results are saved to the specified file. If we do not specify a file with -o, the results are streamed to standard output (the console) by default. The `CookbookTestListener` compiles as is with JDK 1.4 or higher. With JDK 1.3 or earlier you need a JAXP-compliant XML parser implementation such as Xerces (xml.apache.org) and the `org.w3c.dom` classes. Once we've compiled our test listener and runner and added them to the class path along with `junit.jar`, we run them:

```
java -cp %CP% junit.cookbook.reporting.CookbookTestRunner -o junit-
⇒  results.xml junit.tests.framework.AllTests
```

The following XML is the output of a test run with an intentional error and an intentional failure to demonstrate how they appear in the results. Note that passing test methods are just listed with their name. The test listener could be enhanced to print out more information such as timing information for each test method. Counts of one error and one failure appear in the results summary at the bottom, along with a tally of the number of seconds all the tests took to run.

```
<?xml version="1.0" encoding="UTF-8" standalone="yes"?>
<testsuite class="junit.cookbook.tests.reporting.CookbookTestListenerTest">
<test name="testStartTest"/>
<test name="testEndTest"/>
<test name="testAddError">
<error message="Thrown on purpose!"><![CDATA[java.lang.Error: Thrown on purpose!
at junit.cookbook.tests.reporting.CookbookTestListenerTest.testAddError
⇒  (CookbookTestListenerTest.java:38)
    at sun.reflect.NativeMethodAccessorImpl.invoke0(Native Method)
    // several stack frames
]]></error>
</test>
<test name="testAddFailure">
<failure message="Intentional
   failure"><![CDATA[junit.framework.AssertionFailedError: Intentional failure

at junit.cookbook.tests.reporting.CookbookTestListenerTest.testAddFailure
⇒  (CookbookTestListenerTest.java:52)
    at sun.reflect.NativeMethodAccessorImpl.invoke0(Native Method)
    // several stack frames
```

```
]]></failure>
</test>
<summary>
<tests>4</tests>
<errors>1</errors>
<failures>1</failures>
<runtime>0.161</runtime>
</summary>
</testsuite>
```

◆ Discussion

Extending the test runner framework and implementing your own test listener might seem daunting, but there is not that much to it. If you need fast, efficient, and highly customized JUnit results output and you have the team and expertise to do it, extending JUnit to do exactly what you want is a great recipe.

ANT TIP Be sure to consider using Ant to achieve your custom results formatting goals before spending time on extending JUnit yourself. If you don't know about Ant's JUnit reporting capabilities, we strongly suggest looking into them. The `<junit>` task has a `<formatter>` subelement (discussed in recipe 7.5) that can output results as XML (as one option), which you can customize by implementing an interface (see recipe 7.6). The `<junitreport>` task provides HTML formatting of the XML-formatted results by default, but can be used with any XSL stylesheet to produce customized reports.

◆ Related

- 7.5—Customizing <junit> XML reports with XSLT
- 7.6—Extending Ant's JUnit results format

7.8 Reporting a count of assertions

◆ Problem

You need a report of the number of assertions in your test cases.

◆ Background

You might want to measure your testing productivity or progress in quantity of assertions rather than quantity of test case classes or test methods. You might also want to check whether tests have assertions, in case you want to flag them in a test run log or build report.

◆ Recipe

Extend `junit.framework.Assert` with the capability to count the number of assert methods invoked during a test run. Use your assert methods in your test cases instead of the usual assert methods (which `TestCase` inherits from `Assert`). The `CountingAssert` class, as shown in listing 7.12 is mostly a copy and paste of the original `Assert` class, minus some Javadoc comments. The Javadoc comments that we left in (except for the `getAssertCount()` method) document only the methods we've altered by including statements to increment the assertion count total. These methods are important: we only need to instrument these few with calls to increase the counter because all the other assert methods are variations that delegate calls back to these few.

Be warned: this listing is quite long!

Listing 7.12 `CountingAssert`, an extension of `Assert`

```
package junit.cookbook.reporting;

import junit.framework.Assert;
import junit.framework.AssertionFailedError;
import junit.framework.ComparisonFailure;

public class CountingAssert extends Assert {
    private static int assertCount = 0;

    /**
     * getAssertCount() should be called by a TestRunner or
     * TestListener at the end of a test suite execution.
     * It returns a count of how many assertions were executed
     * during the run.
     *
     * @return assertionCounter count of assertions executed
     * during a run.
     */
    public static int getAssertCount() {
        return assertCount;
    }

    protected CountingAssert() {
    }

    /**
     * Asserts that a condition is true. If it isn't, it throws
     * an AssertionFailedError with the given message. Most of
     * the other assert*() methods delegate to this one.
     */
    static public void assertTrue(String message, boolean condition) {
        assertCount++;
        if (!condition)
```

```
        fail(message);
}

static public void assertTrue(boolean condition) {
    assertTrue(null, condition);
}

static public void assertFalse(String message, boolean condition) {
    assertTrue(message, !condition);
}

static public void assertFalse(boolean condition) {
    assertFalse(null, condition);
}

/**
 * Fails a test with the given message.
 */
static public void fail(String message) {
    throw new AssertionFailedError(message);
}

static public void fail() {
    fail(null);
}
/**
 * Asserts that two objects are equal. If they are not,
 * an AssertionFailedError is thrown with the given message.
 */
static public void assertEquals(
    String message,
    Object expected,
    Object actual) {
    assertCount++;
    if (expected == null && actual == null)
        return;
    if (expected != null && expected.equals(actual))
        return;
    failNotEquals(message, expected, actual);
}

static public void assertEquals(Object expected, Object actual) {
    assertEquals(null, expected, actual);
}
/**
 * Asserts that two Strings are equal.
 */
static public void assertEquals(
    String message,
    String expected,
    String actual) {
    assertCount++;
    if (expected == null && actual == null)
        return;
```

```
        if (expected != null && expected.equals(actual))
            return;
        throw new ComparisonFailure(message, expected, actual);
    }

    static public void assertEquals(String expected, String actual) {
        assertEquals(null, expected, actual);
    }
    /**
     * Asserts that two doubles are equal concerning a delta.
     * If they are not, an AssertionFailedError is thrown with
     * the given message. If the expected value is infinity
     * then the delta value is ignored.
     */
    static public void assertEquals(
        String message,
        double expected,
        double actual,
        double delta) {
        assertCount++;
        // handle infinity specially since subtracting
        // to infinite values gives NaN and the
        // the following test fails
        if (Double.isInfinite(expected)) {
            if (!(expected == actual))
                failNotEquals(
                    message,
                    new Double(expected),
                    new Double(actual));
        } else if (!(Math.abs(expected - actual) <= delta))
            // Because comparison with NaN always returns false
            failNotEquals(message, new Double(expected), new Double(actual));
    }

    static public void assertEquals(
        double expected,
        double actual,
        double delta) {
        assertEquals(null, expected, actual, delta);
    }
    /**
     * Asserts that two floats are equal concerning a delta.
     * If they are not, an AssertionFailedError is thrown with
     * the given message. If the expected value is infinity
     * then the delta value is ignored.
     */
    static public void assertEquals(
        String message,
        float expected,
        float actual,
        float delta) {
        assertCount++;
```

```
        if (Float.isInfinite(expected)) {
            if (!(expected == actual))
                failNotEquals(
                    message,
                    new Float(expected),
                    new Float(actual));
        } else if (!(Math.abs(expected - actual) <= delta))
            failNotEquals(message, new Float(expected), new Float(actual));
    }

    static public void assertEquals(
        float expected,
        float actual,
        float delta) {
        assertEquals(null, expected, actual, delta);
    }

    static public void assertEquals(
        String message,
        long expected,
        long actual) {
        assertEquals(message, new Long(expected), new Long(actual));
    }

    static public void assertEquals(long expected, long actual) {
        assertEquals(null, expected, actual);
    }

    static public void assertEquals(
        String message,
        boolean expected,
        boolean actual) {
        assertEquals(message, new Boolean(expected), new Boolean(actual));
    }

    static public void assertEquals(boolean expected, boolean actual) {
        assertEquals(null, expected, actual);
    }

    static public void assertEquals(
        String message,
        byte expected,
        byte actual) {
        assertEquals(message, new Byte(expected), new Byte(actual));
    }

    static public void assertEquals(byte expected, byte actual) {
        assertEquals(null, expected, actual);
    }

    static public void assertEquals(
        String message,
        char expected,
        char actual) {
```

```
    assertEquals(message, new Character(expected), new Character(actual));
}

static public void assertEquals(char expected, char actual) {
    assertEquals(null, expected, actual);
}

static public void assertEquals(
    String message,
    short expected,
    short actual) {
    assertEquals(message, new Short(expected), new Short(actual));
}

static public void assertEquals(short expected, short actual) {
    assertEquals(null, expected, actual);
}

static public void assertEquals(
    String message,
    int expected,
    int actual) {
    assertEquals(message, new Integer(expected), new Integer(actual));
}

static public void assertEquals(int expected, int actual) {
    assertEquals(null, expected, actual);
}

static public void assertNotNull(Object object) {
    assertNotNull(null, object);
}

static public void assertNotNull(String message, Object object) {
    assertTrue(message, object != null);
}

static public void assertNull(Object object) {
    assertNull(null, object);
}

static public void assertNull(String message, Object object) {
    assertTrue(message, object == null);
}
/**
 * Asserts that two objects refer to the same object. If they are not,
 * an AssertionFailedError is thrown with the given message.
 */
static public void assertSame(
    String message,
    Object expected,
    Object actual) {
    assertCount++;
    if (expected == actual)
        return;
```

```
        failNotSame(message, expected, actual);
    }

    static public void assertSame(Object expected, Object actual) {
        assertSame(null, expected, actual);
    }
    /**
     * Asserts that two objects refer to the same object. If they are not,
     * an AssertionFailedError is thrown with the given message.
     */
    static public void assertNotSame(
        String message,
        Object expected,
        Object actual) {
        assertCount++;
        if (expected == actual)
            failSame(message);
    }

    static public void assertNotSame(Object expected, Object actual) {
        assertNotSame(null, expected, actual);
    }

    static private void failSame(String message) {
        String formatted = "";
        if (message != null)
            formatted = message + " ";
        fail(formatted + "expected not same");
    }

    static private void failNotSame(
        String message,
        Object expected,
        Object actual) {
        String formatted = "";
        if (message != null)
            formatted = message + " ";
        fail(
            formatted
                + "expected same:<"
                + expected
                + "> was not:<"
                + actual
                + ">");
    }

    static private void failNotEquals(
        String message,
        Object expected,
        Object actual) {
        String formatted = "";
        if (message != null)
            formatted = message + " ";
```

```
        fail(
            formatted + "expected:<" + expected
                + "> but was:<" + actual + ">");
    }
}
```

Now use CountingAssert's assert methods in your test cases instead of the usual assert methods (which TestCase inherits from Assert). For a simple example, here is a test method with five assertions that CountingAssert will count.

```
    public void testFoo() {
        CountingAssert.assertNotNull(this);
        CountingAssert.assertSame("hello",this,this);
        CountingAssert.assertEquals(1,1);
        CountingAssert.assertEquals(true,true);
        CountingAssert.assertTrue(true);
}
```

Finally, you need to use something similar to the CookbookTestRunner to retrieve the assertion total from the CountingAssert class. Listing 7.13 shows a slightly modified CookbookTestRunner (see recipe 7.7), which obtains the assertion count total from CountingAssert after completing a test run, and then simply prints the total to the console. For brevity, we show only the main() method. For the rest of the class, see listing 7.11.

Listing 7.13 CookbookTestRunner.main() displaying the assertion count

```
public static void main(String args[]) {
    TestResult results = null;
    CookbookTestRunner runner = null;

    if (args.length == 3 && args[0].equals("-o")) {
        try {
            runner = new CookbookTestRunner(args[1], args[2]);
        } catch (FileNotFoundException e) {
            e.printStackTrace();
        } catch (ParserConfigurationException e) {
            e.printStackTrace();
        }
    } else if (args.length == 1) {
        try {
            runner = new CookbookTestRunner(args[0]);
        } catch (ParserConfigurationException e) {
            e.printStackTrace();
        }
    } else {
        throw new RuntimeException(
            "Usage: java TestRunner [-o outputFile] Test "
```

```
                    + System.getProperty("line.separator")
                    + "where Test is the fully qualified name of "
                    + "a TestCase or TestSuite");
        }

        System.out.println("assertion count = "
            + CountingAssert.getAssertCount());
    }
```

◆ Discussion

This recipe describes using `CountingAssert`'s method in your tests in place of the methods that `TestCase` inherits from JUnit's `Assert` class. One alternative to this would be to write your own `TestCase` extension class (a Base Test Case) which extends `CountingAssert`. The alternative is convenient in that you would be able to use `CountingAssert`'s methods without having to refer explicitly to the class name, but *forces* all your test case classes to extend your Base Test Case, rather than JUnit's `TestCase`. Whether you follow the technique in this recipe, try this alternative, or do something else, you will end up reimplementing most of `Assert`.[5] We also prefer to reuse, rather than reimplement, but as you would only need to do it once, it might be worth the effort. It depends on how much you need to be able to count assertions.[6]

A limitation with this recipe is that it won't work transparently with Ant's JUnit test runner. Because our solution depends on a custom test runner (`CookbookTestRunner`) to retrieve and print out the assertion count total after all the tests are run, you have to extend or modify the Ant JUnit test runner class to implement support for retrieving and displaying the assertions total from the `CountingAssert` class. So an alternative worth considering for both the standalone test runner and the Ant test runner context is to write a custom `TestListener` that retrieves the assertion count total from `CountingAssert` and displays it. Either way, you need separate implementations for Ant and for standalone JUnit because Ant uses its own `TestListener` and report-formatting API.

◆ Related

- 7.7—Implementing TestListener and extending TestRunner

---

[5] Worse than that, you might end up copying and pasting a large amount of code, which we frown upon.

[6] J. B. has never wanted nor needed to count assertions, because he sees it as a meaningless metric that is easy to fool. If you measure assertion count, then all you get is more assertions, and not necessarily better tests.

8 Troubleshooting JUnit

This chapter covers

- Problems finding your tests
- Problems executing your custom test suite and test setup
- Problems executing your test after the first assertion fails
- Problems reloading classes between tests
- Problems reloading XML-related classes
- Problems narrowing EJB references in your tests

Wouldn't it be nice if everything worked exactly the way you expected it to work? Come to think of it, if that were so then you wouldn't be reading this book—or maybe *because* you're reading this book, the software you build *will* work exactly the way you expect. At least, that's the idea.

This chapter is about how to handle those situations in which JUnit doesn't do what you expect. Although JUnit is simple, it is a framework, and when you use a framework you always have a learning curve. More than that, the JUnit community pushes the boundaries of what JUnit can do every day. Someone, somewhere is using JUnit to do something it has never done before. Putting software through stress can unearth all sorts of problems, and given the number of people using JUnit these days, it is under considerable stress.

There are two main classes of problems that JUnit users encounter. Beginning JUnit users often have problems implementing their tests according to "the rules." We offer some helpful recipes if you just can't seem to get JUnit to execute your tests the way you expect. It could be that JUnit cannot find your tests, builds the wrong test suite, or fails to set up your test fixture the way you expect. This chapter contains solutions to these problems.

Once you are more comfortable with the fundamentals of writing JUnit tests, you might run into more complex problems with JUnit, many of which center around a class loading problem within JUnit itself. Beyond that, if you override `runTest()` in your tests you should be aware of the problems that can cause.

The goal with this chapter is to address the most common problems we have seen in our years of working with JUnit. We cannot cover them all, and someone seems to have a different problem every week or so. If you cannot find a solution to your problem in this chapter, we recommend joining us at the Yahoo! group for JUnit (http://groups.yahoo.com/group/junit). We will do our best to answer your questions.

The most common problem

Here is the most elementary problem you might encounter with JUnit: when you run your tests, JUnit dies, reporting `NoClassDefFoundError`. The problem here is straightforward: there is something missing on your runtime class path. Simply verify that you have the following items on your runtime class path:

- JUnit's classes, found in `junit.jar`.
- Your test classes, usually as a directory full of loose classes, but alternatively packaged in a *.jar file.

- Your production classes. (You'd be surprised how many times someone forgets those!)
- Any third-party software on which your production and test classes depend.

Managing your class path depends on your environment. Whether you are using the Java Build Path in Eclipse, the `<classpath>` tag in Ant, or the `-classpath` option to the Java interpreter, you can consult your environment's documentation for more details on managing your class path.

A problem with the CLASSPATH environment variable

We recommend against the general practice of using the `CLASSPATH` environment variable because it is global data across an entire system. As a result, anyone can change it at any time, which might cause an application somewhere to begin to fail with class-loading problems. Another reason to avoid using this environment variable is that if you accidentally leave a trailing space in it, then the graphical test runners cannot load classes from the last (far right) location. To summarize the symptom: when you run tests, the graphical test runner (both Swing-based and AWT-based behave the same way) reports "class not found" for a class that you expect to load from the `CLASSPATH` environment variable. Check the environment variable for trailing spaces, and remove them if there are any. The text-based test runner does not exhibit the same problem.[1]

Once you get to the point where the Java Virtual Machine can load all the classes it needs to execute your tests, you should be off and running; but if you continue to have trouble, we hope this chapter has all the solutions you need.

8.1 JUnit cannot find your tests

◆ Problem

When you execute your tests, JUnit either warns you that it cannot find *any* tests in your test case class, or it tells you that it cannot find *one* of your test methods.

◆ Background

These are common problems for people new to JUnit. You might be following our recommendation to let JUnit build a default test suite for you, but you forgot to follow one of the rules for coding your test methods. We enumerate those rules in

[1] Thanks to George Latkiewicz for reporting the problem to us, as we had never seen it before.

recipe 4.1, "Let JUnit build your test suite." You might be building a custom test suite, but have made a minor mistake along the way. You're still getting your bearings with JUnit; these kinds of problems should be expected.

◆ Recipe

First, we will assume that you are letting JUnit build the default test suite for you. In that case, follow this checklist.

- ✔ Does your test method's name start with `test`? If not, rename the test.
- ✔ Does your test method have any parameters? If so, move the parameters into the test fixture and remove the method parameters. See recipe 3.4, "Factor out a test fixture," for details on creating a test fixture.
- ✔ Does your test method return a value? If so, eliminate the return value. JUnit doesn't use it, anyway.
- ✔ Is your test method declared as `public`? If not, make it `public`.
- ✔ Is your test method declared as `final`? If so, remove the declaration.
- ✔ Is your test method declared as `static`? If so, remove the declaration.

By the end of this checklist, JUnit should be able to find your test method. If it can't, then frankly we don't know what the problem might be. We recommend you post your test case class to the JUnit Yahoo! group and we'll see what we can do.[2]

Next, if you are building your own custom test suite, then there is no way to see the warning "No test cases found in *your test case class name*." Instead, you see "Method "*your test name*" not found." If you see this problem, use this checklist to identify the cause:

- ✔ Did you implement the test at all? We *do* occasionally forget, you know.
- ✔ Did you mistype the name of the test method? Check that it matches the test name you specified in your custom test suite.
- ✔ Does your test method have any parameters? If so, follow the advice we gave earlier in this recipe.
- ✔ Does your test method return a value?
- ✔ Did you declare your method as `public`? If not, do that now.

---

[2] We both hang out there: http://groups.yahoo.com/group/junit.

That should be all. If by this point you have addressed all these problems and JUnit *still* does not find your test method, then post your code to the JUnit Yahoo! group, because it might be a problem we've never seen.

◆ Discussion

There are some cases in which JUnit (at least version 3.8.1) is more tolerant of your mistakes than our guidelines here would seem to indicate. These guidelines describe an ideal implementation of the xUnit framework, and JUnit happens to have a few defects in this regard. In particular, JUnit's degree of tolerance changes depending on how it builds the test suite: it tolerates returning a value from a test when you use the `suite()` method (see recipe 4.2, "Collect a specific set of tests"), but ignores methods that return a value when it builds the default test suite (see recipe 4.1, "Let JUnit build your test suite"). With these defects, it is certainly safest to follow all the above guidelines, as defective behavior is always a good candidate to be changed (fixed) in a future release.

The preceding problems have to do with the way JUnit looks for test methods in your test case class and the way it executes those tests. We discuss these issues in detail in chapter 4, "Managing Test Suites," including how to let JUnit automatically extract the tests from your test case class and how to build a custom test suite.

◆ Related

- 3.4—Factor out a test fixture
- 4.1—Let JUnit build your test suite

8.2 JUnit does not execute your custom test suite

◆ Problem

You have written a custom test suite method in your test case, but JUnit ignores your custom suite and builds the default test suite instead.

◆ Background

Usually this problem occurs when you build a suite of suites following our recommendations in recipe 4.3, "Collect all the tests in a package." When you coded the larger suite's custom suite method, you used `addTestSuite()` to add the smaller suite, rather than invoking the smaller suite's own custom suite method. Confused? Here is a simple way to verify that this is the cause of the problem.

Execute the smaller suite on its own. If JUnit executes your custom test suite the way you expect, then you can be sure that this recipe solves your problem.

◆ *Recipe*

Fortunately this is an easy one. Look for any place in your code where you are invoking `TestSuite.addTestSuite()` on the test suite with which you're having trouble. The most common place for this is in any `AllTests` classes you are maintaining. Look for a line of code that appears similar to this:

```
public static Test suite() {
    ...
    suite.addTestSuite(TestListenerTest.class);
    ...
}
```

Change this line of code so that it explicitly invokes the corresponding custom `suite()` method.

```
public static Test suite() {
    ...
    suite.addTestSuite(TestListenerTest.suite());
    ...
}
```

Track down and change any lines of code like this and your problem will disappear.

◆ *Discussion*

This problem occurs because two parts of JUnit behave slightly differently, and frankly it is something that we are surprised has not been fixed by now. It certainly doesn't *feel* like intentional behavior.

When you use a test runner to execute a test suite on its own, the test runner performs these two tasks:

1. It looks for a custom suite method called `suite()`. If found, it invokes this method to obtain the test suite to execute.
2. If there is no custom suite method, it collects all the test methods and builds a test suite from them. These methods have names that start with `test`, are `public`, they occur at the instance level, have no parameters, and return to value.

By contrast, the method `TestSuite.addTestSuite()` does *not* look for a custom suite method. Instead, it simply performs the usual automatic test extraction. This explains why you can execute your test suite correctly on its own, but not when you make it part of a larger test suite. Now you know.

◆ ***Related***

- 4.3—Collect all the tests in a package

8.3 JUnit does not set up your test fixture

◆ ***Problem***

You are trying to use JUnit's test fixture support to create the objects you want to test, but when you execute your test, the fixture is not set up correctly.

◆ ***Background***

This problem is typical for someone still getting acquainted with JUnit. When we started using JUnit, we often had trouble knowing what to do because we were memorizing rules rather than relying on our understanding of how JUnit works. Do not feel bad, as this is the usual learning process for *any* framework. Early on, you plug your classes into the framework as though it were magic—you don't know *how* it works, but it *does* work, and that's good enough for now. Over time, you begin to have problems; you ask questions and learn more about the inner workings of your framework. You become more comfortable with your virtual surroundings. This is as it should be. For now, read this recipe.

◆ ***Recipe***

JUnit invokes the methods `setUp()` and `tearDown()` to create and destroy your test fixture, respectively. A common mistake is to mistype the names of these methods in your test case class. Follow this checklist to see whether you have overridden these methods correctly.

- Are your test fixture methods *really* named `setUp()` and `tearDown()`? Be particularly careful of the uppercase *U* in setUp and the uppercase *D* in tearDown.
- Do your test fixture methods take no parameters and return no value? If you have added method parameters, then you are creating a new method rather than overriding an existing method. JUnit will not invoke your overloaded version of `setUp()` or `tearDown()`.
- If you have a test fixture hierarchy (see recipe 3.5, "Factor out a test fixture hierarchy"), do your test fixture methods invoke their superclass implementations? If part of your fixture is set up, but the rest is not, then you might have forgotten to invoke `super.setUp()`. If you have, then be sure also to call `super.tearDown()`.

These are the most common mistakes we have seen—and made ourselves.

◆ *Discussion*

JUnit provides the test fixture methods `setUp()` and `tearDown()` in the class `junit.framework.TestCase`. That class implements these methods, but the methods have empty bodies—they do nothing. When you subclass `TestCase`, if you type `setup()` rather than `setUp()` the compiler does not notice anything wrong: you have simply written a method that is never invoked. JUnit could perhaps have declared `setUp()` and `tearDown()` as `abstract` methods, but that would have forced you to implement these methods even if your tests had no common fixture. Rather than burden you with something you might not need, JUnit provides you with an empty fixture by default, so it is up to you to implement your custom fixture correctly.

If you want to detect this kind of mistake automatically, you can use style-checking software for which you can create a rule saying, "If you see a method named `setup`, that is probably a mistake. Let me know."[3] You know that it should be `setUp()`, so you ask your style checker to detect the common mistakes you have made in the past. The benefits you gain from this technique depend on your experience with the tool and your propensity to make the same mistake many times. If you find it easy to write such a rule using your favorite style-checking tool, then it can be effective for you; but if not, there is another solution at your disposal: call in a second set of eyes.

If you have access to other JUnit practitioners, don't hesitate to call one over and ask her to look at your code. We speak from experience when we say that this is the most effective way to detect "silly little mistakes" such as mistyping the name of a framework method. The key to making this technique effective is calling in the other person as soon as you realize that you don't see the source of the problem. We programmers have a tendency to want to solve every problem on our own, and while that is commendable, it is not terribly cost efficient. It's not even necessarily effective. We recommend you save your energy for solving such problems[4] as understanding system requirements and writing good tests. When it comes to such little things as, "Why isn't JUnit setting up my test fixture?" the sooner you call in another expert, the sooner you can get on with your *real* work.

---

3 We discuss one such tool in recipe 17.3, "Verify your test case class syntax."

4 Silly things that get in the way of progress are *difficulties*, not *problems*. A *problem* is something worth solving in its own right.

If you think that you'll learn better by solving the problem yourself, then believe us when we say that the minor embarrassment of having someone else see the problem in ten seconds helps you remember not to make the same mistake again.

And of course, if you also practice Pair Programming (www.pairprogramming.com) then you already have the expert with you, ready to catch your error as soon as you make it; but that's a topic for someone else's book.[5]

◆ *Related*

- 17.3—Verify your test case class syntax
- PMD (http://pmd.sourceforge.net)

8.4 Test setup fails after overriding runTest()

◆ *Problem*

You have written a test by overriding the method `runTest()`, rather than letting JUnit identify your test methods. Now JUnit sets up your test fixture only once before all the tests, rather than once before each test.

◆ *Background*

There are a number of reasons to override `runTest()`, not the least of which is implementing a Parameterized Test Case. We described this technique in recipe 4.8, "Build a data-driven test suite." There we suggested overriding `runTest()` so that you could give each of your parameterized tests a meaningful name rather than accepting the default convention of naming the test after the method that implements it.[6] Here you have delved into the inner workings of the framework, with intent to solve a particular problem. We understand that not all forays into the bowels of a framework are done with intent. Sometimes they are done out of desperation, or even just because you didn't quite know what you were doing.

Don't feel bad: we celebrate our ignorance. That might sound strange; good programmers know their limitations and don't feel bad asking for help when they find themselves in over their heads. This is what keeps a programmer from being

---

[5] In particular, Laurie Williams and Robert Kessler, *Pair Programming Illuminated* (Boston: Addison-Wesley Professional, 2003)

[6] In a Parameterized Test Case, each test invokes the same method, but with different parameters. If you used the default naming convention, then it would be difficult to differentiate these tests from one another.

holed up in a room for days, "going dark;" that is, silently making no progress because he doesn't understand some aspect of what he's doing. Faced with an unfamiliar task, we think it's important to put all our energy into finding a good solution, even if it is not our own solution. Don't hide what you don't know: get it out in the open, find someone who *does* know, then learn from that person. In the long run, you'll feel better.

Now what does this have to do with your problem?

It is common for a novice JUnit practitioner to expect the `setUp()` method to be invoked once for the entire test suite, rather than once for each test. She has the same expectation for `tearDown()`. This misunderstanding generally comes from confusing the `TestCase` class with an instance of the test case class. Although you include many test methods on the `TestCase` class, JUnit executes each method in a separate instance of the test case class, invoking `setUp()`, the test method, then `tearDown()`, in that order. If no one has explained this to you, though, then in your quest to get a test to run—any test—you may poke around in the dark a little, stumble upon overriding `runTest()`, get that to work, and claim victory. After all, the "Test Infected" article shows overriding `runTest()` to write a test, so that *must* be the proper technique!

Once you have one test working, you don't see how to add the second test, so you write two methods, invoke them both from `runTest()` and it continues to work. Your tests execute and that's all that matters. Unfortunately, as soon as you try to factor out a common fixture, you will find yourself in trouble, and that is what might have led you here. We think this recipe can help you.

◆ *Recipe*

When you decide to override `runTest()` it is important that you understand that JUnit treats whatever is in `runTest()` *as a single test.* This means that if you invoke multiple methods from inside `runTest()`, expecting each to be its own test, you're in for a surprise, because JUnit treats them all as a single test. Because JUnit invokes `setUp()` and `tearDown()` *once per test,* it only invokes them once each, and not once for each method you invoke from within `runTest()`.

Most of the time—including the case in which you are just trying to execute many tests in a single fixture (test case class)—you do not need to override `run-Test()`, so we recommend you do three things:

1. Create a separate test method for each test you wish to execute.
2. Use the standard JUnit naming rules for your test methods.
3. Do not override `runTest()`.

JUnit will create the default test suite from your test methods, executing `setUp()` before each test and `tearDown()` after each test, just as you were hoping it would do. If you want to execute multiple tests in a single fixture, then you certainly do not want to override `runTest()`. Instead, implement each test as a method following the usual JUnit guidelines, which we describe in recipe 8.1, "JUnit cannot find your tests."

◆ *Discussion*

Here is the method `junit.framework.TestResult.runBare()`, which executes your test:

```
public void runBare() throws Throwable {
    setUp();
    try {
        runTest();
    }
    finally {
        tearDown();
    }
}
```

As you can see, when JUnit executes your test, it first invokes `setUp()`, then your test method, then `tearDown()`. As we wrote previously, JUnit treats whatever code you write inside `runTest()` as a single test. By default, `runTest()` uses reflection to invoke one of your test methods.[7] JUnit expects `runTest()` to execute a single test.

Now that you've seen how JUnit invokes `runTest()`, you can see the effects of overriding it in your test case class. You will not need to do it often, but when you do, you'll know how it fits into the rest of the JUnit framework.

NOTE There are times when it is necessary to override `runTest()`, such as when implementing a Parameterized Test Case (see recipe 4.8, "Build a data-driven test suite"). Typically such a test strategy involves executing a single test for multiple fixtures, rather than multiple tests for a single fixture, which is JUnit's normal mode of operation. If you are building a Parameterized Test Case, then it is unlikely that you will run into the problem this recipe is meant to solve.

◆ *Related*

- 4.8—Build a data-driven test suite
- 8.3—JUnit does not set up your test fixture

---

7 In other words, that is how `TestCase` implements `runTest()`.

8.5 Your test stops after the first assertion fails

◆ Problem

You have written a test with multiple assertions, and JUnit stops executing your test after the first assertion fails. You want to execute all the assertions, even if the first one fails.

◆ Background

This is not so much a problem with JUnit as it is a general misunderstanding of the way JUnit works *or* a misunderstanding of the philosophy behind JUnit's design. Either way, you might have a fundamentally different notion of how JUnit ought to work when compared to the way it does work. JUnit was designed to fail a test at any point that an assertion fails.

◆ Recipe

You have written a test in such a way that you want to execute the entire test even after an assertion has failed. Seeing this, many JUnit practitioners would say, "What you really have is multiple tests, so move each assertion into its own test." The issue is not having multiple assertions in one test, but rather wanting to continue execution even after an assertion has failed. If the assertions are "different enough" that the failure of one does not render the others meaningless (for that test run), then we believe they belong in different tests. In this case, we recommend moving them to separate tests.

Follow these instructions to perform the required change:

1. Factor out your multiassertion test's fixture into the appropriate instance-level fields and `setUp()` code.
2. Move each assertion into its own test method.
3. Remove the old multiassertion method.

We claim that your multiassertion "test" was really a series of tests that share a common fixture. The usual way to implement this in JUnit is to factor out the common fixture into the test case class as we have recommended here. You might find yourself extracting the newly formed tests in a separate test case class, particularly if your test case class contains more tests than just the one you have refactored. See recipe 3.4, "Factor out a test fixture," for further discussion about this technique.

If you really want to allow multiple assertions to fail in a single test, you need to modify a considerable amount of code, so be prepared to dig in and "get a little dirty" with the JUnit source. We outline one approach here:

1. Change `junit.framework.TestResult.run(TestCase test)` so that when it invokes `TestCase.runBare()`, it passes a reference to itself (`this`) to the `TestCase` object.
2. Due to the previous change, you need to add the method `TestCase.runBare(TestResult testResult)`. This method needs to pass the `TestResult` object along when it invokes `TestCase.runTest()`. (Still with us?)
3. Due to the previous change, you need to add the method `TestCase.runTest(TestResult testResult)`. This method does essentially the same thing as `TestCase.runTest()`, but its `InvocationTargetException` handler adds a failure to the `TestResult` object rather than rethrow the originating exception.

This should do the trick. Notice that we say *should* because we have never tried it. We have never tried it because we have never wanted this feature. Such is the nature of open source.[8]

◆ Discussion

First, let us explain our recommendation, because you might feel that it is a comparatively large amount of work for not much gain. For this, remember that JUnit was created to support fine-grained, object-level testing in the style of Test-Driven Development. As such, the goal is to focus each test on a single, predictable behavior. This leads to a larger number of shorter tests with (at times) a considerable amount of common test fixture.[9] This kind of test is desirable because it promotes *orthogonality*: being able to determine the problem by identifying the specific failing test. If each test verifies a single aspect of the system's behavior then it ought to be easier—and it generally is—to pinpoint the problem behind a failing test. In addition, the TDD style of programming naturally lends itself to many tests, each adding features incrementally, so the tendency is for a TDD

---

[8] Open source is built on the notion that he who has an itch ought to be the one to scratch it. Karl Fogel, *Open Source Development with CVS* (freeware document) 9. http://cvsbook.red-bean.com/OpenSourceDevWithCVS_2E. tar.gz

[9] We mean the same fixture as the starting point for each test, and not the case where the second test relies on the results of the first test. Total test isolation is still important!

practitioner to have many small tests, just as a matter of course. We understand that not everyone is a TDD practitioner, but by the same token you need to remember that the people who created JUnit *are* TDD practitioners. It is simply human nature for a person to build software that solves *her* problems according to *her* preferences, even if that goes against what others might do.

There are common situations in which you might want to write some code according to the techniques of TDD but still have multiple assertions fail in a test. We will discuss one such situation here and describe an alternate approach that works *with* JUnit rather than against it. You might be able to find similar solutions to other, similar problems. Consider the case of building a web application. The server handles an HTTP request, passing it to the Controller, which selects the corresponding business logic to execute. As the Controller executes this business logic, it collects any messages that the system decides it should display to the end user. After it has finished this, the Controller bundles these messages into an object. It places that message collection on a web page template (such as a JSP or a Velocity template) and the web page template processor generates the final web page to send to the end user as a response. This pattern is so commonplace in web applications that the Struts (http://jakarta.apache.org/struts) web application framework provides direct support for this. The test you want to write verifies the collection of messages for a particularly complex bit of business logic. Suppose the user of an e-commerce system attempts to check out, that is, submits his order for processing. In so doing, the following is true for this user:

- He qualifies for a 10% discount if he purchases another $25 worth of merchandise.
- He has an item in his shopping cart that might need to be back-ordered.
- He has provided an invalid credit card number.

There are three messages to display to the end user, in addition to the other processing taking place. Your test focuses on those three messages. Your first thought is to verify these messages like so:

```
public void testMessagesForComplexCheckout() {
    // Set up shopcart...
    // Submit order...
    assertEquals("volume.discount", messages.getMessage(0).getKey());
    assertEquals("maybe.backorder", messages.getMessage(1).getKey());
    assertEquals(
        "invalid.credit.card.number",
        messages.getMessage(2).getKey());
}
```

Here you are comparing the message keys you expect to the ones in the corresponding *position* in the list of messages. After you write this test you decide that perhaps it is not a good idea to make an assumption about the order in which the messages appear. This is a brittle test, as it stands: if the messages come out in a different order, the test fails, even though the behavior is as expected. This is a case where your expectations are too specific. All that matters is that each message show up once and that there be three messages. If both those things are correct, then the test should pass. You rewrite the test to look like the following:

```
public void testMessagesForComplexCheckout() {
    // Set up shopcart
    // Submit order
    Collection messageKeys = messages.getKeys();
    assertTrue(messageKeys.contains("volume.discount"));
    assertTrue(messageKeys.contains("maybe.backorder"));
    assertTrue(messageKeys.contains("invalid.credit.card.number"));
    assertEquals(3, messageKeys.size());
}
```

This is clearly better: now the messages can come in any order and the test will pass. When you execute this test, it fails, because the volume discount message does not show up. Once you add the production code to make that pass, the test continues to fail because the credit card number message does not show up. You add the production code to fix *that* problem then the test *still* fails because you are adding each message twice.[10] Finally you fix this last problem and the test passes. You look back and think, *if I could have seen all those failures at once, I could have fixed all those problems at once. That would have been better.* We happen to think it is better to concentrate on one problem at a time, but apart from that, there is an even better way to write this test that shows all the problems at once *and* does not require multiple failures for a single test. Use the technique we recommend in recipe 2.9, "Let collections compare themselves". Rather than verify each item in a collection for correctness, we build the collection we expect, then compare that to the collection we get. The key here is the kind of collection you build: because you don't care about the order of the messages *and* you don't want any duplicate messages, you want to use a `Set` rather than a `List`. We rewrite the test as follows:

```
public void testMessagesForComplexCheckout() {
    // Set up shopcart
    // Submit order
    Set expectedMessageKeys = new HashSet(Arrays.asList(new Object[] {
        "volume.discount",
```

[10] If you wondered why we checked the number of messages, that's why.

```
            "maybe.backorder",
            "invalid.credit.card.number"
        }));
        Set actualMessageKeys = new HashSet(messages.getKeys());
        assertEquals(expectedMessageKeys, actualMessageKeys);
    }
```

The way we have constructed our set of expected message keys might look odd, so here is an explanation. First, we want a `Set`, so we build a `HashSet`, the "default" implementation of `Set`. Next, we want a simple way to define the list of message keys we expect, and the only way to do that in one line of code is by building an array. To build a `Set` requires invoking `add()` multiple times, which is a considerable amount of duplication. Java does not provide a built-in way to get from an array to a `Set`, but it does provide a way to build a `List` from an array: `Arrays.asList()`. Java also provides a way to go from virtually any collection class to another: in this case, making a `Set` from a `List`. So at last we build a `HashSet` from a `List` from an array. This is the only way we know to do this without the unwieldy duplication of invoking `add()` multiple times.[11]

Now it is easy: two `Sets` are equal if they contain the same entries. We use `assertEquals()` to verify the contents of the checkout messages collection, and, if there are any differences, the failure message shows us a string representation of each collection. This allows us to see that we are missing two messages, and the one that *is* there is there twice. We can now take the necessary steps to fix each problem.

The recommendation here is to find ways to implement your tests that *go along with* JUnit's design, rather than *fight against* its design. You might think that this is unfair: "My way or the highway," you might call it. Far from it. If you want multiple assertion failures per test, you have a few choices: you can build the feature yourself[12] or you can find an existing JUnit extension package that already does what you need. JUnitX (www.extreme-java.de/junitx) is one such project. We understand that sometimes you really do want multiple assertion failures per test. Shane Celis has this to say on the subject:

> Having multiple failures per test allows me to provide much more detailed reports. In my environment, running each test is very expensive, so I want to get the most out of it as possible. If the assertion failure means the rest of my assertions aren't run, I'm missing a lot of information. Initially, I broke them all up into separate tests, but that proved to be clumsy, so I modified the code

---

[11] Of course, we should hide this nonsense behind a creation method called `makeSet()` that takes an array. Once we get the test to pass, we can refactor it.

[12] Remember, this is open source.

> to allow for multiple failures (basically, a failed assertion wouldn't throw an exception, it would simply be added to the `TestResult`'s failures), and writing the tests proved much easier and provided much more information than previously available.

We have seen this before and it has always boiled down to the following: someone has a series of tests that are difficult or annoying to implement as separate test methods, that use some expensive external resource (such as a database), and which often fail because of frequent changes in the application's environment (such as continual changes in the data in that database). These people reason that adding multiple assertion failures per test is *the* way to solve the problem. Let us offer another recommendation.

In this particular case, there are a number of tests that share a test fixture and are order dependent. We recommend:

1. Factoring out the test fixture (see recipe 3.4, "Factor out a test fixture")
2. Building a custom test suite (see recipe 4.2, "Collect a specific set of tests") that executes those tests in the required order
3. Using *one-time setup* (see recipe 5.10, "Set up your fixture once for the entire suite") to put the shared fixture into the correct state before the test suite executes
4. Moving each assertion (or block of assertions) into its own test method

We can derive all the benefits that Shane derives from adding the "multiple assertion failures per test" feature to JUnit. The difference? Our approach uses features that JUnit already provides, rather than adding to it. We can implement this kind of test using a smaller framework than Shane.[13] All other things being equal, we prefer to use less code, because that way less can go wrong. Still, if you feel you need this feature, we recommend you try both and measure the difference. If you decide that multiple assertion failures per test is worth the cost, then implement it and share it with the community. If you do, please make it configurable so we can turn it off. Thanks.

◆ *Related*

- 3.4—Factor out a test fixture
- 4.2—Collect a specific set of tests
- 5.10—Set up your fixture once for the entire suite

---

[13] This is not a knock on Shane. We like Shane, really.

8.6 The graphical test runner does not load your classes properly

◆ ***Problem***

When you execute your tests with the graphical test runners, the test fails with either a `ClassCastException` or a `LinkageError`. The text-based test runner does not show the same problem.

◆ ***Background***

There are times when it is particularly convenient to use a text-based test runner, but most people prefer to use a graphical test runner, especially during a Test-Driven Development programming session. The red bar/green bar signal provides a better quality of feedback, though the effect might be purely psychological.[14] Using a graphical test runner, you might have encountered this problem, especially if your tests involve third-party software packages. Some of those packages are designed (if you can call it that) in a way that makes it impossible to reload one of its classes within a Java Virtual Machine.[15] This is incompatible with the graphical test runner, the point of which is to keep the runner open while you are changing your code so you can change your classes, recompile your code, and rerun your tests without having to restart the test runner. This explains why your test executes as expected with the text runner: each test run executes in its own JVM. Not so for the graphical runners. Yes, you could switch to the text runner, but your test *should work*—after all, it works on one test runner, so why not on the other?

◆ ***Recipe***

Identify the class or classes that should not be reloaded within a JVM. Add these classes or packages to the file `excluded.properties` that JUnit provides in its distribution. You will find this file inside `junit.jar`. Your options are either to change the version in your JUnit distribution or create your own version of the file and place it on your class path before `junit.jar`. We recommend the second option, as it is easier to maintain, although it results in a more complex build environment.

The standard version of this file as distributed with JUnit resembles the following, although the actual entries in the file depend on the version you are using. (Later versions generally have more entries.)

---

[14] We do not claim to know anything on the subject; we simply make this observation and move on.

[15] We do not want to name names, but a certain large corporation's JDBC provider is on this list. I believe this is a case of competing priorities, but it's still an annoyance.

```
# The list of excluded package paths for the TestCaseClassLoader
#
excluded.0=sun.*
excluded.1=com.sun.*
excluded.2=org.omg.*
excluded.3=javax.*
excluded.4=sunw.*
excluded.5=java.*
```

Simply add another package filter for the classes you need to exclude from being reloaded. Call the next entry `excluded.6`, and so on, for as many entries as you need. Remember either to put this file back into `junit.jar` or place it on your class path *in front* of `junit.jar`.

◆ Discussion

Each entry in `excluded.properties` is a *filter* that specifies a set of classes—or packages if you use the wildcard character (*) to mean all the classes in this package). When JUnit needs to decide whether to reload a class, it first consults the entries in this list. If the class is in a package that matches any of these filters, then JUnit does not attempt to reload it; otherwise, JUnit reloads it. By default, JUnit does not attempt to reload any classes in any package starting with `sun`, `com.sun`, `org.omg`, `javax`, `sunw`, or `java`. These are standard Java classes, standard Java extensions, other Java extensions from Sun Microsystems, and libraries from the Object Management Group (OMG).[16]

If you keep a separate version of `excluded.properties` file outside `junit.jar`, then you need to know how JUnit loads the file. JUnit expects this file to be in the directory `junit/runner` on the class path, so if you put the file in directory `/home/jbrains/junit/runner`, then be sure to add `/home/jbrains` to the front of your runtime class path when you execute your tests.

If you follow the recommendations in this recipe and you *continue* to have the class loading problem, it might be your IDE. Eclipse's Java Development Toolkit, for example, bundles JUnit. This means that you need to be aware of exactly which copy of `excluded.properties` you are fixing. Be sure to check your runtime class path for unexpected copies of JUnit, then make sure that your edited copy of `excluded.properties` comes before *any* version of JUnit on your class path.

◆ Related

- The JUnit FAQ, item 8, under "Running Tests" (http://junit.sourceforge.net/doc/faq/faq.htm)

---

[16] Among these are early implementations of the Java collections framework and the CORBA libraries.

8.7 JUnit fails when your test case uses JAXP

◆ Problem

You are writing a test that uses the standard Java API for XML, but in spite of what you think is correct code, JUnit fails with a `LinkageError` when it executes your test. The test works when you use the text-based test runner, but fails when you use a graphical test runner.

◆ Background

The Java API for XML includes classes in the package hierarchies `javax.xml.*`, `org.xml.sax.*`, and `org.w3c.dom.*`. These are the standard XML interfaces, the SAX parser interfaces, and the DOM parser interfaces, respectively. Virtually any XML-based testing uses these classes, even if you are not testing XML parsing behavior directly. There might even be cases in which you are not aware that you are using XML parsing. Third-party software with which you might be integrating could use XML for configuration. This has become increasingly common as XML has become the standard, universal data format for text files.[17] Rest assured that the problem is with JUnit's customized class loader and not your tests.

◆ Recipe

The simplest solution is to upgrade to JUnit 3.8.1, which already contains the fix we are about to recommend. If you are not in a position to do that, then read on.

The solution here is the same as in recipe 8.6, "The graphical test runner does not load your classes properly." Add the three package hierarchies we mentioned previously to the file `excluded.properties`: `javax.xml.*`, `org.xml.sax.*`, and `org.w3c.dom.*`. Actually, because `javax.*` is already on the "excluded" list, you only need to add the last two.

Here is an example of adding these two packages to the list of exclusions:

```
# The list of excluded package paths for the TestCaseClassLoader
#
excluded.0=sun.*
excluded.1=com.sun.*
excluded.2=org.omg.*
excluded.3=javax.*
excluded.4=sunw.*
```

[17] We feel that people are using XML in cases where something less complex would work equally well, but that's another issue altogether.

```
excluded.5=java.*
excluded.6=org.w3c.dom.*
excluded.7=org.xml.sax.*
```

JAXP packages

Although this kind of fix gets your hands pretty dirty from playing with the inner workings of JUnit, it's an easy change to make once you become used to it. We recommend keeping your changes in version control somewhere, in case you forget exactly which packages you have added to the list.

◆ *Discussion*

Because this problem seems to materialize a number of times in slightly different settings, there is a detailed description of the problem and its resolution in the JUnit FAQ (junit.sourceforge.net/doc/faq/faq.htm).

◆ *Related*

- 8.6—The graphical test runner does not load your classes properly
- JUnit FAQ (http://junit.sourceforge.net/doc/faq/faq.htm)

8.8 *JUnit fails when narrowing an EJB reference*

◆ *Problem*

You have written a test involving an Enterprise Java Bean (EJB) that fails with a `ClassCastException`. The offending line of code is the one that "narrows" your EJB reference just after a JNDI lookup. The test works when you use the text-based test runner, but fails when you a graphical test runner.

◆ *Background*

It is heartwarming to see that more and more J2EE programmers are looking to JUnit to help test their software. This does present new challenges though, as these programmers find new and interesting ways to use JUnit to do their testing. You are among the programmers that are pushing the envelope, writing JUnit tests that no one else has written before, and in the process you are helping to find problems that no one else has had the opportunity to find yet.

In this case, though, we've seen it before and we know how to help you.

To understand the problem further, consider that when you invoke `InitialContext.lookup()`, this method returns an object loaded and defined by the Java Virtual Machine's standard system class loader,[18] but it was JUnit's `TestCaseClass-`

[18] The class `sun.misc.Launcher$AppClassLoader`, to be precise.

`Loader` that loaded your EJB interface's type. When you invoke `narrow()`, the two fully qualified class names are the same, but the defining class loaders for the two are different. The JVM qualifies a class's runtime type by the identity of the object that loaded the class, so the JVM treats the EJB interface types loaded by the different class loaders as different types, even though *you* know they are the same. The result is a `ClassCastException`.

◆ Recipe

The short version of the story is this: prevent the JUnit custom class loader from loading your EJB interfaces by adding them to `excluded.properties`. We described this solution in recipe 8.6. Although those examples showed adding entire package hierarchies to the "excluded" list, you can specify individual classes and interfaces by their fully qualified name. For example, if you have an EJB called Account in package `com.mycom.model.ejb`, then add the following lines to the excluded list.

```
# We have omitted the preceding lines, for brevity
excluded.10 = com.mycom.model.ejb.Account
excluded.11 = com.mycom.model.ejb.AccountHome
excluded.12 = com.mycom.model.ejb.AccountLocal
excluded.13 = com.mycom.model.ejb.AccountLocalHome
```

Remote interfaces (excluded.10–11)

Local interfaces, EJB 2.x only (excluded.12–13)

◆ Discussion

This solution assumes that your EJB interfaces are in an easily isolated package hierarchy, which is commonly the case: many programmers create a subpackage called `ejb` somewhere in their package hierarchy for EJBs. The good news is that this additional requirement is likely not an issue for you.

The bad news is that if you are testing your EJB implementation, then you cannot add the entire EJB package to the "excluded" list; otherwise, JUnit does not reload your implementation either, and that might be the one part of the package on which you're actually working. There's not much point in using the graphical test runner to help you implement your EJB if the test runner doesn't reload your EJB implementation class! This is why you need to specify the individual interfaces in `excluded.properties`, unless, of course, you want to place your EJB implementation class in a package different from the one containing your interfaces.[19] You might find it necessary to automatically generate `excluded.properties` when you build your application to ensure that it is up to date as you add more EJBs.

---

[19] Nothing in the EJB specification stops you from doing this, and it may not be so bad, but it seems pretty drastic.

Because this problem seems to materialize a number of times in slightly different settings, there are several entries in the JUnit FAQ (junit.sourceforge.net/doc/faq/faq.htm) that describe the problem and solution in detail. We recommend you read the FAQ if you need a more thorough explanation of the problem and its causes.

◆ *Related*

- The JUnit FAQ (http://junit.sourceforge.net/doc/faq/faq.htm)
- 8.6—The graphical test runner does not load your classes properly
- Chapter 11—Testing Enterprise JavaBeans

Part 2

Testing J2EE

Most "serious" Java development these days revolves around J2EE: enterprise components for Java. This part of the book explores testing techniques for the core J2EE technologies: servlets, JavaServer Pages, Velocity templates, Enterprise JavaBeans, and Java Messaging Service. It also covers concepts common to web application platforms: page flow, dynamic content, distributed objects, as well as the separation of application logic, business logic, and persistence. The recipes in this part of the book generally fall into two categories: refactoring towards testing J2EE designs, and dealing with legacy J2EE designs, where *legacy* generally means "you are afraid to change it." From this point forward, recipes build on the foundations in part 1, so you will see numerous references here to earlier recipes. In a way, the goal of the remaining recipes is to reduce every testing problem to a smaller number of recipes from part 1. Enjoy.

Designing J2EE applications for testability

We originally conceived this part as "JUnit and Frameworks," because there are a few general guidelines that govern how to test code that lives in a framework. With J2EE, frameworks are everywhere: servlets, EJBs, JMS message listeners—these are all objects we code within a component framework and execute in the context of containers. This raises two main issues: performance and dependency; and a testable design is one that manages both effectively.

The performance problem

The performance issue stems from the containers or the application server. Executing code inside a container incurs overhead that affects the execution speed of your tests. This has a negative impact on the testing experience, which Kent Beck mentions briefly in *Test-Driven Development: By Example:* "Tests that run a long time won't be run often, and often haven't been run for a while, and probably don't work." Ron Jeffries provides some interesting commentary on how we might behave if we can someday test our entire system, be sure those tests mean the system works, and all in less time than it takes to think about it.[1] One of the key benefits of testing is the refactoring safety net—the ability to make changes confidently because you can always execute the tests to see if your last change broke anything. One of the key practices in refactoring is to execute the tests after every change, to be sure that you have not injected a defect.[2] Because many refactorings involve several changes—say ten or more—a slow test suite discourages you from executing the tests frequently enough to realize most of the benefit of the refactoring safety net. This is all rather a roundabout way of saying that slow tests are more than a nuisance, and their productivity impact is more than just the extra time to execute the tests. It is worth investing considerable amounts of time in making tests fast enough that you will feel free to execute them at any moment. Many of the recipes in the chapters that follow address this issue by guiding you through refactorings that move your code away from the container, allowing you to execute most of your tests without incurring the overhead of an application server. This performance issue is related to the way your J2EE components depend on their environment.

---

1 www.xprogramming.com/xpmag/expUnitTestsat100.htm

2 Martin Fowler describes this in Chapter 4 of *Refactoring: Improving the Design of Existing Code.* See "The Value of Self-testing Code."

The dependency problem

A framework is based on the Hollywood Principle—"don't call us; we'll call you." Framework designers expect you to build components that depend directly on their code: your classes implement their interfaces, or extend their classes. They say, "You worry about the business logic and let us take care of persistence (or a web interface, or transactions)." It looks good on paper, but it leads to testing problems: in particular, if your business logic is built right into a servlet, then you cannot execute that logic without running the application server, which leads us to the performance problems of the previous paragraph.[3] There are two main approaches to this problem: mock objects and reducing dependency. It turns out that this is a source of some controversy among JUnit practitioners.

Mock objects—palliative care

We loosely define a *mock object* as follows: an object that you can use in a test to stand in place of a more expensive-to-use or difficult-to-use object. When people ask about testing and databases, most people offer this advice: "mock the database." That is, rather than use a real database in your tests, you should substitute a mock version of the database objects and let your business logic operate on those. They could use files for persistence, or they could ignore persistence altogether. The benefit is avoiding the expensive, external resource and the test execution speed problems that come with it. We use the term *mock objects approach*, then, to mean a general approach to testing that relies on mock objects to avoid the pain of testing against the real thing. Throughout this book—but especially when discussing J2EE components—we recommend the mock objects approach to test those parts of your application that integrate with expensive, external resources. We do not, however, recommend mock objects as the first and final solution to this problem. (For more about mock objects, see the essay "The mock objects landscape." There is more than meets the eye.)

NOTE *Terminology*—Members of the Programmer Testing community have been trying to converge on a narrow, accurate definition of mock object, as the term seems to mean different things to different people. They have coined the term *testing object* to refer to any object you would use for a test that you would not use in production code, roughly equivalent to the meaning of *mock object* we have just introduced. Using the community's definition, a mock object, then, would be a special kind of testing object—

[3] Altogether accidental alliteration.

one that allows the programmer to set expectations on how it is used and can verify itself against those expectations with a simple method invocation. This matches better with the concept as it was introduced in the Mock Objects paper.[4] The definition we have presented here merely matches the current common usage with which you may already be familiar, but we rather like the term *testing object*, as it more directly describes the underlying concept. We will try to use the two terms appropriately, but will invariably revert to long-standing habits—calling testing objects "mock objects"—from time to time.

Reducing dependency—the cure

Rather than reach for a mock object right away, we recommend reducing your dependency on the frameworks around you. Briefly, code your objects in such a way that you can "plug in" a J2EE-based implementation of the services it provides: persistence, web interface, transactions, and so on. If you store customer information in a database, then create a `CustomerStore` interface and have your business logic depend only on this interface. Now create the class `JdbcCustomerStore`, which implements `CustomerStore` and provides JDBC-specific services, interacting with the database. By separating your business logic from the persistence framework, you make it easy to test the business logic with predictable data and those tests are *fast*. Just provide an in-memory implementation of `CustomerStore`—what some might call a mock object, but we disagree[5]—and test your business logic using the `InMemoryCustomerStore`. If your business logic cannot tell the difference between the two implementations of `CustomerStore`, then by and large it does not matter which implementation you choose for your tests! As always, the devil is in the details, and we get into those details throughout the rest of this book.

It takes an investment in time and effort to make a J2EE design easy to test. The good news is that once you know the general principles, and especially if you let tests drive your work, then it becomes quite natural to build J2EE-independent components, and then integrate them with J2EE later. The goal is to make the integration with J2EE as thin as possible to minimize the number of tests you need to execute against the live container. This maximizes the benefit of testing your code with JUnit. Unfortunately, there are times when this is simply not an option.

---

[4] Steve Freeman, Steve Mackinnon, Philip Craig, "Endo-Testing: Unit Testing with Mock Objects," www.connextra.com/aboutUs/mockobjects.pdf.

[5] If you want the sordid details, then scan the archives of the Test-Driven Development Yahoo! group at groups.yahoo.com/group/testdrivendevelopment/messages. Start at message 5068.

Testing legacy J2EE components

As we wrote previously, we define *legacy* in this context as "code you are afraid to change." In this case "you" might actually be you, or your team lead, your manager, or some other person with a vested interest in keeping you from changing existing code. There are a number of reasons for this, including (but not limited to, as lawyers like to say):

- "We need features; don't waste my time working on stuff that's already done!"
- "It works and we don't know why, so don't touch it."
- "Didn't you get it right the first time?!"
- "If you change John's code, he gets angry, so just leave it alone."
- "You can't change Mary's code without her approval, and she's on vacation this week."

We could go on, but as fun as that is, we need to figure out how to test code that we are not in a position to change. Refactoring towards a more testable design is therefore not an option open to us. What do we do? Recognizing that this situation is more common than we would hope, we have devoted some recipes in this part to testing legacy J2EE components: servlets, JSPs, and EJBs. There are really only two general techniques that you can use in this situation: test from end to end or resort to trickery to substitute mock objects.

End-to-End Tests—tests that execute the end-user interface and involve the entire application—are important, as they establish that the application actually works; however, these tests are expensive to execute, to write, and to maintain. They are slow, because they involve the entire application and all the expensive, external resources it uses. They are difficult to write, because you have to understand how all the components interact in order for the test to verify exactly what you want to verify. It is also difficult to re-create certain obscure error conditions, making it difficult to write tests for how well you handle those error conditions—things such as "disk full" and "graphical resources low."[6] End-to-End Tests are difficult to maintain, because insignificant changes can break them—different screen layout, different button names, translating into German—all these things can lead to changes in the End-to-End Tests. This is the negative feedback loop that drives many development shops to overspend on testing resources rather than use that

---

[6] J. B. worked on a project that spent three weeks hunting down a defect that only occurred when graphical resources were low. It took fifteen minutes of opening windows to recreate the conditions for each test.

money (and time) to eliminate the problem through design improvement. Relying on End-to-End Tests to verify components is a losing proposition.

An alternative is to use virtual machine and bytecode magic to substitute mock objects where you need them. We have always been leery of this approach, mostly because we do not know much about it; however, a recent development in this area looks promising: Virtual Mock Objects (www.virtualmock.org). Their site states, "VirtualMock is a Java unit testing tool which supports the Mock Objects testing approach. Through the use of Aspect-Oriented Programming, it is designed to address some of the limitations of existing Mock Object tools and approaches." Because this is relatively new, much of the advice we offer in this book ignores it. Once we have had the chance to digest it, perhaps our approach will change: the trade-off between mock objects and reducing dependency will certainly change and we will have to change with it. We think that Virtual Mock Objects has the potential to open up new options for people who need to write Object Tests for legacy code—at least in Java. But even so, we recommend reducing dependency over using mock objects. The result is code that is more flexible in addition to being easier to test. It is not a question of disliking mock objects; but in the spirit of the Agile Manifesto (www.agilemanifesto.org), we value reducing dependency over mocking collaborators.

Post script

As we came closer to releasing the book, we discovered that the jMock project (www.jmock.org), together with the CGLib package (http://cglib.sourceforge.net), make it relatively easy to substitute mock implementations of classes (not just interfaces) at runtime in tests. This achieves some of the same goals as Virtual Mock, and so it will be interesting to see how these projects progress in the coming months and years. We strongly recommend you look into both jMock and Virtual Mock to see which approach will best help you apply the mock objects approach to legacy code.

The Coffee Shop application

The Coffee Shop application is a run-of-the-mill online store that we will use to provide examples throughout the remainder of this book. Although we will refer to it frequently in various recipes, it is not the goal of this book to build towards a working online coffee shop. To do that, we would need to make certain design decisions, such as whether to use JavaServer Pages (JSPs), Velocity templates, or

XSL transformations as our presentation engine. Rather than decide on one technology, we will use examples from all these technologies in different recipes to illustrate the techniques they describe. We use the Coffee Shop application simply to provide a context for our J2EE-related recipes, rather than try to talk about testing J2EE applications in abstract terms.

To understand the recipes, it is enough to understand the *requirements* for the Coffee Shop application, so you will not see any architecture or design diagrams here. Throughout part 2 we will introduce those details as we need them. To illustrate a recipe, we will say, "Suppose the Coffee Shop application needs to do *this*; then you might have a design that looks like *that*, and here is how to use JUnit to test it." With this out of the way, we will describe the essential requirements for the Coffee Shop application.

In general terms, this is an online store, in the spirit of amazon.com, although not nearly as rich in features. The users of the store are generally shoppers purchasing coffee beans by the kilogram. The store uses the shopcart[7] metaphor, allowing the shopper to collect different kinds of coffee beans into his cart before completing his purchase. The store has an online catalog of coffee beans that the shopper can browse; the kinds and prices of the coffee are set by the administrator.

As we have already mentioned, we will propose additional features as needed to illustrate the techniques in our recipes. You can assume that the Coffee Shop application always has the very basic features we have mentioned here. Now that we have set the context for part 2, it is time to get to some recipes!

---

[7] Or "shopping cart," if you prefer. Both terms are relatively common, and it just happens that we use "shopcart" more often.

9 Testing and XML

This chapter covers

- Comparing XML documents with XMLUnit
- Ignoring superficial differences in XML documents
- Testing static web pages with XMLUnit
- Testing XSL transformations with XMLUnit
- Validating XML documents during testing

XML documents are everywhere in J2EE: deployment descriptors, configuration files, XHTML and XSL transformations, Web Services Description Language, and on and on. If you are going to test J2EE applications, you are going to need to write tests involving XML documents. Notice the title of this chapter is "Testing and XML," and not "Testing XML." It is not our mission here to test XML parsers, but rather to describe how to write tests involving XML documents and other XML-related technologies, such as XSL transformations. Given that XML documents are everywhere, it looks to us that this is an important skill to have, and we *can* summarize the entire chapter in two words: use XPath.

The XPath language defines a way to refer to the content of an XML document with query expressions that can locate anything from single XML attribute values to large complex collections of XML elements. If you have not seen XPath before, we recommend Elizabeth Castro's *XML for the World Wide Web*, which describes XML, XSL, and XPath in detail.[1] The overall strategy when testing with XML documents is to make assertions about those documents using XPath to retrieve the actual content. You want to write assertions like this:

```
assertEquals("Rainsberger", document.getTextAtXpath("/person/lastName"));
```

This assertion says, "the element `lastName` inside element `person` at the root of the document should have the text `Rainsberger`." Following is an XML document that satisfies this assertion.

Listing 9.1 A simple XML document

```
<?xml version="1.0?">
<person>
    <firstName>J. B.</firstName>
    <lastName>Rainsberger</lastName>
</person>
```

This is perhaps the simplest and most direct way to use XPath in your tests. When testing Java components whose output is an XML document, you want to treat the XML document as a return value and write assertions just as we described back in chapter 2, "Elementary tests." The key difference is that you need some additional tools to help you manipulate XML documents as Java objects, and that is where

[1] Also consider Elliotte Rusty Harold's *Processing XML with Java* (Pearson Education, 2002). Castro's book is a more general introduction, whereas Harold's deals directly with Java. Harold's book is available online at http://cafeconleche.org/books/xmljava/.

XPath comes in. You can use XPath to obtain the text of an element, to obtain the value of an attribute, or to verify whether an element exists. For example, if you have an XML document with many `person` elements and want to verify that there is a `Rainsberger` among them, you can use the same technique but with a different XPath statement:

```
assertFalse(document.getNodesAtXpath(
    "//person[lastName='Rainsberger']").isEmpty());
```

Here, the method `getNodesAtXpath()` works rather like a database query: "find all the `person` elements having a `lastName` element with the text `Rainsberger` and return them as a collection." The assertion says, "The collection of `person` elements with the `lastName` of `Rainsberger` should not be empty." These are the two kinds of XPath statements you will use most often in your tests.

Up to this point we have said little about where to find methods such as `getNodesAtXpath()` and `getTextAtXpath()`, because they are certainly not part of JUnit. There is an XPath API that you can use to execute XPath queries on a parsed XML document. The most widely used implementations of the XPath API are found in Xalan (http://xml.apache.org/xalan-j) and jaxen (http://jaxen.sourceforge.net).[2] You could use this API directly to make assertions about the structure and content of XML documents, but rather than reinventing the wheel, we recommend using XMLUnit (http://xmlunit.sourceforge.net). This package provides `XMLTestCase`, a base test case (see recipe 3.6, "Introduce a Base Test Case") that adds custom assertions (see recipe 17.4, "Extract a custom assertion") built on XPath. To use XMLUnit, create a test case class that extends `org.custommonkey.xmlunit.XMLTestCase`, then write your tests as usual. In your tests you will use the various XMLUnit assertions to verify that XML elements exist, to verify their value, and even to compare entire XML documents. Let's take an example.

Consider XML marshalling, which is the act of turning Java objects into XML documents (and the other way around). Web applications that use XSL transformations (rather than page templates, such as JSPs) as their presentation engine typically need to marshal Java beans to XML so that the transformation engine can present that data to the end user as a web page. Other systems marshal data to and from XML to communicate with other computers in a heterogeneous environment—one involving many computing platforms or programming languages, such as that created by web services. Suppose we are testing a simple XML marshaller

---

[2] Our experience is with Xalan, rather than with jaxen, so when we discuss XPath throughout this book, we are referring to the Xalan implementation.

that creates an XML document from a Value Object. The "person" document in listing 9.1 could have been produced by our XML marshaller operating on a Person object with the String attributes of firstName and lastName. We ought to be able to write out the XML document corresponding to a Person object and verify its contents. Enough words; it is time for a test.

Assume that the XmlMarshaller constructor takes the class object corresponding to our Value Object class and a String that you would like it to use as the name of the XML root element. The remaining XML elements are named according to the attributes of the Value Object. Listing 9.2 shows the resulting test.

Listing 9.2 Testing an XML object marshaller

```
package junit.cookbook.xmlunit.test;

import java.io.StringWriter;
import junit.cookbook.xmlunit.*;
import org.custommonkey.xmlunit.XMLTestCase;

public class MarshalPersonToXmlTest extends XMLTestCase {
    public void testJbRainsberger() throws Exception {
        Person person = new Person("J. B.", "Rainsberger");
        XmlMarshaller marshaller = new XmlMarshaller(
            Person.class, "person");
        StringWriter output = new StringWriter();
        marshaller.marshal(person, output);

        String xmlDocumentAsString = output.toString();

        assertXpathExists("/person", xmlDocumentAsString);

        assertXpathEvaluatesTo(
            "J. B.",
            "/person/firstName",
            xmlDocumentAsString);

        assertXpathEvaluatesTo(
            "Rainsberger",
            "/person/lastName",
            xmlDocumentAsString);
    }
}
```

One thing you will notice about this test is that it makes no mention at all of files. We are very accustomed to thinking of XML documents as files, because we usually use XML documents in their stored format, and we usually store XML in files. Nothing about XML *requires* that documents be processed using files. In fact, web services generally send and receive XML documents over network connections without ever writing that data to file. To keep everything simple, our `XmlMarshaller` writes data to a `Writer`—any `Writer`—and the most convenient kind to use for this kind of test is a `StringWriter`: this way we do not have to load the resulting XML document from disk before parsing and verifying it. It is already in memory!

The assertions we make in this test are the custom assertions that XMLUnit provides. The first we use is `assertXpathExists()`, which executes the XPath query and fails only if there are no nodes in the XML document matching the query. Here we are using this custom assertion to verify the existence of a `person` root element. The other custom assertion we use is `assertXpathEvaluatesTo()`, which executes an XPath query and compares the result to an expected value; the assertion fails if the result and the expected value are different. XPath queries generally return either a list of nodes (in which you can search for the one you expect) or a `String` value (corresponding to the text of an element or attribute).

We could simplify this test, at the risk of making it more brittle, by making an assertion on the entire XML document which we expect the XML marshaller to produce. XMLUnit provides the method `assertXMLEqual()`, which checks whether two XML documents are equal. The way that XMLUnit defines equality in this case, though, requires some explanation. With XMLUnit, documents may be *similar* or *identical*. Documents are identical if the same XML elements appear in exactly the same order. Documents are similar if they represent the same content, but perhaps with certain elements appearing in a different order. Sometimes it matters, and sometimes it does not. As XMLUnit's web site says, "With XMLUnit, you have the control." Referring to listing 9.1, the order in which the `<firstName>` and `<lastName>` elements appear does not affect the meaning of the document. If we compare the document in listing 9.1 to a copy with `<lastName>` before `<firstName>`, we would expect them to be equal, based on the way we interpret the documents. This way of interpreting whether documents are equal–viewing them as data–is common in the kinds of applications we build, so `assertXMLEqual()` compares documents for similarity, rather than identity. As an example, here is a test for our XML object marshaller. We are verifying that the data is marshalled correctly, so we can build the test around `assertXMLEqual()` without having to resort to multiple XPath-based assertions (we have highlighted the differences between this test and the previous one in bold print):

```
public void testJbRainsbergerUsingEntireDocument()
    throws Exception {

    Person person = new Person("J. B.", "Rainsberger");
    XmlMarshaller marshaller =
        new XmlMarshaller(Person.class, "person");
```

```
        StringWriter output = new StringWriter();
        marshaller.marshal(person, output);

        String expectedXmlDocument =
            "<?xml version=\"1.0\" ?>"
                + "<person>"
                + "<firstName>J. B.</firstName>"
                + "<lastName>Rainsberger</lastName>"
                + "</person>";

        String xmlDocumentAsString = output.toString();

        assertXMLEqual(expectedXmlDocument, xmlDocumentAsString);
    }
```

Rather than write an assertion to verify each part of the document that interests us, this second test creates the entire document we expect and compares it with the actual document the XML marshaller gives us. This is how to use XMLUnit in its simplest form. There is, however, one warning to go with this technique: what *you* think of as white space differences are not really mere white space differences in XML.

An XML document consists of a structure of elements—a tag, its attributes, and its content. The content of an XML element can either be text, more elements, or a combination of the two. It is the "combination of the two" that creates problems when comparing XML documents with one another. To illustrate this important point, let us consider what happens when we change the expected XML document in what we believe to be a purely cosmetic way. Another programmer has decided that failure messages would be easier to read if the expected XML document were formatted with line breaks and tabs, so she changes the test to the following:

```
    public void testJbRainsbergerUsingEntireDocument()
        throws Exception {

        Person person = new Person("J. B.", "Rainsberger");
        XmlMarshaller marshaller =
            new XmlMarshaller(Person.class, "person");
        StringWriter output = new StringWriter();
        marshaller.marshal(person, output);

        String expectedXmlDocument =
            "<?xml version=\"1.0\" ?>\n"
                + "<person>\n"
                + "\t<firstName>J. B.</firstName>\n"
                + "\t<lastName>Rainsberger</lastName>\n"
                + "</person>\n";

        String xmlDocumentAsString = output.toString();

        assertXMLEqual(expectedXmlDocument, xmlDocumentAsString);
    }
```

When she executes this test, she fully expects it to continue to pass, so she does so almost absentmindedly.[3] Much to her surprise, she sees this failure message:

```
junit.framework.AssertionFailedError: org.custommonkey.xmlunit.Diff [dif-
   ferent] Expected number of child nodes '5' but was '2' - comparing <per-
   son...> at /person[1] to <person...> at /person[1]
```

Five nodes? By our count there are two: `firstName` and `lastName`. What's the problem? The issue is that what you treat as white space, and therefore not a node, an XML parser treats as a text node with empty content. When you look at the following XML document, you see a `person` element with two elements inside it:

```
<?xml version="1.0" ?>
<person>
    <firstName>J. B.</firstName>
    <lastName>Rainsberger</lastName>
</person>
```

When the XML parser looks inside the `person` element, it finds an empty text element (thanks to the carriage return/linefeed character or characters), a `firstName` element, another empty text element, a `lastName` element, and another empty text element—that makes five. That explains the failure message, although it is not exactly the kind of behavior we want. We would like to ignore those empty text elements altogether. Fortunately, XMLUnit provides a simple way to ignore these kinds of white space differences. We invoke one extra method in our test, telling XMLUnit to ignore white space (we have highlighted the new method invocation in bold print):

```
public void testJbRainsbergerUsingEntireDocument()
    throws Exception {

    Person person = new Person("J. B.", "Rainsberger");
    XmlMarshaller marshaller =
        new XmlMarshaller(Person.class, "person");
    StringWriter output = new StringWriter();
    marshaller.marshal(person, output);

    String expectedXmlDocument =
        "<?xml version=\"1.0\" ?>\n"
            + "<person>\n"
            + "\t<firstName>J. B.</firstName>\n"
            + "\t<lastName>Rainsberger</lastName>\n"
            + "</person>\n";
```

[3] Do not be critical of her for this. Other programmers have concluded in similar cases, "It's a superficial change, so I'm sure it works. I'll just check in my change and go on vacation." At least she ran the tests!

```
        String xmlDocumentAsString = output.toString();

        XMLUnit.setIgnoreWhitespace(true);
        assertXMLEqual(expectedXmlDocument, xmlDocumentAsString);
    }
```

This tells XMLUnit to ignore all those extra elements containing only white space when comparing XML documents. Spaces in an element's content are not affected by this setting. If you need to do this for entire suites of tests, then move this statement into your test case class's `setUp()` method, as it is part of those tests' fixture.

There are other kinds of superficial differences that you may want to ignore on a test-by-test basis. You may, for example, want to compare only the structure of two documents without worrying about the values of attributes and the text. XMLUnit allows you to decide which differences are significant by implementing your own `DifferenceListener`. See recipe 9.3, "Ignore certain differences in XML documents," for details.

As we mentioned previously, many web applications transform XML documents into XHTML using XSLT (http://www.w3.org/TR/xslt) as their presentation engine. If so, you will want to test your XSL transformations in isolation, just as you would test your JSPs or Velocity templates in isolation. See recipe 9.6, "Test an XSL stylesheet in isolation," and also see chapter 12, "Testing Web Components," for recipes addressing JSPs and Velocity templates. The next most common use of XML documents in testing concerns the various J2EE deployment descriptors. There are many cases in which making an assertion on a deployment descriptor is more effective than testing the underlying deployed component. See the other chapters in this part of the book for details on when, how, and why to use the various J2EE deployment descriptors during testing. Finally, it is possible to treat HTML documents as though they are XML documents by writing XHTML (http://www.w3.org/TR/xhtml1/). You can test web pages in isolation in one of two ways: either write them in XHTML and use the techniques we have previously described, or use an HTML-tolerant parser that converts web pages into easy-to-verify XML documents. See recipe 9.5, "Test the content of a static web page," for an example of how to do this.

Validating XML documents provides a way to avoid writing some JUnit tests for your system. We like JUnit, but whenever there is an opportunity to do something even simpler, we take advantage of it. You can validate XML documents using either a DTD or an XML schema, and although this book is not the place to describe how to do that, see recipe 9.7, "Validate XML documents in your tests," for a discussion on making XML document validation part of your testing environment.

9.1 Verify the order of elements in a document

◆ Problem

You want to verify an XML document whose elements need to appear in a particular order.

◆ Background

You have code that produces an XML document, and the order in which the elements appear in the document changes the "value" the document represents. Consider, for example, a DocBook document: the order in which chapters, sections, and even paragraphs appear determines the meaning of the book. If you are marshalling a `List` of objects out to XML (see the introduction to this chapter for a discussion of XML marshalling) then you will want the corresponding XML elements to appear in the same order as they were stored in the `List` (otherwise, why is it a `List`?). If you have tried using `assertXMLEqual()` to compare documents with this sensitivity to order, then you may have seen XMLUnit treat certain unequal documents as equal, and this is not the behavior you want. You need XMLUnit to be stricter in its definition of equality.

◆ Recipe

To verify the order of elements in a document you may need to check whether the actual document is *identical* to the expected document, rather than *similar*. These are terms that XMLUnit defines by default, but allows you to redefine when you need to (see recipe 9.3). By default, documents are identical if their node structures are the same, elements appear in the same order, and corresponding elements have the same value. If you ignore white space (see the introduction to this chapter) then XML documents are identical if the only differences between them are white space.[4] If the elements are at the same level of the node's tree structure, but sibling elements *with different tag names* are in a different order, then the XML documents are not identical, but similar. (See the Discussion section for more on this.) You want to verify that documents are identical, whereas `assertXMLEqual()` only verifies whether they are similar.

Verifying whether documents are identical is a two-step process, compared to just using a customized assertion. First you "take a diff" of the XML documents, then

---

4 Specifically ignorable white space as XML defines the term. This includes spacing of elements, but not white space inside a text node's value. Node text "A B" is still different from "A   B".

make an assertion on that "diff." If you are familiar with CVS or the UNIX toolset, then you know what we mean by a "diff": the UNIX tool computes the differences between two text files, whereas XMLUnit's class `Diff` (`org.custommonkey.xmlunit.Diff`) computes the differences between two XML documents. To take a diff of two XML documents with XMLUnit, you create a `Diff` object from the respective documents, after which you can ask the `Diff`, "Are the documents similar? Are they identical?" Let us look at a simple example.

Consider a component that builds an article, suitable for publication on the web, from paragraphs, sections, and headings that you provide through a simple Java interface. You might use this `ArticleBuilder` as the model behind a specialized article editor that you want to write.[5] As you are writing tests for this class, you decide to add a paragraph and a heading to an article and verify the resulting XML document. Listing 9.3 shows the test using `assertXMLEqual()`.

Listing 9.3 Comparing documents with `assertXMLEqual()`

```
public class BuildArticleTest extends XMLTestCase {
    public void testMultipleParagraphs() throws Exception {
        XMLUnit.setIgnoreWhitespace(true);

        ArticleBuilder builder =
            new ArticleBuilder("Testing and XML");

        builder.addAuthorName("J. B. Rainsberger");
        builder.addHeading("A heading.");
        builder.addParagraph("This is a paragraph.");

        String expected =
            "<?xml version=\"1.0\" ?>"
                + "<article>"
                + "<title>Testing and XML</title>"
                + "<author>J. B. Rainsberger</author>"
                + "<p>This is a paragraph.</p>"
                + "<h1>A heading.</h1>"
                + "</article>";

        String actual = builder.toXml();
        assertXMLEqual(expected, actual);
    }
}
```

[5] Ron Jeffries explores building a specialized article editor in "Adventures in C#" (http://www.xprogramming.com/) as well as his book *Extreme Programming Adventures in C#* (Microsoft Press, 2004).

Here we have "accidentally" switched the heading and the paragraph in our expected XML document: the heading ought to come before the paragraph, not after it. No problem, we say: the tests will catch that problem—but this test passes! It passes because the expected and actual documents are similar, but not identical. In order to avoid this problem, we change the test as shown in listing 9.4 (the change is highlighted in bold print):

Listing 9.4 Testing for identical XML documents

```
public void testMultipleParagraphs() throws Exception {
    XMLUnit.setIgnoreWhitespace(true);

    ArticleBuilder builder =
        new ArticleBuilder("Testing and XML");

    builder.addAuthorName("J. B. Rainsberger");
    builder.addHeading("A heading.");
    builder.addParagraph("This is a paragraph.");

    String expected =
        "<?xml version=\"1.0\" ?>"
            + "<article>"
            + "<title>Testing and XML</title>"
            + "<author>J. B. Rainsberger</author>"
            + "<p>This is a paragraph.</p>"
            + "<h1>A heading.</h1>"
            + "</article>";

    String actual = builder.toXml();

    Diff diff = new Diff(expected, actual);
    assertTrue(
        "Builder output is not identical to expected document",
        diff.identical());
}
```

First we ask XMLUnit to give us an object representing the differences between the two XML documents, then we make an assertion on the `Diff`, expecting it to represent identical documents—specifically that the corresponding elements appear in the expected order. This test fails, as we would expect, alerting us to our mistake. So if we run the risk of this kind of problem, why does `assertXMLEqual()` behave the way it does? It turns out not to be a common problem in practice.

While looking for an example for this recipe, we asked programmers to show us examples of XML documents with a particular property. We wanted to see a document with sibling tags (having the same parent node) with different names, where changing the order of those elements changes the document's meaning. For the most part, they were unable to come up with a compelling example, which surprised us. Far from a proof, let us look at some reasons why.

Consider XML documents that represent books or articles. These documents have sections, chapters, paragraphs—structure that maps very well to XML. In an HTML page, paragraphs merely follow headings, but the paragraphs in a section really *belong* to that section. It makes more sense to represent a section of a document as its own XML element *containing* its paragraphs, as opposed to the way HTML does it. This is the approach that DocBook (http://www.docbook.org/) takes: a section element contains a title element followed by paragraph elements. The paragraph elements are siblings in the XML document tree, the order of the paragraphs matters, and the elements all have the same name. On the other hand, when we use XML documents to represent Java objects, we often render each attribute of the object as its own element. Those elements have *different* names, and most often the order in which those elements appear in the document does not affect the value of the object the document represents. So there appears to be a correlation here:

- If sibling elements have different names, then the order in which they appear likely does not matter.
- If the order in which sibling elements appear matters, then they likely have the same name.

Based on these simple observations, we can conclude that `assertXMLEqual()` behaves in a manner that works as you would expect, most of the time. It may not be immediately obvious, but we thought it was neat once we reasoned it through.

◆ Discussion

When you use `assertXMLEqual()`, XMLUnit ignores the order in which sibling elements with different tag names appear. This is common when marshalling a Java object to XML: we typically do not care whether the first name appears before or after the last name, so long as both appear in the resulting XML document. We emphasize "different tag names" because XMLUnit preserves (and checks) the order of sibling elements with the same tag name, even when checking documents for similarity. If you need to marshal a `Set`, rather than a `List`, to XML, then you will likely represent each element with its own tag and those tags will have the same name, such as `item`. When comparing an expected document with the actual marshalled one, you want to ignore the order of these `item` elements. In order to ignore this difference between the two documents, you need to customize XMLUnit's behavior, which we describe in recipe 9.3.

◆ ***Related***

- 9.3—Ignore certain differences in XML documents
- DocBook (http://www.docbook.org/)

9.2 *Ignore the order of elements in an XML document*

◆ ***Problem***

You want to verify an XML document and the order of certain XML elements within the document does not matter.

◆ ***Background***

In recipe 9.1, "Verify the order of elements in a document," we wrote about a correlation between the names of XML elements and whether it matters in which order the elements appear. We claimed that when there are many tags with the same name, the order in which they appear tends to be important. One exception to this rule that we have encountered is the web deployment descriptor. Servlet initialization parameters, request attributes, session attributes, and other parts of the servlet specification are all essentially `Maps` of data. In particular, a servlet's initialization parameters are stored in a `Map` whose keys are the names of the parameters (as `Strings`) and whose values are the values of those parameters (also as `Strings`). The web deployment descriptor—or `web.xml` as you may know it—represents servlet initialization parameters with the XML element `<init-param>`, which contains a `<param-name>` and a `<param-value>`. It treats the parameters as a `List` of name-value pairs, but those name-value pairs do not logically form a `List`; they form a `Set` instead. The order of the parameters in the deployment descriptor generally does not affect the meaning of those parameters.[6] Accordingly, when we test for the existence of and the correctness of a servlet's initialization parameters, we either have to pay attention to the order in which we specify the parameters in the deployment descriptor or change the test so that it does not take their order into account.

---

[6] If your servlet initialization code depends on the order in which the web container hands you those parameters, then you are in for a surprise one day. Consider yourself warned.

◆ *Recipe*

The most direct way to solve this problem, which we recommend, is to traverse the DOM (Document Object Model) tree for both XML documents. In general, if you are unconcerned about the order of a group of sibling elements with the same tag name, then they represent items in either a `Set` or a `Map`.[7] For that reason, we recommend you collect the data into a `Set` (or a `Map`) using the XPath API, then compare the resulting objects for equality in your test. XMLUnit does not do quite as much for us in this case as we would like, but no tool can be all things to all people. As an example, consider the servlet initialization parameters in a web deployment descriptor for a Struts application, although it could be for any kind of web application. We just chose Struts because we like it. Listing 9.5 shows such a sample:

Listing 9.5 A sample web deployment descriptor

```
<?xml version="1.0" encoding="ISO-8859-1"?>
<!DOCTYPE web-app
    PUBLIC "-//Sun Microsystems, Inc.//DTD Web Application 2.2//EN"
    "http://java.sun.com/j2ee/dtds/web-app_2_2.dtd">

<web-app>
    <display-name>Struts Taglib Exercises</display-name>

    <!-- Action Servlet Configuration -->
    <servlet>
        <servlet-name>action</servlet-name>
        <servlet-class>
            org.apache.struts.action.ActionServlet
        </servlet-class>
        <init-param>
            <param-name>application</param-name>
            <param-value>
                org.apache.struts.webapp.exercise.ApplicationResources
            </param-value>
        </init-param>
        <init-param>
            <param-name>config</param-name>
            <param-value>/WEB-INF/struts-config.xml</param-value>
        </init-param>
        <init-param>
            <param-name>debug</param-name>
            <param-value>2</param-value>
        </init-param>
        <init-param>
            <param-name>detail</param-name>
            <param-value>2</param-value>
```

7 We looked hard—honestly, we did—for a counterexample and could not find one.

```
        </init-param>
        <load-on-startup>2</load-on-startup>
    </servlet>

    <!-- Additional settings omitted for brevity -->
</web-app>
```

We want to focus on the elements in bold print, gather them into `Map` objects in memory, and then compare the corresponding `Map` objects for equality. This makes for rather a simple looking test:

```
public void testActionServletInitializationParameters()
    throws Exception {

    File expectedWebXmlFile =
        new File("test/data/struts/expected-web.xml");
    File actualWebXmlFile = new File("test/data/struts/web.xml");

    Document actualDocument = buildXmlDocument(actualWebXmlFile);
    Document expectedDocument =
        buildXmlDocument(expectedWebXmlFile);

    Map expectedParameters =
        getInitializationParametersAsMap(expectedDocument);

    Map actualParameters =
        getInitializationParametersAsMap(actualDocument);

    assertEquals(expectedParameters, actualParameters);
}
```

The good news is that the test itself is brief and to the point. In words, it says, "get the initialization parameters from the `expected` and `actual` documents and they ought to be equal." The bad news is that, as always, the devil is in the details. Rather than distract you from your reading, we have decided to move the complete solution—which is mostly XML parsing code—to solution A.3, "Ignore the order of elements in an XML document." There you can see how we implemented `getInitializationParametersAsMap()` and `buildXmlDocument()`, the latter of which uses a nice convenience method from XMLUnit.

NOTE *Network connectivity and the DTD*—Notice that the web deployment descriptor in listing 9.5 declares that it conforms to a remotely accessible DTD. XMLUnit tests will attempt to load the DTD from the remote location at runtime, requiring a network connection. If XMLUnit does not find the DTD online, it will throw an `UnknownHostException` with a message reading "Unable to load the DTD for this document," which does not clearly describe the real problem in context. One way to avoid this problem is to execute the tests on a machine that has access to the remote site providing the DTD. Perhaps better, though, is to make the DTD available locally by downloading and storing it on the test machine. Include the location of the local copy in the DTD declaration as follows in bold print:

```
<!DOCTYPE web-app
   PUBLIC "-//Sun Microsystems, Inc.//DTD Web Application 2.2//EN"
   "file:///C:/test/data/struts/web-app_2_2.dtd">
```

This also has the pleasant effect of avoiding the remote connection in the first place, increasing the execution speed of your tests. Of course, now your tests are slightly more brittle, as they depend on files on the local file system. We describe the trade-offs involved in placing test data on the file system in both chapter 5, "Managing Test Data," and chapter 17, "Odds and Ends."

◆ *Discussion*

When we first tried to write this deployment test, we compared the actual web deployment descriptor against a Gold Master we had previously created[8] (see recipe 10.2, "Verify your SQL commands," for a description of the Gold Master concept):

```
public void testStrutsWebDeploymentDescriptor()
    throws Exception {

    File expectedWebXmlFile =
        new File("test/data/struts/expected-web.xml");
    File actualWebXmlFile = new File("test/data/struts/web.xml");

    Document actualDocument = buildXmlDocument(actualWebXmlFile);
    Document expectedDocument =
        buildXmlDocument(expectedWebXmlFile);

    assertXMLEqual(expectedDocument, actualDocument);
}
```

We decided that it was simpler to just compare the entire document, so that is what we did. When we executed this test, all was well until we started generating the web deployment descriptor, rather than handcrafting it. The generator wrote the parameters to XML in a different order than when we wrote the document by hand. We were not concerned about the order of these tags, and when that order changed, our test failed *unnecessarily*. This is when we decided that we needed to change the test to do what this recipe recommends.

Next we tried solving this problem with an XMLUnit `DifferenceListener` (see recipe 9.3), but were not able to do it, at least not always. This is another place

[8] The Gold Master technique is only as good as the correctness of the master copy itself. Be careful! Make sure that the master is absolutely correct and is under strict change control.

where a human's interpretation of the document differs from the software's interpretation. The XMLUnit Diff engine sees four `<init-param>` tags in both the expected and actual documents and says, "Same names and the same number of them, so they are the same." It does not consider the nontext content of the `<init-param>` tags when comparing them to one another, so it does not notice (yet) that they are different. Only when the Diff engine proceeds to compare the `<param-name>` and `<param-value>` tags does it notice a difference, and by that point, it interprets the difference as "`<param-name>` nodes have different text," rather than the much more benign "`<init-param>` nodes are out of order." The former is a failure, but the latter is not, leading to a false negative result in our tests. We could not think of a way to *safely* ignore these differences, short of tracking all the values we have seen so far and comparing them against one another after the Diff engine has processed all the `<init-param>` nodes. That is just too much work. At that point, we thought we may as well just process the nodes in the first place, which is why we recommend the solution in this recipe.

This may not always be a problem, so try using `assertXMLEqual()` before embarking on writing all this extra code. This problem is caused by the document itself: the fact that the differences between the `<init-param>` nodes are found deeper in each node's subtree, and not right at the same level as the `<init-param>` nodes themselves. If, for example, the `<init-param>` nodes had ID attributes and those ID attributes were out of sequence, the Diff engine would have detected that and reported the difference as a *sequence* difference, which we could easily ignore. See recipe 9.3 for details on how to use the `DifferenceListener` feature to ignore those kinds of differences.

◆ Related

- 9.1—Verify the order of elements in a document
- 9.3—Ignore certain differences in XML documents
- A.3—Ignore the order of elements in an XML document (complete solution)

9.3 Ignore certain differences in XML documents

◆ Problem

You want to verify an XML document, but need to ignore certain superficial differences between the actual and expected documents.

◆ *Background*

We generally prefer comparing an expected value to an actual value in our tests, as opposed to decomposing some complex value into its parts and then checking each corresponding part individually. For this reason, we prefer to use `assertXMLEqual()` over individual XPath-based assertions in a test, but sometimes we run into a situation where we want to compare, say, 80% of the content of two XML documents and ignore the rest. We might need several dozen XPath-based assertions, when really all we want to do is to ignore what we might determine to be "superficial" differences between the two documents. We want to ignore a few values here and there, or the order of certain attributes, but compare the rest of the documents for similarity without resorting to a mountain of assertions.

In our Coffee Shop application there is an unpleasant dependency between our tests and the product catalog. Our choice of XSL transformation for the presentation layer prompts us to convert Java objects from the business logic layer into XML suitable for presentation. In particular, we need to convert the `ShopcartModel`, which represents the items in the current shopcart. When the user places a quantity of coffee in her shopcart, the system adds `CoffeeQuantity` objects to the `ShopcartModel`. When it comes time to display the shopcart, the system needs to display the total cost of the items in her shopcart, for which it must consult a `CoffeeBeanCatalog`. The catalog provides each coffee product's unit price from which the system computes the total cost. In summary, we need to convert a `ShopcartModel` into an XML document with prices in it, but in order to do this we need to prime the catalog with whatever coffee products we want to put in the test shopcart. That does not seem right. If we just ignored the prices, trusting that our business logic computes them correctly,[9] we could avoid the problem of having tests depend on a specific catalog.

◆ *Recipe*

The good news is that XMLUnit provides a way to ignore certain differences between XML documents. The even better news is that XMLUnit allows you to change the meaning of "different" from test to test. You can "listen" for differences as XMLUnit's engine reports them, ignoring the superficial differences that do not concern you *for the current test.* To achieve this you create a custom *difference listener*—that is, your own implementation of the interface `org.custommonkey.xmlunit.DifferenceListener`. To use your custom difference listener, you ask XMLUnit for the differences between the actual and expected XML documents,

---

[9] The business logic has comprehensive tests, after all.

then use your listener as a kind of filter, applying it to the list of differences between the documents in order to ignore the ones that do not concern you. We can solve our problem directly using a custom difference listener.

Looking at the `DifferenceConstants` interface of XMLUnit, we can see the way XMLUnit categorizes differences between XML documents. One type of difference is a *text value difference* (represented in `DifferenceConstants` as the constant `TEXT_VALUE`)— that is, the text is different for a given XML tag. We can therefore look for differences of this type, examine the name of the tag, and ignore the difference if the tag name is `unit-price`, `total-price` or `subtotal`. Another type of difference is `ATTR_VALUE`—that is, the values are different for a given tag attribute. We can look for differences of this type, examine the name of the attribute and the element that owns it, and ignore the difference if both the element name is `item` and the attribute name is `id`. (Product IDs depend on the catalog, too.) We now have enough information to write our `IgnoreCatalogDetailsDifferenceListener`. We warn you: the DOM API is rather verbose, so if you are not accustomed to it, read slowly and carefully. First, let us look at the methods we have to implement from the interface `DifferenceListener`, shown here in listing 9.6:

Listing 9.6 An implementation of `DifferenceListener`

```
public class IgnoreCatalogDetailsDifferenceListener
    implements DifferenceListener {

    public int differenceFound(Difference difference) {
        int response = RETURN_ACCEPT_DIFFERENCE;

        int differenceId = difference.getId();
        if (DifferenceConstants.TEXT_VALUE_ID
            == differenceId) {

            String currentTagName =
                getCurrentTagName(difference);

            if (tagNamesToIgnore.contains(currentTagName)) {
                response =
                    RETURN_IGNORE_DIFFERENCE_NODES_SIMILAR;
            }
        }
        else if (DifferenceConstants.ATTR_VALUE_ID
            == differenceId) {

            Attr attribute = getCurrentAttribute(difference);

            if ("id".equals(attribute.getName())
                && "item".equals(
                    attribute
                        .getOwnerElement()
                        .getNodeName())) {
```

```
                response =
                    RETURN_IGNORE_DIFFERENCE_NODES_SIMILAR;
            }
        }

        return response;
    }

    public void skippedComparison(
        Node expectedNode,
        Node actualNode) {

        // Nothing to do here
    }
}
```

XMLUnit invokes `differenceFound()` for each difference it finds between the two XML documents you compare. As a parameter to `differenceFound()`, XMLUnit passes a `Difference` object, providing access to a description of the difference and the DOM `Node` objects in each document so that you can explore them further. Our implementation looks for the two kinds of differences we wish to ignore: text value differences and attribute value differences.

When our difference listener finds a text value difference, it retrieves the name of the tag containing the text, and then compares it to a set of "tags to ignore." If the current tag name is one to ignore, then we respond to XMLUnit with "Ignore this difference when comparing for similarity." (There is another constant we can return to say, "Ignore this difference when comparing for identity.") We declared the `Set` of tag names to be ignored as a class-level constant.[10]

```
public class IgnoreCatalogDetailsDifferenceListener
    implements DifferenceListener {

    // Remaining code omitted

    private static final Set tagNamesToIgnore = new HashSet() {
        {
            add("unit-price");
            add("total-price");
            add("subtotal");
        }
    };
}
```

[10] The coding technique here is to create an anonymous subclass with an instance initializer. It sounds complicated, but the benefit is clear, concise code: one statement rather than four. It looks a little like Smalltalk. See Paul Holser's article on the subject (http://home.comcast.net/~pholser/writings/concisions.html).

We also provided a convenience method to retrieve the name of the "current tag"—the tag to which the current `Difference` corresponds. The method `getTagName()` handles `Text` nodes differently: because a `Text` node does not have its own name, we are interested in the name of its parent node:

```
public class IgnoreCatalogDetailsDifferenceListener
    implements DifferenceListener {

    // Remaining code omitted

    public String getCurrentTagName(Difference difference) {
        Node currentNode =
            difference.getControlNodeDetail().getNode();

        return getTagName(currentNode);
    }

    public String getTagName(Node currentNode) {
        if (currentNode instanceof Text)
            return currentNode.getParentNode().getNodeName();
        else
            return currentNode.getNodeName();
    }
}
```

When our difference listener finds an attribute value difference, it retrieves the current attribute name and the name of the tag that owns it, compares it against the one it wants to ignore, and if there is a match, the difference listener ignores it. Here is the convenience method for retrieving the current attribute name:

```
public class IgnoreCatalogDetailsDifferenceListener
    implements DifferenceListener {

    // ...

    public Attr getCurrentAttribute(Difference difference) {
        return (Attr)
            difference.getControlNodeDetail().getNode();
    }
}
```

If `differenceFound()` does not find any differences to ignore, then it responds "accept this difference," meaning that XMLUnit should count it as a *genuine* difference rather than a *superficial* one. If there remain genuine differences after the superficial ones are ignored, then XMLUnit treats the documents as dissimilar and `assertXMLEqual()` fails. Listing 9.7 shows an example of how we used this difference listener (the lines of code for the difference listener are in bold print):

Listing 9.7 Using the `DifferenceListener`

```
package junit.cookbook.coffee.model.xml.test;

import java.util.Arrays;
import junit.cookbook.coffee.display.*;
import junit.cookbook.coffee.model.*;
import org.custommonkey.xmlunit.*;
import com.diasparsoftware.java.util.Money;

public class MarshalShopcartTest extends XMLTestCase {
    private CoffeeCatalog catalog;

    protected void setUp() throws Exception {
        XMLUnit.setIgnoreWhitespace(true);
        catalog = new CoffeeCatalog() {
            public String getProductId(String coffeeName) {
                return "001";
            }

            public Money getUnitPrice(String coffeeName) {
                return Money.ZERO;
            }
        };
    }

    public void testOneItemIgnoreCatalogDetails() throws Exception {
        String expectedXml =
            "<?xml version='1.0' ?>\n"
                + "<shopcart>\n"
                + "<item id=\"762\">"
                + "<name>Sumatra</name>"
                + "<quantity>2</quantity>"
                + "<unit-price>$7.50</unit-price>"
                + "<total-price>$15.00</total-price>"
                + "</item>\n"
                + "<subtotal>$15.00</subtotal>\n"
                + "</shopcart>\n";

        ShopcartModel shopcart = new ShopcartModel();
        shopcart.addCoffeeQuantities(
            Arrays.asList(
                new Object[] { new CoffeeQuantity(2, "Sumatra")}));

        String shopcartAsXml =
            ShopcartBean.create(shopcart, catalog).asXml();

        Diff diff = new Diff(expectedXml, shopcartAsXml);

        diff.overrideDifferenceListener(
            new IgnoreCatalogDetailsDifferenceListener());

        assertTrue(diff.toString(), diff.similar());
    }
}
```

In the method `setUp()` we faked out the catalog so that we would not have to prime it with data. Every product costs $0 and has ID `001`.

If the documents are not similar, in spite of ignoring all these differences, then the failure message lists the remaining differences. You can then decide whether to change the difference listener to ignore the extra differences or to fix the actual XML document.

◆ *Discussion*

An alternative to this approach is to build a custom Document Object Model from the XML documents, an approach we describe in recipe 9.2, "Ignore the order of elements in an XML document," by loading servlet initialization parameters into a `Map`.[11] It is then easy to compare an expected web deployment descriptor document object against the actual one, because the `Map` compares the servlet entries the way you would expect: ignoring the order in which they appear. We think that this approach is simpler; however, if you doubt us, then as always, try them both and measure the difference.

Remember the two essential approaches to verifying XML documents: using XPath to verify parts of the actual document, or creating an entire expected document and comparing it to the actual document. When working with Plain Old Java Objects, we will generally go out of our way to use the latter approach by building the appropriate `equals()` methods we need. Our experience tells us to expect a high return on investment in terms of making it easier to write future tests. With XML documents the trade-off is less clear.

Building a complex difference listener can take a considerable amount of work, which mostly comes from the difficulty in figuring out exactly which differences to ignore and which to retain. This is not a criticism of XMLUnit, but the way its authors have categorized differences may not map cleanly onto your mental model of the differences between two documents. This complexity is inherent to the problem of describing the difference between two structured text files.[12] From time to time, depending on the complexity of what "similar" and "identical" XML documents mean in your domain, you may find yourself spending an hour trying to build the correct difference listener. If this happens, we recommend you stop, abandon the effort, and go back to using the XPath-based assertions. We also strongly recommend sticking with XPath-based assertions if you find yourself wanting to ignore 80% of the actual document and wanting to check "just this part

---

[11] You do not need to build a custom DOM for the entire document, just the parts you care about.

[12] How many times has your version control system reported the difference between your version of a Java source file and the repository's version "in a strange way?" That is the nature of the problem.

here." It may be more work to describe the parts of the document to ignore than simply to write assertions for the part you want to examine. In that case, you can combine the approaches: use XPath to extract the document fragment that interests you, then compare it with the fragment you expect using `assertXMLEqual()`.

◆ Related

- 9.2—Ignore the order of elements in an XML document

9.4 Get a more detailed failure message from XMLUnit

◆ Problem

You want a more detailed failure message from XMLUnit when documents are different.

◆ Background

The XMLUnit Diff engine stops reporting differences after it finds the first difference, just as JUnit stops reporting failed assertions once the first assertion fails in a test. Although this is consistent with JUnit's core philosophy, it limits the amount of information available to diagnose the causes of the defects in your code. It would certainly be helpful if you had more information from XMLUnit about the differences between the document you have and the one you expect.

◆ Recipe

We recommend placing *all the differences* between the expected and actual XML documents in the failure message of your XMLUnit assertions. To do that, create a `DetailedDiff` object from the original `Diff` then include it in your failure message. Here is an example (our use of `DetailedDiff` is in bold print):

```
public void testMultipleParagraphs() throws Exception {
    XMLUnit.setIgnoreWhitespace(true);

    ArticleBuilder builder =
        new ArticleBuilder("Testing and XML");

    builder.addAuthorName("J. B. Rainsberger");
    builder.addHeading("A heading.");
    builder.addParagraph("This is a paragraph.");

    String expected =
        "<?xml version=\"1.0\" ?>"
            + "<article>"
```

```
            + "<title>Testing and XML</title>"
            + "<author>J. B. Rainsberger</author>"
            + "<p>This is a paragraph.</p>"
            + "<h1>A heading.</h1>"
            + "</article>";

    String actual = builder.toXml();

    Diff diff = new Diff(expected, actual);
    assertTrue(new DetailedDiff(diff).toString(), diff.identical());
}
```

This DetailedDiff lists all the differences between the two documents, rather than just the first difference. In this case, the paragraph and heading elements are mixed up in the test, although we do not realize that right now. (Sometimes we make a mistake when writing a test.) Here is the information that XMLUnit gives us when this assertion fails:

```
[not identical] Expected sequence of child nodes '2' but was '3'
⇒ - comparing <p...> at /article[1]/p[1] to <p...> at /article[1]/p[1]

[not identical] Expected sequence of child nodes '3' but was '2'
⇒ - comparing <h1...> at /article[1]/h1[1] to <h1...> at /article[1]/h1[1]
```

This tells us that the test expects the <p> tag to appear in position 2 and the <h1> tag to appear in position 3, relative to the <article> tag that contains them both. That does not make sense! The heading ought to come before the paragraph! This is the detailed information we need to see that this time it is the test, and not the production code, that needs fixing. Once we reverse the order of the lines in the expected XML document, the test passes:

```
public void testMultipleParagraphs() throws Exception {
    XMLUnit.setIgnoreWhitespace(true);

    ArticleBuilder builder =
        new ArticleBuilder("Testing and XML");

    builder.addAuthorName("J. B. Rainsberger");
    builder.addHeading("A heading.");
    builder.addParagraph("This is a paragraph.");

    String expected =
        "<?xml version=\"1.0\" ?>"
            + "<article>"
            + "<title>Testing and XML</title>"
            + "<author>J. B. Rainsberger</author>"
            + "<h1>A heading.</h1>"
            + "<p>This is a paragraph.</p>"
            + "</article>";
```

```
        String actual = builder.toXml();

        Diff diff = new Diff(expected, actual);
        assertTrue(new DetailedDiff(diff).toString(), diff.identical());
    }
```

That's much better.

◆ *Discussion*

We recommend building a custom assertion (see recipe 17.4, "Extract a custom assertion") called `assertXMLIdentical(String expected, String actual)` with this specialized failure message. We are a little surprised that no one has added it to XMLUnit yet—or perhaps by now they have! That is the essence of open source: if the product is missing something you need, add it yourself, then later submit it for inclusion into the product. You do not need to be stuck with code that falls short of what you need, even if only a little bit. Of course, XMLUnit is an excellent library and we are not out to criticize it, but all software needs improvement.

◆ *Related*

- 17.4—Extract a custom assertion

9.5 Test the content of a static web page

◆ *Problem*

You want to test the content of a web page, but your web pages are not written in XHTML, so they are not valid XML documents.

◆ *Background*

We love XHTML, but it has one fatal flaw: no web browser on the planet enforces it. Browsers are *very* lenient when it comes to HTML, which is why very few people—programmers, web designers, hobbyists—are motivated to write their web pages in XHTML. It is more work for them to do it and, unless they need to parse their web pages as XML, they benefit nothing from the effort. If web design tools were to create XHTML by default (and some at least give you the option to do so) then the story might be different, but as it stands, very few people write XHTML. As a result, unless *you* write every part of every web page you need to test, *you* will have to work a little harder to use the testing techniques we have introduced in this chapter. The alternative is to use another tool to help turn loosely written HTML into well-formed XML.

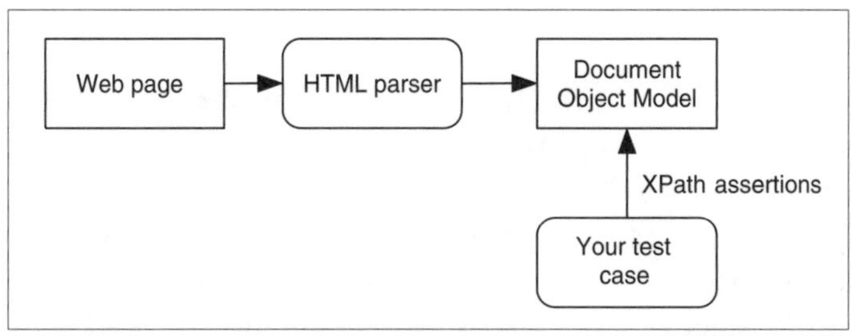

Figure 9.1
Testing a web page by converting it to XML

This recipe works best for verifying static web pages. If you want to verify the content of a dynamically generated web page, see chapter 12, "Testing Web Components," and chapter 13, "Testing J2EE Applications." The former discusses testing web page templates in isolation and the latter describes how to test generated web pages by simulating a web browser. HtmlUnit, the tool of choice for so-called "black box" web application testing, uses the techniques in this recipe to provide a rich set of custom assertions for verifying web page content. This recipe explains some of the machinery behind HtmlUnit, in case you wish to, or need to, get along with HtmlUnit.

There are HTML parsers that you can use to convert HTML documents into equivalent, well-formed XML. These parsers present web pages as DOM trees which you can inspect and manipulate as needed. The two most well-known parsers are Tidy (http://tidy.sourceforge.net/) and NekoHTML (http://www.apache.org/~andyc/neko/doc/html/). Although one can generally use either parser, we favor NekoHTML, as it handles a wider range of badly formed HTML. The general strategy is to load your web page into the HTML parser, which then creates a DOM representation of the page (see figure 9.1). You can then apply the techniques in the preceding recipes to analyze the DOM and verify the parts of it you need to verify. We will use this technique to verify the welcome page for our Coffee Shop application.

Following is the web page we would like to verify. As you can see, it is not quite XHTML compliant: the `link` and `input` start tags do not have corresponding end tags and there is text content without a surrounding paragraph tag.

```
<html>
<head>
<link href="theme/Master.css" rel="stylesheet" type="text/css">
<title>Welcome!</title>
</head>
<body>
<form name="launchPoints" action="coffee" method="post">
Browse our <input type="submit" name="browseCatalog" value="catalog">.
</form>
```

```
</body>
</html>
```

The test we would like to write verifies that there is a way to navigate from this welcome page to our product catalog. We are looking for a `form` whose `action` goes through our `CoffeeShopController` servlet and has a `submit` button named `browseCatalog`. If those elements are present, then the user will be able to reach our catalog from this page. In our test we need to configure the NekoHTML parser, parse the web page, retrieve the DOM object, and use XMLUnit to make assertions about the content of the resulting XML document. Listing 9.8 shows the test we need to write:

Listing 9.8 WelcomePageTest

```
package junit.cookbook.coffee.web.test;

import java.io.FileInputStream;

import org.custommonkey.xmlunit.XMLTestCase;
import org.apache.xerces.parsers.DOMParser;
import org.cyberneko.html.HTMLConfiguration;
import org.w3c.dom.Document;
import org.xml.sax.InputSource;

public class WelcomePageTest extends XMLTestCase {
    private Document welcomePageDom;

    protected void setUp() throws Exception {
        DOMParser nekoParser =
            new DOMParser(new HTMLConfiguration());

        nekoParser.setFeature(
            "http://cyberneko.org/html/features/augmentations",
            true);

        nekoParser.setProperty(
            "http://cyberneko.org/html/properties/names/elems",
            "lower");

        nekoParser.setProperty(
            "http://cyberneko.org/html/properties/names/attrs",
            "lower");

        nekoParser.setFeature(
            "http://cyberneko.org/html/features/report-errors",
            true);

        nekoParser.parse(
            new InputSource(
                new FileInputStream(
                    "../CoffeeShopWeb/Web Content/index.html")));
```

```
        welcomePageDom = nekoParser.getDocument();
        assertNotNull("Could not load DOM", welcomePageDom);
    }

    public void testCanNavigateToCatalog() throws Exception {
        assertXpathExists(
            "//form[@action='coffee']"
                + "//input[@type='submit' and @name='browseCatalog']",
            welcomePageDom);
    }
}
```

The test itself is very simple: it uses a single XPath statement to look for a form with the expected action that also contains the expected submit button. Our web application maps the URI `coffee` to the servlet `CoffeeShopController`, which explains why we compare the form's action URI to `coffee`. We could have written separate assertions to verify that the expected form exists, that it has the expected action URI, that it contains a submit button, and that it contains the expected submit button, as shown here:

```
public void testCanNavigateToCatalog() throws Exception {
    assertXpathExists("//form", welcomePageDom);

    assertXpathEvaluatesTo(
        "coffee",
        "//form/@action",
        welcomePageDom);

    assertXpathExists(
        "//form[@action='coffee']//input[@type='submit']",
        welcomePageDom);

    assertXpathEvaluatesTo(
        "browseCatalog",
        "//form[@action='coffee']"
            + "//input[@type='submit']/@name",
        welcomePageDom);
}
```

There are a few differences with this more verbose test. First, because each assertion verifies only one thing, it is easier to determine the problem from a failure. If the second assertion fails, you can be sure of one of two causes: there is more than one form in the web page *or* the first form on the page has the wrong action. Next, these assertions are more precise: if there are other forms on the page or other buttons in the form, these assertions may fail. Whether this last difference is a benefit or excessive coupling depends on your perspective. We generally prefer to make the weakest assertion that can possibly verify that we have done something right, rather than make the strongest assertion that can possibly eliminate everything we have done wrong. The latter kind of assertion tends to make tests overly brittle.

We should mention the way we have configured NekoHTML for this test. We highlighted in bold print the classes that we imported, because we are not actually using the NekoHTML parser, but rather a Xerces DOM parser with NekoHTML's HTML DOM configuration. This allows us to assume in our tests that all tag names and attribute names are lowercase (the XML standard) even though the web page may not be written that way. This configuration minimizes the disruption that web-authoring tools may introduce into a web design environment. Many tools automatically "fix up" web pages, making them conform to whatever conventions the tool uses when it generates HTML in WYSIWYG mode. These include trying to balance some tags, converting all tag names to uppercase, converting all attribute names to lowercase, and so on. You want your tests to be able to withstand these kinds of changes. We therefore use the NekoHTML `HTMLConfiguration` object to create a Xerces `DOMParser`, which allows us to set various NekoHTML-supported features and properties on the parser, including "convert all tag names to lowercase" and "convert all attribute names to lowercase." We recommend that you consult the NekoHTML documentation for a complete discussion of the available features and properties.

◆ *Discussion*

There are some important configuration notes about NekoHTML, which its web site discusses in detail. First, be sure to put `nekohtml.jar` on your runtime class path *before* your XML parser. Next, you only need `nekohtml.jar`, and not the XNI version of the parser. The most important item, however, has to do with how your web pages are written: specifically, whether the HTML tag names are uppercase or lowercase. It is very important to get this setting right, otherwise none of your XPath-based assertions will work. It is standard practice in HTML for tag names to be uppercase and attribute names to be lowercase, such as in this HTML page:

```
<HTML>
<HEAD>
<LINK href="theme/Master.css" rel="stylesheet" type="text/css">
<TITLE>Welcome!</TITLE>
</HEAD>
<BODY>
<FORM name="launchPoints" action="coffee" method="post">
Browse our <INPUT type="submit" name="browseCatalog" value="catalog">.
</FORM>
</BODY>
</HTML>
```

By default, NekoHTML is configured to expect web pages written this way; so if you write an XPath-based assertion that expects the tag `input`, the assertion fails, because the tag name is `INPUT`. The `DOMParser` object you want for your tests depends on how the web pages have been written. If they follow the HTML DOM standard of uppercase tag names and lowercase attribute names, then simply use Neko's parser with the default `HTMLConfiguration` settings. (No need to set any features.) This means that your XPath-based assertions must use uppercase for tag names and lowercase for attribute names. Listing 9.9 demonstrates:

Listing 9.9 How *not* to use `HTMLConfiguration` for NekoHTML

```
package junit.cookbook.coffee.web.test;

import org.custommonkey.xmlunit.XMLTestCase;
import org.cyberneko.html.parsers.DOMParser;
import org.w3c.dom.Document;

public class WelcomePageTest extends XMLTestCase {
    private Document welcomePageDom;

    protected void setUp() throws Exception {
        DOMParser nekoParser = new DOMParser(new HTMLConfiguration());

        nekoParser.parse(
            new InputSource(
                new FileInputStream(
                    "../CoffeeShopWeb/Web Content/"
                        + "index-DOMStandard.html")));

        welcomePageDom = nekoParser.getDocument();
        assertNotNull("Could not load DOM", welcomePageDom);
    }

    // Tests must expect tag names in UPPERCASE
    // and attribute names in lowercase to work
    // with this configuration of NekoHTML
}
```

It is important to note that if you instantiate the NekoHTML parser this way *you will not be able to set the various DOM parser features or properties.* The NekoHTML site (http://www.apache.org/~andyc/neko/doc/html/) says more about this, so if you need to know more, we suggest visiting the site. The good news is that NekoHTML provides you with a sensible default behavior (matching the HTML DOM standard), and it gives you the control you need to change that behavior when needed. If you want to use NekoHTML to verify that your web pages comply with the XHTML standard, then follow these steps:

1. Create the DOM Parser with the NekoHTML configuration, as we did in this recipe.
2. Change the property configurations for `names/elems` and `names/attrs` to `match`, rather than `lower`.
3. Write your tests to expect all tag names and attribute names to be lowercase.

If you configure your parser this way, then your XPath-based assertions will only pass if the web pages themselves have lowercase tag names and attribute names, per the XHTML standard.

As we were writing this, Tidy is not supported on Windows, although you *can* obtain unsupported binaries and try it out yourself. If you would like to use Tidy outside Java—after all, it is a useful tool on its own—then you need to explore the Tidy web site to examine your options. In spite of its unsupported status, there is a thriving user community around Tidy, so if you have questions, we are confident you can find the help you need. You may simply have to be a bit more patient. Also be aware that as of this writing JTidy had not released new code since August 2001, so you may be better off choosing NekoHTML. That said, please consult NekoHTML's site for its own limitations and problems, one of the most important being *you cannot use Xerces-J 2.0.1 as your XML parser.* At press time, the latest version of NekoHTML does not work with this particular version of the popular XML parser.

NOTE *JTidy is alive!*—Just before we went to press a reviewer brought to our attention that there is activity on the JTidy project. For their development releases—the first ones in about 18 months—the JTidy folks are concentrating on adding tests, which is always a good sign. So far, they have managed to get 63 of their 185 tests to pass. Naturally, we support their efforts and look forward to improved versions of JTidy in the future!

We hope that XHTML grows in popularity, because it is much easier to test web pages written in XHTML than web pages written in straight HTML. However, we are not holding our breath, because what is truly important to users is whether their browser can render a web page. Those browsers are *very* forgiving, and as long as they can process horrendous examples of HTML then we will need solutions such as Tidy or NekoHTML. We suspect that nothing will change until browsers simply stop rendering HTML in favor of XML with cascading stylesheets. Once again, we are not holding our breath.

- ***Related***
  - 9.1—Verify the order of elements in a document
  - 9.2—Ignore the order of elements in an XML document
  - 9.3—Ignore certain differences in XML documents
  - NekoHTML (http://www.apache.org/~andyc/neko/doc/html/)
  - JTidy (http://sourceforge.net/projects/jtidy)
  - Chapter 12—Testing Web Components
  - Chapter 13—Testing J2EE Applications

9.6 Test an XSL stylesheet in isolation

- ***Problem***

You want to verify an XSL stylesheet outside the context of the application that uses it.

- ***Background***

Despite the proliferation of JSPs in the J2EE community, it is not the only way to build a web application's presentation layer. One strong alternative is XSL transformation, which takes data in XML format and presents it as HTML to the end user. We have worked on projects that used this technology and we find that it has one great benefit over JSPs: XSL transformation does not require an application server. We like this a great deal, because it means we can test such a presentation layer entirely outside any kind of J2EE container. All we need are parsers and transformers, such as Xerces and Xalan (http://xml.apache.org/).

If you are working on such a project, you may feel tempted not to test your XSL stylesheets in isolation. You reason, as we have reasoned in the past, "We will test the XSL stylesheets when we test the application end to end." You want to avoid duplicating efforts, which is a laudable goal, so you decide not to treat your XSL stylesheets as independent units worthy of their own tests. Or, you may simply not know how to do it![13] We can tell you from direct, painful, personal experience that this is an error in judgment. Transforming XML is a nontrivial operation fraught with errors. If you need convincing, look at the size of Michael Kay's excellent reference work *XSLT: Programmer's Reference*—it's slightly more than 1,000 pages. That tells us that XSL transformations are complex enough to break, and

[13] That was *our* excuse. Get your own.

when they *do* break, you will be glad to have isolated tests that you can execute to help you determine the cause of the defect. We strongly recommend testing XSL stylesheets in isolation, and this recipe describes two approaches.

◆ Recipe

Testing an XSL stylesheet is about verifying that your templates do what you think they do. The general approach consists of transforming a representative set of XML documents and verifying the result, so the techniques we use here are the XML comparison techniques used in the rest of this chapter. We hard code simple XML documents in our tests—usually as `Strings`—then apply the XSL transformation and make assertions about the resulting XML document. As with any other XML document tests, XMLUnit provides two main strategies for verifying content: XPath-based assertions on parts of the actual document, or comparing an expected document against the actual document. Fortunately, XMLUnit provides some convenience methods to help us do either. To illustrate this technique, we return to our Coffee Shop application and test the XSL stylesheet that displays the content of a shopper's shopcart.

The structure of the "shopcart" document is a simple one: a shopcart contains items and a subtotal. Each shopcart item describes its own details: the coffee name, quantity, unit price, and total price. Listing 9.10 shows a sample XML document showing three items in the shopcart:

Listing 9.10 A shopcart as an XML document

```
<?xml version="1.0" encoding="UTF-8"?>

<shopcart>
    <item id="762">
        <name>Special Blend</name>
        <quantity>1</quantity>
        <unit-price>$7.25</unit-price>
        <total-price>$7.25</total-price>
    </item>
    <item id="903">
        <name>Huehuetenango</name>
        <quantity>2</quantity>
        <unit-price>$6.50</unit-price>
        <total-price>$13.00</total-price>
    </item>
    <item id="001">
        <name>Colombiano</name>
        <quantity>3</quantity>
        <unit-price>$8.00</unit-price>
        <total-price>$24.00</total-price>
```

```
    </item>
    <subtotal>$44.25</subtotal>
</shopcart>
```

NOTE *Effective application design with XSLT*—You may notice that the data in this document is preformatted—the currency values are formatted as such—and that there is derived data that we could have calculated on demand. We recommend delivering data to the presentation layer already formatted and fully calculated. The presentation layer ought not do anything other than decide how to present data; calculations are business logic and formatting currency is application logic. The more we separate responsibilities in this way, the easier it is to write isolated tests.

Now to our first test. We need to verify that our stylesheet correctly renders an empty shopcart. Before we provide the code for this test, we ought to mention that these tests verify *content*, and are not meant to examine the look-and-feel of the resulting web page. In general, nothing is as effective as visual inspection for ensuring that a web page looks the way it should.[14] Moreover, if our tests depend too much on the layout of web pages, then they become overly sensitive to purely cosmetic changes. We are wary of anything that unnecessarily discourages us from changing code. Listing 9.11 shows the test, which expects to see an HTML table for the shopcart, no rows representing shopcart items, and a $0.00 subtotal.

Listing 9.11 DisplayShopcartXslTest

```
package junit.cookbook.coffee.presentation.xsl.test;

import java.io.*;
import javax.xml.transform.*;
import javax.xml.transform.stream.StreamSource;
import org.custommonkey.xmlunit.XMLTestCase;
import org.custommonkey.xmlunit.Transform;
import org.w3c.dom.Document;

public class DisplayShopcartXslTest extends XMLTestCase {
    private String displayShopcartXslFilename =
        "../CoffeeShopWeb/Web Content/WEB-INF/template"
            + "/style/displayShopcart.xsl";

    private Source displayShopcartXsl;
```

[14] Sure, there are automated ways to verify some aspects of a window's layout, but in our experience, the return on investment is low compared to spending the time to just look at the page.

```
    protected void setUp() throws Exception {
        displayShopcartXsl =
            new StreamSource(
                new FileInputStream(displayShopcartXslFilename));
    }

    public void testEmpty() throws Exception {
        String shopcartXmlAsString =
            "<?xml version=\"1.0\" ?>"
                + "<shopcart>"
                + "<subtotal>$0.00</subtotal>"
                + "</shopcart>";

        Document displayShopcartDom =
            doDisplayShopcartTransformation(shopcartXmlAsString);

        assertXpathExists(
            "//table[@name='shopcart']",
            displayShopcartDom);

        assertXpathEvaluatesTo(
            "$0.00",
            "//table[@name='shopcart']//td[@id='subtotal']",
            displayShopcartDom);

        assertXpathNotExists(
            "//tr[@class='shopcartItem']",
            displayShopcartDom);
    }

    public Document doDisplayShopcartTransformation(
        String shopcartXmlAsString)
        throws
            TransformerConfigurationException,
            TransformerException {

        Source shopcartXml =
            new StreamSource(
                new StringReader(shopcartXmlAsString));

        Transform transform =
            new Transform(shopcartXml, displayShopcartXsl);

        return transform.getResultDocument();
    }
}
```

The method `doDisplayShopcartTransformation()` performs the transformation we need to test. It uses the XMLUnit class `Transform` to simplify applying the transformation and to retrieve the resulting document.

The test builds an empty shopcart XML document as a `String`, applies the transformation, then makes XPath-based assertions on the resulting document. In particular, it expects the following things:

- A `table` representing the shopcart, which the test finds by examining its name.
- A table data cell (`td`) inside the `table` containing the shopcart subtotal amount, which the test finds by examining its ID.
- No table rows (`tr`) inside the `table` using the stylesheet class `shopcartItem`, which is how the test detects the existence of shopcart items on the page.

NOTE *Identifying the interesting parts of a web page*—You may have noticed that we use IDs, names, and other identifying text to help the test find the specific part of the web page it needs to verify. Labeling the various "interesting" parts of a web page is a core web-testing technique. Without it, tests would need to verify content by examining the relative positioning of HTML tags on the page. This kind of *physical* coupling makes tests sensitive to layout changes, which makes testing more expensive. Instead, we add a small amount of *logical* coupling by identifying the parts of the web page on which the tests need to do their work. At worst, someone changing the web page needs to make sure that these identifiers continue to identify the same information on the page. This requires some extra attention on the part of the web designer, but is more than worth the effort.

Because XSL stylesheets are generally quite long, we prefer not to distract you by showing the one we use to display the shopcart in its entirety. Refer to solution A.4, "Test an XSL stylesheet in isolation" to see a more complete suite of tests and an XSL stylesheet that makes them pass. As we add more tests, we will begin to repeat some of our XPath-based assertions. We recommend that you be aware of the duplication and extract custom assertions for the ones you use most often. See recipe 17.4, "Extract a custom assertion," for an example of this technique.

◆ *Discussion*

We mentioned an alternative technique, which involves comparing an expected web page against the actual web page that the transformer creates. These tests are easier to write, but can become difficult to maintain, as purely cosmetic changes to the presentation layer require you to update the expected web pages. The tests generally consist of extracting data from a web page, building objects that represent that data, then using `assertEquals()` to compare the expected data against the actual data. Because this amounts to parsing a web page, any change in its layout is likely to affect the parsing code. It is essential that you extract this parsing code to a single place in your class hierarchy, as it is likely to change. Over time, if you refactor the XPath-based assertions mercilessly, you will find yourself building a small library of XPath queries that handle HTML elements such as tables, forms, and paragraphs. If you continue in this direction, you will eventually build another version of HtmlUnit, so once you recognize that you are heading in that direction, we recommend you simply start using HtmlUnit. See chapter 13, "Testing J2EE Applications," for recipes involving this web application-testing package.

In the process of preparing the complete solution for this recipe, we ran into a nasty problem: our XML document was too long to be all on one line. Because we built the XML document as a `String`, we did not pay attention to line breaks, as we would if we were writing a text file. At some point, some component the test uses (maybe XMLUnit, maybe the transformer; we did not bother to find out) began to truncate data. It turns out that we could solve the problem by adding line breaks to the XML document in our test. Very annoying. The good news is this: it might have taken hours and hours to narrow down the problem without all these tests. As it was, it still took over 15 minutes, but at least we found and solved the problem relatively quickly.

◆ *Related*

- Chapter 13—Testing J2EE Applications
- 17.4—Extract a custom assertion
- A.4—Test an XSL stylesheet in isolation (complete solution)

9.7 Validate XML documents in your tests

◆ *Problem*

You want your tests to validate the XML documents your application uses.

◆ *Background*

Most of you began wanting to validate XML documents after being bitten by recurring defects related to invalid XML input to some part of your system. Some teams, for example, validate their Struts configuration file (`struts-config.xml`) in order to avoid discovering configuration errors at runtime. For some configuration errors, the only recovery step is to fix the configuration error and *restart the application server.* During development and testing, restarting the application server is a time-consuming annoyance, and during production it may not be possible until a predetermined time of day, week, or month! If you are in this position yourself, then you can appreciate the desire to prevent these configuration errors before they have the opportunity to adversely affect the system.

◆ *Recipe*

You can either add validation to your JUnit tests or perform validation somewhere else. As this is a book about JUnit, we will describe the second strategy briefly and focus on the first. There are two broad classes of XML documents that you may be using in your application: configuration documents and data transfer documents. We recommend that you validate configuration documents as part of your build process. We also recommend that you validate data transfer documents in your tests, so that you can safely disable validation during production. Let us explain what we mean by each of these recommendations.

A configuration document is generally a file on disk that your system uses to configure itself. The Struts web application framework's `struts-config.xml` is an example of a configuration document. You edit this document to change, for example, the navigation rules of your application, then Struts uses this document to implement those navigation rules. A configuration document typically changes outside the context of your system's runtime environment—that is, the system does not create configuration documents, but merely uses them. It is wise to validate configuration documents against a Document Type Definition (DTD) or XML schema, if one is available, as this helps you avoid discovering badly formed or syntactically incorrect configuration files before your system attempts to use them. For example, if you build and test a Struts-based application using Ant, add a target such as this to your Ant buildfile:

```
<target name="validate-configuration-files">
    <xmlvalidate warn="false">
        <fileset dir="${webinf}" includes="struts-config.xml,web.xml"/>
        <dtd publicId="-//Apache Software Foundation//
        ⇒ DTD Struts Configuration 1.1//EN"
            location="dtd/struts-config_1_1.dtd" />
       <dtd publicId="-//Sun Microsystems, Inc.//DTD Web Application 2.3//EN"
            location="dtd/web-app_2_3.dtd" />
    </xmlvalidate>
</target>
```

This target validates both the Struts configuration file and the application's web deployment descriptor against their respective DTDs. We recommend having your "test" target depend on this one, to ensure that whenever you execute your tests, you also validate these important configuration files. If the configuration files are incorrect, then your test run may mean nothing, as it may attempt to test an incorrectly configured system. Just because you have a testing framework does not mean that that is the *only* place to do testing. Save yourself some irritation and validate configuration files *before* you run your tests.

A data transfer document is a way to transfer data from one tier of your application to another. We commonly use data transfer documents to build an XSLT-based presentation layer. The model executes business logic and returns Java objects to the controller, which then formats that data as an XML document and submits it to the presentation layer. The presentation layer transforms the document into a web page to display to the end user. The system generates data transfer documents at runtime, some of which share a specific, predictable structure. If you find your project having a problem with garbage-in, garbage-out in this part of your application, then we recommend that you add tests that validate that each data transfer document conforms to the structure you expect. You can use either DTDs or XML schemas for this purpose, although there is always the risk of overusing XML schemas. See the Discussion section for details. To validate data transfer documents, locate the XML parsers in your system and make it possible to configure them to validate incoming documents. This generally requires some refactoring on your part.

For example, if you use XSLT as your presentation engine, then some object somewhere is responsible for performing the transformation—it is either your Controller or some object that it uses. In the Coffee Shop application, we can configure the `CoffeeShopController` servlet to perform XSL transformations. We need the ability to enable validation on this XSL transformation service so that, when we execute our tests, we can validate the incoming XML document against its DTD or declared XML schema. This can be as simple as adding a method named `setValidateIncomingDocument()` which, when invoked, causes the underlying service (in this case, our XSL transformation service) to validate the incoming XML document before passing it through the XSL transformer. Implementing this feature involves nothing more complex than creating an XML parser, enabling validation, and parsing a document, but for an example implementation, see solution A.5, "Validate XML documents in your tests." The key part, from our perspective, is enabling this feature in our tests. To do that, we simply make it part of our test fixture. (See recipe 3.4, "Factor out a test fixture," and recipe 3.5, "Factor out a test fixture hierarchy," for details on managing test fixtures.) Here is the test fixture method[15] that performs an XSL translation with document validation enabled:

---

[15] A method can be part of a fixture, just as a variable is part of a fixture. We may eventually refactor the fixture and move such a method into a production class, but sometimes it really is just a tool for the test.

```
public Document doDisplayShopcartTransformation(
    String shopcartXmlAsString)
    throws Exception {

    TransformXmlService service =
        new TransformXmlService(displayShopcartXslReader);

    service.setSourceDocumentValidationEnabled(true);

    DOMResult documentResult = new DOMResult();

    service.transform(
        new StreamSource(
            new StringReader(shopcartXmlAsString)),
        documentResult);

    assertTrue(
        "Incoming XML document failed validation: "
            + service.getValidationProblems(),
        service.isSourceDocumentValid());

    return (Document) documentResult.getNode();
}
```

We used this technique in our tests for presenting shopcart contents. The data transfer document in our tests did not specify the product IDs for the products in the shopcart, which would cause problems for the end user. When we executed the tests with validation enabled, this is the error message we received:

```
junit.framework.AssertionFailedError: Incoming XML document
failed validation: [org.xml.sax.SAXParseException: Attribute
"id" is required and must be specified for element type "item".]
```

This message is certainly more helpful than finding out about the problem at runtime, where the symptom is less obvious: the "Buy!" button on the shopcart page (which uses the product ID in its HTML element name) would not work because there is no way to identify the brand of coffee that the shopper wants to buy. When we added an ID to the `item` tag in the data transfer document, the tests all passed. This recipe provides a way to make problems obvious, which is always a good idea.

NOTE *Make problems obvious*—Rather than infer the cause of a defect from a secondary symptom, write your tests in such a way that the problem becomes obvious. Without validating the shopcart data transfer document, all we would know is that one of our end-to-end tests fails because the "Buy!" button does not work. There are a few reasons this could fail: the XSL stylesheet could be wrong, the "Add Coffee to Shopcart" action could be wrong, there could be data corruption, or there might be no coffee matching that particular product ID. By validating the data transfer document in the tests, the cause of the defect becomes obvious and, most importantly, inexpensive to fix.

Now whenever we execute our tests, we add another layer of problem isolation. If the XML document we pass as input to our test is invalid, then document validation fails before the object under test tries to process it, making it clear whether the problem is bad input or an incorrectly behaving XML-processing component.

◆ Discussion

Bear in mind that validating XML is expensive, particularly if doing so forces you to parse the same XML document more than once. If your system is passing data transfer documents to other components in your system, then you can feel safe turning validation off in production. After all, your tests will catch the vast majority of problems that you might have with those documents (at least the problems you know about). If, instead, you are receiving data transfer documents from a component outside your control—either from another group in your organization or someone outside your organization—then we recommend leaving validation enabled, even in production. If nothing else, it quickly settles the question of who is responsible for a problem: you or them.[16]

There is one trap to avoid when validating data transfer documents against XML schemas. The power of the XML schema is its expressiveness: it can validate structure *and* data, leveraging the power of regular expressions. As in any similar situation, you need to be ever aware of the power you have available and be careful not to overstep your bounds. In particular, it becomes tempting to validate every little thing you can in your XML schemas. For example, you may be tempted to verify that the shipping charge in a Purchase Order document is less than $10 when the order contains over $300 worth of goods. After all, XML schemas allow you to do this, so why not? The problem is simple: that is a business rule, and a data transfer document—a simple data structure that your system passes between layers—is the wrong place to validate business rules. Why? Because changes in business rules ought not to affect the system's ability to generate XML documents from a `PurchaseOrder` object! This is a clear sign that the design needs work.

[16] We are not concerned with assessing blame, but it is important to assess responsibility, because someone has to fix it. Better it be the programmer whose component is actually broken.

Validate business rules by testing your business rules; stick to just validating structure and formatting in your data transfer document tests.[17]

◆ Related

- 3.4—Factor out a test fixture
- 3.5—Factor out a test fixture hierarchy
- A.5—Validate XML documents in your tests

[17] Of course, if you process business rules using an XML-based engine then you may perform XML schema validation in your tests. It is better to separate the tests rather than have one try to do two things.

10 Testing and JDBC

This chapter covers

- Which parts of your JDBC client code *not* to test
- Testing your mapping between domain objects and ResultSets
- Verifying SQL commands with the Gold Master technique
- Using database meta data to write simpler tests
- Managing test data in different databases and using DbUnit
- Testing legacy JDBC code

There are those who would say that the database is the core of any "real" Java application. Although applications need data, many people have designed applications *around* the database, as though it were the center of the universe. This leads to high coupling between the application and its data sources and, as we have been saying throughout, high coupling and duplication are primary sources of frustration during Programmer Testing. In this chapter we present strategies and techniques for testing data components as well as offering ways to refactor your application towards a more testable design.

As of this writing, one of the greatest stumbling blocks in testing Java database code—that is, JDBC clients—is that there appears not to be any mature, standalone SQL parsers for Java. When we looked for one, there were two promising candidates: HSQLDB and Mimer. HSQLDB (hsqldb.sourceforge.net) is an all-Java database platform, so we thought it would be possible to use its parser directly. Although we could have looked at the source to see how HSQLDB parsed SQL statements before execution, the parser is so tightly coupled with the database and its SQL query executer, that (as is) it is impossible to parse an SQL statement by itself. This is not to disparage HSQLDB or its authors—perhaps they had no requirement for a standalone parser. If we could work with them to extract it, that would be nice.

Upright Database Technology provides an online SQL query validator based on its Mimer (www.mimer.com) database engine; but at press time only offered its validation feature as a web service, rather than in embedded mode, which is really what we want. Several more hours on Google proved fruitless, so we are left to conclude that as of this writing there is no standalone SQL parser that you can use to verify your SQL statements. We present alternative techniques for handling this issue until a suitable SQL parser/validator comes along.

As a community, test-driven programmers have written a great deal about testing against the database. It is often the first complex bit of testing that a programmer attempts. You can find some excellent guiding principles in Richard Dallaway's article "Unit Testing Database Code."[1] Among the guidelines you will find there is "you need four databases," which we include here to give you a taste of the article:

1 The production database. Live data. No testing on this database.
2 Your local development database, which is where most of the testing is carried out.
3 A populated development database, possibly shared by all developers so you can run your application and see it work with realistic amounts of

[1] www.dallaway.com/acad/dbunit.html. Excerpted with permission.

data, rather than the handful of records you have in your test database. You may not strictly need this, but it's reassuring to see your app work with lots of data (a copy of the production database's data).

4 A deployment database, or integration database, where the tests are run prior to deployment to make sure any local database changes have been applied. If you're working alone, you may be able to live without this one, but you'll have to be sure any database structure or stored procedure changes have been made to the production database before you go live with your code.

The recipes in this chapter fall into two essential categories: how to write Object Tests for both your data components and their clients, and how to test your data access layer as a unit. The recipes in the former category will be most helpful for programmers who are either building data components or are able (and willing) to refactor existing data components to make them easier to test. The recipes in the latter category are for those who have inherited data components that they cannot change or are at a point in their project where refactoring is not an option. (Even Martin Fowler himself described situations in which one ought *not* to refactor in his *Refactoring: Improving the Design of Existing Code.*)

We have some early advice for the reader. Many programmers new to JUnit choose their data access code as the first bit of complex code to try to test. They begin writing tests for every JDBC call they make: every create, retrieve, update, and delete. Before too long they build up a collection of tests replete with both duplication and mutual dependence. For each table, they often follow this pattern:

1. First put a row into the database "through the back door."[2]
2. Verify that the data access object can retrieve the row.
3. Create a row through the data access object.
4. Verify through the back door that the row is there.

All this in a single test! Doing this for every table is repetitive; and the second part of the test (which ought to be its own test!) depends on the first part passing. Please notice that these tests verify your vendor's implementation of its JDBC provider as much as—if not more than—they verify your data access code. Concentrate on testing the code you have written. *Don't test the platform*; conserve your testing energy to apply to *your own code.*

---

[2] The "back door" is plain JDBC itself. The test first creates data using a straight JDBC method invocation to avoid using the data access object to test itself. A noble effort, but more trouble than it is worth.

To illustrate the point, let us test a `DELETE` statement. In our Coffee Shop application, we store data representing discounts and promotional offers in a database table called `catalog.discount`. On an ongoing basis, the marketing department gives the go-ahead for new discounts and promotional offers, usually for a limited time. Once an offer has expired, we want to be able to remove it from the `catalog.discount` table. We also want to be able to cancel any kind of offer on demand, in case something goes wrong—for example, we want to avoid accidentally offering coffee beans at $1 per kilogram. We need a simple utility that deletes all discounts that expired by some date that the user chooses. Eventually we want to write a test for that utility's data access code, including the following "happy path" test. This test assumes an empty `catalog.discount` table, removes all discounts that have expired by January 1, 2003, and then searches for all discounts that expire by January 1, 2003, expecting there to be none.

```
public class DeleteDiscountsTest extends CoffeeShopDatabaseFixture {
    // other code omitted
    public void testDiscountsExpiredThirtyDaysAgo() throws Exception {
        // FIXTURE: getDataSource() returns our test data source
        // FIXTURE: Table cleanup occurs in setUp() and tearDown()
        DiscountStore discountStore =
            new DiscountStore(getDataSource());

        Date expiryDate = DateUtil.makeDate(2003, 1, 1);

        discountStore.removeExpiredDiscountAsOf(expiryDate);

        Collection expiresByDate =
            discountStore.findExpiresNoLaterThan(expiryDate);

        assertTrue(expiresByDate.isEmpty());
    }
}
```

We have decided that `DiscountStore` should use JDBC to talk to a database, so this class contains the following general categories of behavior:

- `DiscountStore` translates Value Object properties to `PreparedStatement` parameters to use in a `PreparedStatement` that executes the corresponding SQL command.
- `DiscountStore` executes SQL commands using the JDBC API.
- For `SELECT` statements (queries), `DiscountStore` translates `ResultSet` columns into Value Object properties, so as to return Value Objects (business objects) to the business logic layer.

A test such as the one in our `DeleteDiscountTest` example has one troubling dependency: it relies on data *in the database* to determine the correctness of the "delete discount" feature. This dependency couples our tests to a working, live database, which not only slows the tests down but also makes them more brittle. (What happens when someone accidentally adds data to the test database?) More to the point, in order to verify any part of this class, we are *forced* to execute an SQL command, which is the one part of the class's behavior over which we have no control: we are unwittingly testing the JDBC driver, which is code we did not write. We ought to treat the JDBC API and our database vendor's JDBC provider as "trusted libraries," meaning that we ought not to test them—or at a minimum, we ought to test them at most once to verify that they work in general, and then worry about testing *our* code instead.

NOTE *Do you trust the library?*—If you do not trust your JDBC provider implementation, then either use one you do trust *or* write Learning Tests that verify the JDBC provider's behavior against your expectations. This is especially useful if you are frequently upgrading the JDBC provider or you need to support multiple databases with the same JDBC code.

Many veterans of JUnit are quick to suggest using a mock JDBC provider to decouple you from the production JDBC provider, but we recommend an alternative approach: refactor your dependency on the JDBC API to a minimum, and thus reduce the number of tests that require a live database. We love mock objects, but there is always the risk that the mock JDBC provider differs from your production JDBC provider in some important way. If the JDBC provider you use has a defect, you could complain about it; but in the end, you have to live with that defect, upgrade, or switch vendors. The fact that the mock JDBC provider works correctly does not help you in production. It is certainly possible to manage these risks, but we prefer to avoid them. We do this by testing the above behaviors separately, minimizing the number of tests that depend on having a live database available.

The first kind of test verifies that we create `PreparedStatements` correctly from a `Discount` Value Object. We need one of these tests per `PreparedStatement`. Proceed with this task until fear turns to boredom. We tried to test this behavior directly by creating the `PreparedStatement` for the `DELETE` statement we wanted to test, but quickly ran into a roadblock in the JDBC API. This test uses the hypothetical class `DiscountStoreJdbcImpl`, a JDBC-specific discount store. We are just trying out a design idea for now:

```
public class DiscountStorePreparedStatementTest
    extends CoffeeShopDatabaseFixture {
```

```
    public void testCreate_RemoveExpiredDiscountAsOf()
        throws Exception {

        DiscountStoreJdbcImpl discountStoreJdbcImpl =
            new DiscountStoreJdbcImpl(getDataSource());

        PreparedStatement removeExpiredDiscountAsOf =
            discountStore.prepareJdbcStatement(
                "removeExpiredDiscountAsOf",
                expiryDate);

        // How do we check the PreparedStatement?
    }
}
```

Unfortunately for us, the people who designed the JDBC API provided no way to ask a `PreparedStatement` about its parameters. It is a very secretive object that way.[3] Although a `MockPreparedStatement` would provide us with the extra information we need, we prefer to try another approach. Rather than actually creating the `PreparedStatement`, we verify the parameters we plan to pass to it. Rather than testing a JDBC implementation of `DiscountStore`, we test a JDBC *query builder* for the `DiscountStore`. We write the following test for a new class we plan to introduce:

```
public void testParametersForRemoveExpiredDiscountAsOf()
    throws Exception {

    Date expiryDate = DateUtil.makeDate(2003, 1, 1);
    List domainParameters = Collections.singletonList(expiryDate);

    DiscountStoreJdbcQueryBuilder discountStoreJdbcQueryBuilder =
        new DiscountStoreJdbcQueryBuilder();

    List removeExpiredDiscountAsOfParameters =
        discountStoreJdbcQueryBuilder
            .createPreparedStatementParameters(
                "removeExpiredDiscountAsOf",
                domainParameters);

    List expectedParameters =
        Collections.singletonList(
            JdbcUtil.makeTimestamp(expiryDate));

    assertEquals(
        expectedParameters,
        removeExpiredDiscountAsOfParameters);
}
```

[3] George Latkiewicz informs us that starting with a recent version of JDBC (bundled with JDK 1.4), one can ask a `PreparedStatement` for parameter type information through its meta data, but that is not enough for our purposes.

The new class is DiscountStoreJdbcQueryBuilder, which knows how to create the PreparedStatement parameters for each feature that the DiscountStore supports, mapping domain-level parameters, which are Java-based business objects, to SQL-level parameters, which match the various SQL data types. We have decided to name the feature we want to test removeExpiredDiscountAsOf, so the DiscountStore can ask its query builder for the PreparedStatement parameters that go with the removeExpiredDiscountAsOf feature (or as we are implementing the feature in JDBC, its SQL command).

Notice that although this is a DiscountStore *JDBC* query builder, there is no actual dependency on the JDBC API. This test does not use a database fixture and there is no need for PreparedStatements and the like. The production code that passes this test is quite simple:

```
public List createPreparedStatementParameters(
    String statementName,
    List domainParameters) {

    Date expiryDate = (Date) domainParameters.get(0);
    return Collections.singletonList(
        JdbcUtil.makeTimestamp(expiryDate));
}
```

You may not feel as though you have made much progress writing this simple test, but we *did* convert a domain object (java.util.Date) into a database object (java.sql.Timestamp) and that is what needed to happen. We can cross number one off our list, although you *should* write tests for the error case—domainParameters might not have the expected Date object in it—if you are concerned that someone might pass bad data into this method.

The second behavior is the correct execution of the query: that is, creating the correct DiscountStore prepared statement and executing the statement. Because this is JDBC-specific behavior, we now rename the class to DiscountStoreJdbcImpl and extract the interface DiscountStore from it [Refactoring, 341]. At the same time, we change our DeleteDiscountsTest to use the JDBC implementation of DiscountStore.

```
public void testDiscountsExpiredThirtyDaysAgo() throws Exception {
    DiscountStore discountStore =
        new DiscountStoreJdbcImpl(getDataSource());

    Date expiryDate = DateUtil.makeDate(2003, 1, 1);

    discountStore.removeExpiredDiscountAsOf(expiryDate);

    assertTrue(
        discountStore.findExpiresNoLaterThan(expiryDate).isEmpty());
}
```

Nothing else changes, but the test still passes. We change the implementation of `DiscountStoreJdbcImpl.removeExpiredDiscountAsOf()` so that it asks the query builder for the prepared statement parameters and sets them in a loop:

```
public void removeExpiredDiscountAsOf(Date expiryDate) {
    // Define variables
    try {
        connection = getDataSource().getConnection();

        deleteStatement =
            connection.prepareStatement(
                "delete from "
                    + "catalog.discount "
                    + "where ("
                    + "catalog.discount.toDate <= ?"
                    + ")");

        List parameters =
            queryBuilder.createPreparedStatementParameters(
                "removeExpiredDiscountAsOf",
                Collections.singletonList(expiryDate));

        deleteStatement.clearParameters();

        int columnIndex = 1;
        for (Iterator i = parameters.iterator();
            i.hasNext();
            columnIndex++) {

            Object eachParameter = (Object) i.next();
            deleteStatement.setObject(columnIndex, eachParameter);
        }

        deleteStatement.executeUpdate();
    }
    // Handle exceptions and clean up resources
}
```

We can extract the code printed in bold into a method that executes the prepared statement. The resulting method depends *not one bit* on a domain object. It is pure JDBC client code:

```
private void executeDeleteStatement(
    PreparedStatement deleteStatement, List parameters)
    throws SQLException {

    deleteStatement.clearParameters();

    int columnIndex = 1;
    for (Iterator i = parameters.iterator();
        i.hasNext();
        columnIndex++) {
```

```
            Object eachParameter = (Object) i.next();
            deleteStatement.setObject(columnIndex, eachParameter);
        }

        deleteStatement.executeUpdate();
    }
```

We can move this into a new class, which we call a JDBC query executer, *and never have to test this behavior again!* Let that sink in a little, because it is surprising.

We can take this a few steps further. Here is an outline of what we did:

1. Notice that the only discount-specific code left in `removeExpiredDiscountAsOf()` is the string representing the `DELETE` query.
2. After the previous step, we were able to move *all* the exception-handling code into `executeDeleteStatement()`.
3. After that we noticed poor alignment of responsibilities: `DiscountStoreJdbcImpl` provided the SQL query string, but the `DiscountStoreJdbcQueryBuilder` processed the parameters. That did not seem right, so we moved the SQL query string into the query builder.

The code for `removeExpiredDiscountAsOf()` as of now looks like this.

```
public void removeExpiredDiscountAsOf(Date expiryDate) {
    String deleteExpiredDiscountsSql =
        queryBuilder.getSqlString("removeExpiredDiscountAsOf");

    List parameters =
        queryBuilder.createPreparedStatementParameters(
            "removeExpiredDiscountAsOf",
            Collections.singletonList(expiryDate));

    executeDeleteStatement(deleteExpiredDiscountsSql, parameters);
}
```

Pretty short, don't you think? But now there is duplication: the literal string `"removeExpiredDiscountAsOf"` appears twice. To remove the duplication, the query builder needs to provide a single method, returning the query string and the prepared statement parameters together in a single object. No problem: we introduce the class `PreparedStatementData` to store both those pieces of information. We also introduce the class `JdbcQueryExecuter` to execute queries and change `DiscountStoreJdbcImpl` to use it:

```
public class DiscountStoreJdbcImpl implements DiscountStore {
    // Some code omitted for brevity

    private DiscountStoreJdbcQueryBuilder queryBuilder =
        new DiscountStoreJdbcQueryBuilder();
```

```
    private JdbcQueryExecuter queryExecuter;

    public DiscountStoreJdbcImpl(DataSource dataSource) {
        queryExecuter = new JdbcQueryExecuter(dataSource);
    }

    public void removeExpiredDiscountAsOf(Date expiryDate) {
        PreparedStatementData removeExpiredDiscountAsOfStatementData =
            queryBuilder.getPreparedStatementData(
                "removeExpiredDiscountAsOf",
                Collections.singletonList(expiryDate));

        queryExecuter.executeDeleteStatement(
            removeExpiredDiscountAsOfStatementData);
    }
}
```

Look at how little code is left in the actual `DiscountStore`! Building the SQL query string and marshalling the parameters—converting them from domain parameters to SQL parameters—is all done in the query builder, *which you can test without using a database.* Executing the delete statement is done in the query executer, *for which you only need a handful of tests that use a database.* That is all. You might have 100 different `DELETE` statements, but there is only *one method* that actually uses the JDBC API to execute those statements. This means that you may have a few hundred tests running in memory and a handful of tests—less than ten—running against the database. There is a savings both in complexity and in the time it takes to execute your tests. You win twice!

No more testing the JDBC provider. Test *your* code.

10.1 Test making domain objects from a ResultSet

◆ Problem

You want to verify that you are correctly making domain objects from the JDBC `ResultSet` objects returned by your `SELECT` queries.

◆ Background

There are really only two things that can go wrong when executing a query with JDBC. You might issue the wrong SQL command. You might unmarshal data into objects incorrectly. The straightforward way to test this is to do it all in one go: prime the database with data, create the `SELECT` statement, execute it, and then verify that you `SELECT`ed what you expected. (That rhymes; how nice!) While this is straightforward, it does not scale very well.

After a while, every `SELECT` test looks the same: the differences are in the query string and whether you invoke `getString()`, `getInt()`, `getBlob()` or ... you `get` the picture. There must be a way to remove all that duplication. Surely there is, because we described how to do exactly that in the introduction to this chapter! Once you have applied those techniques and only one part of your data access layer executes the SQL command, you are left with the responsibility of testing just those two things mentioned previously: the command and the unmarshalling logic. This recipe handles the latter; see recipe 10.2, "Verify your SQL commands," for details on testing the former.

◆ *Recipe*

We need to test turning a `ResultSet` into the `Set` of domain objects that the `ResultSet` represents. A direct approach is to populate a `ResultSet` object with known data, invoke the "make domain objects from this" method, and then compare the results with the expected values. Unfortunately for us, JDBC does not provide a standalone implementation of `ResultSet` to which we can start adding data. This is one situation in which mock objects are simple and work well. Fortunately for us, the Mock Objects project (www.mockobjects.com) provides a couple of easy-to-use `ResultSet` implementations: `MockMultiRowResultSet` for result sets with multiple rows of data and `MockSingleRowResultSet` for result sets with a single row of data. The latter provides a simpler interface and can perform better than the former.

NOTE *The Mock Objects project*—This project began as an embodiment of the ideas that Tim Mackinnon, Steve Freeman, and Philip Craig described in their paper "Endo-Testing: Unit Testing with Mock Objects."[4] It contains mock implementations of various J2SE and J2EE library classes and interfaces. We do not rely heavily on this package—we mostly use EasyMock to implement mock objects—but the Mock Objects project does provide a useful collection of prefabricated mock objects. We recommend using their objects while you "get the feel" of mock objects (or testing objects in general) before building your own. It is important to experience the effect that mock objects have on the style of the tests that use them. As the authors themselves point out, Mock Objects (their implementation of the concept) help you focus on the *interactions* between objects, without worrying about every little implementation detail for each test.

---

4 www.connextra.com/aboutUs/mockobjects.pdf

Now that we have a result set whose data we can hard code, we can write our test for turning a `ResultSet` object into a domain object. We will verify that we can create a `Discount` object from the `catalog.discount` table. Listing 10.1 shows a good first test.

Listing 10.1 A test for unmarshalling `ResultSet` data

```
public void testDiscountJoinWithDiscountDefinition()
    throws Exception {

    PercentageOffSubtotalDiscountDefintion
        expectedDiscountDefinition =
            new PercentageOffSubtotalDiscountDefintion();
    expectedDiscountDefinition.percentageOffSubtotal = 25;

    Date expectedFromDate = DateUtil.makeDate(1974, 5, 4);
    Date expectedToDate = DateUtil.makeDate(2000, 5, 5);

    Discount expectedDiscount =
        new Discount(
            expectedFromDate,
            expectedToDate,
            expectedDiscountDefinition);

    DiscountStoreJdbcMapper mapper = new DiscountStoreJdbcMapper();

    Map rowData = new HashMap();    <-- Store the name/value pairs for a single row

    rowData.put(
        "typeName",
        PercentageOffSubtotalDiscountDefintion.class.getName());

    rowData.put("fromDate", JdbcUtil.makeTimestamp(1974, 5, 4));
    rowData.put("toDate", JdbcUtil.makeTimestamp(2000, 5, 5));
    rowData.put("percentageOffSubtotal", new Integer(25));
    rowData.put("suspended", null);

    MockSingleRowResultSet resultSet = new MockSingleRowResultSet();
    resultSet.addExpectedNamedValues(rowData);    <-- Stuff the hard coded data into a ResultSet

    assertTrue(resultSet.next());    <-- Point the ResultSet at the first row

    Discount actualDiscount = mapper.makeDiscount(resultSet);
    assertEquals(expectedDiscount, actualDiscount);
}
```

Ignoring the additional complexity of using mock objects, the test follows the usual pattern: we create the `Discount` object we expect, create a `ResultSet` with the JDBC data we want to process, and then check the mapper's behavior. We used the `MockSingleRowResultSet` because our test only used a single row of data. You can use the corresponding `MockMultiRowResultSet` if your test needs to operate on multiple rows of data. We present the `DiscountStoreJdbcMapper` that passes this test in listing 10.2.[5]

Listing 10.2 DiscountStoreJdbcMapper

```
package junit.cookbook.coffee.jdbc;

import java.sql.ResultSet;
import java.sql.SQLException;
import junit.cookbook.coffee.data.*;
import com.diasparsoftware.jdbc.JdbcMapper;

public class DiscountStoreJdbcMapper extends JdbcMapper {
    public Discount makeDiscount(ResultSet discountResultSet)
        throws SQLException {

        Discount discount = new Discount();

        discount.fromDate = getDate(discountResultSet, "fromDate");
        discount.toDate = getDate(discountResultSet, "toDate");   <-- Part of JdbcMapper

        discount.discountDefinition =
            makeDiscountDefinition(discountResultSet);

        return discount;
    }

    public DiscountDefinition makeDiscountDefinition(
        ResultSet resultSet)
        throws SQLException {

        String discountClassName = resultSet.getString("typeName");
        if (PercentageOffSubtotalDiscountDefintion
            .class.getName().equals(discountClassName)) {

            PercentageOffSubtotalDiscountDefintion
                discountDefinition =
                    new PercentageOffSubtotalDiscountDefintion();
            discountDefinition.percentageOffSubtotal =
                resultSet.getInt("percentageOffSubtotal");
            return discountDefinition;
        }
        else
            throw new DataMakesNoSenseException(   <-- DataMakesNoSenseException is a new custom exception we created
                "Bad discount definition type name: '"
                    + discountClassName + "'");
    }
}
```

[5] The method `getDate()` appearing in this listing is defined in the superclass `JdbcMapper`. It does what you would expect: retrieves a `Date` value for the specified column.

◆ *Discussion*

We ought to warn you that when using this technique it is *crucial* that the data in your hard-coded result set match the data you would retrieve from the production database. Be aware of trouble spots common to database programming in general (and not just JDBC), such as time zone differences, number formats and strings that are too big for a column. For example, some databases silently truncate oversized strings, while others throw an exception to indicate that the string is too long. It is important both to understand the behavior of your live database and to identify any differences between the mock JDBC objects and your vendor's JDBC implementation. You may need to create custom mock objects to achieve a more faithful simulation of your vendor's JDBC provider's idiosyncrasies.

Also, this recipe shows us that high coupling means less reuse. The JDBC `ResultSet` is an excellent example of an object with too many responsibilities. It does at least three important things: represents a single table row, provides an iterator over a collection of table rows, and interacts with the underlying database to fetch those rows. This is too much work for a single object. Often when we write Object Tests we want to use just one of the features such an object provides without its other responsibilities "getting in the way." A class with high internal coupling thwarts attempts at reusing the "smaller object" that we feel is trying to get out of the "bigger object." The task this recipe sets out to perform is a fine example of this struggle.

We only want the data; we do not want to talk to a database to get it. If JDBC were to provide a separate class representing the *rows* in a `ResultSet` then we could use the production quality implementation in place of a mock object in our tests. We would be able to test the way we map SQL data types onto Java data types and relational column names onto Value Object properties. Unfortunately there is no such separation of data from its source, forcing us to use a mock `ResultSet` object. We can appreciate the value of this mock object by looking at the size of the interface it implements. To write a custom mock object for the `ResultSet` interface requires a considerable amount of work, even if we only need a small part of that interface! The `MockResultSet` implementations represent the data that a live `ResultSet` would fetch from a database without actually doing so. If JDBC had only separated those responsibilities in the first place, we would not need to use a `MockResultSet` at all; and all things being equal, we prefer to test with production code, rather than simulators.

◆ *Related*

- 10.2—Verify your SQL commands

10.2 Verify your SQL commands

◆ Problem

You would like to verify your SQL commands without necessarily involving the database each time.

◆ Background

The three ingredients[6] for correct JDBC code are:

1. Correct SQL commands
2. Correctly converting domain objects to `PreparedStatement` parameters
3. Correctly converting a `ResultSet` to domain objects

We have shown that the rest of the interaction with the JDBC API can be isolated to a single place, tested once, and then trusted forever. Verifying your SQL commands with JUnit is strange. When we try to write such a test, it seems to reduce to this assertion:

```
assertEquals(
    expectedSqlString,
    queryBuilder.getSqlString(statementName);
```

This is equivalent—*isomorphic*, really—to putting a key-value pair into a `Map`, and then verifying that you can retrieve the value with the key. It only tests the key's `hashCode()` method and Java's implementation of `HashMap` or `TreeMap`, which has nothing to do with JDBC and SQL. Is there a point to using JUnit to verify SQL commands? We do not think so.

◆ Recipe

We recommend not writing JUnit tests to verify your SQL commands against a database. This is one case where JUnit is not the best tool for the job. Instead we recommend simply executing your SQL commands using your database's command-line tool, such as Mimer's BatchSQL.

Yes, you read that correctly: we recommend manual tests in this case. Have we gone mad?

---

[6] There are more issues to handle, including connection pooling and transactions, but those are more infrastructure issues and should only be coded once in an application. Here we are referring to JDBC code you would need to write throughout an application, handling various tables, queries and updates.

No, although you may disagree with that assessment. Generally speaking, the best way to verify SQL commands is to try them out a few times, become comfortable with them, and then treat them as "correct." You may then write tests that verify that the SQL commands still match the "last known correct version." In short, apply the *Golden Master* technique.

NOTE *Gold(en) Master*—Also known as "golden results," a Golden Master—or Gold Master, depending on whom you ask—is a test result that you verify once by hand, and then use as the baseline for future test runs. Future executions of that test pass if the results match the Gold Master output. Do not confuse this technique with the well-known anti-pattern *Guru Checks Output*. We are talking about checking output by hand *once* then using that output to implement a self-verifying test. With Guru Checks Output, you need the guru to check the output of each test run, and when the guru is not around, no testing can happen. With Gold Master, we capture the guru's knowledge once and keep it in the test for all time.

To illustrate the point, here is an example from the Coffee Shop application. While shoppers are purchasing coffee from the online store, a product manager somewhere is updating the catalog. She needs to add products to the database when we decide to launch a new type of coffee bean. Somewhere in the system there is a line of code that creates the corresponding SQL statement to insert a new coffee bean product into the appropriate table. Let us treat this as a legacy coding scenario, meaning that the code already exists and "is correct"—at least as far as our basic observations of the system are concerned. We want to add a test to help stop us from changing the SQL statement without seeing the effects immediately. In a legacy code situation this is the first line of defense.

First we locate the method that performs the SQL update:

```
public void addProduct(Product toAdd) {
    Connection connection = null;
    PreparedStatement insertStatement = null;

    try {
        connection = dataSource.getConnection();
        insertStatement =
            connection.prepareStatement(
                "insert into catalog.beans "
                + "(productId, coffeeName, unitPrice) values "
                + "(?, ?, ?)");

        insertStatement.clearParameters();
        insertStatement.setString(1, toAdd.productId);
        insertStatement.setString(2, toAdd.coffeeName);
        insertStatement.setInt(3, toAdd.unitPrice.inCents());
```

```
            if (insertStatement.executeUpdate() != 1)
                throw new DataMakesNoSenseException(
                    "Inserted more than 1 row into catalog.beans!");
        }
        catch (SQLException e) {
            throw new DataStoreException(e);
        }
        finally {
            try {
                if (insertStatement != null)
                    insertStatement.close();

                if (connection != null)
                    connection.close();
            }
            catch (SQLException ignored) {
            }
        }
    }
```

If we are able to refactor this method, we can extract the SQL command into a method similar to the following:

```
public String getAddProductSqlString() {
    return "insert into catalog.beans "
        + "(productId, coffeeName, unitPrice) values "
        + "(?, ?, ?)";
}
```

Note that we generally favor extracting these strings to methods rather than to symbolic constants, because it is easier to refactor the method in something more general purpose, such as a key-based lookup method. This is just a special case of interface/implementation separation...but we digress.[7]

Now that we have extracted out the SQL string, we can write the following test:

```
public void testAddProductSqlString() throws Exception {
    CatalogStoreJdbcImpl store = new CatalogStoreJdbcImpl(null);
    assertEquals("", store.getAddProductSqlString());
}
```

Notice that we expect an empty string here, which is obviously *not* the string we really expect the catalog store to execute against the database. We write this test because we are unsure about the actual SQL command we are going to get, and yet the JUnit API requires that we expect *something*. Because we have decided to treat the actual SQL command as correct, we need to let the store tell *us* what that

[7] It is also a small amount of Smalltalk influence, which we think is generally a Good Thing.

string is, rather than guess at it. It is much easier this way. We execute the test and receive this failure message:

```
expected:<> but was:<insert into catalog.beans
➾  (productId, coffeeName, unitPrice) values (?, ?, ?)>
```

Now we know the SQL command to expect, so we place it in the test for future reference, using trusty old copy-and-paste:

```
public void testAddProductSqlString() throws Exception {
    CatalogStoreJdbcImpl store = new CatalogStoreJdbcImpl(null);
    assertEquals(
        "insert into catalog.beans "
            + "(productId, coffeeName, unitPrice) values "
            + "(?, ?, ?)",
        store.getAddProductSqlString());
}
```

This test now passes, allowing us to do some future refactoring such as generating this statement from database schema information. If our refactoring changes the SQL command in any way, this test lets us know immediately, at which point we can either update the Gold Master string or decide that something we have done has introduced a defect.

◆ *Discussion*

The next step is to externalize the Gold Master string to a file, in which case a properties file suffices. Once all your SQL commands are externalized to a file you can use *that* as the *source* for your SQL queries, rather than hard coding them in your JDBC client. This refactoring adds considerable flexibility to your design. If tomorrow the database group decides to reorganize the tables using a different schema name or a different table-naming scheme, you only need to change a single file and rerun all the tests.

Now what if you are unable to refactor the SQL command as we did here? How do you determine the Gold Master string? The answer is to substitute a `DataSource` implementation that collects that information for you. Rather than reinvent the wheel, you can use Mock Objects to write essentially the same test as we have already described:

```
public void testAddProductSqlString() throws Exception {
    String expectedSqlString = "";  <---- Store the Gold Master string

    MockDataSource dataSource = new MockDataSource();
    MockConnection2 connection = new MockConnection2();
    MockPreparedStatement expectedStatement =
        new MockPreparedStatement();
    expectedStatement.addUpdateCount(1);
```

```
        dataSource.setupConnection(connection);
        connection.setupAddPreparedStatement(
            expectedSqlString,
            expectedStatement);    <-- Tell the Mock Connection
                                       which SQL string to expect
        CatalogStoreJdbcImpl store =
            new CatalogStoreJdbcImpl(dataSource);

        Product product =
            new Product(
                "762",
                "Expensive New Coffee",
                Money.dollars(10, 50));

        store.addProduct(product);    <-- The production code will supply the SQL string

        expectedStatement.verify();   <-- Check the Gold Master against the production code
    }
```

When we executed this test, we received this message:

```
junit.framework.AssertionFailedError: com.mockobjects.sql.
   CommonMockConnection2.preparedStatements does not contain insert into
   catalog.beans (productId, coffeeName, unitPrice) values (?, ?, ?)
```

This is the Gold Master string! Now we can place this in the test, assigning it to the variable `expectedSqlString` above. After we make that change and execute the test again, it passes! The Gold Master string is now in the test to guard against future unexpected changes. Notice that there is a bit more work to do here, as clients cannot gain direct access to the SQL string, but the technique is the same: execute the test once without knowing what to expect, let the test tell you what value to expect, and then change the test so that it expects that value from this point forward.

Remember the important distinction between Gold Master (which we like) and Guru Checks Output (which we like much less): in the former case you check the output by hand *once*, after which point the test becomes self-verifying; in the latter case, you have to check the output *each time you execute the test.* If you use Guru Checks Output, and if *you* are the guru, then we hope you have no plans for a vacation any time soon.

◆ *Post script*

One of our reviewers, George Latkiewicz, suggested an alternative technique using JUnit. Because we have not tried this technique in a real project yet, we cannot really recommend it, but it *sounds* good and is worth trying.

The technique is simple. Ask the JDBC driver to compile your SQL command by creating a `PreparedStatement` from a live connection to the database. When you invoke `prepareStatement()`, the `Connection` object should throw an `SQLException` if the statement is incorrect. The amount of validation is not limited in this case merely to SQL syntax, but the JDBC driver should also report incorrect column and table names. You could create a Parameterized Test Case (see recipe 4.8, "Build a data-driven test suite") to test each SQL command your application might need to execute. The test would simply invoke `prepareStatement()` on each command without actually executing it.[8] George has found this particularly useful when the statements change frequently or when he has had to support multiple database systems or JDBC drivers (including differences among platforms). In particular, George has found this technique invaluable when generating SQL commands dynamically.

Now we still think that the Gold Master approach, on the whole, provides better return on both the investment of effort and the investment in time executing tests, but we are only speculating. To be fair, we would need to try George's technique before drawing any conclusions. For that reason, we offer it to you as an alternative and hope that it works well for you.

◆ *Related*

- Keith Stobie, "Test Result Checking Patterns" for a description of Gold Master, also known as Batch Check, Golden Results, and Reference Checking (various web references)

10.3 Test your database schema

◆ *Problem*

You want to test your database schema, verifying such things as nullable columns, indices, foreign key constraints, and triggers.

◆ *Background*

We Agilists love to live in a dream world where *the team*[9] collectively owns the database. This is a world in which programmers and database administrators work together in harmony to build the perfect database for our collective customer (or boss). The database schema is flexible and everyone is responsive to change.

---

[8] This is one kind of test that does not require any assertions. Just invoke the method, and if it does not throw any exceptions, then the test passes. Not all tests require explicit assertions to be useful.

[9] http://groups.yahoo.com/group/extremeprogramming/files. Look for the document called "One Team."

When change happens, everyone knows about it immediately. When this happens, it is a beautiful thing.

The reality is that in most organizations there are large walls between "the database group" and "the developers," making such harmonious collaboration nearly impossible. Even if not the result of some nefarious management control strategy, if your application has grown around the database, then the chances are good that a separate team maintains the database and acts as gatekeeper: all changes go through them. Whenever you submit a request to change the database schema, you need to be sure that your change was received correctly and processed correctly, and what better way to do that than with tests?

NOTE *It actually happened...* Before you believe that nothing could ever go wrong submitting database schema changes to a separate team, consider this story. A programmer—we'll name him Joe—builds his component against an in-memory data model before translating that model into a relational database schema. He creates the schema, right down to the necessary DDL, and then submits a schema change request to the database team. One week later, after his schema changes are integrated into the weekly test driver, he runs his tests against the new database schema. Lo and behold—one of them fails! Surprised, Joe examines the test driver's database creation script—only to find that the database team has misplaced a unique index on one of the tables. Even more surprised, Joe asks the database team lead what happened. "We maintain the schema using ERwin,"[10] the team lead says, "so we imported your DDL into the tool, and then exported the entire database schema into the test driver. ERwin must have messed up somewhere." Even though Joe thought he was being precise by submitting a DDL for the database tables, something was lost in the translation. Joe learned a valuable lesson: the database schema *could* break!

If Joe's experience resonates with you, then you need to add some tests to protect yourself against these kinds of surprises.

◆ Recipe

Perhaps the best solution to this problem has nothing to do with testing: create a single, unambiguous description of your application's data model from which the DDL scripts are generated. Martin Fowler describes using XML documents—easy to parse and therefore easy to verify using XPath (see chapter 9, "Testing and

[10] A relational database modeling tool, part of the AllFusion Modeling Suite, from Computer Associates (www3.ca.com).

XML")—as the single description of the application's data layout from which a database schema may be generated [PEAA, 49]. You can find tools for parsing XML today, but we could not find tools for parsing DDL for Java.

Let us now assume that you need to test the database schema without being able (or allowed) to use XML documents to represent it. In this case the general strategy is to write a test for each of the following aspects of your database schema. Verify that:

- Tables and columns exist.
- Primary key columns are correct.
- Foreign key constraints are correct, including cascade properties.
- Triggers are correct.
- Default values and `check` constraints are correct.
- Stored procedures are correct.
- Database object privileges are correct.

For any of these kinds of tests, there are two general strategies to consider: either make assertions on database meta data or test against the database judging the correctness of the schema by performing queries and checking the results. We prefer the meta data strategy, because it does not depend on any data in the database, but meta data support is different from database vendor to database vendor. Our Coffee Shop application uses a Mimer (www.mimer.se) database to store business data, and we were not sure how well its JDBC provider supports database meta data, so we tried the Learning Test in listing 10.3.

Listing 10.3 A Learning Test for the database

```
public void testTablesAndColumnsExist() throws Exception {
    MimerDataSource coffeeShopDataSource = new MimerDataSource();
    coffeeShopDataSource.setDatabaseName("coffeeShopData");
    coffeeShopDataSource.setUser("admin");
    coffeeShopDataSource.setPassword("adm1n");

    Connection connection = coffeeShopDataSource.getConnection();
    DatabaseMetaData databaseMetaData = connection.getMetaData();
    ResultSet schemasResultSet = databaseMetaData.getSchemas();

    Map databaseSchemaDescriptors = new HashMap();
    while (schemasResultSet.next()) {
        databaseSchemaDescriptors.put(
            schemasResultSet.getString("TABLE_SCHEM"),
            schemasResultSet.getString("TABLE_CATALOG"));
    }
```

```
        schemasResultSet.close();
        connection.close();

        fail(databaseSchemaDescriptors.toString());   <-- What do we get?
    }
```

This is essentially a "printf," but it has the side effect of being easily transformed into a regression test that we can use to uncover incompatibilities or other changes in future versions of the Mimer JDBC provider. After looking at the output from the `fail()` statement, we can decide what to assert. The first thing we learned was that the column `TABLE_CATALOG` is not in the result set—something that the Javadoc for `DatabaseMetaData.getSchemas()` says ought to be there. We need a closer look at the schema meta data. Fortunately, we can use Diasparsoft Toolkit's `JdbcUtil` to get a human-readable representation of a JDBC result set. We placed this line of code before trying to process the result set:

```
fail(JdbcUtil.resultSetAsTable(schemasResultSet).toString());
```

The result set only has one column: `TABLE_SCHEM`, and sure enough, the `CATALOG` schema we expect to be there is there. We change the test to reflect this knowledge and remove this bit of trace code. Listing 10.4 shows the new test.

Listing 10.4 Our Learning Test after having learned something

```
public void testTablesAndColumnsExist() throws Exception {
    MimerDataSource coffeeShopDataSource = new MimerDataSource();
    coffeeShopDataSource.setDatabaseName("coffeeShopData");
    coffeeShopDataSource.setUser("admin");
    coffeeShopDataSource.setPassword("adm1n");

    Connection connection = coffeeShopDataSource.getConnection();
    DatabaseMetaData databaseMetaData = connection.getMetaData();
    ResultSet schemasResultSet = databaseMetaData.getSchemas();

    List schemaNames = new LinkedList();
    while (schemasResultSet.next()) {
        schemaNames.add(schemasResultSet.getString("TABLE_SCHEM"));
    }

    schemasResultSet.close();
    connection.close();

    assertTrue(schemaNames.contains("CATALOG"));   <-- A more direct assertion
}
```

We changed the "schema descriptors"—which we thought would have more than one property—to "schema names," which are just `Strings`. We no longer need a `Map`, because each item we want to store in the collection is now a single value—a `List` will do. Our assertion is more direct and easier to understand: we expect there to be a schema called `CATALOG`. Now this test is *slightly* brittle, because it assumes that the schema meta data will come back in uppercase. If you are concerned about this, then use Diasparsoft Toolkit's `CollectionUtil`, which provides a case-insensitive search capability for collections of strings. Replace the assertion above with the following code:

```
assertTrue(
    CollectionUtil.stringCollectionContainsIgnoreCase(
        schemaNames,
        "catalog"));
```

Both of the two preceding tests now pass and we have successfully verified the existence of the schema `CATALOG` in our database. You can use the remaining parts of the `ResultSetMetaData` API to verify the existence of tables, columns, and constraints—as always, depending on the degree to which your database vendor supports these features. Not all do, including at least one of the big players in the industry. What to do when meta data lets you down? Return to the basics: describe the expected behavior for a database with the desired characteristic and write the corresponding test. The one in listing 10.5 verifies that `coffeeName` is unique within the table `CATALOG.BEANS`, even though `coffeeName` is not a primary key.

Listing 10.5 Verifying a unique index

```
public void testCoffeeNameUniquenessConstraint() throws Exception {
    MimerDataSource coffeeShopDataSource = new MimerDataSource();
    coffeeShopDataSource.setDatabaseName("coffeeShopData");
    coffeeShopDataSource.setUser("admin");
    coffeeShopDataSource.setPassword("adm1n");

    Connection connection = coffeeShopDataSource.getConnection();

    PreparedStatement createBeanProductStatement =
        connection.prepareStatement(
            "insert into catalog.beans "
                + "(productId, coffeeName, unitPrice) "
                + "values (?, ?, ?)");

    createBeanProductStatement.clearParameters();
    createBeanProductStatement.setString(1, "000");
    createBeanProductStatement.setString(2, "Sumatra");
    createBeanProductStatement.setInt(3, 725);
```

```
    assertEquals(1, createBeanProductStatement.executeUpdate());

    // How will Mimer react to the duplicate entry?
}
```

Check only one row inserted

Because we are new to Mimer, we are unsure how it will react to the duplicate entry, so we do not know which exception to expect—or whether to expect one at all. (You never know.) This means that we start again with a Learning Test. Let us execute the same update a second time and see what happens. We replace the comment with this line of code:

```
createBeanProductStatement.executeUpdate();
```

When we execute the test, Mimer tells us `java.sql.SQLException: UNIQUE constraint violation`, so we know to expect an `SQLException`, but we don't know which `SQLState` corresponds, so we refine the Learning Test and replace the preceding line with this block:

```
try {
    createBeanProductStatement.executeUpdate();
}
catch (SQLException expected) {
    fail(expected.getSQLState());
}
```

When we execute the test, we get another `UNIQUE constraint violation` message. What?!

Oh yes, the data is in the database from the previous test run. This is why we recommend writing as many tests as possible without involving an actual database—even in a simple case such as this we have the complication of setting up and tearing down the data. See recipe 10.6, "Manage external data in your test fixture," for some strategies for managing a test fixture that includes a database. Now back to our test. We add code at the start of the test to delete all data from table `CATALOG.BEANS`, then we execute the test. The `SQLState` is 23000. We consult the Mimer documentation quickly and determine that this `SQLState` code represents an "integrity constraint violation." Bingo. See listing 10.6 for the final version of this test.

Listing 10.6 `CoffeeShopDatabaseSchemaTest`, the final version

```
package junit.cookbook.coffee.jdbc.test;

import java.sql.*;
import java.util.LinkedList;
import java.util.List;
import junit.framework.TestCase;
```

```
import com.diasparsoftware.java.util.CollectionUtil;
import com.mimer.jdbc.MimerDataSource;

public class CoffeeShopDatabaseSchemaTest extends TestCase {
    public void testCoffeeNameUniquenessConstraint()
    throws Exception {
        MimerDataSource coffeeShopDataSource = new MimerDataSource();
        coffeeShopDataSource.setDatabaseName("coffeeShopData");
        coffeeShopDataSource.setUser("admin");
        coffeeShopDataSource.setPassword("adm1n");

        Connection connection = coffeeShopDataSource.getConnection();
        connection.createStatement().executeUpdate(
            "delete from catalog.beans");

        PreparedStatement createBeanProductStatement =
            connection.prepareStatement(
                "insert into catalog.beans "
                    + "(productId, coffeeName, unitPrice) "
                    + "values (?, ?, ?)");

        createBeanProductStatement.clearParameters();
        createBeanProductStatement.setString(1, "000");
        createBeanProductStatement.setString(2, "Sumatra");
        createBeanProductStatement.setInt(3, 725);

        assertEquals(1, createBeanProductStatement.executeUpdate());

        try {
            createBeanProductStatement.executeUpdate();
            fail("Added two coffee products with the same name?!");
        }
        catch (SQLException expected) {
            assertEquals(
                String.valueOf(23000),
                expected.getSQLState());
        }
    }

    // JDBC resource cleanup code omitted for brevity
}
```

One thing to bear in mind is that this test assumes some information about the database schema. In particular, the failure message assumes that the duplicate key field is the coffee name, as opposed to, perhaps, the product ID. This is the kind of subtle dependency that tends to creep into tests for JDBC code, especially when testing against a live database. Suppose that three months from now the uniqueness constraints on the table change, and this test fails. The failure message, while *trying* to be helpful by being precise, is now possibly misleading. For a small table of three columns, that may not be a great problem; however, for a table with dozens of columns, this could waste considerable debugging time by throwing the programmer off track. We tend to err on the side of putting more information in failure messages, but like any habit, there are times when it becomes a *bad* habit. If you are aware of the potential problem, then you are in a better position to handle it should it arise.

◆ Discussion

We have encountered a few issues to consider when testing against a live database, even when you have the database all to yourself. To achieve test isolation you need to clean the database before each test. There are two key consequences to this practice:

- *Table dependencies grow quickly*—You must add logic to clean all the tables, and the more complex your foreign key constraints, the more complex this logic becomes. It is not uncommon in a medium-sized application to have upwards of 40 database tables, all but a few of which have foreign key constraints that determine the order in which the tables must be deleted.
- *The database is an expensive external resource*—The more tests you write that exercise the database, the more slowly your tests will execute. Remember that one of the goals of Programmer Testing is that tests be *fast* so that you can and will execute them frequently while programming. This is what provides the refactoring safety net you need to keep your design flexible and reduce the cost of adding features.

NOTE *Crunch the numbers*—It is more straightforward to write tests against a live database, especially to the programmer not accustomed to decoupling JDBC client code from a physical database. It is important to crunch the numbers and realize the benefit of refactoring away from the database. We wrote two tests to verify which columns in a table were nullable. The first approach was to take Martin Fowler's advice and move the database definition to XML; the second approach was to use database meta data as we have described here. On a Pentium-4 1.7 GHz computer with 512 MB of RAM, the former test took an average of 0.05 seconds to execute, while the latter test took 0.5 seconds. The difference appears miniscule, but this is to check seven database columns in the same table. Assume there are 1000 such columns to check—and about 50 to 200 tables, depending on the database designer's philosophy and design sense. Multiply by 143 (1000/7) and the difference is 143 * 0.45 = 64.35 seconds or more than one minute! Now as your test suite grows, startup costs such as establishing database connections cease to dominate the suite's execution time as much as for a smaller suite. Even if we are overstating the difference, and it is closer to only 30 seconds, that is 30 seconds per test execution per member of the team per day for, on average, half the lifetime of your project. Pull out your calculator and see how that adds up.

So while we wanted to provide you with examples of verifying the database schema against a live database, it is *generally* worth the effort to exclude the database from the equation. If you are truly concerned that the database does not work, write a few Learning Tests against the database, and then run them as part of your background build—say using Anthill or Cruise Control. At a minimum, you will have End-to-End Tests that verify that your application talks to the database correctly by testing through your application's user interface.[11] If the tests for your data access layer also verify the way you integrate with a live database, then you are duplicating efforts between the two kinds of tests. This is a waste. Focus your Object Tests on individual objects instead.

◆ Related

- 10.6—Manage external data in your test fixture

10.4 Verify your tests clean up JDBC resources

◆ Problem

You have written some tests that create JDBC objects such as connections, statements, and result sets. You want to avoid leaking resources by ensuring that your tests clean themselves up.

◆ Background

There are a number of problems with leaking JDBC resources. For one, you can easily defeat the purpose of JDBC connection pooling by holding on to connections until the database gives up waiting for you and orphans them, rendering them unusable. This article we found on the Web describes the problem in more detail.[12]

---

[11] Object Tests on their own are not enough to verify that you have implemented the features your end users need. That is what the End-to-End Tests are for.

[12] From "WebSpherePro System Admin Tips," May 28, 2003 issue (www.e-promag.com/epnewsletters). Use search keywords "connection pooling performance".

NOTE *Connection pool performance*—Many users report that JDBC connection pooling enhances performance for a short time, but then actually degrades user response times significantly after a few hundred user transactions. The problem seems to be a server performance issue, but it's actually a coding flaw: failure to close JDBC sessions and release JDBC resources.

Opening JDBC resources is an expensive process, which is why JDBC connection pooling exists in the first place. Without pooling, if you fail to close and release JDBC connections you're not really consuming, there is no obvious performance drain. Eventually you may run out of memory, but often that situation doesn't occur during the life of the server.

But with connection pooling, if you fail to close JDBC sessions, you'll eventually exhaust the pool, at which point your application will experience long waits until connections get freed by other instances.

The first place to look for such problems is in the cleanup phase of an individual HTTP transaction. Even though you may have an application-level session open, you must close JDBC sessions to return them to the pool for reuse by other HTTP sessions.

If you don't see any obvious failures to close JDBC sessions, you may be "leaking" sessions in exception code. Any exception handler that ends the HTTP interaction needs to release JDBC resources. This is a particularly insidious failure mode because you may experience such exceptions infrequently, allowing a long time to lapse between server startup and application slowdown.

Although the above words were written in the context of IBM's WebSphere Application Server, it applies to a much broader context: no matter what your platform, the more JDBC resources you leak, the more memory you leak, which impacts performance. You will experience frequent garbage collection and slow, silent erosion of the memory your application needs to do its job.

The bad news is that if you do not clean up JDBC resources, the JDBC API will simply let you continue not cleaning up after yourself. We imagine it sits there laughing at you while it watches your code consume every available byte of memory. Fortunately, cleaning up JDBC resources in your code is not a problem. In your tests, you allocate a connection at the top of the test and close it at the bottom. If you allocate a statement, you close it at the bottom. What could go wrong?

The problem is that you need to clean up *even if your test fails!* You have no doubt coded your JDBC resource cleanup in `finally` statements. Those `finally` statements are ugly: they themselves may throw `SQLExceptions` all over the place. It is not pretty. There must be a better way.

◆ Recipe

You can use the following as a checklist to ensure that any test using JDBC resources cleans up after itself properly, not only in terms of cleaning up the database, but also in cleaning up the Java objects the test uses to talk to the database.

- ✔ Create the data source in `setUp()`.
- ✔ Allocate connections in `setUp()`—you may only need one, unless you are testing transactional behavior with multiple connections.
- ✔ Create collections in `setUp()` to store any result sets, statements, and connections you want to clean up on your way out—one collection for each kind of resource.
- ✔ As you create JDBC resources in your test, add them to the "clean me up later" collections you created in the preceding step.
- ✔ In `tearDown()`, invoke `close()` on any of the resources you used in the test. Be sure to test for `null` first, because you never know when the test ended!

After you have done this two or three times, you will notice a definite code pattern that you can likely refactor up into a Base Test Case (see recipe 3.6, "Introduce a Base Test Case"). There is also some duplication that can be pushed out to utility classes, but we're getting ahead of ourselves. First, let's look at an example. We have written two tests for the Coffee Shop database schema: one that verifies the existence of a catalog and table, another that verifies the existence of a uniqueness constraint on a table column. Both tests run against the database. Listing 10.7 shows the code for both tests, with some extraneous code removed.

Listing 10.7 Two database schema tests

```
public class CoffeeShopDatabaseSchemaTest extends TestCase {
    public void testTablesAndColumnsExist() throws Exception {
        MimerDataSource coffeeShopDataSource = new MimerDataSource();
        coffeeShopDataSource.setDatabaseName("coffeeShopData");
        coffeeShopDataSource.setUser("admin");
        coffeeShopDataSource.setPassword("adm1n");

        Connection connection = coffeeShopDataSource.getConnection();
        DatabaseMetaData databaseMetaData = connection.getMetaData();
        ResultSet schemasResultSet = databaseMetaData.getSchemas();

        List schemaNames = new LinkedList();
        while (schemasResultSet.next()) {
            schemaNames.add(schemasResultSet.getString("TABLE_SCHEM"));
        }

        assertTrue(
```

```
            CollectionUtil.stringCollectionContainsIgnoreCase(
                schemaNames,
                "catalog"));

        schemasResultSet.close();
        connection.close();
    }

    public void testCoffeeNameUniquenessConstraint() throws Exception {
        MimerDataSource coffeeShopDataSource = new MimerDataSource();
        coffeeShopDataSource.setDatabaseName("coffeeShopData");
        coffeeShopDataSource.setUser("admin");
        coffeeShopDataSource.setPassword("adm1n");

        Connection connection = coffeeShopDataSource.getConnection();
        connection.createStatement().executeUpdate(
            "delete from catalog.beans");

        PreparedStatement createBeanProductStatement =
            connection.prepareStatement(
                "insert into catalog.beans "
                    + "(productId, coffeeName, unitPrice) "
                    + "values (?, ?, ?)");

        createBeanProductStatement.clearParameters();
        createBeanProductStatement.setString(1, "000");
        createBeanProductStatement.setString(2, "Sumatra");
        createBeanProductStatement.setInt(3, 725);

        assertEquals(1, createBeanProductStatement.executeUpdate());

        try {
            createBeanProductStatement.executeUpdate();
            fail("Added two coffee products with the same name?!");
        }
        catch (SQLException expected) {
            assertEquals(String.valueOf(23000), expected.getSQLState());
        }
    }
}
```

The code printed in bold is duplicated in the two tests, so we extract these lines into a test fixture (see recipe 3.4, "Factor out a test fixture").

Now that we have taken care of the connection, we need to handle the statements. Here is our general approach:

1. We create an instance-level collection of statements to close.
2. We identify all the places in a test where we have created a statement and, just before executing it, place it in the list of statements to close.
3. We add code in `tearDown()` to iterate over the list of statements to close, closing each one.

We repeat these three steps for result sets as well. Listing 10.8 shows the resulting code.

Listing 10.8 Handling JDBC resources in the test fixture

```
public class CoffeeShopDatabaseSchemaTest extends TestCase {
    public void testTablesAndColumnsExist() throws Exception {
        DatabaseMetaData databaseMetaData = connection.getMetaData();
        ResultSet schemasResultSet = databaseMetaData.getSchemas();
        resultSetsToClose.add(schemasResultSet);      <-- Will be closed after each test

        List schemaNames = new LinkedList();
        while (schemasResultSet.next()) {
            schemaNames.add(schemasResultSet.getString("TABLE_SCHEM"));
        }

        assertTrue(
            CollectionUtil.stringCollectionContainsIgnoreCase(
                schemaNames,
                "catalog"));
    }

    public void testCoffeeNameUniquenessConstraint() throws Exception {
        Statement statement = connection.createStatement();
        statementsToClose.add(statement);   <-- Will be closed after each test

        statement.executeUpdate("delete from catalog.beans");

        PreparedStatement createBeanProductStatement =
            connection.prepareStatement(
                "insert into catalog.beans "
                    + "(productId, coffeeName, unitPrice) "
                    + "values (?, ?, ?)");

        statementsToClose.add(createBeanProductStatement);   <-- Will be closed after each test

        createBeanProductStatement.clearParameters();
        createBeanProductStatement.setString(1, "000");
        createBeanProductStatement.setString(2, "Sumatra");
        createBeanProductStatement.setInt(3, 725);

        assertEquals(1, createBeanProductStatement.executeUpdate());

        try {
            createBeanProductStatement.executeUpdate();
            fail("Added two coffee products with the same name?!");
        }
        catch (SQLException expected) {
            assertEquals(String.valueOf(23000), expected.getSQLState());
        }
    }

    private Connection connection;
    private MimerDataSource dataSource;
    private List statementsToClose = new LinkedList();    | Store object
    private List resultSetsToClose = new LinkedList();    | to close
```

```
    protected void setUp() throws Exception {
        dataSource = new MimerDataSource();
        dataSource.setDatabaseName("coffeeShopData");
        dataSource.setUser("admin");
        dataSource.setPassword("adm1n");

        connection = dataSource.getConnection();
    }

    protected void tearDown() throws Exception {
        for (Iterator i = statementsToClose.iterator(); i.hasNext();) {
            Statement each = (Statement) i.next();
            each.close();
        }

        for (Iterator i = resultSetsToClose.iterator(); i.hasNext();) {
            ResultSet each = (ResultSet) i.next();
            each.close();
        }

        if (connection != null)
            connection.close();
    }

    public MimerDataSource getDataSource() {
        return dataSource;
    }
}
```

Close each "closable" object

Once this fixture is in place, you can take it a step further and extract the JDBC resource cleanup into its own class. Your database test fixture only needs to hold an instance to this new class—call it `JdbcResourceRegistry`, where you can register JDBC resources to be cleaned up. In `setUp()`, create a new resource registry; in `tearDown()`, invoke `JdbcResourceRegistry.cleanup()`.

You can finally move the database fixture code up into a database fixture class. This code is generally application- or component-specific, as it involves using *your* data source and priming it with specific fixture data. We pushed the `CoffeeShopDatabaseSchemaTest` fixture objects up to a new test fixture we called `CoffeeShopDatabaseFixture`, which we show in listing 10.9.

Listing 10.9 CoffeeShopDatabaseFixture

```
package junit.cookbook.coffee.jdbc.test;

import java.sql.*;
import junit.framework.TestCase;
import com.diasparsoftware.java.sql.JdbcResourceRegistry;
import com.mimer.jdbc.MimerDataSource;

// You should only need one database fixture for the entire project
```

```
public abstract class CoffeeShopDatabaseFixture extends TestCase {
    private Connection connection;
    private MimerDataSource dataSource;
    private JdbcResourceRegistry jdbcResourceRegistry;

    protected void setUp() throws Exception {
        dataSource = new MimerDataSource();
        dataSource.setDatabaseName("coffeeShopData");
        dataSource.setUser("admin");
        dataSource.setPassword("adm1n");

        jdbcResourceRegistry = new JdbcResourceRegistry();

        connection = dataSource.getConnection();
        getJdbcResourceRegistry().registerConnection(connection);
    }

    protected void tearDown() throws Exception {
        getJdbcResourceRegistry().cleanUp();     <-- Simple, no?
    }

    public MimerDataSource getDataSource() {
        return dataSource;
    }

    protected Connection getConnection() {
        return connection;
    }

    protected JdbcResourceRegistry getJdbcResourceRegistry() {
        return jdbcResourceRegistry;
    }

    protected void registerConnection(Connection connection) {
        jdbcResourceRegistry.registerConnection(connection);
    }

    protected void registerStatement(Statement statement) {      Convenience
        jdbcResourceRegistry.registerStatement(statement);        methods
    }

    protected void registerResultSet(ResultSet resultSet) {
        jdbcResourceRegistry.registerResultSet(resultSet);
    }
}
```

Let us review how far we have come. By refactoring our database test, we have built a database fixture class from which all other database-related tests can extend. If you are testing legacy JDBC code, then this is a particularly useful design. If you plan to refactor your JDBC code in the direction of a small JDBC engine, this fixture helps you write the tests that support that refactoring effort. All in all, a good thing. You can see the difference in listing 10.10, which shows `CoffeeShopDatabaseSchemaTest` using the new fixture.

Listing 10.10 CoffeeShopDatabaseSchemaTest using the new fixture

```
package junit.cookbook.coffee.jdbc.test;

import java.sql.*;
import java.util.LinkedList;
import java.util.List;

import com.diasparsoftware.java.util.CollectionUtil;

public class CoffeeShopDatabaseSchemaTest
    extends CoffeeShopDatabaseFixture {

    protected void tearDown() throws Exception {
        Statement statement = getConnection().createStatement();
        registerStatement(statement);

        statement.executeUpdate("delete from catalog.beans");

        super.tearDown();    <-- Invoke super to do the regular cleanup
    }

    public void testTablesAndColumnsExist() throws Exception {
        DatabaseMetaData databaseMetaData =
            getConnection().getMetaData();
        ResultSet schemasResultSet = databaseMetaData.getSchemas();
        registerResultSet(schemasResultSet);    <-- Register objects to be closed after each test

        List schemaNames = new LinkedList();
        while (schemasResultSet.next()) {
            schemaNames.add(schemasResultSet.getString("TABLE_SCHEM"));
        }

        assertTrue(
            CollectionUtil.stringCollectionContainsIgnoreCase(
                schemaNames,
                "catalog"));
    }

    public void testCoffeeNameUniquenessConstraint() throws Exception {
        Statement statement = getConnection().createStatement();
        registerStatement(statement);    <-- Register objects to be closed after each test

        statement.executeUpdate("delete from catalog.beans");

        PreparedStatement createBeanProductStatement =
            getConnection().prepareStatement(
                "insert into catalog.beans "
                    + "(productId, coffeeName, unitPrice) "
                    + "values (?, ?, ?)");

        registerStatement(createBeanProductStatement);    <-- Register objects to be closed after each test

        createBeanProductStatement.clearParameters();
        createBeanProductStatement.setString(1, "000");
        createBeanProductStatement.setString(2, "Sumatra");
```

```
        createBeanProductStatement.setInt(3, 725);

        assertEquals(1, createBeanProductStatement.executeUpdate());

        try {
            createBeanProductStatement.executeUpdate();
            fail("Added two coffee products with the same name?!");
        }
        catch (SQLException expected) {
            assertEquals(String.valueOf(23000), expected.getSQLState());
        }
    }
}
```

◆ Discussion

If you need this (almost) automatic cleanup facility, then take a look at GSBase's JDBC resource wrappers, available at gsbase.sourceforge.net. These resource wrappers clean up after themselves, which is quite nice of them! If you can change the JDBC code you need to test, then we recommend using these resource wrappers, even as a substitute for the techniques in this recipe.

◆ Related

- 3.4—Factor out a test fixture
- 3.6—Introduce a Base Test Case
- GSBase (http://gsbase.sourceforge.net)

10.5 Verify your production code cleans up JDBC resources

◆ Problem

You want to test your production code, verifying that it closes all the JDBC resources it allocates: result sets, statements, and connections.

◆ Background

The good news is that if your application moves all query execution into one place, just as we have recommended and described in this chapter, then there is not much work to do. The only production code that needs to clean up JDBC resources is that query execution code, so in this case you would only need to apply this recipe to a handful of methods.

The bad news is that if your application—and this is still the most common case—has JDBC calls all over the place, then you have much more work to do. You need to evaluate very carefully whether it is more effort to write all the tests you need or throw away all your data access code (but not the knowledge you gained in writing and reading it!) and replace it with the JDBC framework we have developed here. Take some time and estimate—apply this recipe a few times and measure how long it takes. Rewrite one data access class and measure how long it takes. Compare the results.

If you have decided to forge ahead and test all the scattered JDBC client code, rather than using a JDBC framework, then this recipe can point you in the right direction.

◆ *Recipe*

You can use the Mock Objects JDBC implementations to verify that `close()` has been invoked (or not, as the case might be) for the various JDBC resources you need to use. Listing 10.11 shown an example of such a test.

Listing 10.11 Verify that the `CatalogStore` closes its `PreparedStatement`

```
package junit.cookbook.coffee.jdbc.test;

import java.sql.*;
import junit.cookbook.coffee.data.*;
import junit.cookbook.coffee.data.jdbc.CatalogStoreJdbcImpl;
import junit.framework.*;
import com.diasparsoftware.java.util.Money;
import com.mockobjects.sql.*;

public class AddProductTest extends TestCase {
    public void testHappyPathWithPreparedStatement() {
        Product toAdd =
            new Product("999", "Colombiano", Money.dollars(9, 0));

        final MockPreparedStatement addProductStatement =
            new MockPreparedStatement();
        addProductStatement.addUpdateCount(1);
        addProductStatement.setExpectedCloseCalls(1);   <—— Set expectation

        MockConnection2 connection = new MockConnection2();
        connection.setupAddPreparedStatement(
            "insert into catalog.beans "
                + "(productId, coffeeName, unitPrice) values "
                + "(?, ?, ?)",
            addProductStatement);

        CatalogStore store = new CatalogStoreJdbcImpl(connection);
        store.addProduct(toAdd);
```

```
        addProductStatement.verify();
        connection.verify();
    }
}
```

Verify expectations

We have drawn attention to the code that sets and verifies our expectations, using a common Mock Objects coding pattern. First we invoke `setExpectedCloseCalls()` to indicate how many times the code we are testing should close the `PreparedStatement`—once. At the end of the test we invoke `verify()` to allow both the mock `PreparedStatement` and mock `Connection` the chance to fail if the expectations we have set have not been met. That is, the test fails if we do not close the `PreparedStatement` exactly once, or if we try to close the `Connection` at all.[13] We do not want the `CatalogStore` to close the `Connection` for two reasons: first, whoever obtains the `Connection` ought to close it, and the `CatalogStore` did not obtain the connection; and second, we want multiple data stores to be able to participate in the same transaction, and to do that they must be able to use the same `Connection`, which means they had better not close it!

◆ *Discussion*

We have not included an example test that verifies that we have closed our `ResultSet` objects, but that is easy to add. Also remember that it is important to close the result set, and *then* the statement, and *then* the connection, in that order. This technique does not ensure that we have cleaned up our resources in the order required: Mock Objects do not provide direct support for verifying the order in which methods on different objects have been invoked.

To be complete you need to write this kind of test for every distinct piece of JDBC client code. Think about how your JDBC client code is designed: you may need to write *hundreds* of tests. The good news is that if you notice coding patterns in the tests themselves, you can always refactor to a Parameterized Test Case (see recipe 4.8, "Build a data-driven test suite") and, if the design contains actual *duplication*, you may be able to extract a handful of representative test cases from your system and write just those tests. If you do not yet appreciate the power of refactoring, you will once you get to avoid writing all those tests. Walk over to your manager and say, "I just saved us about 150 hours of work." With luck, she will ask you how.

[13] Because we have not set an expected number of `close()` calls on the mock `Connection`, it expects `close()` not to be invoked at all. It is the same as invoking `setExpectedCloseCalls(0)`.

We see JDBC client code littered throughout applications on a regular basis and we view this as a serious design problem. You may have the sense that we look down on the people who create these designs problems, and that could not be further from the truth. If you are the one who wrote the data access code that led to having to write hundreds of tests like the ones in this recipe, do not feel bad about it. Instead, see how you can refactor your way out of it. You wrote the best code you could at that time under those conditions with what you knew then. Don't feel bad because you didn't do what you did not *know* how to do. Who can? Learn from the experience, and maybe laugh about it a little. We do.

◆ Related

- 4.8—Build a data-driven test suite

10.6 Manage external data in your test fixture

◆ Problem

You want to test against a database, but after each test the database is in a slightly different state.

◆ Background

JUnit practitioners often say that "shared test setup smells." This is our cute way of saying that the desire to share fixture data between tests is an indication of a design problem; if not now, then soon (but not for the rest of your life—you can always refactor). By "shared fixture" we mean the case when test #1 updates the fixture by adding some data, and then test #2 sees the data that test #1 has added. This breaks test isolation and, by now, our opinion on that point should be clear. If not, then please keep reading.

Instead of sharing fixture data, code your tests so that they share a common starting point, and then add or remove data as needed for the individual test. Sometimes that common starting point is a clean slate, and sometimes it is a known set of data. It is possible to organize your fixture so that it is easy to extract into a separate class and reuse in many tests. This recipe describes how to do that.

◆ Recipe

First things first: extract any tests you write against a live database to its own fixture. See recipe 3.4, "Factor out a test fixture," for details on how to do that. Once you have a fixture for your database tests, the general strategy is this.

1. In `setUp()`, connect to the database and prime it with whatever data you need.
2. In `tearDown()`, delete all data from the database.

If you would like to do something a little tricky, you can start a transaction in `setUp()`, and then roll it back in `tearDown()` so that JDBC never actually commits the data to the database. No data to clean up! Listing 10.12 shows an example that puts everything together.

Listing 10.12 Using the "rollback" trick

```
package junit.cookbook.coffee.jdbc.test;

import java.sql.*;

public class SelectCoffeeBeansTest extends CoffeeShopDatabaseFixture {
    protected void setUp() throws Exception {
        super.setUp();    <-- Need to set up superclass fixture

        Connection connection = getConnection();
        connection.setAutoCommit(false);    <-- Enable "rollback" trick

        PreparedStatement insertStatement =
            connection.prepareStatement(
                "insert into catalog.beans "
                    + "(productId, coffeeName, unitPrice) values "
                    + "(?, ?, ?)");

        registerStatement(insertStatement);

        insertCoffee(insertStatement, "001", "Sumatra", 750);    <-- Hide PreparedStatement details
        insertCoffee(insertStatement, "002", "Special Blend", 825);
        insertCoffee(insertStatement, "003", "Colombiano", 810);
    }

    protected void tearDown() throws Exception {
        getConnection().rollback();    <-- Don't commit the data!
        super.tearDown();
    }

    public void testFindExpensiveCoffee() throws Exception {
        Connection connection = getConnection();
        PreparedStatement findExpensiveCoffeeStatement =
            connection.prepareStatement(
                "select * from catalog.beans where unitPrice > 2000");

        registerStatement(findExpensiveCoffeeStatement);

        ResultSet expensiveCoffeeResults =
            findExpensiveCoffeeStatement.executeQuery();
        registerResultSet(expensiveCoffeeResults);

        assertFalse(expensiveCoffeeResults.next());
    }
```

```
    public void testFindAllCoffee() throws Exception {
        Connection connection = getConnection();
        PreparedStatement findAllCoffeeStatement =
            connection.prepareStatement("select * from catalog.beans");

        registerStatement(findAllCoffeeStatement);

        ResultSet allCoffeeResults =
            findAllCoffeeStatement.executeQuery();
        registerResultSet(allCoffeeResults);

        int rowCount = 0;
        while (allCoffeeResults.next())
            rowCount++;

        assertEquals(3, rowCount);

    }

    private void insertCoffee(
        PreparedStatement insertStatement,
        String productId,
        String coffeeName,
        int unitPrice)
        throws SQLException {

        insertStatement.clearParameters();
        insertStatement.setObject(1, productId);
        insertStatement.setObject(2, coffeeName);
        insertStatement.setObject(3, new Integer(unitPrice));
        insertStatement.executeUpdate();
    }
}
```

If the JDBC code you test needs to commit data to the database—for example to test transactional behavior—then in `tearDown()` replace `Connection.rollback()` with the necessary JDBC code to remove the data you may have inserted, or undo any updates you may have made. This "on-the-fly undo" can become complicated very quickly, so do not go overboard. If it takes more than one minute to write the data cleanup code for a test, then try something else, because the effort is not worth it. Speaking from painful experience, once you have about 40 to 50 tests in place, some with complex "undo changes" code, the maintenance cost begins to outweigh the benefit of using the trick, and at that point you have trouble.[14]

Your best bet is to have a database instance that you can destroy and rebuild at any time, so that in the worst case your `tearDown()` code can include deleting

[14] A former colleague, with his distinctive accent, always liked to say, "You are going to have trouble!"

entire tables. As one reviewer wrote, "If rebuilding the database is not easy, then make it easy." Still, if you do not have this luxury, we will not leave you in the dark—see recipe 10.7, "Manage test data in a shared database."

◆ *Discussion*

Like many of the other live database testing recipes in this chapter, this technique is most useful when you have legacy JDBC code that you cannot change or when you want to create a refactoring safety net. If you have the opportunity to replace your JDBC access code, we recommend applying the techniques we describe in the opening of this chapter. Ideally, you would not write so many tests against a live database, but rather isolate the code that needs the database, and test the rest without one. The other recipes in this chapter discuss the relevant techniques.

Be aware of `IDENTITY` or auto-increment columns. The more you run your tests, the higher and higher the next available row ID becomes. If you run your tests as often as we hope you will, then you might eventually run out of IDs! If you think this is a serious problem, then the simplest thing you can do is rebuild the database schema periodically, which resets the next available row ID. If you do not "own the plug"[15] on your test database, then you need a more sophisticated strategy. See recipe 10.7 for suggestions.

◆ *Related*

- 3.4—Factor out a test fixture
- 10.7—Manage test data in a shared database

10.7 Manage test data in a shared database

◆ *Problem*

You want to test against a database, but you do not have access to a dedicated database against which to test.

◆ *Background*

There are a number of reasons why you are stuck sharing a test database.

Consider the cost issues around licenses for the database platform your project uses. It may be quite expensive to procure additional licenses, and management is

---

[15] See the end of recipe 10.7, "Manage test data in a shared database" for a discussion of "owning the plug."

usually unclear on the cost/benefit trade-off, preferring to minimize the costs they can easily quantify (the exact price of a license) rather than attempting to minimize the costs they have difficulty quantifying (how much less productive the team is because programmers have to share a database), even though the latter cost may well be much higher than the former. We can complain all we want, but until we can provide a definite cost/benefit analysis *and* convince management of the accuracy of our analysis, things are not likely to change.

There may be political issues of "ownership" surrounding the database. There are those managers who feel that if the database group does not maintain total control over the database then there will be chaos. They are often afraid of programmers telling database administrators how to structure the database, which has the tendency to create tension between the two groups. Past experience has told these managers that, in order to keep the peace, the database group must both own and tightly control the databases. It is unclear whether there is any point to try to overcome this roadblock.

Whatever the reason, you may feel yourself stuck with a shared test database and you would like to know how to deal with it.

◆ Recipe

Before diving into the painful world of bobbing and weaving around data you absolutely cannot destroy, consider some alternatives.

- Download a free database product and have your own database. You can select from Mimer, MySQL, HSQLDB, and others. There are a number of companies providing free database products (at least for development) that give you the freedom to write the tests you need.
- Create a separate tablespace or schema in the shared database for your tests. Although you are sharing a database, you are really only sharing disk space; other than that you can do what you need to do. This option has the nice property of forcing your SQL code to be tablespace or schema independent, which eliminates an implicit dependency on the identity of the logged-in user, making it additionally worth the extra effort.
- Execute your database tests during off hours, when there is less likelihood of colliding with other testers. Here, we assume that you are sharing a test database[16] with other programming groups. By staggering your testing times, you

[16] If your organization lets you test on the production database, frankly it deserves what it gets. Nothing is worth that.

can share a license without incurring the cost of trampling on each others' data. Restricting yourself to off hours reduces how often you can execute your tests *and* makes it difficult to write them in the first place.

If you are forced to share a single database, tablespace, and schema with other groups and need to run your tests while they are running theirs, then you do not have much of an option left: every group must ensure that its test data does not collide with any other group's test data. This means things like "For customer names, we'll take A through D; and for coffee product IDs we'll use 000-099." You will want to make sure to capture each of these decisions in a big chart and make it visible, preferably on a web site. When some rogue programmer causes a conflict, calmly point them to the web site and politely ask him to be more careful. If he does it a second time....[17]

◆ Discussion

Although carving up the database into slices is workable, there are a few constraints to consider:

- *Excluding large classes of data may lead to burying subtle defects*—If you are writing tests for retrieving and processing contracts, you may have a special rule for contracts that expire in the first quarter of the year. If your test data consists only of contracts from October to December, then you will never test that special rule.
- *You might run out of data*—What happens when you want to write a stress test with customers buying from among 1,000 coffee bean products? If you only have 100 product IDs to choose from, then you cannot write that test—or at a minimum, you have to coordinate with the other teams about executing that test, probably only during off-peak hours.
- *You might run out of row IDs*—If your database provides `IDENTITY` columns (also known as auto-increment columns), then you may overflow the next available row ID after executing your tests 10 to 20 times per day every day. Admittedly, sharing a test database may force you to execute your tests less often, but even if you manage to overcome that hurdle, this issue presents another one.
- *You cannot test certain edge cases*—How can you verify your code in the presence of an empty table if you cannot empty the table? You *can* take a mock objects approach (see recipe 10.9, "Test legacy JDBC code without the database") but not everyone finds that solution satisfying. We do not mind so much.

[17] http://c2.com/cgi/wiki?RolledUpNewspaper

- *Data collisions are notoriously difficult to diagnose*—When two tests collide there can only be chaos. The result is nearly impossible to diagnose beyond, "Someone else is running tests right now." Whom should you call? How bad is the damage? Those questions are not readily answered, which wastes time and effort that could be spent executing the tests and preventing defects.

We recommend having separate test databases by any means necessary. We feel that it is impossible to understate its importance.

NOTE *You need to own the plug*—Ward Cunningham wrote about the importance of "owning the plug" in his afterword to Kent Beck's *Sorted Collection*, which you can find at http://c2.com/doc/forewords/beck2.html. Ward starts by writing, "While a program expresses intent, it is the computer, the hardware, that brings that intent to life. In order to have full control over your program's expression you must control the computer that runs it. Therefore: Write your program for a computer with a plug. Should you be dissatisfied with the behavior of the computer, unplug it." The same is true with databases. In order to be best able to realize code that talks to a database, you need to be able to "unplug"—or destroy—the database. The resulting tests take longer to execute, but you save an *unbounded amount of time* not having to deal with the problems you incur by sharing a test database with others.

◆ *Related*

- 10.9—Test legacy JDBC code without the database

10.8 Test permissions when deploying schema objects

◆ *Problem*

You have noticed a defect pattern when deploying any new schema object: the first user that tries it tells you that it does not work.

◆ *Background*

We received this e-mail from Carl Manaster, describing the defect pattern in only sixty words.

"I write a stored procedure in the development database, test it, and call it good. I copy it into the production database, test it there, find it still good, and release it. But I never granted regular users execute permission on it, so I get a call from the first user to try it, telling me it doesn't work."

If you have this pattern,[18] then you need more tests, and this recipe describes the test you need.

◆ Recipe

It is common to forget to grant permission for users to actually *use* a schema object, such as a stored procedure or table. Unfortunately, the SQL standard does not provide a way to ask a database object whether a given user has sufficient authority to perform an operation on that object. As a result, your test should just try to use the object and fail only if there is a permissions problem. One question: how does your database vendor report permission problems?

In order to find that out, start with a Learning Test. Create a stored procedure (Carl's particular problem), revoke your privilege to execute it, and then try to execute it. Let the JDBC provider show you how it reports a permission problem. Listing 10.13 shows the test.

Listing 10.13 Testing privileges on stored procedures

```
public class StoredProcedurePrivilegesTest
    extends CoffeeShopDatabaseFixture {

    protected void setUp() throws Exception {
        super.setUp();

        Statement statement = getConnection().createStatement();
        registerStatement(statement);

        try {
            statement.executeUpdate("drop procedure NOT_ALLOWED");
        }
        catch (SQLException doesNotExist) {
            if ("42000".equals(doesNotExist.getSQLState()) == false) {
                throw doesNotExist;
            }
        }

        statement.executeUpdate(
            "create procedure NOT_ALLOWED() begin end");
    }

    protected void tearDown() throws Exception {
        Statement statement = getConnection().createStatement();
        registerStatement(statement);
        statement.executeUpdate("drop procedure NOT_ALLOWED");
        super.tearDown();
    }
```

[18] Geek shorthand for "If you have noticed that this pattern also applies to you..."

```
    public void testSeePermissionProblem() throws Exception {
        Connection connection =
            getDataSource().getConnection("programmer", "pr0grammer");
        Statement statement = connection.createStatement();
        registerStatement(statement);

        statement.execute("call NOT_ALLOWED()");   <-- Should throw SQLException
    }
}
```

We executed this test and received the message `java.sql.SQLException: The procedure NOT_ALLOWED does not exist (or no execute privilege)`, which told us to catch an `SQLException` and look at the error code and SQL state. We added that to the test, which you can see in listing 10.14.

Listing 10.14 Adding code to expect an `SQLException`

```
public void testSeePermissionProblem() throws Exception {
    Connection connection =
        getDataSource().getConnection("programmer", "pr0grammer");
    Statement statement = connection.createStatement();
    registerStatement(statement);

    try {
        statement.execute("call NOT_ALLOWED()");
        fail("User 'programmer' allowed to call NOT_ALLOWED?!");
    }
    catch (SQLException e) {
        assertEquals(0, e.getErrorCode());      | Change expected values
        assertEquals("", e.getSQLState());      | after we see them
    }
}
```

We are quite certain that the assertions we have just added will fail, but once they do we can replace the expected values with the correct ones. This is a miniature version of the Gold Master technique. After discovering the two values—both of which are highly vendor dependent, so do not copy these into your code—we fixed the catch block of the test.

```
try {
    statement.execute("call NOT_ALLOWED()");
    fail("User 'programmer' allowed to call NOT_ALLOWED?!");
}
catch (SQLException e) {
    assertEquals(-12743, e.getErrorCode());
    assertEquals("42000", e.getSQLState());
}
```

Now we have a test that fails if a user attempts to call the specified stored procedure and they *have* permission. We did this to learn how Mimer (in this case) reports permission problems. Now we can write the test we really want, which uses this information to distinguish a test failure from the test "blowing up." Listing 10.15 shows a test that verifies a user *has* permission to call a stored procedure.

Listing 10.15 StoredProcedurePrivilegesTest

```
package junit.cookbook.coffee.jdbc.test;

import java.sql.*;

public class StoredProcedurePrivilegesTest
    extends CoffeeShopDatabaseFixture {

    // setUp and tearDown omitted

    public void testCanCall() throws Exception {
        Connection connection =
            getDataSource().getConnection("programmer", "pr0grammer");
        Statement statement = connection.createStatement();
        registerStatement(statement);

        try {
            statement.execute("call NOT_ALLOWED()");
        }
        catch (SQLException e) {
            if (isNoPrivilegesException(e))
                fail("User 'programmer' cannot call procedure "
                    + "NOT_ALLOWED");
            else
                throw e;   <-- Signal "unexpected exception"
        }
        finally {
            connection.close();
        }
    }

    private boolean isNoPrivilegesException(SQLException e) {   | Move to
        return (-12743 == e.getErrorCode())                     | reusable
            && ("42000".equals(e.getSQLState()));               | library
    }
}
```

This is one of those rare times that we decide to catch an unexpected exception—well, a reasonably unexpected one—and fail, rather than let the exception be propagated up to the JUnit framework. This is really a question of taste: in this case we would rather report simply that the user does not have the expected permission. We could rely on Mimer's error message to tell us that, but this way if Mimer changes, our message remains as informative as it ever was.

The next step is to extract the bare test "engine" from this test and execute it for all the stored procedures and against all the users you expect to have permission. The input to the test consists of a user name, a stored procedure, and your expectation regarding their authority to execute it. You can see a short example access control list in table 10.1. This is the data for your tests.

Table 10.1 Sample access control list for stored procedures

User	Description	Stored procedure	Allowed to execute?
`admin`	Administrator	`addProduct`	Yes
`csr`	Customer service representative	`addProduct`	No
`clerk`	Data entry clerk	`addProduct`	No
`marketing`	Marketing professional	`addProduct`	Yes

Now that you have tabular data you can create a Parameterized Test Case (see recipe 4.8, "Build a data-driven test suite") where the data for each test is a row in this table. Externalize the tabular data, such as to a file, in order to make it easy to keep up to date alongside your evolving list of stored procedures.

◆ *Discussion*

The one large stumbling block in this recipe is that management may strictly forbid you from even *attempting* to execute these tests on the production server, which is where you need to test them most! Frankly, we have no idea how to help you here, because we still have much to learn about negotiating effectively. The best you can do is to ask very nicely and emphasize the number of support calls that these tests will save. Of course, if executing the test runs any risk whatsoever of harming the database, then they are right to not let you execute it. This is a case where it may be necessary to test the tests.

Although our example here was testing permissions on a stored procedure, remember that you should test permissions on *all* your schema objects, not just stored procedures.

◆ *Related*

- 10.12—Test stored procedures

10.9 Test legacy JDBC code without the database

◆ ***Problem***

You have inherited legacy JDBC code and would like to test it without dragging a database along with you.

◆ ***Background***

Your big problem—and it's not your fault, but it *is* your problem—is that you cannot apply the refactorings that we have described in this chapter to the JDBC code you need to test. We feel bad for you, but rather than just feel bad, we can help.[19] This recipe describes how to use Mock Objects (www.mockobjects.com) to test those JDBC calls without a database.

◆ ***Recipe***

Before we begin, we would like to refer you to the Mock Objects article "Developing JDBC Applications Test First" (www.mockobjects.com/wiki/DevelopingJdbcApplicationsTestFirst). Even if you are not writing your application test-first, the article provides good examples on the various parts of the Mock JDBC API that Mock Objects provides. We have no desire to repeat good documentation in print, where it may become stale. Instead, we will show you one example of testing the JDBC implementation of our `CatalogStore` using the Mock JDBC API. After all, you may not have the Web in front of you just now.

Let us reprise the example we used in recipe 10.2, "Verify your SQL commands." This time, rather than verifying just the SQL string, we will add assertions pertaining to using the JDBC API correctly. We will also assume that the JDBC code we want to test is not subject to change, being legacy code that management is deathly afraid to touch.[20] We submit a mock data source to the JDBC implementation of our `CatalogStore`. This mock data source is primed with a mock connection and a mock prepared statement, and despite all these mocks—which might eventually make you wonder what *exactly* you are testing—the point is to verify that the JDBC implementation of the `CatalogStore` knows how to talk to the classes in the JDBC API. Listing 10.16 shows the test for adding a coffee bean product to the catalog.

---

[19] That same colleague, in his distinctive accent, liked to say, "All you can do is cry." In this case, you can do more.

[20] We hope that, as you continue reading this book, you realize—and perhaps are able to convince your management of the fact—that when you have tests as a safety net, change is not painful, but rather beneficial.

Listing 10.16 A database test using the Mock Objects JDBC API

```
public void testAddProduct() {
    Product toAdd =
        new Product("999", "Colombiano", Money.dollars(9, 0));

    MockDataSource dataSource = new MockDataSource();

    MockConnection2 connection = new MockConnection2();
    connection.setExpectedCloseCalls(1);

    final MockPreparedStatement addProductStatement =
        new MockPreparedStatement();
    addProductStatement.setExpectedClearParametersCalls(1);
    addProductStatement.addExpectedSetParameters(
        new Object[] { "999", "Colombiano", new Integer(900)});
    addProductStatement.addUpdateCount(1);
    addProductStatement.setExpectedCloseCalls(1);

    dataSource.setupConnection(connection);
    connection.setupAddPreparedStatement(
        "insert into catalog.beans "
            + "(productId, coffeeName, unitPrice) values "
            + "(?, ?, ?)",
        addProductStatement);

    CatalogStore store = new CatalogStoreJdbcImpl(dataSource);
    store.addProduct(toAdd);

    addProductStatement.verify();
    connection.verify();
    dataSource.verify();
}
```

The majority of this test is setup work, which is common for mock objects-based tests. We create a mock data source, mock connection, and mock prepared statement. We tell the prepared statement to expect to be used in the following fashion:

1. The `CatalogStore` will invoke `clearParameters()` once.
2. The `CatalogStore` will set the parameters that correspond to the `Product` object we want to add to the catalog. Notice the mapping of the unit price property from a `Money` object to the equivalent amount of money in cents.
3. The `CatalogStore` will update one row, represented by the property `MockPreparedStatement.updateCount`.
4. The `CatalogStore` will close the statement once.

Similarly, we tell the connection how to expect to be used, and even the data source itself. After we perform the operation—`addProduct()` in this case—that uses these JDBC objects, we ask them to verify themselves and complain if their expectations are not met. All this without involving a real database.

◆ *Discussion*

The one thing we do not like about these tests is that although the database is not involved, the tests themselves remain brittle: each test depends on both the correctness of your JDBC client code and its ability to map the data correctly. Code that tries to serve two masters is easily distracted.[21] We prefer to test different behaviors separately, but we understand that with true legacy code—code without tests that you cannot change—you have no choice. Using mock objects provides a coping mechanism for the problem, but if you have the opportunity, you ought not to stop here.

We recommend that you take the JDBC client code and, if the design makes this feasible, extract business-oriented interfaces from them. That is, extract interfaces whose methods and parameters and return types *only express domain concepts*. For example, if you have a data access object that finds all customers whose accounts are 30 days past due, then extract the interface `CustomerStore` with method `findPastDue(int days)` and place your legacy JDBC client code inside an implementation of `CustomerStore`, perhaps called `CustomerStoreLegacyImpl`.[22] You can then treat your legacy implementation of the "Store" interfaces as a giant black box. Over time you can replace parts of it with implementations you can actually test! Moreover, you can do that *at your leisure*. No hurry. It may take a long time to refactor completely away from the legacy code, but at least you know that you *can* do it—that it is only a matter of time.

◆ *Related*

- 10.2—Verify your SQL commands
- Mock Objects project (www.mockobjects.com)
- "Developing JDBC Applications Test First" (www.mockobjects.com/wiki/DevelopingJdbcApplicationsTestFirst)

---

[21] A liberal paraphrase of Irving Chernev, the great chess writer, in *Logical Chess: Move by Move*.

[22] "Impl" is one of those rare times when we do not mind using an abbreviation. The exception proves the rule.

10.10 Test legacy JDBC code with the database

◆ Problem

You have inherited legacy JDBC code and would like to test it against a live database.

◆ Background

If you have decided to test your legacy JDBC code against a live database, be sure you own the data. See recipe 10.7 for a discussion of the issues involved. Next, you need a mechanism to cope with the complexity of test data setup. We have tried setting up test data using JDBC code itself, and our experience was forgettable. We needed to maintain so much code *just for setting up fixtures* that it was clearly an unworkable situation. Fortunately we have learned from the experience, and we would like to pass that wisdom on to you.

◆ Recipe

For this recipe we will assume that you want to test your JDBC code as is without refactoring and that you have a test database at your disposal. The approach is straightforward: create a data set for each suite of tests you would like to execute, and then use DbUnit (http://dbunit.sourceforge.net) to organize that test data on the file system.

DbUnit provides the ability to store test data in simple file formats. This alleviates the need to duplicate JDBC code just to set up the database with data, because you only need one copy of the test data file. You can specify that data in XML documents or build up a dataset with code inside your test. Here is an example using the "flat XML format"—that is, a simplified XML format where each tag represents a table and the attributes represent column names.

```
<?xml version="1.0" ?>
<dataset>
    <catalog.beans productId="000"
                   coffeeName="Sumatra"
                   unitPrice="750" />

    <catalog.beans productId="001"
                   coffeeName="Special Blend"
                   unitPrice="825" />

    <catalog.beans productId="002"
                   coffeeName="Colombiano"
                   unitPrice="925" />
</dataset>
```

This small example shows specifying three coffee products. Each product is a row in the table `catalog.beans` with the columns `productId`, `coffeeName`, and `unitPrice`. Your dataset is not limited in its size or complexity in any way, except (of course) by your ability to understand it.

To use a DbUnit dataset in a JUnit test, you can write a test case class that extends `org.dbunit.DatabaseTestCase`, and then override two methods to help the framework extract your data: `getConnection()`, which returns a connection to your database; and `getDataSet()`, which returns the description of your dataset. Before executing each test in your test case class, DbUnit populates the database with exactly those rows in your dataset. Listing 10.17 shows the `DatabaseTestCase` to go with the example dataset.

Listing 10.17 A test case using a DbUnit dataset

```
public class FindProductsTest extends DatabaseTestCase {
    private DataSource dataSource;
    private JdbcResourceRegistry jdbcResourceRegistry;

    public FindProductsTest(String name) {
        super(name);
    }

    protected void setUp() throws Exception {
        jdbcResourceRegistry = new JdbcResourceRegistry();
        super.setUp();
    }

    protected void tearDown() throws Exception {
        jdbcResourceRegistry.cleanUp();
        super.tearDown();
    }

    private DataSource getDataSource() {
        if (dataSource == null)
            dataSource = CoffeeShopDatabaseFixture.makeDataSource();
        return dataSource;
    }

    private Connection makeJdbcConnection() throws SQLException {
        Connection connection = getDataSource().getConnection();
        jdbcResourceRegistry.registerConnection(connection);
        return connection;
    }

    protected IDatabaseConnection getConnection() throws Exception {
        Connection connection = makeJdbcConnection();
        return new DatabaseConnection(connection);
    }
                                                         DbUnit methods
    protected IDataSet getDataSet() throws Exception {
```

```
        return new FlatXmlDataSet(
            new File("test/data/datasets/findProductsTest.xml"));
    }

    public void testFindAll() throws Exception {
        Connection connection = makeJdbcConnection();
        CatalogStore store = new CatalogStoreJdbcImpl(connection);
        Set allProducts = store.findAllProducts();
        assertEquals(3, allProducts.size());
    }
}
```

For a discussion of the `JdbcResourceRegistry` see recipe 10.4, "Verify your tests clean up JDBC resources." The key methods are `getDatabaseConnection()`, which asks our data source for a connection, and `getDataSet()` which loads the dataset from disk in "flat XML" format. We recommend storing your datasets on disk if the corresponding code to build a `DefaultDataSet` would exceed, say, ten lines.[23] The forces that are in conflict are the desire to have the test data in the test and a conflicting desire to keep "noise" out of the test. Although test data is decidedly not noise, the code you need to write to express it may well be, so as always, we recommend that you try both and measure the difference. We think you will end up on the side of pushing all but the simplest datasets to disk.

◆ *Discussion*

If you currently have tests that set up test data using JDBC code, we recommend you change one of those tests to use DbUnit, then compare the two approaches. It should be clear that DbUnit is the way to go, especially when you consider the impact of not being able to refactor the JDBC code under test. The only way to avoid duplication between the test setup code and the JDBC code under test is to expose the production code's SQL statements to your test classes, but if you are unable to refactor the code under test then there is no direct way to make those SQL statements available. This forces you to duplicate this SQL code, and the accompanying JDBC code, in your tests! It is certainly not worth the effort.

NOTE *DbUnit Limitation*—If you have auto-increment or `IDENTITY` columns on your database tables, you may need to disable those before using DbUnit to prime your tables with data. At press time, DbUnit only supported `IDENTITY` columns on MS SQL Server. For details, consult the DbUnit site's FAQ section.

[23] We recommend consulting the DbUnit site for examples of building a `DefaultDataSet` in your test.

◆ ***Related***

- 10.4—Verify your tests clean up JDBC resources
- 10.7—Manage test data in a shared database
- DbUnit (http://dbunit.sourceforge.net)

10.11 Use schema-qualified tables with DbUnit

◆ ***Problem***

You want to use DbUnit to store data sets to test a legacy database with tables in multiple schemas. When you execute the tests, DbUnit does not find your tables.

◆ ***Background***

Although the solution to this is clearly posted on the DbUnit web site (http://dbunit.sourceforge.net), your impatience may have gotten the better of you when you first tried to use DbUnit on a database where tables are organized into multiple schemas. It is also possible that after using DbUnit successfully on a database with a single schema—the default schema—you may be moving to a database with multiple schemas, and what *used* to work no longer appears to work.

◆ ***Recipe***

You need to enable qualifying table schemas through a Java system property called `dbunit.qualified.table.names`.[24] You need to set this property to `true` before the test retrieves your database connection, so we recommend placing this in your test's `setUp()` method, as follows:

```
public class FindProductsTest extends DatabaseTestCase {
    // other code omitted

    protected void setUp() throws Exception {
        System.setProperty("dbunit.qualified.table.names", "true");
        super.setUp();
    }

    protected IDatabaseConnection getConnection() throws Exception {
        return new DatabaseConnection(
            CoffeeShopDatabaseFixture.makeDataSource().getConnection());
    }
```

[24] Unfortunately, DbUnit 2.0 no longer supports setting system properties for this feature. This recipe works with DbUnit 1.5.6. The new version uses configuration parameters similar to XML parsers. See the DbUnit site for details.

```
    protected IDataSet getDataSet() throws Exception {
        return new FlatXmlDataSet(
            new File("test/data/datasets/findProductsTest.xml"));
    }

    // tests omitted
}
```

You can now specify schema-qualified table names in your dataset, just as we did here with our flat XML dataset.

```
<?xml version="1.0" ?>
<dataset>
    <catalog.beans productId="000"
                   coffeeName="Sumatra"
                   unitPrice="750" />

    <catalog.beans productId="001"
                   coffeeName="Special Blend"
                   unitPrice="825" />

    <catalog.beans productId="002"
                   coffeeName="Colombiano"
                   unitPrice="925" />
</dataset>
```

And for completeness, listing 10.18 shows a simple test that uses this dataset.

Listing 10.18 Using a schema-qualified dataset

```
public class FindProductsTest extends DatabaseTestCase {
    private DataSource dataSource;
    private JdbcResourceRegistry jdbcResourceRegistry;

    public FindProductsTest(String name) {
        super(name);
    }

    protected voJcid setUp() throws Exception {
        System.setProperty("dbunit.qualified.table.names", "true");
        jdbcResourceRegistry = new JdbcResourceRegistry();
        super.setUp();
    }

    protected void tearDown() throws Exception {
        jdbcResourceRegistry.cleanUp();
        super.tearDown();
    }

    private DataSource getDataSource() {
        if (dataSource == null) {
            dataSource = CoffeeShopDatabaseFixture.makeDataSource();
        }
```

Compatible with older versions of JUnit (constructor `FindProductsTest(String name)`)

Tracks JDBC resources and cleans them up (`new JdbcResourceRegistry()` / `jdbcResourceRegistry.cleanUp()`)

```
        return dataSource;
    }

    private Connection makeJdbcConnection() throws SQLException {
        Connection connection = getDataSource().getConnection();
        jdbcResourceRegistry.registerConnection(connection);
        return connection;
    }

    protected IDatabaseConnection getConnection() throws Exception {
        return new DatabaseConnection(makeJdbcConnection());
    }

    protected IDataSet getDataSet() throws Exception {
        return new FlatXmlDataSet(
            new File("test/data/datasets/findProductsTest.xml"));
    }

    public void testFindAll() throws Exception {
        Connection connection = makeJdbcConnection();
        CatalogStore store = new CatalogStoreJdbcImpl(connection);
        Set allProducts = store.findAllProducts();
        assertEquals(3, allProducts.size());
    }
}
```

◆ *Discussion*

This is just one of those features that one encounters by accident. The longer you have been using DbUnit successfully without having run into this problem, the more annoying it is when you finally encounter it, because by that point you have probably developed a certain sense of security in your knowledge of the package. This is the kind of situation in which having a pair partner with whom to program[25] helps considerably: she challenges your assumptions about your working environment, often leading you to discover the problem sooner than you would if left to your own devices. We have all experienced "going down the rathole" as the result of an all-consuming compulsion to find—on our own—the solution to a silly problem. It is important to cultivate in yourself the ability to recognize when this is happening and seek help immediately so that you can move from wallowing in the problem to working towards a solution.

◆ *Related*

- DbUnit (http://dbunit.sourceforge.net)

[25] www.pairprogramming.com

10.12 Test stored procedures

◆ Problem

You want to test stored procedures.

◆ Background

When your application implements some of its business logic in stored procedures then you *need* to test against a live database in order to test that business logic. We recognize that this allows the database to optimize executing business rules for improved response time; however, this makes it more difficult to test business logic both by placing it in a difficult-to-test resource and potentially splitting business logic between the database and application objects. We recommend keeping business logic where it can more easily be tested. It is, after all, one of the most important aspects of your software.

If, instead, your application uses stored procedures only as a way to hide database schema details through a CRUD-style interface, then we applaud the people who made that decision. These stored procedures relieve the data access layer of the burden of generating correct SQL commands, leaving only data mapping. We think this is a wise choice, as it makes testing easier!

It may not be possible for you to do so at this time, but if you can refactor away from the first case towards the second case, we recommend it.

◆ Recipe

If you can help it, do not test the behavior of a stored procedure with JUnit. We find that JDBC is too verbose for such a simple task; instead, use shell scripts and your vendor's SQL command-line tool to run tests. Do not worry whether you have a framework for your shell. Instead, simply start with a test that feeds some SQL into your database, queries the result, compares against some known value, and uses return codes or error levels to signal pass or fail. We recommend such books as Timothy Hill's *Windows NT Shell Scripting* and David Tansley's *Linux and Unix Shell Programming* for a thorough treatment of using shell scripts do to testing.

NOTE *BashUnit?*—Curtis Cooley tells the story of writing tests for a Unix shell. The moral of the story is this: you do not need a framework; you need tests. The framework will appear.

> "I just got done with a fun experiment. I was working with a DBA who groks [Extreme Programming]...and he was trying to get a bunch of shell scripts working. The scripts were part of the install and backup procedures for the database.

> He was struggling with trying to figure out how they worked and what their intent was. I joked, 'We should unit test these. It shouldn't be that hard to write a shell framework.'
>
> After a couple of minutes of frustration he said, 'Let's go for it.'
>
> So for the next day and a half, we wrote unit tests for `bash` scripts, developing a little (unit test) framework along the way.
>
> The tests found many minor errors in the scripts that would have taken quite a while to track down.
>
> In a day and a half we completely rewrote and tested a bunch of scripts that originally took another DBA a couple of weeks to write.

Should you be required for some reason to test your stored procedures from Java, the best you can do is set up some data, invoke the `CallableStatement`, and then check the results. See recipe 10.10, "Test legacy JDBC code with the database," for an example of such a test. Be careful to maintain your test data and clean up your JDBC resources.

If you want to verify that your business logic *invokes* a stored procedure correctly, then we recommend testing with `MockCallableStatement` objects. Verify that the callable statement receives the appropriate parameters and that the invoking code was able to handle the different kinds of parameters the callable statement passes back. Listing 10.19 shows an example, where we verify that the `CatalogStore` adds a product by invoking the expected stored procedure.

Listing 10.19 `AddProductTest` using a stored procedure

```
public class AddProductTest extends TestCase {
    public void testHappyPath() {
        Product toAdd =
            new Product("999", "Colombiano", Money.dollars(9, 0));

        MockDataSource dataSource = new MockDataSource();

        final MockCallableStatement addProductStatement =
            new MockCallableStatement();
        addProductStatement.setExpectedClearParametersCalls(1);
        addProductStatement.setExpectedCloseCalls(1);
        addProductStatement.addExpectedSetParameters(
            new Object[] { "999", "Colombiano", new Integer(900)});
        addProductStatement.addUpdateCount(1);

        MockConnection2 connection = new MockConnection2() {
            public CallableStatement prepareCall(String sql)
                throws SQLException {

                Assert.assertEquals("call addProduct(?, ?, ?)", sql);
```

Check setting parameters correctly

Verify the SQL string

```
                return addProductStatement;    Verify the
            }                                   SQL string
        };
        connection.setExpectedCloseCalls(1);

        dataSource.setupConnection(connection);

        CatalogStore store =
            new CatalogStoreStoredProcedureImpl(dataSource);
        store.addProduct(toAdd);   <-- Execute business logic

        addProductStatement.verify();
        connection.verify();
        dataSource.verify();
    }
}
```

We can break this test up into three parts:

1. *Set up the Data Source*—Create a mock data source, preprogrammed to return a mock callable statement. The statement is set up with the expected parameters, which tests `CatalogStoreStoredProcedureImpl`'s ability to map the domain object `Product` to the stored procedure parameters, including converting the `Money` to an `Integer`. Notice that with mock objects, there is a considerable amount of work to do here.
2. *Execute the business logic*—Invoke `addProduct()`. This eventually invokes `MockConnection2.prepareCall()` which verifies the SQL string. In addition, `addProduct()` *should* set the appropriate parameters on the `MockCallableStatement` we set up in the previous step.
3. *Verify the JDBC objects*—This is standard for mock objects: ask each one to verify all the expectations you set at the beginning of the test.

The various expectations we set on the mock JDBC objects ensure that our catalog store resets the callable statement parameters, executes the statement, updates one row, and then closes both the statement and the connection.

◆ Discussion

We do not recommend using JUnit to test stored procedures, simply because writing them in Java at all puts an unnecessary layer of complexity between the tester (you) and the code being tested. This extra layer of complexity takes effort to build, as we have illustrated throughout this chapter. A JUnit test for a stored procedure will include either: (1) inserting data into the database, calling the procedure, and then cleaning up the database, *or* (2) setting up mock JDBC objects, calling the procedure, and then verifying the mock JDBC objects.

The resulting JDBC and mock objects code present nothing of value: just a verbose layer around SQL that includes translating data types, handling `null` values, and so on—all the things about JDBC that annoy many Java programmers. On the whole, testing stored procedures is best left to database-centered tools and approaches, such as shell scripting.

Hey, if you *need* to write the tests in Java because it is the path of least resistance, then by all means go ahead, but we have experienced more return on investment from implementing these tests as shell scripts.

Do not, however, mistake the preceding statement as "do not test your stored procedures." Code is code and you need to test it; otherwise, when the application fails, how will you know whether it is the application or the stored procedures at fault? Test them with JUnit if you do not have the skill to do it through shell scripting, but we believe you will save effort by learning to write shell scripts for these tests.

◆ Related

- 10.10—Test legacy JDBC code with the database
- Timothy Hill, *Windows NT Shell Scripting*.
  Published by Que. ISBN 1578700477
- David Tansley, *Linux and Unix Shell Programming*.
  Published by Addison-Wesley. ISBN 0201674726

11 Testing Enterprise JavaBeans

This chapter covers

- Testing session bean methods without the EJB container
- Testing legacy session bean methods with MockEJB
- Testing legacy session bean methods with Cactus
- Testing entity beans both with and without the EJB container
- Testing message-driven beans and JMS components
- Verifying components deployed to a JNDI directory

It has become commonplace to design enterprise applications in accordance with the Model View Controller design pattern, so our discussion generally assumes the presence of this pattern. MVC advocates separating business logic and data (the Model), screen-to-screen navigation rules (the Controller), and how to display information to the user (the View). Even though we agree that the benefits of using MVC vary considerably from application to application, it is convenient to talk about Enterprise JavaBeans as Model components, because for the most part, that is how the J2EE community sees them. A typical J2EE application, then, does much of its work in the Model components: executing business logic and providing access to business data. When adding features to your application, you will likely do twice as much work building new Model component features than you will building new View component features (such as JSPs or Velocity templates), although this is only a rule of thumb and depends mostly on how "slick" the application's appearance needs to be. Because we will spend a majority of our effort on the Model, we ought to make it as easy to test as we can. Beyond the effort to fix problems in the Model, those problems tend to have more of an impact on the system.

Consider the impact of a defect in a presentation object: if we display information incorrectly, it is an inconvenience, but this kind of defect does not usually corrupt business data. The business might receive angry phone calls from its customers, but data is safe. When we programmers sit down to fix this kind of defect, we tend not to worry about its impact on the rest of the system. By contrast, when the Model shows incorrect behavior, the problem is more severe: the application might make incorrect business decisions that could corrupt data and cost the business money. Fixing the problem tends to involve correcting the corrupted data (we hope the business performs frequent and thorough backups) as well as changing a part of the system on which multiple units of business logic might depend. These dependencies create enough uncertainty to make us uncomfortable fixing something we know we must fix immediately. The result is a positive feedback loop of bad feelings: we are afraid to fix the problem, which worries the business, so they put more pressure on us to fix the problem, which makes us even more afraid to make a mistake. This is a recipe for ulcers, heart attacks, and early graves for everyone involved. It should be clear, then, the importance of making the Model as easy to test as possible.

It is common for J2EE application architects to choose Enterprise JavaBeans (EJB) technology for implementing Model components. This book is not the appropriate forum to discuss the suitability of EJB to a given application,[1] although we

---

[1] Current suitable forums include www.theserverside.com and http://groups.yahoo.com/group/VirtualPair.

generally believe that a majority of projects using EJB would be better off without it: they need only a small portion of EJB's feature set, but have to contend with all of EJB's complexity in both design and deployment. Let us say that architects ought to be certain that they *need* the special features that EJB provides before deciding to integrate EJB into their application, because, as this chapter will show, we have to work quite hard to make our EJB-based Model components easy to test. That is not to say that the work we do is necessarily *difficult*, but the most flexible design strategy for making EJB components easy to test is to make the EJBs themselves as "thin" as possible, just as one might do with View components. That is, place most of the code in Plain Old Java Objects[2] and use EJBs as simple wrappers that do little more than plug in to the EJB container and delegate to other Java objects. The overall strategy is to be able to execute as much Model component code as possible without involving an EJB container, because that allows tests to be simple and execute quickly. In spite of this general strategy, there are times when testing an EJB does not make sense *without* the container. As this might be confusing, let us provide you with some guiding principles for testing EJBs. The recipes in this chapter elaborate on these principles and provide examples of implementing tests that adhere to them.

Stateless session beans

One often implements each discrete unit of business logic as a method on a session bean. Our "discrete unit" is usually the Transaction Script, as Martin Fowler defines it in *Patterns of Enterprise Application Architecture* [PEAA, 110].[3] Briefly, a Transaction Script is a procedure the system invokes to handle a user request. One usually builds a different Transaction Script for each different kind of request—often one per form the user can submit. Because each Transaction Script is meant to execute in isolation from the others, it makes sense to test each session bean method independently. The general principles of EJB design dictate that we should create stateless services where possible, so we consider stateless session beans first. We recommend starting with a separate test fixture (see recipe 3.4, "Factor out a test fixture") for each Transaction Script. Write a test for every scenario you can imagine and place them all in the same fixture. If you identify a special case (or a number of them) that requires fixture objects that the other "main

---

2 This is commonly abbreviated as *POJO*. See www.martinfowler.com/bliki/POJO.html.

3 It is *common*, but it is not a universal solution. Read further on in PEAA about when and why to use Transaction Script, Domain Model or Table Model. Since Transaction Script is easy to implement, you will encounter it often, and so you will need to know how to test it—and how to refactor away from it.

line" cases do not need, move those special case tests to a new fixture (see recipe 3.7, "Move special case tests to a separate test fixture"). Organizing your tests this way emphasizes the fact that stateless session bean methods are discrete and independent units of business logic. The fact that these methods are implemented on the same class is, mostly, a coincidence of where we happened to type them in, although we *do* try to group them with more care than that—for example, methods with similar parameter lists might belong in the same session bean class.

Notice that we recommend creating a separate fixture for each *method*, rather than for each *class*. You do *not* need to have a one-to-one correspondence between test case classes and production classes. The fact that you might package several Transaction Scripts into a single session bean class does not imply that their tests should be similarly organized. The general rule of "one test case class per production class" makes sense when the classes participate in object-oriented relationships and implement cohesive objects; however, stateless session beans are not really objects in the pure object-oriented sense—they are collections of procedures. The only reason we implement session beans as classes is that the Java language requires it. If this were C++, we might well consider implementing session bean methods as global functions. Session bean classes are different, so we recommend treating them differently. There is no natural way to group session bean tests into a common test fixture. Instead, you should start with separate fixtures, identify the identical ones as you build them, and then consider moving the corresponding tests into a single fixture after you have built three or four fixtures.

Among the different types of Enterprise JavaBeans, stateless session beans may well be the easiest to test. They are excellent candidates for refactoring: the goal is to extract all the business logic out of the session bean method and into a Plain Old Java Object. It then becomes possible to test that logic without involving a container (see recipe 11.1, "Test a session bean method outside the container"). The session bean in this case plays the role of a Bridge between EJB behavior and your business logic, adding distributed computing services to objects without their being aware of it. Objects that do not know about their environment—particularly when that environment is as complex as an EJB container—are the easiest objects to test.

Some session beans invoke other objects they retrieve through JNDI lookups. For these beans, first perform the lookup in the session bean method and then pass the resulting object as a parameter to the newly extracted POJO's business logic method. This is another way to keep your business logic unaware of its environment. See the Discussion section of recipe 11.1 for an example of this technique.

If you have inherited "junk drawer" session beans—you know, everything jammed in the method because that was the easiest place to put it—you need to add tests to it either by simulating the container (see recipe 11.2, "Test a legacy session bean") or by deploying it in a real container (see recipe 11.3, "Test a session bean method in a real container"). We highly recommend writing tests against a simulated container, but if you prefer testing your session bean in a production-quality environment, then by all means test the deployed session bean. Keep in mind that the second technique leads to slower-to-execute tests than the first, and you *might* be overestimating the value of testing your session bean in a real container, compared to a simulated container. If you are unsure of the difference, then do the sensible thing: try both, measure the difference, and let that help you decide.

Stateful session beans

We generally use stateful session beans only in those cases where we cannot assume access to an HTTP session object, such as when building a rich client (Swing or AWT) application that communicates with our business logic through RMI/IIOP rather than over HTTP. If your application only requires a web-based presentation layer, then we highly recommend implementing business logic as stateless session bean methods that accept session data through method parameters. The Controller is then responsible for providing that information when it invokes the business logic. See chapter 12, "Testing Web Components" for information on testing web components and their interaction with HTTP sessions. In general, testing a stateful session bean is not much different than testing a stateless session bean.

One fundamental difference between testing a stateful session bean and a stateless session bean has to do with scale: we tend to treat each stateless session bean method as a separate unit to test; whereas we tend to test a stateful session bean (and all its methods together) as a separate unit to test. The techniques for writing these tests remain the same as for stateless session beans: decouple the business logic from the session bean when possible, test by simulating the container when needed, and test by deploying the session bean into a live container only when nothing else will do. You can use the recipes we mentioned in the previous section to test your stateful session beans as well.

Entity beans

First, we strongly recommend that you use container-managed persistence (CMP) entity beans when possible and bean-managed persistence (BMP) entity beans only where necessary. We make this recommendation because CMP entity beans are easier to build *even though they are more expensive to test.* This is one trade-off we make that incurs additional testing costs, and we do not make this trade-off lightly. As you will see in this chapter, we advocate testing CMP entity beans in a real container and *only* in a real container. For BMP entity beans, we recommend the usual approach: decoupling business logic from EJB services. The benefits of leveraging the container's services outweigh the benefits of making CMP entity beans easy to test. Because CMP entity beans are more expensive to test than the rest of our application, we have the tendency to execute those tests less frequently, using an "offline" continuous integration tool such as Cruise Control. (Here we mean "offline" in the sense that you do not execute these tests as part of your normal programming activity, unless you are working specifically on the CMP entity beans themselves.)

Next, if you have business logic in your entity beans, remove it immediately. In order to maintain the flexibility of pluggable persistence—something very useful for testing, at a minimum—you need to place all business logic in a single application layer. If you insist on having simple business logic in your entity beans, extract an abstract superclass of the bean implementation class and push the logic up there. The goal is to have that business logic available to *any* implementation of your entity class, whether it is an entity bean, a Hibernate component, or an object in a *prevalent system.*[4]

In addition to these general entity bean guidelines, we have provided specific recipes for testing CMP and BMP entity beans. We recommend testing CMP entity beans mainly inside the container (see recipe 11.4, "Test a CMP entity bean"). If your CMP entity bean also has business logic to test, extract that business logic to its own method, then adapt the techniques in recipe 11.1 to test the new method.

If you use container-managed relationships (CMR) and test your CMP entity beans in a live container, then the testing complexity increases considerably. The issues mirror those of testing against a live database, as that is essentially what you need in order to test container-managed relationships. See chapter 10, "Testing and JDBC," for a discussion of the issues in testing against a live database and why we work so hard (well, not so hard as it turns out) to avoid it. We recommend against testing container-managed relationships, because this service is provided entirely within the EJB container itself, and we d*on't test the platform.* Instead, let your End-to-End Tests catch any potential defects related to incorrectly specified container-managed relationships. If you do not find this advice satisfying, or if you have already been bitten by problems in this area, we recommend using XMLUnit to verify the various parts of your container-managed relationship meta data. Use the CMR specification—or a good book on EJBs—to help you decide what your meta data ought to look like, and then write some XMLUnit tests to codify that.

---

4 That is, a system based on Prevayler (www.prevayler.org), an alternative to a database for object persistence.

If you describe your relationships to the container correctly, then the container cannot get them wrong.

Finally we come to BMP entity beans, which we test using a two-pronged attack: we use the session bean recipes in this chapter to test the business logic and the recipes in chapter 10 to test the persistence logic. A BMP entity bean consists only of these two parts: hand-coded persistence logic and simple business logic, and we do not much care for entity beans that contain their own business logic. We recommend using BMP entity beans only as a Bridge between EJBs and persistence logic. They ought to do little more than invoke persistence components (JDBC, Hibernate, Torque, however you implement them) that you have tested—or will test—separately. We show an example of this and discuss the fine points in recipe 11.6, "Test a BMP entity bean." Of course, if you have inherited "junk drawer"-designed entity beans and need to test them as they are, then you might as well treat them like CMP entity beans and test them that way. See recipe 11.4 for our recommended approach.

Message-driven beans

Message-driven beans are just JMS message consumers (or message *listeners*, if you prefer) wrapped inside an EJB. The EJB part of a message-driven bean is quite similar to a session bean, so many of the testing strategies you apply to session beans also make sense for message-driven beans. The most notable of these strategies is refactoring the message-driven bean so that it interacts directly with only the EJB container by extracting a separate JMS message consumer class [Refactoring, 149]. This newly extracted class handles the message without needing access to EJB container-related resources, such as a JNDI directory, so we can easily test the most important behavior of the message-driven bean without involving an EJB container.

Because JMS is asynchronous by nature, it makes sense to test the message producer and the message consumer separately. Because JMS is a framework and its runtime is an expensive external resource (a JMS server), it makes sense to separate the message-processing logic from the message-receiving logic. Put the two together and you need this recipe: test JMS message processing without a JMS server, and don't worry about the JMS details.

If your web application sends JMS messages, you first ought to extract that capability from the Controller and isolate it in a separate component. This gives you the flexibility to move away from a messaging architecture when the need arises. If you have done this or are planning to do this, then you need to test the isolated JMS message producer, and it is always more pleasant to do so without getting a server involved. (See recipe 11.12, "Test a JMS message producer.")

After extracting the JMS message consumer logic from your message-driven bean, you can further separate reading the message (unmarshalling its contents) from processing the message (performing the requisite action). There are three kinds of behavior involved here, which are easier to test when separated:

1. *Reading the message*—You can test receiving and unmarshalling the message contents without worrying about whether the corresponding application logic works. As long as this logic turns the message into the correct message-processing method parameters, you know you can read the message correctly.
2. *Processing the message*—There is some business logic method you need to execute in response to the message you have received. You *could* process a dummy message, but why build a message just to unmarshal it into Java objects? Instead, directly create the Java objects corresponding to that dummy message and use a mock objects approach to ensure that the message-processing method chooses the correct business logic method.
3. *Business logic*—Eventually the application invokes some business logic method in response to the message it has received, but you can easily test the business logic method by simply invoking it directly. At this point, the business logic has no idea that it is responding to a JMS message, so you do not need JMS messages to test it.

Although this appears to be extra work, you are actually investing time writing more tests that will pay off with faster, simpler tests that are easier to understand. It may take twice as long to write them, but you will save time and energy every day thereafter until the end of the project. In our experience, the return on investment is more than high enough to justify the effort.

When all else fails

It is possible that, due to design constraints or fear of the unknown, you cannot test your EJBs in the manner we describe in these recipes. You are unable to refactor the EJBs you need to test, or you are feeling pressure to start testing *now.* If that is the case, then you can take the most straightforward approach to testing EJBs: deploy them in a live container, and then write your tests directly against the EJB's home and component interfaces. These tests are easy to write, but require a live environment, so they are slow to execute and might require complex configuration for each machine that needs to execute them. We understand the pressure to start getting results, so if you feel this pressure, or if you are otherwise unsure where to start, then test your EJBs directly through their interfaces.

We provide the recipes in this chapter to make your EJB testing experience better: faster tests that require less setup to execute and that lead to a more flexible design. Some of these recipes mean extra work up front, but the effort pays off for the rest of the project's lifetime.

11.1 Test a session bean method outside the container

◆ Problem

You want to test a session bean method without involving the container.

◆ Background

If you have previous experience trying to test EJBs in a live container, you understand the issues involved. It takes time to start and stop the container: we have worked on projects where starting the EJB server took fifteen minutes! So even in the days before we practiced Test-Driven Development, or indeed automated testing at all, we were sometimes only able to test our EJB logic about three times per hour. This constrained our ability to program incrementally and forced us to write more code in between testing sessions, which made it difficult to know where a newly injected defect was, slowing us down even more. This is a positive feedback loop of negative feelings, and if nothing else, is bad for morale.

Next, there is the complexity of deployment. Especially in the days before we understood EJBs (but were nevertheless expected to write them), deploying EJBs happened as if by magic. It is quite similar to seeing `public static void main(String[] args) {}` for the first time. If you did not have a background in the C language when you learned Java, then this statement must have looked like a strange way to say, "This is the entry point of my application." There is also a fair amount of strange machinery that one needs to use even to deploy the simplest "Hello, World" session bean. This creates a barrier for the programmer trying to take their first small step in building a new session bean method. Even when you become experienced enough that deploying EJBs is a familiar task, it is slow, so you would like to defer deploying your EJB to the last possible moment. This recipe can help.

◆ Recipe

The general strategy of this recipe, as with many of the J2EE-related recipes in this book, is to refactor towards a more testable design. We recommend that you extract your business logic from the session bean method and place it in a Plain

Old Java Object (POJO). The resulting session bean, with its business logic removed, then plays the role of Remote Facade [PEAA, 388], and generally becomes *too simple to break* (see the essay B.1, "Too simple to break"). At this point, you can use the techniques in part 1 to test the business logic POJO entirely in memory. You can achieve all this by applying a refactoring similar to Move Method [Refactoring, 142].

Rather than move the session bean method, you move the *implementation* of the method (but not the method itself) into a new Domain Model class, and then change the session bean method to delegate its work to the new Domain Model class. To illustrate this we return to our Coffee Shop application and the feature that displays the shopcart, which has been implemented by a `ShopcartOperations` session bean. We have a method that adds coffee to the shopcart and another method that retrieves the shopcart on demand. The Controller is now blissfully ignorant of where or how the shopcart is stored. Listing 11.1 shows the code for the session bean implementation, with some of the irrelevant code omitted. The `create()`method creates an empty shopcart and the methods `addToShopcart()` and `getShopcartItems()` behave as their names suggest.

Listing 11.1 ShopcartOperationsBean

```
package junit.cookbook.coffee.model.ejb;

import java.util.*;
import junit.cookbook.coffee.model.CoffeeQuantity;

public class ShopcartOperationsBean
    implements javax.ejb.SessionBean {

    private Map coffeeQuantities;

    public void ejbCreate() throws javax.ejb.CreateException {
        coffeeQuantities = new HashMap();
    }

    public void addToShopcart(Vector requestedCoffeeQuantities) {
        for (Iterator i =
            requestedCoffeeQuantities.iterator();
            i.hasNext();
            ) {

            CoffeeQuantity each = (CoffeeQuantity) i.next();

            String eachCoffeeName = each.getCoffeeName();
            CoffeeQuantity currentQuantity;

            if (coffeeQuantities
                .containsKey(eachCoffeeName)) {
```

```
                currentQuantity =
                    (CoffeeQuantity) coffeeQuantities.get(
                        eachCoffeeName);

            }
            else {
                currentQuantity =
                    new CoffeeQuantity(0, eachCoffeeName);

                coffeeQuantities.put(
                    eachCoffeeName,
                    currentQuantity);
            }

            coffeeQuantities.put(
                eachCoffeeName,
                currentQuantity.add(each));
        }
    }

    public Vector getShopcartItems() {
        return new Vector(coffeeQuantities.values());
    }
}
```

The test we have in mind simulates two transactions, adding coffees A and B to the shopcart first, and then adding coffees A and C second. This is perhaps the most complex test we can imagine for adding coffee to the shopcart, because the second transaction adds a new product *and* adds more of a product already in the shopcart. If this test passes, then we feel confident that the others will pass. This is the test we want to write:

```
public void testComplexCase() throws Exception {
    // Create a shopcart somehow!

    Vector coffeeQuantities1 = new Vector();
    coffeeQuantities1.add(new CoffeeQuantity(2, "A"));
    coffeeQuantities1.add(new CoffeeQuantity(3, "B"));

    shopcart.addToShopcart(coffeeQuantities1);
    assertEquals(coffeeQuantities1, shopcart.getShopcartItems());

    Vector coffeeQuantities2 = new Vector();
    coffeeQuantities2.add(new CoffeeQuantity(1, "A"));
    coffeeQuantities2.add(new CoffeeQuantity(2, "C"));

    shopcart.addToShopcart(coffeeQuantities2);

    Vector expectedTotalQuantities = new Vector();
    expectedTotalQuantities.add(new CoffeeQuantity(3, "A"));
    expectedTotalQuantities.add(new CoffeeQuantity(3, "B"));
```

```
        expectedTotalQuantities.add(new CoffeeQuantity(2, "C"));

        assertEquals(expectedTotalQuantities, shopcart.getShopcartItems());
    }
```

Notice that there is nothing in this test that mentions EJBs. Also notice that we have not yet been able to write the line of code that creates the shopcart object we want to test. This is the point at which we create a new Domain Model object representing the shopcart business logic and add to it the appropriate methods. We call this new class `ShopcartLogic`, which allows us to replace the opening comment in the code with this line of code:

```
ShopcartLogic shopcart = new ShopcartLogic();
```

We now copy the two methods, `addToShopcart()` and `getShopcartItems()` from the session bean implementation class into `ShopcartLogic`. When we do this, we realize that we also need to copy the session bean's client state (the variable `coffeeQuantities`) into `ShopcartLogic`, or the latter does not compile. The result is the class shown in listing 11.2.

Listing 11.2 `ShopcartLogic`

```
package junit.cookbook.coffee.model;

import java.util.*;

public class ShopcartLogic {
    private Map coffeeQuantities;

    public void addToShopcart(Vector requestedCoffeeQuantities) {
        for (Iterator i =
            requestedCoffeeQuantities.iterator();
            i.hasNext();
            ) {

            CoffeeQuantity each = (CoffeeQuantity) i.next();

            String eachCoffeeName = each.getCoffeeName();
            CoffeeQuantity currentQuantity;

            if (coffeeQuantities
                .containsKey(eachCoffeeName)) {

                currentQuantity =
                    (CoffeeQuantity) coffeeQuantities.get(
                        eachCoffeeName);

            }
            else {
                currentQuantity =
                    new CoffeeQuantity(0, eachCoffeeName);
```

```
                coffeeQuantities.put(
                    eachCoffeeName,
                    currentQuantity);
            }

            coffeeQuantities.put(
                eachCoffeeName,
                currentQuantity.add(each));
        }
    }

    public Vector getShopcartItems() {
        return new Vector(coffeeQuantities.values());
    }
}
```

When we execute our test, it fails with a `NullPointerException`. We do not initialize the `coffeeQuantities` collection in `ShopcartLogic`. To fix this problem, we copy the body of the session bean's `ejbCreate()` method into a new constructor for `ShopcartLogic`. Here is the resulting constructor:

```
public ShopcartLogic() {
    coffeeQuantities = new HashMap();
}
```

We execute the test one more time and receive the following failure:

```
junit.framework.AssertionFailedError: expected:
  <[<3, A>, <3, B>, <2, C>]> but was:<[<3, A>, <2, C>, <3, B>]>
```

Looking at the failure, we see that the expected shopcart contents and the actual shopcart contents are the same, but that the items appear in a different order. This test *should* pass, but when we compare `Vector` objects for equality, the index at which each element is stored affects whether the collections are equal (see recipe 2.9, "Let collections compare themselves"). We can immediately think of two ways to fix this problem:

- Compare the expected and actual shopcart contents in a way that ignores the index of each element.
- Return the shopcart items as a `Set`, rather than as a `Vector`.

When we implemented the session bean we chose `Vector` because `Vector` is serializable, and the EJB specification requires all method parameters and return types for remote EJB methods to be serializable at runtime.[5] To keep confusion to a minimum, we specified `Vector` rather than rely on ourselves to get the runtime

[5] This is a slight simplification. These types may be `String`, primitives, implementations of `javax.rmi.Remote` or of `java.io.Serializable`. See the EJB specification for details.

type right.[6] The `Set` interface does not extend `Serializable`, so there is no *guarantee* that all `Set` implementations are serializable, in spite of the fact that `HashSet` and `TreeSet`—the two basic implementations of `Set` in Java—are each serializable. While deciding whether to change the return type of `getShopcartItems()` from `Vector` to `Set` (which has a slight ripple effect in our design), we can get to a "quick green" by wrapping both the expected and actual shopcart items in `Set` objects and comparing those. This is one of those tricks that Java programmers typically learn about through experience, rather than through a tutorial. We change the final assertion of our test to the following:

```
assertEquals(
    new HashSet(expectedTotalQuantities),
    new HashSet(shopcart.getShopcartItems()));
```

Finally the test passes. We can now change the session bean method to delegate to this Domain Model object. Listing 11.3 shows the final session bean implementation code, or at least the relevant parts. We have highlighted the changes in bold print.

Listing 11.3 The final version of `ShopcartOperationsBean`

```
package junit.cookbook.coffee.model.ejb;

import java.util.Vector;
import junit.cookbook.coffee.model.ShopcartLogic;

public class ShopcartOperationsBean
    implements javax.ejb.SessionBean {

    private javax.ejb.SessionContext mySessionCtx;
    private ShopcartLogic shopcart;

    public void ejbCreate()
        throws javax.ejb.CreateException {

        shopcart = new ShopcartLogic();
    }

    public void addToShopcart(Vector requestedCoffeeQuantities) {
        shopcart.addToShopcart(requestedCoffeeQuantities);
    }

    public Vector getShopcartItems() {
        return shopcart.getShopcartItems();
    }
}
```

[6] If we were doing it all again, we would change the `public` interface to `List` or `Collection`, rather than `Vector`. The good news is that we can always refactor.

This session bean implementation class is *too simple to break*: it does nothing more than delegate method invocations to another object. Such a class cannot break unless there is a defect in the class to which it delegates, which is `ShopcartLogic` in our case. If it cannot break, why test it? Test the underlying business logic, instead, as we have done.

Let us summarize what we did, so that you can apply this technique to your own session beans:

1. We created a new Domain Model class that implements the same methods that are on the session bean's remote component interface.
2. We wrote a test that uses the new Domain Model class rather than the session bean implementation class.
3. We copied the body of the methods we wanted to test from the session bean implementation class into the Domain Model class.
4. We copied the relevant instance variables (fields) into the Domain Model class.
5. We copied the body of any relevant `ejbCreate()` method into a corresponding constructor in the Domain Model class.
6. We tested the Domain Model methods until we were satisfied that they work.
7. We removed the body of each session bean implementation method, replacing it with a simple invocation of the Domain Model's corresponding method. Those session bean methods are now *too simple to break*.

From here we simply repeat this process until we have moved all business logic from the session bean implementation classes into the Domain Model classes. You can apply this same technique to all your session bean methods, whether stateless or stateful. After you do, you can test all your business logic entirely outside the container, with tests that execute at a rate of *hundreds* per second rather than *a few* per second, as we have experienced in past projects.

◆ Discussion

If you use this technique to refactor an existing session bean layer, you might be put off by the extra classes you begin to write. You will feel as though you are doubling a large part of your code base "just for testing." First, we feel that testing is important enough to warrant the extra code: we would rather have twice as much tested code than a smaller amount of untested code. Still, we recognize that extra code of any kind introduces its own costs: the programmers need to read it and understand it. All things being equal, less code is better. Can we avoid this extra code somehow? Yes. In many cases it is possible to instantiate your session bean implementation class directly and test its methods just as you test any other method that returns a value. In particular, any session bean method that does not invoke services the EJB container provides (such as a JNDI lookup) can be tested this way. In our Coffee Shop example, we might write the test as follows:

```
package junit.cookbook.coffee.model.logic.test;

// import statements omitted

public class AddToShopcartSessionBeanTest extends TestCase {
    public void testComplexCase() throws Exception {
        ShopcartOperationsBean shopcart = new ShopcartOperationsBean();
        shopcart.ejbCreate();

        // Rest of the test as written previously
    }
}
```

If you choose this technique, *do not forget to invoke* `ejbCreate()`! This method acts as the implementation class's "second constructor," so calling only its (Java) constructor is insufficient. One drawback to this approach is that the test now depends on part of the J2EE interface: namely `CreateException`, which `ejbCreate()` might throw. This makes it necessary to add a part of the J2EE library (in our case it was `j2ee.jar`) to your class path when building and executing your tests. Is this a small price to pay for a simpler design? We leave it up to you to try them both and judge for yourself. If someone decides tomorrow that your business logic layer ought to use Jini for object distribution rather than EJB, then you will need to perform the refactoring this recipe suggests, anyway.

NOTE *A testable design is a better design*—George Latkiewicz, one of our most prolific reviewers, emphasized to us the point underlying the previous paragraph: this is yet another case where designing for testability *naturally* improves the design in other ways. He wrote, "By following the refactoring recommended in this recipe, the EJBs become what they should have been all along—merely wrappers that provide the benefits and services of the container to the guts of your application. Now an EJB guru can make sure that the wrappers do the 'right thing the right way' without being distracted by lots of application logic code, and similarly, the application developer can inspect the domain classes without needing to understand all the intricacies of EJB.

"If it weren't for all the hype that led to the EJB bandwagon, one wouldn't have even *considered* a framework which required such an invasive solution to the problems that EJB addresses (distribution, transactions). So, what this recipe reminds us of is that EJB doesn't really force us to do what we shouldn't be doing. It is interesting to note that many of the new emerging frameworks (Spring, JDO, JBoss 4) have, as a central design goal, the theme: "leave my POJO alone."

We could not agree more.

Some of your session bean methods retrieve objects through JNDI. Because this is a service that your application server provides, you cannot move this code into a Plain Old Java Object and expect it to work outside the application server runtime environment. We suggest you treat this object as a parameter to your business logic, and it is up to your application (and the distributed objects services it uses) to decide how to retrieve it. Add that object to the Domain Model business method interface as a parameter, and then have the session bean retrieve the object using JNDI and pass it into the Domain Model business method. Your test can provide that object any way it likes, including passing in hard-coded values, an in-memory implementation, or a mock object (see recipe 11.6). You will use this technique when your session bean uses an entity bean to provide business data persistence. The session bean retrieves the entity bean by JNDI and passes it as a parameter to the Domain Model. In your test, provide some dummy implementation of the entity bean's component interface (remote or local, depending on your needs) so that you can test the business logic without worrying about the correctness of your persistence mechanism. Test your entity beans on their own, using the other recipes in this chapter.

It is important to understand why we use EJB technology. We introduce EJBs into our J2EE application designs to provide object distribution, declarative security, and declarative transactions—and nothing more. When we incorporate EJBs into an application, the goal is to add these features to existing business logic, so we should be able to test the business logic without worrying about EJBs. Even if it is "too late" for the session beans that someone has already written, if you decide to write all new session beans to be mere Remote Facades, then you will find yourself building those session beans more quickly than you did before.

That is all well and good when considering future session beans, but what if you need to test existing session beans that you are not allowed to refactor? In that case, you need to either simulate the container (see recipe 11.2) or test in a live environment (see recipe 11.3). The resulting tests are slower to execute and often more complex to write, but you have no choice. Good luck.

◆ Related

- 2.9—Let collections compare themselves
- 11.2—Test a legacy session bean
- 11.3—Test a session bean method in a real container
- 11.6—Test a BMP entity bean
- B.1—Too simple to break

11.2 Test a legacy session bean

◆ Problem

You need to test a legacy session bean, which appears to require being tested in a container. You are hoping that there is a better way.

◆ Background

You have inherited session beans that you are not allowed to change, for whatever reason. As a result, you need to test them in a container, but doing so is costly in at least two ways:

- The tests are slower to execute, costing you time every time you execute the tests.
- The tests are more complicated to write, adding effort to writing the tests.

Nevertheless, if the session bean in question embeds the business logic directly inside it, you have no choice but to test it within a container. The good news is that it need not be a *real* container, saving you some time, if not effort.

◆ Recipe

If your session bean depends on other objects it obtains through a JNDI lookup—and that is the most likely case—then your best option is to use the MockEJB (www.mockejb.org) framework.[7] This allows you to substitute fake implementations of those collaborators at runtime, which further isolates the session bean's behavior from the behavior of its collaborators. This way you can test just the session bean. You will test its collaborators in isolation as well, but not right now. (One thing at a time.) Consider the common example of a session bean that con-

[7] There were some major changes between version 0.4 (August 2003) and 0.5 (December 2003) of MockEJB. We use version 0.5 in this book.

tains some business logic and uses an entity bean for object persistence. Say that we have inherited an implementation of a session bean to manage a shopper's shopcart, shown in listing 11.4. Here, `LegacyShopcart` is an entity bean representing a single shopcart.

Listing 11.4 A session bean using an entity bean

```
package junit.cookbook.coffee.model.ejb;

import java.util.*;
import javax.ejb.CreateException;
import javax.naming.*;
import javax.rmi.PortableRemoteObject;
import junit.cookbook.coffee.model.CoffeeQuantity;

public class LegacyShopcartOperationsBean
    implements javax.ejb.SessionBean {

    private javax.ejb.SessionContext mySessionCtx;
    private LegacyShopcart shopcart;

    public javax.ejb.SessionContext getSessionContext() {
        return mySessionCtx;
    }

    public void setSessionContext(javax.ejb.SessionContext ctx) {
        mySessionCtx = ctx;
    }

    public void addToShopcart(Vector requestedCoffeeQuantities) {
        for (Iterator i = requestedCoffeeQuantities.iterator();
            i.hasNext();
            ) {

            CoffeeQuantity each = (CoffeeQuantity) i.next();

            String eachCoffeeName = each.getCoffeeName();

            int currentQuantity;
            if (shopcart.containsCoffeeNamed(eachCoffeeName)) {
                currentQuantity = shopcart.getQuantity(eachCoffeeName);
            }
            else {
                currentQuantity = 0;
            }

            shopcart.setQuantity(
                eachCoffeeName,
                currentQuantity + each.getAmountInKilograms());
        }
    }

    public void ejbCreate() throws javax.ejb.CreateException {
        try {
```

```
            Context context = new InitialContext();
            Object homeAsObject = context.lookup("ejb/legacy/Shopcart");

            LegacyShopcartHome home =
                (LegacyShopcartHome) PortableRemoteObject.narrow(
                    homeAsObject,
                    LegacyShopcartHome.class);

            shopcart = home.findByUserName("jbrains");
        }
        catch (NamingException e) {
            throw new CreateException(
                "Naming exception: " + e.getMessage());
        }
    }

    public void ejbActivate() {
    }

    public void ejbPassivate() {
    }

    public void ejbRemove() {
        shopcart = null;
    }
}
```

Unfortunately for us, this is legacy code, which we define as "code without tests."[8] Adding to our bad fortune, we have been instructed to test this code and not refactor it, because of time constraints and project pressures. Here is our approach:

1. Use MockEJB and the Self-Shunt Pattern[9] to "fake out" looking up a shopcart using `LegacyShopcartHome`. Without this, we would need test data and a live database to execute this test. No thanks!
2. Use EasyMock to create a mock `LegacyShopcart`. Without this, the test would depend on the correctness of the `LegacyShopcart` EJB, which we plan to test separately, anyway. One thing at a time.
3. Use MockEJB to deploy our fake `LegacyShopcartHome`, which will return our mock `LegacyShopcart` when our session bean invokes `findByUserName()`.

[8] Some people find this definition amusing, but others have commented how apt it is. You decide. Apparently Alan Francis also defines legacy code this way, and said so at Agile Scotland 2003. Strictly speaking, we wrote these words here before he spoke them there, but I suppose we can call it a draw. (See www.scottishdevelopers.com/modules/news/article.php?storyid=11)

[9] www.objectmentor.com/resources/articles/SelfShunPtrn.pdf, written by Michael Feathers.

With these Test Objects in place, we can write our test. First, let us look at the code that deploys all the objects we are *not* testing, shown in listing 11.5.

Listing 11.5 Deploying some objects with MockEJB

```
package junit.cookbook.coffee.model.ejb.test;

import java.util.*;

import javax.ejb.*;
import javax.naming.*;
import javax.rmi.PortableRemoteObject;

import junit.cookbook.coffee.model.CoffeeQuantity;
import junit.cookbook.coffee.model.ejb.*;
import junit.framework.TestCase;

import org.easymock.MockControl;
import org.mockejb.*;
import org.mockejb.jndi.*;
import org.mockejb.jndi.MockContext;

public class AddToShopcartTest
    extends TestCase
    implements LegacyShopcartHome {

    private static final String SESSION_BEAN_JNDI_NAME =
        "ejb/legacy/ShopcartOperations";
    private static final String ENTITY_BEAN_JNDI_NAME =
        "ejb/legacy/Shopcart";

    private LegacyShopcart mockShopcart;
    private MockControl shopcartControl;
    private MockContainer mockContainer;

    protected void setUp() throws Exception {
        MockContextFactory.setAsInitial();
        Context context = new InitialContext();
        context.bind(ENTITY_BEAN_JNDI_NAME, this);

        shopcartControl =
            MockControl.createNiceControl(LegacyShopcart.class);
        mockShopcart = (LegacyShopcart) shopcartControl.getMock();

        mockContainer = new MockContainer(context);
        deployLegacyShopcartOperationsEjb(mockContainer);
    }

    private void deployLegacyShopcartOperationsEjb(
        MockContainer mockContainer)
        throws NamingException {
```

Mock-deploy test case as entity bean home

Use EasyMock to generate mock entity bean

Mock-deploy session bean

```
        SessionBeanDescriptor shopcartOperationsBeanDescriptor =
            new SessionBeanDescriptor(
                SESSION_BEAN_JNDI_NAME,
                LegacyShopcartOperationsHome.class,
                LegacyShopcartOperations.class,
                LegacyShopcartOperationsBean.class);

        mockContainer.deploy(shopcartOperationsBeanDescriptor);
    }

    public LegacyShopcart findByUserName(String userName) {
        return mockShopcart;
    }

    public void remove(Object object)
        throws RemoveException, EJBException {

        // Intentionally do nothing
    }
}
```

Mock-deploy session bean

"Self-Shunt" methods

We use the Self-Shunt pattern here so that we can easily substitute our mock `LegacyShopcart` for the actual `LegacyShopcart` entity bean that the EJB container will return in production. You might be tempted to write a small, in-memory version of `LegacyShopcartHome`, complete with a `Map` of user names to shopcart objects, but for this test there is no need. We do not care where the shopcart entity bean comes from, or even if it is a real entity bean! Instead, we are concerned with testing the session bean in isolation. That is the motivation for using MockEJB. Now that we have all the Test Objects in place, let us look at the test, which we add to class `AddToShopcartTest`:

```
public void testEmptyShopcart() throws Exception {
    final String coffeeName = "Sumatra";

    mockShopcart.containsCoffeeNamed(coffeeName);
    shopcartControl.setReturnValue(false);

    mockShopcart.setQuantity(coffeeName, 1);
    shopcartControl.setVoidCallable();

    shopcartControl.replay();

    LegacyShopcartOperationsHome home =
        lookupShopcartOperationsHome();

    Vector requestedQuantities = new Vector() {
        {
            add(new CoffeeQuantity(1, coffeeName));
        }
    };
```

```
        home.create().addToShopcart(requestedQuantities);

        shopcartControl.verify();
    }
```

The majority of this test is concerned with setting expectations on the mock `LegacyShopcart` entity bean. Because we do not have access to what the original programmer was thinking at the time she wrote this code, we are forced to treat the code as the *specification* on which to base our tests. If you have access to a documented specification and can verify that that specification still makes sense for the current needs of the project, then use that to write your tests. Here, we are trying to add a single coffee product to an empty shopcart, so we expect `LegacyShopcartOperationsBean` to do the following:

- Ask the shopcart if it contains any Sumatra coffee.
- Set the current quantity of Sumatra to be 1 kg, since there was no Sumatra in the shopcart.

Because the shopcart is empty, we need to tell the mock shopcart to return `false` when asked whether it contains any Sumatra coffee, so we invoke `setReturnValue(false)` to do that. This is the way we *simulate* an empty shopcart, rather than *duplicate* an empty shopcart using an in-memory implementation of a shopcart (probably just a wrapper around a `Map` of product names to quantities). It is a bad idea to duplicate the essential logic of a shopcart—once in the test and once in the production entity bean. We would use the production entity bean if we could do so without dragging that big ugly EJB container with it.

As with most mock object approaches, we invoke `mockShopcart.verify()` at the end of our test to verify that the expectations we set at the beginning of the test are met by the production code. In this case, they are, and the test passes! First, notice that we were able to test the session bean without changing any of its code, but also notice the amount of effort that went into mocking the behavior of all the session bean's collaborators: its home interface, an entity bean, and the EJB container. If we were able to separate the business logic from the session bean, we would at least be able to eliminate the need to simulate the EJB container. Compare this to recipe 11.1 to see how avoiding the EJB container (and JNDI service) can simplify testing as well as improve the flexibility of your design.

◆ *Discussion*

If your session bean does not interact with the application server's services at all, then there is a more straightforward approach. In this case, just instantiate the EJB implementation class in your test and invoke methods on it. With this approach, you need to simulate the container to a certain extent, invoking the EJB lifecycle methods to ensure that each does what it should. The good news is that, for example, you can test your bean's passivation behavior by simply invoking `ejbCreate()` followed by `ejbPassivate()`. There is no need for the complex test environment setup of starting a container. You merely simulate that small part of the container's behavior germane to the current test. We recommend using the EJB lifecycle diagrams in the EJB specification as a guideline in order to determine which lifecycle methods to invoke for a given test. When you take this approach, you are treating the EJB implementation class just like any other Java class, so you can apply whatever testing techniques are appropriate. You can forget for the moment that you are testing an EJB, and that just makes the tests easier.

If you are able to test your session bean using MockEJB, then keep in mind that your job is not quite finished. In using MockEJB you are mocking up your session bean's collaborators, *including* how they are deployed into a JNDI directory. This means that in spite of your good work, it is still possible for the session bean to fail in production: if you incorrectly deploy the objects on which the session bean depends, then the session bean will appear to fail. To avoid this rather unpleasant problem—one which you usually discover after you think you have finished your task—be sure to include those dependent objects in a test that verifies that they are correctly deployed into the live JNDI directory. See recipe 11.13, "Test the content of your JNDI directory" for details.

At the time we write this, MockEJB supports session beans and message-driven beans, but not yet entity beans. We do not fully understand the limits of testing with MockEJB, but if you are testing legacy EJBs then *you* might be the one to find those limits. If you find you cannot get past them, then your next choice is to test the EJBs using Cactus, as we describe in 11.3 Test a session bean method in a real container. We favor MockEJB over Cactus, but recognize that MockEJB does not solve all our problems, so use MockEJB when you can and Cactus when you must.[10]

◆ *Related*

- 11.1—Test a session bean method outside the container
- 11.13—Test the content of your JNDI directory
- MockEJB (www.mockejb.org)
- Self-Shunt Pattern (www.objectmentor.com/resources/articles/SelfShunPtrn.pdf)

---

[10] Do not mistake this to mean that we dislike Cactus. Rather, we dislike testing domain logic inside a container, since domain logic should be separate from implementation details. We are glad that Cactus is there when we need it!

11.3 Test a session bean method in a real container

◆ Problem

You want to test a session bean method inside a real target container.

◆ Background

There are a number of reasons why this might be necessary, including the possibility that your application server supports a particular feature or extension, or has a particular defect that you need to take into account during testing. We refuse to name names, but life can be interesting moving from application server to application server, and it is possible to uncover production code "defects"—even when they merely expose platform defects—running against a live container that you might not find through simulation. You might also want to execute performance tests, the results of which depend on being executed in a real environment.[11] If you need to test your session bean in a real container, then this recipe can help you do it.

◆ Recipe

Put simply, use Cactus (http://jakarta.apache.org/cactus). Cactus is a JUnit-based test framework that executes tests in a J2EE application server. More than that, Cactus allows you to pretend that you are executing tests on the client side—that is, outside the application server—by executing them transparently on the server side. It is an evolutionary step beyond the idea of simply executing server-side tests on the server (see the Discussion section for more). Let us return to our Coffee Shop application and the `ShopcartOperations` session bean. Recall that this session bean performs shopcart-oriented operations, such as adding items to it. We want to test adding a single coffee product to an empty shopcart. With Cactus, the test is straightforward—almost indistinguishable from a plain-vanilla JUnit test case. We show the test in listing 11.6.[12]

Listing 11.6 A Cactus test for adding a product to a shopcart

```
package junit.cookbook.coffee.model.ejb.test;

import java.util.Vector;

import javax.naming.*;
```

[11] You can execute performance tests outside the application server; however, you would then only be able to interpret the results relative to one another. Those results offer limited feedback.

[12] This test requires Cactus on the class path. We recommend adding the entire contents of the Cactus `lib` directory, just to be safe.

```
import javax.rmi.PortableRemoteObject;

import junit.cookbook.coffee.model.CoffeeQuantity;
import junit.cookbook.coffee.model.ejb.*;
import junit.cookbook.coffee.model.ejb.ShopcartOperationsHome;

import org.apache.cactus.ServletTestCase;

public class AddToShopcartTest extends ServletTestCase {
    public void testEmptyShopcart() throws Exception {
        Context context = new InitialContext();
        Object homeAsObject = context.lookup("ejb/ShopcartOperations");

        ShopcartOperationsHome home =
            (ShopcartOperationsHome) PortableRemoteObject.narrow(
                homeAsObject,
                ShopcartOperationsHome.class);

        Vector requestedCoffeeQuantities = new Vector() {
            {
                add(new CoffeeQuantity(2, "Sumatra"));
            }
        };

        ShopcartOperations shopcartOperations = home.create();
        shopcartOperations.addToShopcart(requestedCoffeeQuantities);

        Vector items = shopcartOperations.getShopcartItems();
        assertEquals(1, items.size());
        assertEquals(new CoffeeQuantity(2, "Sumatra"), items.get(0));
    }
}
```

Use Cactus's server-side TestCase class

The only real difference between this test and a regular JUnit test is that this test case class extends Cactus's `ServletTestCase`, rather than `junit.framework.TestCase`. The class `ServletTestCase` provides the transparent server-side test execution service, so you only need to write your test, deploy it into the application server, and then execute the tests from any test runner. Cactus transparently delegates executing the test to a server-side component—at least it is transparent when your test *passes.* When your test fails, you receive an "Internal Error" message, HTTP Status Code 500, followed by a description of the problem that occurred on the server. Aside from this extra error message, though, test failure reporting occurs as it does when executing tests locally. Cactus is truly a wonderful tool for server-side testing.

We recommend deploying your tests in a separate J2EE application (*.ear file) so that they remain isolated from your production web application resources, and are not subject to any unnecessary security policies. This simplifies the test environment considerably. In addition, you should read all about the integration between Cactus and Ant on the Cactus web site. If you are using Ant to build your product and run your tests, then it is easy to integrate Cactus into that environment.

◆ ***Discussion***

This technique helps you cope with having to test session beans in a real container. If you can, we recommend refactoring the session bean instead. Extract the business logic and test it outside the container, as we describe in recipe 11.1. We recognize that you are not always able to do this, but if you can, then you should. Your next alternative is to simulate the container, as we describe in recipe 11.2, using MockEJB.

If you need to test your EJB in the container, but do not wish to use Cactus, then we suggest you write a simple servlet that executes tests on the server on your behalf and reports the results as a web page. Before you run off and write that yourself, keep in mind that this is exactly how Cactus began, so we recommend you simply use it. Still, if you find that Cactus is more than you need, then you can start with your own, simpler solution. When you reach the point where you realize you are reimplementing Cactus, stop. There is little point in doing that.

One last comment about testing a session bean in a container: be aware of *all* the costs of testing within the container, because they add up. First, you have the complex test environment: you need to start and stop the application server as needed, you have to configure the application server correctly and, in many cases, you have to deal with licensing issues. Next, you have a slow test environment: remote communications, JNDI lookups, database access; these things all add to test execution time. When you consider that the goal of Programmer Testing is to execute the tests *after every change* to ensure you have not broken anything, it becomes obvious that these tests are simply too slow to support this goal. Perhaps the most insidious cost, though, is an indirect one: most session beans interact (eventually) with the database. Testing these session beans in a live environment means setting up test data for each and every test. We discussed in chapter 10, "Testing and JDBC," the cost of setting up test data, whether you try setting up fresh data for each test or, worse, try to have all your tests share a common test data set. These are costs that just keep climbing throughout the lifetime of the project, and which grow superlinearly—that is, costs which accelerate. That is bad news. These are the reasons we recommend that you limit the amount of EJB testing you do in a live environment. The costs just add up far too quickly for our liking.

◆ ***Related***

- 11.1—Test a session bean method outside the container
- 11.2—Test a legacy session bean
- Chapter 10—Testing and JDBC
- Cactus (http://jakarta.apache.org/cactus)

11.4 Test a CMP entity bean

◆ ***Problem***

You would like to test a container-managed persistence (CMP) entity bean.

◆ ***Background***

Part of the point of using container-managed persistence is to let the application server—specifically the EJB container—provide the vast majority of entity bean code for you. Because we recommend that you *don't test the platform,* it seems quite reasonable not to test CMP entity beans at all. It *seems* reasonable, but it is not. Even though you might not need to write much code for CMP entity beans—simply declare interfaces and methods—you still need to specify your CMP entity bean at least in enough detail that the container can fill in the rest. This is why we recommend that you try testing the CMP entity bean meta data, rather than the bean itself (see recipe 11.5, "Test CMP meta data outside the container"). We have found that, much of the time, this is enough, but we recognize that there are times when you need more confidence than that.

If you have encountered specific, recurring defects with CMP entity beans, then we recommend writing at least *some* tests to guide future work. You might be working with a slightly defective application server, you might be working with CMP entity beans that someone else wrote (and for which there are no tests), or perhaps you are learning to write CMP entity beans and would like to use tests to provide ongoing feedback while you learn.[13] Whatever the reason, we understand that some programmers want to test "the real thing" and not "just the meta data." If you fall into that category, then this recipe is for you.

---

[13] This is an excellent technique for learning a new programming language. When J. B. took his first steps in Squeak Smalltalk, he wrote Learning Tests using SUnit, the Smalltalk equivalent to (and predecessor of) JUnit.

◆ *Recipe*

The most direct way to test a CMP entity bean is to test it inside the container. If you wish to do this, then we highly recommend using Cactus. In this recipe we will describe the kinds of tests you likely need to write. To write them, use the same techniques we describe in recipe 11.2. To test a CMP entity bean requires testing these features:

- The mapping between the entity bean class and the database table
- The mapping between the entity bean container-managed fields and the table columns
- Container-managed relationships, if any
- All the finder methods

We discuss testing security and transaction attributes elsewhere (chapter 13, "Testing J2EE applications") because these issues apply to more than just CMP entity beans.

You can test both levels of mappings (class/table and field/column) by storing a few objects and loading them back. Be sure to exercise each field of the entity bean at least once. You can test relationships by storing an empty collection of related objects, loading it back, adding an object or two, and then storing it once again. As for the finder methods, unfortunately there is no substitute for setting up test data, invoking the finder, and verifying the results.

In chapter 10 we discussed the exorbitant cost of testing against live data from a database, so we implore you to keep this in mind as you test your CMP entity bean finder methods. Once you gain some confidence writing EJBQL queries—or even if you have that confidence already—move your live-container tests to a separate test suite. Execute those tests using a background automated build tool such as Cruise Control. When someone changes a finder method, he *must* execute those tests to verify the change; otherwise, let Cruise Control run them in the background as a safety net against unexpected changes.

Finder methods are the one part of CMP entity beans that are the most prone to error, so we recommend that you test them thoroughly. At the same time, we recognize that those tests are expensive to execute, which is why we recommend executing them in the background. Aside from finder methods, though, we recommend testing just CMP entity bean meta data, since *that* is what you write. See recipe 11.5 for details.

◆ *Discussion*

You will notice that this list of tests does not include, for example, verifying the entity bean in the presence of null values, its unique indices, duplicate keys, or invalid foreign keys. The application server writes code to handle those situations, and not you, so you ought to focus on testing how you react to these conditions. Presumably you have session beans that invoke this CMP entity bean. Rather than test whether the EJB container correctly throws `DuplicateKeyException` (which is outside your control, anyway), test how your session bean reacts when the entity bean throws a `DuplicateKeyException`.[14] *Don't test the platform.*

We have been on projects where it has been suggested to test CMP entity beans "through the End-to-End Tests." This would mean using black-box—"from the GUI, to the back end, and back"—tests to verify that the entity beans fit into the overall application correctly. We *strongly* recommend that you resist the urge to do this. First, End-to-End Tests are not well-suited to isolate defects, as they involve the entire application. These tests are meant to show that you have implemented features the way they were specified. Next, consider the variety of tests you might want to write for a single entity bean, checking all the finder methods for various boundary conditions and so on. Imagine how *slow* a test suite you would have if you tested all these boundary conditions with a web container, an EJB container, EJB-to-EJB communication, *and* all the business logic executing around it. Do not go down that road, as it will only lead you to pain and misery. We have been that way. If you are going to test CMP entity beans in a live container, then test them in isolation.

One more note, related to deployment: if your tests themselves are going to set up and tear down test data in the database, be careful with your choice of entity bean commit options. If your test uses JDBC (whether directly, or indirectly through a tool such as DbUnit) to create and remove test data while your EJBs are running, then do *not* deploy your entity beans using "exclusive database access," also known as "commit option A." Certainly your entity beans do not have exclusive access to the database, so especially if your tests change the live data in the middle of a transaction, you will not be able to assume exclusive access to the database for your entity beans. You can detect this problem if your tests fail because of unexpected duplicate key or foreign key problems, or your entity beans appear to have stale data during your tests but not in production. Consult the EJB specification or

---

[14] We recommend using MockEJB and deploying a crash test dummy version of the entity bean that always throws the desired exception. See recipe 11.1 for details.

an EJB-specific book such as *Mastering Enterprise JavaBeans*[15] for details on the various commit options.

◆ Related

- 11.1—Test a session bean method outside the container
- 11.5—Test CMP meta data outside the container
- Chapter 10—Testing and JDBC
- Chapter 13—Testing J2EE Applications

11.5 Test CMP meta data outside the container

◆ Problem

You want to test a CMP entity bean, but outside the container.

◆ Background

There was a project on which J. B. worked that used a database overrun with referential integrity. There were foreign key chains—that is, I have a foreign key to you, you have a foreign key to him, who has a foreign key to her, and so on—spanning seven or eight tables. The end result was absolute chaos for testing: to populate the data to test one entity bean required populating dozens of rows in eight different tables. Not only did this make tests slow to execute, but they were a nightmare to maintain. The team had to choose between isolated test data for each test—and the 45 seconds-per-test execution speed that came with it—and one big suite of test data for a large number of tests, whose cost of change turned out to be aptly modeled by an exponential curve—and a *steep* one at that. If this sounds like your situation, and if you absolutely *must* use entity beans, and if you absolutely cannot do away with a majority of those referential integrity constraints,[16] then you need another plan. This recipe is your other plan.

---

[15] Ed Roman, Scott Ambler and Tyler Jewell. *Mastering Enterprise JavaBeans, 2nd Edition.* John Wiley & Sons, 2001. This book is freely available online at www.theserverside.com/books/wiley/masteringEJB/index.tss.

[16] Show this sentence to the nearest Database Administrator. He may find it funny... or upsetting. Either way, you are sure to get a reaction.

◆ *Recipe*

If testing the entity bean in a live container is taking too much time, then what you *can* do is test the entity bean meta data instead. The good news is that this meta data is typically expressed in XML, so it is quite easy to test. For a typical CMP entity bean, you can test any of the following without the container:

- The container-managed fields are specified correctly.
- The mapping between the entity bean class and a database table is correct.
- The mapping between container-managed fields and table columns is correct.
- A table column mapping exists for each container-managed field.
- The entity bean uses the correct data source.
- EJBQL queries are correctly specified.
- Container-managed relationships are correctly specified.

There are probably others, but this list is a good place to start. You can use XMLUnit (see chapter 9, "Testing and XML") to write tests for all the various deployment descriptors and server configuration files. Note that the way you test your server configuration depends on how your application server stores that information. For example, JBoss stores it all in XML documents, making it easy to test with XMLUnit. Specifically, we could test the mapping between our `CoffeeCatalogItem` entity bean, representing an item in the Coffee Shop's catalog, and the `catalog.beans` database table that provides persistent storage for it. Listing 11.7 shows the test we would write for JBoss 3.2.4.[17] Note that it extends `XMLTestCase`, part of the XMLUnit package.

Listing 11.7 CoffeeCatalogItemEntityBeanMetaDataTest

```
package junit.cookbook.coffee.model.ejb.test;

import java.io.FileReader;
import org.custommonkey.xmlunit.*;
import org.w3c.dom.Document;
import org.xml.sax.InputSource;

public class CoffeeCatalogItemEntityBeanMetaDataTest
    extends XMLTestCase {
```

[17] This test uses an XML document that declares a DTD, so you'll either need a network connection to execute it, or you'll have to edit the XML document to point to your local copy of the JBoss DTD in question.

```
    private static final String META_DATA_FILENAME =
        "../CoffeeShopEJB/ejbModule/META-INF/jbosscmp-jdbc.xml";

    private static final String ENTITY_BEAN_XPATH =
        "/jbosscmp-jdbc/enterprise-beans/"
            + "entity[ejb-name='CoffeeCatalogItem']/";

    private Document metaDataDocument;

    protected void setUp() throws Exception {
        XMLUnit.setIgnoreWhitespace(true);

        metaDataDocument =
            XMLUnit.buildTestDocument(
                new InputSource(new FileReader(META_DATA_FILENAME)));
    }

    public void testTableMapping() throws Exception {
        assertXpathEvaluatesTo(
            "catalog.beans",
            ENTITY_BEAN_XPATH + "table-name",
            metaDataDocument);
    }

    public void testFieldMapping() throws Exception {
        assertXpathEvaluatesTo(
            "productId",
            ENTITY_BEAN_XPATH
                + "cmp-field[field-name='productId']/column-name",
            metaDataDocument);

        assertXpathEvaluatesTo(
            "coffeeName",
            ENTITY_BEAN_XPATH
                + "cmp-field[field-name='coffeeName']/column-name",
            metaDataDocument);

        assertXpathEvaluatesTo(
            "unitPrice",
            ENTITY_BEAN_XPATH
                + "cmp-field[field-name='unitPrice']/column-name",
            metaDataDocument);
    }

    public void testDataSource() throws Exception {
        assertXpathEvaluatesTo(
            "java:/jdbc/mimer/CoffeeShopData",
            "/jbosscmp-jdbc/defaults/datasource",
            metaDataDocument);
    }
}
```

All the XPath expressions in this test come from reading the Document Type Definition (DTD) for configuring container-managed persistence for JBoss. You need to consult the corresponding documentation for your application server of choice to obtain the same results—and that assumes that your vendor stores that information in XML as JBoss does. For those of you using JBoss, after you write this test, you might not be clear what the XPath expressions in the test mean. We decided to apply a few refactorings to this example. Here is a summary of what we did:

1. We revealed the intent behind the XPath expressions by introducing appropriately named methods.
2. We removed duplication in the XPath-based assertions, particularly involving substrings that the XPath expressions have in common.
3. We introduced a new class named `EntityBeanMetadataTest` and made it part of Diasparsoft Toolkit.[18]
4. We pulled up [Refactoring, 322] all the newly created, generic methods into the new class, leaving only the original tests behind, and with much less "noise" to distract the programmer.

The end result is the test case class in listing 11.8. Notice that `setUp()` invokes `setEntityBeanUnderTest()` so that the tests do not need to duplicate the name of the entity bean under test throughout. We tend to test each entity bean in its own test fixture, so this makes the most sense to us at the moment. We have shown the changes highlighted in bold print.

Listing 11.8 The refactored test

```
package junit.cookbook.coffee.model.ejb.test;

import java.io.FileReader;
import javax.xml.transform.TransformerException;
import org.custommonkey.xmlunit.XMLUnit;
import org.w3c.dom.Document;
import org.xml.sax.InputSource;
import com.diasparsoftware.util.jboss.testing.EntityBeanMetaDataTest;

public class CoffeeCatalogItemEntityBeanMetaDataTest
    extends EntityBeanMetaDataTest {

    protected void setUp() throws Exception {
        setMetaDataFilename(
            "../CoffeeShopEJB/ejbModule/META-INF/jbosscmp-jdbc.xml");
        setEntityBeanUnderTest("CoffeeCatalogItem");
```

[18] www.diasparsoftware.com/toolkit

```
        super.setUp();
    }

    public void testTableMapping() throws Exception {
        assertBeanMappedToTable("catalog.beans");
    }

    public void testFieldMapping() throws Exception {
        assertFieldMappedToColumn("productId", "productId");
        assertFieldMappedToColumn("coffeeName", "coffeeName");
        assertFieldMappedToColumn("unitPrice", "unitPrice");
    }

    public void testDataSource() throws Exception {
        assertDefaultDataSource("java:/jdbc/mimer/CoffeeShopData");
    }
}
```

What about `EntityBeanMetaDataTest`? Listing 11.9 shows an early version of this class. It will evolve over time to meet the needs of whoever might use it. As you write tests for other types of J2EE meta data, you might find yourself extracting classes [Refactoring, 149] similar to this one. If you do, please make those classes available to the rest of the J2EE programming community. We would appreciate it!

Listing 11.9 An early version of `EntityBeanMetaDataTest`

```
package com.diasparsoftware.util.jboss.testing;

import java.io.FileReader;
import javax.xml.transform.TransformerException;
import org.custommonkey.xmlunit.*;
import org.w3c.dom.Document;
import org.xml.sax.InputSource;

public abstract class EntityBeanMetaDataTest extends XMLTestCase {
    private String metaDataFilename;
    private Document metaDataDocument;
    private String entityBeanName;

    protected void setUp() throws Exception {
        parseMetaData();
    }

    protected void setMetaDataFilename(String metaDataFilename) {
        this.metaDataFilename = metaDataFilename;
    }

    protected void setEntityBeanUnderTest(String entityBeanName) {
        this.entityBeanName = entityBeanName;
    }

    protected void parseMetaData() throws Exception {
```

```
        XMLUnit.setIgnoreWhitespace(true);

        metaDataDocument =
            XMLUnit.buildTestDocument(
                new InputSource(new FileReader(metaDataFilename)));
    }

    protected void assertBeanMappedToTable(String expectedTableName)
        throws TransformerException {

        assertXpathEvaluatesTo(
            expectedTableName,
            getXpathRelativeToEntityBean(entityBeanName, "table-name"),
            metaDataDocument);
    }

    protected void assertFieldMappedToColumn(
        String fieldName,
        String expectedColumnName)
        throws TransformerException {

        assertXpathEvaluatesTo(
            expectedColumnName,
            getColumnMappingForField(entityBeanName, fieldName),
            metaDataDocument);
    }

    protected void assertDefaultDataSource(
        String expectedDataSourceJndiName)
        throws TransformerException {

        assertXpathEvaluatesTo(
            expectedDataSourceJndiName,
            "/jbosscmp-jdbc/defaults/datasource",
            metaDataDocument);
    }

    private String getColumnMappingForField(
        String entityBeanName,
        String fieldName) {

        return getXpathRelativeToEntityBean(
            entityBeanName,
            "cmp-field[field-name='" + fieldName + "']/column-name");
    }

    private String getXpathRelativeToEntityBean(
        String entityBeanName,
        String relativeXpath) {

        return getEntityBeanXpath(entityBeanName) + relativeXpath;
    }

    private String getEntityBeanXpath(String entityBeanName) {
        return "/jbosscmp-jdbc/enterprise-beans/"
            + "entity[ejb-name='"
```

```
                + entityBeanName
                + "']/";
        }
    }
```

◆ *Discussion*

We should emphasize at this point that implementing referential integrity in the database is not necessarily everything people claim it is. In fairly specific circumstances it is more of a hindrance than an aid. In particular, if there is only one application accessing the database, then it is possible to place all referential integrity rules in the application and leave them out of the database. Aside from purist arguments against this practice, it makes testing easier by reducing the size and complexity of the data sets you need for testing. This is a sizable benefit and should not be discounted right away. Referential integrity constraints do help keep invalid data out of the database—data which could come from places entirely out of your control—but they come at a cost, and you need to balance that cost against the benefits. There is no free lunch. (See the post script to this recipe for an opposing view.)

Another way to reduce the cost of testing entity beans against a live database is to execute those tests (and *only* those tests) against a version of the database schema without referential integrity rules. This gives you the best of both worlds: the safeguard of referential integrity in production without the shackles of *too much* referential integrity during testing. If you choose this direction, do be careful of any defects that "slip through" as a result. If you find that this strategy leads to defects that only occur because you are using the strategy, then either rethink the strategy or try to learn from your mistakes. Every benefit has its price.

You might wonder about using this technique to test EJBQL queries; after all, the only way to be certain that an EJB query works is to try it against a live application server. We agree with this, but that does not necessarily make it a good idea to test *every* query against a live application server. This is another case where you need to balance cost and benefit. One maxim among test-oriented programmers (such as those who practice Test-Driven Development) is "test until fear turns to boredom." That is, keep writing tests until you are confident that the code works, then stop. On the other hand, if you are afraid that the code does not work, then keep writing tests until the fear subsides. When we follow this guideline we tend to work in cycles: we test everything down to the smallest detail, and then boredom (even complacency!) sets in, we relax our guard, a defect pops up that embarrasses us, and we turn the testing knob back up to 11. This appears to hit the sweet spot in the trade-off between the cost and benefit of testing.

You should apply this principle to testing EJBQL queries. You want to minimize the number of these tests and execute them less frequently, such as in a background continuous build process using Cruise Control or Anthill. At the beginning, write in-container tests for all EJBQL queries. Over time, as you become more comfortable, write fewer tests for those queries; however, *and this is the important part,* whenever you introduce a defect through an EJBQL query you *must* write a test for it. Without this important feedback, you will begin to feel as though you never make a mistake, and if you truly felt that way, then we would wonder why you need this book![19] Remember that the goal is still to produce defect-free code, so if you introduce a defect because you forgot to write a test, then write the test. Over time, this will occur less frequently. When a problem arises, your End-to-End Tests will catch them (or QA if you are less lucky) and alert you to the problem. You can then execute your in-container tests to isolate the problem and help you fix it.

◆ Post script

Our intrepid reviewer, George Latkiewicz, dislikes databases without referential integrity constraints. "If I had a choice I wouldn't shake a stick at a database that didn't have RI. I have personally worked on a project where a whole team spent over a year attempting to reverse engineer the RI that should have been defined in a DBMS and cleaning up the data that violated those constraints ('What do we do when there is no matching person for the transaction and no matching product, but the accounting information records that the amount was actually paid?' and 'Can you figure out the person from the credit card number?'). Literally millions of dollars and thousands of hours spent because of a handful of missing RI constraints." Obviously we ought to take George's experience to heart, but we tend to take an extreme position on these issues because that is usually when we learn the most, and the more we know, the better for our clients. Here, we ask, "How much are these constraints helping us, anyway? Let us get rid of them all and see." We have worked on several projects that use referential integrity sparingly, if at all, and have walked away from them unharmed. Whose position is better—George's or ours? As usual, even better would be someplace in between, which is why we recommend you try both and measure the results. If nothing else, this recipe reminds us not to bear the cost of referential integrity (or anything else, for that matter) without understanding the benefit.

◆ Related

- Chapter 9—Testing and XML

---

[19] Just kidding. Thank you for picking up this book. No hard feelings.

11.6 Test a BMP entity bean

◆ *Problem*

You want to test a bean-managed persistence (BMP) entity bean.

◆ *Background*

If you are using entity beans, then why would you choose to use bean-managed persistence? Whereas there might in the past have been performance- or design-related reasons to use BMP entity beans, we have seen those issues melt away for the most part. You might have inherited an application that uses BMP entity beans because it has survived from the days before CMP began to perform acceptably on most application servers. Now nobody wants to change those entity beans because "they work."[20] It is also possible that you have inherited a newer application, but one written by programmers that fell victim to the myth that CMP entity beans were "too slow." Whatever the reason, a BMP entity bean has many more moving parts in it than a CMP entity bean, making it considerably more difficult to test. As a result, this recipe is among the most involved in the book. That just reflects the complexity of BMP: you have an *EJB* using *JDBC* to talk to a database. That means two layers of complexity to contend with, so it is no surprise that there is essentially double the work involved in building isolated tests around BMP entity beans.

◆ *Recipe*

The strategy you can use to test a BMP entity bean depends on your ability to move the persistence code out of the entity bean and into other classes. First, we will consider what to do when you can refactor the BMP entity beans you need to test. This makes testing BMP entity beans much simpler, because a BMP entity bean consists of little more than JDBC client code, JNDI lookups, and primary key management. To that end, here is the general strategy:

1. Create a new class, which we will call the Bean Logic class.
2. Pick an EJB lifecycle method and identify the places where it performs a JNDI lookup or obtains the primary key.
3. Create a new method in the EJB that takes as parameters the primary key (if needed) and any objects the EJB looks up with JNDI.

[20] As soon as you are afraid of changing code, throw it away. You may not always be able to do this, but if you do it when you can, you will notice an improvement in the code you write. Trust us.

4 Move this new method into the Bean Logic class and name it appropriately. You can make the code easier to read by naming the new method after the lifecycle method.

5 Presumably the Bean Logic class now contains mostly JDBC client code, which you can test using the techniques in chapter 10, "Testing and JDBC."

6 Use a mock objects approach to verify that the BMP entity bean correctly supplies the primary key to any Bean Logic method that requires it. This recipe relies rather heavily on mock objects, so if you are not already familiar with them, read essay B.4, "The mock objects landscape," and then visit the EasyMock site (www.easymock.org) to help you get started.

7 Create a Deployment Test—which will have to run within the container—to verify that the BMP entity bean retrieves its data source correctly.

8 Use a mock objects approach to test any programmatic security the bean might perform. The most direct approach is to instantiate the entity bean, give it a mock `EntityContext` and a fake version of the Bean Logic class, and then invoke the various lifecycle methods and verify that they perform the appropriate security checks.

To illustrate this strategy, let us return to our Coffee Shop application. We have a BMP entity bean that represents order information: an order has an ID and belongs to a customer. (An order also contains order items, but we ignore that for now to simplify the example.) Imagine that you have inherited a "junk-drawer" BMP entity bean: one that does everything directly inside its lifecycle methods. (See solution A.7, "Test a BMP entity bean," for the complete source of the original entity bean.) Testing this bean requires a live container, Cactus, setting up live test data in a database—all this is much more complex than it needs to be. Applying the technique of this recipe, we move the vast majority of the entity bean code into a new class, which we name `OrderBmpBeanLogic`. To illustrate how little is left in the entity bean, here is what remains of the method `ejbLoad()`:

```
public void ejbLoad() throws EJBException, RemoteException {
    logic.ejbLoad(getOrderId());
}
```

It really does not get much simpler than that. The variable `logic` stores an instance of the class `OrderBmpBeanLogic`. The method `getOrderId()` reveals the intent behind retrieving the primary key, because the primary key *is* the order ID:

```
private Integer getOrderId() {
    return (Integer) context.getPrimaryKey();
}
```

Returning to `ejbLoad()`, notice the difference between this method's signature and that of the Bean Logic class's `ejbLoad()` method: the Bean Logic class's version of the method takes the order ID as a parameter. Managing the primary key remains the entity bean's job, so that code stays with the entity bean. This makes it easier to test the Bean Logic class because the test can provide the order ID *directly*, rather than use an `EntityContext`, something *else* the EJB container instantiates (and not us). As it stands, the Bean Logic class—despite the fact that it is called a *bean* logic class—does not depend at all on EJBs or an application server. We merely call it the "Bean Logic class" in the absence of a better name.[21] As it stands, `OrderBmpBean.ejbLoad()` looks to be *too simple to break*, so we do not need to test it. The only way it can fail is if either the primary key is incorrect or if `OrderBmpBeanLogic.ejbLoad()` is broken.

Now the only way the primary key could be incorrect would be if the EJB container were broken. The EJB container provides the entity context, so unless we *forget* to invoke `EntityContext.getPrimaryKey()`, we will have our primary key. Well, then, our next test should verify that we do not forget to invoke that method. Listing 11.10 shows the test.

Listing 11.10 `OrderBmpBeanTest`

```
package junit.cookbook.coffee.model.ejb.test;

import javax.ejb.EntityContext;
import javax.naming.*;
import javax.naming.Context;
import javax.sql.DataSource;

import junit.cookbook.coffee.model.ejb.OrderBmpBean;
import junit.framework.TestCase;

import org.easymock.MockControl;
import org.mockejb.jndi.MockContextFactory;

public class OrderBmpBeanTest extends TestCase {
    private OrderBmpBean bean;
    private Object actualPrimaryKey;

    protected void setUp() throws Exception {
        MockContextFactory.setAsInitial();

        new InitialContext().bind(
            "java:comp/env/jdbc/OrderData",
            mockDataSource);
```

21 If you think of a better name, then use it. Do not inherit our laziness.

```
        bean = new OrderBmpBean();
    }

    public void testGetOrderId() throws Exception {
        Integer orderId = new Integer(0);

        MockControl entityContextControl =
            MockControl.createNiceControl(EntityContext.class);

        EntityContext mockEntityContext =
            (EntityContext) entityContextControl.getMock();

        mockEntityContext.getPrimaryKey();
        entityContextControl.setReturnValue(orderId);

        entityContextControl.replay();

        bean.setEntityContext(mockEntityContext);
        assertEquals(orderId, bean.getOrderId());

        entityContextControl.verify();
    }
}
```

Here we have used EasyMock to create a mock `EntityContext`. We then instantiate the EJB implementation class (`OrderBmpBean`), invoke `setEntityContext()` passing in our mock entity context, and then verify the value returned by `getOrderId()`. To be certain that this value is not just hard coded somewhere, we take advantage of EasyMock's API for verifying method invocation sequences. We set up the mock entity context, "record" the expected invocation of `getPrimaryKey()`, and then pass the mock entity context to our entity bean. When we invoke `verify()` at the end of the test, the mock entity context verifies that its `getPrimaryKey()` method was indeed invoked once. When we execute this test, it passes, so we can conclude that `OrderBmpBean` correctly retrieves the primary key from its entity context. We can further conclude that as long as `OrderBmpBeanLogic.ejbLoad()` works, then so will `OrderBmpBean.ejbLoad()`, as the latter merely invokes the former. You can test `OrderBmpBeanLogic` entirely outside the container, using the techniques in the first part of this book. Rather than complicate this discussion, we refer you to solution A.7, "Test a BMP entity bean," to see the final refactored version of our entity bean and its collaborators, including some of its tests. The next step is to verify that our entity bean correctly finds the data source in a JNDI directory.

If the data source is bound to part of the global JNDI namespace, then we can use `MockContext`, part of MockEJB, to verify that that entity bean looks up the data source using the correct JNDI name. This would be the test:

```
public void testLookupDataSource() throws Exception {
    assertSame(mockDataSource, OrderBmpBean.lookupDataSource());
}
```

We deploy a MockDataSource at the expected JNDI name so that the entity bean will retrieve it, rather than be forced to check the contents of the live JNDI directory. Yes, we *do* need to verify that the production JNDI directory has the data source, but not for this test. See recipe 11.13 for details on testing the production JNDI service. Finally, we make lookupDataSource() publicly available so we can easily test it. This is *one* advantage of EJBs: we can make methods public at will; and as long as they do not show up on an EJB interface, only our tests will ever invoke them. There is a slight problem, however, if our entity bean uses a resource reference to look up the data source. See the Discussion section of this recipe for how to test looking up JNDI resources outside the global JNDI namespace.

That would appear to be all for this entity bean. To summarize our approach, we extracted from the entity bean all the code *except* the code that depended directly on the EJB container: using the EntityContext and looking up resources in the JNDI directory. We tested the remaining EJB code using various mock object techniques, incorporating a mock entity context and a mock JNDI directory. What is left now is to test the Bean Logic class, a flexibly designed class that makes it easy to use Test Objects to test it in isolation from the database. See solution A.7, "Test a BMP entity bean," if you are interested in seeing all the code involved.

◆ Discussion

If your entity bean uses resource references, then you need to know a couple of extra details to use MockEJB properly. The first is relatively simple: deploy your mock object at the resource reference address, and not the JNDI name to which the reference resolves. For example, our entity bean might use the resource reference jdbc/OrderData to refer to the data source deployed at jdbc/mimer/CoffeeShopData in the global JNDI namespace. The entity bean would then look up the data source with the JNDI name java:comp/env/jdbc/OrderData. To deploy a mock data source for the entity bean, you must add your deploy at *this* address, and not at jdbc/mimer/CoffeeShopData. A future version of MockEJB will support resolving this resource reference for you, but in the meantime, it is not much of a problem.[22] The second extra detail you need to know relates to a defect in J2EE 1.3.

We tried to use MockContext to deploy a mock data source to java:comp/env/jdbc/OrderData, and then let the entity bean find the mock data source with this

---

[22] That is, a version after 0.5, which still does not support resolving resource references.

JNDI name. It did not work. We asked MockEJB author Alexander Ananiev if there was anything we could do, and he told us about an apparently well-known defect in J2EE 1.3 that affects JNDI lookups outside the global namespace. The file j2ee.jar, part of the J2EE distribution, contains a copy of jndi.properties, the properties file used to configure the `InitialContextFactory`. This file specifies the property `java.naming.factory.url.pkgs`, and even if you try to override that property by invoking `System.setProperty()`, the initial context factory insists on delegating all nonglobal namespace lookups to the system default initial context factory, rather than the MockEJB context factory. This causes the test to look up resource references in a live JNDI directory, rather than the `MockContext`. To work around this problem, which has been fixed in J2EE 1.4, *delete* the file jndi.properties from your copy of j2ee.jar. You need to apply this workaround to any machine that might execute your tests. It is a drastic measure, but once we did it, our tests passed! Because the file was removed in J2EE 1.4, it is safe to remove the file from your distribution. Your application server vendor will use its own j2ee.jar with its own vendor-specific jndi.properties, anyway.

We admit that to someone new to JUnit, this looks like much more work than simply deploying the EJB and testing it in the container. We ought to mention that the merciless refactoring we performed to make the EJB easier to test did yield some utility classes that we can reuse for *any* entity bean, making it easier to create new ones and reducing the complexity of all BMP entity beans considerably. If, after reading this recipe, you remain unconvinced, then all we can do is say, "We tried," and encourage you to try testing your BMP entity beans in a live container, against live data. We have spent a considerable amount of space (and time) in this book enumerating the drawbacks of testing all your database-aware code against a live database. The drawback to running tests inside a container should be equally clear. What you have *not* seen, however, are the hours of effort it took to write this recipe, due to problems with Cactus (a defect that had already been fixed in a more recent unreleased version), hot redeployment in JBoss (dynamic class-loading problems are *difficult* to recognize), and the other technical challenges intrinsic to a complex test environment. The lesson is obvious: keep it simple. Design your system so that the vast majority of your tests can run in a plain-vanilla JVM. Following this one piece of advice for all your testing is guaranteed to save you a sizable amount of grief. Trust us.

◆ Related

- 11.13—Test the contents of your JNDI directory
- Chapter 10—Testing and JDBC

- A.7—Test a BMP entity bean
- B.1—Too simple to break
- MockEJB (www.mockejb.org)
- EasyMock (www.easymock.org)
- jMock (www.jmock.org), an alternative to EasyMock

11.7 Test a message-driven bean inside the container

◆ Problem

You want to test a message-driven bean as it executes in production: inside a live EJB container.

◆ Background

The asynchronous nature of message-driven beans makes it difficult for the test to make assertions on the result. A typical test follows the three A's: arrange, act, assert. Because that typical test has access to all the objects involved, writing assertions is not difficult: simply invoke methods on the object and verify their return values. In recipe 2.2, "Test a method that returns nothing," we discuss how to cope with testing a method that returns no value. The same issues there also apply to testing a message-driven bean, as the message-handling method `onMessage()` returns no value; but, in the case of a message-driven bean, you do not even invoke the method under test—you send the container a message, and then the container invokes the appropriate message-driven bean. There is no way to obtain a reference to the message-driven bean through a JNDI lookup, so there is no way to observe the side effects `onMessage()` has. The object under test is in another JVM, executing on another thread, and there is no way for you to obtain a reference to it. This is the severest kind of testing blind.

◆ Recipe

This is perhaps the worst case scenario for Object Testing. We know of no way to write an isolated object test for a message-driven bean running in a live container. All you can do is send a message to the appropriate destination, wait long enough for the message to be delivered and processed, and then observe whatever external side effect comes from processing the message. If your message-driven bean updates the database, then you need to test against a live database. If your message-driven bean sends e-mail, then you need to test against a live e-mail server.

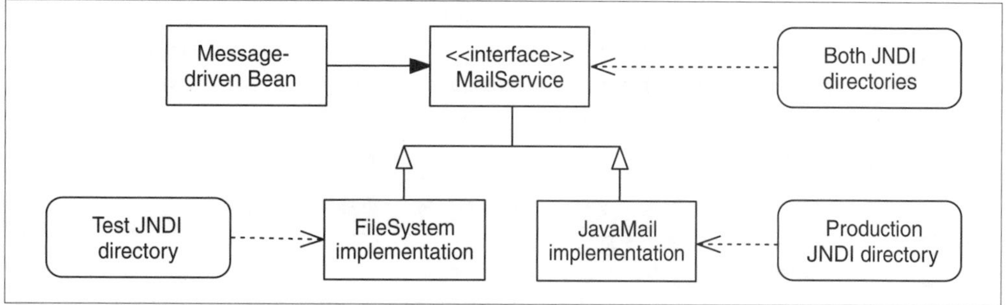

Figure 11.1 Implement `MailService` differently for tests and for production

This brings with it all the problems inherent in testing with expensive, external resources. We strongly recommend you test message-driven beans outside the container (see recipe 11.8, "Test a message-driven bean outside the container"). There are some coping mechanisms that you can try, but sometimes the cure is worse than the disease.

You could try substituting a simpler implementation of the external resource in your JNDI directory. As an example, you could extract a `MailService` interface [Refactoring, 341], and then implement that interface twice: once with a `FileSystem` implementation that writes incoming messages to the file system, and once with a `JavaMail` implementation that sends messages over a real SMTP transport (see figure 11.1). Your message-driven bean looks up the `MailService` object in your JNDI directory, and your deployment descriptors decide which implementation of `MailService` it finds: a production deployment includes the `JavaMail` implementation and a test deployment includes the `FileSystem` implementation. The details depend entirely on your application server, so we do not present them here.

Now your tests can verify that the message-driven bean has processed a message by waiting for a given file to appear on the file system. The test remains coupled to an expensive, external resource (the file system), but at least you do not need a fully functioning SMTP and POP server. This is a case of introducing a separating interface to hide the implementation details of the service you want to use.[23] We ought to mention at this point that if you are happy to do *that*, then you could save yourself a considerable amount of headache by simply factoring out the message-processing logic from the message-receiving logic and testing each separately, as we suggest in recipe 11.8.

[23] Robert C. Martin, "The Interface Segregation Principle." (www.objectmentor.com/publications/isp.pdf) When an object depends on another, it should depend on the narrowest interface possible.

Assuming you perform these refactorings, here is the kind of test you would write. The test in listing 11.11 submits an order to the appropriate message queue, waits for the `ProcessOrderSubmissionBean` to process the incoming message and write a reply to the file system, and then the test looks at the file system for the reply and analyzes it.

Listing 11.11 `ProcessOrderSubmissionBeanTest`

```
package junit.cookbook.coffee.model.ejb.test;

import java.io.*;

import javax.jms.*;
import javax.naming.*;
import org.apache.cactus.ServletTestCase;
import com.diasparsoftware.java.io.ReaderUtil;

public class ProcessOrderSubmissionBeanTest extends ServletTestCase {
    private File tmpDirectory;
    private FilenameFilter testMailFilenameFilter;

    protected void setUp() throws Exception {
        tmpDirectory = new File(System.getProperty("java.io.tmpdir"));

        testMailFilenameFilter = new FilenameFilter() {
            public boolean accept(File dir, String name) {
                return (name.startsWith("test-mail"));
            }
        };

        File[] testMailFiles =
            tmpDirectory.listFiles(testMailFilenameFilter);

        for (int i = 0; i < testMailFiles.length; i++) {
            testMailFiles[i].delete();
        }

        super.setUp();
    }

    public void testHappyPath() throws Exception {
        String jbossQueueConnectionFactoryJndiName =
            "ConnectionFactory";

        String orderQueueJndiName = "queue/Orders";

        Context context = new InitialContext();
        QueueConnectionFactory queueConnectionFactory =
            (QueueConnectionFactory) context.lookup(
                jbossQueueConnectionFactoryJndiName);

        QueueConnection connection =
            queueConnectionFactory.createQueueConnection();

        Queue orderQueue =
```

```
            (Queue) context.lookup(orderQueueJndiName);

        QueueSession session =
            connection.createQueueSession(
                false,
                QueueSession.AUTO_ACKNOWLEDGE);

        connection.start();

        MapMessage message = session.createMapMessage();
        String customerEmailAddress = "jbr@diasparsoftware.com";
        message.setString("customer-email", customerEmailAddress);

        QueueSender sender = session.createSender(orderQueue);
        sender.send(message);

        connection.stop();
        session.close();
        connection.close();

        Thread.sleep(500);

        File[] testMailFiles =
            tmpDirectory.listFiles(testMailFilenameFilter);

        assertEquals(
            "Too many test files. I don't know which one to look at.",
            1,
            testMailFiles.length);

        File testMailFile = testMailFiles[0];
        String testMailText =
            ReaderUtil.getContentAsString(new FileReader(testMailFile));

        assertTrue(
            "Cannot find customer's e-mail address in the reply: "
                + testMailText,
            testMailText.indexOf(customerEmailAddress) >= 0);
    }
}
```

In the middle of this test we invoke `Thread.sleep(500)` just to give the message-driven bean enough time to finish its work. We dislike having to pause like this, partly because it introduces an unnecessary delay, but mostly because there is no guarantee that 500 milliseconds is enough time. No amount of "sleep time" is guaranteed to be enough. As a result, this test's behavior is somewhat random: it is possible for the production code to behave correctly and for this test to fail, because perhaps garbage collection occurs on the application server JVM at exactly the wrong moment. This is another small issue that leads us away from testing message-driven beans in the container. The little things, given enough time, can really add up.

◆ *Discussion*

This test is rather brittle, which is the nature of in-container testing. Here are some of the things that could go wrong with the test:

- Someone could move the Orders queue to another JNDI name. This would stop the message-driven bean from receiving the message. You would not know that this was the problem until you looked at the application server log and saw that the bean had not done anything.
- Someone could incorrectly configure the `FileSystemMailService`. You would not know that this was the problem until you looked at the application server log and *perhaps* saw nothing! Of course, if you test with a real e-mail address, you will know the production system works when you see the e-mail pile up in that address' inbox.
- Someone could change the directory to which the `FileSystemMailService` writes the e-mails and forget to change the tests. This is one problem whose symptoms are clear, although the cause might not be so obvious. With so many things to go wrong, you might check five different configuration settings before thinking of this particular problem.
- The message-driven bean could slow down momentarily, due either to garbage collection or other machine activity. This is the worst kind of problem, because of the potential for false failures. There are two big problems with false failures: first, they waste your time, hunting down nonexistent problems; and second, the more false failures you handle, the less sensitive you become to test failures, and this second problem is by far more serious than the first. If a failing test becomes nothing to get excited about, then why test at all?

> **NOTE** *Be careful testing against "the real thing"*—If you want to test code that sends a fax, be careful testing with a real fax machine. Imagine injecting an infinite loop into your production code, sending the same fax over and over again. Now imagine the fax machine is not nearby *and no one notices the problem for hours!* We found it funny, but some people definitely did *not* find it funny. (It was not our fax machine.)

You can see now why we emphasize testing outside the container. For message-driven beans in particular, it is very important, because your test is not a direct client of the object it tests. This means that there is no direct way for the message-driven bean to communicate its behavior back to the test, unless, of course, you consider adding a response message just for testing. We really do not think that is a good idea. If there is absolutely no other reason to return a response message from your message-driven bean, then it makes little sense to add one simply to examine the response. This is one case where the cost outweighs the benefit.

We have suggested in other parts of this book that testing is so important that it is worth adding methods to an interface (as an example) just for testing. We stand by that statement, mostly because creating methods "just for testing" tends to mask a deeper design problem that you might wish or need to solve. We agree that an ideal design can be tested as is, but if we all created ideal designs, there would be no need for this book! The methods we tend to add to these interfaces, though, are "query" methods in the sense of the Command/Query Separation Principle.[24] As such, they have no potential side effects to disturb the system. Sending a response message when the system did not originally require one has the potential to significantly disturb the system.

At a minimum, using this practice for all message-driven beans could double the overall message traffic, which might have strong performance implications. You would also need to configure an extra message queue, and set the `JMSReplyTo` and `CorrelationID` properties on your outgoing messages. This is too much to add just to write tests. Because writing tests is important, the only option left is to do some refactoring without a safety net. This is one case where we believe the rewards outweigh the risk. We would even be tempted to test-drive the message-driven bean from scratch, but that would depend on the specific situation. We would rather test-drive a new class than try to refactor one without tests. See recipe 11.8 for the details.

This book is little more than a snapshot of what we know at this particular time. Since we first wrote this recipe, we discovered an article that described integrating a Simple SMTP server into a test environment.[25] If you like their approach, then you can integrate it into your system by creating a custom JavaMail Provider—assuming your application server supports this feature—and having it ask the Simple SMTP server for a JavaMail `Session`. As long as both the message-driven bean and the test use the default `Session` instance, the message-driven bean can send messages to that `Session` and the test can verify the messages using that `Session`. As always, we recommend you try out the various approaches and use what works well for you.

◆ Related

- 11.8—Test a message-driven bean outside the container
- Command/Query Separation (http://c2.com/cgi/wiki?CommandQuerySeparation)

---

[24] http://c2.com/cgi/wiki?CommandQuerySeparation

[25] www.javaworld.com/javaworld/jw-08-2003/jw-0829-smtp_p.html.

11.8 Test a message-driven bean outside the container

◆ Problem

You would like to test a message-driven bean without involving the container.

◆ Background

Message-driven beans are notoriously difficult to test, mostly because the EJB container hides them entirely from clients wanting to use them. We describe these issues in detail in recipe 11.7, "Test a message-driven bean inside the container." Beyond this visibility problem, message-driven beans fall victim to the same testing difficulties for any container-bound component. We explore these issues in several of the recipes in this chapter. It would appear that in the case of message-driven beans there is a kind of "double whammy"—two different kinds of roadblocks to testing, each merely making the other worse. This is enough to convince us to test message-driven beans outside the container, and we hope it is enough to convince you.

◆ Recipe

A message-driven bean is two things at once: a JMS message consumer and an EJB. For that reason, this recipe essentially refers you to two other recipes to find the solution.[26] The first thing you should do is identify code that requires the container—code that performs a JNDI lookup, for example—and separate it from the rest of the code. Keep the container-specific code in the message-driven bean and move the rest into a new class. The remaining code either performs a JNDI lookup or uses the `MessageDrivenContext` object provided by the container. You can use MockEJB to test the JNDI lookups and a take a mock objects approach to testing whatever the message-driven bean does with the `MessageDrivenContext`. See recipe 11.6 for an example of both this overall refactoring and of the remaining EJB behavior to test. The newly created class is now only a JMS message consumer, and you can use it entirely outside the EJB container.

The next step is to separate the JMS message consumer's behavior into three main tasks: receiving the message, processing the message, and replying to the message. Here, by "replying," we specifically mean *replying with another JMS message*. If your bean processes the incoming message and writes information out to the

[26] We even avoid duplication in writing, when we can.

database, then we consider that act part of processing the message and not replying to it. Extract the message-processing code into a separate class and leave the rest behind [Refactoring, 110]. The newly created class has methods that are entirely unaware of messaging or EJBs—it is just a Plain Old Java Object, so you can test it like one, using all the techniques from part 1. We discuss this in detail and provide an example in recipe 11.10, "Test a JMS message consumer without the messaging server."

The resulting design is essentially a paper-thin EJB wrapper around a medium-sized JMS wrapper around the message-receiving logic. See figure 11.2 for a sequence diagram showing the overall flow of control.

◆ Discussion

The JMS message consumer, although merely a wrapper around the message-processing logic, is almost never *too simple to break*. The most common case has the JMS message consumer casting the `Message` to the appropriate type and unpacking

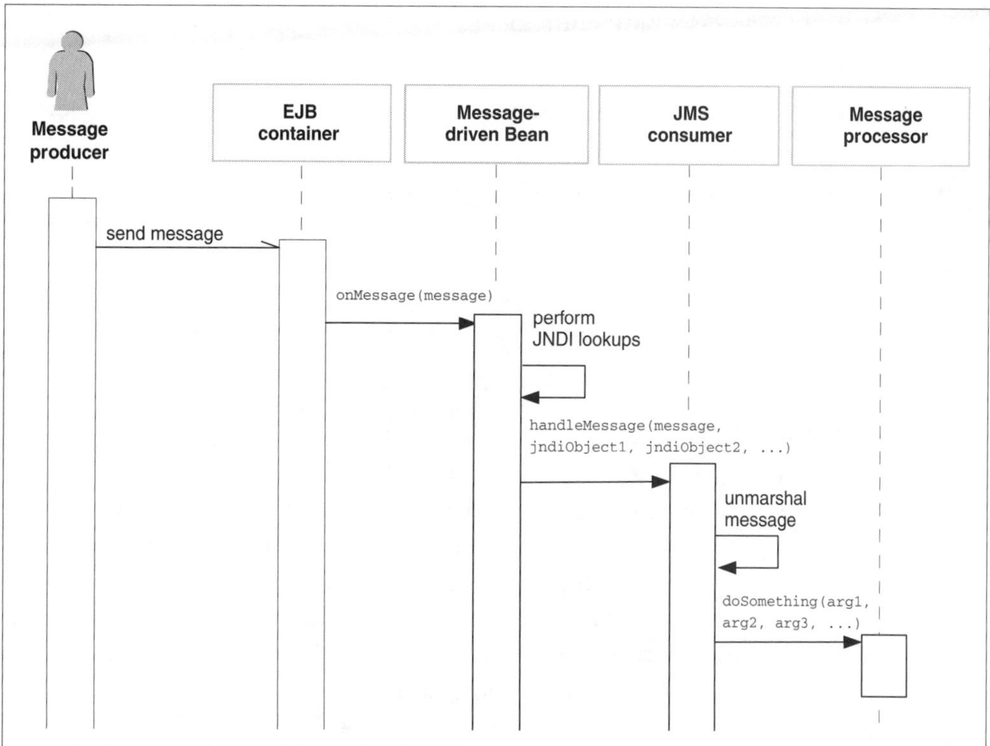

Figure 11.2 A layered approach to sending a JMS message

data from the message. If you are afraid that the type-cast will fail, then *test the message producer* and not the consumer—after all, the consumer is saying, "I only process messages of *this* type," so it is up to the message producer to comply. If you are afraid that unpacking the data might fail, then test that logic by invoking `YourMessageConsumer.handleMessage()` and passing in a Spy version of the message-processing logic class. Verify that the JMS message consumer invoked the message-processing logic method with the expected parameters. If many JMS message consumers unpack the same kind of message, then of course we recommend moving that code into a separate class and testing it separately: create some messages, invoke `YourMessageUnmarshaler.unmarshal()`, and verify the object it returns. This approach nudges you in the direction of having an object model for your messages, which lays the groundwork for future refactorings that ultimately simplify your asynchronous messaging design. Less code means fewer tests to write, which is always a good thing.

◆ Related

- 11.6—Test a BMP entity bean
- 11.7—Test a message-driven bean inside the container
- 11.10—Test a JMS message consumer without the messaging server

11.9 Test a legacy message-driven bean

◆ Problem

You want to test a message-driven bean outside the container, but do not want to refactor it (yet).

◆ Background

Throughout this chapter we have discussed the forces that lead you to testing a legacy J2EE component *as is*—that is, without refactoring it towards a more testable design. The most notable ones are fear of the unknown and creating the safety net. The first is a manifestation of the common fear, "It works and I don't understand how, so I won't touch it." The second is the chicken-and-egg problem of, "I don't know how to test it without refactoring; I ought not to refactor without tests." A message-driven bean, being an EJB, requires an EJB container to test in its natural habitat, and we have already described the difficulties inherent in testing an EJB in a live container. The good news is that if the message-driven bean itself is simple, then the fact that it is an EJB does not make it any more difficult to test than it already is.

The complexity of the tests you need depends only on the complexity of the message-driven bean itself. Being an EJB does not make the matter worse. The EJB machinery for a message-driven bean is quite simple, but because the EJB container maintains the message-driven bean's lifecycle, the bean has to obtain its collaborators either by instantiating them (see recipe 2.11, "Test an object that instantiates other objects") or retrieving them from a JNDI directory (see recipe 11.13). This latter issue is the source of most of the testing complexity and is the key stumbling block to testing a message-driven bean. This recipe tells you how to cope with the EJB container-related complexity, but you need to find other recipes to help you deal with the rest. The good news is that this book is full of them.

◆ *Recipe*

We recommend using MockEJB to simulate deploying your message-driven bean and to provide a mock JNDI directory. With this in place, you simply need to instantiate a `Message` object and invoke `onMessage()` directly. For most message-driven beans, this is the easy part. Returning to our order-processing example, listing 11.12 shows a MockEJB-based test for processing an order submission.

Listing 11.12 Testing order submission with MockEJB

```
package junit.cookbook.coffee.model.ejb.test;

import javax.jms.*;
import javax.naming.InitialContext;

import junit.cookbook.coffee.model.ejb.ProcessOrderSubmissionBean;
import junit.cookbook.coffee.service.MailService;
import junit.framework.TestCase;
import org.mockejb.*;
import org.mockejb.jndi.*;
import com.sun.jms.MapMessageImpl;

public class ProcessOrderSubmissionLegacyBeanTest
    extends TestCase
    implements MailService {

    private MessageListener processOrderSubmissionBean;
    private boolean invoked;

    protected void setUp() throws Exception {
        invoked = false;

        MockContextFactory.setAsInitial();
        InitialContext rootContext = new InitialContext();
        rootContext.bind("java:comp/env/service/Mail", this);
```

```
        MockContainer mockContainer = new MockContainer(rootContext);
        MockEjbObject mockEjbObject =
            mockContainer.deployMessageBean(
                ProcessOrderSubmissionLegacyBean.class);

        processOrderSubmissionBean =
            mockContainer.createMessageBean(mockEjbObject);
    }

    public void testHappyPath() throws Exception {
        final MapMessage message = new MapMessageImpl();
        message.setString(
            "customer-email",
            "jbr@diasparsoftware.com");

        processOrderSubmissionBean.onMessage(message);

        assertTrue("Did not invoke MailService", invoked);
    }

    public void sendMessage(
        String fromAddress,
        String toAddress,
        String subject,
        String bodyText) {

        invoked = true;
        assertEquals("jbr@diasparsoftware.com", toAddress);
    }
}
```

This test uses MockEJB to deploy and create the message-driven bean. The test simply instantiates a `MapMessage` (using the standard implementation from the J2EE library, `MapMessageImpl`),[27] adds data to it, and then invokes `onMessage()`. To explain the rest requires looking at the code for the message-driven bean itself. Because `onMessage()` is the only interesting part, we show it in listing 11.13 and omit the rest.

Listing 11.13 ProcessOrderSubmissionLegacyBean

```
package junit.cookbook.coffee.model.ejb;

import javax.ejb.*;
import javax.jms.*;
import javax.naming.*;
```

[27] Sadly, `com.sun.jms.MapMessageImpl` is not part of J2EE 1.4. We wanted to reuse someone else's POJO-style implementation of `MapMessage` to avoid having to build our own. If you are running J2EE 1.4 then you will have to look for an alternative, or build one yourself. Sorry about that.

```
import junit.cookbook.coffee.service.MailService;

public class ProcessOrderSubmissionLegacyBean
    implements MessageDrivenBean, MessageListener {

    // Lifecycle methods omitted

    public void onMessage(Message message) {
        try {
            MapMessage incomingMessage = (MapMessage) message;

            Context rootContext = new InitialContext();
            Object object =
                rootContext.lookup("java:comp/env/service/Mail");

            MailService mailService = (MailService) object;

            String customerEmailAddress =
                incomingMessage.getString("customer-email");

            mailService.sendMessage(
                "ordering@coffeeShop.com",
                customerEmailAddress,
                "We received your order",
                "Hello, there! We received your order.");
        }
        catch (NamingException logged) {
            logged.printStackTrace();
        }
        catch (JMSException logged) {
            logged.printStackTrace();
        }
    }
}
```

Here, `onMessage()` tells us that it expects a `MapMessage`, that it retrieves a `MailService` object from JNDI, and then invokes `MailService.sendMessage()` using the e-mail address it retrieved from the message. We can use MockEJB to deploy a spy `MailService` object with the appropriate JNDI name, and then verify that the "To address" parameter passed in to the `MailService` is the same as the one retrieved from the incoming message. Because `MailService` is an interface, we applied the Self-Shunt Pattern (see recipe 11.2) and had the test case class implement `MailService` itself. The Spy implementation of this method verifies two things: that the message-driven bean invoked the `MailService` at all, and that it invoked `sendMessage()` with the appropriate "To address."

As we wrote previously, using MockEJB to deploy the message-driven bean is the easy part. The difficult part—and it only gets worse as your message-driven beans become more complex—is dealing with the fact that the object under test manages its own collaborators. You need to attack this testing problem on a case-by-case basis using perhaps any technique from the rest of this book.

◆ *Discussion*

MockEJB makes it simple to simulate deploying and to invoke your message-driven bean, and for simple beans that is enough; but, most message-driven beans need to collaborate with other objects, which complicates matters. To cope with that complexity, we recommend moving the remaining message-consuming and message-processing logic out to separate classes, as we describe in recipe 11.8. The alternative is to test the message-driven bean in a live container, with all the additional issues that it raises (see recipe 11.7).

One thing you will notice about our MockEJB test is that it does not actually depend on the message-driven bean class `ProcessOrderSubmissionLegacyBean`. Instead, it treats the message-driven bean as just a `MessageListener`. As the test only ever invokes `onMessage()`, part of the generic `MessageListener` interface, there is no need to cast the object to the specific message-driven bean class. Unusual perhaps, but true. Anything to make the tests simpler.

◆ *Related*

- 2.11—Test an object that instantiates other objects
- 11.7—Test a message-driven bean inside the container
- 11.8—Test a message-driven bean outside the container

11.10 Test a JMS message consumer without the messaging server

◆ *Problem*

You would like to test a JMS message consumer without running the messaging server.

◆ *Background*

You can overcome one of the major difficulties in testing a message-driven bean by testing it in isolation as a JMS message consumer. Simply instantiate the message listener directly, and use a mock objects approach to substitute Test Objects in place of the message consumer's collaborators. Even with this simplification, there are some issues with message consumers that you need to be aware of during testing:

- *Communication via JMS is still entirely asynchronous*—This means that, for example, a message consumer cannot throw an exception and expect the message producer to receive it. Error handling is trickier with JMS message consumers, so it is important to focus more energy on ensuring that the message producers never send invalid messages.
- *JMS message consumers are typically deployed in a J2EE application as message-driven beans*—Although it is not strictly necessary to do so, wrapping your message consumer in a message-driven bean helps you leverage the EJB container's services, such as participating in transactions, guaranteed delivery, and so on. Even if you are building a standalone JMS message consumer class, the odds are good that you will (eventually) wrap it in a message-driven bean.

Testing a JMS message consumer carries with it essentially the same issues as testing a message-driven bean, so it is no accident that this recipe resembles the message-driven bean recipes in this chapter.

◆ Recipe

Most message-driven beans are 95% JMS message consumer and 5% EJB. Perhaps the most EJB-like thing your message-driven beans do is implement `ejbCreate()` to lookup collaborators in a JNDI directory and cache them. Aside from that, though, you can test a message-driven bean and a JMS message consumer in essentially the same way. For that reason, the tests in this recipe are similar in approach to the ones in recipe 11.9, "Test a legacy message-driven bean."

In recipe 11.8 we described an overall design for a message-driven bean. It describes a kind of Decorator-like approach, starting with message-processing logic, wrapping that in a JMS message consumer, and then finally wrapping that in a message-driven bean (see figure 11.2 for the relevant sequence diagram). You can apply that design pattern here, ignoring the last layer of wrapping. This allows you to test the message-receiving logic—interaction with the JMS API—without having to rely on the correctness of the business logic that responds to the message. Returning to our order-processing example, our JMS message consumer, `ProcessOrderSubmissionMessageListener`, retrieves a collaborator from the JNDI directory, unmarshals the message, and then executes a `ProcessOrderSubmissionAction`. Because we instantiate the message listener in our test, we can substitute a Spy version of the action. This allows us to verify that the message consumer invokes the action with the parameters it received from the message. Listing 11.14 shows the relevant test.[28]

---

[28] This test uses `com.sun.jms.MapMessageImpl`, which is not part of J2EE 1.4. See the end of listing 11.13 for an explanation.

Listing 11.14 ProcessOrderSubmissionMessageListenerTest

```
package junit.cookbook.coffee.model.jms.test;

import javax.jms.MapMessage;
import javax.naming.InitialContext;
import
  junit.cookbook.coffee.model.jms.ProcessOrderSubmissionMessageListener;
import junit.cookbook.coffee.model.logic.ProcessOrderSubmissionAction;
import junit.cookbook.coffee.service.MailService;
import junit.framework.TestCase;
import org.mockejb.jndi.MockContextFactory;
import com.sun.jms.MapMessageImpl;

public class ProcessOrderSubmissionMessageListenerTest
    extends TestCase
    implements MailService {

    private boolean invoked;

    protected void setUp() throws Exception {
        invoked = false;

        MockContextFactory.setAsInitial();
        new InitialContext().bind("java:comp/env/service/Mail", this);
    }

    public void testHappyPath() throws Exception {
        ProcessOrderSubmissionAction spyAction =
            new ProcessOrderSubmissionAction() {
            public void processOrder(
                MailService mailService,
                String customerEmailAddress) {

                invoked = true;
                assertEquals(
                    "jbr@diasparsoftware.com",
                    customerEmailAddress);
            }
        };

        ProcessOrderSubmissionMessageListener consumer =
            new ProcessOrderSubmissionMessageListener(spyAction);

        MapMessage message = new MapMessageImpl();
        message.setString(
            ProcessOrderSubmissionMessageListener
                .CUSTOMER_EMAIL_PARAMETER_NAME,
            "jbr@diasparsoftware.com");

        consumer.onMessage(message);
        assertTrue("Did not invoke the processing action.", invoked);
    }

    public void sendMessage(
```

```
        String fromAddress,
        String toAddress,
        String subject,
        String bodyText) {

        fail("No-one should ever invoke me.");
    }
}
```

The test creates a Spy version of the "process submitted order" action, passes it to the JMS message consumer, simulates sending a message, and then verifies that the message consumer invoked the action with the correct customer e-mail address. We decided to use the Self-Shunt pattern to implement `MailService`, because we find the resulting test to be a little easier to read. The alternative is to create a separate `DoNotUseMeMailService` that simply throws an exception whenever some tries to invoke it (a crash test dummy). We have the `MailService` behave this way to emphasize the point that we are *overriding* the message-processing logic and therefore do not expect to actually try to use the `MailService` passed into it. If it did, then our test would not be testing what we think it would be testing, and we would want to know that so we can correct it.

To substitute our Spy version of the message-processing logic we used the technique we described in recipe 2.11, "Test an object that instantiates other objects." We could have extracted an interface [Refactoring, 341] around the action, but given how simple the class is, we felt it was sufficient to merely subclass it and override its only method.

We have verified that our message consumer sends the correct parameters to the message-processing logic. We still need to test that logic itself, which we describe in recipe 11.11, "Test JMS message-processing logic."

◆ Discussion

The test in this recipe is very similar to the one we wrote in recipe 11.9, except that we substitute a Spy version of the message-processing logic, rather than a Spy version of the `MailService`. The distinction is subtle, but important. This test does *not* rely on the correctness of the business logic that the application wants to invoke in response to the message, whereas our legacy message-driven bean test does. This is common in testing legacy code: it is typically more tightly coupled to its environment, making it more difficult to write the kind of focused, isolated test we generally prefer to write. Part of this is a perception problem: project managers, architects, and technical leads often see EJBs as complicated components that are best left alone as much as possible. We have observed a kind of psychological barrier to refactoring EJBs that we do not see as strongly when we suggest refactoring other kinds of components. Even though message-driven beans are quite similar to their JMS message consumer counterparts, it is common to think of message-driven beans as more complex, simply because they are EJBs. Whatever the reason, we find it easier to convince others to let us refactor a JMS message consumer than a message-driven bean. This allows us to write simpler tests, such as the one in this recipe, which verifies that the message consumer specifies the correct e-mail address for processing. This is simpler than the legacy message-driven test, which verifies that an *e-mail was sent* to the correct e-mail address. The test in this recipe is more focused and less easily perturbed by, say, a failure in the JNDI directory or a temporary problem with the mail server. Your deployment tests can check the contents of the JNDI directory (see recipe 11.13).

◆ Related

- 2.11—Test an object that instantiates other objects
- 11.9—Test a legacy message-driven bean
- 11.11—Test JMS message-processing logic
- 11.13—Test the content of your JNDI directory
- Self-Shunt pattern (www.objectmentor.com/resources/articles/SelfShunPtrn.pdf)

11.11 Test JMS message-processing logic

◆ Problem

You want to test the logic for processing a JMS message without worrying about how that message is delivered.

◆ Background

The JMS API is complicated, or at least, verbose. It takes several lines of code just to send a simple text message using a live JMS server. If you try to mock all the objects involved, a single test can run between 50 and 100 lines, depending on your code formatter—all that just to test the business logic triggered by a specific kind of message. When discussing how to test J2EE applications we have emphasized the importance of testing business logic entirely in isolation from J2EE components.

This affords you maximum flexibility in your design as well as making it much easier to test the most important part of your application: how well it solves your business problem. For that reason, it is important to test your business logic separately—the logic that you plan to execute when you receive a particular JMS message. This recipe describes how to do that.

◆ *Recipe*

In recipe 11.8 we describe the design we recommend: the EJB container delivers the message to a message-driven bean, which performs JNDI lookups, and then passes the message to a JMS message consumer, which unmarshals the message and passes it to a message processor. This recipe focuses on the message processor. There is one key principle to make these tests simple: the message processor should have no knowledge of JMS or messaging. If you can refactor towards that design, then you can treat your message processor like any other Plain Old Java Object and test it in a straightforward manner.

Returning to our example of receiving and processing an order, we want to send e-mail to the customer saying that we have received her order. Fortunately, we have already isolated the e-mail feature into an interface named `MailService`. (See recipe 11.7 for a description of when and why we created this interface.) This simplifies the corresponding tests. The test in listing 11.15 verifies that we used the correct (customer's) e-mail address for the "To" address in our "We received your order" e-mail.

Listing 11.15 Verifying the "To" address in an e-mail

```
package junit.cookbook.coffee.model.logic.test;

import junit.cookbook.coffee.model.logic.ProcessOrderSubmissionAction;
import junit.cookbook.coffee.service.MailService;
import junit.framework.TestCase;

public class ProcessOrderSubmissionActionTest extends TestCase {
    private boolean spyMailServiceInvoked = false;

    public void testToAddress() throws Exception {
        ProcessOrderSubmissionAction action =
            new ProcessOrderSubmissionAction();

        MailService spyMailService = new MailService() {
            public void sendMessage(
                String fromAddress,
                String toAddress,
                String subject,
                String bodyText) {
```

```
                assertEquals("jbr@diasparsoftware.com", toAddress);
                spyMailServiceInvoked = true;
            }
        };

        action.processOrder(spyMailService, "jbr@diasparsoftware.com");
        assertTrue(spyMailServiceInvoked);
    }
}
```

Here we decided to use a hand-coded Spy implementation of `MailService`, rather than an all-out EasyMock mock object. This test is only concerned with whether we get the "To" address right; we will write other tests to verify the content of the e-mail and what happens if `MailService.sendMessage()` throws an exception. For this test, however, the simplest approach is the one you see here. We need to check a flag representing "the Spy mail service was invoked" to avoid a false positive[29] in the case where nothing invoked `sendMessage()`. If it did not invoke our Spy mail service's method, then nothing would execute its assertion either.

The key point to note is that these tests have nothing to do with EJBs, JMS, or anything else. We are merely testing a Plain Old Java Object—the easiest tests to write.

◆ Discussion

This test is very simple—almost *too* simple. Fear not: it is this way on purpose. The idea is to test the action, and not the objects with which the action collaborates! Elsewhere we have tested our production implementation of `MailService`, the one that uses JavaMail to send e-mail. We do not even need to concern ourselves with which `MailService` implementation is passed into our action class—that is up to the object that invokes this action, and we will test that too. (See the JMS message consumer and message-driven bean recipes in this chapter for examples.) The simplicity of the test comes from the simplicity of the action, and *that* is good design.

One note on the test itself: because `MailService` is an interface, we could have used the Self-Shunt pattern and had the test case implement `MailService` itself, rather than use an anonymous implementation bound to the test method. If many tests want to use the same Spy `MailService` implementation, then we recommend moving those tests into a separate fixture and using the Self-Shunt pattern. This removes duplication from the tests.

[29] That is, a test that passes even though the production code does not behave correctly. Such tests are very bad for you: they give you a false sense of progress, and problems jump up at you unexpectedly, and much later on.

◆ **Related**

- 11.7—Test a message-driven bean inside the container
- 11.8—Test a message-driven bean outside the container

11.12 Test a JMS message producer

◆ **Problem**

You want to test a JMS message producer.

◆ **Background**

The vast majority of the code you write to send a JMS message is what we sometimes call "JMS noise." There is this large, repetitive structure of code to write before you can send a simple text message such as "Hello." Especially for novice JMS programmers writing code with an open book next to the keyboard, it is easy to start practicing "copy and paste reuse," which does nothing except duplicate this JMS noise throughout an application. The most direct way to test a JMS producer is to start a messaging server, connect a listener to the appropriate queue, create a message, send it, and then verify that the listener received it. Although this kind of test is excellent for verifying that you have configured your JMS messaging server correctly, it gets in the way of testing the important part: what you *do* with the messaging server—the messages you send. After writing one small set of deployment and configuration tests, you ought to focus on the key questions: are we sending the right messages? Are we sending them to the right place? After that, you can trust your application server's JMS server implementation to work. If not, then we recommend that you do not use it. Either way, *don't test the platform.*

◆ **Recipe**

There are essentially two parts to this recipe. First, we strongly recommend you refactor the JMS noise out to a separate class [Refactoring, 149, 345]. There really ought to be a simpler API for sending simple messages—convenience methods set up for just that purpose. If it were up to us, the JMS API would include a convenience API that allows the programmer to send a message with a single method invocation. As there is no such standard API, you either need to find someone who has implemented one or build your own.[30] We built the interface `MapMessage-`

[30] You may be tempted to build a utility class with class-level methods for sending the various kinds of messages you need. We recommend avoiding class-level methods. See recipe 14.4, "Test a Singleton's client."

Sender which does just that: it sends a MapMessage to a particular destination—in our case, a Queue. Listing 11.16 shows the result.

Listing 11.16 MapMessageSender

```
package com.diasparsoftware.javax.jms;

import java.util.Map;

public interface MapMessageSender {
    void sendMapMessage(
        String destinationQueueJndiName,
        Map messageContent)
        throws MessagingException;
}
```

This is a simplifying interface: its job is to hide some of the details—the "JMS noise"—behind simpler method invocations. To send a MapMessage we only need to indicate the JNDI name of the destination Queue and provide a Map containing the message contents. An implementation of this interface does the rest for us. Although we omit it here for brevity, we implemented MapMessageSender for JBoss to use the JBoss JMS server. By inserting an interface between our message producers and our JMS server, we remove the potential for duplicating JMS client code throughout the application. This is the first step in testing a JMS message producer.

In order to test your message producer without running the messaging server, you need to separate its key responsibilities: creating the message content (not the Message object, but what it contains), specifying the message's destination, and using the JMS server. Here is a quick summary of how to test each of these responsibilities.

Creating the message content

We prefer testing message content-generating code separately; the more complex the content, the more important this testing becomes. With a MapMessage, for example, you could extract the ability to add data to a MapMessage from a Map into a separate method (or class), test it once, and use it forever [Refactoring, 110]. You will want to test this behavior in isolation for all but the simplest cases. With MapMessage, for example, it is easy to forget that MapMessage.setObject() only supports the primitive wrapper classes (Integer, Long, and so on) and String, but not arbitrary objects. This is enough to get wrong, so it is enough to test on its own. Listing 11.17 shows an example of such a test, which tries to add an ArrayList object to a MapMessage.

Listing 11.17 BuildMapMessageTest

```
package com.diasparsoftware.javax.jms.test;

import java.util.*;
import javax.jms.*;
import junit.framework.TestCase;
import com.diasparsoftware.javax.jms.*;
import com.sun.jms.MapMessageImpl;

public class BuildMapMessageTest extends TestCase {
    private MapMessageImpl mapMessage;
    private MessageBuilder messageBuilder;

    protected void setUp() throws Exception {
        mapMessage = new MapMessageImpl();
        messageBuilder = new MessageBuilder();
    }

    public void testGenericObject() throws Exception {
        Map singleton = Collections.singletonMap("b", new ArrayList());
        try {
            messageBuilder.buildMapMessage(mapMessage, singleton);
            fail("Added a generic object to a MapMessage!");
        }
        catch (MessagingException expected) {
            Throwable throwable = expected.getCause();
            assertTrue(
                "Wrong exception type",
                throwable instanceof MessageFormatException);
        }
    }
}
```

You will find similar tests useful, depending on what types of messages you use in your system. When building an `ObjectMessage`, be sure the `Object` is `Serializable`. When building a `StreamMessage`, be sure you are streaming the contents in the expected order. These are the kinds of tests you ought to write for the different kinds of messages you build. The test we have written here helps us be sure that we can build a `MapMessage` correctly. All that is left is to verify that each message producer passes in the correct content (`Map` object) depending on the content of the message they want to send. Listing 11.18 shows the "happy path" test.

Listing 11.18 The "happy path" test for submitting an order

```
package junit.cookbook.coffee.model.logic.test;

import java.util.*;
import junit.cookbook.coffee.model.*;
```

```
import junit.cookbook.coffee.model.logic.SubmitOrderCommand;
import junit.framework.TestCase;
import org.easymock.MockControl;
import com.diasparsoftware.javax.jms.MapMessageSender;

public class SubmitOrderTest extends TestCase {
    private MockControl mapMessageSenderControl;
    private MapMessageSender mapMessageSender;
    private Customer jbrains;
    private Order order;

    protected void setUp() throws Exception {
        mapMessageSenderControl =
            MockControl.createControl(MapMessageSender.class);

        mapMessageSender =
            (MapMessageSender) mapMessageSenderControl.getMock();

        jbrains = new Customer("jbrains");
        jbrains.emailAddress = "jbr@diasparsoftware.com";

        Set orderItems =
            Collections.singleton(
                new CoffeeQuantity(3, "Special Blend"));

        order = new Order(new Integer(762), jbrains, orderItems);

    }

    public void testHappyPath() throws Exception {
        Map expectedMessageContent =
            Collections.singletonMap(
                "customer-email",
                jbrains.emailAddress);

        mapMessageSender.sendMapMessage(
            "queue/Orders",
            expectedMessageContent);
        mapMessageSenderControl.setVoidCallable();

        mapMessageSenderControl.replay();

        SubmitOrderCommand command = new SubmitOrderCommand();
        command.setOrder(order);
        command.execute(mapMessageSender);

        mapMessageSenderControl.verify();
    }
}
```

Here we use EasyMock to mock the `MapMessage` sender, because we have already tested it separately. We verify the message content (the `Map` object) by examining the parameter that the `SubmitOrderCommand` passes to the `MapMessageSender`.

Of course, we should add other tests to cover various error cases, such as an invalid `Order` object.

Verifying the message destination

The previous test killed two birds with one stone, as it were: in addition to verifying the message content parameter, we used EasyMock to verify the destination queue for the message. Once again, we have already tested whether `MapMessageSender` uses that destination parameter when sending a message, so all the message producer needs to do is to specify the destination correctly. This is one area where error-case testing is important: JMS implementations have a large number of moving parts, so you want to be sure that you handle JMS exceptions properly. In our design, the implementations of `MapMessageSender` wrap JMS exceptions in a more general `MessagingException`. The latter is an unchecked exception, which reduces unnecessary coupling between message clients and our JMS-integration objects. We may, for example, want to verify that if the destination we specify does not exist, then the `SubmitOrderCommand` reports the exception in a useful way. Here is such a test. We use EasyMock to simulate `MapMessageSender` throwing a `MessagingException`:

```
public void testQueueDoesNotExist() throws Exception {
    Map expectedMessageContent =
        Collections.singletonMap(
            "customer-email",
            jbrains.emailAddress);

    mapMessageSender.sendMapMessage(
        "queue/Orders",
        expectedMessageContent);

    MessagingException destinationNotExistException =
        new MessagingException(
            "Unable to send message",
            new JMSException("Destination does not exist"));

    mapMessageSenderControl.setThrowable(
        destinationNotExistException);

    mapMessageSenderControl.replay();

    try {
        SubmitOrderCommand command = new SubmitOrderCommand();
        command.setOrder(order);
        command.execute(mapMessageSender);
        fail("Did not throw exception?");
    }
    catch (CommandException expected) {
        assertEquals(
```

```
                "Unable to submit order " + order,
                expected.getMessage());

            assertSame(
                destinationNotExistException,
                expected.getCause());
        }

        mapMessageSenderControl.verify();
    }
```

Here we verify that the `SubmitOrderCommand` reports the problem from the domain's perspective: "unable to submit order." If it were merely to report "Queue does not exist: `queue/Orders`," then it might or might not be clear to the person reading the message where the problem lies. Yes, the stack trace would help, but in a production environment there might not be any line numbers to help, even if one could retrieve that particular revision of the source code![31] The more the errors communicate, the better. This test helps improve the way in which the system communicates this kind of problem.

Using the messaging server

Now we need to verify that the JMS-integration code works as we would expect. In our case, this is an implementation of `MapMessageSender` that actually sends the message using the JMS API. We recommend testing this behavior with a live container, as only then can you be certain that the results are meaningful. The tests can be simple, they have nothing to do with your problem domain and you can use them almost exclusively to help isolate defects reported from outside the programming team. Best of all, the `MapMessageSender` is something you can use across projects, and so if you test it once, you can treat it as a trusted component on future projects. If you can get the same quality with fewer tests, then so much the better. The technique is straightforward: start the JMS server, register a `MessageListener`, send the message, and verify that it was received. There are few enough of these tests that you can accept the cost of testing against an expensive, external resource. This is another case in which we choose simpler tests over faster tests.

◆ *Discussion*

If you are adamant about testing the message-sending behavior without a messaging server, then you can use EasyMock and MockEJB's JNDI implementation (`MockContext`) to verify that your message-sending code invokes the appropriate

[31] Many organizations we have worked with have not been disciplined in their configuration management. How quickly could you get the source for the third-to-last release of your product?

API methods. Just be aware that this requires *five* mock objects: the queue connection factory, queue connection, queue session, queue sender, and the queue itself. Not only that, the test virtually duplicates the underlying code, so it proves little *and* is easy to get wrong. Using the JMS API correctly is the point of the entire test: invoking the correct methods in the correct order to make the JMS server send your message. The process is complex enough that we recommend against this kind of test. When an external resource requires that much code to simulate its behavior, take it as a sign that too much can go wrong to make it worth writing a simulator. The more you need to mock, the more risk you run in getting the test wrong—after all, how would you know? If you set up your mock JMS objects incorrectly, how would you discover the problem? Probably not until you tried to run your JMS-integration code against a live messaging server. If that is the case, then test against the live server, but keep the integration as small as possible. This is the approach we take in this recipe and a general approach we have recommended elsewhere in this book. See chapter 10, "Testing and JDBC," for details on minimizing the size of a JDBC integration layer.

By the way, although we have focused the discussion on map messages and queues, the underlying principles apply just as well to the other message types and topics. We would not want to make you feel as though they need to be handled any differently.

◆ Related

- Chapter 10—Testing and JDBC
- 14.4—Test a Singleton's client

11.13 Test the content of your JNDI directory

◆ Problem

You want to test the content of your JNDI directory as part of a Deployment Test suite.

◆ Background

Many of the J2EE testing techniques that we recommend throughout this part of the book have one goal: to minimize the amount of testing you do inside J2EE containers. The logic is straightforward: the less you test inside the container, the more quickly the tests execute and the less complex your testing environment. In particular, if fewer of your tests require a container, then the complexity of in-container testing affects you less. If you have a problem with the in-container tests, then they do not block progress as much as they would if you did, say, all your business logic testing in the container. The idea is to minimize the impact of this complexity. In spite of this, you still eventually need to verify that you have configured the container correctly.

Suppose you use the MockEJB approach to testing a session bean that uses an entity bean, as we described in recipe 11.2. That recipe recommends using an in-memory JNDI directory so that your test can deploy a mock entity bean for the session bean to use. This way you avoid the complexity of deploying several EJBs just to test the one session bean. We like this approach; however, it is not enough to ensure that your session bean will work *in production.* It is a fact of J2EE-based software development that the JNDI directory is nothing more than a big, glorified Singleton, and that J2EE components use this Singleton all over the place. The fact that you can override this Singleton by setting JVM properties (as MockEJB does) does not change the fact that you need to verify that the production Singleton is configured correctly. That is the problem we are trying to solve here.

◆ Recipe

Write a single test that verifies the content of the production JNDI directory by connecting to it and looking up all the objects you expect to find. This part is easy. Doing this effectively is the hard part, and we will get to that. First, let us consider an example from our Coffee Shop application. An early version of the application had only two objects in the JNDI directory: the business data source and a session bean for performing shopcart-based operations. We first wrote a simple test to perform the JNDI lookup on the JNDI name for our business data source, narrowed the object the directory returned, and then verified that it is indeed a `DataSource` object. Next we wrote a second test to do the same thing for the `ShopcartOperations` EJB. We extracted what the tests had in common into a method named `doTestObjectDeployed()`. Listing 11.19 shows the resulting code.

Listing 11.19 JndiDirectoryContentsTest

```
package junit.cookbook.coffee.deployment.test;

import javax.naming.*;
import javax.rmi.PortableRemoteObject;
import javax.sql.DataSource;

import junit.cookbook.coffee.model.ejb.ShopcartOperationsHome;

import org.apache.cactus.ServletTestCase;
```

```
public class JndiDirectoryContentsTest extends ServletTestCase {
    public void testBusinessDataSource() throws Exception {
        doTestObjectDeployed(
            "business data source",
            "java:/jdbc/mimer/CoffeeShopData",
            DataSource.class);
    }

    public void testShopcartOperationsEjb() throws Exception {
        doTestObjectDeployed(
            "shopcart operations EJB",
            "ejb/ShopcartOperations",
            ShopcartOperationsHome.class);
    }

    public void doTestObjectDeployed(
        String jndiObjectDescription,
        String jndiName,
        Class expectedClass)
        throws Exception {

        Context context = new InitialContext();
        Object jndiObject = context.lookup(jndiName);

        String failureMessage =
            "Unable to find "
                + jndiObjectDescription
                + " at "
                + jndiName;

        assertNotNull(failureMessage, jndiObject);

        Object narrowedObject =
            PortableRemoteObject.narrow(jndiObject, expectedClass);

        assertTrue(expectedClass.isInstance(narrowedObject));
    }
}
```

This is a Cactus test, as it extends `ServletTestCase`. We did not need to make this a Cactus test in particular, but it *does* need to run inside the container, as not all objects are deployed to the global JNDI namespace. When we consulted the JBoss documentation, we learned that any data source we configure is only available inside the application server JVM, so to obtain the data source from the JNDI directory, we need to execute the test inside the application server JVM. Cactus is an easy way to make that happen—indeed, that is the point of Cactus. You could certainly just deploy this test and execute it from within a hand-crafted servlet, if you decided that you did not want to use Cactus, but we usually try to reuse the good work of others.

◆ *Discussion*

We included the JNDI object description to make the failure message more informative. We will typically run this test right after deploying to a live application server, and if any object is not correctly deployed, we will want to know exactly which object with which the JNDI name is missing. Especially when we deploy to production, we want to be able to solve any configuration problems as quickly as possible, so we want as much information as we can get.

You will notice that as you add more tests to this test suite, each test is a one-liner: it invokes `doTestObjectDeployed()` with different parameters. You may think, "This ought to be a Parameterized Test Case," as we described in recipe 4.8, "Build a data-driven test suite." Yes, it ought to be; however, Cactus 1.5 does not allow us to use the Parameterized Test Case technique. Cactus instantiates test cases on the server side, rather than using the test case objects we specify in the `suite()` method; there is no way to pass the test parameters into the server-side test objects. Perhaps by the time you read this, Cactus will have changed to accommodate this approach, but if it has not, then your next best alternative is perhaps to generate the source code for this kind of test.

Remember, if you employ a mock objects approach to testing any J2EE component that uses JNDI, then all you have to do is verify that those objects are bound to the correct names in your JNDI directory, and those components will just work. This is another example of isolating the expensive external resource to make testing easier.

◆ *Related*

- 4.8—Build a data-driven test suite
- Chapter 10—Testing and JDBC

12 Testing web components

This chapter covers

- Testing HTTP session data
- Testing static and dynamic web pages
- Testing JSP components
- Testing servlet code
- Testing dynamic data *before* it is displayed
- Using ServletUnit to simulate the web container

In this chapter we provide recipes for testing web components in isolation, rather than testing the web application as a whole. We divided the chapters this way because we use different technologies and approaches to test a web application than we do to test its components—the servlets, JSPs, Velocity templates, and what have you that make up the application. In short, we test web applications from end to end using HtmlUnit, something described in detail in chapter 13, "Testing J2EE Applications," but we use plain old JUnit and ServletUnit[1] to test web components in isolation—that is, without a container and, if we can, without invoking any business logic. How do we do it?

We test business logic entirely outside the context of the web components that invoke it. It does not matter how complex this business logic is, nor which technologies this business logic uses; we can test it without any mention whatsoever of a servlet or a JSP, so we do. As Mark Eames wrote to us, "If business logic is placed in Java objects that are tied to the web container or any container service, then that logic is only accessible within that container." There is no good reason for business logic—by definition, something that belongs to the *business*—to be tied down to a particular application or its technology. We already implement the business logic in Java, constraining the business's ability to use it in another context, so we prefer not to make it any worse than that.

To test business logic separately from the web components that invoke it requires some refactoring. Our general approach is as follows:

1. Write business logic *entirely* in terms of business objects.
2. Move business logic into an object that can execute outside the context of a servlet (the usual web application Controller).
3. Change the servlet to invoke the new, separate business logic object.

If you have existing servlet code whose business logic you need to test, extracting the business logic out of the servlet makes it possible to apply the "building block" techniques we have discussed in part 1 without having to mess about with web component-related test tools. Keep those tools for the jobs they are designed to do. See recipe 12.1, "Test updating session data without a container," for an example of the testing approach you can take when one extracts the business logic from a servlet.

[1] Part of the HttpUnit project (http://httpunit.sourceforge.net). Do not confuse this with the defunct project of the same name.

Once you have isolated your business objects from the web components that use them you can use web component-related test tools to test them. At this point there are at least three viable options.

Test the components in a container

Your tests initialize a web container and invoke servlet methods as needed. These servlet methods are small and decoupled enough from the business logic that you can test what they do without invoking the business logic. If you *want* to use the business logic in your test, then please consult chapter 13, "Testing J2EE Applications," as those recipes involve testing the application more from end to end, rather than testing its parts in isolation.

Simulate the container

Rather than use a live web container, your tests can use lightweight container simulation to manage your web components. The two primary benefits of this approach are faster tests and more control. The tests execute more quickly because the simulated container does not provide all the same value-added features that an industrial-strength container provides. You have more control because the simulated container provides you with access to the HTTP objects that a production container would not provide. You can use these objects both to set up your test fixture and to verify the results. We generally prefer this approach to test handling a request and rendering a response.

Avoid the container

The web components we use in our web applications are just Java objects, so we can certainly test them without a container. The tricky part is knowing which parts of a servlet are easy to test without a container and which parts are just not worth the effort. The same is true of presentation layer technologies such as JSP or Velocity. Our first instinct is to try to test a web component in isolation, but our experience told us when to throw in the towel and reach for a simulated container.

Our simulated container of choice is ServletUnit, which provides `ServletRunner` as its lightweight container, capable of processing your web deployment descriptor and registering servlets programmatically. In this chapter, whenever we identify the need to simulate the container we will use ServletUnit. The recipes are organized according to the component you need to test and the problems you might encounter along the way.

Finally, if you are stuck testing web components that you cannot refactor, but still want to write out-of-container tests, all is not lost. You can still use ServletUnit, and we provide some recipes that describe how.

12.1 Test updating session data without a container

◆ Problem

You have logic that updates an HTTP session and you would like to test it.

◆ Background

You have chosen to store temporary, client data in the HTTP session, as opposed to a stateful session bean or some other mechanism. You would like to verify that the session is updated correctly, without involving the entire web application in the process. End-to-End Tests are typically quite long, as they can require many steps just to get the application to the desired point. Once you reach that point, you have to rely on the application to correctly interpret the session data just to verify that the session data is correct. What if there is a defect when displaying session data? How do you know which part works?

The *real* problem is that many applications scatter their interaction with the session all over the place, either duplicated within the servlet or in a variety of places outside the servlet. Duplication, as always, is the enemy. The question is how to refactor to make this logic available outside the container, yet allow it to interact with the session.

◆ Recipe

There are two key responsibilities at play in this interaction: updating session data and then updating the HTTP session object. The distinction between the session and its data is the key point for this recipe. Your business logic does not need to know where the data comes from: some from the request, some from the session, some from a hole in the wall—to the business logic it is not important. Therefore, we recommend you do the following:

1. Move the logic that updates the *session data* to its own class, usually called an *action*.
2. Keep the logic that updates the *HTTP session* with the *session data* in the servlet.
3. At each request, have the servlet take a snapshot of the session data and pass that to the *action* for processing.

To illustrate this, we will follow a time-honored tradition: implementing a shopping cart with an HTTP session. Of course, in a real e-commerce application you would *never* store the shopping cart in a user's session; but much as "Hello, World" is the obligatory example of a first program, so is the shopping cart the obligatory HTTP session example. Our store is a coffee shop, selling coffee beans of different varieties and, one hopes, in copious quantities. You can surf our online store and purchase coffee beans by the kilogram.[2] When you submit the form to add a few kilograms of Sumatra to your shopcart, this code takes over:

```
HttpSession session = request.getSession(true);

for (Iterator i = requestedQuantities.iterator(); i.hasNext();) {
    CoffeeQuantity each = (CoffeeQuantity) i.next();
    Integer currentQuantityInKilograms =
        (Integer) session.getAttribute(each.getCoffeeName());

    if (currentQuantityInKilograms == null) {
        session.setAttribute(
            each.getCoffeeName(),
            new Integer(each.getAmountInKilograms()));
    }
    else {
        int newQuantityInKilograms =
            currentQuantityInKilograms.intValue()
                + each.getAmountInKilograms();

        session.setAttribute(
            each.getCoffeeName(),
            new Integer(newQuantityInKilograms));
    }
}
```

This codes lives inside the servlet[3] and is invoked by the method `doPost()`. Here, `requestedQuantities` is a collection of `CoffeeQuantity` objects, each of which describes the amount of a certain type of coffee. For example, if you ask for 3 kg of Special Blend, the corresponding `CoffeeQuantity` object has the values in table 12.1.

Table 12.1 Sample `CoffeeQuantity` properties

Property name	Property value
`amountInKilograms`	3
`coffeeName`	"Special Blend" (`java.lang.String`)

[2] With a Canadian author, you get kilograms. If you want pounds, multiply by 2.2.

[3] We are talking about a hypothetical servlet that stores session information this way. The actual servlet in our Coffee Shop application, CoffeeShopController, has already been refactored according to this recipe.

Then when it is time to display your shopcart, this code takes over:

```
public static ShopcartBean create(
    HttpSession session,
    CoffeeCatalog catalog) {

    ShopcartBean shopcartBean = new ShopcartBean();
    for (Enumeration e = session.getAttributeNames();
        e.hasMoreElements();
        ) {

        String eachCoffeeName = (String) e.nextElement();
        Integer eachQuantityInKilograms =
            (Integer) session.getAttribute(eachCoffeeName);

        ShopcartItemBean item =
            new ShopcartItemBean(
                eachCoffeeName,
                eachQuantityInKilograms.intValue(),
                catalog.getUnitPrice(eachCoffeeName));

        shopcartBean.shopcartItems.add(item);
    }

    return shopcartBean;
}
```

This code lives within the `ShopcartBean`, the object that contains all the shopcart data to be displayed on a web page. Notice that it too interacts directly with the HTTP session, in spite of the fact that this object has the potential to be used outside the context of a web application. This is an indicator of high coupling in the design. If you are not in a position to extract the business logic from this code, then you can use ServletUnit to test it, which we describe in recipe 12.2, "Test updating the HTTP session object."

We want to test the logic that updates the shopcart, pure and simple. We want to write this test:

```
public void testAddToEmptyShopcart() {
    String coffeeProductId = "0";
    String coffeeName = "Sumatra";
    int requestedQuantity = 5;

    CoffeeCatalog catalog = new CoffeeCatalog();
    catalog.addCoffee(
        coffeeProductId, coffeeName, Money.dollars(7, 50));

    ShopcartModel model = new ShopcartModel();

    List requestedQuantities =
        Collections.singletonList(
            new CoffeeQuantity(
                requestedQuantity,
```

```
                catalog.lookupCoffeeById(coffeeProductId)));

        model.addCoffeeQuantities(requestedQuantities);

        assertEquals(5, model.getQuantity("Sumatra"));
        assertEquals(5, model.getTotalQuantity());
    }
```

This test primes the catalog with data, creates a new shopcart, adds a certain quantity of coffee to the shopcart, then verifies both the amount of Sumatra coffee and the amounts of all coffees. The last assertion ensures that the Sumatra is the only coffee in the shopcart. This is much more to the point. To write this test, we need to make the design change indicated in figure 12.1.

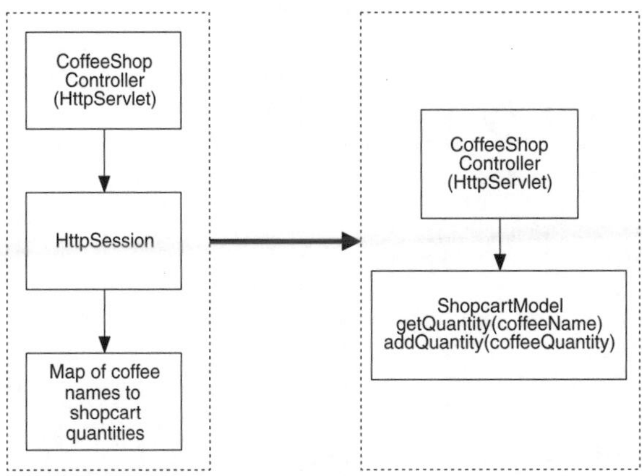

Figure 12.1 Changing the design to encapsulate session data in a model object

Notice that the preceding test says nothing whatsoever about HTTP session, requests, or servlets. It is a pure test of business logic. You can see the final `ShopcartModel` code in listing 12.1:

Listing 12.1 `ShopcartModel`

```
package junit.cookbook.coffee.model;

import java.io.Serializable;
import java.util.*;

import com.diasparsoftware.java.util.Quantity;

public class ShopcartModel implements Serializable {
    private Map coffeeQuantities = new HashMap();

    public void addCoffeeQuantities(List requestedQuantities) {
        for (Iterator i = requestedQuantities.iterator();
            i.hasNext();
            ) {
```

```
            CoffeeQuantity each = (CoffeeQuantity) i.next();

            String coffeeName = each.getCoffeeName();
            CoffeeQuantity currentQuantity
                = getCoffeeQuantity(coffeeName);

            Quantity sum = each.add(currentQuantity);
            coffeeQuantities.put(coffeeName, sum);
        }
    }

    private CoffeeQuantity getCoffeeQuantity(String coffeeName) {
        CoffeeQuantity currentQuantity =
            (CoffeeQuantity) coffeeQuantities.get(coffeeName);

        return (currentQuantity == null)
            ? new CoffeeQuantity(0, coffeeName)
            : currentQuantity;
    }

    public int getQuantity(String coffeeName) {
        return getCoffeeQuantity(coffeeName)
            .getAmountInKilograms();
    }

    public int getTotalQuantity() {
        int totalQuantity = 0;
        for (Iterator i = coffeeQuantities.values().iterator();
             i.hasNext();
             ) {

            CoffeeQuantity each = (CoffeeQuantity) i.next();
            totalQuantity += each.getAmountInKilograms();
        }
        return totalQuantity;
    }

    public Iterator items() {
        return coffeeQuantities.values().iterator();
    }

    public boolean isEmpty() {
        return coffeeQuantities.isEmpty();
    }

    public boolean equals(Object other) {
        if (other != null && other instanceof ShopcartModel) {
            ShopcartModel that = (ShopcartModel) other;
            return this.coffeeQuantities
                .equals(that.coffeeQuantities);
        }
        else {
            return false;
        }
    }
```

```
    public int hashCode() {
        return coffeeQuantities.hashCode();
    }

    public String toString() {
        return "a ShopcartModel with " + coffeeQuantities;
    }
}
```

We have changed the servlet so that interaction with the HTTP session is reduced to a single method.

```
public ShopcartModel getShopcartModel(HttpServletRequest request) {
    HttpSession session = request.getSession(true);

    ShopcartModel model =
        (ShopcartModel) session.getAttribute("shopcartModel");

    if (model == null) {
        model = new ShopcartModel();
        session.setAttribute("shopcartModel", model);
    }

    return model;
}
```

This is the entire interface between your business logic and HTTP session, and although it is not *too simple to break*, it is so simple that defects in your business logic will not affect your interaction with the session. To test your interaction with the session, you only need the following tests:

- Start with an empty session. Issue a request. Expect a shopcart model in the session.
- Start with a session containing a shopcart model. Issue a request. Expect the shopcart model to be there.

With these two tests in place, you can ignore HTTP session interaction when testing the rest of your application.

◆ *Discussion*

The original design was simple from one perspective, but there were two properties of the design preventing us from writing the test we wanted to write.

- The logic to update the shopcart was tightly coupled to the Controller—the servlet.
- The logic to update the shopcart was in a different place than the logic to retrieve the shopcart.

The first design property made it difficult to execute the update logic on its own, forcing us to drag the servlet along for the ride. We should be able to test the update logic no matter how the application delivers the data to it, and our final test reflects that statement, because the test provides the data.

The second design property made it difficult to have confidence in the servlet's ability to update the session correctly with the session data. Keeping the HTTP session up to date after changing the underlying session data should almost be automatic. At a minimum, it should only occur in one place. If you find that your session data object works correctly, but you still have session problems, then the problem lies in the code that takes your single session model object (like our `ShopcartModel`) and stuffs it into the HTTP session. In this case, we recommend writing a few tests to ensure that your session data object makes it into the `HttpSession` properly (see recipe 12.2 for details on how to do this). You can then refactor to a design where this "glue code" appears in only one place. After that, you can concentrate on having the right session data object without worrying about whether it actually gets into the session.

◆ *Related*

- 12.2—Test updating the HTTP session object
- B.1—Too simple to break

12.2 Test updating the HTTP session object

◆ *Recipe*

You want to verify the contents of an HTTP session, but the code that triggers updating the session is not available to invoke directly from a test.

◆ *Background*

You will most typically arrive at this situation if you have inherited servlet code that was not designed to be tested easily. The methods that update a servlet session could be anywhere in the system, rather than refactored into a centralized service. This makes writing these tests a little more difficult than it needs to be. Still, even if updating servlet session is done entirely within the servlet class itself, it might be hidden in non-`public` methods, meaning that you would need to either move those methods into another class or use some means of getting around the Java visibility rules in your tests.

◆ *Recipe*

Fortunately, ServletUnit provides a way to gain access to the servlet session so that you can verify its contents. Returning to our Coffee Shop application, listing 12.2 shows the test we write to verify the contents of the HTTP session when putting 5 kilograms of Sumatra coffee beans into an empty shopcart.

Listing 12.2 Verifying the contents of the HTTP session

```
package junit.cookbook.coffee.test;

import javax.servlet.http.*;

import junit.cookbook.coffee.CoffeeShopController;
import junit.cookbook.coffee.model.ShopcartModel;
import junit.framework.TestCase;

import com.diasparsoftware.java.util.Money;
import com.meterware.HttpUnit.*;
import com.meterware.servletunit.*;

public class AddToShopcartControllerTest extends TestCase {
    private static final String webApplicationRoot =
        "../CoffeeShopWeb/Web Content";

    public void testAddToEmptyShopcart() throws Exception {
        ServletRunner servletRunner =
            new ServletRunner(                                      ❶
                webApplicationRoot + "/WEB-INF/web.xml",
                "/coffeeShop");

        String coffeeName = "Sumatra";
        String coffeeProductId = "1";
        int expectedQuantity = 5;

        CoffeeShopController coffeeShopController                  ❷
            = new CoffeeShopController();
        coffeeShopController.init();

        coffeeShopController.getCatalog().addCoffee(
            coffeeProductId,
            coffeeName,
            Money.dollars(7, 50));

        WebRequest addToShopcartRequest = makeAddCoffeeRequest(   ❸
            coffeeProductId, expectedQuantity);

        ServletUnitClient client = servletRunner.newClient();     ❹

        InvocationContext invocationContext =
            client.newInvocation(addToShopcartRequest);

        coffeeShopController.service(                             ❺
            invocationContext.getRequest(),
            invocationContext.getResponse());
```

```
        ShopcartModel shopcartModel =
            checkShopcartModel(invocationContext.getRequest());     6

        assertEquals(
            expectedQuantity,
            shopcartModel.getQuantity(coffeeName));
    }

    public ShopcartModel checkShopcartModel(
        HttpServletRequest request) {

        HttpSession session = request.getSession();
        assertNotNull(session);

        ShopcartModel shopcartModel =
            (ShopcartModel) session.getAttribute("shopcartModel");
        assertNotNull(shopcartModel);

        return shopcartModel;
    }

    private static WebRequest makeAddCoffeeRequest(
        String coffeeProductId,
        int expectedQuantity) {

        WebRequest addToShopcartRequest = new PostMethodWebRequest(
            "http://localhost/coffeeShop/coffee");   <-- Always use localhost and port 80 with ServletUnit

        addToShopcartRequest.setParameter(
            "quantity-" + coffeeProductId,
            String.valueOf(expectedQuantity));

        addToShopcartRequest.setParameter(
            "addToShopcart-" + coffeeProductId,
            "Buy Now!");

        return addToShopcartRequest;
    }
}
```

The general steps for writing such a test are:

1. Initialize the container—the `ServletRunner`—with your web deployment descriptor.
2. Instantiate and initialize the servlet, so that you can invoke its methods directly. You might wonder why one does not ask the container for the servlet, as that is the container's job. The "container" in this case provides context information, such as the servlet context root path, but it does not actually handle servlet requests. It is in this respect that it is a container *simulator*, rather than a lightweight container.
3. Create a request, for which you use HttpUnit's `WebRequest` hierarchy: usually either a `GetMethodWebRequest` or a `PostMethodWebRequest`.

4 Ask the container for a `ServletUnitClient` from which you obtain an `InvocationContext`. It is this invocation context that provides access to the raw HTTP request and response that the servlet processes.

5 Invoke the servlet's `service()` method passing the raw HTTP request and response as parameters, just as though the container were doing the work.

6 Ask the invocation context for the raw HTTP request, retrieve the `HttpSession` object, then verify its contents.
It is really only this last step that is specific to the needs of this test; you can use the others to build *any* servlet-based test with ServletUnit.

◆ *Discussion*

If you are testing a servlet that you cannot change, then we recommend writing End-to-End Tests with HtmlUnit rather than Object Tests with ServletUnit. To justify our recommendation, here are a few things we experienced while writing the test in this example, compared to the corresponding HtmlUnit test.

Because the ServletUnit test deals with raw HTTP requests, we entered some of the HTML element names incorrectly. When we read the test code to determine the problem, it was not clear which element name corresponded to which HTML form element. We find the corresponding HtmlUnit test (see chapter 13, "Testing J2EE Applications") is clearer because we code it in terms of text fields and buttons, rather than request parameters.

When we first tried to execute this test we found that we needed to involve Jasper (a JSP compiler) and Ant (which *shocked* us). We needed this because our servlet forwards to a JSP. We think that this is only more complexity without much gain, so we recommend you separate the act of *choosing* which JSP to forward to from the act of *executing* that forward operation. Doing so allows you to avoid the work (and expense) of actually compiling and "displaying" the JSP. Your test only needs to examine the HTTP session, so it might not even look at the rendered page, anyway.

The fact that the servlet forwards to a JSP *also* meant that we needed a real web deployment descriptor, rather than being able to register the servlet programmatically in the test. This separates test data from the test itself, which can make the test difficult to understand. If you do not need to forward or redirect to another URI/URL then you can invoke `ServletRunner.registerServlet()` to register your servlet. ServletUnit still provides you with the necessary invocation context to check your session object, but none of the web component-to-URL mapping you might expect would work. If your test does not need it, then do not worry about it.

The test is still quite long: almost fifty lines. Some of that is code that can be extracted into a test fixture (see recipe 3.4, "Factor out a test fixture"), and that includes statements stretching onto multiple lines, but even conceptually the test is "long." It would be nice to focus on the one aspect of the test we really care about—updating the session.

Do not take this to mean that we dislike ServletUnit. Far from it. We intend these comments to mean that one should use ServletUnit judiciously, to test those aspects of web container interaction that cannot be extracted along with business logic. In other words, to test the "glue code" between your servlet and the code around it. When you first reach for ServletUnit, ask yourself whether you can extract the code in question and test it separately. If you honestly answer "no," then *that* is the time to use ServletUnit.

Before we leave this discussion, here is an advisory from the ServletUnit documentation on using the invocation context feature. "Note first that you must do all of the processing that the `service()` method would have done if you take this approach. You may either call the `service()` method itself, or a combination of other calls that will prepare the response in the fashion you wish to test." The pattern we have found most useful is to have `doGet()` or `doPost()` invoke `processRequest()`, then format the request (forward to JSP or write raw HTML). The method `processRequest()`, which we add, does all the real work. Using this little implementation pattern avoids rendering the JSP, which we leave to a different test (see recipe 12.3, "Test rendering a JavaServer Page").

◆ *Related*

- 3.2—Create a separate source tree for test code
- 3.3—Separate test packages from production code packages
- 3.4—Factor out a test fixture
- 12.3—Test rendering a JavaServer Page

12.3 Test rendering a JavaServer Page

◆ *Problem*

You want to verify the output of a JavaServer Page.

◆ *Background*

Testing JSPs in isolation—that is, without simply writing End-to-End Tests—is one of those activities that many people find too difficult to be worth the effort. We find that strange, especially in light of the way many people write JSPs in the first place. It is commonplace for a web author to start with a static web page containing dummy data. This makes it easy to work on both layout and general look-and-feel using web authoring tools such as Dreamweaver. After the page looks good, it is time to replace the static content with placeholders for dynamic content which the application will provide. These placeholders correspond to JavaBean properties, so now the "only way" to see the rendered JSP is to get real data from the application, which is most easily done by executing the application end to end.

◆ *Recipe*

Rather than test your application from end to end, we recommend hard coding some data for the JSP, then rendering it directly using a JSP engine. You can compare the JSP engine's output with a Gold Master—a version of the JSP output that you have checked by hand *once* and then filed away as "correct."

The general strategy is to use ServletUnit along with Jasper[4] to render the JSP in question. ServletUnit also allows you to intercept the request on the way to the JSP so that you can add data to it in the form of request or session attributes. Finally, you will apply the Gold Master technique, comparing the current JSP output to known, correct output.[5]

The example that follows consists of a fair amount of code, so we will explore it in pieces. Much of this code is reusable, and so represents a one-time effort, leaving surprisingly little code to write for the dozens of tests you need to test all your JSPs. In listing 12.3 we start with the "easy" part: the tests themselves.

Listing 12.3 `RenderShopcartJspTest`

```
package junit.cookbook.jsp.test;

import java.io.File;

import javax.servlet.http.HttpServletRequest;

import junit.cookbook.coffee.display.*;
import junit.cookbook.coffee.presentation.test.JspTestCase;
```

4 Here we are using the Apache Tomcat web container, which includes Jasper as its JSP engine.

5 We discuss the Gold Master technique in recipe 10.2, "Verify your SQL commands."

```
import com.diasparsoftware.java.util.Money;
import com.diasparsoftware.javax.servlet.ForwardingServlet;
import com.diasparsoftware.util.junit.GoldMasterFile;
import com.meterware.servletunit.*;

public class RenderShopcartJspTest extends JspTestCase {     <-- JspTestCase contains some convenience methods
    private ShopcartBean shopcartBean;
    private ServletRunner servletRunner;
    private ServletUnitClient client;

    protected void setUp() throws Exception {
        shopcartBean = new ShopcartBean();

        servletRunner =
            new ServletRunner(
                getWebContentPath("/WEB-INF/web.xml"),
                "/coffeeShop");     <-- Register an entire Web Deployment Descriptor
        servletRunner.registerServlet(
            "/forward",
            ForwardingServlet.class.getName());     <-- A dummy servlet to help serve up JSPs

        client = servletRunner.newClient();
    }

    public void testEmptyShopcart() throws Exception {
        checkShopcartPageAgainst(
            new File(
                "test/gold",
                "emptyShopcart-master.txt"));     <-- Check against the Gold Master
    }

    public void testOneItemInShopcart() throws Exception {
        shopcartBean.shopcartItems.add(
            new ShopcartItemBean(
                "Sumatra",
                "762",
                5,
                Money.dollars(7, 50)));

        checkShopcartPageAgainst(
            new File(
                "test/gold",
                "oneItemInShopcart-master.txt"));
    }

    // Helper code omitted for now
}
```

The superclass JspTestCase provides some useful methods for locating JSPs on the file system and deciding where on the file system the JSP engine should generate servlet source code. If you are interested in the details, see the Discussion section of this recipe, but we recommend reading on first, and then coming back to the details when the rest of this recipe is in focus.

The tests are tiny: add some items to a shopcart (or not, in the case of the empty shopcart case) then check the resulting page against a Gold Master. This method —`checkShopcartPageAgainst()`—is where all the magic happens, but before we get to that, we first look at `ForwardingServlet`. This is a simple servlet that does two things: lets a test put data into a request (or session) and forwards the request to the URI we specify. This simulates what our `CoffeeShopController` does in production *after* all the business logic and database updates are complete. Our strategy here is to eliminate the business logic because what we want has nothing to do with business logic: we simply want to verify that a JSP "looks right." We write the `ForwardingServlet` once—or hope that someone else provides one for us[6]—then use it for the rest of these kinds of tests. Listing 12.4 shows the result.

Listing 12.4 `ForwardingServlet`

```
package com.diasparsoftware.javax.servlet;

import java.io.IOException;

import javax.servlet.ServletException;
import javax.servlet.http.*;

public class ForwardingServlet extends HttpServlet {
    private String forwardUri = "";

    protected void doGet(
        HttpServletRequest request,
        HttpServletResponse response)
        throws ServletException, IOException {

        handleRequest(request, response);
    }

    protected void doPost(
        HttpServletRequest request,
        HttpServletResponse response)
        throws ServletException, IOException {

        handleRequest(request, response);
    }

    protected void handleRequest(
        HttpServletRequest request,
        HttpServletResponse response)
        throws ServletException, IOException {
```

6 Diasparsoft Toolkit (www.diasparsoftware.com/toolkit) includes ForwardingServlet for use in tests.

```
        getServletContext().getRequestDispatcher(
            getForwardUri()).forward(
            request,
            response);
    }

    public void setForwardUri(String forwardUri) {      Specify which URI
        this.forwardUri = forwardUri;                    to forward to when
    }                                                    invoking service()

    public String getForwardUri() {
        return forwardUri;
    }
}
```

The next part is rendering the JSP and retrieving its content—that is, using the `ForwardingServlet` in combination with ServletUnit, then reading the JSP output as text.

```
public String getActualShopcartPageContent()
    throws Exception {

    InvocationContext invocationContext =                  We created the
        client.newInvocation(                              ServletUnitClient
            "http://localhost/coffeeShop/forward");  <--  in setUp()

    ForwardingServlet servlet =
        (ForwardingServlet) invocationContext.getServlet();

    servlet.setForwardUri("/shopcart.jsp");      Put the shopcart    Invoke the
                                                 data on the request Forwarding-
    HttpServletRequest request =                                     Servlet
        invocationContext.getRequest();

    request.setAttribute("shopcartDisplay", shopcartBean);  <--     Get the
    servlet.service(request, invocationContext.getResponse());  <-- JSP output
    return invocationContext.getServletResponse().getText();  <--   as text
}
```

This is a direct translation of the steps we needed to test the JSP: put data in the request, render the JSP, and look at the resulting web page. Notice that we do not worry about where the data comes from—we just hard code the data we want to display and stuff it into the request, where the JSP expects it to be. We *know* that the shopcart data comes from the user's session object and we *know* that we have to translate that session object into a `ShopcartBean`, but *we do not care* about those details for this test. Tomorrow, when it turns out we need to store shopcart data in the database and retrieve it using a `ShopcartStore` (see chapter 10, "Testing and JDBC"), *this test remains unaffected.* That is one indicator of a good design: no ripple effect. Good work!

The last piece of the puzzle comes in two parts: the Gold Master. We say two parts because to use the Gold Master technique requires first creating the Gold Master and checking it by visual inspection, then verifying future output against that Gold Master. To create the Gold Master you need to write the JSP text out to a file:

```
public void generateGoldMaster(File goldMasterFile)
    throws Exception {

    String responseText = getActualShopcartPageContent();
    new GoldMasterFile(goldMasterFile).write(responseText);
    fail("Writing Gold Master file.");
}
```

When you first code your test, have it invoke `generateGoldMaster()`. This method creates the Gold Master file *and fails the test* as a reminder that you have not finished yet. This last point is important. If you let the test pass it is possible for someone to run the test, believe it is actually testing something, and not realize that there is work to do. You can ignore a passing test, but not a failing test![7] So your test will look like this the first time you execute it:

```
public void testEmptyShopcart() throws Exception {
    generateGoldMaster(
        new File(
            "test/gold",
            "emptyShopcart-master.txt"));
}
```

Execute the test, then inspect the output yourself:

```
<!DOCTYPE HTML PUBLIC "-//W3C//DTD HTML 4.01 Transitional//EN">
<html>
<head>
<meta http-equiv="Content-Type"
      content="text/html; charset=ISO-8859-1" />
<meta name="GENERATOR" content="IBM WebSphere Studio" />
<meta http-equiv="Content-Style-Type" content="text/css" />
<link href="theme/Master.css" rel="stylesheet" type="text/css" />
<title>shopcart.jsp</title>
</head>
<body>
<h1>your shopcart contains</h1>
<table name="shopcart" border="1">
    <tbody>
        <tr>
            <td><b>Name</b></td>
```

7 Some people might use this opportunity to "ignore" the test (see recipe 6.6, "Ignore a test") rather than have it fail. We recommend the latter, but it is largely a question of personal taste. Do what works for you.

```
                <td><b>Quantity</b></td>
                <td><b>Unit Price</b></td>
                <td><b>Total Price</b></td>
            </tr>

            <tr>
                <td colspan="3"><b>Subtotal</b></td>
                <td><b>$0.00</b></td>
            </tr>
        </tbody>
    </table>

<form action="coffee" method="POST"><input type="submit"
    name="browseCatalog" value="Buy More Coffee!" /></form>
</body>
</html>
```

This looks right: displaying an empty shopcart means no items in the cart and a zero subtotal. There is your Gold Master file. Now that you have written it to disk, change the test so that it checks the response from the server against the Gold Master:

```
public void testEmptyShopcart() throws Exception {
    checkShopcartPageAgainst(
        new File(
            "test/gold",
            "emptyShopcart-master.txt"));
}
```

such that `checkShopcartPageAgainst()` looks like this:

```
public void checkShopcartPageAgainst(File goldMasterFile)
    throws Exception {

    String responseText = getActualShopcartPageContent();
    new GoldMasterFile(goldMasterFile).check(
        responseText);
}
```

The class `com.diasparsoftware.util.junit.GoldMasterFile` is also part of Diasparsoft Toolkit and provides convenience methods for generating and checking against a Gold Master. Listing 12.5 shows the source for this class.

Listing 12.5 GoldMasterFile

```
package com.diasparsoftware.util.junit;

import java.io.*;
import junit.framework.Assert;

public class GoldMasterFile extends Assert {
    private File file;

    public GoldMasterFile(String directory, String file) {
```

```
        this(new File(directory, file));
    }

    public GoldMasterFile(File file) {
        this.file = file;
    }

    public void write(String content) throws IOException {
        file.getParentFile().mkdirs();
        FileWriter goldMasterWriter = new FileWriter(file);
        goldMasterWriter.write(content);
        goldMasterWriter.close();
    }

    public void check(String actualContent)
        throws IOException {

        assertTrue(
            "Gold master [" + file.getAbsolutePath() + "] not found.",
            file.exists());

        StringWriter stringWriter = new StringWriter();
        PrintWriter printWriter = new PrintWriter(stringWriter);

        BufferedReader goldMasterReader =
            new BufferedReader(new FileReader(file));
        while (true) {
            String line = goldMasterReader.readLine();
            if (line == null)
                break;
            printWriter.println(line);
        }

        assertEquals(stringWriter.toString(), actualContent);
    }
}
```

So that is everything: to write a new test, simply add items to the shopcart, write the JSP output to disk, inspect the results by hand, make it a Gold Master, then change the test to check against that Gold Master. If the test ever fails—and it will whenever you change the JSP—just inspect the Gold Master by hand again.

◆ Discussion

We tried to find a standalone JSP engine that we could use to execute these tests and came up empty. We did try to use Jasper—the JSP engine embedded in Apache Tomcat—but we had to write a considerable amount of code, mostly faking context objects, just to get to the point where we could *compile* a JSP, let alone execute it. For that reason we abandoned this approach, preferring instead to use an actual container to process the JSPs. Perhaps by the time you read this there will be a standalone JSP engine that you can use in its place. If so, you can compile and execute the JSP directly rather than going through a web container. So much the better.

Test performance is always an issue to consider, so we feel it is important to mention the cost of executing these tests. In terms of time expense, the cost to execute these tests is approximately 2 seconds of startup cost and 2 seconds per test. These numbers are based on a P4-2.4 GHz machine with all operations occurring in memory (no swapping). This means that a site with 100 JSPs might need a total of 10 minutes (3 test scenarios per JSP times 100 JSPs, times 2 seconds each) to execute an exhaustive test suite for its JSPs. We recommend that you use a background-running continual build system such as Cruise Control to execute these tests regularly, rather than trying to make them part of the Programmer Test suite that you execute whenever you change the production code. The bulk of the cost comes from rendering the JSP and comparing the resulting web page against content we retrieve from disk. In order to speed up these tests, we need to eliminate these costly operations.

We can verify that the JSP has the correct data to display, but that has *nothing* to do with the JSP. Instead, see recipe 12.12, "Verify the data passed to a page template," which, in spite of its title, only tests the servlet.

We can verify that the JSP displays the correct data without worrying about layout or look and feel by using XMLUnit. See chapter 9, "Testing and XML," for recipes involving XMLUnit.

For the sake of completeness, here is the code for `JspTestCase`:

```
public abstract class JspTestCase extends TestCase {
    protected static final String webApplicationRoot =
        "../CoffeeShopWeb/Web Content";      | #1

    protected String getWebContentPath(String relativePath) {
        return new File(
            webApplicationRoot, relativePath).getAbsolutePath();
    }

    protected String getCoffeeShopUrlString(String uri)
        throws Exception {

        return "http://localhost/coffeeShop" + uri;   <-- Change these values for your project
    }

    protected String getJspTempDirectory() {
        return System.getProperty("java.io.tmpdir");
    }
```

```
        protected void tearDown() throws Exception {
            File[] files =
                new File(getJspTempDirectory()).listFiles(
                    new FilenameFilter() {

                public boolean accept(File dir, String name) {
                    return name.endsWith(".java")
                        || name.endsWith(".class");
                }
            });

            for (int i = 0; i < files.length; i++) {
                File file = files[i];
                file.delete();
            }
        }
    }
```

One final note: we do not recommend using the Gold Master technique for output that constantly changes. This technique is best used to detect inadvertent or unexpected changes in output. If cosmetic changes such as look-and-feel or layout enhancements are likely to happen, we strongly recommend that you verify just the dynamic content parts of the JSP, as in the Discussion section of recipe 12.10, "Verify web page content without a web server." Those tests tend to be much less brittle than tests that use the Gold Master technique.

◆ Related

- 12.4—Test rendering a Velocity template
- 12.10—Verify web page content without a web server

12.4 Test rendering a Velocity template

◆ Problem

You are using Velocity as your presentation engine and want to verify that the page renders correctly.

◆ Background

If you are using Velocity rather than JSP as your presentation engine there is much less work involved in testing your templates compared to testing JSPs—at least when writing Object Tests. This recipe describes how simple it is to test rendering a Velocity template.

◆ Recipe

Testing a Velocity template consists of these steps:

1. Initialize the Velocity engine, pointing to the location of the templates on the file system.
2. Add display JavaBeans to a `VelocityContext` object.
3. Merge the Velocity template with the data in the `VelocityContext`.
4. Compare the results against a Gold Master or parse the results in some way.

We return to the shopcart example and use the Gold Master technique. The Velocity template test is much the same as the JSP-based test (see listing 12.3 in recipe 12.3 to compare). We have highlighted the differences in bold print in listing 12.6.

Listing 12.6 RenderShopcartDisplayTemplateTest

```
public class RenderShopcartDisplayTemplateTest extends TestCase {
    private File contentDirectory =
        new File("../CoffeeShopWeb/Web Content"
            + "/WEB-INF/template/velocity");

    private ShopcartBean shopcartBean;

    protected void setUp() throws Exception {
        contentDirectory.mkdirs();

        Properties properties = new Properties();
        properties.put(
            RuntimeConstants.FILE_RESOURCE_LOADER_PATH,
            contentDirectory.getAbsolutePath());

        Velocity.init(properties);

        shopcartBean = new ShopcartBean();
    }

    public void testEmptyShopcart() throws Exception {
        File goldMasterFile =
            new File("test/gold/velocity", "emptyShopcart-master.txt");
        checkShopcartPageAgainst(goldMasterFile);
    }

    public void testOneItemInShopcart() throws Exception {
        shopcartBean.shopcartItems.add(
            new ShopcartItemBean(
                "Sumatra", "762", 5, Money.dollars(7, 50)));

        checkShopcartPageAgainst(
            new File("test/gold/velocity", "oneItemInShopcart-master.txt"));
    }
```

Specify the location of the Velocity templates

```
    public void checkShopcartPageAgainst(File goldMasterFile)
        throws Exception {

        String responseText = getActualShopcartPageContent();
        new GoldMasterFile(goldMasterFile).check(responseText);
    }

    public String getActualShopcartPageContent() throws Exception {
        Context templateAttributes = new VelocityContext();
        templateAttributes.put("shopcartDisplay", shopcartBean);

        StringWriter webPageWriter = new StringWriter();

        Velocity.mergeTemplate(
            "shopcart.vm",
            "UTF-8",
            templateAttributes,
            webPageWriter);

        String responseText = webPageWriter.toString();
        return responseText;
    }

    public void generateGoldMaster(File goldMasterFile)
        throws Exception {

        String responseText = getActualShopcartPageContent();
        new GoldMasterFile(goldMasterFile).write(responseText);
        fail("Writing Gold Master file.");
    }
}
```

Provide data to the template

Write the resulting web page to a String

Merge the template with the template attributes

These tests use the Velocity engine in standalone mode, which eliminates the need to mock anything around you. We believe that this is a considerable improvement over the work we need to do to write the same test for a JSP.

◆ *Discussion*

There is one difference between JSP and Velocity that we consider an annoyance, but you might consider a blessing. The display JavaBeans we have used on our JSPs expose properties as `public` fields, rather than as *get* methods. When we tried to use those JavaBeans on a Velocity template, Velocity did not behave the way we expected. It turns out that Velocity *requires* you to expose JavaBean properties through *get* methods, so we added the ones we needed. We see this as more code without an obvious justification, but perhaps it is a small price to pay for the simplicity of Velocity over JSP. And, of course, if you believe that `public` fields are pure evil, then you probably do not mind this additional requirement.

If you do not want to use the Gold Master technique, but prefer instead to make assertions about the structure and content of the resulting web page, then see recipe 12.10 for details.

◆ Related

- 12.3—Test rendering a JavaServer Page
- 12.10—Verify web page content without a web server

12.5 Test a JSP tag handler

◆ Problem

You would like to write Object Tests for a JSP tag handler.

◆ Background

Because the JSP framework invokes the JSP tag handler, it is not obvious how to test the tag handler in isolation. The approach you take depends on whether you want to involve a JSP engine. As we have written previously, there is no mature, standalone JSP engine that you can use outside the context of a web container, so if you want to avoid a JSP engine, your best bet is to simulate it in your test. Although a little annoying, it only takes a little research to get all the information you need.

◆ Recipe

To test a JSP tag handler in isolation, you must write a test that invokes the tag handler's methods in the same order that the JSP engine would. Now that *sounds* like a lot of work, but it is surprisingly simple. Not only that, but you can certainly recuperate the effort you invest in writing this kind of test by refactoring your mini-JSP engine and using it for future work. Perhaps one is available in a publicly available toolkit somewhere.

In order to simulate the JSP engine, at least the part that executes your tag handler, we searched the web and found a presentation by Doris Chen of Sun Microsystems.[8] It includes lifecycle graphs for the various kinds of JSP tag handler objects. We used these lifecycle graphs as specifications to build our tests, as they told us the order in which to invoke the various JSP tag handler methods. For our

[8] http://developers.sun.com/dev/evangcentral/presentations/customTag.pdf

example, we consider a custom tag that iterates over the items in a shopcart, presenting each shopcart item as a JavaBean that the JSP can then render as it wants. Listing 12.7 shows you how to use such a tag.

Listing 12.7 Using an `IterationTag`

```
<table name="shopcart" border="1">
    <tbody>
        <tr>
            <td><b>Name</b></td>
            <td><b>Quantity</b></td>
            <td><b>Unit Price</b></td>
            <td><b>Total Price</b></td>
        </tr>
        <coffee:eachShopcartItem shopcartBean="shopcartDisplay"
                                 each="item">
            <tr>
                <td><%= item.coffeeName %></td>
                <td id="product-<%= item.productId %>">
                    <%= item.quantityInKilograms %> kg
                </td>
                <td><%= item.unitPrice %></td>
                <td><%= item.getTotalPrice() %></td>
            </tr>
        </coffee:eachShopcartItem>
        <tr>
            <td colspan="3"><b>Subtotal</b></td>
            <td>
                <b><jsp:getProperty name="shopcartDisplay"
                                    property="subtotal" /></b>
            </td>
        </tr>
    </tbody>
</table>
```

We have highlighted the relevant parts of this JSP fragment in bold print. The tag `<coffee:eachShopcartItem>` defines an iterator over the shopcart items, placing each in the scripting variable named by the attribute `each`. In this case, we named that scripting variable `item` and use that variable to display a single row. We could certainly further hide the `<tr>` tag for each shopcart item behind *another* JSP tag, but that is not germane to the point we want to make here. We see that this as an `IterationTag`, and so refer to the lifecycle for an `IterationTag`, which we have translated into pseudocode in listing 12.8. The parts in bold print are the actual method and constant names.

Listing 12.8 Pseudocode for a generic IterationTag handler

```
initialize page context
initialize tag attributes

whatNext := doStartTag()
if (whatNext == EVAL_BODY_INCLUDE)
    do
        evaluate body
    until (doAfterBody() == SKIP_BODY)
endif

whatNext := doEndTag()
if (whatNext == EVAL_PAGE)
    evaluate rest of page
endif
```

We need to know the essential strategy behind the tag's behavior before we know what to test. The tag takes the specified shopcart and iterates over the items in it. The tag stores each item in a scripting variable—implemented as a page context attribute—so that the JSP can display its properties. We can describe the behavior we need to test, then, in terms of the way we expect the JSP engine to invoke the tag handler.

1. Set the tag attribute values, `shopcartBean` and `each`.
2. Invoke `doStartTag()`. If the shopcart is empty, we should skip the tag body; otherwise, we should store the first shopcart item in the scripting variable named by the attribute `each`, and then process the body.
3. If the shopcart is not empty, invoke `doAfterBody()`. If there are more shopcart items, store the next shopcart item in the scripting variable named by the attribute `each`, then process the body again; otherwise, skip the body.
4. Now that all the shopcart items have been processed, invoke `doEndTag()`, then evaluate the rest of the page.

We are essentially simulating a JSP engine—a theoretical one that follows the JSP specification correctly. If your vendor supports the specification differently,[9] your End-to-End Tests will reveal that, at which point you should feed that information back into your Object Tests with the appropriate comments. This is one case

[9] A euphemism for "has a defect."

where comments are certainly appropriate in code: when third-party software does not conform to specifications to which it is meant to conform. We can translate these steps into code relatively easily, as in listing 12.9.

Listing 12.9 EachShopcartItemHandlerTest

```
package junit.cookbook.coffee.jsp.test;

import java.util.*;
import javax.servlet.jsp.tagext.*;

import junit.framework.*;
import junit.cookbook.coffee.display.*;
import junit.cookbook.coffee.jsp.EachShopcartItemHandler;

import com.diasparsoftware.java.util.Money;

import com.mockobjects.servlet.MockJspWriter;
import com.mockobjects.servlet.MockPageContext;

public class EachShopcartItemHandlerTest extends TestCase {
    private EachShopcartItemHandler handler;
    private ShopcartBean shopcartBean;
    private MockPageContext pageContext;

    protected void setUp() throws Exception {
        shopcartBean = new ShopcartBean();
        handler = new EachShopcartItemHandler();

        pageContext = new MockPageContext() {    <-- MockPageContext does not store attributes by default
            private Map attributes = new HashMap();

            public Object getAttribute(String name) {
                return attributes.get(name);
            }

            public void setAttribute(String name, Object value) {
                attributes.put(name, value);
            }

            public void removeAttribute(String name) {
                attributes.remove(name);
            }
        };

        MockJspWriter out = new MockJspWriter();    <-- You can set the expected output and verify it against a String
        pageContext.setJspWriter(out);

        handler.setPageContext(pageContext);
        handler.setParent(null);    <-- We do not need the parent tag for this test

        handler.setShopcartBean(shopcartBean);    | Set the tag attributes
        handler.setEach("item");

    }
```

```
    public void testEmptyShopcart() throws Exception {
        assertEquals(Tag.SKIP_BODY, handler.doStartTag());
        assertNull(getTheEachAttribute());
        assertEquals(Tag.EVAL_PAGE, handler.doEndTag());
    }

    public void testOneItem() throws Exception {
        ShopcartItemBean shopcartItem1 = new ShopcartItemBean(
            "Sumatra", "762", 1, Money.dollars(10, 0));
        shopcartBean.shopcartItems.add(shopcartItem1);

        List shopcartItemAsList = new LinkedList(
            shopcartBean.shopcartItems);        <- Allows us to refer to each shopcart item by index

        assertEquals(Tag.EVAL_BODY_INCLUDE, handler.doStartTag());

        assertEquals(shopcartItemAsList.get(0), getTheEachAttribute());
        assertEquals(Tag.SKIP_BODY, handler.doAfterBody());

        assertNull(getTheEachAttribute());

        assertEquals(Tag.EVAL_PAGE, handler.doEndTag());
    }

    public void testTwoItems() throws Exception {
        shopcartBean.shopcartItems.add(
            new ShopcartItemBean(
                "Sumatra", "762", 1, Money.dollars(10, 0)));
        shopcartBean.shopcartItems.add(
            new ShopcartItemBean(
                "Special Blend", "768", 1, Money.dollars(10, 0)));

        List shopcartItemAsList = new LinkedList(
            shopcartBean.shopcartItems);

        assertEquals(Tag.EVAL_BODY_INCLUDE, handler.doStartTag());

        assertEquals(shopcartItemAsList.get(0), getTheEachAttribute());
        assertEquals(
            IterationTag.EVAL_BODY_AGAIN,
            handler.doAfterBody());

        assertEquals(shopcartItemAsList.get(1), getTheEachAttribute());
        assertEquals(Tag.SKIP_BODY, handler.doAfterBody());

        assertNull(getTheEachAttribute());
        assertEquals(Tag.EVAL_PAGE, handler.doEndTag());
    }

    public Object getTheEachAttribute() {    <- A strange name, only because getEachAttribute() could mean something different
        return pageContext.getAttribute("item");
    }
}
```

This test shows iterating over an empty shopcart, a single-item shopcart, and a multiple-item shopcart. These are the three distinct cases we need to test, although if it would make you more comfortable, you could test for ten items rather than two. The next step is to turn this into a Parameterized Test Case (see recipe 4.8, "Build a data-driven test suite") that allows you to test against a variety of values for the tag input attributes.

Notice that we do not test the output of the `JspWriter` our tag uses. In this case, the tag does not write any output, but simply sets a page context attribute and processes whatever body it might have. If your tag writes output using the `JspWriter`, then add these lines of code to the end of your test:

```
MockJspWriter out = new MockJspWriter();
pageContext.setJspWriter(out);
handler.setPageContext(pageContext);
// The rest of the test
out.setExpectedData("The output you expect");
out.verify();
```

When you execute the test, the `MockJspWriter` verifies its actual output against the expected data you specify here. You will use this technique for tags that write directly to the JSP.

◆ *Discussion*

We have built our own `MockPageContext` implementation (as an anonymous class) because the version that comes with Mock Objects v0.09 does not store page context attributes. The tag we want to test sets those attributes, so we need to add enough behavior to `MockPageContext` to store, retrieve and remove page context attributes. This is a candidate to move to a reusable library (such as Mock Objects itself). If your tag does not manipulate the page context in this way, then you can use `MockPageContext` as is. Try it and see.

Compare the logic in each of the three tests with the `IterationTag` lifecycle to see how the two match up. To help you see what we mean, consider the empty shopcart case. The JSP engine should invoke `doStartTag()`, which should skip the tag body. The JSP engine should then invoke `doEndTag()`, which should evaluate the rest of the page. This case entirely avoids processing the body and invoking `doAfterBody()`.

We do not generally recommend writing your own platform simulators. We strongly recommend against, for example, writing your own servlet processing engine for the sake of writing tests like this. We made an exception here for two key reasons: it turns out to be simpler than we thought and there does not appear to be a viable alternative for writing Object Tests for a JSP tag handler. Our next option would have been to write an End-to-End Test involving a JSP that uses this tag (see recipe 12.3); so we compared the effort of writing this small JSP tag processor, executing and maintaining the corresponding tests against writing, and executing and maintaining the corresponding End-to-End Tests. We judged that it was worth taking an hour or so to learn how to write these tests. We were right this time. As always, be aware of the alternatives *and* the overall cost of each option before you make your choice. If you do not know, then ask; the JUnit community is only too happy to help you.

◆ Related

- 4.8—Build a data-driven test suite
- 12.3—Test rendering a JavaServer Page

12.6 Test your JSP tag library deployment

◆ Problem

You want to verify that your JSP tag library has been deployed correctly.

◆ Background

It is possible to write all the right Object Tests for your web components but have the system fail an End-to-End Test. It is easy to forget to write the deployment descriptors for your web components when you do the majority of your web component testing outside of a web container. The approach you take to deal with this problem depends in part on how often you make the mistake and how much it hurts you when you do. (Do not feel bad: it happens to the best of us.)

◆ Recipe

Let us first recommend you use your End-to-End Tests to detect this kind of problem. If you are executing End-to-End Tests ("Customer Tests" in the Extreme Programming vernacular) as you complete features or as you execute your Object Tests, then you can easily let your End-to-End Tests detect any defect arising from deploying your web components incorrectly. For example, if you deploy a JSP tag library incorrectly, your Object Tests will pass but your End-to-End Tests will fail. As a result, when this failure happens, the first question to ask yourself is, "Did I deploy this stuff correctly?"

We understand that this solution might not satisfy you. It might seem unnecessarily informal or haphazard. If you feel that way *or* decide for any other reason that you need some more focused tests in place, then we recommend verifying the deployment descriptors themselves, either using the Gold Master technique (which we discussed in chapter 10, "Testing and JDBC") or by parsing the XML documents and making assertions about them (see chapter 9, "Testing and XML"). We recommend the latter approach over the former. You might even wish to compare the Gold Master file against the current deployment descriptor using XMLUnit rather than performing a straight text-content comparison. If you use XMLUnit you will not be bothered by false failures resulting from purely innocuous differences in formatting: tabs or spaces, different white space, different line breaks.

The files you need to verify are the tag library descriptors (*.tld) and the web deployment descriptor itself (web.xml). Check the former to ensure that you have specified the tag name, attributes, requirements, and tag handler class name correctly. Check the latter to ensure that your application has access to all the tag libraries it needs.

The following is an example of using XMLUnit to verify that you have specified a custom tag correctly in your tag library descriptor. The entire test revolves around checking the existence of a number of increasingly specific XPath expressions. Listing 12.10 is an example.

Listing 12.10 CoffeeTagLibraryDeploymentTest

```
package junit.cookbook.coffee.deployment.test;

import java.io.File;

import javax.xml.parsers.DocumentBuilder;
import javax.xml.parsers.DocumentBuilderFactory;
import junit.cookbook.coffee.display.ShopcartItemBean;

import org.apache.crimson.jaxp.DocumentBuilderFactoryImpl;
import org.custommonkey.xmlunit.XMLTestCase;
import org.w3c.dom.Document;

public class CoffeeTagLibraryDeploymentTest
    extends XMLTestCase {
    private Document tagLibraryDescriptorDocument;

    protected void setUp() throws Exception {
        DocumentBuilderFactory factory =
            new DocumentBuilderFactoryImpl();

        factory.setNamespaceAware(true);
```

```
        factory.setValidating(false);

        DocumentBuilder documentBuilder =
            factory.newDocumentBuilder();

        documentBuilder.setEntityResolver(
            new StringEntityResolver(""));

        File file =
            new File(
                "../CoffeeShopWeb/Web Content",
                "WEB-INF/coffeeShop.tld");

        tagLibraryDescriptorDocument =
            documentBuilder.parse(file);
    }

    public void testShopcartTagDeployedCorrectly()
        throws Exception {

        String[] expectedRelativeXpaths =
            new String[] {
                "",
                "/attribute[name='shopcartBean']",
                "/attribute[name='each']",
                "/attribute[name='each' and required='true']",
                "/variable[name-from-attribute='each']",
                "/variable[name-from-attribute='each' and "
                    + "variable-class='"
                    + ShopcartItemBean.class.getName()
                    + "']" };

        for (int i = 0;
            i < expectedRelativeXpaths.length;
            i++) {

            assertXpathExists(
                "/taglib/tag[name='eachShopcartItem']"
                    + expectedRelativeXpaths[i],
                tagLibraryDescriptorDocument);
        }
    }
}
```

Avoid loading the DTD

Verify each expected XPath expression

You now have the skeleton from which you can make two main enhancements. First, add more XPath-based assertions to cover the other parts of the tag library descriptor that you expect to find. Next, build a customized Document Object Model for this document, similar to the work that Mike Bowler has done in creating a domain-oriented Document Object Model for HTML in HtmlUnit. If you get that far, consider sharing it with the rest of the world through the medium of open source!

◆ ***Discussion***

In our example we avoided loading the DTD for our tag library descriptor[10] because that was not part of the problem we were trying to solve. XMLUnit provides support for validating documents against a DTD, and you should use them in testing wherever you can. Validating XML documents—either against a DTD or a schema—catches perhaps 90% of the silly mistakes we make when writing XML by hand or when generating it. See chapter 9, "Testing and XML" for more information on testing with XMLUnit.

We recommend building a Deployment Test Suite that you execute when you deploy the application. This suite would include all manner of tests that verify deployment descriptors, including checking for tag libraries. Not only will the programmers find this useful during development, but the deployers will find it useful to avoid silly problems during deployment. Everyone wins.

If you are test-driving your JSP tag library, then you will typically use XMLUnit to build the content of your tag library descriptor and web deployment descriptor as you write the tag library. In that case, you are more likely to use XMLUnit directly on the deployment descriptor and place the expected contents in your test method than you would be to use the Gold Master technique. If you are adding deployment tests to an existing application, you will probably find the Gold Master technique sufficient until you notice a pattern in the kinds of deployment defects your organization tends to make. If that happens, we recommend adding the more direct-style tests to cover those "blind spots."

◆ ***Related***

- Chapter 9—Testing and XML
- Chapter 10—Testing and JDBC

12.7 Test servlet initialization

◆ ***Problem***

You want to verify that your servlet initializes correctly.

[10] We created the class `StringEntityResolver` and used it in a rather trivial manner, because that was quick and easy.

◆ *Background*

If you have trouble verifying a servlet's initialization behavior, this is most likely the reason: the behavior has no directly observable side effect. Often the servlet reads some startup data or builds some internal lookup tables and that information is not available outside the servlet object—instead they are `private` parts. Other times, servlet initialization consists of initializing other resources, such as a data source, messaging server, or security server. It is often difficult to verify that the servlet initializes those resources correctly, as doing so involves both having those resources online *and* making assertions on their state. You would be surprised how difficult it can be to ask a messaging server, "Are you initialized properly?" They are not accustomed to answering such simple questions!

◆ *Recipe*

The most direct approach is best: invoke `init()` and verify the results. Listing 12.11 provides an example.

Listing 12.11 Verifying the behavior of `init()`

```
public class InitializeCoffeeShopControllerTest extends TestCase {
    public void testCatalogInitialized() throws Exception {
        final Map initParameters = new HashMap();
        initParameters.put("A", "$7.25");

        CoffeeShopController controller = new CoffeeShopController() {
            public Enumeration getInitParameterNames() {
                return new Vector(initParameters.keySet()).elements();
            }

            public String getInitParameter(String name) {
                return (String) initParameters.get(name);
            }
        };

        controller.init();
        assertEquals(1, controller.getCatalog().size());
    }
}
```

Annotations: **Hard code initialization parameters** (initParameters lines); **Substitute hard-coded data** (anonymous subclass methods); **Verify servlet processed hard-coded data** (assertEquals line)

NOTE *A question of style?*—Our hard-working reviewer George Latkiewicz pointed out that, "realistically" there would be an additional assertion in this test verifying the values of the item in the catalog. After all, it is *possible* for the catalog to have one item, but the wrong item, masking a defect. We have to admit that to be true in general, but definitely not in this case.

The only way the catalog could have the wrong item would be if `getInitParameter()` were broken, and returned the wrong values. In this case, we're *faking* `getInitParameter()`, so really we do not care what it returns—we only care that the servlet `init()` method invokes it. As long as `getInitParameter()` returns something meaningful that the servlet can then add to its catalog, that does the job. Adding the assertion George suggests is not only superfluous, but increases the test's coupling to its data. Not this time, George!

To invoke `init()`, you might need to pass a `ServletConfig` object to this method, in which case you need a simple implementation of this interface: either an off-the-shelf mock or your own, hand-coded implementation.[11] You can find an easy-to-use implementation of `ServletConfig` in the reference implementation of J2EE,[12] called `org.apache.catalina.core.StandardWrapper`. With this class, you can set initialization parameters by invoking `addInitializationParameter(key, value)`, then verify that your servlet processes those parameters correctly. Listing 12.12 shows an example.

Listing 12.12 Test processing initialization parameters

```
public void testProcessedParameters() throws Exception {
    FrontControllerServlet servlet = new FrontControllerServlet() {
        public void log(String message) {
            // Intentionally disable logging
        }
    };                                                        ❶

    StandardWrapper config = new StandardWrapper();
    config.addInitParameter(
        "serverImplementationClass",
        "junit.cookbook.servlet.RmiServerImpl");

    servlet.init(config);

    assertEquals(
        "junit.cookbook.servlet.RmiServerImpl",
        servlet.getServerImplClassName());                    ❷
}
```

❶ *Override log()*—If you use this technique, you will need to override the method `GenericServlet.log(String)` just to avoid a `NullPointerException` when executing

[11] Fortunately, it is a small interface: only four methods as of this writing. Unfortunately, one of those returns a `ServletContext`, which you would also need to mock—sometimes once you mock, you can't stop!

[12] Only in J2EE 1.3.1, apparently. It is not included in J2EE 1.4, but *is* part of Catalina, the Tomcat 4.0 web container.

the test. This test is quite brittle, as it depends on a particular implementation of `GenericServlet` and might change from application server to application server. Try instantiating your servlet directly *without* overriding this method to see what changes you need to make to get around whatever your implementation does in `GenericServlet.init()`.

❷ *Add query method for testing*—If you do not have a way to ask the servlet for this property, then you will have to add this method. If none such exists, then you might need to ask the servlet for its `private` parts. See recipe 17.6, "Test a private method if you must," for details on using JUnitX.

To summarize, if your servlet implements `init()` with no parameters then you need to override the servlet methods that retrieve initialization parameters. This is the most direct way to control the initialization parameters your servlet tries to process during a test. If your servlet implements `init(ServletConfig)` then you can use the `StandardWrapper` to hard code initialization parameters. This second option is generally less confusing, so we recommend implementing `init(ServletConfig)` in your servlets, rather than the no-parameter version. Doing so makes your servlet easier to test.

◆ Discussion

If you would also like to verify the behavior of `destroy()`, then you can apply the above technique and invoke `destroy()` directly. You might need to invoke `init()` first, but as the two methods go together, that is perfectly reasonable. Do be sure to test `init()` first if you are going to rely on its behavior to test `destroy()`. If you *can* find a way to avoid calling `init()` in your `destroy()` test—without merely duplicating `init()`'s code in the test—so much the better. (Test isolation is important, test isolation is important, test isolation is important, ...)

◆ Related

- 17.6—Test a private method if you must

12.8 Test the ServletContext

◆ Problem

Your servlet stores lookup data in the `ServletContext` during initialization. You want to verify its behavior without running the servlet in a container.

◆ Background

It is common, although perhaps not necessarily recommended, to store lookup tables in the `ServletContext`.[13] In applications with multiple servlets that look up data at initialization, it is common to cache this data in the `ServletContext`, as this object is available to all servlets in a web application. Certainly if the cache is incorrect on startup, the application does not stand much of a chance of working.

◆ Recipe

There are really two behaviors here that you want to test: the servlet asks an object to load the data, and that indeed the object loads the data correctly. Test them separately, if you can. We will start with the second behavior and return to the first.

Testing the ability to load the lookup data depends on how it is stored. If you store it on disk, simply load the file into memory, present the data as objects, then verify that you load the right objects. You will generally provide a "lookup data provider" with methods to look up data by some key. In our Coffee Shop application we want to be able to find the unit price for a given kind of coffee. We build this interface to provide that service:

```
package junit.cookbook.coffee.model;

import com.diasparsoftware.java.util.Money;

public interface CoffeeBeanUnitPriceProvider {
    Money getUnitPrice(String coffeeName);
}
```

Let us say we want to load this data from a database. In that case, we use the techniques in chapter 10, "Testing and JDBC," to build a `CatalogStoreJdbcImpl`, which not only implements `CatalogStore`—providing more catalog-related features—but also implements `CoffeeBeanUnitPriceProvider`. We test it according to the JDBC testing techniques we have already described, and the result is a database-aware lookup table for the unit price of coffee products. So far, so good. On to the other part of the equation: verifying that the servlet asks to load this data during initialization and stores it in the `ServletContext`. For that, we use ServletUnit and servlet context initialization parameters.

In the web deployment descriptor for our web application, we specify which implementation of the `CoffeeBeanUnitPriceProvider` to instantiate and place in the `ServletContext`. The application can then obtain this object and ask it for

---

[13] The ServletContext is essentially global data, after all.

unit prices whenever such are needed. We therefore need to test that the servlet instantiates the unit price provider and stores it in the `ServletContext`. Listing 12.13 shows the test we need.

Listing 12.13 `InitializeUnitPricesTest`

```
public class InitializeUnitPricesTest {
    private ServletRunner servletRunner;
    private ServletUnitClient client;

    public void testInitializeUnitPrices() throws Exception {
        servletRunner =
            new ServletRunner(
                getWebContentPath("/WEB-INF/web.xml"),
                "/coffeeShop");

        client = servletRunner.newClient();

        WebRequest request = new PostMethodWebRequest(
            "http://localhost/coffeeShop/coffee");    <-- Any request that goes through the servlet
        request.setParameter("browseCatalog", "catalog");

        client.sendRequest(request);

        InvocationContext invocationContext =
            client.newInvocation(request);

        CoffeeShopController controller =
            (CoffeeShopController) invocationContext
                .getServlet();

        assertTrue(
            controller.getServletContext().getAttribute(
                "unitPriceProvider")
                instanceof CoffeeBeanUnitPriceProviderJdbcImpl);    <-- No need to be more specific
    }
}
```

The key parts to this test are triggering servlet initialization and verifying what *kind* of unit price provider ends up in the servlet context. By passing this test you know that a unit price provider is available on servlet startup. By testing the JDBC implementation of `CoffeeBeanUnitPriceProvider` on its own, you know that it works. In this case you do not even need a mock unit price provider! We always like it when that happens.

◆ ***Discussion***

If you are unable to refactor (or design!) your application in the manner we describe here, you will need to combine the two kinds of tests: the ones that verify the lookup data provider and the one that verifies initializing the `ServletContext`. Do not despair: just use the initialization code as the test fixture. Move the initialization test into your test case class's `setUp()` method, then use that as the fixture for the rest of your tests. Certainly if the fixture code fails then the tests that depend on it will fail and you will know right away. We could even have written this entire recipe that way, but we prefer more and smaller tests, where possible. This is another instance where less coupling makes for simpler tests.

We describe `JspTestCase` elsewhere in this chapter, particularly in recipe 12.3, so if you want to know more about it, look there.

◆ Related

- Chapter 10—Testing and JDBC
- 12.3—Test rendering a JavaServer page

12.9 Test processing a request

◆ Problem

You would like to verify that your servlet correctly processes incoming requests.

◆ Background

The typical way one tests a servlet is manually, and through the end-user interface. Often, the general strategy is to click through a maze of pages until you arrive at the right one, fill in some text, push a button, and determine from the end result whether the servlet did the right thing. There are two principal downfalls with this approach. First, the tests are manual, so they are expensive to execute and prone to error. Second, you verify the result *indirectly* by observing side effects of correct behavior, rather than making assertions on the servlet itself. Clearly some automated tests are in order: tests that verify the correct handling of the request without relying on the correctness of the rest of the application.

◆ Recipe

In a typical web application, a servlet behaves as follows:

1. Receive a request from the web container.
2. Choose some business logic to execute based on the request.
3. Extract data from the request and pass it to the business logic as parameters.

This recipe is about testing each of these aspects of a servlet's behavior. Because we want these to be isolated Object Tests, there are a few principles that guide our approach. The first is "the servlet does not know where the request comes from." We ought to be able to simulate the request without involving a live web container. The next is "the business logic does not need to behave correctly." We should not have to invoke the production business logic corresponding to the request, but rather verify that we choose the appropriate method and send it the correct parameters. We will test the business logic elsewhere, if we have not done so already. We will use these as the guiding principles for our tests.

If your servlet is already well factored, with application logic and business logic separate from the servlet class itself, then most of the work is done: simply test all those pieces in isolation and trust the web container to do its job correctly. At this point, the servlet is nothing more than a data transfer bus between the network and your objects. Use the techniques in part 1 of this book plus a mock objects approach between the application logic and the business logic. The rest of this recipe deals with the majority of web applications: ones where the servlet is more than just a gateway to your application.

If you have a "kitchen sink" servlet—all the logic is in the request handler methods[14]—then you must approach testing it like any other method that has no return value. The best you can do is invoke the method and observe its behavior by examining its side effects. See recipe 2.2, "Test a method that returns nothing," for a more detailed discussion of the issues. Now for a servlet, those side effects likely include invoking business logic, something we expressly wish to avoid; therefore, we need to extract the code that processes the request parameters into a separate method [Refactoring, 110]. We then test the new method in isolation, in addition to verifying that the servlet correctly invokes it. Testing the former is straightforward, whereas the latter is best done with a mock objects approach.

Returning to our Coffee Shop application, consider a shopper adding a quantity of coffee to his shopcart. Our application presents the catalog information to the user with a text field to specify the quantity of a given coffee and a button to add it to the shopcart. When the shopper presses the "Buy!" button, the servlet instantiates an `AddToShopcartCommand`, containing the `ShopcartModel` for the shopper's shopcart and the `CoffeeQuantity` object that corresponds to their choice of coffee name and amount in kilograms. It then executes this command to update the shopcart. We want to test creating that command from a request, without actually executing the command. To do this, we extract the command-creating logic

---

[14] `doGet(), doPost(), ....`

into a new method named `makeAddToShopcartCommand()`. Rather than take the `HttpServletRequest` as a parameter, it takes as parameters the request parameters (as a `Map`) and the session attributes (as a `Map`). This makes the method very easy to test, because by the time the servlet invokes `makeAddToShopcartCommand()`, there are no servlet-related interfaces to deal with. Listing 12.14 shows the test.[15]

Listing 12.14 Test making the "add to shopcart" command

```
public void testMakeCommandValidRequest() {
    CoffeeShopController controller = new CoffeeShopController();

    CoffeeShopModel coffeeShopModel = new CoffeeShopModel();
    coffeeShopModel.getCatalog().addCoffee(
        "0",
        "Sumatra",
        Money.dollars(7, 50));

    controller.setModel(coffeeShopModel);

    Map parameters = new HashMap();
    parameters.put("quantity-0", new String[] { "2" });
    parameters.put("addToShopcart-0", new String[] { "Buy!" });
    ShopcartModel shopcartModel = new ShopcartModel();
    Map sessionAttributes =
        Collections.singletonMap("shopcartModel", shopcartModel);

    AddToShopcartCommand actualCommand =
        controller.makeAddToShopcartCommand(
            parameters,
            sessionAttributes);

    AddToShopcartCommand expectedCommand =
        new AddToShopcartCommand(
            new CoffeeQuantity(2, "Sumatra"),
            shopcartModel);

    assertEquals(expectedCommand, actualCommand);
}
```

We set the request parameter values as arrays of `String` objects, because that is how the servlet API presents them when we invoke `HttpServletRequest.getParameterMap()`. We also substitute our own coffee catalog for the one the servlet would initialize to avoid an unpleasant dependency between this test and the servlet. If someone were to change the default data in the coffee catalog, this test

[15] Find all these tests in `junit.cookbook.coffee.test.AddToShopcartParametersTest`.

might fail even though the logic it tests is correct. For this, we needed to add the method `setModel()` to our servlet. We could alternatively have made the `CoffeeShopModel` object an optional constructor parameter, as we described in recipe 2.11, "Test an object that instantiates other objects." Adding this method is easier, but if we find we want to add more of these kinds of methods, we will consider refactoring towards optional constructor parameters.

The next step is to verify that given a request to add coffee to the shopcart, the servlet attempts to invoke `makeAddToShopcartCommand()` with the expected parameters. To determine how to create that request, we consult the page that presents the appropriate form: the catalog page. It turns out that the names of the request parameters we need depend on the product ID of the coffee the shopper wants to buy. If he chooses coffee with product ID 762, then the name of the quantity parameter is `quantity-762` and the name of the submit button for adding that coffee to the shopcart is `addToShopcart-762`. We already know from working with the code that the shopcart is stored in the session under the name `shopcartModel`, so that is all the information we need to simulate an incoming request. We create a mock request and response, invoke `doPost()` then verify that `makeAddToShopcartCommand()` is eventually invoked. To do that, we simply subclass the class under test, intercept that method invocation, assert that it happened, and that the parameters were the correct ones. Listing 12.15 shows the test in question. Because we are faking the servlet API, our fake objects are more complex than we would like.

Listing 12.15 Verifying the servlet invokes the new command

```
public void testServletInvokesMakeAddToShopcartCommand()
    throws Exception {

    final Map expectedRequestParameters = new HashMap() {
        {
            put("quantity-0", new String[] { "2" });
            put("addToShopcart-0", new String[] { "Buy!" });
        }
    };

    ShopcartModel shopcartModel = new ShopcartModel();
    final Map expectedSessionAttributes =
        Collections.singletonMap("shopcartModel", shopcartModel);

    CoffeeShopModel coffeeShopModel = new CoffeeShopModel();
    coffeeShopModel.getCatalog().addCoffee(
        "0",
        "Sumatra",
        Money.dollars(7, 50));
```

```
    CoffeeShopController controller = new CoffeeShopController() {
        public AddToShopcartCommand makeAddToShopcartCommand(
            Map parameters,
            Map sessionAttributes) {

            makeAddToShopcartCommandInvoked = true;
            assertEquals(expectedRequestParameters, parameters);
            assertEquals(
                expectedSessionAttributes,
                sessionAttributes);

            return null;
        }
    };

    controller.setModel(coffeeShopModel);

    MockControl httpServletResponseControl =
        MockControl.createNiceControl(HttpServletResponse.class);

    HttpServletResponse httpServletResponse =
        (HttpServletResponse) httpServletResponseControl.getMock();

    final HttpRequestBase httpServletRequest =
        new HttpRequestBase() {

        public HttpSession getSession(boolean create) {
            return new FakeHttpSession(expectedSessionAttributes);
        }

        public RequestDispatcher getRequestDispatcher(String path) {
            return new RequestDispatcherAdapter();
        }
    };

    httpServletRequest.clearParameters();

    CollectionUtil
        .forEachDo(
            expectedRequestParameters,
            new MapEntryClosure() {
        public void eachMapEntry(Object key, Object value) {
            httpServletRequest.addParameter(
                (String) key,
                (String[]) value);
        }
    });

    controller.doPost(httpServletRequest, httpServletResponse);
    assertTrue(
        "Did not invoke makeAddToShopcartCommand()",
        makeAddToShopcartCommandInvoked);
}
```

Fake making the command

Use EasyMock to mock the HttpServletResponse

An easy way to fake HttpServletRequest

Copy the request parameters into the fake request

Was the method invoked?

The are two key parts to this test: intercepting the invocation of makeAddToShopcartCommand() and asserting that the method was invoked at all. We create a field in our test case class named makeAddToShopcartCommandInvoked to store whether the method was invoked, set it to false in setUp(), set it to true when the method is invoked, and then verify it at the end of the test. When the test invokes doPost() on the servlet, our spy version of makeAddToShopcartCommand() says "Someone invoked me," and then makes assertions about the parameters passed into it. The rest of the test contains some mock objects noise: the servlet API is notoriously annoying to fake out, which indicates that using ServletUnit for these tests might be easier, but that is a decision you can only make on a case-by-case basis. If you feel that hand rolling Test Objects is too much work, then try the various packages (ServletUnit, EasyMock, MockMaker, and jMock) and learn what works best in which situation.

These tests combine to give us the confidence that the servlet correctly extracts the relevant data from the request (product ID, quantity, and shopcart) and chooses the correct business logic to execute (AddToShopcartCommand). Now we need to verify that it actually invokes the command. We can use the same technique as for makeAddToShopcartCommand(): extract the method executeCommand(), intercept the method invocation, assert that it happened, and that the correct command was executed. Listing 12.16 shows the test.

Listing 12.16 testServletInvokesExecuteCommand()

```
public void testServletInvokesExecuteCommand() throws Exception {
    final AddToShopcartCommand expectedCommand =
        new AddToShopcartCommand(
            new CoffeeQuantity(200, "Special Blend"),
            new ShopcartModel());

    CoffeeShopController controller = new CoffeeShopController() {
        public AddToShopcartCommand makeAddToShopcartCommand(        ❶
            HttpServletRequest request) {

            return expectedCommand;
        }

        public void executeCommand(AddToShopcartCommand command) {     ❷
            executeCommandInvoked = true;
            assertEquals(expectedCommand, command);
        }
    };

    final HttpRequestBase httpServletRequest =
        new HttpRequestBase() {
```

```
            public HttpSession getSession(boolean create) {
                return new FakeHttpSession(Collections.EMPTY_MAP);
            }

            public RequestDispatcher getRequestDispatcher(String path) {
                return new RequestDispatcherAdapter();
            }
        };

        httpServletRequest.clearParameters();

        Map requestParameters = new HashMap() {
            {
                put("quantity-0", new String[] { "2" });
                put("addToShopcart-0", new String[] { "Buy!" });
            }
        };

        CollectionUtil
            .forEachDo(requestParameters, new MapEntryClosure() {

            public void eachMapEntry(Object key, Object value) {
                httpServletRequest.addParameter(
                    (String) key,
                    (String[]) value);
            }
        });

        MockControl httpServletResponseControl =
            MockControl.createNiceControl(HttpServletResponse.class);

        HttpServletResponse httpServletResponse =
            (HttpServletResponse) httpServletResponseControl.getMock();

        controller.doPost(httpServletRequest, httpServletResponse);
        assertTrue(                                                    ❸
            "Did not invoke executeCommand()",
            executeCommandInvoked);
    }
```

❶ *Fake making the command*—Fake `makeAddToShopcartCommand()` to return a hard-coded command. This avoids worrying about whether the servlet does this correctly—we test that elsewhere.

❷ *Record the invocation of executeCommand()*—Intercept `executeCommand()` so that the test knows whether the servlet invoked it. We store this information in the field `executeCommandInvoked`, which we declare on the test case class.

❸ *The actual test*—Invoke `doPost()` and verify that the servlet invoked `executeCommand()`

NOTE The classes `RequestDispatcherAdapter` and `FakeHttpSession` are both part of Diasparsoft Toolkit. Each one merely makes it easier to fake out the corresponding objects: the request dispatcher and the HTTP session. You might want to use these in your own projects.

Altogether now, we have verified that the servlet executes the "add to shopcart" business logic when given an "add to shopcart" request. There are boundary cases and error conditions to check, but they are split into two categories: invalid request data and exceptions thrown when executing the command. To test the former, create an invalid request—say leave out one of the parameters—invoke `doPost()`, and then verify that the servlet reports the necessary error messages. Extract this behavior to a method named, for example, `signalError()`, and then test it by intercepting the method invocation—the same technique we have used throughout this recipe. To test the latter, override `executeCommand()` to throw an exception that your commands might throw, then verify how the servlet reacts: it should add error messages, so you can intercept `signalError()` again and verify the method invocations.

◆ *Discussion*

You will notice that testing a servlet this way leads to intercepting a number of the servlet's methods, substituting some test-only behavior in their place. Repeatedly subclassing the class under test indicates that it is time to consider moving that behavior to a separate class by applying the refactoring Replace Subclass with Collaborator.[16] We generally use the three-strike rule [Refactoring, 58]: "three strikes and you refactor." Let your conscience—and your experience in deferring a refactoring for too long—be your guide. When you apply this refactoring, you end up with a servlet providing a thin wrapper around a main Controller class that does not depend on the servlet specification. This controller class is a Plain Old Java Object, and therefore easier to test. If your servlet is not yet designed this way, then start adding tests to it: the tests will nudge you in the direction of having a standalone Front Controller, which you then integrate into your Front Controller servlet.[17] This not only makes your application easier to test, but easier to wrap in a different user interface, such as a standalone application.

Finally, be careful! Even if you pass all the tests you write using this approach, there is no guarantee that your front end—usually HTML pages—provides form

---

[16] www.diasparsoftware.com/articles/refactorings/replaceSubclassWithCollaborator.pdf

[17] Front Controller is one of the Core J2EE patterns. See http://java.sun.com/blueprints/corej2eepatterns.

attributes that match the request parameters from your tests. You will need more tests to verify that your web form has the expected attributes. See recipe 12.11, "Verify web form attributes," for details.

◆ ***Related***

- 2.2—Test a method that returns nothing
- 2.11—Test an object that instantiates other objects
- 12.3—Test rendering a JavaServer Page
- 12.11—Verify web form attributes
- J. B. Rainsberger, "Replace Subclass with Collaborator" (www.diasparsoftware.com/articles/refactorings/replaceSubclassWithCollaborator.pdf)

12.10 Verify web page content without a web server

◆ ***Problem***

You want to verify the content of a web page using HtmlUnit, rather than XPath-based assertions, but without running a web server.

◆ ***Background***

You have used HtmlUnit in End-to-End Tests, and you like the way it works. Its customized assertion library is designed specifically for analyzing web pages, making it an ideal tool to use when testing all kinds of web pages without a web server: static web pages, rendered Velocity templates, possibly even rendered JSPs. The problem is that, out of the box, HtmlUnit is coupled to its HTTP client: there is no way to create an `HtmlPage` object without retrieving it through a `WebConnection`, so you cannot use HtmlUnit unless you test against a live web server or web container.

◆ ***Recipe***

Out of the box, HtmlUnit expects to retrieve web pages from a remote server, but with only a few lines of code it is possible to load web pages from the file system. Listing 12.17 shows an example of how to use that code.[18]

---

[18] The code the test is using—`FileSystemWebResponse` and `FileSystemWebConnection`—is part of Diasparsoft Toolkit, and should one day be submitted as a patch to HtmlUnit.

Listing 12.17 Loading web pages from the file system with FileSystemWebResponse

```
public void testContent() throws Exception {
    URL loginPageUrl =
        new URL("http://localhost/coffeeShop/login.html");   <-- Just a label here
    File loginPageFile =
        new File(webContentDirectory, "login.html");   <-- Point to the page on the file system
    WebClient webClient = new WebClient();
    FileSystemWebResponse webResponse =
        new FileSystemWebResponse(loginPageUrl, loginPageFile);   <-- Set up a mock WebResponse from the file system
    webResponse.setContentType("text/html");
    FileSystemWebConnection fileSystemWebConnection =
        new FileSystemWebConnection(webClient);
    fileSystemWebConnection.setResponse(webResponse);   <-- Prime a mock WebConnection with the mock WebResponse
    webClient.setWebConnection(fileSystemWebConnection);   <-- Register the mock WebResponse with the WebClient
    HtmlPage loginPage =
        (HtmlPage) webClient.getPage(loginPageUrl);   <-- Ask HtmlUnit to create the HtmlPage
    assertEquals("Login", loginPage.getTitleText());
    assertTrue(
        loginPage.asText().indexOf(
            "Enter your user name and password")
            >= 0);
    HtmlForm loginForm = loginPage.getFormByName("loginForm");
    assertNotNull(loginForm);
    assertEquals("/coffeeShop", loginForm.getActionAttribute());
    assertTrue(
        "post".equalsIgnoreCase(loginForm.getMethodAttribute()));
    HtmlInput usernameInput = loginForm.getInputByName("username");
    assertNotNull(usernameInput);
    assertEquals(
        12,
        Integer.parseInt(usernameInput.getSizeAttribute()));
    assertTrue(usernameInput instanceof HtmlTextInput);   <-- Better than checking the "type" attribute
    assertEquals("", usernameInput.getValueAttribute());
    HtmlInput passwordInput = loginForm.getInputByName("password");
    assertNotNull(passwordInput);
    assertTrue(passwordInput instanceof HtmlPasswordInput);
    assertEquals(
        12,
        Integer.parseInt(passwordInput.getSizeAttribute()));
    assertEquals("", passwordInput.getValueAttribute());
    HtmlInput loginInput = loginForm.getInputByName("login");
    assertNotNull(loginInput);
    assertTrue(loginInput instanceof HtmlSubmitInput);
    assertEquals("Login", loginInput.getValueAttribute());
}
```

The `instanceof` check in this code bears some explanation. Rather than verify the value of the `type` attribute, we recommend using `instanceof` to verify the `input` tag's type without resorting to a case-insensitive string comparison. The alternative is to write this assertion:

```
assertTrue("text".equalsIgnoreCase(myInput.getTypeAttribute());
```

If you try to use `assertEquals()`, you run the risk of typing `TEXT` in the web page and having the test fail while the browser is satisfied. This makes the test unnecessarily brittle, adds the risk of "false failures" and those are bad things. You have enough problems to handle without creating more for yourself!

◆ Discussion

This technique works very well for static web pages, but what about dynamic ones? You cannot simply retrieve them from the file system, because as page templates (JSPs or Velocity templates) they need to be merged with some set of data to produce a final result. No need to worry, though: just render the page, then obtain its content as either an `InputStream` or a `String`. If you can do this, then HtmlUnit can create an `HtmlPage` object from it, and that is all you need to be able to use its HTML assertion library in your tests.

If you are using JSPs, apply the technique in recipe 12.3, after which point you will have the rendered web page as a `String`. You can create an `InputStream` from that String using HtmlUnit's utility method `TextUtil.toInputStream(String)`. You can then create an `InputStreamWebResponse` and the corresponding `InputStreamWebConnection`, substituting them in this recipe's sample code, like so:[19]

```
FileInputStream webPageAsInputStream
    = new FileInputStream(loginPageFile);

TextUtil.toInputStream("Web page content as a string");

WebClient webClient = new WebClient();

InputStreamWebConnection inputStreamWebConnection =
    new InputStreamWebConnection(webClient);

InputStreamWebResponse webResponse =
    new InputStreamWebResponse(
        loginPageUrl,
        webPageAsInputStream);
webResponse.setContentType("text/html");

inputStreamWebConnection.setResponse(webResponse);
```

[19] These classes are also part of Diasparsoft Toolkit.

```
webClient.setWebConnection(inputStreamWebConnection);
HtmlPage loginPage = (HtmlPage) webClient.getPage(loginPageUrl);
```

After this point, make the same kinds of assertions that we made in our example.

If you are using Velocity templates, then apply the technique we describe in recipe 12.4, "Test rendering a Velocity template." This involves writing the resulting web page to a `String`, from which point you can use the same code as we have just provided to obtain an `HtmlPage`.

No matter how you render a web page—from the file system, through a template engine, some other way—if you can get either an `InputStream` or a `String` with that web page's contents, you can use HtmlUnit to verify its structure and contents. To verify its look and feel, however, generally requires human intervention, at least at first. See recipe 12.3 for an example of comparing a rendered dynamic web page against a Gold Master. This technique ensures that the page looks right, in addition to merely having all the right content.

◆ Related

- 12.3—Test rendering a JavaServer Page
- 12.4—Test rendering a Velocity template
- Chapter 9—Testing and XML
- HtmlUnit (http://HtmlUnit.sourceforge.net)

12.11 Verify web form attributes

◆ Problem

You want to verify that a web form contains the attributes your request processor—usually a servlet—expects.

◆ Background

You might have written Object Tests for your servlet, verifying that it correctly handles various requests. When you execute your End-to-End Tests, however, the system does not work. You have just seen for yourself the importance of *complete* object-level testing: your web form is wrong, so you need a test for it. It seems fairly straightforward to load the page and inspect the form visually, but any approach you take is likely to require a great deal of work. You hope that someone has done the work for you.

◆ Recipe

You can use HtmlUnit to verify the attributes of the web form, but that usually assumes the existence of a server to serve up those pages. (It might be overkill to apply recipe 12.10 at this point.) Assuming that you do not want to run an actual server—that leads to slow tests—you can use Jetty[20] in embedded mode and serve the page up that way *or* simply load the page from disk. Once you have the page, you can obtain the form and make assertions about its elements using XMLUnit. We describe this technique in recipe 9.5, "Test the content of a static web page," and the example we use is a login form, so this recipe is (as much as anything) a pointer to that one. Enjoy.

◆ Discussion

Once you have tests such as this in place, you can pass hard-coded `HttpServlet-Request` objects to your request processor and verify that it chooses the appropriate business logic, or *action*, to execute. The interface for such a request processor can be small and simple: `getAction(HttpServletRequest)` returning an `Action`. The `Action` can provide the method `execute()`, which performs the action, then returns a URI corresponding to the page to show next. You could easily test all these parts in isolation, then use ServletUnit to verify that the controller wires them all together properly. If you think this all sounds suspiciously like Struts, you are right. There are some parts of Struts applications that are delightfully easy to test.

◆ Related

- 9.5—Test the content of a static web page

12.12 Verify the data passed to a page template

◆ Problem

You want to test the data passed into a page template without having to involve the web component that forwards to that page template. The page template could be a JSP, Velocity template, or some other page template mechanism.

[20] A Java-based HTTP server that is easy to embed in applications. Vincent Massol and Ted Husted describe using Jetty in *JUnit in Action* (Manning, 2003) and you can find the project at http://jetty.mortbay.org/jetty/.

◆ *Background*

In many ways, a page template is only as good as the data you pass into it. It is easiest, and therefore most common, to test passing data to a page template by rendering the page and inspecting it. When errors occur, the page often dies in some spectacular manner, and as a result you might fall into the trap of seeing the page templates as the problem, rather than the rest of the application around it. As you investigate defects in the application, if you notice that the page template itself is not often to blame, then you might want to write tests to verify the data that you passed into them.

◆ *Recipe*

Your JSPs use data to present dynamic content to the end user. You find this dynamic data in as many as five sources: the HTTP request, the HTTP session, the page itself, the application context, or an external data source from which the page template pulls data.

The first four of these data sources[21] are the familiar servlet API objects: `request`, `response`, `page`, and `application`, and have one thing in common: the servlet places data into these objects, and then the page template pulls the data out of these objects. They represent a kind of shared memory space between the Controller and the View. The general strategy to test this interaction is to verify that the Controller supplies the correct data for a given request.

The last of these five data sources is most commonly a JDBC data source—the page template either includes JDBC code directly or uses a data-aware component such as an Enterprise JavaBean or Data Bean. With this design, the Controller provides primary key information to the page template, which then pulls the rest of the data from "the database" using that primary key information. In addition to verifying that the Controller supplies the correct primary key data, you need to test that the page template invokes the data-aware component properly.

In either case, you certainly need to test the data retrieval code separately, and we invite you to refer to chapter 10, "Testing and JDBC," for details.

We now return to the Coffee Shop application and consider the shopcart display JSP. Listing 12.18 shows the page template.

---

[21] We do *not* mean J2EE Data Sources, such as relational databases. We just mean "sources of data."

Listing 12.18 Shopcart Display page template (JSP)

```
<%@page import="java.util.*" %>
<%@page import="junit.cookbook.coffee.display.*" %>

<jsp:useBean id="shopcartDisplay"
             class="junit.cookbook.coffee.display.ShopcartBean"
             scope="request" />

<!DOCTYPE HTML PUBLIC "-//W3C//DTD HTML 4.01 Transitional//EN">
<html>
<head><title>Your Coffee Shop Shopcart</title></head>
<body>
<h1>Your Shopcart Contains</h1>
<table name="shopcart" border="1">
    <tbody>
        <tr>
            <td><b>Name</b></td>
            <td><b>Quantity</b></td>
            <td><b>Unit Price</b></td>
            <td><b>Total Price</b></td>
        </tr>
<%
for (Iterator i = shopcartDisplay.shopcartItems.iterator();
     i.hasNext(); ) {

    ShopcartItemBean item = (ShopcartItemBean) i.next();
%>
        <tr>
            <td><%= item.coffeeName %></td>
            <td id="product-<%= item.productId %>">
                <%= item.quantityInKilograms %> kg
            </td>
            <td><%= item.unitPrice %></td>
            <td><%= item.getTotalPrice() %></td>
        </tr>
<%
}
%>
        <tr>
            <td colspan="3"><b>Subtotal</b></td>
            <td><b><%= shopcartDisplay.getSubtotal() %></b></td>
        </tr>
    </tbody>
</table>

<form action="coffee" method="POST">
    <input type="submit"
           name="browseCatalog" value="Buy More Coffee!" />
</form>
</body>
</html>
```

This JSP expects a `ShopcartBean` containing `ShopcartBeanItems` and displays a subtotal for the items in the shopcart. You compute shipping and taxes when the user submits the order for processing. What do we need to test, then? The JSP expects to see a `ShopcartBean` in the HTTP request as an attribute with the name `shopcartDisplay`. Those are the assertions for our first test.

```
public void testControllerProvidesShopcartBean() {
    // This does not yet compile

    // Arrange?
    // Act?

    Object shopcartDisplayAttribute =
        request.getAttribute("shopcartDisplay");

    assertNotNull(shopcartDisplayAttribute);
    assertTrue(shopcartDisplayAttribute instanceof ShopcartBean);
}
```

We need more code here. Specifically, we need to initialize our test environment and request the shopcart page. It seems reasonable to start with a user who does not yet have a shopcart, then verify that the act of requesting the shopcart places an empty shopcart in the request. If the Controller does its job—and that is what we plan to test here—then we can separately test that the JSP displaying the shopcart does indeed display the data as expected. As for checking the layout, nothing beats good, old-fashioned visual inspection. There are some things you just have to see before you can be confident that they are right.

As for the rest of this code, you have two choices, depending on whether you have access to the source code of the Controller. If you need to test the Controller as is, then you need to send an HTTP request to the servlet and verify the contents of the request after invoking the `service()` method. For this, use ServletUnit. Listing 12.19 shows an example.

Listing 12.19 `testControllerProvidesShopcartBean()`

```
public void testControllerProvidesShopcartBean() throws Exception {
    ServletRunner servletRunner = new ServletRunner();
    servletRunner.registerServlet(
        "CoffeeShopController",
        CoffeeShopController.class.getName());

    CoffeeShopController coffeeShopController =
        new CoffeeShopController() {
            public void log(String message) {
                // Intentionally disable logging
            }
        };
```

```
        ServletUnitClient client = servletRunner.newClient();

        WebRequest addToShopcartRequest =
            new PostMethodWebRequest(
                "http://localhost:9080/coffeeShop/coffee");
        addToShopcartRequest.setParameter("displayShopcart", "shopcart");

        InvocationContext invocationContext =
            client.newInvocation(addToShopcartRequest);

        coffeeShopController.handleDisplayShopcart(
            invocationContext.getRequest());

        Object shopcartDisplayAttribute =
            invocationContext.getRequest().getAttribute("shopcartDisplay");

        assertNotNull(shopcartDisplayAttribute);
        assertTrue(shopcartDisplayAttribute instanceof ShopcartBean);
    }
```

The "arrange" part of this test involves the usual ServletUnit set up: creating a `ServletRunner`, registering the servlet and creating a client.[22] The "act" part of this test involves creating the "display shopcart" request, creating the invocation context (to convert the `WebRequest` into an `HttpServletRequest`) and invoking the request handler. Notice that we do *not* invoke `doPost()`, but just invoke the correct handler for the request. If we try to invoke `doPost()`, ServletUnit throws a `NullPointerException` deep inside. That should not worry you: after all, you want to test the request handler, and not the rest of the servlet. If the request handler puts the right data in the request, then the JSP works as expected. That is the point of this test. We extracted the method `handleDisplayShopcart()`[23] and made it public in order to invoke it for this test. If you prefer, leave `handleDisplayShopcart()` protected and put your test in the same package, but a different source tree. (See recipe 3.3, "Separate test packages from production code packages," for details.)

◆ *Discussion*

This test does not need to change *at all* if you use Velocity templates as your presentation layer. Because the test prepares the data to be displayed but does not actually invoke the presentation layer, it does not matter what presentation layer

[22] There is a clue in that last sentence—perhaps we need to extract this into a test fixture. See recipe 3.4, "Factor out a test fixture."

[23] This method has since been refactored out of the class, so if you look at the code online, you will not see it. Do not worry about that, because it is the concept, and not the code, that matters here.

you use: forward to a JSP or merge with a Velocity template. Any way you do it, the test remains the same. You can even use this technique to verify data passed to any component, such as a web resource filter. (See recipe 12.13, "Test a web resource filter," for a total strategy for testing a filter.)

As a general design rule, we recommend that page templates not pull data from a data source, but rather display the data the Controller sends to it. The Controller ought to retrieve all the data to be displayed, and then pass it to the page template through session attributes, request attributes, or template context, whatever the appropriate underlying mechanism. This design reduces the coupling between your presentation layer and the business layer, allowing you to substitute a different presentation layer when a new technically minded manager joins your project and declares, "From this point forward, we use Velocity templates rather than JSPs!" You might doubt that, but it happens.

◆ Related

- 3.3—Separate test packages from production code packages
- 3.4—Factor out a test fixture
- 12.13—Test a web resource filter

12.13 Test a web resource filter

◆ Problem

You want to test a web resource filter.

◆ Background

Filters can make a web application difficult to understand. Runtime behavior appears as if by magic, because you do not see that behavior in the servlet, the most logical place to start looking. Moreover, debugging a filter can be quite annoying: typically you end up executing manual, End-to-End Tests with a browser, and logging information to the web application log. This is very time consuming, and one instance where adding a few tests can save hours of headache.

◆ Recipe

A filter has two responsibilities: execute certain logic, and do it at the appropriate time. That is, not only do you need to test *what* the filter does, but you need to test *when* it does that work in relation to when it invokes the rest of the filter chain. Testing the logic is the easy part, so let us start with that.

As with any other framework component, a filter consists of two parts: its logic and its integration to the framework. In general, you should separate those two parts, refactoring the logic to a separate class where possible, leaving behind in the `Filter` implementation only its integration to the web container. For all but the simplest filters, we recommend performing this refactoring. We describe this technique in recipe 12.1 as well as throughout chapter 11, "Testing Enterprise JavaBeans." It so happens that the filter we use as an example is simple enough that we can take a shortcut.

Our Coffee Shop application contains an annoying bit of behavior. Due to the way the HTTP session API behaves, our `CoffeeShopController` needs to verify on every request whether the user has a session and, if so, whether that session contains a `ShopcartModel` object. It would simplify the servlet if we could extract that check to a filter. Not only does it make the servlet easier to understand, but also easier to test: for tests that have nothing to do with session data, there is no need to mock up the method `HttpServletRequest.getSession()`. The less we need to do, the better. Our filter, then, ensures that the user has a shopcart in her session. As such, we call it `EnsureShopperHasShopcartFilter`.

The logic our filter executes, then, can be summarized as follows: *create a session, if needed, and if it has no shopcart, add an empty one.* Because we have no reason to do otherwise, we decide to execute this logic before invoking the rest of the filter chain. There are essentially three tests that we need to pass:

1. If the user has no session to start with, then after invoking the filter, she has a session and a shopcart.
2. If the user has a session without a shopcart to start with, then after invoking the filter, she has a session with a shopcart.
3. If the user already has a shopcart, the filter does not change the session in any way.

This appears to be sufficient to test the filter's logic. We can easily implement this in a single method, so we decide to implement it directly on the filter class and make it `public`, rather than extracting it to a separate class as we recommend doing in general. This is one of those make-as-you-go trade-offs: we cannot really reuse this logic outside the context of a web application, anyway, so moving it to a separate class does not appear to make sense yet. Perhaps something else—a new feature or a design change elsewhere—will change the balance of pros and cons here. We will take that as it comes. Listing 12.20 shows the three tests.

Listing 12.20 EnsureShopperHasShopcartFilterLogicTest

```
package junit.cookbook.coffee.test;

import junit.cookbook.coffee.EnsureShopperHasShopcartFilter;
import junit.cookbook.coffee.model.ShopcartModel;
import junit.framework.TestCase;

import com.diasparsoftware.javax.servlet.http.HttpSessionAdapter;
import com.mockobjects.servlet.*;

public class EnsureShopperHasShopcartFilterLogicTest
    extends TestCase {

    private FakeHttpSession session;
    private MockHttpServletRequest request;
    private MockHttpServletResponse response;
    private EnsureShopperHasShopcartFilter filter;

    protected void setUp() throws Exception {
        session = new FakeHttpSession();
        request = new MockHttpServletRequest();
        response = new MockHttpServletResponse();
        filter = new EnsureShopperHasShopcartFilter();

        request.setSession(session);
    }

    public void testAlreadyHasShopcart() throws Exception {
        ShopcartModel shopcartModel = new ShopcartModel();
        session.setAttribute("shopcartModel", shopcartModel);

        filter.addShopcartIfNeeded(request);

        assertSame(
            shopcartModel,
            request.getSession(true).getAttribute("shopcartModel"));
    }

    public void testEmptySession() throws Exception {
        filter.addShopcartIfNeeded(request);
        assertNotNull(session.shopcartModelAttribute);
        assertTrue(session.shopcartModelAttribute.isEmpty());
    }

    public void testNoSession() throws Exception {
        request.setExpectedCreateSession(true);

        filter.addShopcartIfNeeded(request);
        assertNotNull(session.shopcartModelAttribute);
        assertTrue(session.shopcartModelAttribute.isEmpty());
    }

    public static class FakeHttpSession extends HttpSessionAdapter {
        public ShopcartModel shopcartModelAttribute;
```

```
            public Object getAttribute(String name) {
                return shopcartModelAttribute;
            }

            public void setAttribute(String name, Object value) {
                shopcartModelAttribute = (ShopcartModel) value;
            }
        }
    }
```

Notice the use of `assertSame()` in the "already has shopcart" test. If the user already has a shopcart in her session, we want the filter to leave that shopcart alone. To implement this assertion, we invoke the filter logic, then verify that the session contains the same shopcart *object* that it had before invoking the filter logic, and not just an equivalent one. We could take this test one step further: clone the "before" shopcart, apply the filter logic, assert that the session has the same shopcart object, then assert that the "after" shopcart is equal to (contains the same items as) the "before" shopcart. If you want to be certain that the filter logic does not place 50 items in the shopcart, then this is a good idea. It all depends on the level of confidence you need in the correctness of that logic. Next, we need to test that the filter invokes its logic before invoking the filter chain.

This test is more complex, requiring a more complex fixture, so we create a separate one. We need to test when the method `doFilter()` invokes `addShopcartIfNeeded()` and `filterChain.doFilter()`, so we need to be a little sneaky here. The simplest solution we imagined involves doing something we ordinarily dislike: subclassing the class under test. The idea is to override the method `addShopcartIfNeeded()` and store in a flag if the method has been invoked. We then create a mock `FilterChain` that fails when *its* method `doFilter()` is invoked when this flag is `false`. Listing 12.21 shows the test, with the "sneaky parts" highlighted in bold print.

Listing 12.21 EnsureShopperHasShopcartFilterIntegrationTest

```
package junit.cookbook.coffee.test;

import java.io.IOException;
import javax.servlet.*;
import javax.servlet.http.HttpSession;
import junit.cookbook.coffee.EnsureShopperHasShopcartFilter;
import junit.framework.TestCase;
import com.diasparsoftware.javax.servlet.http.HttpSessionAdapter;
import com.mockobjects.servlet.*;
```

```
public class EnsureShopperHasShopcartFilterIntegrationTest
    extends TestCase {

    private HttpSession session;
    private MockHttpServletRequest request;
    private MockHttpServletResponse response;
    private MockFilterChain filterChain;
    private EnsureShopperHasShopcartFilter filter;
    private boolean invokedFilterChainDoFilter;
    private boolean filterLogicDone;

    protected void setUp() throws Exception {
        filterLogicDone = false;
        invokedFilterChainDoFilter = false;

        session = new HttpSessionAdapter();

        request = new MockHttpServletRequest();
        request.setSession(session);

        response = new MockHttpServletResponse();

        filterChain = new MockFilterChain() {
            public void doFilter(
                ServletRequest request,
                ServletResponse response)
                throws IOException, ServletException {

                assertTrue(
                    "Something invoked filterChain.doFilter "
                        + "before the filter logic was done",
                    filterLogicDone);

                invokedFilterChainDoFilter = true;
            }
        };

        filter = new EnsureShopperHasShopcartFilter() {
            public void addShopcartIfNeeded(ServletRequest request) {
                super.addShopcartIfNeeded(request);
                filterLogicDone = true;
            }
        };
    }

    public void testInvokesFilterChain() throws Exception {
        filter.doFilter(request, response, filterChain);
        assertTrue(invokedFilterChainDoFilter);
    }
}
```

If we needed to invoke the filter chain before the filter logic, we would use the same technique, but in reverse: `FilterChain.doFilter()` would have to set the "someone invoked me" flag, then we would override `addShopcartIfNeeded()` to assert that that flag had been set. Now that we have tested the filter logic and its integration with the filter chain, what remains is to test that it has been correctly deployed.

It is important to verify that your web application actually invokes the filter; otherwise the rest of your testing effort goes for naught. One approach is to test the servlet in a live container, another is to use ServletUnit, but these approaches have a common weakness: they test the web container, rather than the information you provide to the web container. *Don't test the platform.* Instead, use XMLUnit to verify that you have specified the deployment descriptor correctly, a technique we describe in detail in the introduction to chapter 9, "Testing and XML." Listing 12.22 shows a few simple tests.

Listing 12.22 Some simple filter tests

```
package junit.cookbook.coffee.deployment.test;

import java.io.*;
import junit.cookbook.coffee.EnsureShopperHasShopcartFilter;
import org.custommonkey.xmlunit.*;
import org.w3c.dom.Document;
import org.xml.sax.InputSource;

public class FiltersTest extends XMLTestCase {
    public void testEnsureShopperHasShopcartFilterConfigured()
        throws Exception {

        String webDeploymentDescriptorFilename =
            "../CoffeeShopWeb/Web Content/WEB-INF/web.xml";

        Document webDeploymentDescriptorDocument =
            XMLUnit.buildTestDocument(
                new InputSource(
                    new FileReader(
                        new File(webDeploymentDescriptorFilename))));

        String filterNameMatch =
            "[filter-name='EnsureShopperHasShopcartFilter']";

        assertXpathExists(
            "/web-app/filter" + filterNameMatch,
            webDeploymentDescriptorDocument);

        assertXpathEvaluatesTo(
            EnsureShopperHasShopcartFilter.class.getName(),
            "/web-app/filter" + filterNameMatch + "/filter-class",
            webDeploymentDescriptorDocument);

        assertXpathExists(
            "/web-app/filter-mapping" + filterNameMatch,
            webDeploymentDescriptorDocument);
```

```
        assertXpathEvaluatesTo(
            "/coffee",
            "/web-app/filter-mapping"
                + filterNameMatch
                + "/url-pattern",
            webDeploymentDescriptorDocument);
    }
}
```

The first assertion verifies that a filter is configured at all; the next verifies the class name implementing the filter. The third assertion verifies that the filter is mapped to some URL; the next verifies the URL to which it is mapped. This is the beginning of a general pattern for testing the deployment of web resource filters and probably ought to be refactored into its own class. At a minimum, this test is an excellent candidate to refactor towards a Parameterized Test Case (see recipe 4.8, "Build a data-driven test suite"); so if we were to add more tests, we would likely perform the refactoring.

Finally, for the sake of completeness, listing 12.23 shows a filter that passes these tests.

Listing 12.23 `EnsureShopperHasShopcartFilter` (final version)

```
package junit.cookbook.coffee;

import java.io.IOException;

import javax.servlet.*;
import javax.servlet.http.*;

import junit.cookbook.coffee.model.ShopcartModel;

public class EnsureShopperHasShopcartFilter implements Filter {
    public void doFilter(
        ServletRequest request,
        ServletResponse response,
        FilterChain filterChain)
        throws ServletException, IOException {

        addShopcartIfNeeded(request);
        filterChain.doFilter(request, response);
    }

    public void addShopcartIfNeeded(ServletRequest request) {
        HttpSession session =
            ((HttpServletRequest) request).getSession(true);

        ShopcartModel shopcartModel =
            (ShopcartModel) session.getAttribute("shopcartModel");
```

```
            if (shopcartModel == null) {
                session.setAttribute("shopcartModel", new ShopcartModel());
            }
        }

        public void init(FilterConfig config) {
        }

        public void destroy() {
        }
    }
```

◆ Discussion

If we were *really* concerned about subclassing the class under test—and ordinarily we are—we could easily have extracted the filter logic to a separate class. In this case, for the above test we would substitute a Spy implementation of the filter logic that kept track of whether it had yet been invoked. As we wrote previously, this example is simple enough that the risk of subclassing the class under test is low. It is worth noting, however, that the desire to subclass the class under test tends to indicate a need to perform the refactoring Extract Class [Refactoring, 149]. You will typically move the methods you override into the new class.

If your web resource filter requires information from the outside world, such as input from a servlet, then use the techniques in recipe 12.12. In this case, the web resource filter plays the same role that a page template plays: it is the recipient of data that some component (the servlet) has passed into the request object.

◆ Related

- 4.8—Build a data-driven test suite
- Chapter 9—Testing and XML
- Chapter 11—Testing Enterprise Java Beans
- 12.1—Test updating session data without a container
- 12.12—Verify the data passed to a page template

13 Testing J2EE applications

This chapter covers

- Testing web application page flow, including Struts
- Testing your site for broken links
- Testing web and EJB resource security
- Testing container-managed transactions

As you read this book it should become clear that we advocate testing an application by testing its components thoroughly, and then integrating those components as simply as possible. Specifically, "integration" for us is little more than choosing which implementations of various interfaces to use, and then creating an application entry point object with references to those implementations. Which logging strategy do we use? How about Log4J! We know that our components work with any implementation of the logging strategy interface. What kind of model? A JDBC-based one, although our Controller really only knows about our Model interface, so an in-memory implementation, or one based on Prevayler (www.prevayler.org) will do. To us, this is integration. As a result, we tend not to emphasize End-to-End Testing for correctness, but rather to give us confidence that we have built the features we needed to build. Object Tests tell you whether you built the thing right; whereas End-to-End Tests help you decide whether you built the right thing.

There are certain aspects of J2EE applications that people associate with End-to-End Tests rather than Object Tests. These include page flow—or navigating a web application—and using container services, such as security and transactions. We discuss these topics in recipes in this chapter, showing you how to test these behaviors in isolation—as Object Tests. We do not want to give the impression that we shy away from End-to-End Tests—that is, testing an application by simulating the way an end user interacts with it through its end-user interface. As we wrote previously, we use End-to-End Tests to play a different role than other programmers do: we use End-to-End Tests to help us determine whether what we have built actually does what our customers need. We do discuss using HtmlUnit to write End-to-End Tests for a web application (see recipe 13.1), but we no longer see JUnit as the best tool available for testing an application from end to end. We use Fit (http://fit.c2.com) and its companion tool, FitNesse (www.fitnesse.org).

NOTE We are certainly not the only people who see End-to-End Tests in this role: we got the idea from the Agile community (www.agilealliance.org) at large. Still, while Agile developers remain in the minority, organizations will continue to see End-to-End Tests as their primary tool for validating software, an approach that we feel ultimately wastes resources that could be better spent ensuring correctness from the inside out through Programmer Tests.

Because this is a book on JUnit, and not Fit, we will describe Fit only briefly. Imagine writing tests entirely as spreadsheets and word-processor documents. You could annotate your tests with plain-language descriptions of what they verify—mix code and text together so that both the programmers and the nonprogrammers can follow them. Now imagine running those tests through software that decorates your documents green for the parts that are right (tests pass) and red for the parts that are wrong (tests fail). That is Fit, and it allows those with business knowledge to write *executable* tests, even if they are not programmers. FitNesse[1] is a Wiki (www.wiki.org) that can execute Fit tests, providing an excellent way to organize them and collaborate on them. Many people have designated FitNesse as "the way they do End-to-End Tests." We are among them.

But this is a book about JUnit, and this is a chapter on writing Object Tests for aspects of J2EE applications that one usually tests from end to end. In here is a collection of recipes that will help you test certain aspects of J2EE applications more effectively. These are behaviors that tend to be sprinkled throughout the application: page flow, broken links, security, transactions, and JNDI. We have added a recipe related to the Struts application framework (http://jakarta.apache.org/struts), but for more on testing Struts applications, we recommend the `StrutsTestCase` project (http://strutstestcase.sourceforge.net). It provides both a mock objects approach (testing outside the application server) and a Cactus approach (testing inside the application server). It embodies many of the techniques we have described in this book, and rather than duplicate their fine work, we refer you to them.

13.1 Test page flow

◆ Problem

You want to verify that a user can navigate through your web application's pages correctly, and you want to make the verification without involving all the machinery of the application itself.

◆ Background

Even though you[2] will execute End-to-End Tests that can help uncover problems with page flow, it is generally easier to verify page flow without involving your application's business logic, presentation layer, external resources, and so on. What we recommend you do is translate your web application into a large state diagram where moving from page to page depends on two things: (1) the action the user took, and (2) the result of the action the user took. We provide a sample diagram in figure 13.1. The boxes are pages and the arrows represent actions.

[1] Pronounced "fit-NESS." Micah Martin, cocreator of FitNesse, tells the story how Uncle Bob (Robert C. Martin) was tired of executing Fit tests from the command line and wanted to execute them "with finesse."

[2] Well, *someone* will. Who does it is largely a matter of organizational culture.

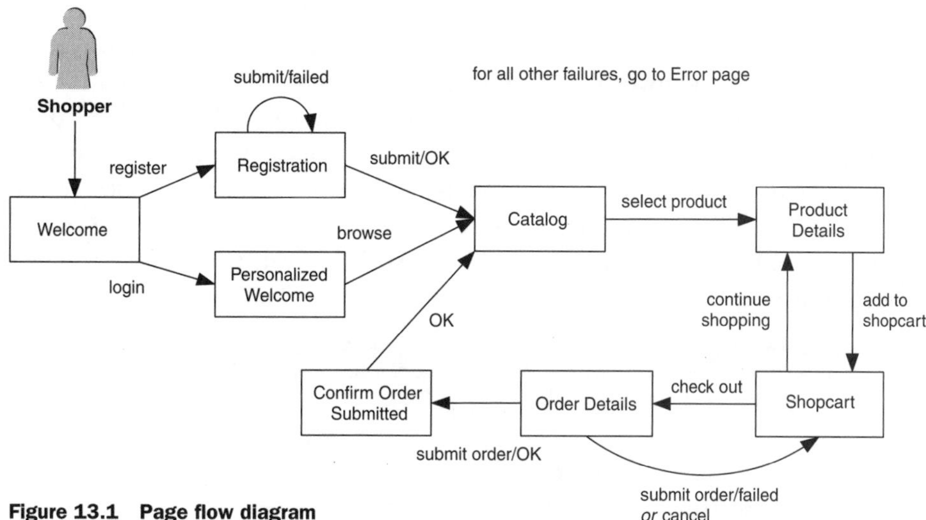

Figure 13.1 Page flow diagram

Some actions have a single outcome, such as clicking the link to browse the catalog. For the most part, that action cannot fail—when you click that link, you end up at the catalog page. Some actions have multiple outcomes, such as "OK" and "failed." In the diagram, at the registration page, if submitting the registration form fails, then the shopper stays at the registration page. We label those arrows using a format of *action/result*, so that "submit/OK" means "follow this arrow if submitting the form is successful." When we model page flow this way, it does not look very complex, and so it ought to be relatively easy to test—after all, they are just names of pages, names of actions, and names of results. They are all strings! How hard can that be?

Not hard at all. If you can focus your attention like this on just the page flow of your system, then certainly you can extract the page-to-page navigation code from your system into a single navigation "engine"that operates on navigation data. The Struts web application framework[3] works on this principle, and we discuss how much simpler it is to verify page flow on a Struts application in recipe 13.2. This recipe shows a simple example of how to create a refactoring safety net, refactor navigation logic to a single class, and then verify the resulting data.

---

[3] We recommend James Turner and Kevin Bedell, *Struts: Kick Start* (SAMS, 2002) as well as Ted Husted et al., *Struts in Action* (Manning, 2002). The former is an excellent tutorial and the latter shows you what Struts can *really* do.

◆ *Recipe*

We will start with what seems to be the simpler test: an End-to-End Test that verifies the ability to move from one page to another. Returning to our Coffee Shop application, we first verify that we can move from the welcome page to the catalog page. We can use HtmlUnit to first load the welcome page, and then push the browse catalog button and verify that the resulting web page is indeed the coffee catalog page. Of course, before we execute this test, we need to deploy the application to a live application server and start the server. You can see the test in question in listing 13.1.

Listing 13.1 NavigationTest, a sample page flow test

```
package junit.cookbook.coffee.endtoend.test;

import java.net.URL;
import junit.framework.TestCase;
import com.gargoylesoftware.htmlunit.*;
import com.gargoylesoftware.htmlunit.html.*;

public class NavigationTest extends TestCase {
    private WebClient webClient;

    protected void setUp() throws Exception {
        webClient = new WebClient();
        webClient.setRedirectEnabled(true);
    }

    public void testNavigateToCatalog() throws Exception {
        Page page =
            webClient.getPage(
                new URL("http://localhost:8080/coffeeShop/"));

        assertTrue(
            "Welcome page not an HTML page",
            page instanceof HtmlPage);

        HtmlPage welcomePage = (HtmlPage) page;
        HtmlForm launchPointsForm =
            welcomePage.getFormByName("launchPoints");

        HtmlInput htmlInput =
            launchPointsForm.getInputByName("browseCatalog");

        assertTrue(
            "'browseCatalog' is not a submit button",
            htmlInput instanceof HtmlSubmitInput);

        HtmlSubmitInput browseCatalogSubmit =
            (HtmlSubmitInput) htmlInput;

        Page page2 = browseCatalogSubmit.click();
```

```
        assertTrue(
            "Catalog page not an HTML page",
            page2 instanceof HtmlPage);

        HtmlPage catalogPage = (HtmlPage) page2;
        assertEquals(
            "Coffee Shop - Catalog",
            catalogPage.getTitleText());
    }
}
```

There are a number of things about this test that are worthy of concern.

We need to deploy the application and start the application server in order to execute it. Although this seems like a reasonable requirement to verify page flow, any number of unrelated problems can make it impossible to execute this test: EJB deployment problems, servlet/URL mapping problems, and so on. That is not to say that these problems are not important enough to fix, but we generally prefer to verify them separately. *These* tests are meant to verify page flow and nothing else.

The test hard codes information about the server to which the application is deployed (`localhost`) and the port on which it is listening (8080). Both of these pieces of information vary from environment to environment, so at a minimum, you ought to refactor the information to some external source, such as a configuration file. This makes the tests slightly more complex to configure and execute correctly.

The test depends on the correctness of the web pages themselves, which is not guaranteed. If there is a problem with either the welcome page or the catalog page, then this test might fail, even though the problem is not navigation related. Certainly you will test the pages themselves in isolation using the techniques in chapter 12, "Testing Web Components," so there is no need to duplicate that effort here.

This test hard codes information about the structure of the web pages—the form named `launchPoints` and the submit button named `browseCatalog`. If someone changes these names, then these tests will fail, making them somewhat brittle. A web author ought to be able to change that button to a link, get the URL right, and the only tests to fail would be the ones for the page itself. This test does not allow that to happen.

Now please do not get us wrong: the foregoing is *not* an indictment of HtmlUnit. Far from it. HtmlUnit is an excellent package that does a very good job of automating End-to-End Tests. With its focus on analyzing the result of a web request—its comprehensive HTML page object model—HtmlUnit is an ideal choice for automating End-to-End Tests for web applications, so HtmlUnit is not the issue here. The issue is using a hammer to kill a fly, as it were: using End-to-End Tests (no matter how you write them) to verify page flow invites the kinds of problems we have just described. Instead, we ought to write tests that focus on the navigation rules themselves.

This is the kind of test we want to write, assuming the existence of an object representing a "navigation engine."

```
public void testNavigateToCatalog() {
    assertEquals(
        "Catalog Page",
        navigationEngine.getNextLocation(
            "Browse Catalog",
            "OK"));
}
```

This test simply says, "If I push the button marked Browse Catalog and everything goes OK, then I should be taken to the catalog page." The test is expressed in a somewhat abstract fashion in terms of locations, actions, and results: a *location* is usually a web page, an *action* is usually either submitting a form or clicking a link, and a *result* is a description of result of the action. If we want to talk in terms of a finite state machine, the locations are the machine's states and the action/result pairs are the machine's transitions. We can model navigating through our site entirely in terms of locations and actions.

A location corresponds to the URI of a web page or a web page template (Velocity template or JSP). An action corresponds to the URI of a form submit button or of a hypertext link. This means that we need some way to translate incoming request URIs into locations and actions, and vice versa. Once we give each URI the name of either a location or an action, we can ignore the details of which JSP displays the catalog page or which request parameter indicates "add a product to the shopcart." We can test that all separately.

First, listing 13.2 shows our Coffee Shop Controller using a separate "request-to-action" mapper.

Listing 13.2 `CoffeeShopController` using an Action Mapper

```
private void handleRequest(
    HttpServletRequest request,
    HttpServletResponse response)
    throws IOException, ServletException {

    String forwardUri = "index.html";
    String userName = "jbrains";

    try {
```

```
            String actionName = actionMapper.getActionName(request);
            log("Performing action: " + actionName);

            if ("Browse Catalog".equals(actionName)) {
                CoffeeCatalog catalog = model.getCatalog();

                CatalogView view = new CatalogView(request);
                view.setCatalog(catalog);

                forwardUri = view.getUri();
            }
            else if ("Add to Shopcart".equals(actionName)) {
                AddToShopcartCommand command =
                    makeAddToShopcartCommand(request);
                executeCommand(command);
            }
            else {
                log("I don't understand action " + actionName);
            }
        }
        catch (Exception wrapped) {
            throw new ServletException(wrapped);
        }

        request.getRequestDispatcher(forwardUri).forward(
            request,
            response);
    }
```

Here, actionMapper is an object of type HttpServletRequestToActionMapper, for which we have started with the tests in listing 13.3.

Listing 13.3 MapRequestToActionTest

```
package junit.cookbook.coffee.web.test;

import java.util.*;
import java.util.regex.*;
import java.util.regex.Pattern;
import javax.servlet.RequestDispatcher;
import javax.servlet.http.*;
import junit.cookbook.coffee.HttpServletRequestToActionMapper;
import junit.framework.TestCase;
import org.apache.catalina.connector.HttpRequestBase;
import com.diasparsoftware.java.util.*;
import com.diasparsoftware.javax.servlet.http.*;

public class MapRequestToActionTest extends TestCase {
    private HttpServletRequestToActionMapper actionMapper;

    protected void setUp() throws Exception {
```

```
            actionMapper = new HttpServletRequestToActionMapper();
        }

        public void testBrowseCatalogAction() throws Exception {
            Map parameters =
                Collections.singletonMap(
                    "browseCatalog",
                    new String[] { "catalog" });

            doTestMapAction(
                "Browse Catalog",
                "/coffeeShop/coffee",
                parameters);
        }

        public void testAddToShopcart() throws Exception {
            HashMap parameters = new HashMap() {
                {
                    put("addToShopcart-18", new String[] { "Buy!" });
                    put("quantity-18", new String[] { "5" });
                }
            };

            doTestMapAction(
                "Add to Shopcart",
                "/coffeeShop/coffee",
                parameters);
        }

        private void doTestMapAction(
            String expectedActionName,
            String uri,
            Map parameters) {

            HttpServletRequest request =
                HttpUtil.makeRequestIgnoreSession(uri, parameters);

            assertEquals(
                expectedActionName,
                actionMapper.getActionName(request));
        }
    }
```

These tests create a fake `HttpServletRequest` using `HttpUtil` from Diasparsoft Toolkit. As the method name implies, we create a request without worrying about keeping track of session information, as we do not care about session information for these tests. The more variables you can eliminate in a test, the better. The request-to-action mapper is simple: turn a request into the name of an action. This test case is a good candidate to be turned into a Parameterized Test Case (see recipe 4.8, "Build a data-driven test suite").

We have built a location-to-URI mapper in a similar style: it turns location names into URIs. After adding that into the equation, our servlet's request handler method can now be seen in listing 13.4.[4]

Listing 13.4 CoffeeShopController using the location mapper

```
private void handleRequest(
    HttpServletRequest request,
    HttpServletResponse response)
    throws IOException, ServletException {

    String userName = "jbrains";
    String nextLocationName = "Welcome";

    try {
        String actionName = actionMapper.getActionName(request);
        log("Performing action: " + actionName);

        if (knownActions.contains(actionName) == false) {
            log("I don't understand action " + actionName);
        }
        else {
            String actionResult = "OK";
            if ("Browse Catalog".equals(actionName)) {
                CoffeeCatalog catalog = model.getCatalog();

                CatalogView view = new CatalogView(request);
                view.setCatalog(catalog);
            }
            else if ("Add to Shopcart".equals(actionName)) {
                AddToShopcartCommand command =
                    makeAddToShopcartCommand(request);
                executeCommand(command);
            }

            nextLocationName =
                navigationEngine.getNextLocation(actionName, "OK");
        }

    }
    catch (Exception wrapped) {
        throw new ServletException(wrapped);
    }

    String forwardUri = locationMapper.getUri(nextLocationName);
    request.getRequestDispatcher(forwardUri).forward(
        request,
        response);
}
```

[4] You can find this code online in the class `CoffeeShopControllerDecoupledNavigator`, because `CoffeeShopController` undergoes more refactorings as the book progresses.

The overall behavior of the request handler is straightforward:

1. Interpret the incoming request to determine which action the user wants to perform.
2. Perform the action, assuming it goes "OK." If the action fails for some reason, set the value of `result` to some short description of the failure. For example, if the user tries to add -1 kg of Sumatra to his shopcart, set `result` to `invalid quantity`.
3. Ask the navigator for the next location, based on the action performed and the result of that action.
4. Determine the URI that corresponds to the next location.
5. Provide that URI to the request dispatcher.

This design makes it possible to test the rest of your application's navigation rules—no matter how complex they might be—without actually running the servlet! Of course, you should write at least one test suite that verifies that the servlet invokes the mappers and the navigator. Use either ServletUnit or mock objects, depending on the technique with which you feel most comfortable. We describe both techniques throughout chapter 12, "Testing Web Components."

◆ *Discussion*

Once you have written these tests and extracted the navigation rules into an easily tested object, you might notice a striking similarity to the Struts web application framework. With Struts, you specify navigation rules as data in struts-config.xml and the "navigation engine" operates on that data, rather than having navigation rules strewn about the site, as is common. Not only is the Struts approach easy to understand and maintain, it is easy to test: one can substitute dummy `Actions` programmed to return the desired `ActionForward` to verify the expected navigation path. See recipe 13.2 for more.

◆ *Related*

- 4.8—Build a data-driven test suite
- 13.2—Test navigation rules in a Struts application

13.2 Test navigation rules in a Struts application

◆ Problem

You want to test page-to-page navigation in your Struts application, preferably without starting Struts.

◆ Background

Testing navigation rules using End-to-End Tests is expensive. We described the issues in recipe 13.1. Here, we are interested in verifying the navigation rules for a Struts application. Using End-to-End Tests to do this is no less expensive for a Struts application than for any other type of web application. Using a framework does not make End-to-End Tests any simpler than not using a framework. What Struts does, however, is provide a way to test navigation rules without resorting to End-to-End Tests, something that makes isolated navigation tests remarkably easy.

◆ Recipe

The most direct approach you can use is to verify the content of struts-config.xml using XMLUnit. Here we will show a few example tests, but for more details on verifying XML documents, see chapter 9, "Testing and XML." We will use the sample struts-config.xml currently posted at the Struts web site (http://jakarta.apache.org/struts/index.html). Listing 13.5 shows some tests.[5]

Listing 13.5 XMLUnit tests for struts-config.xml

```
package junit.cookbook.coffee.web.test;

import java.io.*;
import junit.extensions.TestSetup;
import junit.framework.*;
import org.custommonkey.xmlunit.XMLUnit;
import org.w3c.dom.Document;
import org.xml.sax.InputSource;

public class StrutsNavigationTest extends StrutsConfigFixture {
    private static Document strutsConfigDocument;

    public static Test suite() {
        TestSetup setup =
```

[5] The tests here will fail without an internet connection, because XMLUnit will try to validate the XML document against its DTD. For further details, see recipe 9.2, "Ignore the order of elements in an XML document," and read the section entitled, "Network connectivity and the DTD."

```
            new TestSetup(new TestSuite(StrutsNavigationTest.class)) {
            private String strutsConfigFilename =
                "test/data/sample-struts-config.xml";

            protected void setUp() throws Exception {
                XMLUnit.setIgnoreWhitespace(true);
                strutsConfigDocument =
                    XMLUnit.buildTestDocument(
                        new InputSource(
                            new FileReader(
                                new File(strutsConfigFilename))));
            }
        };

        return setup;
    }

    public void testLogonSubmitActionExists() throws Exception {
        assertXpathExists(
            getActionXpath("/LogonSubmit"),
            strutsConfigDocument);
    }

    public void testLogonSubmitActionSuccessMappingExists()
        throws Exception {

        assertXpathExists(
            getActionForwardXpath("/LogonSubmit"),
            strutsConfigDocument);
    }

    public void testLogonSubmitActionSuccessMapsToWelcome()
        throws Exception {

        assertXpathEvaluatesTo(
            "/Welcome.do",
            getActionForwardPathXpath("/LogonSubmit", "success"),
            strutsConfigDocument);
    }
}
```

The Struts configuration file combines navigation rules with the mapping between locations and URIs. When an action forwards to another action, it uses a navigation rule; whereas, actions that forward to page templates (a JSP or a Velocity template) are location/URI mapping rules. In this way, the Struts configuration file plays the role of navigation engine as well as location mapper, as we described them in recipe 13.1. You can use the same approach to test location mappings as for navigation rules.

◆ *Discussion*

There are a few things to notice about the tests in this recipe. First, notice that we load the Struts configuration file using one-time setup (see recipe 5.10, "Set up your fixture once for the entire suite," for more about how to use `TestSetup`). Next, notice the methods `getActionXpath()`, `getActionForwardXpath()`, and `getActionForwardPathXpath()`. These methods translate the concepts of "action" and "action forward" to the corresponding XPath locations in struts-config.xml. Not only do you *not* need to remember the various XPath expressions for actions and action forwards, but you also avoid duplicating those expressions in case of future changes in the Struts Configuration file DTD. We extracted a fixture class `StrutsConfigFixture` and pulled those methods up into the new fixture class for reuse (see recipe 3.4, "Factor out a test fixture" for more about extracting test fixtures). Listing 13.6 shows these methods.

Listing 13.6 A sample fixture for struts-config.xml tests

```
package junit.cookbook.coffee.web.test;

import org.custommonkey.xmlunit.XMLTestCase;

public abstract class StrutsConfigFixture extends XMLTestCase {
    protected String getActionForwardPathXpath(
        String action,
        String forward) {

        return getActionXpath(action)
            + "/forward[@name='" + forward + "']/@path";
    }

    protected String getActionXpath(String path) {
        return "/struts-config/action-mappings/action[@path='"
            + path + "']";
    }

    protected String getActionForwardXpath(String action) {
        return getActionXpath(action) + "/forward";
    }
}
```

Notice the incremental style of the tests. This is a good approach to take when verifying XML documents with XPath, because when an XPath-based assertion fails, there is no easy way to determine the cause. Perhaps you mistyped the name of an XML element three levels down in the expression, or you forgot to include an "at" sign (@) for an attribute. By writing many small, increasingly specific tests, it is easier to determine the problem by observing which tests fail. For an action mapping, consider these three tests:

1. Is the action configured at all?
2. Does it have any forwards?
3. Are its forwards correct?

Writing three tests rather than just the third one makes it possible to say that, for example, if the second and third tests both fail, then there is a problem with the Struts configuration file—there is an action without a forward.

◆ ***Related***

- 3.4—Factor out a test fixture
- 5.10—Set up your fixture once for the entire suite
- 13.1—Test page flow (navigation rules)

13.3 Test your site for broken links

◆ ***Problem***

You want to verify that all the links on your site lead somewhere.

◆ ***Background***

A typical web application end user will leave your site *and never come back* if he is annoyed by clicking a link that leads him nowhere. You need to avoid letting end users see "404 File Not Found" at essentially any cost. Fortunately, it is quite simple to use JUnit to test your entire site.

◆ ***Recipe***

Here, HtmlUnit can come to the rescue: a fairly simple recursive algorithm makes this test surprisingly easy to write. The key parts of the algorithm are:

1. Retrieve a page by invoking `WebClient.getPage()`.
2. If the page is an `HtmlPage`, get all the anchors (`<a>` tags) on it and try to follow each one.
3. If you reach a page outside your domain, do not bother checking any further.
4. If something goes wrong when following a link, identify that link as broken.

This leads to a recursive algorithm; however, as we tried to execute the test, we ran into some specific details of which you need to be aware.

The Jakarta Commons HttpClient does not handle `mailto` links, so we cannot check those. The best you can do is verify that they represent valid e-mail addresses, perhaps. We recommend you check them by hand.

There is a defect in HtmlUnit 1.2.3 that does not handle linking to page targets (`<a href="#Hello" />`) correctly. We have submitted the issue to Mike Bowler with a fix, and more than likely by the time you read this sentence, it will already have been fixed. If not, lean on him a little.[6]

Many links lead back to a page the test has already checked. To avoid infinite recursion, keep track of every URL the test has checked so far, and then skip those URLs if they come up again.

There are the occasional false failures—that is, the test fails, you check the link, and it is not broken. Part of that is the nature of the web: sometimes a URL is unavailable for a few seconds. Other than that, we do not know why this would happen. You would have to run the test more often to notice a pattern. Because you will likely run this test say, once per week, these false negative are not a hot issue.

Also be aware that we are not checking form submission, which would be very complex to do in general. Instead, see chapter 12, "Testing Web Components," for a discussion on how to verify web forms, one by one, in isolation.

Let us look at the code in listing 13.7. Simply change `domainName` to whatever URL you would like to start with. We do not recommend running this test against `yahoo.com`–that would take an awfully long time.

Listing 13.7 LinksTest

```
package junit.cookbook.applications.test;

import java.io.IOException;
import java.net.URL;
import java.util.*;

import junit.framework.TestCase;

import com.gargoylesoftware.HtmlUnit.*;
import com.gargoylesoftware.HtmlUnit.html.*;

public class LinksTest extends TestCase {
    private WebClient client;
    private List urlsChecked;
    private Map failedLinks;
    private String domainName;
```

[6] No need. We received e-mail from Mike that our fix was checked in and will be part of the next release of HtmlUnit. Ah, open source!

```
    protected void setUp() throws Exception {
        client = new WebClient();
        client.setJavaScriptEnabled(false);
        client.setRedirectEnabled(true);
        urlsChecked = new ArrayList();
        failedLinks = new HashMap();
    }

    public void testFindABrokenLink() throws Exception {
        domainName = "yahoo.com";
        URL root = new URL("http://www." + domainName + "/");

        Page rootPage = client.getPage(root);
        checkAllLinksOnPage(rootPage);

        assertTrue(
            "Failed links (from => to): " + failedLinks.toString(),
            failedLinks.isEmpty());
    }

    private void checkAllLinksOnPage(Page page) throws IOException {
        if (!(page instanceof HtmlPage))
            return;

        URL currentUrl = page.getWebResponse().getUrl();
        String currentUrlAsString = currentUrl.toExternalForm();

        if (urlsChecked.contains(currentUrlAsString)) {
            return;
        }

        if (currentUrlAsString.indexOf(domainName) < 0) {
            return;
        }

        urlsChecked.add(currentUrlAsString);
        System.out.println("Checking URL: " + currentUrlAsString);

        HtmlPage rootHtmlPage = (HtmlPage) page;
        List anchors = rootHtmlPage.getAnchors();
        for (Iterator i = anchors.iterator(); i.hasNext();) {
            HtmlAnchor each = (HtmlAnchor) i.next();

            String hrefAttribute = each.getHrefAttribute();

            boolean isMailtoLink = hrefAttribute.startsWith("mailto:");
            boolean isHypertextLink = hrefAttribute.trim().length() > 0;

            if (!isMailtoLink && isHypertextLink) {
                try {
                    Page nextPage = each.click();
                    checkAllLinksOnPage(nextPage);
                }
```

```
                catch (Exception e) {
                    failedLinks.put(currentUrlAsString, each);
                }
            }
        }
    }
}
```

◆ ***Discussion***

A few warnings about this test:

- It is slow to execute, as it is checking URLs over a live network.
- If one of your broken links is to a nonexistent domain or a domain with its server entirely down, the test's network connection might have to time out before registering a failure, which makes it even slower. Although our version of the test only checks pages in the desired domain, you could certainly remove that restriction in your test. If you do, then this becomes an issue.
- The whole thing executes as one big test, rather than as a test for each URL to check. We cannot see a way to get around this without implementing Test directly, which we could certainly do; however, the idea of creating a `TestSuite` in memory while the test is running gave us a headache, so we chose not to try it.

Still, we think it is a good starting point for common use.

◆ ***Related***

- Chapter 12—Testing Web Components

13.4 Test web resource security

◆ ***Problem***

You want to verify that you have protected your web resources correctly.

◆ ***Background***

The typical way to verify security is with End-to-End Tests: deploy the application, log in as different users, and verify that you receive "Authorization Failure" or "Forbidden" at the expected moment. In this recipe we will describe how to automate this kind of testing, but bear in mind that these tests might violate our principle of *don't test the platform.* If you are using J2EE's declarative security feature—

and we would be surprised if you were not—then you can test your security settings without getting the container involved.

◆ Recipe

First, let us look at how to test security from the outside, using an End-to-End Test. HtmlUnit provides support for specifying credentials along with a request, so that you can simulate having a user logged in. You can also use HtmlUnit to test the login procedure itself. Returning to our Coffee Shop application, imagine an administrative interface for such simple day-to-day things as changing products and prices.[7] Obviously, these features need to be protected behind some resource security. In particular, we want to be sure that if a user tries to access this page without logging in, that the application forces them to identify themselves. The test in listing 13.8 verifies that very condition. All the administrative pages are under the URI `admin` inside our application.

Listing 13.8 Test the authorization rules for administrative web resources

```
package junit.cookbook.coffee.endtoend.test;

import java.net.URL;
import junit.framework.TestCase;
import com.gargoylesoftware.HtmlUnit.*;
import com.gargoylesoftware.HtmlUnit.html.HtmlPage;

public class AdminWelcomePageTest extends TestCase {
    private static final int AUTHORIZATION_FAILED = 401;

    private WebClient webClient;

    protected void setUp() throws Exception {
        webClient = new WebClient();
    }

    public void testWithoutCredentials() throws Exception {
        try {
            Page page =
                webClient.getPage(
                    new URL("http://localhost:8080/coffeeShop/admin/"));

            fail("Got through without a challenge?!");
        }
```

[7] You are right: no company in its right mind would dare make pricing changes available to the web. Nevertheless, we need an example, and this is the one we have chosen. Suspend your disbelief for a few pages.

```
        catch (FailingHttpStatusCodeException expected) {
            assertEquals(
                AUTHORIZATION_FAILED,
                expected.getStatusCode());
        }
    }
}
```

Here we use HtmlUnit to try to retrieve the page, expecting a 401 response code: "Authorization Failed." In order to make this test work, we had to configure security in our application's web deployment descriptor. Listing 13.9 shows the relevant portion.

Listing 13.9 A web deployment descriptor that passes the tests in AdminWelcomePageTest

```
<?xml version="1.0" encoding="UTF-8"?>
<!DOCTYPE web-app PUBLIC "-//Sun Microsystems, Inc.//DTD Web Application 2.3/
  /EN" "http://java.sun.com/dtd/web-app_2_3.dtd">
<web-app id="WebApp">

    <!-- Most of the file omitted for brevity -->

    <display-name>CoffeeShopWeb</display-name>
    <security-constraint>
        <web-resource-collection>
            <web-resource-name>CatalogAdministration</web-resource-name>
            <url-pattern>/admin/*</url-pattern>
        </web-resource-collection>
        <auth-constraint>
            <role-name>administrator</role-name>
        </auth-constraint>
    </security-constraint>
    <login-config>
        <auth-method>BASIC</auth-method>
    </login-config>
</web-app>
```

Now that we know these pages require the requester to log in, we need to limit access to those users that play the administrator role. Our next test uses HtmlUnit's `CredentialProvider` API to simulate having a particular user logged in. The class `SimpleCredentialProvider` allows you to specify the user name and password to simulate for all requests originating from the same `WebClient` object. Suppose that `admin` is the user name of an administrator who should have access to the administrative part of the online store. Here is the test we need to verify that `admin` can log in and see the welcome page.

```
public void testAdminLoggedIn() throws Exception {
    webClient.setCredentialProvider(
        new SimpleCredentialProvider("admin", "adm1n"));

    Page page =
        webClient.getPage(
            new URL("http://localhost:8080/coffeeShop/admin/"));

    assertEquals(
        HttpServletResponse.SC_OK,
        page.getWebResponse().getStatusCode());

    assertTrue(page instanceof HtmlPage);

    HtmlPage welcomePage = (HtmlPage) page;
    assertEquals(
        "Coffee Shop - Administration",
        welcomePage.getTitleText());
}
```

You will notice two differences with this test: first, we invoke `WebClient.setCredentialProvider()` to simulate user `admin` logging in with password `adm1n`. From this point, until you change the `CredentialProvider`, all requests from this `WebClient` object will pass those credentials, the behavior you would expect from such an API.[8] The other difference to note is that we verify that we receive the response code 200, meaning "OK." We need this because we have made a small but useful change to our `WebClient`. In the `setUp()` method we have added the line highlighted in bold print:

```
protected void setUp() throws Exception {
    webClient = new WebClient();
    webClient.setThrowExceptionOnFailingStatusCode(false);
}
```

This line configures how the `WebClient` reacts when it receives a failing status code from the server—that is, a code outside of the range 200–299. By default, the `WebClient` throws an exception, which explains our first test: because it expected status code 401, a failing status code, the test expects its `WebClient` to throw a `FailingHttpStatusCodeException`. By turning this behavior off we can avoid having to catch all these exceptions, but in return, we need to check the status code of every request—even the ones we expect to pass. It is a small price to pay to simplify tests that generally expect the server to respond with a failing status code.

[8] Remember that each test executes in its own object, and so uses a different `WebClient` object. Do not expect those credentials to remain set for other tests in your suite.

As an example, this next test tries to log in to the administrative application as shopper. We expect the server to answer with "forbidden."

```
public void testShopperLoggedIn() throws Exception {
    webClient.setCredentialProvider(
        new SimpleCredentialProvider("shopper", "sh0pper"));

    Page page =
        webClient.getPage(
            new URL("http://localhost:8080/coffeeShop/admin/"));

    assertEquals(
        HttpServletResponse.SC_FORBIDDEN,
        page.getWebResponse().getStatusCode());
}
```

We *were* using hard-coded status code in the original version of our tests, but remembered later that HttpServletResponse defines constants for them all, so we use the constants instead. The resulting tests are much easier to read. You have seen how to simulate having no credentials (not being logged in), being logged in as a user with the required access, and being logged in as a user without the required access. These are the building blocks you need to write as sophisticated a test as you need, centered on authentication and authorizationfor web resources.

◆ Discussion

Be aware of one downside to testing application resource security "from the outside" as we have described here. If you verify the container's enforcement of your security policies for all user roles on all resources, there is a real danger of duplicating your entire access control list in the tests. This defeats, at least in part, the point of *declarative* security.[9] As a result, we recommend that you test the way you declare security information, rather than whether your application server applies it correctly. To test the latter would require essentially duplicating the application server's assembly descriptor-processing algorithm. If you are building an application server, then that effort is appropriate; however, if you are only building an enterprise application to execute on an application server, then it goes too far. *Don't test the platform.* Instead, verify the content of each of your deployment descriptors using the techniques we described in chapter 9, "Testing and XML."

The specific techniques you need to test your server-side security settings depend on the application server: some servers are not open enough to make

[9] You know: security *without* a large pile of code.

server configuration data available to outside components.[10] With JBoss, for example, a combination of XMLUnit and Plain Old JUnit can help you verify your settings in `jboss-web.xml`, `login-config.xml`, and—in the case of the user registry (which is based on properties files)—`users.properties` and `roles.properties`. With other application servers, check your local documentation.

◆ ***Related***

- Chapter 9—Testing and XML

13.5 Test EJB resource security

◆ ***Problem***

You want to test your EJB security settings.

◆ ***Background***

Manual EJB security testing is generally even more annoying than manual web resource security testing (see recipe 13.4). The typical approach is to build a web front end just to be able to invoke the EJBs directly, or you might be using a development environment that provides test client applications for this purpose.[11] Such test clients are essentially interactive Java interpreters, in which you execute code by clicking hypertext links; and while it can be useful for quickly verifying that your EJBs are not entirely broken, they are not a substitute for or—at least in our opinion—a good tool for testing. What you need is a way to write security-based tests that simply provide credentials, look up the EJB, and try to use it. These tests are easy to automate. This recipe describes how.

◆ ***Recipe***

We recommend starting with Cactus, which helps you simulate having a specific user logged in on a per test basis. It uses a mechanism quite similar to HtmlUnit (see recipe 13.4). The general strategy is to provide Cactus with the appropriate authentication information to simulate a user being logged in, and then trying to invoke the protected EJB method. Remember that because we are using Cactus, these tests execute in the container. We will come back to that in the Discussion

[10] We do not have any specific product in mind. The culprits know who they are.

[11] IBM's WebSphere Studio, for example, provides the Universal Test Client for this purpose.

section of this recipe. Listing 13.10 shows the first test: if there are no credentials (no one has logged in), then invoking an EJB method ought to fail. The EJB in question is a session bean that can provide the business logic for our Coffee Shop administrative application. This EJB performs pricing changes.

Listing 13.10 PricingOperationsSecurityTest, a server-side Cactus test

```
package junit.cookbook.coffee.model.ejb.test;

import java.rmi.ServerException;
import javax.ejb.EJBException;
import javax.naming.*;
import javax.rmi.PortableRemoteObject;
import junit.cookbook.coffee.model.ejb.*;
import org.apache.cactus.*;

public class PricingOperationsSecurityTest extends ServletTestCase {
    public void testNoCredentials() throws Exception {
        Context context = new InitialContext();
        Object object = context.lookup("ejb/PricingOperations");
        PricingOperationsHome home =
            (PricingOperationsHome) PortableRemoteObject.narrow(
                object,
                PricingOperationsHome.class);

        try {
            PricingOperations pricingOperations = home.create();
            fail("No credentials and you got through?!");
        }
        catch (ServerException expected) {
            Throwable serverExceptionCause = expected.getCause();
            assertTrue(
                "This caused the ServerException: "
                    + serverExceptionCause,
                serverExceptionCause instanceof EJBException);

            EJBException ejbException =
                (EJBException) serverExceptionCause;

            Exception ejbExceptionCause =
                ejbException.getCausedByException();

            assertTrue(
                "This caused the EJBException: " + ejbExceptionCause,
                ejbExceptionCause instanceof SecurityException);

        }
    }
}
```

All the code in bold print verifies that the server-side exception is indeed a security exception, and not some incidental problem. It is common practice in Java to wrap exceptions within exceptions when propagating them up through the various layers of an application, which explains all the unwrapping here in the test. We will refactor this into a separate method when we add another test or two. Otherwise, this uses the technique we describe in recipe 2.8, "Test throwing the right exception." Our next test verifies that a user with the required authorization can create a `PricingOperations` bean.

You need to follow a few simple instructions from the Cactus web site to be able to provide authentication information along with a request.[12] After we augmented our web deployment descriptor, we added the following test, which verifies that an administrator (user `admin`) can invoke methods on both the home interface and on the bean itself.

```
public void beginAdministrator(WebRequest request) {
    request.setRedirectorName("ServletRedirectorSecure" );
    request.setAuthentication(
        new BasicAuthentication("admin", "adm1n"));
}

public void testAdministrator() throws Exception {
    PricingOperations pricingOperations = home.create();
    pricingOperations.setPrice("762", Money.dollars(12, 50));
}
```

The Cactus web site instructed us to implement a "begin" method in order to set authentication for this test. Our test then simply creates a `PricingOperations` bean and invokes a method on it. As long as this test does not throw any security-related exceptions, it passes—that is why there are no assertions in it. If the test *did* throw an exception, we might want to add logic to verify exactly which exception it is throwing, and have the test fail only if it threw a security-related exception. We believe that the extra reward is not worth the extra effort, so we leave the test as it is. We have moved `home` into the test fixture and initialize it in `setUp()`, as follows:

```
public class PricingOperationsSecurityTest extends ServletTestCase {
    private PricingOperationsHome home;

    protected void setUp() throws Exception {
        Context context = new InitialContext();
        Object object = context.lookup("ejb/PricingOperations");
        home =
            (PricingOperationsHome) PortableRemoteObject.narrow(
```

[12] See http://jakarta.apache.org/cactus/writing/howto_security.html

```
                object,
                PricingOperationsHome.class);
    }

    // Tests omitted
}
```

The last test we include here tries to log in as a shopper and invoke the `PricingOperations` EJB, which ought to fail with "user not authorized." When we wrote this test, we realized that we wanted the Cactus test redirector to work for *any* authenticated user, because the EJB layer was going to perform the stricter security check. After failing to figure out how to do that, we settled on a role that no user played, and named it `test`. We configured our test web application—the web application containing our Cactus tests—with a security constraint, but authorized all users to use the web application (by not preventing anyone from using it). This forces the user to be authenticated for purposes of testing the user's authority to invoke EJBs, but any user can execute the tests. We think this is a good design for security-based tests.

We refactored the "no credentials" test, extracting the code that tries to invoke `PricingOperationsHome.create()`, unwraps the expected exception, and verifies that it is a `SecurityException`. We even added some code to check the `SecurityException` message—now we need to distinguish between "no credentials provided" and "user not authorized." Listing 13.11 shows that method.

Listing 13.11 Verifying the `SecurityException` message

```
private void doTestExpectingSecurityException(
    String testFailureMessage,
    String expectedSecurityExceptionMessageContains)
    throws Exception {

    try {
        PricingOperations pricingOperations = home.create();
        fail(testFailureMessage);
    }
    catch (ServerException expected) {
        Throwable serverExceptionCause = expected.getCause();
        assertTrue(
            "This caused the ServerException: "
                + serverExceptionCause,
            serverExceptionCause instanceof EJBException);

        EJBException ejbException =
            (EJBException) serverExceptionCause;

        Exception ejbExceptionCause =
            ejbException.getCausedByException();
```

```
            assertTrue(
                "This caused the EJBException: " + ejbExceptionCause,
                ejbExceptionCause instanceof SecurityException);

            SecurityException securityException =
                (SecurityException) ejbExceptionCause;

            String securityExceptionMessage =
                securityException.getMessage();

            assertTrue(
                securityExceptionMessage,
                securityExceptionMessage.matches(
                    ".*"
                        + expectedSecurityExceptionMessageContains
                        + ".*"));
        }
    }
```

We have highlighted in bold print the extra code to check the `SecurityException` message. With this change, the "no credentials" test now looks as follows:

```
public void testNoCredentials() throws Exception {
    doTestExpectingSecurityException(
        "No credentials and you got through?!",
        "principal=null");
}
```

And the new test, which tries to invoke the EJB as a shopper, looks as follows.

```
public void beginShopper(WebRequest request) {
    request.setRedirectorName("ServletRedirectorSecure");
    request.setAuthentication(
        new BasicAuthentication("shopper", "sh0pper"));
}

public void testShopper() throws Exception {
    doTestExpectingSecurityException(
        "Only administrators should be allowed to do this!",
        "Insufficient method permissions");
}
```

As with the "administrator" test, first we implement the Cactus method `beginShopper()` to impersonate a shopper, and then we implement the test itself, expecting to see "Insufficient method permissions" in the `SecurityException` message. This message text is specific to JBoss 3.2.2, and if we wrote any more of these tests, we would certainly extract that text into either a property file or at least a symbolic constant, to avoid massive duplication. If in JBoss 4.0, that message text changes, we do not want to have to change 25 strings scattered throughout our tests.

So here we have examples of the three typical kinds of security tests: no user logged in, an authorized user logged in, and an unauthorized user logged in. You can use these as templates to write your own tests.

◆ *Discussion*

The Cactus tests are complex, but only in the sense that the runtime environment is complex. Writing the tests themselves involves a slight learning curve—in our opinion, not too steep a curve, either—and the usual tentative experiment or two while trying to figure out whether you have followed the instructions correctly. The good news is that once you get going, the only real problem is that the tests are slower to execute than we would like. Certainly that is not the fault of Cactus,[13] but rather is intrinsic to any kind of in-container testing strategy. The only drawback is that writing an exhaustive security test suite this way—trying all permutations of roles and so on—leads to an unhealthy amount of duplicated code.

If you refactor mercilessly, eventually you will end up with an engine that generates the tests from a text-based description of the security roles. You could imagine an XML document that describes which roles are authorized to perform which actions, and that could be used to generate the tests. Does this sound familiar? We recognize it as a description of the declarative security feature of J2EE! To get your tests right, then, would be equivalent to getting your test-generating XML document right. Instead of this, we recommend just verifying the deployment descriptors themselves. Use XMLUnit to verify that you have specified the security settings correctly, and then use whatever strategies you need to verify the configuration files that are specific to your application server. These tests provide a warning system whenever someone changes security settings: the tests will fail, and then it will be up to the team to decide whether that change is correct. No more accidental security holes caused by someone who changed a file at 2 a.m. and neglected to warn anyone about it.[14]

◆ *Related*

- Chapter 9—Testing and XML
- 13.4—Test web resource security
- Cactus Security HOWTO (http://jakarta.apache.org/cactus/writing/howto_security.html)

---

[13] It must be Chet's fault.

[14] We do not recommend working when tired, anyway, but we recognize that some people are pressured into doing it.

13.6 Test container-managed transactions

◆ Problem

You want to verify your container-managed transactions.

◆ Background

Transaction-based programming can be complex, which is one of the reasons for the J2EE container-managed transaction feature. The goal of this feature is to allow you to specify transactions without having to code all the dirty details. The simplicity of container-managed transactions often leaves programmers feeling as though it were "too easy," and they sometimes worry that the application will not behave as expected under a large, concurrent load. Because they know that transaction-based programming is complex, they feel as though they should have to "do more" to add transactional behavior to an application. Testing container-managed transactions is not complex at all, once you put some trust in the container. This recipe helps you focus on testing *your* work, and not the work of the container.

◆ Recipe

The most direct approach you can take involves verifying the container-managed transaction attributes set in your deployment descriptors. When you do this, you are not testing whether your transaction settings make sense for the application, but rather that the transaction settings are what you *think* they should be. This kind of test largely protects against someone unknowingly (or carelessly) changing the settings. This kind of test alerts you to any changes so that you can make a sound judgment whether the change is appropriate. It merely avoids the unpleasant task of debugging a test or production problem and tracing it all the way back to a transaction isolation level that could not possibly work. Avoid the problem by verifying your deployment descriptors. You can do this using the techniques in chapter 9, "Testing and XML."

You may develop additional Deployment Tests to enforce your own deployment rules. As an example, you might decide that all entity bean component methods (on the remote and local interfaces) must be deployed with the transaction attribute `Required`.[15] In this case, you could certainly write a test to verify those settings, such as the one that follows. The test in listing 13.12 verifies that the

[15] This is not a suggestion; rather just an example.

transaction attribute for any container transaction involving the component methods of a particular EJB is `Required`. Note how complex it is.[16]

Listing 13.12 EntityBeanTransactionAttributeTest

```
package junit.cookbook.coffee.model.ejb.test;

import java.io.*;

import org.apache.xpath.XPathAPI;
import org.custommonkey.xmlunit.*;
import org.w3c.dom.*;
import org.xml.sax.InputSource;

public class EntityBeanTransactionAttributeTest extends XMLTestCase {
    protected void setUp() throws Exception {
        XMLUnit.setIgnoreWhitespace(true);
    }

    public void testOrder() throws Exception {
        doTestTransactionAttribute(
            "../CoffeeShopLegacyEJB/META-INF/ejb-jar.xml",
            "Order");
    }

    private void doTestTransactionAttribute(
        String ejbDeploymentDescriptorFilename,
        String ejbName)
        throws Exception {

        Document ejbDeploymentDescriptor =
            XMLUnit.buildTestDocument(
                new InputSource(
                    new FileInputStream(
                        new File(ejbDeploymentDescriptorFilename))));

        String transactionAttributeXpath =
            "/ejb-jar/assembly-descriptor/container-transaction"
                + "[method/ejb-name='" + ejbName + "' and "
                + "(method/method-intf='Remote' or "
                + "method/method-intf='Local')]"
                + "/trans-attribute";

        NodeList transactionAttributeNodes =
            XPathAPI.selectNodeList(
                ejbDeploymentDescriptor,
                transactionAttributeXpath);
```

16 The tests here will fail without an internet connection, because XMLUnit will try to validate the XML document against its DTD. For further details, see recipe 9.2, "Ignore the order of elements in an XML document," and read the section entitled, "Network connectivity and the DTD."

```
            assertTrue(
                "No transaction attribute setting for " + ejbName + " EJB",
                transactionAttributeNodes.getLength() > 0);

            for (int i = 0;
                i < transactionAttributeNodes.getLength();
                i++) {

                Node each = transactionAttributeNodes.item(i);
                Text text = (Text) each.getFirstChild();

                Node assemblyDescriptorNode =
                    each.getParentNode().getParentNode();

                assertEquals(
                    "Transaction attribute incorrect at "
                        + assemblyDescriptorNode.toString(),
                    "Required",
                    text.getData());
            }
        }
    }
```

We have already factored out a generic version of the test so that you can convert this into a Parameterized Test Case (see recipe 4.8, "Build a data-driven test suite"), looping over all the entity beans in your system. Due to the inherent flexibility in describing container-managed transactions, we need a particularly long and convoluted XPath expression to match them all: any `container-transaction` node that contains the `ejb-name` we are looking for and either the Remote or Local `method-intf`. It would take even seasoned XPath users a moment or two to realize what this test is doing, so naming it is particularly important. As we wrote previously, you *could* write this kind of test, but we find it to be too complex. Instead, we recommend generating your EJB deployment descriptors from a process that can more easily enforce this deployment rule. If you use XDoclet (http://xdoclet.sourceforge.net/) to generate your EJB deployment descriptors, then you could use XJavaDoc—the standalone JavaDoc engine—to parse your entity bean implementation class source files and make assertions as to the value of each entity bean's `@ejb.transaction type` property. We recommend that you try a few different approaches and see what works best for you.

◆ Discussion

In this recipe we made it clear what we were testing: that the transaction attribute set in your deployment descriptors is what you think it should be. There is the other question: how do you test that such a transaction attribute produces the desired results? Typically one chooses transaction attributes and transaction isolation levels based on reasoning about the system and live experiments. We will not discuss how to discern which transaction settings are appropriate, as that is the not the goal of this book.[17] As for live experiments, there are several commercial—and perhaps some viable noncommercial—tools that one can use to simulate heavy load for web applications. There are performance testing packages built on JUnit, such as JUnitPerf (www.clarkware.com/software/JUnitPerf.html); and the combination of JUnitPerf and HtmlUnit can help you implement load tests driving a web application. Whatever tools you choose, there is no substitute for deploying your application on a production quality machine, letting 1000 simulated users loose on it and monitoring the error log. Or, as Ron Jeffries said, "Speculation or experimentation—which is more likely to give the correct answer?"

◆ *Related*

- 4.8—Build a data-driven test suite
- Chapter 9—Testing and XML
- JUnitPerf (www.clarkware.com/software/JUnitPerf.html)
- XDoclet (http://xdoclet.sourceforge.net/)

---

[17] See Greg Barish, *Building Scalable and High-Performance Java Web Applications Using J2EE Technology* (Addison-Wesley, 2001). The title is a mouthful, but the content is well worth it.

Part 3

More JUnit techniques

Up to this point we have discussed the building blocks of JUnit tests, as well as how to apply those building blocks in testing J2EE components and applications. There is more to Java than J2EE, and there is much more to JUnit than the basics; so we wanted to look at some of the more advanced JUnit techniques that we had not had the opportunity to introduce up to now. This part contains recipes related to design patterns, popular JUnit extensions, and a few other recipes that did not seem to fit into other chapters.

14 Testing design patterns

This chapter covers

- Testing the Observer/Observable pattern
- Testing the Singleton pattern
- Testing the Factory pattern
- Testing the Template Method pattern

Design Patterns have been around for quite a long time, now—enough time to have become part of the common vocabulary of Java programmers. As we become more comfortable discussing designs in terms of the patterns we apply, we begin to wonder what kinds of tests are most appropriate when we apply those patterns. For example, if there is a special set of cases that one typically needs to cover in order to effectively test the Flyweight pattern,[1] then we would like to know about them. As we plan to apply the pattern, we can be sure to include the corresponding tests. Some of these patterns present challenges to testing, and we would like to have guidelines for how to meet those challenges. The Singleton presents a test isolation problem, whereas it is not obvious how to test the Observer without the Observable. Are there any special shortcuts to testing designs using other patterns? The Decorator and Abstract Factory patterns each provide an opportunity to see abstract test cases in action. While we cannot possibly treat all the classic Design Patterns in this single chapter, we can examine how to test some of the elementary patterns. Our approach is to point out how the tests for each pattern relate to the recipes in the first part of this book. This provides the road map to writing the appropriate tests.

Not only do certain Design Patterns suggest certain testing strategies, but the opposite might be true as well. If you notice yourself writing a particular class of tests, this can be a sign that your design is converging towards a well-known pattern. For example, you might use abstract test cases to test a number of classes in a "wide, but shallow" hierarchy—that is, a large number of sibling classes, but perhaps only one superclass. In this case, look closely at the classes under test. Could these classes decorate one another? Refactor towards the Decorator pattern. Could there be a node/leaf relationship among them? Refactor towards the Composite pattern. Do you notice four or five parallel abstract test case hierarchies? Perhaps the objects under test are the "families of objects" one creates using the Abstract Factory pattern, so consider refactoring in that direction. To learn more about the notion of refactoring towards Design Patterns, we refer you to Joshua Kerievsky's work on the topic.[2] As you gain more experience writing tests, you will see the relationships between the structure of test code and the structure of the objects it tests. You will recognize how the two types of code influence one another: how certain test code structure leads you towards a given Design Pattern

---

1 http://c2.com/cgi/wiki?FlyweightPattern

2 www.industriallogic.com/xp/refactoring/, as well as Joshua Kerievsky, *Refactoring to Patterns* (Addison-Wesley, 2004).

and the other way around. This chapter starts you on that road with an essential collection of tests for various elementary Design Patterns.

14.1 Test an Observer (Event Listener)

◆ Problem

You want to test an event listener.

◆ Background

The power of the Observer (or Event Listener) is that it is not coupled to the Observable (or Event Source). The nature of their collaboration makes it possible to test the Observer in perfect isolation, although on the surface it seems strange to use the Observer without the Observable. When considering how to test an Observer, the first idea that might come to one's mind is to create a fake Observable—an object that plays the role of the real Observable, but does something simpler. It turns out that testing an Observer is even easier than that.

◆ Recipe

The simplest way to test an Observer is simply to invoke its event handler methods directly and make assertions about what they do. There is no need to create a fake Observable: the test case class itself is good enough.[3] You can take advantage of the fact that the Observer does not care about the origin of the events it is listening for, by merely invoking the event handler method directly with a variety of events. You can easily simulate any condition you like in this way.

We look to JUnit itself for an example. One of its core interfaces is `junit.framework.TestListener`. A test listener registers with the test runner to find out when tests begin, when they end, and when they fail. The text-based test runner registers a `TestListener` to print out a dot (.) for each test, an "F" for each failure and an "E" for each error. Although JUnit has already implemented `junit.textui.ResultPrinter`, in this example we will build our own implementation.

Because event handler methods typically do not return values, we need to observe some side effect to verify their correctness. In this case, the side effect is

[3] This approach is not quite the Self-Shunt Pattern, although it is similar in spirit. Sometimes we want to add labels to things to make them sound important, but not here—we're simply invoking methods, just as we did way back in chapter 2.

whatever the test listener prints out...*somewhere.* In production, this test listener should print to the console, but that would be an invisible side effect for the tests. Referring to the techniques in recipe 2.2, "Test a method that returns nothing," we make the side effect visible by providing the `TextBasedTestListener` a `PrintWriter` to which to print. In our tests, we use a `PrintWriter` that wraps a `StringWriter`, so we can retrieve the output as a `String`, while in production we use a `PrintWriter` that redirects to `System.out`, the console. Look at the tests in listing 14.1, the first few of which invoke each event handler method in isolation to verify its basic behavior.

Listing 14.1 Tests for a text-based `TestListener` implementation

```
package junit.cookbook.patterns.test;

import java.io.*;
import junit.cookbook.patterns.TextBasedTestListener;
import junit.framework.*;

public class TextBasedTestListenerTest extends TestCase {
    private TextBasedTestListener testListener;
    private StringWriter stringWriter;

    protected void setUp() throws Exception {
        stringWriter = new StringWriter();
        testListener =
            new TextBasedTestListener(new PrintWriter(stringWriter));
    }

    public void testStartTestEvent() throws Exception {
        testListener.startTest(this);
        assertEquals(".", stringWriter.toString());
    }

    public void testAddFailureEvent() throws Exception {
        testListener.addFailure(this, new AssertionFailedError());
        assertEquals("F", stringWriter.toString());
    }

    public void testAddErrorEvent() throws Exception {
        testListener.addError(this, new RuntimeException());
        assertEquals("E", stringWriter.toString());
    }

    public void testEndTestEvent() throws Exception {
        testListener.endTest(this);
        assertEquals("", stringWriter.toString());
    }
}
```

These tests are straightforward: at the start of a test, we ought to see a dot; when a test fails, we ought to see an "F", and so on. We write the production code to make these tests pass.[4] Now we know that our `TextBasedTestListener` correctly handles the various events occurring on their own. There are no special case variations on these events that we can think of, but do we need any other tests? Just to be sure, in listing 14.2, we try out the various "end-to-end" scenarios that occur when executing a test.

Listing 14.2 Further text-based `TestListener` tests

```
package junit.cookbook.patterns.test;

import java.io.*;
import junit.cookbook.patterns.TextBasedTestListener;
import junit.framework.*;

public class TextBasedTestListenerTest extends TestCase {
    private TextBasedTestListener testListener;
    private StringWriter stringWriter;

    protected void setUp() throws Exception {
        stringWriter = new StringWriter();
        testListener =
            new TextBasedTestListener(new PrintWriter(stringWriter));
    }

    // Basic event handler tests omitted

    public void testCompletePassingTestScenario() throws Exception {
        testListener.startTest(this);
        testListener.endTest(this);
        assertEquals(".", stringWriter.toString());
    }

    public void testCompleteTestFailureScenario() throws Exception {
        testListener.startTest(this);
        testListener.addFailure(this, new AssertionFailedError());
        testListener.endTest(this);
        assertEquals(".F", stringWriter.toString());
    }

    public void testCompleteTestErrorScenario() throws Exception {
        testListener.startTest(this);
        testListener.addError(this, new RuntimeException());
        testListener.endTest(this);
        assertEquals(".E", stringWriter.toString());
    }
}
```

[4] For this recipe we have decided to work in Test-Driven Development mode. If you do not like TDD, then pretend we wrote the code first—whichever you prefer.

These tests verify that `TextBasedTestListener` handles the typical event flows the way we would expect. The last feature we need to add makes it easier to eyeball how many tests have executed: insert a line break every forty tests so that as we see a row of dots we know that forty tests have executed. Here is that test.

```
public void testAddLineBreakAfterFortyTests() throws Exception {
    for (int i = 0; i < 41; i++) {
        testListener.startTest(this);
    }

    assertEquals(
        "........................................\r\n.",
        stringWriter.toString());
}
```

Count them if you like: there are forty dots, a line break, and then one more dot. If we had to generate more long lines of dots, we would extract a method like `StringUtil.repeat()` to do it; but until then, we'll live with the duplication, or lack of abstraction, however you prefer to see it. This is the test that forces the `TextBasedTestListener` to keep a count of the number of tests and invoke `println()` at the right time. We did not need any test runner, real or fake, to generate the events for these tests. Instead, we simply invoke the event handler methods with some sample events and verify the way the methods respond.

◆ Discussion

The event-handling logic for `TextBasedTestListener` was very simple: print some characters to a `PrintWriter`. Some event-handling logic is complex enough to present its own testing challenges, making it difficult to use as the "observable side effect" to test the event handlers. Observer tests *should* be very simple, and if they are not, then that is generally a sign that the Observer is "working too hard." It might be violating the Single Responsibility Principle. For example, consider an event handler that sends a JMS message when it receives an event notification. Verifying that the event handler sent the appropriate JMS message involves JMS servers, message marshalling and unmarshalling, and on and on—quite a complex test environment for something that ought to be much simpler. Instead, we recommend separating the event handler's key responsibilities, which are probably:

- Determine the message content and destination, depending on the event received.
- Marshal the content into a JMS message and send it to its destination.

Extract the second responsibility and move it into a separate class and introduce an interface containing a method that takes the message content and destination as a parameter. Name the new interface MessageSender.[5] Your event handler now creates the message content, determines the destination, and invokes its MessageSender. This is a much simpler side effect to observe during testing: you can use a mock objects approach to verify that your event handler invokes MessageSender correctly. Listing 14.3 shows an example that uses EasyMock to verify this method invocation.

Listing 14.3 Testing MessageSender with EasyMock

```
package junit.cookbook.patterns.test;

import junit.cookbook.patterns.*;
import junit.framework.TestCase;

import org.easymock.MockControl;

public class MessageSendingObserverTest extends TestCase {
    private MessageSendingObserver observer;
    private MessageSender messageSender;
    private MockControl messageSenderControl;

    protected void setUp() throws Exception {
        messageSenderControl =
            MockControl.createControl(MessageSender.class);

        messageSender = (MessageSender) messageSenderControl.getMock();

        observer = new MessageSendingObserver(messageSender);
    }

    public void testAbcEvent() throws Exception {
        messageSender.sendMessage(
            "ABC-related content", "ABC destination");

        messageSenderControl.replay();

        observer.handle(new AbcEvent());

        messageSenderControl.verify();
    }
}
```

We have highlighted in bold print the two main parts of the test. The first is recording the method invocation you expect: that *someone* will invoke sendMessage() with the correct message content and destination. The second is simulating the event by invoking the event handler directly. This verifies that when the

[5] Not a great name, we know, but you will think of something better later.

`MessageSendingObserver` receives an `AbcEvent`, it asks the `MessageSender` to send the right message. Now no matter how many different events might result in sending a message, you only need one small set of tests for the JMS-based `MessageSender` implementation you use in production. (We discuss testing JMS message producers in recipe 11.12, "Test a JMS message producer.") By separating the event handler's two main responsibilities, we can ignore the complexity of sending a real JMS message when all we need to verify is how our Observer determines the content and destination of a message based on the event it receives. The resulting tests are simpler and faster, and the resulting design is more flexible.

◆ Related

- 2.2—Test a method that returns nothing
- 11.12—Test a JMS message producer

14.2 Test an Observable (Event Source)

◆ Problem

You want to test an event source.

◆ Background

You might be wondering how to test an Observable (or Event Source) without involving the Observer (or Event Listener). After all, how are you supposed to verify that an object generates the right events if you do not listen for those events? Well, yes, without an event listener there is no way to verify that the event source works; however, just because you need *an* event listener does not mean you need the *production* event listener. On the contrary, *any* event listener will do. The simplest kind of event listener does nothing important when it receives an event, except possibly remember the events it received. This recipe shows you how to leverage this observation—pun intended—to test an event source.

◆ Recipe

To test an Observable, you need to recreate the conditions under which you expect an event to be generated, and then verify that it notified its listeners. We often implement this kind of test using the Self-Shunt Pattern. In particular, the *test case class* implements the event listener interface, collects the events it receives in a `List`, and then verifies the received events against a `List` of expected events.

To illustrate this, we look once again to JUnit for an example. In recipe 14.1 we tested a text-based implementation of `TestListener`, which printed information in response to various test-execution events. Now it is time to verify that JUnit generates those events correctly. To generate those events requires executing a test—the `TestResult` object we pass into the `TestCase` when executing the test acts as the Observable. *We warn you:* testing JUnit with JUnit is a little like trying to chase your own tail, but it is a worthy exercise.[6] First, we set up the Self-Shunt: the test case class implements `TestListener` and collects the various method invocations as events. Because `TestResult` does not generate event objects, we collect the information about each event handler method invocation in a convenient package: a `List`. Listing 14.4 shows our test, with the Self-Shunt bits highlighted in bold print.

Listing 14.4 Verifying the events generated when running a JUnit test

```
package junit.cookbook.patterns.test;

import java.util.*;

import junit.framework.*;

public class TestCaseEventsTest
    extends TestCase
    implements TestListener {

    private List events;

    protected void setUp() throws Exception {
        events = new ArrayList();
    }

    public void addError(Test test, Throwable throwable) {
        events.add(
            Arrays.asList(
                new Object[] { "addError", test, throwable }));
    }

    public void addFailure(Test test, AssertionFailedError failure) {
        events.add(
            Arrays.asList(
                new Object[] {
                    "addFailure",
                    test,
                    failure.getMessage()}));
    }
```

6 Consider that JUnit was built using JUnit, and done so test-first. See Kent Beck's *Test-Driven Development: By Example* (Addison-Wesley, 2002) to see how to build a Python-based xUnit framework using itself!

```
    public void endTest(Test test) {
        events.add(Arrays.asList(new Object[] { "endTest", test }));
    }

    public void startTest(Test test) {
        events.add(Arrays.asList(new Object[] { "startTest", test }));
    }
}
```

With this in place, we need to test executing a test. (We warned you it would sound weird.) The simplest kind of test to execute is a passing test. We create a passing test, attach our Spy `TestListener` to a `TestResult`, and then execute the test using our `TestResult`. Get it? Maybe not. The code in listing 14.5 makes it more clear.

Listing 14.5 Adding a dummy passing test

```
public class TestCaseEventsTest
    extends TestCase
    implements TestListener {

    // code from previous listing omitted

    public TestCaseEventsTest(String name) {
        super(name);
    }

    public void dummyPassingTest() {
    }

    public void testPassingTestCase() throws Exception {
        final TestCase testCase =
            new TestCaseEventsTest("dummyPassingTest");

        TestResult testResult = new TestResult();
        testResult.addListener(this);

        testCase.run(testResult);

        List expectedEvents = new ArrayList();
        expectedEvents.add(
            Arrays.asList(new Object[] { "startTest", testCase }));
        expectedEvents.add(
            Arrays.asList(new Object[] { "endTest", testCase }));

        assertEquals(expectedEvents, events);
    }
```

What better test case class to use to create our dummy passing test than the current class? (Again, we warned you about how it would sound.) We create a dummy passing test and *intentionally* name it in such a way that the default test suite will not pick it up. Why? When we execute the default `TestCaseEventsTest` suite, we do not want to include the dummy tests. Instead, we want the `TestCaseEventTest` tests to execute the dummy tests.[7] In `testPassingTestCase()` we instantiate the test, pass it a `TestResult` with our `TestListener` attached, and execute the test case expecting the "start" and "end" events and nothing else. This test passes. So far, so good, but does our test listener handle failing tests? To find out, write a dummy failing test, as in listing 14.6.

Listing 14.6 Adding a dummy failing test

```
public class TestCaseEventsTest
    extends TestCase
    implements TestListener {

    // code from previous listings omitted

    public void dummyFailingTest() {
        fail("I failed on purpose");
    }

    public void testFailingTestCase() throws Exception {
        final TestCase testCase =
            new TestCaseEventsTest("dummyFailingTest");

        TestResult testResult = new TestResult();
        testResult.addListener(this);

        testCase.run(testResult);

        List expectedEvents = new ArrayList();
        expectedEvents.add(
            Arrays.asList(new Object[] { "startTest", testCase }));

        expectedEvents.add(
            Arrays.asList(
                new Object[] {
                    "addFailure",
                    testCase,
                    "I failed on purpose" }));

        expectedEvents.add(
            Arrays.asList(new Object[] { "endTest", testCase }));

        assertEquals(expectedEvents, events);
    }
```

[7] By now you must realize that we are just trying to have fun with you. If the words are confusing, then look at the code. Take your time and try to keep it all straight. If you understand this, then you *really* understand JUnit.

We have highlighted in bold print both the failing test and the extra event we expect as a result: a "test failure" event between the "start" and "end" events. Notice that we compare the failure messages, too—we want `TestResult` to report the *exact* failure we expect, or at a minimum, a failure indistinguishable from the one we expect. Either will do. This test also passes. That makes two out of three scenarios—the last occurs when a test throws an exception. This is trickier (as if it has not been tricky enough), so first we present the code in listing 14.7, and then follow it with an explanation.

Listing 14.7 Adding a test that throws an exception

```
public class TestCaseEventsTest
    extends TestCase
    implements TestListener {

    // code from previous listings omitted

    private Exception expectedException;

    protected void setUp() throws Exception {
        events = new ArrayList();
        expectedException = new Exception("I threw this on purpose");
    }

    public void dummyExceptionThrowingTest() throws Exception {
        throw expectedException;
    }

    public void testError() throws Exception {
        final TestCaseEventsTest testCase =
            new TestCaseEventsTest("dummyExceptionThrowingTest");

        TestResult testResult = new TestResult();
        testResult.addListener(this);

        testCase.run(testResult);

        List expectedEvents = new ArrayList();
        expectedEvents.add(
            Arrays.asList(new Object[] { "startTest", testCase }));

        expectedEvents.add(
            Arrays.asList(
                new Object[] {
                    "addError",
                    testCase,
                    testCase.expectedException }));

        expectedEvents.add(
            Arrays.asList(new Object[] { "endTest", testCase }));

        assertEquals(expectedEvents, events);
    }
```

We have highlighted in bold print the new additions. First the easy part: we expect an "add error" event between the start and end events. So far, so good. To verify that it is the right "add error" event, we need to know which exception (or `Throwable`, to be precise) prompted the `TestResult` to report the error. The exception object we want to verify is the one belonging to the `dummyExceptionThrowingTest` and not to the `testError` test, which is why we use `testCase.expectedException` and not just `expectedException`. The latter would be an object belonging to `testError`'s fixture, whereas the former belongs to `dummyExceptionThrowingTest`'s fixture. Got it? If not, do not worry—it took us a while to get it too. The point is that we have verified that JUnit generates the four `TestListener` events correctly by attaching our own `TestListener`, and then verifying that it receives the events we expected it to receive.

At this point, we can safely conclude that if one listener is correctly notified, then so would any number of registered listeners; however, if you are at all unsure, write one test that registers three event listeners, generates an event, and verifies that all three event listeners were notified. The odds are slim that this would work for one type of generated event and not the others; but if you think there is a greater chance that this might fail, then by all means, write more tests. Our experience has shown that more tests are warranted when testing legacy Observables and fewer are needed when we are building our own. *Test until fear turns to boredom.*

◆ *Discussion*

If for some reason you cannot use the Self-Shunt Pattern for this kind of test—and that is rare—we recommend using EasyMock. Each incoming event corresponds to invoking a particular event handler method with certain parameters, and EasyMock is optimized for recording and verifying method invocation sequences. Set up a mock event listener with EasyMock, record the event handler method invocations you expect, invoke `yourMockControl.replay()`, invoke the Observable so that it generates its events, and then invoke `yourMockControl.verify()`. Once you get the implementation pattern down, it is easy to test more and more events. That said, the Self-Shunt Pattern is simpler in that it results in less test code, and so we prefer it.

If you find an Observable difficult to test, then the principle cause is violating the Single Responsibility Principle. The most common symptom of this is writing a large amount of code to recreate the situation in which a given event is generated—or worse, being unable to recreate that situation at all. If you find yourself trying to test such an Observable, then you need to refactor the Observable, extracting the smallest amount of code that will generate the expected event. You can typically achieve this by extracting a method [Refactoring, 110]. Your test would then attach itself as an event listener, invoke the newly extracted method, and then verify the event received. The details of the refactoring you need depend entirely on the specifics of your design, so we are unable to give you more specific advice. As usual, testing difficulties usually point to objects with too many responsibilities.

◆ *Related*

- 14.1—Test an Observer
- Self-Shunt Pattern (www.objectmentor.com/resources/articles/SelfShunPtrn.pdf)
- Robert C. Martin, "The Single Responsibility Principle," (www.objectmentor.com/resources/articles/srp)

14.3 Test a Singleton

◆ *Problem*

You want to test a Singleton.

◆ *Background*

There are a number of things that make testing a Singleton difficult, only some of which are related to the pattern itself. Perhaps the most notable problem is that the Singleton retains state from test to test, making it difficult to isolate tests that use it. Worse, when Singletons collaborate with one another, they often force you to write long, complex test fixtures. These fixtures are not only difficult to understand, but also difficult to maintain. They become brittle. The slightest change in one Singleton's behavior causes the kind of ripple effect that Object-Oriented Design is meant to minimize. Let us be frank: a Singleton is a big, fancy global variable, and global variables get in the way of the kind of simple, predictable behavior that makes Object Testing possible. Beyond the Singleton's design characteristics, it is the simplest of the Design Patterns to understand and, as a result, the most commonly used pattern. When a programmer reads *Design Patterns* for the first time, she often proceeds to "solve" design problems by introducing Singletons.[8] You don't know where objects of this type should be stored? Make it a

[8] When all you have is a hammer, everything looks like a nail—the "Golden Hammer" antipattern. William J. Brown et al., *AntiPatterns: Refactoring Software, Architectures and Projects in Crisis.* (Wiley, 1998).

Singleton! You only need one of those objects for now? Make it a Singleton! This causes the very proliferation of Singletons that compounds their negative effects on isolated Object Testing, and there are always more programmers around the corner just itching to build more Singletons. What can we do?

◆ *Recipe*

Not surprisingly, the only scenario in which a Singleton *does not* make Object Testing difficult is when there is only one test. The choice of the Singleton design is not an impediment in that case: you simply invoke `MySingleton.getInstance()` rather than `new MySingleton()` in the "arrange" part of your test.[9] Where you get into trouble is in trying to write a second test, a third test, and so on.

Because the object under test is a Singleton, it retains state from test to test. This is a test isolation problem, related to the danger of having one big data set for tests against a live database. (See chapter 10, "Testing and JDBC" for a discussion of this problem.) When you test a Singleton, your tests are seemingly forced to share a fixture: this is one of the reasons why Singletons and isolated object testing do not mix well. Unless your Singleton never changes state, you need to either solve the shared test fixture problem or live with it. Guess which one we recommend? You could *try* to live with it, but we have too many "war wounds" to make that choice again. There are several ways to handle this:

1. Change the Singleton class so that it is no longer a Singleton. Perhaps your application entry point simply needs to instantiate one object, maintain a reference to it, and then hand that reference to any components that need it. This is our preferred way to solve the problem, but it affects every client of the class, and that sounds like real work.
2. Make the Singleton constructors `public` so that your tests can instantiate the class, but all your production clients can continue using the class as a Singleton. This solves the problem, but defeats the purpose of designing the class as a Singleton in the first place.[10] If you think that the class ought not to be a Singleton, then this is all right; however, you run the risk of

---

9 Remember Bill Wake's three "A"s—arrange, act, assert. This is the essential rhythm of a test. Kent Beck starts Chapter 19 of *Test-Driven Development: By Example* (Addison-Wesley, 2002) with an explanation of the pattern.

10 We would argue that the tests are telling you that the class should not be a Singleton. Nay-sayers often respond, "Are you saying that a Singleton is *never* appropriate?!" Frankly we don't have the energy to take up that debate any longer.

allowing production code to use the newly visible constructors. If that weren't an issue then you likely wouldn't have designed the class as a Singleton in the first place. (You *must* have had a reason.) We recommend using this technique as the first step towards refactoring the Singleton into a Plain Old Java Object. If you do not intend to do that, then choose another approach.

3. Add a `reset()` method to the Singleton, which resets the unique instance to its original state. This is essentially the same as making the constructors `public`, although it does continue to limit the number of instances of the class, which is at least in keeping with the spirit of the Singleton pattern. As with making the constructors `public`, we recommend this as the first step towards a refactored system.
4. If the Singleton has a `protected` constructor, then subclass the Singleton, place `public` constructors in your subclass, and then test the subclass. (Do not override *any* methods!) This subverts the Singleton design, "just for testing." If you keep your test classes in a separate source tree from your production classes (see recipe 3.3, "Separate test packages from production code packages"), then your production code will not see the Singleton's subclass, so there is no way for the production code to bypass the Singleton and instantiate the class on its own. Of course, if your Singleton's constructors are `private`, then you cannot use this technique.
5. Execute each test in its own JVM (or at least class loader). This is one way to ensure that each test executes a freshly initialized Singleton. We describe how to do this in recipe 6.4, "Execute each test in its own JVM." It is a very heavyweight solution and so, while viable, it is the not the first solution we would try, and likely not the solution we would use over the long term.

If you are unable or unwilling to refactor the system and change the Singleton into a Plain Old Java Object, then you have decided to live with the shared fixture problem and the associated high coupling of all the Singleton's clients to the Singleton. We warned you, but we cannot stop you; so if you choose to proceed this way, then you need an effective strategy for testing the Singleton's clients. Fortunately, we have a recipe for just that case in this chapter.

◆ Discussion

Sometimes a class really does make sense designed as a Singleton, but it happens a great deal less frequently than you might think. See J. B.'s article, entitled "Use

Your Singletons Wisely,"[11] for a thorough discussion of how Singletons affect your approach to testing. The article concludes by identifying some rules of thumb to help you decide whether a class really ought to be designed as a Singleton. The shared fixture problem intrinsic to testing a Singleton is a direct example of the kinds of problems you have writing any code that uses a Singleton. After all, your tests are just another bunch of clients for the Singleton.

◆ ***Related***

- 3.3—Separate test packages from production code packages
- Chapter 10—Testing and JDBC
- J. B. Rainsberger, "Use Your Singletons Wisely," (www-106.ibm.com/developerworks/webservices/library/co-single.html)

14.4 Test a Singleton's client

◆ ***Problem***

You want to a test a class that uses a Singleton.

◆ ***Background***

The problem with using a Singleton is that it introduces a certain amount of coupling into a system—coupling that is almost always unnecessary. You are saying that your class can only collaborate with one particular implementation of a set of methods—the implementation that the Singleton provides. You will allow no substitutes. This makes it difficult to test your class in isolation from the Singleton. The very nature of test isolation assumes the ability to substitute alternate implementations—Test Objects, as we call them—for an object's collaborators. If an object hard codes the class name of its collaborator, then one has to resort to some kind of meta code, such as aspects, to substitute a Test Object version of that collaborator in a test. If you are not comfortable with aspects, then unless you change your design, you are forced to rely on the correct behavior of the Singleton in order to test any of its clients. We have been there and done that and prefer never to go back.

[11] www-106.ibm.com/developerworks/webservices/library/co-single.html

◆ *Recipe*

First let us clarify one point: when we refer to a client of a Singleton, we mean any class that invokes the Singleton's `getInstance()` method. Many of the testing issues around a Singleton's client reduce to problems we explored in recipe 2.11, "Test an object that instantiates other objects." Although a Singleton's client does not instantiate the Singleton class (by the definition of Singleton) it does hard-code how it obtains one of its collaborators, a design point equivalent to instantiating the Singleton object directly. With a Singleton's client, an extra layer of complexity comes from the shared test fixture problem we described in recipe 14.3. There is no easy way to reset a Singleton's state from test to test, which violates the principle of test isolation. We have mentioned throughout this book how important test isolation is to testing your object effectively.[12] So how do we solve this problem?

There are two main approaches from which to choose. The first is to change the interface of the Singleton's client so that it does not invoke `getInstance()` directly. We describe this in detail in recipe 2.11, "Test an object that instantiates other objects," using a Singleton as the example. If you follow that recipe, then you will have solved the problem. Here is a recap of the technique:

1. Change the Singleton's clients so that they accept an instance of the Singleton through either a constructor or as an additional method parameter.
2. Extract an interface [Refactoring, 341] with the Singleton methods that your client needs to use. Change the constructor or method parameter to be the interface's type, rather than the Singleton's type.
3. Implement a mock version of the newly created interface, perhaps using EasyMock, to use in your tests.

You could, alternatively, change your Singleton to a Plain Old Java Object by making its constructors available to your client—usually by changing their visibility to `public`. In your tests, instantiate the ex-Singleton object with whatever state you need for each test, but use the Singleton version in the rest of your production code. The vast majority of the Singletons we have seen were not really Singletons. Instead they were Plain Old Java Objects, of which a particular application only needed one instance. In that case, let the application instantiate just one of them and have it pass that object to the other objects that need it. Only your application's entry point needs to know that there is one and only one instance of the

[12] We mentioned it specifically in chapter 4, "Managing Test Suites," but it is a principle that pervades our approach to testing, and in many cases is an unspoken assumption in our recommendations.

class, and you entirely avoid the tight coupling that comes with using a Singleton. Everyone wins.

◆ Discussion

We do recognize, however, that it might not be desirable to change the production code without having the safety net of running tests. It is a bit of a chicken-and-egg problem that faces the intrepid Test-Infected Programmer:[13] *I need to refactor to test the current design, but I ought not to refactor without tests.* These opposing forces are as mutually contradictory as they come. You could walk the tightrope of refactoring without a net, but an exciting and (as we write this) new idea has come along that changes the story considerably: Virtual Mock Objects.

We had intended to include an example of Virtual Mock Objects here; however, the idea is relatively new and implementations are still changing quite rapidly. As a result, we would rather refer you to the Virtual Mock site (www.virtualmock.org) than write something here, only to have it become out of date before the book even goes to press. Such is the nature of writing about quickly changing technology! To give you a sneak peek, Virtual Mock allows you to mock—that is, substitute in your tests—invocations to class-level (`static`) methods without having to modify the design of the code under test. Virtual Mock achieves this through aspect-oriented programming and bytecode manipulation. If you are in a situation where refactoring is not a reasonable option—at least not at present—then Virtual Mock enables you to work around your current design and add tests to it. Virtual Mock does more than just make it easy to mock class-level methods, so we recommend you visit the Virtual Mock site to learn more about its features.

We recommend using this technique as a way to enable you to refactor safely, rather than as a substitute for refactoring. At the slightest sign of trouble, we recommend employing this technique to add at least a thin covering of tests for your Singleton client code. Later, when the current design *really* begins to hurt, at least the tests will be in place to support the refactoring that will ease your pain. Otherwise, you will experience twice the pain: the ill effects of the design itself and the difficulty of adding tests to fix the problem—all this under tight deadline pressure and while you are in a bad mood. If you need to test large amounts of legacy code, riddled with coupling between objects and class-level methods, then we strongly recommend that someone on your team spend a few days exploring Virtual Mock. You will be glad that you did.

---

[13] A term named after this article: http://junit.sourceforge.net/doc/testinfected/testing.htm.

◆ ***Related***

- 2.11—Test an object that instantiates other objects
- 14.3—Test a singleton
- Virtual Mock (www.virtualmock.org)

14.5 Test an object factory

◆ ***Problem***

You want to test an object factory. More specifically, you would like to test a factory method.[14]

◆ ***Background***

First, there is some general confusion as to what a factory method is. There is a small, but important, difference between a *factory method* and a *creation method.* A creation method is simply a method that creates an object. This method usually just delegates to a specific class's constructor. In this situation, the creation method is *too simple to break* and you should focus on deciding whether to test the underlying constructor. See recipe 2.3, "Test a constructor," for details. A factory method is a kind of creation method that applies some logic to decide which class to instantiate. Most commonly, the factory method chooses among many subclasses of a class or many implementations of an interface. The code using a factory method often knows nothing about the specific implementation it receives. When we say "factory," we refer to a class that provides a factory method, and not just creation methods.

Testing an object factory generally creates all kinds of wonderful problems to solve. A typical object factory implementation involves:

1. Reading data from either the file system or a database
2. Using that data to decide which subclass or implementation to create
3. Passing a variable list of parameters to the constructor
4. Answering the result

[14] See the "Gang of Four" book for details on the Factory design pattern. Erich Gamma, Richard Helm, Ralph Johnson, John Vlissides, *Design Patterns* (Addison Wesley, 1995).

As you can see, there are a lot of moving parts and those moving parts present serious challenges to someone new to JUnit.

When writing tests for an object factory, you see—perhaps for the first time—how a design with *high coupling* is difficult to test. You need to get the right data into the database, make sure that the database is up and running, and just when you get *that* to work, the test you write looks like a perfect duplication of the code you are trying to test. This kind of duplication is *always* a signal that something is not quite right.

◆ Recipe

The basic approach is to test the two concrete behaviors of a factory method separately.

- Choose the *creation method* to invoke. This is the rule that decides which implementation to instantiate.
- Invoke the *creation method* correctly. The factory method needs to send the correct parameters to the creation method it has decided to use.

To test the first of these behaviors, use a test similar to the following. Paying homage to the classics, we use the time-tested polymorphism example: making shapes.

```
public void testChooseMakeSquare() {
    SpyShapeMaker spyShapeMaker = new SpyShapeMaker();
    ShapeFactory factory = new ShapeFactory(spyShapeMaker);
    double[] dummyParameters = new double[0];
    factory.makeShape("square", dummyParameters);
    assertEquals(1, spyShapeMaker.getShapesMadeCount());
    assertEquals(1, spyShapeMaker.getSquaresMadeCount());
}
```

Here we see the Spy technique in use: a spy collects information about how other objects invoke its methods, so if you want to verify that the `ShapeFactory` uses the `ShapeMaker` properly, give the factory a spy shape maker, let the spy collect its "intelligence," and then ask it what it learned. "The factory asked me to make one shape: a square." This is about as cloak-and-dagger as we get in programming.

A seemingly simpler design would be for the `ShapeFactory` to own the `ShapeMaker`–that is, the factory not only holds a reference to a maker, but manages its lifecycle, creating and destroying it. If the factory is the only class using the maker, then why make it visible to the outside? We have two answers. First, the *tests* talk to the maker, testing it directly; therefore, more than just the factory uses it. Second, and more importantly, in order to achieve test isolation—where each object is tested without relying on the behavior of its collaborators—it is necessary to be able to substitute alternate implementations of an object's collaborators at run time. In the tests, pass the factory a spy shape maker in order to test it; in production, pass the factory a *real* shape maker, where "real" is in the eye of the application.

Now that you know that the `ShapeFactory` requests the correct kind of shape, you need a production-quality class that can make that kind of shape. The tests for `ShapeMaker` are very simple. Here is a test for making a square (for real):

```
public void testMakeSquare() {
    ShapeMaker shapeMaker = new ShapeMaker();
    Square expected = new Square(5.0d);
    assertEquals(expected, shapeMaker.makeSquare(5.0d));
}
```

Sometimes it is difficult to believe that a test this simple is actually doing anything to give you confidence in the code, but it really *is* this simple! By separating concerns effectively, the tests become simple and the production code even simpler.

Now you have a test for choosing the creation method: the `ShapeFactory` correctly asks the `ShapeMaker` for a `Square`. You also have a test for the creation method itself: the `ShapeMaker` makes the expected `Square` when asked to make a `Square`. To test making new kinds of shapes, add a "choose the right creation method" test to the `ShapeFactory`. To test making different instances of existing kinds of shapes, such as the different kinds of triangles, simply add a "creation method" test for the `ShapeMaker`.

◆ *Discussion*

Commonly, the two responsibilities of an object factory are coded directly inside the factory class. Using our example, the object factory would simply call `new Square()` inside the `if` statement that checked which kind of shape the client wanted. A test for this might look like:

```
public void testMakeSquare() {
    double[] parameters = new double[] {5.0d};
    Square expected = new Square(5.0d);
    ShapeFactory factory = new ShapeFactory();
    assertEquals(expected, factory.makeSquare("square", parameters);
}
```

Now this test looks simpler than what we've written, but it has some duplication. Because duplication is the root of all evil[15], we should remove it. Here is the resulting test:

---

[15] If you don't think that it is, then please consult Martin Fowler, *Refactoring: Improving the Design of Existing Code* (Addison-Wesley, 1999).

```
public void testMakeSquare() {
    double sideLength = 5.0d;
    Square expected = new Square(sideLength);
    ShapeFactory factory = new ShapeFactory();
    double[] parameters = new double[] {sideLength};
    assertEquals(expected, factory.makeSquare("square", parameters);
}
```

So far so good, but consider what happens in the rest of the system. You will feel compelled to test the constructors for `Square`. Those assertions will duplicate some of the work that you have done here. This duplication is not only wasted effort, but the resulting tests are brittle: if the shape-making behavior needs to change, you will need to change not only the `SquareTest`, but also the `ShapeMakerTest`. Worse, the changes you make will *essentially* be the same, but still have small differences. Nothing creates defects in code more easily than having to make "almost the same change" in multiple places. Confusion abounds. By separating concerns, you can avoid the confusion.

Worse, *the only way* to verify that the factory creates the correct *kind* of shape is to have it create the actual shape. What if, rather than creating shapes, your factory created connectors to back-end systems? What if those connectors required a live connection to the corresponding back-end system *just to be created*? Now you cannot test your connector factory without having each of your supported back-end systems up and running. Those tests will be slow, brittle, and there will be times when you'll want to run them and you cannot, because some other department has borrowed the back-end systems you need. This recipe makes it possible to verify choosing the correct connector without even having to create the connector!

Finally, listing 14.8 shows an implementation of `SpyShapeMaker`, able to count how many squares and shapes it has been asked to create.

Listing 14.8 `SpyShapeMaker`

```
package junit.cookbook.common.test;

import junit.cookbook.common.ShapeMaker;
import junit.cookbook.common.Square;

public class SpyShapeMaker extends ShapeMaker {
    private int squaresMade = 0;

    public int getShapesMadeCount() {
        return squaresMade;
    }

    public int getSquaresMadeCount() {
        return squaresMade;
    }
```

```
    public Square makeSquare(double sideLength) {
        squaresMade++;
        return super.makeSquare(sideLength);
    }
}
```

Related

- 2.3—Test a constructor

14.6 Test a template method's implementation

Problem

You want to test a template method, but you cannot instantiate the class that defines the method, because the class is `abstract`.

Background

We generally create template methods from classes in an existing class hierarchy. We extract them when we notice that each subclass implements a method to perform the same minitasks (or "primitive operations") in the same order, even though each subclass might implement some of those primitive operations differently. First, we extract each primitive operation into an appropriately named method [Refactoring, 110]. Next, we pull the larger method up into the superclass [Refactoring, 322], along with any operations that all the subclasses implement the same way. Next, we create abstract methods for the operations that each subclass implements differently, pulling them up into the superclass. The result is a superclass with some abstract methods, declaring abstract operations. We want to test that the template method works, no matter how any subclass decides to implement these abstract operations. We could simply test all the existing subclasses, but that duplicates testing effort, overestimates our testing progress,[16] and misses the point: we want to test *all possible subclasses* no matter how they implement the abstract operations.

[16] If you have 10 subclasses, then you will test the template method 10 times, even though each test verifies the same thing. Verifying it 10 times does not make it more correct!

◆ Recipe

There are two aspects of a template method to test: behavior and structure. We will describe testing the behavior later in this recipe, but first we will test the structure by verifying that it invokes the expected primitive operations in the expected order. To invoke a template method we need concrete implementations of the abstract operations, which means that we have to create a particular implementation of our abstract class. This appears to contradict our stated goal of testing all possible subclasses, which makes it seem like we cannot do what we have set out to do. In spite of this, there is a straightforward solution.

Consider that a template method consists of invoking a desired set of methods in a desired order. In order to verify this, we need to record the method invocations in order, which we can do with a simple Spy object. The general strategy is to override all the primitive operations to say "I was invoked," and to collect the order in which the operations report that they were invoked into a `List`. You can then verify the `List` of method invocations. This technique is similar to the one Kent Beck calls "Log String."[17] To illustrate the technique, let us verify part of JUnit's own behavior: the way it runs a test.

Recall that JUnit first invokes `setUp()`, and then your test method, and then `tearDown()`. In particular, this is the method that runs your test, from the class `junit.framework.TestCase`:

```
public void runBare() throws Throwable {
    setUp();
    try {
        runTest();
    }
    finally {
        tearDown();
    }
}
```

We want to verify that JUnit does indeed invoke these methods in the correct order. We will implement a `SpyTestCase` which collects the method names `runBare`, `setUp`, `runTest`, and `tearDown` in the order in which they are invoked. Our test will verify the order of those methods. First, here is the test:

```
public class TestCaseTest extends TestCase {
    public void testRunBareTemplate() throws Throwable {
        SpyTestCase spyTestCase = new SpyTestCase();
        spyTestCase.runBare();
```

[17] Kent Beck, *Test-Driven Development: By Example* (Addison-Wesley, 2002), p. 146.

```
        List expectedMethodNames = new ArrayList() {
            {
                add("setUp");
                add("runTest");
                add("tearDown");
            }
        };

        assertEquals(
            expectedMethodNames,
            spyTestCase.getInvokedMethodNames());
    }
}
```

Next, here is our SpyTestCase, which overrides the methods of interest and records the name of each method as it is invoked:

```
public class SpyTestCase extends TestCase {
    private List invokedMethodNames = new ArrayList();

    protected void runTest() throws Throwable {
        invokedMethodNames.add("runTest");
    }

    protected void setUp() throws Exception {
        invokedMethodNames.add("setUp");
    }

    protected void tearDown() throws Exception {
        invokedMethodNames.add("tearDown");
    }

    public List getInvokedMethodNames() {
        return invokedMethodNames;
    }
}
```

We override each primitive operation method and have it just add its name to the list of invoked methods. We also add a method to provide access to the list of invoked method names so that the test can compare that to its expectations. Our SpyTestCase is a "spy" in that it records information about what happened (the order in which the primitive operations were invoked) and provides that "intelligence" to the test. This is the essence of the Spy testing pattern, a mock object-related technique. We provide a survey of mock objects in essay B.4, "The mock objects landscape." You can use this test as a template (yes, we intended the pun) for testing your own template methods.

We started this recipe by describing two types of template method tests: behavioral and structural. The Spy technique helps you test the structure of a template method, but you still need to verify that, in general, the template method does what it should. You can use the techniques in recipe 2.6, "Test an interface," to write tests for the general behavior you expect from your template method. Returning to our example, we could verify that invoking `TestCase.runBare()` causes a test to be executed, throwing an `AssertionFailedError` in the event of a failure.[18] To illustrate the difference, here is one of those tests. This test only verifies that `runBare()` reports a failure by throwing an `AssertionFailedError`, and does not concern itself with the order in which the other methods are invoked, such as `setUp()` or `tearDown()`.

```
public void testRunBareExecutesAFailingTest() throws Throwable {
    TestCase testCase = new TestCase() {
        protected void runTest() throws Throwable {
            fail("Intentional failure");
        }
    };

    try {
        testCase.runBare();
        fail("Test should have failed!");
    }
    catch (AssertionFailedError expected) {
        assertEquals("Intentional failure", expected.getMessage());
    }
}
```

We recommend that you separate the behavioral and structural tests, as combining the two can be confusing for particularly complex template methods. As with any of our other recommendations, feel free to try both and measure the results for yourself.

◆ *Discussion*

It is generally a good idea to test how your template method reacts when one of the primitive operations fails. Because the template method has no control over how a subclass implements a primitive operation, you should assume that the primitive operations can fail. The general strategy for writing this kind of test involves overriding your Spy and having it simulate the desired failure in the appropriate primitive operation. The result is a combination of the Spy technique and the Crash Test Dummy technique. (See essay B.4, "The mock objects landscape" for more on these mock object techniques.) Returning to JUnit, we want to verify that `runBare()` invokes `tearDown()` even when the test fails. To simulate test

---

[18] We searched through JUnit to see which methods invoke `runBare()` and the only one is `TestCase.runProtected()`. We used this method to decide how `runBare()` should behave.

failure, we can simply override `SpyTestCase.runTest()` and have it invoke `fail()`! Listing 14.9 shows the resulting test. We have highlighted in bold print the key differences between this test and the previous one.

Listing 14.9 TestCaseTest

```
public void testRunBareInvokesTearDownOnTestFailure()
    throws Throwable {

    SpyTestCase spyTestCase = new SpyTestCase() {
        protected void runTest() throws Throwable {
            super.runTest();
            fail("I failed on purpose");
        }
    };

    try {
        spyTestCase.runBare();
    }
    catch (AssertionFailedError expected) {
        assertEquals("I failed on purpose", expected.getMessage());
    }

    List expectedMethodNames = new ArrayList() {
        {
            add("setUp");
            add("runTest");
            add("tearDown");
        }
    };

    assertEquals(
        expectedMethodNames,
        spyTestCase.getInvokedMethodNames());
}
```

First, we override `SpyTestCase.runTest()` and have it do two things: invoke `super.runTest()` to record that the method was invoked, and then invoke `fail()` to simulate a generic test failure. Next, we catch the expected `AssertionFailedError` when we invoke `runBare()`; otherwise, that failure will propagate up the call chain and make it look like our `TestCase` test failed. When we catch `AssertionFailedError`, we check its message so that we can be sure that it is the failure we expect, and not some other failure occurring in the process of executing our test. Otherwise, our expected result is the same: we expect `runBare()` to invoke `setUp()`, `runTest()`, and then `tearDown()`. We execute the test and indeed, it passes. If you write a third test and have `setUp()` throw an exception, you will see that JUnit does *not* invoke `tearDown()` in that case. While that piece of information is not germane to this recipe, it is useful to know. As you can see, testing how a template method handles the failure of one of its primitive operations is just like testing the more general "what happens when this method throws an exception," which we described in recipe 2.8, "Test throwing the right exception."

Finally, we could have made our above test stricter by implementing more of our `SpyTestCase`. We can actually change the production implementation of `runBare()` by having it invoke another method (say, `setName("blah blah blah")`, which could be harmful), and our test would be none the wiser. This is a case where we should consider testing not only that the template method does what we expect, but that it also does not do what we do not expect. We could simply override all the methods in `TestCase` *except* `runBare()` to add their name to `invokedMethodNames`. This "more nosy" version of `SpyTestCase` would detect `runBare()` invoking methods that it should not be invoking. The problem is that whenever we add a method to `TestCase`, we would have to override it accordingly in `SpyTestCase` to avoid an "incomplete intelligence report." This makes our test quite brittle, and we are skeptical of anything that gets in the way of refactoring. There is an aspect-oriented solution to this problem: intercept every `TestCase` method invocation and record the name of each method in `invokedMethodNames`. This solution does not depend on knowledge of the specific methods that `TestCase` declares, so it is not susceptible to change the way the hand-coded `SpyTestCase` is. We present a complete solution in solution A.6, "Aspect-based universal Spy."

◆ Related

- 2.3—Test a constructor
- 2.6—Test an interface
- 2.8—Test throwing the right exception
- A.6—Aspect-based Universal Spy

15 GSBase

This chapter covers

- Testing event sources with EventCatcher
- Testing object serialization and cloning
- Testing legacy objects for equality

GSBase (http://gsbase.sourceforge.net) is an open source project maintained by Mike Bowler. Mike is also the lead programmer for HtmlUnit, which we highlighted in chapter 13, "Testing J2EE Applications." Mike decided to take his toolkit of useful Java classes—ones he had developed for his own use and found handy—and create a public project around it, so GSBase contains some general-purpose classes that you might be able to use in your own projects. In this toolkit are a few utilities to make testing with JUnit easier. Mike is a long-time JUnit user and a proponent of Test-Driven Development.

An experienced Java programmer, Mike has been writing Swing applications since, as he puts it, "before Swing 1.0." As a result, GSBase contains some utilities for Swing programming, among which is `EventCatcher`, a way to verify Swing UI events. If you write Swing applications—and they are making a comeback as we write these words—then you can use `EventCatcher` to verify that your event listener receives the events you *think* it ought to receive. We include a recipe on using `EventCatcher` in this chapter.

Mike has also given several presentations to Java user groups and at conferences on object serialization. In addition to his in-depth knowledge of the topic, he has built a universal serializability test, which helps you verify that you have properly identified your serializable objects as such. We include a recipe for using GSBase's `SerializabilityTest`. This is especially important for J2EE applications, where object serialization plays a key role in providing distributed object services.

GSBase also provides a simple test for the `clone()` method. It is still very common for programmers—in their haste—to forget to make their `clone()` method `public` or to forget to add `Cloneable` to the list of interfaces their class implements. We include a recipe for using `TestUtil.testClone()`, which not only tests your implementation, but optionally verifies whether it is consistent with `equals()`.

Finally, GSBase provides a test utility for JavaBeans: "appears equal." If you have used JavaBeans provided by another programmer or package that do *not* implement the `equals()` method, then you can use "appears equal" on those Java beans in your tests. Although it is not a perfect replacement for `equals()`, it is generally good enough for the vast majority of intended uses, so we include a recipe for using this utility.

There is more to GSBase than we describe here, so we recommend visiting the GSBase site and incorporating this excellent toolkit into your projects. You can also find in table 15.1 the other recipes in this book that use GSBase as part of their solutions.

Table 15.1 Other recipes in this book that feature GSBase

Recipe	GSBase feature
2.1—Test your equals method	`EqualsTester`
2.9—Let collections compare themselves	`BaseTestCase.assertCollectionsEqual()`
4.5—Scan the file system for tests 4.6—Separate the different kinds of test suites	`RecursiveTestSuite, TestFilter`
4.7—Control the order of some of your tests	`OrderedTestSuite`

15.1 Verify events with EventCatcher

◆ Problem

You want a simple way to verify the events that an Observable generates.

◆ Background

Verifying that an Observable generates the expected events is not a difficult task, but when programming Swing applications in particular, event sources are *everywhere.* It is easy to fall into the trap of duplicating test code throughout your application, when instead you ought to create a single object that knows how to listen for events and verify them against the events you expect to receive. In short: you *could* write your own Spy listener, but why not leverage good work already done by others?

◆ Recipe

GSBase provides the utility class `EventCatcher` which you can attach to any object. It is a universal event listener that collects every event it "hears" and provides access to those events as a `List`. Your typical test scenario will be the following, using a GUI widget as an example:

1. Create the GUI widget whose behavior you want to verify.
2. Create an `EventCatcher` and tell it to listen to the GUI widget.
3. Make the widget do something interesting.
4. Iterate over the list of events caught by the `EventCatcher` and verify each one—or even just the ones of interest.

Of course, the GUI widget could really be *any* event source, but because Mike originally wrote `EventCatcher` to use on Swing applications, it was written specifically with that context in mind.

Listing 15.1 shows an example of using `EventCatcher` to verify receiving the `HierarchyEvent` that a Swing component produces when the component hierarchy changes—that is, when one component is added to the content pane of another. To test more complex scenarios, you only need to make more assertions about the events which you expect your Swing components to generate.

Listing 15.1 Using `EventCatcher` on a Swing component

```
package junit.cookbook.gsbase.test;

import java.awt.event.HierarchyEvent;

import javax.swing.JFrame;
import javax.swing.JOptionPane;

import junit.framework.TestCase;

import com.gargoylesoftware.base.testing.EventCatcher;

public class ConfirmationDialogTest extends TestCase {

    public void testEvents() throws Exception {
        JOptionPane optionPane =
            new JOptionPane(
                "Are you sure?!",
                JOptionPane.QUESTION_MESSAGE,
                JOptionPane.YES_NO_CANCEL_OPTION);

        EventCatcher eventCatcher = new EventCatcher();
        eventCatcher.listenTo(optionPane);

        JFrame mainFrame = new JFrame("The Main Frame");
        mainFrame.getContentPane().add(optionPane);          ❶

        assertEquals(1, eventCatcher.getEventCount());
        Object eventAsObject = eventCatcher.getEventAt(0);
        assertTrue(eventAsObject instanceof HierarchyEvent);   ❷
    }
}
```

❶ *Generates a `HierarchyEvent`*—Adding a Swing component to another component generates a `HierarchyEvent`, indicating that the hierarchy of components has changed.

❷ *Cannot try `assertEquals()`*—Most Swing events do not implement `equals()` the way a Value Object should, so there is little point in trying to compare an expected `HierarchyEvent` with the one that Swing generated.

◆ Discussion

Although Mike Bowler originally built EventCatcher to help him test Swing components, it is useful to help with any event listener design. The EventCatcher is a universal event listener, relying on time-honored naming conventions to discover the events an object might generate at runtime. This means that as long as your event source adheres to the usual Java naming conventions for the event listener implementation pattern, you can use EventCatcher to help verify the behavior of any event source.

When you invoke EventCatcher.listenTo(), the event catcher scans the methods on the event source you specify, looking for the types of events it might generate. Specifically, the EventCatcher searches for methods whose names start with add and end with Listener, and which take exactly one argument, assuming that such a method signals a type of event the object might generate. The EventCatcher then invokes addEventListener() for each Event, registering itself with the event source as an EventListener.[1]

When the event source generates an event, it notifies its listeners by invoking a method on them. The EventCatcher's dynamic invocation handler intercepts this method invocation and remembers the event so that you can ask for it later. How does EventCatcher know that these method invocations are event notifications? Once again, conventions to the rescue. An event notification is typically implemented as a method invocation with one parameter: the event; therefore, EventCatcher assumes that the first parameter to any method invocation is an EventObject. Also, because it is uncommon to invoke any method on an event listener *other than* the event notification method, it is quite safe to assume that any method invocation is an event notification.

NOTE *Sometimes it's not an event notification*—By default, EventCatcher handles equals() and hashCode() differently, as you might have other tests that invoke those methods. Any other method invocation is assumed to be an event notification. If this fails for you, then subclass EventCatcher and augment the dynamic invocation handler to handle any other special cases you might have. As of press time, the method getListener() returns a listener for a given event type. Override that method to substitute your specialized invocation handler for the one that EventCatcher creates by default.

Finally, we noted above that most event objects do not implement equals() in a manner consistent with a Value Object. That means that we are typically unable to

---

[1] Here, Event is any subclass of java.util.EventObject, such as AWTEvent or PropertyChangedEvent.

compare an expected event object with the actual event object using the `equals()` method. `EventCatcher` provides the next best thing. The method `assertEvents-AppearEquals()` accepts a `List` of expected event objects and compares them with the `EventCatcher`'s internal `List` using a simple, clever algorithm. Two event objects "appear" to be equal if they come from the same class and if their corresponding JavaBean properties have the same values. For a more thorough discussion of the notion of "appears equal," see recipe 15.4.

Certainly, the `EventCatcher` provides a wealth of features for testing components that use the event/listener design, something rampant in the Swing UI framework.

◆ Related

- 15.4—Compare JavaBeans using "appears equal"

15.2 Test serialization

◆ Problem

You want to test that your serializable classes implement the feature correctly without writing custom test code for each class.

◆ Background

Especially when working in J2EE it is important to implement serialization correctly. It is one of the cornerstones of remote method invocation (RMI), and therefore of J2EE. One of the difficulties in implementing this feature correctly and completely is that the compiler helps you very little and the rules for serialization are not straightforward. Serialization is not as well understood by the general Java programming population as it should be, given its importance in J2EE programming. Any help you can get in implementing serialization correctly should be welcome.

◆ Recipe

GSBase provides the utility method `TestUtil.testSerialization()` to execute a simple yet effective serialization test. Writing a serialization test is simple, as listing 15.2 shows.

Listing 15.2 Testing serialization

```
package junit.cookbook.gsbase.test;

import com.gargoylesoftware.base.testing.TestUtil;

import junit.cookbook.util.Money;
```

```
import junit.framework.TestCase;

public class SerializabilityTest extends TestCase {
    public void testSerializable() throws Exception {
        Money money = Money.dollars(1000);
        TestUtil.testSerialization(money, true);
    }
}
```

The first parameter to `testSerialization()` is the object to serialize. `TestUtil` serializes and then deserializes the object, and if that proceeds without throwing an exception, the test passes. The second parameter is a `boolean` flag indicating whether to compare the deserialized object with the original for equality. The test passes if the object is successfully serialized and then deserialized, and the deserialized object is equal to the original object according to `equals()`. This is useful for testing the serialization of Value Objects, such as `Money`.

◆ *Discussion*

One aspect of serialization that this utility does not cover is the "serial version UID." This is a number that identifies different versions of a serializable class. This is important for objects serialized to disk, as it is necessary to know whether the object on disk can be deserialized using the current (and presumably newer) version of the class. If the class has changed in a backward-compatible way, then it might keep its serial version UID; and if it has changed in an incompatible way, then it should change its serial version UID to avoid attempting a deserialization operation that is doomed to fail.[2] There is no way to test this in a generic manner, so GSBase has not attempted to provide a generic solution for this problem.

Worse, the only way to test serial versioning effectively is to serialize objects to disk using different versions of a class, change the class, and then attempt deserializing that object using the newer version of the class. Although you can use the Gold Master technique to do this, you can only verify whether the most recent version of your serializable class has correctly decided whether to change its serial version UID. Going back to older versions of the class requires reverting source code to previous revisions, which is an entirely manual process.

◆ *Related*

- 15.3—Test object cloning

[2] Serialization can be a dicey subject and is worthy of its own complete tutorial. You can find Sun's own tutorial at http://java.sun.com/docs/books/tutorial/essential/io/providing.html.

15.3 Test object cloning

◆ Problem

You want to verify that your class implements `clone()` correctly without writing custom test code each time you need it.

◆ Background

The most common mistake in implementing `clone()` is to do so in a way that is inconsistent with `equals()`.[3] Typically, when you `clone()` an object you want the clone to be indistinguishable from the original, and yet a different object in memory, often to avoid the aliasing problem with mutable objects. In most cases, your implementation of `equals()` defines objects that are interchangeable—indeed, that is the point of the `equals()` method. It would be nice to verify that you have implemented `clone()` consistently with `equals()` without having to implement the same tedious test over and over again.

◆ Recipe

GSBase provides the method `TestUtil.testClone()` which verifies your implementation of `clone()`. The parameters to `testClone()` are the object to clone and a `boolean` flag indicating whether to compare the cloned object to the original using `equals()`. The following is an example of using `testClone()`.

```
public void testCloneMoney() throws Exception {
    Money moneyToClone = Money.dollars(1000);
    TestUtil.testClone(moneyToClone, true);
}
```

This test passes if `Money` provides a visible `clone()` method *and* the resulting cloned `Money` object is equal to the original according to `equals()`. For any class that needs to be `Cloneable`, you want to write a test like this one.

NOTE *Cloneable considered harmful*—Sometimes language designers get it wrong, and the Java mechanism for cloning is an instance of this. We refer you to Joshua Bloch's book *Effective Java*, chapter 3, for discussions on the various methods of the class `Object` that we are expected to override in our subclasses.[4] To summarize, `clone()` is not worth the effort; use copy

---

[3] That and forgetting to implement the `Cloneable` interface and make `clone()` a `public` method.

[4] http://java.sun.com/developer/Books/effectivejava/Chapter3.pdf. See item 10: Override `clone()` judiciously. The book was published by Addison-Wesley in 2001.

constructors or creation methods based on the Prototype pattern instead. The Java way of implementing object cloning is strange, confusing, and prone to error. The only reason you should bother with `clone()` is because you *have* to, such as the framework you are using relies heavily on `clone()` and you cannot get away from it.

◆ *Discussion*

Now we will demonstrate how you would develop a `clone()` implementation test-first using `testClone()`. We continue with our `Money` class, which already has a correct implementation of `equals()`, and allows us to check for equality after cloning. Let us start with the test we wrote in the Recipe section and a `Money` object that does not implement `clone()` at all. When we execute the test, the result is a failure: `Object is not cloneable`. This indicates that `Money` does not implement the `Cloneable` interface.

We change `Money` to implement this interface, execute the test again, and this time the result is a different failure: `Object does not have a public clone() method`. We declare this method on `Money` as follows, with a simple implementation that will appease the compiler.[5]

```
public class Money implements Cloneable {
    // remaining code omitted

    public Object clone() {
        return new Object();
    }
}
```

We execute the test once more and the result is another, different failure: `Objects are different: original=[$1,000.00] copy=[java.lang.Object@10ef90c]`. At this point we need to change our implementation of `clone()` to return a `Money` object representing the expected amount of money. The final implementation follows.

```
public Object clone() {
    return new Money(cents);
}
```

We execute the test one last time and verify that it passes. Let us summarize the conditions that `testClone()` verifies:

- Your class implements the interface `java.lang.Cloneable`.

[5] Many test-drivers use the default implementation `return null;` in this situation. We prefer to return a valid object to avoid `NullPointerExceptions`, which only leads to confusion.

- Your class provides a public `clone()` method—the default implementation is protected!
- (Optional) Your class implements `clone()` in a manner consistent with `equals()`—only if you invoke `testClone()` with the check equality parameter set to `true`.

This is the complete contract of `Object.clone()`, as described in the Javadoc for class `java.lang.Object`. (Well, the Javadoc is a bit lax on this issue, but we interpret the general intent as a contract, just to be safe.)

◆ Related

- 15.2—Test serialization

15.4 Compare JavaBeans using "appears equal"

◆ Problem

You want like to use `assertEquals()` to compare two JavaBeans to one another, but the JavaBean class does not implement `equals()` in a manner consistent with a Value Object.

◆ Background

In spite of repeated suggestions to do so, many programmers do not implement `equals()` correctly for their Value Objects. This is bad news for JUnit practitioners, as so many of their tests use `assertEquals()` to verify the result of a given behavior. If you are adding tests to legacy code or third-party code that you cannot change, you might have no direct way to use `assertEquals()` on objects that, by all rights, are Value Objects. JavaBeans typically fall into this category.

If you are not able to use `assertEquals()` then you are forced to compare your expected values and the actual values on a property-by-property basis, making tests longer than they need to be. There must be a better way.

◆ Recipe

GSBase allows you to determine whether two Java objects appear to be equal. Although not a perfect equality test, this facility makes it possible to at least approximate the equality of JavaBeans by automating the property-by-property comparison you would otherwise need to code by hand. You can find this feature in the class `com.gargoylesoftware.base.testing.TestUtil` with the methods `appearsEqual()`, `assertAppearsEqual()`, and `assertAppearsNotEqual()`.

The first method, `appearsEqual()`, takes two `Objects` and compares them for apparent equality, returning `true` when they appear to be equal and `false` otherwise. The assertion methods simply wrap `appearsEqual()` in the appropriate manner, asserting either that the two objects appear equal or do not.

Listing 15.3 shows an example of using "appears equal" along with the `EventCatcher` (see recipe 15.1). As a convenience, `EventCatcher` provides the method `assertEventsAppearEquals()` so that you do not need to ask for the actual events and make the comparison yourself.

Listing 15.3 Verifying events with "appears equal"

```
package junit.cookbook.gsbase.test;

import java.awt.Container;
import java.awt.event.HierarchyEvent;
import java.util.Arrays;
import java.util.List;
import javax.swing.JFrame;
import javax.swing.JOptionPane;
import junit.framework.TestCase;
import com.gargoylesoftware.base.testing.EventCatcher;

public class ConfirmationDialogTest extends TestCase {

    public void testEvents() throws Exception {
        JOptionPane optionPane =
            new JOptionPane(
                "Are you sure?!",
                JOptionPane.QUESTION_MESSAGE,
                JOptionPane.YES_NO_CANCEL_OPTION);

        EventCatcher eventCatcher = new EventCatcher();
        eventCatcher.listenTo(optionPane);

        JFrame mainFrame = new JFrame("The Main Frame");
        Container mainContentPane =
            mainFrame.getContentPane();
        mainContentPane.add(optionPane);

        HierarchyEvent expectedHierarchyEvent =
            new HierarchyEvent(
                optionPane,
                HierarchyEvent.HIERARCHY_CHANGED,
                optionPane,
                mainContentPane,
                HierarchyEvent.PARENT_CHANGED);

        List expectedEvents =
            Arrays.asList(
                new Object[] { expectedHierarchyEvent });
```

The event we expect

```
        eventCatcher.assertEventsAppearEquals(
            expectedEvents);
    }
}
```

Did we catch the expected events?

◆ *Discussion*

Although it is a handy construct, do not mistake "appears equal" for actual equality. The "appears equal" algorithm is simple and reasonable, but even the relatively benign use of `public` fields can make a liar of it. The algorithm works as follows. Each object is inspected for any readable properties by scanning for methods that take no parameters. The method `appearsEqual()` invokes each of these methods on the two objects to compare them, and it fails if they return different values. As usual with JUnit, if no assertion fails, then `appearsEqual()` declares that the two objects appear to be equal. For any reasonably coded JavaBean, this algorithm works very nicely, but if your objects contain `public` fields, rather than conform to the JavaBean specification, then "appears equal" simply will not work at all for those objects.

NOTE *An important detail about "appears equal"*—The *idea* behind "appears equal" is to find all the methods that could reasonably be property accessors, invoke them on each of the two objects in question, and then compare the return values for equality. As implemented in GSBase 2.0, `appearsEqual()` invokes all no-parameter methods, rather than just ones that follow the JavaBean property-naming conventions of `getX()` or `isX()` for readable properties. This means that `appearsEqual()` invoke such methods as `init()` and `clear()`, which would cause problems for certain objects, creating unintended side effects.

All we can say on the matter is that `appearsEqual()` is intended to be invoked with eventlike objects, which tend to be immutable bags of data, having little or no behavior. Mike designed and built this method to use on GUI events along with `EventCatcher`, so if you need to apply the idea to other objects, and `appearsEqual()` is invoking the wrong methods on those objects, then use `appearsEqual()` as a model to build your own version, and then submit it to GSBase as a patch. Mike will consider it.

It is possible, we suppose, for JavaBeans to appear equal through their `public`, readable properties, and yet have additional fields whose values differ.[6] In this case, it is up to you to decide the correct semantics: because the outside world

[6] Perhaps this is largely a theoretical concern. Real-life examples are welcome, but we expect they are rare.

cannot tell the difference between the two objects—at least from a value perspective—perhaps they ought to be treated as apparently equal. Perhaps not. That is a judgment call that you need to make, and often you will take one of two stances. You might be conservative and not consider the two objects apparently equal until you are certain that it is the case, or you might instead plunge ahead, assume that they are apparently equal, and not worry about that assumption until it is proven false. Without considering this issue in context—in other words, without having to write a specific test—we cannot know what the answer is. The approach you take depends on the goals of the test.

◆ *Related*

- 15.1—Verify GUI events with EventCatcher

16 JUnit-addons

This chapter covers

- Testing Comparable classes
- Collecting tests from within archives
- Organizing test data and sharing test resources
- Ensuring that shared test fixtures clean themselves up
- Reporting the name of each test as it executes

Vladimir Bossicard is a long-time member of the JUnit community, and one of its most vocal members as well. Perhaps the one trait that identifies him most easily within the community is his insistence that we not content ourselves with whatever feature set JUnit provides. If JUnit does not do something you need, then Vladimir simply tells you to build it yourself, and then share it with the world through open source. It is in this spirit that he has led the evolution of JUnit-addons: a collection of helper classes for JUnit. Visit the JUnit-addons site at http://junit-addons.sourceforge.net. In this chapter we describe some problems that JUnit-addons solves.

In the first chapter of recipes we described how to test your implementation of the `equals()` method. Related to the concept of object equality is object *order*, which defines less-than and greater-than relationships on your objects. If you have classes that implement the `Comparable` interface, then you will want to use `ComparabilityTestCase` to verify your implementation of the `compareTo()` method. This test case class provides a simple, standard set of tests for `compareTo()` so you can avoid writing them for yourself—and possibly forgetting some part of the `Comparable.compareTo()` contract.

In chapter 3, "Organizing and Building JUnit Tests," we describe various ways to automatically collect test case classes into a large test suite. These techniques have generally assumed that your tests are sitting on the file system, either as loose class files or as Java source files. JUnit-addons provides a number of `SuiteBuilder` classes, including an implementation that collects tests from Java archives and *.zip files. This chapter includes a recipe describing how to collect tests from within a *.jar file.

In chapter 5, "Working with Test Data," we describe how to manage test data with properties files. If you would like to use this technique without duplicating (yet again) the code to integrate the properties files into your tests, this chapter contains a recipe for managing your properties file-based test data with `PropertyManager`. If you need to go beyond properties files to manage shared test resources, we describe how to use the `ResourceManager` to tame the proliferation of global access to test resources, such as a database. If you use shared test resources, then you might have problems with those resources correctly cleaning up after themselves. JUnit has a minor flaw in its implementation of `TestSetup` (see recipe 5.10, "Set up your fixture once for the entire suite") that JUnit-addons corrects with its version of this class. In this chapter we describe how to *ensure* that your shared test fixture cleans itself up, even when its test suite ends badly.

Finally, going beyond merely augmenting JUnit, Vladimir has built his own JUnit test runner. Among its additional features is an open test listener architecture that allows you to monitor test execution and generate customized test reports. To help you get started, we describe another technique for displaying the name of each test as it executes, using JUnit-addons Test Runner. You can adapt this technique to write test results in any format you need: XML, comma-delimited text, even to a database table for sophisticated report generation. Never one to accept things the way they are, Vladimir has provided a rich library of JUnit utilities with his JUnit-addons that make any JUnit practitioner's job easier.

16.1 Test your class for compareTo()

◆ Problem

You want to verify your implementation of the `Comparable` interface without writing custom tests for each `Comparable` class you have.

◆ Background

Any class that you store in a sorted collection (`SortedSet`, `SortedList`, the keys in a `SortedMap`) needs to implement `java.lang.Comparable`; otherwise, the collection cannot know how to keep the objects in sorted order. The behavior of `Comparable.compareTo()` can be checked with a "universal `compareTo()` test," much the way we have described testing your implementation of `equals()` in recipe 2.1, "Test your equals method." Because a domain model might have dozens of `Comparable` classes, it would be nice to have one way of ensuring that they all implement `Comparable` correctly.

◆ Recipe

JUnit-addons provides `junitx.extensions.ComparabilityTestCase` to provide the framework for testing your `Comparable` classes. It defines the tests your class needs to pass and you provide the test data through an Abstract Test Case design (see recipe 2.6, "Test an interface" for a discussion of the Abstract Test Case pattern). Listing 16.1 shows the "abstract" part of this universal comparability test.

Listing 16.1 `ComparabilityTestCase` (abstract methods)

```
public abstract class ComparabilityTestCase
    extends TestCase {

    protected abstract Comparable createLessInstance()
        throws Exception;

    protected abstract Comparable createEqualInstance()
        throws Exception;
```

```
    protected abstract Comparable createGreaterInstance()
        throws Exception;
}
```

To use this comparability test, create a subclass of `ComparabilityTestCase` and then implement the required methods to return objects that you expect to be ordered as follows: `lessInstance`, which is less than `equalInstance`, which is less than `greaterInstance`.

Each invocation of these methods must return a new object. The Abstract Test Case class provides all the tests: it verifies that the class under test respects the contract of `Comparable`. Listing 16.2 shows one of the tests it provides.

Listing 16.2 A test from `ComparabilityTestCase`

```
public abstract class ComparabilityTestCase
        extends TestCase {

    public final void testReturnValues() {
        ComparableAssert.assertLesser(equal1, less);
        ComparableAssert.assertLesser(equal2, less);
        ComparableAssert.assertGreater(less, greater);
        ComparableAssert.assertEquals(equal1, equal2);
        ComparableAssert.assertGreater(equal1, greater);
        ComparableAssert.assertGreater(equal2, greater);
    }
}
```

Perhaps these assertions are a little confusing. They were to us, at first. Note that in each one, the *expected* (or *limit*) value is the first parameter and the *actual* value is the second. To read these assertions we have to work backwards, in a sense. For example, read the first assertion as "`less` (the actual value) should be less than `equal1` (the limit value)," even though this goes against the common-sense convention of reading parameters from left to right. Vladimir is simply using the same coding convention as JUnit's `assertEquals()`, where the value we are comparing is on the right, but the expected (or limit) value against which to compare is on the left.

This test checks various pairs of objects for the appropriate lesser than, equal to, or greater than relationship. Notice that it does not verify whether `compareTo()` is consistent with `equals()`. It is common for the two methods to be consistent, but it is not strictly necessary. To be consistent, `compareTo()` would have to return `0` when comparing objects that are equal according to `equals()`. If you need to verify this additional constraint, then continue to the Discussion section of this recipe. Listing 16.3 contains a sample comparability test, verifying `String` comparisons. Notice that the "create" methods return a new `String` each time, as the `ComparabilityTestCase` documentation indicates is needed.

Listing 16.3 Comparability test for class `String`

```
package junit.cookbook.addons.test;

import junitx.extensions.ComparabilityTestCase;

public class StringCompareToTest extends ComparabilityTestCase {
    public StringCompareToTest(String name) {
        super(name);
    }

    protected Comparable createLessInstance() throws Exception {
        return new String("abc");
    }

    protected Comparable createEqualInstance() throws Exception {
        return new String("abcd");
    }

    protected Comparable createGreaterInstance() throws Exception {
        return new String("abcde");
    }
}
```

◆ *Discussion*

`ComparabilityTestCase` uses custom assertion methods from `ComparableAssert`, also part of JUnit-addons (see recipe 17.4, "Extract a custom assertion"). These custom assertion methods provide a uniform, informative failure message that looks quite a bit like the failure message for JUnit's own `assertEquals()`.

If you need to further verify that `compareTo()` is consistent with `equals()`, you need to add another test.

```
public void testConsistentWithEquals() throws Exception {
    assertEquals(
        "compareTo() is inconsistent with equals",
        0,
        createEqualInstance().compareTo(createEqualInstance()));
}
```

Perhaps by the time you read this, someone will have submitted this as a patch to JUnit-addons.

◆ ***Related***

- 2.1—Test your equals method
- 2.6—Test an interface
- 17.4—Extract a custom assertion

16.2 Collect tests automatically from an archive

◆ ***Problem***

You want to deploy your tests in a *.jar file, and then execute them without unpacking them.

◆ ***Background***

It is becoming increasingly common to ship the tests along with the production code when releasing an application. You want to do this, too, but are having trouble automatically collecting all the tests in a *.jar file. GSBase's `RecursiveTestSuite` scans a file system directory tree for Java source files. JUnit-addons `DirectorySuiteBuilder` scans a file system direction tree for Java class files. What about classes packaged in a *.jar file? JUnit-addons provides a way to collect those tests too.

◆ ***Recipe***

JUnit-addons provides the class `junitx.util.ArchiveSuiteBuilder` to collect tests from a *.jar file. All you do is instantiate one and tell it to browse either a `ZipFile` object or the filename of a *.jar or *.zip file. We packaged up the JUnit tests in junit-test.zip and put them somewhere on our file system to illustrate how to use it.[1] Listing 16.4 shows our `AllTests` class.

Listing 16.4 Collecting the tests in a JAR file

```
package junit.cookbook.addons.test;

import junit.framework.Test;
import junitx.util.ArchiveSuiteBuilder;

public class AllJUnitTestsInJar {
    public static Test suite() throws Exception {
```

[1] To try this yourself, create a *.zip file from the junit folder inside the JUnit distribution. It contains both the samples and JUnit's own tests.

```
        return new ArchiveSuiteBuilder().suite(
            "d:/junit3.8.1/junit-tests.jar");
    }
}
```

◆ **Discussion**

Of course, do not forget to place the *.jar file in your class path (along with all its dependencies) when you execute `AllTests`! If you do not, then you will see `ClassNotFoundExceptions` on the test case classes you are trying to execute. That is really all there is to it.

You could add this to your suite of Deployment Tests so that when the application is deployed in the target environment, the deployment script tests your application in that environment. You can package the tests as a *.jar file to avoid littering your deployment package with hundreds of extra Java class files. All it takes is an extra `<jar>` task in your Ant buildfile to package the tests in a *.jar and include them in your main deployment package. No one would be able to complain that shipping the tests is too intrusive or unnecessarily complicates deployment. There are no excuses not to execute the tests.

◆ **Related**

- Chapter 4—Managing Test Suites

16.3 Organize test data using PropertyManager

◆ **Problem**

You have a growing collection of system properties that you are using to pass data into your tests. You are looking for a good way to manage these properties as your tests evolve.

◆ **Background**

In recipe 5.4, "Using a properties file" we described how and why to use a properties file to store test data. If your test data consists of simple key-value pairs, then the properties file is an excellent choice to store this data. Using properties, however, leads to duplicating the code to retrieve those properties: creating the `Properties` object, loading from a file, specifying the file name, specifying the root directory for all the files in your test suite, and on and on. It would be nice to write this code *once*—or even better, to use something already written to manage all this from a central location.

◆ Recipe

Use JUnit-addons `PropertyManager` to manage your properties file-based test data. It is very simple to use: specify the properties filename as a system property, and then invoke class-level methods on the `PropertyManager` class to retrieve your data. To specify your properties filename, set the `propertyManager.file` system property.

```
java -DpropertyManager.file=/home/jbrains/projects/props.properties
⇒  junit.textui.TestRunner AllTests
```

Now you can retrieve your test data by invoking the method `PropertyManager.getProperty()`. The `PropertyManager` utility eliminates the need to code the support for reading a properties file yourself. Stand on the shoulders of giants![2]

◆ Discussion

One disadvantage to `PropertyManager` is that it manages one properties file at a time. If you need to manage multiple properties files, then you need to switch to JUnitPP (see recipe 5.9, "Using JUnitPP"), manage those properties files yourself, or consolidate them in order to use `PropertyManager`. Fortunately one can always consolidate many properties files into one: create a "namespace" for each file's properties, and then change each property in the file from `xyz` to `thisFileNamespace.xyz`. As long as the prefix `thisFileNamespace` is different for each file, you can safely consolidate the properties files into one large one. This might make maintaining the data easier, or it might make that task more confusing, depending on the amount and nature of the data. Try both and measure the results. A sufficiently powerful text editor, such as emacs or jEdit can make it easy to perform the necessary search-and-replace operations to switch back between the two approaches.

◆ Related

- 5.4—Using a properties file
- 5.9—Using JUnitPP

---

[2] Although this phrase is generally attributed to Sir Isaac Newton, apparently it goes back to the twelfth century. It is amazing the trivia you can find on the Web. (www.warble.com/jherbert/giants.html)

16.4 Manage shared test resources

◆ Problem

You want a simple way to manage a resource that all your tests share—such as a database— without duplicating custom lookup code throughout your tests.

◆ Background

Duplication is the root of all evil in programming. Expensive, external resources make Object Testing difficult. Put the two together...well, we would rather not put the two together. Duplicating expensive, complex code is about as bad as it gets in object-oriented design, and it is entirely avoidable. If you use a testing resource (a data source, a JNDI directory, or some data files) in multiple test case classes, and if you refactor mercilessly the code that gains access to those resources, then you can end up with a design very similar to the solution we propose in this recipe. If that is true, then you might as well just follow this recipe and cut out the middle man.

◆ Recipe

There is one straightforward solution: use a central Registry [PEAA, 480] of resources. There are essentially two ways to use a Registry: either register a resource the first time you use it or register all the resources you need in one big `TestSetup` that you execute for your entire test suite (see recipe 5.10, "Set up your fixture once for the entire suite"). There are good and bad points with each.

- *Register each resource as you use it*—This makes it easy to start using new resources; however, it can make it more difficult to understand where objects are coming from. If a test dies because of a resource problem, you have to search all the tests to find the test suite that initializes that resource.
- *Register all resources in one TestSetup wrapper*—This solves the key problem with the other approach by keeping all your shared resources in one place; however, you need to wrap *any test suite you execute* in this `ResourceTestSetup`, otherwise the tests fail. This generally requires a customized test execution script and might be incompatible with IDE-based test runners such as the one in Eclipse.

Whichever approach you take, JUnit-addons provides the class `junitx.util.ResourceManager` to help you manage your test sources. The class itself is simple enough: it is a collection of named resources, and you have access to the usual operations: add, remove, get and contains. Any kind of object can be a resource.

Listing 16.5 shows an example of using a `DataSource` as a resource, adapted from recipe 10.10, "Test legacy JDBC code with the database." We opt for the second approach for initializing the `ResourceManager`. We have highlighted our use of the `ResourceManager` in bold print.

Listing 16.5 Using `ResourceManager` to manage a `DataSource`

```
package junit.cookbook.addons.jdbc.live.test;

import java.io.File;
import java.sql.*;
import java.util.Set;
import javax.sql.DataSource;
import junit.cookbook.coffee.data.CatalogStore;
import junit.cookbook.coffee.data.jdbc.CatalogStoreJdbcImpl;
import junit.framework.*;
import junitx.util.ResourceManager;
import org.dbunit.DatabaseTestCase;
import org.dbunit.database.*;
import org.dbunit.dataset.IDataSet;
import org.dbunit.dataset.xml.FlatXmlDataSet;
import com.diasparsoftware.jdbc.JdbcResourceRegistry;

public class FindProductsTest extends DatabaseTestCase {
    private JdbcResourceRegistry jdbcResourceRegistry;

    public FindProductsTest(String name) {
        super(name);
    }

    public static Test suite() {
        return new ResourceManagerTestSetup(
            new TestSuite(FindProductsTest.class));
    }

    protected void setUp() throws Exception {
        System.setProperty("dbunit.qualified.table.names", "true");
        jdbcResourceRegistry = new JdbcResourceRegistry();
        super.setUp();
    }

    protected void tearDown() throws Exception {
        jdbcResourceRegistry.cleanUp();
        super.tearDown();
    }

    public void testFindAll() throws Exception {
        Connection connection = makeJdbcConnection();
        CatalogStore store = new CatalogStoreJdbcImpl(connection);
        Set allProducts = store.findAllProducts();
        assertEquals(3, allProducts.size());
    }
```

```
    public void testFindByName() throws Exception {
        Connection connection = makeJdbcConnection();
        CatalogStore store = new CatalogStoreJdbcImpl(connection);
        Set allProducts = store.findBeansByName("Sumatra");
        assertEquals(1, allProducts.size());
    }

    private DataSource getDataSource() {
        return (DataSource) ResourceManager.getResource("dataSource");
    }

    private Connection makeJdbcConnection() throws SQLException {
        Connection connection = getDataSource().getConnection();
        jdbcResourceRegistry.registerConnection(connection);
        return connection;
    }

    protected IDatabaseConnection getConnection() throws Exception {
        Connection connection = makeJdbcConnection();
        return new DatabaseConnection(connection);
    }

    protected IDataSet getDataSet() throws Exception {
        return new FlatXmlDataSet(
            new File("test/data/datasets/findProductsTest.xml"));
    }
}
```

As you can see we did not make any significant coding changes to introduce the `ResourceManager`, so you ought to have little trouble incorporating it into your project. For completeness, we show our `ResourceManagerTestSetup` in listing 16.6.

Listing 16.6 ResourceManagerTestSetup

```
package junit.cookbook.addons.jdbc.live.test;

import junit.cookbook.coffee.jdbc.test.CoffeeShopDatabaseFixture;
import junit.extensions.TestSetup;
import junit.framework.Test;
import junitx.util.ResourceManager;

public class ResourceManagerTestSetup extends TestSetup {
    public ResourceManagerTestSetup(Test test) {
        super(test);
    }

    protected void setUp() throws Exception {
        ResourceManager.addResource(
            "dataSource",
            CoffeeShopDatabaseFixture.makeDataSource());
    }
```

```
    protected void tearDown() throws Exception {
        ResourceManager.removeResource("dataSource");
    }
}
```

This is all it takes to get started using the JUnit-addons `ResourceManager`, and as you can see, it is quite handy, and you can register as many resources as your tests need. For testing against a live database—if you *must*—the combination of `ResourceManager` and DbUnit is quite powerful.

◆ Discussion

Now because we only have one test suite that uses the `ResourceManager`, we wrapped it directly in a `ResourceManagerTestSetup` to execute it. Without `ResourceManagerTestSetup`, any invocation of `getResource()` returns `null`. When we add a second test suite that uses the `ResourceManager`, we need to ensure that it too executes within a `ResourceManagerTestSetup`. How to do this depends on the environment.

If you use Eclipse and execute your tests with the built-in test runner, you have a few options, none of which are encouraging. You could create a `suite()` method in each test case class that wraps itself in a `ResourceManagerTestSetup`; you could create an `AllTests` class (see recipe 4.3, "Collect all the tests in a package") and wrap it in a `ResourceManagerTestSetup`; or you could use the register-as-you-go design, but then each test would need to be able to register the resource it needs in case you do not execute the test that initializes the resource for you. Looking for something even better than the best of these options leads you in the direction of using the JUnit-addons test runner, which we describe towards the end of this recipe.

If you use Ant and `<batchtest>` to collect all the tests in your source tree, then you have at least two options. You can extend the `<batchtest>` task to wrap a `ResourceManagerTestSetup` around the suite it would otherwise collect. If you do this, please publish it as open source, because the community could certainly use it. If you do not want to learn about Ant tasks at this moment, you can convert your `<batchtest>` task into to a special `AllTests` class. This class's `suite()` method just wraps a `ResourceManagerTestSetup` around a suite collected using `DirectorySuiteBuilder`. If you also use `<junitreport>` to report your test results, then you can duplicate `<batchtest>`'s XML output by writing a custom XML-based `TestListener` and registering it to the JUnit-addons test runner. After some thought, perhaps the custom Ant task is easier! Do whichever makes you more comfortable.

Finally, you should consider using JUnit-addons test runner, which provides a natural integration for the `ResourceManager`. No surprise there, as they came from the same project! You can let this custom test runner manage your resources automatically by doing the following:

1. Create a resource wrapper class that implements `junitx.runner.Resource`. This is a resource factory class.
2. Override `Resource.init()` to initialize your resource.
3. Add an entry to `test.properties` such as `junitx.resource.1=com.mycom.MyResourceFactory`.

The number at the end of the property name controls the order in which the resources are initialized. Now when you execute any test suite with the JUnit-addons test runner and this `test.properties` file, the test runner manages your resources and you can obtain them using `ResourceManager`. If you have more than two or three resources to manage, we highly recommend this last approach.

◆ Related

- 4.3—Collect all the tests in a package
- 5.10—Set up your fixture once for the entire suite

16.5 Ensure your shared test fixture tears itself down

◆ Problem

You have a test suite whose tests share a common fixture. When something goes wrong in the middle of executing the suite, JUnit does not invoke your shared fixture's `tearDown()` method and you have no way to force it to do so.

◆ Background

The more complex your test fixtures become, the more likely it is that you will encounter this problem. If you are writing tests against a database, for example, you might decide to set up your test data in your one-time `setUp()` and delete your test data in your one-time `tearDown()`. If your database administrators decide to add more referential integrity constraints to the database while you are not looking, then the next time you execute your database tests, you might not be able to clean up the test data. This might cause all future database tests to fail, even though those tests—and the production code they test—might be perfectly fine. Test isolation is important! Perhaps your best solution is to eliminate the need for one-time setup, but you might not be in a position to perform the considerable refactorings that you need to reach that point. You need to cope with this problem *now.*

◆ *Recipe*

JUnit-addons provides an alternative implementation of `TestSetup` that executes `tearDown()` inside a `finally` block, ensuring that it is invoked even in the presence of errors during fixture setup. The difference between the two `TestSetup` classes is slight, but important. Listing 16.7 shows the standard JUnit implementation of `TestSetup.run()`.

Listing 16.7 The standard JUnit implementation of `TestSetup.run()`

```
package junit.extensions;

public class TestSetup extends TestDecorator {
    public void run(final TestResult result) {
        Protectable p= new Protectable() {
            public void protect() throws Exception {
                setUp();
                basicRun(result);
                tearDown();
            }
        };
        result.runProtected(this, p);
    }
}
```

Listing 16.8 shows the the JUnit-addons version.

Listing 16.8 The JUnit-addons implementation of `TestSetup.run()`

```
package junitx.extensions;

public class TestSetup extends TestDecorator {
    public void run(final TestResult result) {
        Protectable p = new Protectable() {
            public void protect() throws Exception {
                try {
                    setUp();
                    basicRun(result);
                } finally {
                    tearDown();
                }
            }
        };
        result.runProtected(this, p);
    }
}
```

We have highlighted the difference in bold print: the JUnit-addons version invokes `tearDown()` *even if the test suite fails somehow.* This ensures that your shared test fixture tears itself down properly, no matter what happens during your test run. When you need a shared test fixture, use the JUnit-addons version of `TestSetup`, rather than the standard JUnit version. It could be as simple as replacing imports for `junit.extensions.TestSetup` with imports for `junitx.extensions.TestSetup` throughout your test source.

◆ Discussion

It is commonly held in the JUnit community that a shared test fixture is a "smell." That is, if you find yourself wanting to have many tests share a fixture, then there is a design issue that you have not fully addressed. In the case of testing against a live database, the problem is, well, the database: we believe that the majority of your testing ought to be done without a live database, as we described throughout Chapter 10, "Testing and JDBC." You can minimize the amount of testing you perform against a live database through some aggressive refactoring. Still, we recognize that it is not always easy to perform these refactorings: there is urgent work to do, and although we find these refactorings important, not everyone shares our opinion, perhaps including your project manager. The shared test fixture is a coping strategy for these situations, and JUnit-addons provides a better way to implement shared test fixtures with their version of `TestSetup`. We recommend using this version over the one that ships with standard JUnit.

◆ Related

- 5.10— Set up your fixture once for the entire suite

16.6 Report the name of each test as it executes

◆ Problem

You want a real-time report of the tests as they execute, perhaps including the name of the test, the suite to which it belongs, and the result.

◆ Background

The text-based test runner that comes with JUnit provides only a compact and very brief report of the test run as it happens. Specifically, it prints a dot for each test it executes and adds an "E" for an error or an "F" for a failure. It does not report the name of each test as the execution proceeds. You might decide that you want this feature, if for no other reason than to have a sense that the tests you expect to execute are actually doing so.

Beyond this there is one situation we have encountered where we needed to know the names of the tests as they executed.[3] If you write a test that uncovers a deadlock situation, it is impossible to use the JUnit text-based test runner to determine which test reproduces the deadlock. At this point you have a few options, none of them particularly nice.

- Use a graphical test runner, wait for the deadlock situation to happen, and then look at the test runner's status bar. It shows you name of the last test to execute completely, from which you might be able to deduce which test contains the deadlock.[4]
- Remove test suites from and add them back to your test run, hoping to isolate the test suite that contains the offending test. From there you can remove test methods from and add them back to the one test suite, hoping to isolate the test method that contains the offending test. Binary search will not help you here: you cannot rely on the order of execution of tests.
- Isolate the test suite that contains the offending test, as in the previous option, and then add `System.out.println(getName());` into the `setUp()` method so that the name of the test prints to the console before the test executes. Remember to take it out when you have finished! Remember to put it back when you need it next time!

Forget it! None of these is useful on an ongoing basis, and each requires specialized knowledge of JUnit to do. You want a solution that lasts, that's easy to turn on and off and that anyone can use.

◆ Recipe

What you need is a better test runner. Gathering information about which test is currently executing is not the responsibility of the test itself, but of the test runner, so you should add this feature to the test runner. Fortunately, you can add a simple `TestRunListener` to the JUnit-addons `TestRunner` whose job is to print to the console the name of the test about to be executed. Listing 16.9 shows a quick-and-dirty implementation of such a test run listener.

---

[3] Undoubtedly there are more, but we prefer to recount our experience rather than speculate.

[4] Of course, Murphy's Law says that the next test—the one that uncovers the deadlock—is in a different test suite, and you have no idea which test suite the test runner is executing now!

Listing 16.9 DumpTestNameListener

```
package junit.cookbook.addons.listener;

import junit.framework.Test;
import junit.framework.TestResult;
import junitx.runner.listener.AbstractRunListener;

public class DumpTestNameListener
    extends AbstractRunListener {

    public void testStarted(Test test, TestResult result) {
        System.out.println("> " + test);    <-- toString() includes the test name
    }

    // The remaining event handler methods do nothing
}
```

To use this extra listener, specify it in a "runner properties" file. This is a properties file that the JUnit-addons runner uses to register listeners at runtime. Because we want the default output *as well as* our small amount of customized reporting, we want the following runner properties file:

```
# runner.properties
junitx.runner.listener.0=junitx.runner.listener.DefaultConsole
junitx.runner.listener.1=junit.cookbook.addons.listener.DumpTestNameListener
```

The `DefaultConsole` listener is the one that the JUnit-addons runner registers if you do not specify your own listeners. If you specify custom listeners but still want the default listener to run, then you need to include it, probably in the first position in the listener list.

Now that you have created the listener and placed it in the runner properties file, you need to specify that properties file when you launch the JUnit-addons test runner. You specify a runner properties file by passing the option `-runner.properties <filename>` to the test runner, as in the following command.

```
> java -classpath <your classpath> junitx.runner.TestRunner
⇒  -runner.properties <runner properties file>
⇒  -class <test suite or test case class>
```

NOTE *A minor defect in the JUnit-addons test runner documentation*—Unfortunately, at press time, the JUnit-addons test runner documentation was incorrect in describing how to specify the `runner.properties` file. It mentions using `-runner.properties=<filename>`, but our experiments showed that this does not work. The way we specify the runner properties in this recipe is correct. Other than this minor problem, the JUnit-addons documentation is quite good!

The following is some sample output from a test run using the `DumpTestNameListener`.

```
> testRunHeader(junit.cookbook.listener.test.TestRunReporterTest)
*> testRunFooter_RunEnds(junit.cookbook.listener.test.TestRunReporterTest)
*> testRunFooter_RunStops(junit.cookbook.listener.test.TestRunReporterTest)
*> testTestStarted_TestCase(junit.cookbook.listener.test.TestRunReporterTest)
*> testTestIgnored(junit.cookbook.listener.test.TestRunReporterTest)
*> testTestFailure(junit.cookbook.listener.test.TestRunReporterTest)
*> testTestError(junit.cookbook.listener.test.TestRunReporterTest)
*> testTestSuccess(junit.cookbook.listener.test.TestRunReporterTest)
*> testTestStarted_TestSuite(junit.cookbook.listener.test.TestRunReporterTest)
*> testTestStarted_TestSuite_TwoTests
⇒  (junit.cookbook.listener.test.TestRunReporterTest)
*> testTestStarted_TestSuite_ZeroTests
⇒  (junit.cookbook.listener.test.TestRunReporterTest)
*

Elapsed time: 0.061 sec (11 tests)
```

The default run listener `DefaultConsole` provides the asterisks (*) and the "Elapsed time" message. The run listener `DumpTestNameListener` provides the name of each test as it executes.

◆ *Discussion*

The architecture of the JUnit-addons test runner is very similar to JUnit's standard test runners, with one key exception that interests us now: JUnit's test runners do not provide a method to register additional `TestListeners` when running tests. Internally, JUnit's test runners send events to a `TestListener`, which can report on each test as it executes. The text-based test runner prints dots and "E"s and "F"s to the console; the graphical test runner advances the progress bar and decides whether to turn it red (the result of a failure or error). You could certainly write your own test runner to report test execution the way you want, but it would take much more work than it should: you just want to add one more `TestListener` to the `TestRunner`!

◆ *Related*

- 6.1—See the name of each test as it executes
- 6.2—See the name of each test as it executes with a text-based test runner

17 Odds and ends

This chapter covers

- Testing file-based features without disrupting the file system
- Testing the syntax of your tests
- Customizing assertions for test readability
- Testing hidden behavior

There are always a few more things that authors want to say, but cannot find the appropriate chapter in which to say them. At that point, there are essentially two options: leave those things out of the book or create a catchall chapter in which to put them. We opted for the latter. This chapter contains recipes that simply did not make their way into one of the other chapters, for one reason or another.

We do not recommend writing tests that rely heavily on the file system; but if you need to do it, then we provide a recipe that describes some of the unexpected problems with cleaning up files between tests (see recipe 17.1, "Clean up the file system between tests"). We further describe one way to reduce the degree to which your tests depend on the file system in recipe 17.2, "Test your file-based application without the file system."

Some of the problems that novice JUnit users experience have to do with incorrect JUnit syntax. We see at least one or two such messages on the mailing lists per month. In recipe 17.3, "Verify your test case class syntax," we describe a tool that helps you avoid spending time hunting down a problem related to a typo, rather than a "real" problem. If you have to program alone, then this recipe helps eliminate *one* source of problems.

The more tests you write, the more complex your assertions become. Patterns emerge. Some people have questions about refactoring test code, wondering if it is any different from refactoring production code. Read recipe 17.4, "Extract a custom assertion" to see that there really is no difference: a *custom assertion* is simply the result of removing certain kinds of duplication from your tests.

Finally, we offer some recipes that use JUnitX (www.extreme-java.de/junitx/), a package that allows you to test the non-`public` parts of your classes. While we *strongly* recommend that you test entirely through publicly accessible methods, we recognize that not everyone agrees with this sentiment. Moreover, especially when testing legacy code, it is often advantageous to write tests for `private` methods before extracting them to a `public` interface or refactoring them some other way. This chapter contains a few recipes about testing non-`public` parts: testing a legacy method with no return value and testing a `private` method. Relying on `private` implementation details is discouraged, in general, but if you need to do it, then JUnitX helps you do it.

17.1 Clean up the file system between tests

◆ Problem

You want to write isolated tests for code that writes to the file system, so you need to clean up the file system between tests, but that does not appear to work as you would expect.

◆ Background

When a Java application writes to the file system using the file I/O libraries, file system changes occur asynchronously relative to the Java application. In other words, the Java application does not wait for the file system operations to complete. Ordinarily, the file system operation takes so little time to complete that this slight drift in execution time has no impact on your application; however, it easily affects well-isolated tests.

Consider a test fixture whose `tearDown()` method cleans up the directory you used for the test. (Which directory that is does not concern us for the moment.) The fixture is something similar to that found in listing 17.1.

Listing 17.1 A fixture that tries to delete its files

```
public class FileSystemOutputStrategyTest extends TestCase {
    private File expectedOutputFile;

    protected void setUp() throws Exception {
        expectedOutputFile = new File("./test/output/a/b/c/d.html");
    }

    public void testWriteOutputToDirectory() throws Exception {
        // Try writing output to file
        // Verify the file exists
    }

    protected void tearDown() throws Exception {
        if (expectedOutputFile.exists())
            expectedOutputFile.delete();    <-- delete() complains when
    }                                           a file does not exist
}
```

When you have about five tests using this fixture, you begin to notice that the file created in test #3 has not been deleted by the time test #4 executes, causing the latter to fail. You do not have the test isolation you think you have.

The next impulse is to clean up the file in both `setUp()` and `tearDown()`, which is not a bad idea, anyway. Listing 17.2 shows the new code.

Listing 17.2 Cleaning up the file in `setUp()` and `teardown()`

```
public class FileSystemOutputStrategyTest extends TestCase {
    private File expectedOutputFile;

    protected void setUp() throws Exception {
        expectedOutputFile = new File("./test/output/a/b/c/d.html");

        if (expectedOutputFile.exists())
            expectedOutputFile.delete();        <-- Ugh! Duplication
    }

    public void testWriteOutputToDirectory() throws Exception {
        // Try writing output to file
        // Verify the file exists
    }

    protected void tearDown() throws Exception {
        if (expectedOutputFile.exists())
            expectedOutputFile.delete();        <-- Ugh! Duplication
    }
}
```

This does not seem to solve the problem, particularly if your tests are short and execute quickly. Anything else seems like a hack, so what do you do?

◆ *Recipe*

Sadly, we only see two options.

1. Change the production code to eliminate the file system from the equation, a strategy we discuss in recipe 17.2, "Test your file-based application without the file system."
2. Slow the tests down.

That's right, folks: slow the tests down. It pains us even to type those words.

If your test involves asynchronous communication—such as invoking file system operations—and it does not stop to acknowledge the other party completing their part of the test, then you need to slow the test down. This is what we mean:

```
protected void tearDown() throws Exception {
    if (expectedOutputFile.exists()) {
        expectedOutputFile.delete();
        pauseSoTheFileHasTimeToDelete();
    }
}
```

You can implement this pause method with something as simple as `Thread.sleep(250)`—sleep for 250 milliseconds. Although this might work, there are a few drawbacks. First, the time to sleep depends on several factors, including CPU speed, hard drive speed, file size, and disk fragmentation. (This is not an exhaustive list, either.) Next, this pause slows your test suite down, discouraging you from executing it as often as you otherwise would. Finally, the decision to pause or not to pause *has nothing to do with the test!* It is a constraint of your production code's implementation details. It ought to be irrelevant. Now if you are testing code that you built strictly to use with a file system, such as Prevayler (www.prevayler.org), then the rules are different. For most business applications, though, the file system is an incidental tool and not an integral part of the architecture. Your tests ought not to have to worry about these low-level details. This is why we recommend factoring out the file system.

Nevertheless, if you inherit legacy code coupled to the file system and you need to add tests—possibly to enable future refactoring—then you need to apply this little hack until you can move to something better. This is another of those recipes that is good to know, not because you want to apply the technique, but because you might be forced to apply it at some point so that you can eventually phase out the need for it, similar to recipe 4.7, "Control the order of some of your tests."

◆ Discussion

If you apply this technique, you need to be aware of the possibility for spurious "false failures." That is, from time to time your file system tests fail only because `tearDown()` did not pause long enough before the next test began to execute. This wastes time in two ways: either you will carefully investigate each such failure and find it was a false alarm or, *much worse*, you will begin to ignore those failures and decide not to investigate a real defect in the same part of the code. One of the goals of Programmer Testing is to minimize the mean time between injecting a defect and discovering it. If you ignore failures, you defeat this purpose.

When we trade the cost of having these false failures against the cost of factoring out the file system, we tend to lean in the direction of the refactoring as soon as is feasible. Of course we do not want to sacrifice delivering business value to make the tests slightly better, but that depends on the number of tests. Five? Twenty? Two hundred? The more file system tests there are, the higher the cost of leaving the dependency on the file system in place. As always, crunch the numbers, and if they do not convince you, then leave the dependency in and log how much time you spend dealing with the problems that arise as a result. It is better to measure the impact than speculate about it.

- ***Related***
  - 4.7—Control the order of some of your tests
  - 17.2—Test your file-based application without the file system

17.2 Test your file-based application without the file system

- ***Problem***

You have an application that interacts with the file system and you want to test it without involving the file system.

- ***Background***

It is a common question: "I have a class that reads data from a file. How do I test it?" The straightforward answer is to read the data from the file and verify it against the data you expect. The bad news is that in applications *not* designed to be tested, this approach has some serious disadvantages. First, it is common to see the file name hard coded in the class. A simple test involves putting known data in a file, pointing the file-reading object at the file, and then verifying the data it reads. If the test cannot tell the file-reading object which file to use, then there is no way to write this test without disturbing the production application we are trying to test. Next, it is common to see one class with two responsibilities: reading raw text from the file and parsing that text into objects. Remember the Single Responsibility Principle?[1]

- ***Recipe***

The file system is yet another expensive, external resource. As an external resource, it is sensitive to changes occurring outside your Java application and its tests, so you want to depend on it as little as possible. It is fortunate, then, that the Java class libraries were designed with this in mind: its I/O libraries make it easy to separate the act of reading and writing data from the data sources. The data might come from a file, a network connection, another Java Virtual Machine, or even just a `String` in memory. The key to testing file-based components is to separate them from the file system as much as possible. Make your integration to the file system as thin as possible.

---

[1] J. B., in particular, finds it difficult to do more than one thing at a time, which is one reason he is so keen on respecting the Single Responsibility Principle. His objects ought not to be more capable than he is.

Let us return to the Coffee Shop application we examined in part 2. Suppose we would like to read the coffee catalog data as comma-delimited text stored in a file. We would need a class to read the file, parse the text, and create a `CoffeeCatalog` object. We might end up with the simple class in listing 17.3.

Listing 17.3 `CoffeeCatalogFileReader`

```
package junit.cookbook.coffee.data;

import java.io.*;
import java.util.regex.*;

import junit.cookbook.coffee.model.CoffeeCatalog;

import com.diasparsoftware.java.util.Money;

public class CoffeeCatalogFileReader {
    private Pattern catalogLinePattern = Pattern
        .compile("(.+),(.+),(.+)");

    public CoffeeCatalog load() throws IOException {
        CoffeeCatalog catalog = new CoffeeCatalog();

        BufferedReader reader = new BufferedReader(
            new FileReader(new File("data/catalog.txt")));

        while (true) {
            String line = reader.readLine();

            if (line == null) break;

            Matcher matcher = catalogLinePattern.matcher(line);
            if (matcher.matches()) {
                String productId = matcher.group(1);
                String coffeeName = matcher.group(2);
                String unitPriceAsString = matcher.group(3);
                Money unitPrice = Money
                    .parse(unitPriceAsString);

                catalog.addCoffee(productId, coffeeName,
                                  unitPrice);
            }
        }

        return catalog;
    }
}
```

We typed this all in without even testing it. (Calm down.) Because we have not tested it at all, we want to do that now, but the only way to test this code *as is* involves using the real catalog file and verifying the data it contains. This is straightforward, so let us test it. Here is our production coffee catalog file.

```
762,Sumatra,$7.50
800,Special Blend,$9.50
900,Colombiano,$10.00
```

Listing 17.4 shows our test.

Listing 17.4 `CoffeeCatalogFileTest`

```
package junit.cookbook.coffee.data.test;

import junit.cookbook.coffee.data.CoffeeCatalogFileReader;
import junit.cookbook.coffee.model.CoffeeCatalog;
import junit.framework.TestCase;

import com.diasparsoftware.java.util.Money;

public class CoffeeCatalogFileTest extends TestCase {
    public void testReadCatalogFile() throws Exception {
        CoffeeCatalogFileReader reader = new CoffeeCatalogFileReader();

        CoffeeCatalog expected = new CoffeeCatalog();
        expected.addCoffee("762", "Sumatra", Money.dollars(7, 50));
        expected.addCoffee("800", "Special Blend", Money.dollars(9, 50));
        expected.addCoffee("900", "Colombiano", Money.dollars(10, 0));

        assertEquals(expected, reader.load());
    }
}
```

There is one little problem with our test: it cannot pass. The problem is simple: we keep our tests in a separate Eclipse project *and* the `CoffeeCatalogFileReader` hard codes a relative filename—relative to the directory in which *its* Eclipse project is located. Either we move `CoffeeCatalogFileReader` into the test's project or the test into the file reader's project. Neither option is particularly good, so we need to refactor. We add a parameter to `CoffeeCatalogFileReader.load()` so that it can accept the file from which to load. Listing 17.5 shows the new version of the test.

Listing 17.5 `CoffeeCatalogFileTest` with a relative filename

```
package junit.cookbook.coffee.data.test;

import java.io.File;

import junit.cookbook.coffee.data.CoffeeCatalogFileReader;
import junit.cookbook.coffee.model.CoffeeCatalog;
import junit.framework.TestCase;

import com.diasparsoftware.java.util.Money;

public class CoffeeCatalogFileTest extends TestCase {
    public void testReadCatalogFile() throws Exception {
```

```
        CoffeeCatalogFileReader reader = new CoffeeCatalogFileReader();

        CoffeeCatalog expected = new CoffeeCatalog();
        expected.addCoffee("762", "Sumatra", Money.dollars(7, 50));
        expected.addCoffee("800", "Special Blend", Money.dollars(9, 50));
        expected.addCoffee("900", "Colombiano", Money.dollars(10, 0));

        assertEquals(
            expected,
            reader.load(
                new File("../CoffeeShopEngine/data/catalog.txt")));
    }
}
```

Now the test passes, but there is still a problem: what happens when, next week, someone adds a few new coffee products to the catalog? When this happens, the test will fail, and really for no good reason. In order to avoid this, we ought to use a different file. We copy the production catalog file to a local directory and change our test accordingly, to the version in listing 17.6.

Listing 17.6 `CoffeeCatalogFileTest` using a test data directory

```
package junit.cookbook.coffee.data.test;

import java.io.File;

import junit.cookbook.coffee.data.CoffeeCatalogFileReader;
import junit.cookbook.coffee.model.CoffeeCatalog;
import junit.framework.TestCase;

import com.diasparsoftware.java.util.Money;

public class CoffeeCatalogFileTest extends TestCase {
    public void testReadCatalogFile() throws Exception {
        CoffeeCatalogFileReader reader = new CoffeeCatalogFileReader();

        CoffeeCatalog expected = new CoffeeCatalog();
        expected.addCoffee("762", "Sumatra", Money.dollars(7, 50));
        expected.addCoffee("800", "Special Blend", Money.dollars(9, 50));
        expected.addCoffee("900", "Colombiano", Money.dollars(10, 0));

        assertEquals(
            expected,
            reader.load(new File("test/data/catalog.txt")));
    }
}
```

Even better, but now we have a complex test environment. If someone moves our test file, or forgets to copy it to the right place, or someone decides to change its contents—any of these things results in a false failure. It would be better just to put the test data right next to the test itself, to essentially eliminate the possibility of someone changing one without the other. The simplest solution is to parse the information from a `String`. In order to do this, we need `CoffeeCatalogFileReader.load()` to accept a `Reader`, not a `File`, as its parameter. It is nice to see that with Java's well-designed I/O library, this is an easy change. Listing 17.7 shows the new test.

Listing 17.7 `CoffeeCatalogFileTest` with an inline file

```
package junit.cookbook.coffee.data.test;

import java.io.StringReader;

import junit.cookbook.coffee.data.CoffeeCatalogFileReader;
import junit.cookbook.coffee.model.CoffeeCatalog;
import junit.framework.TestCase;

import com.diasparsoftware.java.util.Money;

public class CoffeeCatalogFileTest extends TestCase {
    public void testReadCatalogFile() throws Exception {
        String catalogText =
            "762,Sumatra,$7.50\r\n"
                + "800,Special Blend,$9.50\r\n"
                + "900,Colombiano,$10.00\r\n";

        CoffeeCatalog expected = new CoffeeCatalog();
        expected.addCoffee("762", "Sumatra", Money.dollars(7, 50));
        expected.addCoffee("800", "Special Blend", Money.dollars(9, 50));
        expected.addCoffee("900", "Colombiano", Money.dollars(10, 0));

        CoffeeCatalogReader reader = new CoffeeCatalogReader();

        assertEquals(
            expected,
                reader.load(new StringReader(catalogText)));
    }
}
```

We have not had to change the production code much, either, except to rename the class. After all, it does not read from a file any more. Listing 17.8 shows the final version, with the changes highlighted in bold print.

Listing 17.8 `CoffeeCatalogReader`

```
package junit.cookbook.coffee.data;

import java.io.*;
```

```
import java.util.regex.*;
import com.diasparsoftware.java.util.Money;
import junit.cookbook.coffee.model.CoffeeCatalog;

public class CoffeeCatalogReader {
    private Pattern catalogLinePattern =
        Pattern.compile("(.+),(.+),(.+)");

    public CoffeeCatalog load(Reader catalogDataReader)
        throws IOException {

        CoffeeCatalog catalog = new CoffeeCatalog();
        BufferedReader reader = new BufferedReader(catalogDataReader);

        while (true) {
            String line = reader.readLine();

            if (line == null)
                break;

            Matcher matcher = catalogLinePattern.matcher(line);
            if (matcher.matches()) {
                String productId = matcher.group(1);
                String coffeeName = matcher.group(2);
                String unitPriceAsString = matcher.group(3);
                Money unitPrice = Money.parse(unitPriceAsString);

                catalog.addCoffee(productId, coffeeName, unitPrice);
            }
        }
        return catalog;
    }
}
```

But what about reading from a file? The newly named `CoffeeCatalogReader` now has no dependency at all on the source of the data, but only its format. Whichever object uses the `CoffeeCatalogReader` is now responsible for providing it with a valid `Reader` object configured to read well-formed catalog data. Perhaps the `CoffeeShopController` servlet should have this responsibility. If so, we can use a mock objects approach to verify that it provides the proper parameter to `CoffeeCatalogReader.load()`. Not only is the test very robust (no dependency on external resources), but the design is more flexible. If someone needs to read catalog data from a network connection, they can do it without changing `CoffeeCatalogReader` at all. The Open/Closed Principle at work![2]

[2] www.objectmentor.com/resources/articles/ocp.pdf

◆ *Discussion*

If you are given a legacy system that interacts with files, then you might not be able to apply this recipe. In that case, you need to cope with the application's dependency on the file system. See recipe 17.1 to achieve test isolation in the face of such a dependency.

◆ *Related*

- 17.1—Clean up the file system between tests
- Open/Closed Principle (www.objectmentor.com/resources/articles/ocp.pdf)
- Single Responsibility Principle (www.objectmentor.com/resources/articles/srp)

17.3 Verify your test case class syntax

◆ *Problem*

You want to verify that your test case classes adhere to the basic syntax rules of JUnit, but many common problems cannot be caught by the compiler.

◆ *Background*

You have a large suite of test cases, including dozens or even hundreds of test case classes. It is virtually impossible—at least highly undesirable—to inspect all your test case classes by hand or execute each individually to uncover problems such as incorrectly overriding `setUp()` and `tearDown()`, or not providing a proper `suite()` method. Moreover, whenever someone changes the tests, she runs the risk of reintroducing the kind of problem that can easily go unnoticed. You would like to run some sanity check on your tests to give you some confidence that they at least "make sense."

◆ *Recipe*

JUnit-addons provides a nifty tool to help: the `TestClassValidator`. The idea behind this tool is to examine the source of a test case class and highlight any potential defects in it that compilers cannot catch, such as typing `setup()` rather than `setUp()` or failing to make the `suite()` method class level. Listing 17.9 shows a test case class with a number of problems (or potential problems) we have highlighted in bold print.

Listing 17.9 A test case class in need of validation

```
public class ValidationExample
        extends TestCase {

    public ValidationExample(String name) {
        super(name);
    }

    public Test suite() {
        return null;
    }

    public void setup() {
    }

    public void tearDown() {
    }

    public void atestDummy() {
        assertTrue( true );
    }
}
```

To execute the `TestClassValidator`, issue the following command.

```
java junitx.tool.TestClassValidator classname
```

For the above class, `TestClassValidator` provides the following report.

```
TestClassValidator, by Vladimir R. Bossicard
    WARN > junitx.example.ValidationExample: method potentially misspelled
   <setup>
    ERROR> junitx.example.ValidationExample: method 'suite' must be static
    INFO > junitx.example.ValidationExample: method seems to be a test
   <atestDummy>
```

The method potentially misspelled is `setup()`, which ought to be `setUp()`. This is a common source of questions on the JUnit mailing lists. The next problem is clear enough: the `suite()` method must be class level (`static`) in order for JUnit to use it to collect your tests. Finally, the method `atestDummy()` *looks* like a test: after all, it has test in the name and makes an assertion, so you probably just slipped on the keyboard just before running your build process. The `TestClassValidator` notices when you make the kind of mistake that a compiler does not catch, but that might affect your tests. It is not as good as having someone program with you, but it helps.

◆ *Discussion*

If you validate your test classes before executing them, you can save yourself the embarrassment of hiding a defect for weeks (months!) before finding it. The point of ongoing testing is to find defects as soon as you inject them into the code. If you mistype a test method name and that test does not execute, and that is the only test that exposes a certain defect...well, you might finally uncover the defect later—much later. The longer you wait to uncover a defect after creating it, the more effort it takes to understand the defect and to fix it. If you are going to spend time writing tests, you want them to execute. They are not there to "look pretty."

If you have other test case validation rules you would like to enforce with `TestClassValidator`, then you can subclass `ClassValidator` and add your own rules. If you would like to report the errors differently, you can provide your own implementation of `ClassValidatorListener` and listen for validation events of various severities: warning, information, or error. This is another example of the commitment of JUnit-addons to simple, flexible design.

Another way to verify these kinds of coding issues is to use a style checker, such as PMD (http://pmd.sourceforge.net/) or checkstyle (http://checkstyle.sourceforge.net/). Although one generally thinks of these tools as ways to enforce a team's coding style, they simply verify that source code conforms to some standard, so we can certainly use them to verify that source code conforms to the demands of a framework such as JUnit. As this is not a book about coding standards, we recommend you visit the various web sites of these coding standards tools to see whether they might help you on your project. They have become part of the standard toolkit for Java Open Source projects, particularly the Jakarta projects (http://jakarta.apache.org).

Robert Wenner provided a more clever solution to the specific problem of mistyping `setup()` and `teardown()`. It is not a general-purpose solution, but if you make this mistake often enough, then you might want to try it. He recommends adding these two methods to your Base Test Case class (see recipe 3.6, "Introduce a Base Test Case").

```
private final void setup() {
}

private final void teardown() {
}
```

Now in your test case class if you accidentally type `setup()` rather than `setUp()`, the compiler catches the error. Is this solution too clever? We do not think so.

If you happen to have considerable trouble with this kind of mistake—we all have our blind spots—then we think it is worth trying.

◆ Related

- PMD (http://pmd.sourceforge.net/)
- checkstyle (http://checkstyle.sourceforge.net/)

17.4 Extract a custom assertion

◆ Problem

You notice repetition in the assertions you write and want to remove that duplication.

◆ Background

As you write more and more tests for your system, you begin to develop a kind of *application testing language* wherein you express larger, more complex thoughts in your assertions. These assertions have both a structural aspect and a domain-oriented aspect. The structural aspect has to do with data structures: you expect this list to contain that item, or you expect this Value Object to have those properties. The domain-oriented aspect gives meaning to your data structures: this customer's order should contain those items, or the subtotal of the shopcart should be $157. You can manage domain complexity by building a rich object model and, in particular, designing good Value Objects. The more complex are the values they represent, the more compact are the assertions you can make about the return value of a method. As your design becomes more structurally complex, you begin to require three or four actual assertions to make what you logically consider a single, "macroassertion." One way to manage this complexity is through custom assertions, the topic of this recipe.

◆ Recipe

Just as you extract any duplicate code into a method, you should extract repetitive assertions into a custom assertion. There are a number of kinds of duplication that we recommend extracting into a customized assertion. Some of the duplication is obvious and some is not so obvious. The *real* talent is in identifying obscure duplication and dealing with it. The programmers who can do this are the master designers. We will start with an example from a discussion on the JUnit Yahoo!

group, with some obvious duplication. We are verifying that a collection contains a specific object: that a rainbow contains the color orange. Here is our assertion.

```
assertTrue(rainbow.contains(Color.orange));
```

As long as this assertion passes, all is well; however, when it fails, the first question we usually ask is, "All right, which colors are in the rainbow?!" To find that out, we add a failure message to the assertion, which would print the contents of rainbow. The new assertion might look like this:

```
assertTrue(
    "Rainbow " + rainbow.colorListAsString()
        + " unexpectedly does not contain " + Color.orange,
    rainbow.contains(Color.orange));
```

Aside from the fact that this failure message makes the assertion more difficult to read, the method `colorListAsString()` looks quite suspect here, as it is not necessarily a method the rest of your application needs. In a Yahoo! group discussion, Vladimir Bossicard expressed it best when he asked, "Do you really need the method `colorListAsString()`? If this method is not in your public API, you're writing an additional method just in the case of a *failing* test. It doesn't help your design at all." We have discussed elsewhere in this book and out in the public discussion groups whether one ought to add methods to a `public` interface "just for testing." While we do not mind adding methods to support testing, we have to admit that adding a method to support a *failing* test just does not feel right. But Vladimir is not through. He goes on to say, "Let's finish the tests—and be careful when you're copying/pasting the code!"

```
assertTrue(
    "Rainbow " + rainbow.colorListAsString()
        + " unexpectedly does not contain " + Color.orange(),
    rainbow.contains(Color.orange));
assertTrue(
    "Rainbow " + rainbow.colorListAsString()
        + " unexpectedly does not contain " + Color.blue(),
    rainbow.contains(Color.blue));
assertTrue(
    "Rainbow " + rainbow.colorListAsString()
        + " unexpectedly does not contain " + Color.yellow(),
    rainbow.contains(Color.yellow));
assertTrue(
    "Rainbow " + rainbow.colorListAsString()
        + " unexpectedly does not contain " + Color.red(),
    rainbow.contains(Color.red));
assertTrue(
    "Rainbow " + rainbow.colorListAsString()
```

```
        + " unexpectedly does not contain " + Color.green(),
    rainbow.contains(Color.green));
```

The duplication is quite obvious, and we certainly need to rid ourselves of it. We can apply a purely mechanical refactoring, noticing that only the color changes from assertion to assertion. We extract the following method into our test case class:

```
public static void assertRainbowContains(Color color) {
    assertTrue(
        "Rainbow " + rainbow.colorListAsString()
            + " unexpectedly does not contain " + color,
        rainbow.contains(color));
}
```

And now our assertions are much easier to read:

```
assertRainbowContains(Color.orange);
assertRainbowContains(Color.blue);
assertRainbowContains(Color.yellow);
assertRainbowContains(Color.red);
assertRainbowContains(Color.green);
```

Or, as Vladimir reminds us, we could simply use the JUnit-addons `ListAssert`:

```
import junitx.framework.ListAssert;
...
ListAssert.assertContains(rainbow, Color.orange);
ListAssert.assertContains(rainbow, Color.blue);
ListAssert.assertContains(rainbow, Color.yellow);
ListAssert.assertContains(rainbow, Color.red);
ListAssert.assertContains(rainbow, Color.green);
```

Either way, we have removed duplication in our assertions by applying the Extract Method refactoring [Refactoring, 110], perhaps the most fundamental refactoring of them all. Moreover, much of the power of the various JUnit extensions, including HtmlUnit, JUnit-addons, GSBase, and XMLUnit, comes from their extensive libraries of custom assertions. It is a simple, but powerful technique.

◆ *Discussion*

Here are a few tips for writing your custom assertions:.

Make them class-level (`static`) methods. Because they are just algorithms that do not operate on any particular instance of a class, this makes sense. Remember, too, that if you are using XMLUnit and your test case class extends `XMLTestCase`, then you will not be able to also extend the class that defines your custom assertions. If your custom assertions are class-level methods, then this does not present a problem.

Even if your custom assertions build customized failure messages, provide an optional parameter for an additional failure message. For example, when using `ListAssert`, you automatically get a failure message telling you that the list does not contain the expected item, but that does not tell you what the list and expected item *mean* in your object model. You will likely want to add some domain-specific detail to your failure message.

After you have collected a good number of custom assertions—say five or more—move them into either a `CustomAssert` class (such as `StringAssert`, `FileAssert`, or `ListAssert`, which are all part of JUnit-addons) or into a Base Test Case (as GSBase does). This makes it easier to find the custom assertion when you want to use it.

◆ *Related*

- Chapter 15—GSBase
- Chapter 16—JUnit-addons

17.5 Test a legacy method with no return value

◆ *Problem*

You need to test a method with no return value. You would like to be able to apply recipe 2.2, "Test a method that returns nothing," but you are unable to change the production code to create an observable side effect. You need an alternative.

◆ *Background*

Perhaps the most annoying aspect of working with legacy code is that if the original authors did not design for testability, then you have to jump through hoops to write effective tests. In particular, there might be no publicly observable side effect for a given behavior—that is, you want to test a class feature, but its behavior can only be observed from within the class itself. Perhaps only privately accessible data is affected with no way to query that data. In this situation you typically have three options:

1. Make the `private` data visible by adding a query method.
2. Write a higher-level (or more coarsely grained) test that involves other production objects.
3. Bypass the Java protection mechanism in your tests.

JUnitX provides a way to do the latter, which might be the solution you need.

◆ *Recipe*

Create a `PrivateTestCase` using JUnitX that allows you to execute non-`public` methods and gives you access to non-`public` data. Use this extra power to make assertions about the state of the object before and after you invoke the desired methods. Following are the steps to create a `PrivateTestCase`:

1. Create a subclass of `PrivateTestCase`.
2. In the package containing the class under test, create a subclass called `TestProxy` of `junitx.framework.TestProxy`. You can find the code for this class in listing 17.3. The code for this class is the same for every package that requires it.
3. Write the test in your subclass of `PrivateTestCase`, which invokes the method with no return value.
4. Use the `PrivateTestCase` methods `get()`, `getInt()`, `getLong()`, `getBoolean()`, and so on to make assertions about the private data that the method changes.

There is one common design that creates a need to use this technique: the Observer/Observable pattern as it is often implemented in Java. Even though Java provides its own implementation of this in the `java.util` package, many programmers feel the need to reproduce this design themselves. Because we are talking about legacy code, let us first consider the code we wish to test, shown in listing 17.10.

Listing 17.10 An implementation of `Observable`

```
package junit.cookbook.patterns;

public class Observable {
    private Observer[] observers = new Observer[9];
    private int totalObs = 0;
    private int state;

    public void attach(Observer o) {
        observers[totalObs++] = o;
    }

    public int getState() {
        return state;
    }

    public void setState(int in) {
        state = in;
        notifyObservers();
    }
```

```
    private void notifyObservers() {
        for (int i = 0; i < totalObs; i++)
            observers[i].update();
    }
}
```

In its current state, the only way to verify that an `Observer` is correctly attached is to attach one, trigger an update, and then verify that it was correctly notified. While that does not sound like much to do, it is important to realize the implementation detail you need to know to write that simple test: that the way to trigger an update is to invoke the method `setState()`. Your test depends on the mechanism for notifying observers, even though all you want to verify is that `Observable` registers your `Observer` correctly. We ought to be able to test that behavior independently of the way observers are notified.

Listing 17.11 shows the test that uses JUnitX's facility for gaining access to `private` data. We have highlighted the key line of code in bold print. This is the line that uses JUnitX's `get()` method to retrieve the value of the private variable `observers`.

Listing 17.11 ObservableTest

```
package junit.cookbook.patterns.test;

import junit.cookbook.patterns.Observable;
import junit.cookbook.patterns.Observer;
import junitx.framework.PrivateTestCase;
import junitx.framework.TestAccessException;

public class ObservableTest
    extends PrivateTestCase
    implements Observer {          <-- Self-Shunt pattern

    public ObservableTest(String name) {
        super(name);
    }

    public void testAttachObserver()
        throws TestAccessException {

        Observable observable = new Observable();
        observable.attach(this);

        Observer[] observers =
            (Observer[]) get(observable, "observers");    <-- Read private instance variable

        assertTrue(arrayContains(observers, this));
    }

    private boolean arrayContains(          <-- Refactor to utility class
        Object[] objects,
```

```
        Object object) {

        for (int i = 0; i < objects.length; i++)
            if (object.equals(objects[i]))
                return true;

        return false;
    }

    public void update() {    <-- Intentionally empty
    }
}
```

This test implements the Self-Shunt pattern: the test case class itself implements a required interface—in this case, `Observer`—to avoid the need to create an anonymous implementation and use it in the test case. We recommend reading Michael Feathers' "The 'Self-Shunt' Unit Testing Pattern" for details on this useful technique.

For the sake of completeness, listing 17.12 shows the standard implementation of `TestProxy`. To gain access to non-`public` parts of a class, you must write a version of this class in the same package as that class. The class *must* be named `TestProxy`—JUnitX's rules, not ours.

Listing 17.12 `TestProxy`

```
package junit.cookbook.patterns;    <-- Place in package containing production code

import junitx.framework.TestAccessException;

public class TestProxy extends junitx.framework.TestProxy {    <-- Class must be named TestProxy

    public Object newInstance(Object[] arguments)
        throws TestAccessException {

        try {
            return getProxiedClass()
                .getConstructor(arguments)
                .newInstance(arguments);
        }
        catch (Exception e) {
            throw new TestAccessException(
                "could not instantiate "
                    + getTestedClassName(),
                e);
        }
    }

    public Object newInstanceWithKey(
        String constructorKey,
        Object[] arguments)
        throws TestAccessException {
```

```
            try {
                return getProxiedClass()
                    .getConstructor(constructorKey)
                    .newInstance(arguments);
            }
            catch (Exception e) {
                throw new TestAccessException(
                    "could not instantiate "
                        + getTestedClassName(),
                    e);
            }
        }
    }
```

◆ Discussion

We have already advised the reader against using non-`public` parts of a class to write tests. Although there are varying opinions on the matter—as a search of the Web certainly illustrates—we believe that in judging the trade-off between encapsulation and testability, we lean towards testability. What is the point of a good design if we cannot directly verify the code's behavior? If we have to choose between working code and well-designed code, we opt for working code, because we know that we can refactor working code. Now with JUnitX, there is another option: we can maintain the production code's design by writing more complicated tests, such as the ones we have seen using JUnitX. We prefer simpler code to more complicated code, and we hold tests to the same standards as production code in this respect. For that reason, we tend to favor good designs that allow for simple tests over (arguably) better designs that require more complicated tests. You have to live with your own decision here, so do what you think is right.

We recommend the technique in this recipe either as a last resort or as a stepping-stone towards a more testable design.[3] The idea here is to "jam in" the tests you need so that you can feel confident refactoring the design towards something more testable. You might think that adding a query method for the `private` data you need violates encapsulation "just for testing." Although we cannot argue with that statement, we believe that making a class easier to test is worth a temporary violation of encapsulation.[4] Our typical approach is to break encapsulation, write

[3] See recipe 4.7, "Control the order of some of your tests," for another example of using a testing tool as a temporary refactoring aid.

[4] We say "temporary" because there is almost always another well-encapsulated solution to the same problem that is easier to test. We have a wonderful proof, but there is not enough space here to explain it.

the tests we need, and then refactor back towards a well-encapsulated solution using the tests as a safety net. We think it's better than nothing.

We also mentioned the possibility of writing Integration Tests in place of Object Tests in this situation. It might be possible to use a collaborating class to observe the side effect of the behavior you want to test. We prefer not to resort to a less isolated test, because we lose the ability to identify the cause of a problem from the particular test that fails. The decision to treat the legacy system as a black box depends on your intent to change its design. If you plan to replace the legacy system with another implementation (which you test thoroughly with JUnit), then it might be wise to freeze some portion of the legacy system's API, capture it in an interface, and write tests against the new interface. As you build the replacement system, you can verify its behavior against the interface-level tests to ensure its behavior is consistent with the legacy system. If, however, you plan to refactor the legacy system towards a more testable design, then JUnitX provides you the means to begin creating a refactoring-friendly safety net. We applaud your courage and advise that you proceed with caution.

◆ *Related*

- 2.2—Test a method that returns nothing
- Michael Feathers, "The 'Self-Shunt' Unit Testing Pattern" (www.objectmentor.com/resources/articles/SelfShunPtrn.pdf)

17.6 Test a private method if you must

◆ *Problem*

You would like to test a `private` method and prefer not to *or* are unable to make the method `public` "just for testing."

◆ *Background*

Not everyone agrees with the philosophy of testing classes entirely through a `public` interface. We respectfully agree to disagree. You have a `private` method that is complex enough to warrant its own tests, but nevertheless is not important enough to promote to the `public` interface or refactor to a collaborating class. You could test the method indirectly through the `public` methods that invoke it, but you would rather test it in isolation, which is a laudable goal.

It is also possible that you've been painted into this corner, inheriting code that was not designed to be tested. In that case, your goal might be to create a refactoring safety net before attempting to move code around. In that case, you might have no choice but to test the private method before deciding how to refactor the class.

◆ Recipe

JUnitX provides the ability to gain access to private methods. See recipe 17.5, "Test a legacy method with no return value," for instructions on how to enable JUnitX to access the private parts of the class you want to test. After you have done that, invoke the method invoke() which is described in table 17.1.

Table 17.1 Parameters to JUnitX's PrivateTestCase.invoke() method

Parameter	Description
`Object object`	The object on which to invoke the method
`String methodKey`	The name of the method to invoke
`Object[] arguments`	An array of the arguments to pass to the method. The array must be the same length as the number of parameters the method expects.

We can return to the example from recipe 17.5. In the previous recipe, we used JUnitX to gain access to the private variable observers to verify that the method attach() works. Here we invoke the private method notifyObservers() to verify that it indeed notifies its observers. Here is the test, which uses EasyMock to implement a Spy Observer:

```
public void testNotifyListeners() throws Exception {
    MockControl observerControl =
        MockControl.createControl(Observer.class);
    Observer observer = (Observer) observerControl.getMock();

    observer.update();
    observerControl.setVoidCallable();

    observerControl.replay();

    Observable observable = new Observable();
    observable.attach(observer);

    invoke(observable, "notifyObservers", new Object[0]);

    observerControl.verify();
}
```

We have highlighted in bold print the line of code that uses JUnitX to invoke the `private` method `notifyObservers()` with no parameters. This test passes, telling us that `Observable` works with a single observer. We could next attach the observer more than once, and then expect the observable to invoke `update()` more than once. With EasyMock, that is easy.

```
public void testMultipleListeners() throws Exception {
    MockControl observerControl =
        MockControl.createControl(Observer.class);
    Observer observer = (Observer) observerControl.getMock();

    observer.update();
    observerControl.setVoidCallable(5);

    observerControl.replay();

    Observable observable = new Observable();
    for (int i = 0; i < 5; i++)
        observable.attach(observer);

    invoke(observable, "notifyObservers", new Object[0]);

    observerControl.verify();
}
```

Using EasyMock, we say that we expect `observer.update()` to be invoked five times. Next, we attach the same observer five times to the observable, in order to receive five notifications. This test also passes, so we can be certain that the observable supports five observers. Change five to whatever number you like, if you feel you need to test further. We are satisfied and stop here. The key to this recipe is seeing how to use JUnitX to invoke private methods. If you *must* do it—and we recommend against it—then at least you know an easy way to do it.

◆ *Discussion*

So what's so bad about testing `private` methods, anyway? Perhaps the greatest problem is that `private` methods are `private` for a reason: the author intended for nothing but this one class to have any knowledge of the particulars of its implementation. Most notably, `private` methods might change—both their behavior and their interface—with no expected impact to any other part of the system. That is the power of `private` methods.[5] In that sense, `private` methods support refactoring very well by providing the design with a degree of freedom of

---

[5] It is interesting, of course, that this notion of privacy is not universal and that other languages get along swimmingly without it. It must be a matter of taste, because somehow people manage to write good software in Smalltalk.

change. When we invoke a `private` method directly, though, we destroy this degree of freedom. With each test we add for a `private` method, we introduce a dependency: when the production code changes, the test has to change. In this way, the `private` method introduces the same kind of dependency that a `public` method introduces: if the method changes, then the tests must change. You might as well make the method `public` at that point.

You can achieve `private/public` access control by placing `public` methods on an interface and `private` methods on an implementation, much the way that an EJB is designed. If you want to test a particular implementation of the interface, then write tests for that implementation class; and if you want to test adherence to the behavior of methods on the interface, then introduce an Abstract Test Case (See recipe 2.6, "Test an interface"). Client code uses each implementation only through its interface, restricting the methods it can invoke while allowing you to test the implementation details as thoroughly as you need. In a sense, we can do away with `private/public` access entirely by introducing the appropriate interfaces. We don't recommend changing all your code tomorrow, but this is an idea worth considering for new code.

◆ Related

- 2.6—Test an interface
- 17.5—Test a legacy method with no return value

A Complete solutions

Here you can find complete solutions to some of the problems we raise in the recipes. We did not want to confuse these recipes with code samples that are hundreds of lines long, but we thought it important to include the complete solutions, so we have done so here. Consult table A.1 to see the recipes to which these solutions correspond.

Table A.1 The complete solutions, and the recipes to which they correspond

Complete solution	Follow up to recipe
A.1—Define a test in XML	4.9—Define a test suite in XML
A.2—Parameterized Test Case overriding runTest()	4.8—Build a data-driven test suite
A.3—Ignore the order of elements in an XML document	9.2—Ignore the order of elements in an XML document
A.4—Test an XSL stylesheet in isolation	9.6—Test an XSL stylesheet in isolation
A.5—Validate XML documents in your tests	9.7—Validate XML documents in your tests
A.6—Aspect-based universal Spy	14.6—Test a Template Method's implementation
A.7—Test a BMP entity bean	11.6—Test a BMP entity bean

A.1 Define a test suite in XML

◆ Solution

We first present the Parameterized Test Case that tests the `split()` method. The custom test suite method in listing A.1 specifies the location of the XML document containing the test data.

Listing A.1 AllocateMoneyXmlBasedTest

```
package junit.cookbook.suites.test;

import java.util.*;

import junit.cookbook.util.Money;
import junit.framework.*;

public class AllocateMoneyXmlBasedTest extends TestCase {
    private Money amountToSplit;
    private int nWays;
    private Map expectedCuts;
    private Map actualCuts;

    public AllocateMoneyXmlBasedTest(Money amountToSplit,
        int nWays, Map expectedCuts) {
```

```
        super("testAllocate");

        this.amountToSplit = amountToSplit;
        this.nWays = nWays;
        this.expectedCuts = expectedCuts;
    }

    public static Test suite() throws Exception {
        TestSuite suite = new TestSuite();

        String testFileName
            = "/junit/cookbook/suites/test"
                + "/allocate-money-tests.xml";       See listing 4.6

        List tests = AllocateMoneyTestBuilder
            .makeTests(testFileName);

        for (Iterator i = tests.iterator(); i.hasNext();) {
            AllocateMoneyTest eachTest = (AllocateMoneyTest) i
                .next();
            suite.addTest(eachTest);
        }
        return suite;
    }

    public void testAllocate() {
        List allocatedAmounts = amountToSplit.split(nWays);
        Map actualCuts = organizeIntoBag(allocatedAmounts);
        assertEquals(expectedCuts, actualCuts);
    }

    private Map organizeIntoBag(List allocatedAmounts) {
        Map bagOfCuts = new HashMap();

        for (Iterator i = allocatedAmounts.iterator(); i
            .hasNext();) {

            Money eachAmount = (Money) i.next();
            incrementCountForCutAmount(bagOfCuts, eachAmount);
        }
        return bagOfCuts;
    }

    private void incrementCountForCutAmount(Map bagOfCuts,
        Money eachAmount) {

        Object cutsForAmountAsObject = bagOfCuts
            .get(eachAmount);

        int cutsForAmount;
        if (cutsForAmountAsObject == null) {
            cutsForAmount = 0;
        } else {
            cutsForAmount = ((Integer) cutsForAmountAsObject)
                .intValue();
        }
```

```
        bagOfCuts.put(eachAmount,
            new Integer(cutsForAmount + 1));
    }
}
```

Next is the code for the object that builds the tests by parsing an XML document, and converting each test element into an `AllocateMoneyTest` object.

Listing A.2 AllocateMoneyTestBuilder

```
package junit.cookbook.suites.test;

import java.io.*;
import java.text.ParseException;
import java.util.*;

import javax.xml.parsers.*;
import javax.xml.transform.TransformerException;

import junit.framework.Assert;

import org.apache.xpath.XPathAPI;
import org.w3c.dom.*;
import org.xml.sax.SAXException;

import com.diasparsoftware.java.util.Money;

public class AllocateMoneyTestBuilder extends Assert {
    private String testFileName;

    public AllocateMoneyTestBuilder(String testFileName) {
        this.testFileName = testFileName;
    }

    public static List makeTests(String testFileName)
        throws Exception {

        return new AllocateMoneyTestBuilder(testFileName)
            .makeTests();
    }

    private List makeTests() throws Exception {
        List tests = new ArrayList();

        Document document = makeDocument(testFileName);

        NodeList testNodes = XPathAPI.selectNodeList(      // Test data elements
            document, "/tests/test");

        for (int i = 0; i < testNodes.getLength(); i++) {
            Node eachTestNode = testNodes.item(i);

            AllocateMoneyTest eachAllocateMoneyTest
                = makeAllocateMoneyTest(eachTestNode);
```

```
        tests.add(eachAllocateMoneyTest);
    }

    return tests;
}

private AllocateMoneyTest makeAllocateMoneyTest(Node eachTestNode)
    throws TransformerException, ParseException {

    Money amountToSplit = parseAsMoney(eachTestNode,
        "input/amount-to-split");

    int nWays = parseAsInt(eachTestNode,
        "input/number-of-ways");

    NodeList expectedCutNodes = XPathAPI.selectNodeList(
        eachTestNode, "expected-result/cut");

    Map expectedCuts = parseExpectedCuts(expectedCutNodes);

    AllocateMoneyTest eachAllocateMoneyTest = new AllocateMoneyTest(
        amountToSplit, nWays, expectedCuts);

    return eachAllocateMoneyTest;
}

private Document makeDocument(String documentFileName)
    throws FactoryConfigurationError,
    ParserConfigurationException, SAXException, IOException {

    DocumentBuilderFactory factory = DocumentBuilderFactory
        .newInstance();
    DocumentBuilder builder = factory.newDocumentBuilder();

    InputStream testDataAsStream = AllocateMoneyTestBuilder.class
        .getResourceAsStream(documentFileName);

    Document document = builder.parse(testDataAsStream);
    return document;
}

private Map parseExpectedCuts(NodeList expectedCutNodes)
    throws TransformerException, ParseException {

    Map expectedCuts = new HashMap();

    for (int i = 0; i < expectedCutNodes.getLength(); i++) {
        Node eachCutNode = expectedCutNodes.item(i);

        Money cutAmount = parseAsMoney(eachCutNode,
            "amount");
        int numberOfCuts = parseAsInt(eachCutNode, "number");

        expectedCuts.put(cutAmount, new Integer(
            numberOfCuts));
    }
```

Make a test from each test data element

```
        return expectedCuts;
    }

    private static int parseAsInt(Node fromNode,
        String xpathToInt) throws TransformerException {

        String intAsString = getNodeText(fromNode, xpathToInt);
        return Integer.parseInt(intAsString);
    }

    private static String getNodeText(Node fromNode,
        String xpath) throws TransformerException {

        Text text = (Text) XPathAPI.selectSingleNode(fromNode,
            xpath).getFirstChild();

        return text.getData();
    }

    private static Money parseAsMoney(Node fromNode,
        String xpathToMoneyObject) throws TransformerException,
        ParseException {

        String moneyAsString = getNodeText(fromNode,
            xpathToMoneyObject);

        return new Money(moneyAsString);
    }
}
```

A.2 Parameterized Test Case overriding runTest()

◆ Solution

This is a Parameterized Test Case that overrides `runTest()` and provides a meaningful name for each test. The test data is hard coded directly into the `suite()` method, although it could easily be extracted into a file.

NOTE *Be careful!*—Overriding `runTest()` does not work if you are using a JUnit-related framework that already overrides this method for its own purpose. For example, you cannot employ this technique with Cactus, because its test case classes override `runTest()` to determine whether to execute the test entirely on the client or on the server. If your test case class extends something other than `junit.framework.TestCase`, then we recommend you look at the source for that customized test case class and ensure that this approach is compatible with those customizations.

Listing A.3 AllocateMoneyTestOverridesRunTest

```
package junit.cookbook.suites.test;

import java.util.Collections;
import java.util.HashMap;
import java.util.Iterator;
import java.util.List;
import java.util.Map;

import junit.cookbook.util.Money;
import junit.framework.Test;
import junit.framework.TestCase;
import junit.framework.TestSuite;

public class AllocateMoneyTestOverridesRunTest extends TestCase {
    private Money amountToSplit;
    private int nWays;
    private Map expectedCuts;
    private Map actualCuts;

    public AllocateMoneyTestOverridesRunTest(
        String testName,
        Money amountToSplit,
        int nWays,
        Map expectedCuts) {

        super(testName);

        this.amountToSplit = amountToSplit;
        this.nWays = nWays;
        this.expectedCuts = expectedCuts;
    }

    public static Test suite() throws Exception {
        TestSuite suite = new TestSuite();

        Map oneGSixWays = new HashMap();
        oneGSixWays.put(new Money(166, 66), new Integer(2));
        oneGSixWays.put(new Money(166, 67), new Integer(4));
        suite.addTest(
            new AllocateMoneyTestOverridesRunTest(
                "testAllocate/Requires Rounding",
                new Money(1000, 0),
                6,
                oneGSixWays));

        Map oneGTwoWays =
            Collections.singletonMap(
                new Money(500, 0),
                new Integer(2));
        suite.addTest(
            new AllocateMoneyTestOverridesRunTest(
                "testAllocate/Goes Evenly",
                new Money(1000, 0),
```

```
                2,
                oneGTwoWays));

        Map oneGOneWay =
            Collections.singletonMap(
                new Money(1000, 0),
                new Integer(1));
        suite.addTest(
            new AllocateMoneyTestOverridesRunTest(
                "testAllocate/One Way",
                new Money(1000, 0),
                1,
                oneGOneWay));

        return suite;
    }

    protected void runTest() throws Throwable {
        List allocatedAmounts = amountToSplit.split(nWays);
        Map actualCuts = organizeIntoBag(allocatedAmounts);
        assertEquals(expectedCuts, actualCuts);
    }

    private Map organizeIntoBag(List allocatedAmounts) {
        Map bagOfCuts = new HashMap();

        for (Iterator i = allocatedAmounts.iterator();
            i.hasNext();
            ) {

            Money eachAmount = (Money) i.next();
            int cutsForAmount =
                getNumberOfCutsForAmount(bagOfCuts, eachAmount);

            bagOfCuts.put(
                eachAmount,
                new Integer(cutsForAmount + 1));
        }
        return bagOfCuts;
    }

    private int getNumberOfCutsForAmount(Map cuts, Money amount) {

        Object cutsForAmountAsObject = cuts.get(amount);
        int cutsForAmount;
        if (cutsForAmountAsObject == null) {
            cutsForAmount = 0;
        }
        else {
            cutsForAmount =
                ((Integer) cutsForAmountAsObject).intValue();
        }
        return cutsForAmount;
    }
}
```

The greatest difference between this and the other Parameterized Test Case is that it overrides `runTest()`, allowing you to give the tests meaningful names.

A.3 Ignore the order of elements in an XML document

◆ Solution

As we prepared the complete code solution, we noticed that the test itself contained some duplication, so we refactored a little further and the test is now about as compact (yet still expressive) as it can be. This test, and the accompanying methods, compares two web deployment descriptors to see whether the "action servlet"has the expected initialization parameters.

Listing A.4 StrutsDeploymentTest

```
package junit.cookbook.xmlunit.test;

import java.io.*;
import java.util.*;

import javax.xml.transform.TransformerException;

import org.apache.xpath.XPathAPI;
import org.custommonkey.xmlunit.*;
import org.w3c.dom.*;
import org.xml.sax.InputSource;

public class StrutsDeploymentTest extends XMLTestCase {
    public void testActionServletInitializationParameters()
        throws Exception {

        assertEquals(
            getInitializationParametersAsMapFromFile(
                "test/data/struts/expected-web.xml"),
            getInitializationParametersAsMapFromFile(
                "test/data/struts/web.xml"));
    }

    private Map getInitializationParametersAsMapFromFile(
        String filename) throws Exception {

        File webXmlFile = new File(filename);
        Document webXmlDocument = buildXmlDocument(webXmlFile);
        return getInitializationParametersAsMap(webXmlDocument);
    }

    private Document buildXmlDocument(File file)
        throws Exception {

        return XMLUnit.buildTestDocument(new InputSource(
```

```
                new FileInputStream(file)));
        }

        private Map getInitializationParametersAsMap(
            Document webXmlDocument) throws TransformerException {

            Map initializationParameters = new HashMap();

            NodeList initParamNodes = XPathAPI
                .selectNodeList(
                    webXmlDocument.getDocumentElement(),
                    "/web-app/servlet[servlet-name='action']/init-param");

            int matchingNodes = initParamNodes.getLength();

            assertFalse(
                "Found no nodes. Something wrong with XPath statement",    ❶
                matchingNodes == 0);

            for (int i = 0; i < matchingNodes; i++) {
                Node currentNode = initParamNodes.item(i);

                addInitializationParameter(
                    initializationParameters, currentNode);
            }

            return initializationParameters;
        }

        private void addInitializationParameter(
            Map initializationParameters, Node currentNode) {

            String name = null;
            String value = null;

            NodeList childNodes = currentNode.getChildNodes();
            for (int i = 0; i < childNodes.getLength(); i++) {
                Node each = childNodes.item(i);
                if ("param-name".equals(each.getNodeName())) {
                    name = getText(each);
                } else if ("param-value".equals(each.getNodeName())) {
                    value = getText(each);
                }
            }

            initializationParameters.put(name, value);
        }

        private String getText(Node each) {
            String nodeText = each.getFirstChild().getNodeValue();

            // What a shame we have to innoculate ourselves
            // against the DOM API returning us a null!
            return (nodeText == null) ? null : nodeText.trim();
        }
    }
```

❶ Verify that there are indeed matching nodes to check; otherwise, your XPath statement could be wrong and the test will not notice it! Instead, it will happily match empty node lists against each other and pass.

To make this code more reusable, simply extract the String `action` from the XPath expression that finds the initialization parameter nodes. This is the name of the Struts Action servlet, so it is a "magic value" for our purposes. Note, however, that `param-name` and `param-value` are (arguably) not magic values, as they are part of the well-known and slow-to-change servlet specification. We suppose that if the servlet specification changed tomorrow, you would have much bigger problems than having hard coded those two values.

Notice that we used the XMLUnit convenience method `buildTestDocument()` to parse our XML from a file. If your application uses a different parser than your tests, then you can register the two parsers with XMLUnit so that it can parse your control (expected) document with one parser and your test (actual) document with the other. If, as in this example, there is no difference, then you can use either `buildControlDocument()` or `buildTestDocument()` to parse XML, and rather arbitrarily, we chose the latter.

A.4 Test an XSL stylesheet in isolation

◆ Solution

We have taken the solution that we presented in recipe 9.6, "Test an XSL stylesheet in isolation," and expanded and refactored it. We added two tests: one for the case of one item in the shopcart and another for the case of three items in the shopcart. In the process, we decided to verify the content of the shopcart using plain XPath, rather than XMLUnit. Here is the entire test case class, followed by the reasoning behind our approach.

Listing A.5 DisplayShopcartXslTest

```
package junit.cookbook.coffee.presentation.xsl.test;

import java.io.FileInputStream;
import java.io.StringReader;

import javax.xml.transform.*;
import javax.xml.transform.stream.StreamSource;
import junit.cookbook.coffee.display.ShopcartItemBean;

import org.apache.xpath.XPathAPI;
```

```
import org.custommonkey.xmlunit.Transform;
import org.custommonkey.xmlunit.XMLTestCase;
import org.w3c.dom.*;

import com.diasparsoftware.java.util.Money;

public class DisplayShopcartXslTest extends XMLTestCase {
    private String displayShopcartXslFilename =
        "../CoffeeShopWeb/Web Content/WEB-INF"
            + "/style/displayShopcart.xsl";

    private Source displayShopcartXsl;

    protected void setUp() throws Exception {
        displayShopcartXsl =
            new StreamSource(
                new FileInputStream(displayShopcartXslFilename));
    }

    public void testEmpty() throws Exception {
        String shopcartXmlAsString =
            "<?xml version=\"1.0\" ?>"
                + "<shopcart>"
                + "<subtotal>$0.00</subtotal>"
                + "</shopcart>";

        Document displayShopcartDom =
            doDisplayShopcartTransformation(shopcartXmlAsString);

        assertShopcartTableExists(displayShopcartDom);
        assertSubtotalEquals("$0.00", displayShopcartDom);

        assertXpathNotExists(
            "//tr[@class='shopcartItem']",
            displayShopcartDom);
    }

    public void testOneItem() throws Exception {
        String shopcartXmlAsString =
            "<?xml version=\"1.0\" ?>"
                + "<shopcart>"
                + "<item id=\"762\">"
                + "<name>Special Blend</name>"
                + "<quantity>1</quantity>"
                + "<unit-price>$7.25</unit-price>"
                + "<total-price>$7.25</total-price>"
                + "</item>"
                + "<subtotal>$7.25</subtotal>"
                + "</shopcart>";

        Document displayShopcartDom =
            doDisplayShopcartTransformation(shopcartXmlAsString);

        assertShopcartTableExists(displayShopcartDom);
        assertSubtotalEquals("$7.25", displayShopcartDom);
```

```
        assertShopcartItemAtRowIndexEquals(
            new ShopcartItemBean(
                "Special Blend",
                "762",
                1,
                Money.dollars(7, 25)),
            displayShopcartDom,
            1);
    }

    public void testThreeItems() throws Exception {
        // NOTE: Be sure to put line breaks after each <item>
        // tag to avoid overstepping the limit for characters
        // on a single line.

        String shopcartXmlAsString =
            "<?xml version=\"1.0\" ?>"
                + "<shopcart>\n"
                + "<item id=\"762\">"
                + "<name>Special Blend</name>"
                + "<quantity>1</quantity>"
                + "<unit-price>$7.25</unit-price>"
                + "<total-price>$7.25</total-price>"
                + "</item>\n"
                + "<item id=\"001\">"
                + "<name>Short</name>"
                + "<quantity>2</quantity>"
                + "<unit-price>$6.50</unit-price>"
                + "<total-price>$13.00</total-price>"
                + "</item>\n"
                + "<item id=\"803\">"
                + "<name>Colombiano</name>"
                + "<quantity>4</quantity>"
                + "<unit-price>$8.00</unit-price>"
                + "<total-price>$32.00</total-price>"
                + "</item>\n"
                + "<subtotal>$52.25</subtotal>"
                + "</shopcart>";

        Document displayShopcartDom =
            doDisplayShopcartTransformation(shopcartXmlAsString);

        assertShopcartTableExists(displayShopcartDom);
        assertSubtotalEquals("$52.25", displayShopcartDom);

        assertShopcartItemAtRowIndexEquals(
            new ShopcartItemBean(
                "Special Blend",
                "762",
                1,
                Money.dollars(7, 25)),
            displayShopcartDom,
            1);
```

```
        assertShopcartItemAtRowIndexEquals(
            new ShopcartItemBean(
                "Short",
                "001",
                2,
                Money.dollars(6, 50)),
            displayShopcartDom,
            2);

        assertShopcartItemAtRowIndexEquals(
            new ShopcartItemBean(
                "Colombiano",
                "803",
                4,
                Money.dollars(8, 0)),
            displayShopcartDom,
            3);
    }

    public void assertSubtotalEquals(
        String expectedSubtotal,
        Document displayShopcartDom)
        throws TransformerException {

        assertXpathEvaluatesTo(
            expectedSubtotal,
            "//table[@name='shopcart']//td[@id='subtotal']",
            displayShopcartDom);
    }

    public void assertShopcartTableExists(
        Document displayShopcartDom)
        throws TransformerException {

        assertXpathExists(
            "//table[@name='shopcart']",
            displayShopcartDom);
    }

    public void assertShopcartItemAtRowIndexEquals(
        ShopcartItemBean expectedShopcartItemBean,
        Document displayShopcartDom,
        int rowIndex)
        throws TransformerException {

        Node productIdAttributeNode =
            XPathAPI.selectSingleNode(
                displayShopcartDom,
                "//tr[@class='shopcartItem']["
                    + rowIndex
                    + "]/@id");   ❶

        assertNotNull(
```

```
                "Cannot find product ID at row index " + rowIndex,
                productIdAttributeNode);

        String productId =
            ((Attr) productIdAttributeNode).getValue();

        NodeList columnNodes =                                    ❷
            XPathAPI.selectNodeList(
                displayShopcartDom,
                "//tr[@class='shopcartItem']["
                    + rowIndex
                    + "]/td");

        String actualCoffeeName =
            getTextAtNode(columnNodes.item(0));
        String actualQuantityAsString =
            getTextAtNode(columnNodes.item(1));
        String actualUnitPriceAsString =
              getTextAtNode(columnNodes.item(2));

        ShopcartItemBean actualShopcartItemBean =
            new ShopcartItemBean(
                actualCoffeeName,
                productId,
                Integer.parseInt(
                    actualQuantityAsString),
                Money.parse(
                    actualUnitPriceAsString));

        assertEquals(
            "Wrong shopcart item in row #" + rowIndex,
            expectedShopcartItemBean,
            actualShopcartItemBean);  ❸
    }

    public String getTextAtNode(Node tableDataNode) {
        return tableDataNode.getFirstChild().getNodeValue();
    }

    public Document doDisplayShopcartTransformation(
        String shopcartXmlAsString)
        throws
            TransformerConfigurationException,
            TransformerException {

        Source shopcartXml =
            new StreamSource(
                new StringReader(shopcartXmlAsString));

        Transform transform =
            new Transform(shopcartXml, displayShopcartXsl);

        return transform.getResultDocument();
    }
}
```

1. Because the coffee product ID is not something we want to display to the end user, but is something we want to verify, we need to include it in the table row as the table row's ID.

2. Rather than write four separate assertions for the information in the four columns, we use plain XPath to retrieve the table data cells in this table row and create a `ShopcartItemBean` from the data we display on the page.

3. This is the simpler assertion we can make as a result of the previous design decision. The alternative was to invoke `assertXpathEvaluatesTo()` for each column in the row. We did not like the resulting duplication, which is the reason for our design choice.

For completion, listing A.6 shows an XSL stylesheet that passes these tests.

Listing A.6 XSL stylesheet for displaying a shopcart

```
<?xml version="1.0" encoding="UTF-8"?>
<xsl:stylesheet xmlns:xsl="http://www.w3.org/1999/XSL/Transform"
    version="1.0"
    xmlns:xalan="http://xml.apache.org/xslt">

<xsl:template match="/">
    <html>
    <head>
    <meta http-equiv="Content-Type"
          content="text/html; charset=ISO-8859-1" />
    <meta name="GENERATOR" content="IBM WebSphere Studio" />
    <meta http-equiv="Content-Style-Type" content="text/css" />
    <link href="theme/Master.css" rel="stylesheet" type="text/css" />
    <title>Your Shopcart</title>
    </head>
    <body>

    <xsl:apply-templates />

    </body>
    </html>
</xsl:template>


<xsl:template match="shopcart">
    <h1>your shopcart contains</h1>
    <table name="shopcart" border="1">
        <thead>
            <tr>
                <th>Name</th>
                <th>Quantity</th>
                <th>Unit Price</th>
                <th>Total Price</th>
            </tr>
```

```
        </thead>
        <tbody>

    <xsl:apply-templates />

            <tr>
                <td colspan="3">Subtotal</td>
                <td class="subtotal" id="subtotal">
                    <xsl:value-of select="subtotal" />
                </td>
            </tr>
        </tbody>
    </table>

    <form action="coffee" method="POST"><input type="submit"
        name="browseCatalog" value="Buy More Coffee!" /></form>
</xsl:template>

<xsl:template match="item">
            <tr class="shopcartItem" id="{@id}">
                <td><xsl:value-of select="name" /></td>
                <td><xsl:value-of select="quantity" /></td>
                <td><xsl:value-of select="unit-price" /></td>
                <td><xsl:value-of select="total-price" /></td>
            </tr>
</xsl:template>

</xsl:stylesheet>
```

Even for such a relatively simple web page we have had to write approximately 100 lines of custom assertions and XML parsing code to implement our tests. It would likely be less effort to switch to HtmlUnit at this point, as we describe in recipe 12.10, "Verify web page content without a web server."

A.5 Validate XML documents in your tests

◆ Solution

The following is an example of an XSL transformation service that validates incoming XML documents on demand. Although this solution validates only the XML document to transform, you could easily use the same approach to validate the XSL stylesheet as well. The keys to the solution are:

1. Provide a method to enable document validation.
2. Provide a method to ask whether the document is valid.
3. Provide a method to return a collection of validation problems, if any.

Listing A.7 TransformXmlService

```
package junit.cookbook.xmlunit;

import java.io.*;
import java.util.ArrayList;
import java.util.Collection;

import javax.xml.transform.*;
import javax.xml.transform.dom.DOMSource;
import javax.xml.transform.stream.StreamResult;
import javax.xml.transform.stream.StreamSource;

import org.apache.xerces.parsers.DOMParser;
import org.w3c.dom.Document;
import org.xml.sax.*;

public class TransformXmlService {
    private Transformer transformer;
    private Reader stylesheetReader;
    private boolean sourceDocumentValidationEnabled;
    private Collection validationProblems = new ArrayList();

    public TransformXmlService(Reader stylesheetReader) {
        this.stylesheetReader = stylesheetReader;
    }

    public void transform(StreamSource source, Result result)
        throws TransformerException, SAXException, IOException {    ❶

        if (sourceDocumentValidationEnabled) {
            Document sourceDocument =
                validateAndReturnSourceDocument(source);

            getTransformer().transform(
                new DOMSource(sourceDocument),
                result);
        }
        else {
            getTransformer().transform(source, result);
        }
    }

    private Document validateAndReturnSourceDocument(
        StreamSource source)
        throws
            SAXNotRecognizedException,
            SAXNotSupportedException,
            SAXException,
            IOException {

        DOMParser parser = new DOMParser();
        parser.setFeature(
            "http://xml.org/sax/features/validation",
            true);    ❷
```

```
    validationProblems.clear();

    parser.setErrorHandler(new ErrorHandler() {   ❸
        public void error(SAXParseException exception)
            throws SAXException {

            validationProblems.add(exception);
        }

        public void fatalError(SAXParseException exception)
            throws SAXException {

            validationProblems.add(exception);
        }

        public void warning(SAXParseException exception)
            throws SAXException {
        }
    });

    parser.parse(new InputSource(source.getReader()));
    Document sourceDocument = parser.getDocument();
    return sourceDocument;
}

public void setTransformer(Transformer transformer) {
    this.transformer = transformer;
}

public Transformer getTransformer() {
    if (transformer == null) {
        try {
            transformer =
                TransformerFactory.newInstance().newTransformer(
                    new StreamSource(stylesheetReader));
        }

        catch (TransformerConfigurationException e) {
            throw new RuntimeException(
                "Unable to create transformer",
                e);
        }
    }
    return transformer;
}

public void transform(
    String xmlDocumentAsString,
    Writer resultWriter)
    throws TransformerException, SAXException, IOException {

    transform(
        new StreamSource(new StringReader(xmlDocumentAsString)),
        new StreamResult(resultWriter));
}
```

```
    public void setSourceDocumentValidationEnabled(
        boolean sourceDocumentValidationEnabled) {

        this.sourceDocumentValidationEnabled =
            sourceDocumentValidationEnabled;
    }

    public boolean isSourceDocumentValid() {
        if (sourceDocumentValidationEnabled)
            return validationProblems.isEmpty();
        else
            return true;
    }

    public Collection getValidationProblems() {
        return validationProblems;
    }
}
```

1. We must demand the incoming XML document as a `StreamSource`, rather than just a `Source`, in order to be able to run it through an XML parser. This adds a constraint to clients using this solution. If you need to process documents from a `SAXSource` or a `DOMSource`, then you need to adapt this solution slightly.

2. Consult your XML parser's documentation—or write some Learning Tests—to verify that your XML parser supports this feature. We verified this with the Xerces 2.5.0 parser.

3. The key to the solution: this is the standard way to collect errors during XML parsing, including validation errors. You can choose here which kinds of messages to collect. In particular, we ignore warnings, although you might wish to treat them as errors worth reporting.

The last three methods are the ones your tests will use to enable validation and verify that incoming XML documents are valid. Your XML processing service, whatever it does, should then decide whether to invoke `validateAndReturnSourceDocument()`. This performs the actual validation. Although we have used this technique in the context of XSL transformation, you can use this technique anywhere you process XML documents. In the interest of performance, however, do not parse and validate the XML document unless the client has enabled validation, as validating large XML documents is particularly expensive.

A.6 Aspect-based universal Spy

◆ Solution

We need an aspect to intercept every method invocation in a test and record those invocations so that we can verify them later. This is much like method tracing, which is a core application of Aspect-Oriented Programming. Many thanks to Ramnivas Laddad, author of *AspectJ in Action* (Manning, 2003) for his solution, which uses the Wormhole pattern in chapter 8 of that book.

First, let us look at the class under test. To illustrate the power of this technique, we want to verify that a `public` method invokes a `private` method, something we would ordinarily need to do by observing some side effect of the `private` method. In the case of this trivial class, there *is* no side effect to observe!

```
package com.mycompany;

public class SomeClass {
    public void publicMethod() {
        privateMethod();
    }

    private void privateMethod() { }
}
```

We choose to test this using the "Log String" technique that Kent Beck describes in *Test-Driven Development: By Example*. First we collect the names of the invoked methods, and then we verify the contents of that collection for the methods we expect. Unlike Kent's implementation, however, we do not need to implement a mock version of `SomeClass` that collects the name of each invoked method. Here is the test we want to write.

Listing A.8 Testing `SomeClass` with the universal Spy

```
package com.mycompany.tests;

import com.mycompany.SomeClass;
import java.util.*;
import junit.cookbook.patterns.test.aspectj.UniversalSpyFixture;
import junit.framework.TestCase;

public class SomeClassTest extends UniversalSpyFixture {
    public void testPublicInvokesPrivate()
        throws Exception {

        setExpectedMethodNames(
            Arrays.asList(
            new Object[]{"publicMethod", "privateMethod"}));
```

```
        new SomeClass().publicMethod();
    }
}
```

Here we simply specify the names of the methods we expect to be invoked, then invoke the *one* method that causes the other to be invoked. Think of a long line of dominoes: we expect them all to fall after we topple only the first one. We achieve this method tracing without having to write a mock version of `SomeClass`. Instead, we use a universal Spy consisting of three parts.

- The Spy itself, which contains the list of methods invoked during a test
- The `UniversalSpyFixture`, a test fixture that contains a universal Spy capturing all the relevant method invocations for each test
- An aspect that intercepts method invocations and records the name of the invoked method (If you are not familiar with AspectJ, we recommend Ramnivas's excellent book on the subject.)

In decreasing order of complexity (and therefore interest), let us first look at the aspect in question.

Listing A.9 The universal Spy aspect

```
package junit.cookbook.patterns.test.aspectj;

import java.util.*;
import junit.framework.*;

public aspect RecordTestCaseInvokedMethodNames {
    public pointcut testExecution(UniversalSpyFixture testCase)
        : execution(* UniversalSpyFixture+.test*(..))
          && this(testCase);

    public pointcut anyMethodInvocation(UniversalSpyFixture testCase)
        : execution(* *.*(..))
      && cflowbelow(testExecution(testCase))
      && !within(junit.cookbook.patterns.test.aspectj.*);

    before(UniversalSpyFixture testCase)
        : anyMethodInvocation(testCase) {

        testCase.getSpy().signalInvokedMethod(
            thisJoinPointStaticPart.getSignature().getName());
    }

    after(UniversalSpyFixture testCase) returning
        : testExecution(testCase) {

        Assert.assertEquals(
```

```
            testCase.getExpectedMethodNames(),
            testCase.getSpy().getInvokedMethodNames());
    }
}
```

The pointcut[1] `anyMethodInvocation()` intercepts any method invoked within a test case, excluding methods of the universal Spy machinery itself, which do not interest us anyway. The two pieces of advice are simple enough: before invoking *any* method within the execution of a test, have the universal Spy record the name of the method about to be invoked. After the test finishes executing, verify that the expected method names (which the test itself sets at some point) matches the collection of methods actually invoked.

The `UniversalSpyFixture` simply provides a fixture with a universal Spy and a placeholder for the list of method names you expect each test to invoke.

Listing A.10 `UniversalSpyFixture`

```
package junit.cookbook.patterns.test.aspectj;

import java.util.*;
import junit.framework.TestCase;

public abstract class UniversalSpyFixture extends TestCase {
    private List expectedMethodNames;
    private UniversalSpy spy = new UniversalSpy();

    public List getExpectedMethodNames() {
        return expectedMethodNames;
    }

    public void setExpectedMethodNames(List names) {
        expectedMethodNames = names;
    }

    public UniversalSpy getSpy() {
        return spy;
    }
}
```

And finally the `UniversalSpy` itself is a collector for invoked method names.

[1] A pointcut is a construct that selects execution points in a program as well as their surrounding context. For a more detailed definition, and more information about cross-cutting elements in Aspect-Oriented Programming, see Ramnivas Laddad, *AspectJ in Action* (Manning, 2003), section 2.1.2.

Listing A.11 `UniveralSpy`

```
package junit.cookbook.patterns.test.aspectj;

import java.util.*;

public class UniversalSpy {
    private List invokedMethodNames = new ArrayList();

    protected void signalInvokedMethod(String methodName) {
        invokedMethodNames.add(methodName);
    }

    public List getInvokedMethodNames() {
        return Collections.unmodifiableList(invokedMethodNames);
    }
}
```

You can reuse this code *as is* in your tests, as long as you do not mind recording *all* method invocations inside each test. If you need to narrow your focus to, say, an individual class, then you need to change the aspect `RecordTestCaseInvokedMethodNames`, making its pointcuts match only those methods or objects in which you have an interest.

NOTE *Building the solution*—Compiling aspects and weaving them into source code is a little different than compiling plain vanilla Java code. In particular, you need to compile *all* the source files and *all* the desired aspects together at one time.[2] If you attempt to compile them separately, then you will not get the desired result.[3] You need to compile the code with this command (the important part is the `sourceroots` value, and not the directory to which the compiled code is to be written):

```
ajc -sourceroots "com/mycompany;
⇒ junit/cookbook/patterns/test/aspectj" -d .
```

[2] See Ramnivas Laddad, *AspectJ in Action* (Manning, 2003), section 3.4, "Tips and tricks."

[3] Worse, as we found out, the test passes even when the required aspect is not weaved into the code. The simplest solution we found was to move the assertion from the aspect into the test to ensure that the assertion is executed and fails when the aspect is not weaved into the code.

A.7 Test a BMP entity bean

◆ Solution

Starting with a BMP entity bean that implements everything in one place, we applied a few refactorings to reach a final design that is significantly easier to test. Here is where we started—this is the original BMP entity bean. This listing is particularly long at about 250 lines, and it is just the beginning. There is a *large* amount of code in this solution.

Listing A.12 A BMP entity bean for orders

```
package junit.cookbook.coffee.model.ejb;

import java.rmi.RemoteException;
import java.sql.*;

import javax.ejb.*;
import javax.naming.*;
import javax.sql.DataSource;
import junit.cookbook.coffee.data.*;

public class OrderBmpBean implements EntityBean {
    private EntityContext context;
    private DataSource dataSource;

    private Integer customerId;

    public Integer getCustomerId() {
        return customerId;
    }

    public Integer ejbFindByPrimaryKey(Integer orderId)
        throws FinderException, RemoteException {

        Connection connection = null;
        PreparedStatement statement = null;

        try {
            connection = getConnection();

            statement =
                connection.prepareStatement(
                    "select orderId from orders.orders "
                        + "where orderId = ?");

            statement.setInt(1, orderId.intValue());
            ResultSet resultSet = statement.executeQuery();

            if (resultSet.next() == false) {
                throw new ObjectNotFoundException(
                    "Order ID <" + orderId.toString() + ">");
            }
```

```
            return orderId;
        }
        catch (NamingException report) {
            throw new FinderException(report.toString());
        }
        catch (SQLException report) {
            throw new FinderException(report.toString());
        }
        finally {
            try {
                if (statement != null)
                    statement.close();

                if (connection != null)
                    connection.close();
            }
            catch (SQLException ignored) {
            }
        }
    }

    public Integer ejbCreate(Integer orderId, Integer customerId)
        throws CreateException, RemoteException {

        this.customerId = customerId;

        Connection connection = null;
        PreparedStatement statement = null;

        try {
            connection = getConnection();

            statement =
                connection.prepareStatement(
                    "insert into orders.orders (orderId, customerId) "
                        + "values (?, ?)");

            statement.setInt(1, orderId.intValue());
            statement.setInt(2, customerId.intValue());

            statement.executeUpdate();

            return orderId;
        }
        catch (Exception wrap) {
            throw new EJBException(
                "Unable to create order with ID <" + orderId + ">",
                wrap);
        }
        finally {
            try {
                if (statement != null)
                    statement.close();

                if (connection != null)
```

```
                connection.close();
            }
            catch (SQLException ignored) {
            }
        }
    }

    public void ejbPostCreate(Integer orderId, Integer customerId) {
    }

    private Connection getConnection()
        throws SQLException, NamingException {
        return getDataSource().getConnection();
    }

    private DataSource getDataSource() throws NamingException {
        if (dataSource == null) {
            Context rootContext = new InitialContext();
            Object object =
                rootContext.lookup("java:/comp/env/jdbc/OrderData");
            dataSource = (DataSource) object;
        }
        return dataSource;
    }

    public void ejbLoad() throws EJBException, RemoteException {
        Connection connection = null;
        PreparedStatement statement = null;
        ResultSet resultSet = null;

        Integer orderId = (Integer) context.getPrimaryKey();

        try {
            connection = getConnection();

            statement =
                connection.prepareStatement(
                    "select * from orders.orders where orderId = ?");

            statement.setInt(1, orderId.intValue());

            resultSet = statement.executeQuery();
            resultSet.next();

            customerId = new Integer(resultSet.getInt("customerId"));
        }
        catch (Exception wrap) {
            throw new EJBException(
                "Unable to load order with ID <" + orderId + ">",
                wrap);
        }
        finally {
            try {
                if (resultSet != null)
                    resultSet.close();
```

```
                if (statement != null)
                    statement.close();

                if (connection != null)
                    connection.close();
            }
            catch (SQLException ignored) {
            }
        }
    }

    public void ejbRemove()
        throws RemoveException, EJBException, RemoteException {
        Connection connection = null;
        PreparedStatement statement = null;

        Integer orderId = (Integer) context.getPrimaryKey();

        try {
            connection = getConnection();

            statement =
                connection.prepareStatement(
                    "delete from orders.orders where orderId = ?");

            statement.setInt(1, orderId.intValue());

            statement.executeUpdate();
        }
        catch (Exception wrap) {
            throw new EJBException(
                "Unable to remove order with ID <" + orderId + ">",
                wrap);
        }
        finally {
            try {
                if (statement != null)
                    statement.close();

                if (connection != null)
                    connection.close();
            }
            catch (SQLException ignored) {
            }
        }
    }

    public void ejbStore() throws EJBException, RemoteException {
        Connection connection = null;
        PreparedStatement statement = null;

        Integer orderId = (Integer) context.getPrimaryKey();

        try {
            connection = getConnection();
```

```
            statement =
                connection.prepareStatement(
                    "update orders.orders set customerId = ? "
                        + "where orderId = ?");

            statement.setInt(1, customerId.intValue());
            statement.setInt(2, orderId.intValue());

            statement.executeUpdate();
        }
        catch (Exception wrap) {
            throw new EJBException(
                "Unable to store order with ID <" + orderId + ">",
                wrap);
        }
        finally {
            try {
                if (statement != null)
                    statement.close();

                if (connection != null)
                    connection.close();
            }
            catch (SQLException ignored) {
            }
        }
    }

    public void setEntityContext(EntityContext context)
        throws EJBException, RemoteException {

        this.context = context;
    }

    public void unsetEntityContext()
        throws EJBException, RemoteException {

        this.context = null;
    }

    public void ejbActivate() throws EJBException, RemoteException {
    }

    public void ejbPassivate() throws EJBException, RemoteException {
    }
}
```

In its current state, this entity bean needs to be tested in the container, and so it requires working test data, a correctly populated JNDI directory, and all the associated startup and shutdown costs. First, we moved almost all the code out to a new class, leaving behind only JNDI lookups and managing the primary key. Here is the entity bean after this refactoring.

Listing A.13 A thinner BMP entity bean for orders

```
package junit.cookbook.coffee.model.ejb;

import java.rmi.RemoteException;

import javax.ejb.*;
import javax.naming.*;
import javax.sql.DataSource;

import junit.cookbook.coffee.data.OrderRow;
import junit.cookbook.coffee.data.jdbc.*;

public class OrderBmpBean implements EntityBean {
    private EntityContext context;
    private OrderBmpBeanLogic logic;

    public String getCustomerId() {
        return logic.getCustomerId();
    }

    public void setCustomerId(String customerId) {
        logic.setCustomerId(customerId);
    }

    public void setEntityContext(EntityContext context)
        throws EJBException, RemoteException {

        this.context = context;
        makeBeanLogicObject();
    }

    protected void makeBeanLogicObject() {
        DataSourceConnectionProvider connectionProvider =
            new DataSourceConnectionProvider(lookupDataSource());

        OrderStoreCommandExecuter orderStoreCommandExecuter =
            new OrderStoreCommandExecuterJdbcImpl(
                new OrderStoreCommandExecuterEjbImpl(
                    new SimpleOrderStoreCommandExecuter()),
                connectionProvider);

        this.logic =
            new OrderBmpBeanLogic(
                new OrderStoreJdbcImpl(),
                orderStoreCommandExecuter);
    }

    public void unsetEntityContext()
        throws EJBException, RemoteException {

        this.context = null;
    }

    public Integer ejbFindByPrimaryKey(Integer orderId)
        throws FinderException, RemoteException {
```

```
        return logic.ejbFindByPrimaryKey(orderId);
    }

    public Integer ejbCreate(Integer orderId, String customerId)
        throws CreateException, RemoteException {

        return logic.ejbCreate(orderId, customerId);
    }

    public void ejbPostCreate(Integer orderId, String customerId) {
    }

    public void ejbLoad() throws EJBException, RemoteException {
        logic.ejbLoad(getOrderId());
    }

    public void ejbRemove()
        throws RemoveException, EJBException, RemoteException {

        logic.ejbRemove(getOrderId());
    }

    public void ejbStore() throws EJBException, RemoteException {
        logic.ejbStore();
    }

    public void ejbActivate() throws EJBException, RemoteException {
    }

    public void ejbPassivate() throws EJBException, RemoteException {
    }

    public static DataSource lookupDataSource() {
        try {
            Context rootContext = new InitialContext();
            Object object =
                rootContext.lookup("java:comp/env/jdbc/OrderData");
            return (DataSource) object;
        }
        catch (NamingException wrap) {
            throw new EJBException(
                "Unable to retrieve data source",
                wrap);
        }
    }

    public Integer getOrderId() {
        return (Integer) context.getPrimaryKey();
    }
}
```

There is a combination of paper-thin EJB lifecycle methods, a JNDI lookup, and a considerable amount of work to create the `OrderBmpBeanLogic` object, which we have highlighted in bold print. This is where most of the action now takes place. This Bean Logic class uses an `OrderStore`—a persistent store for order objects—and a specialized `OrderStoreCommandExecuter`, which hides the ugliness of handling JDBC exceptions and generating EJB exceptions. The `OrderStore` is modeled after the `CatalogStore` we developed in chapter 10, "Testing and JDBC," so we simply present the interface first, and then the JDBC implementation that our entity bean needs to store order objects in the database. The `OrderStore` operates on `OrderRow` objects—each represents a row in the `orders.orders` table, relating each order to the customer who placed it, using their primary keys.

```
package junit.cookbook.coffee.data;

public interface OrderStore {
    boolean exists(Integer orderId);
    void create(OrderRow orderRow);
    OrderRow findByOrderId(Integer orderId);
    void remove(Integer orderId);
    void update(final OrderRow orderRow);
}
```

Each of these methods corresponds to an EJB lifecycle method. For example, `OrderBmpBean.ejbFindByPrimaryKey()` needs to check that the `OrderRow` exists using `OrderStore.exists()`. The JDBC implementation of `OrderStore` uses the Diasparsoft Toolkit JDBC classes to simplify its implementation. The result is the following class named `OrderStoreJdbcImpl`.

Listing A.14 JDBC implementation of `OrderStore`

```
package junit.cookbook.coffee.data.jdbc;

import java.sql.*;
import java.util.*;

import junit.cookbook.coffee.data.*;
import junit.cookbook.coffee.model.*;

import com.diasparsoftware.java.sql.PreparedStatementData;
import com.diasparsoftware.jdbc.*;

public class OrderStoreJdbcImpl implements OrderStore {
    private JdbcQueryExecuter executer;

    public void open(Connection connection) {
        this.setExecuter(new JdbcQueryExecuter(connection));
    }

    public void close() {
        this.executer = null;
    }
```

```
private JdbcQueryExecuter getExecuter() {
    if (executer == null) {
        throw new IllegalStateException(
            "Please provide me with a database connection first.");
    }
    return executer;
}

private void setExecuter(JdbcQueryExecuter executer) {
    this.executer = executer;
}

public boolean exists(Integer orderId) {
    PreparedStatementData countOrdersByIdStatementData =
        new PreparedStatementData(
            "select count(orderId) from orders.orders "
                + "where orderId = ?",
            Collections.singletonList(orderId));

    int rowCount =
        getExecuter().executeCountStatement(
            countOrdersByIdStatementData);

    return (rowCount > 0);
}

public void create(final OrderRow orderRow) {

    List parameters = new ArrayList() {
        {
            add(orderRow.orderId);
            add(orderRow.customerId);
        }
    };

    PreparedStatementData insertStatementData =
        new PreparedStatementData(
            "insert into orders.orders (orderId, customerId) "
                + "values (?, ?)",
            parameters);

    getExecuter().executeInsertStatement(insertStatementData);
}

public OrderRow findByOrderId(final Integer orderId) {
    PreparedStatementData selectStatementData =
        new PreparedStatementData(
            "select * from orders.orders where orderId = ?",
            Collections.singletonList(orderId));

    List orders =
        getExecuter().executeSelectStatement(
            selectStatementData,
            new OrderRowMapper());
```

```
        return (OrderRow) orders.get(0);
    }

    public void remove(Integer orderId) {
        PreparedStatementData deleteStatementData =
            new PreparedStatementData(
                "delete from orders.orders where orderId = ?",
                Collections.singletonList(orderId));

        getExecuter().executeDeleteStatement(deleteStatementData);
    }

    public void update(final OrderRow orderRow) {
        List parameters = new ArrayList() {
            {
                add(orderRow.customerId);
                add(orderRow.orderId);
            }
        };

        PreparedStatementData updateStatementData =
            new PreparedStatementData(
                "update orders.orders set customerId = ? "
                    + "where orderId = ?",
                parameters);

        getExecuter().executeUpdateStatement(updateStatementData);
    }

    public static class OrderRowMapper extends JdbcRowMapper {
        public Object makeDomainObject(ResultSet row)
            throws SQLException {

            Integer orderId = (Integer) row.getObject("orderId");
            String customerId = row.getString("customerId");

            return new OrderRow(orderId, customerId);
        }
    }
}
```

Each of the methods of this class follows the same basic rhythm: collect the parameters, create a `PreparedStatementData` object, and then execute the corresponding SQL statement. To enable transactional behavior, we want the JDBC connection to be passed in from outside. For this reason, we originally had a constructor that took a connection as a parameter; however, to avoid unnecessary object creation and to simplify other code, we moved to an open/close design: to use the JDBC-based `OrderStore`, you "open" it with a database connection, then "close" it when you have finished. Closing the JDBC-based `OrderStore` does *not* close the database connection—never close connections you do not own—but causes it to release its reference to the connection, so as not to leak connections. So much for `OrderStore` and its JDBC-based implementation.

Next are the `OrderStoreCommandExecuters`. These evolved when we extracted duplication out of the original entity bean's lifecycle methods. Notably, each method was doing two things:

- Obtaining a database connection, invoking some JDBC client code, and closing the database connection.
- Invoking some `OrderStore` code, and wrapping all `DataStoreExceptions` into `EJBExceptions`.

We wanted to remove this duplication, so we extracted the first pattern into its own method, then moved that method into its own class. Here is the result. Whenever we see "invoke some code" inside a recurring implementation pattern, we know that the Command pattern is lurking in there, and sure enough, as we refactored, the class `OrderStoreCommand` appeared, as if out of nowhere. We had originally implemented the JDBC client code in `Closure` objects,[4] but realized that a Command is essentially just a type-safe `Closure`, so we created the class `OrderStoreCommand` and the associated command executers. This first one ensures that when we execute an `OrderStoreCommand` on a JDBC-based `OrderStore`, we manage the database connection correctly.

Listing A.15 `OrderStoreCommand`

```
package junit.cookbook.coffee.data.jdbc;

import java.sql.*;

import junit.cookbook.coffee.data.*;

public class OrderStoreCommandExecuterJdbcImpl
    implements OrderStoreCommandExecuter {

    private OrderStoreCommandExecuter executer;
    private ConnectionProvider connectionProvider;

    public OrderStoreCommandExecuterJdbcImpl(
        OrderStoreCommandExecuter executer,
        ConnectionProvider connectionProvider) {

        this.executer = executer;
        this.connectionProvider = connectionProvider;
    }
```

[4] See the Jakarta Commons Collections package for more about the interface `Closure`. (http://jakarta.apache.org/commons/collections.html)

```
    public void execute(
        OrderStore orderStore,
        OrderStoreCommand orderStoreCommand,
        String exceptionMessage) {

        OrderStoreJdbcImpl orderStoreJdbcImpl =
            (OrderStoreJdbcImpl) orderStore;

        Connection connection = connectionProvider.getConnection();
        orderStoreJdbcImpl.open(connection);

        try {
            executer.execute(
                orderStoreJdbcImpl,
                orderStoreCommand,
                exceptionMessage);
        }
        finally {
            try {
                orderStoreJdbcImpl.close();
                connection.close();
            }
            catch (SQLException ignored) {
            }
        }
    }
}
```

You can see how this class implements the pattern: obtain a connection, open the JDBC-based `OrderStore`, execute the JDBC client code (the "order store command"), and then ensure (with a `finally` block) that the connection is closed. We also implemented the second pattern—wrapping a `DataStoreException` inside an `EJBException`—as a command executer. Here is the code.

Listing A.16 EJB-based `OrderStoreCommand` executer

```
package junit.cookbook.coffee.model.ejb;

import javax.ejb.EJBException;

import junit.cookbook.coffee.data.*;

import com.diasparsoftware.store.DataStoreException;

public class OrderStoreCommandExecuterEjbImpl
    implements OrderStoreCommandExecuter {

    private OrderStoreCommandExecuter executer;

    public OrderStoreCommandExecuterEjbImpl(
        OrderStoreCommandExecuter executer) {

        this.executer = executer;
    }
```

```
    public void execute(
        OrderStore orderStore,
        OrderStoreCommand orderStoreCommand,
        String exceptionMessage) {

        try {
            executer.execute(
                orderStore,
                orderStoreCommand,
                exceptionMessage);
        }
        catch (DataStoreException wrap) {
            throw new EJBException(exceptionMessage, wrap);
        }
    }
}
```

These command executers implement the Decorator pattern: each performs its specific work, then asks the next command executer to do its work, eventually ending with a command executer that simply executes the command. This pattern makes it simpler to add behavior to the act of executing a command by literally adding behavior on top of behavior. We can reuse the JDBC Decorator without the EJB Decorator when we abandon BMP entity beans and move to plain-vanilla Java objects using JDBC. All we have to do is create a JDBC-based command executer that wraps the "just execute the command" command executer, which we named `SimpleOrderStoreCommandExecuter`. Here is the code:

```
package junit.cookbook.coffee.data;

public class SimpleOrderStoreCommandExecuter
    implements OrderStoreCommandExecuter {

    public void execute(
        OrderStore orderStore,
        OrderStoreCommand orderStoreCommand,
        String exceptionMessage) {

        orderStoreCommand.execute(orderStore);
    }
}
```

We think this is worthy of a name starting with "simple." It even ignores the exception message, as it does not handle any exceptions. Returning to `OrderBmpBeanLogic`, we see how these command executers fit together.

```
OrderStoreCommandExecuter orderStoreCommandExecuter =
    new OrderStoreCommandExecuterJdbcImpl(
        new OrderStoreCommandExecuterEjbImpl(
```

```
            new SimpleOrderStoreCommandExecuter()),
        connectionProvider);
```

When OrderBmpBeanLogic uses this command executer to execute an OrderStoreCommand, it first manages the database connection properly (JDBC command executer), then wraps any exceptions in an EJBException (EJB command executer), then finally executes the command. If we were to reuse the OrderBmpBeanLogic outside the context of an EJB (and really at that point we should invent a better name), then we could change the above code to the following, removing the EJB command executer and thereby letting DataStoreExceptions be reported as they are. If you were to remove EJBs from a typically designed J2EE application, think of all the exception handlers you would have to change! Here, it is a one-line change.

```
OrderStoreCommandExecuter orderStoreCommandExecuter =
    new OrderStoreCommandExecuterJdbcImpl(
        new SimpleOrderStoreCommandExecuter()),
        connectionProvider);
```

No more EJBExceptions! It really is that simple. Now enough is enough: let us look at OrderBeanBmpLogic. It contains methods that correspond to the entity bean lifecycle methods, and to create one of these, you supply an OrderStore and a command executer. This class essentially does what the corresponding entity bean would do without relying on an EJB container or even a database-aware OrderStore. It would work entirely in memory too!

Listing A.17 Business logic POJO for orders

```
package junit.cookbook.coffee.model.ejb;

import java.rmi.RemoteException;

import javax.ejb.*;

import junit.cookbook.coffee.data.*;

public class OrderBmpBeanLogic {
    private OrderStore orderStore;
    private OrderStoreCommandExecuter executer;
    private OrderRow orderRow;

    public OrderBmpBeanLogic(
        OrderStore orderStore,
        OrderStoreCommandExecuter executer) {

        this.orderStore = orderStore;
        this.executer = executer;
    }

    public Integer ejbFindByPrimaryKey(final Integer orderId)
        throws ObjectNotFoundException {
```

```
    OrderStoreCommand orderStoreLogic = new OrderStoreCommand() {
        private boolean orderExists;

        public void execute(OrderStore orderStore) {
            orderExists = orderStore.exists(orderId);
        }

        public Object getReturnValue() {
            return new Boolean(orderExists);
        }
    };

    String failureMessage =
        "Unable to find order with ID <" + orderId + ">";

    executer.execute(orderStore, orderStoreLogic, failureMessage);

    boolean orderExists =
        ((Boolean) orderStoreLogic.getReturnValue())
            .booleanValue();

    if (orderExists)
        return orderId;
    else
        throw new ObjectNotFoundException(failureMessage);
}

public Integer ejbCreate(Integer orderId, String customerId) {
    orderRow = new OrderRow(orderId, customerId);

    OrderStoreCommand command = new OrderStoreCommand() {
        public void execute(OrderStore orderStore) {
            orderStore.create(orderRow);
        }
    };

    String failureMessage =
        "Unable to create order with ID <"
            + orderRow.orderId
            + ">";

    executer.execute(orderStore, command, failureMessage);

    return orderId;
}

public void ejbLoad(final Integer orderId) {
    OrderStoreCommand command = new OrderStoreCommand() {
        private OrderRow orderRow;

        public void execute(OrderStore orderStore) {
            orderRow = orderStore.findByOrderId(orderId);
        }

        public Object getReturnValue() {
            return orderRow;
```

```
            }
        };

        String failureMessage =
            "Unable to load order with ID <" + orderId + ">";

        executer.execute(orderStore, command, failureMessage);

        orderRow = (OrderRow) command.getReturnValue();
    }

    public void ejbStore() {
        OrderStoreCommand command = new OrderStoreCommand() {
            public void execute(OrderStore orderStore) {
                orderStore.update(orderRow);
            }
        };

        String failureMessage =
            "Unable to store order with ID <"
                + orderRow.orderId
                + ">";

        executer.execute(orderStore, command, failureMessage);
    }

    public void ejbRemove(final Integer orderId) {
        OrderStoreCommand command = new OrderStoreCommand() {
            public void execute(OrderStore orderStore) {
                orderStore.remove(orderId);
            }
        };

        String failureMessage =
            "Unable to remove order with ID <" + orderId + ">";

        executer.execute(orderStore, command, failureMessage);
    }

    public String getCustomerId() {
        return orderRow.customerId;
    }

    public void setCustomerId(String customerId) {
        orderRow.customerId = customerId;
    }

    public OrderRow getOrderRow() {
        return orderRow;
    }
}
```

Each method has the same rhythm: create an `OrderStoreCommand`, create a failure message in case any exceptions are thrown, and then execute the command.

Some commands have return values for those methods that return a value. Look at how simple the commands are: they merely delegate their work to the OrderStore, which defines a method for each command. The nice thing about this class is that it works with *any* kind of OrderStore (not just ones that use a database) and provides maximum flexibility for executing the OrderStoreCommands. In particular, testing OrderBeanBmpLogic is a breeze. Here are a few tests, using EasyMock to fake out the OrderStore and the command executer.

Listing A.18 Testing the POJO for orders

```
package junit.cookbook.coffee.model.ejb.test;

import java.sql.SQLException;

import javax.ejb.*;

import junit.cookbook.coffee.data.*;
import junit.cookbook.coffee.model.ejb.OrderBmpBeanLogic;
import junit.framework.TestCase;

import org.easymock.MockControl;

import com.diasparsoftware.store.DataStoreException;

public class OrderBmpBeanLogicTest extends TestCase {
    private OrderBmpBeanLogic logic;
    private MockControl orderStoreControl;
    private OrderStore mockOrderStore;

    protected void setUp() throws Exception {
        orderStoreControl =
            MockControl.createNiceControl(OrderStore.class);

        mockOrderStore = (OrderStore) orderStoreControl.getMock();

        OrderStoreCommandExecuter simpleExecuter =
            new OrderStoreCommandExecuter() {
            public void execute(
                OrderStore orderStore,
                OrderStoreCommand orderStoreCommand,
                String exceptionMessage) {

                orderStoreCommand.execute(orderStore);
            }
        };

        logic =
            new OrderBmpBeanLogic(mockOrderStore, simpleExecuter);
    }

    public void testFindByPrimaryKey_Found() throws Exception {
        mockOrderStore.exists(new Integer(762));
        orderStoreControl.setReturnValue(true);
```

```
        orderStoreControl.replay();

        assertEquals(
            new Integer(762),
            logic.ejbFindByPrimaryKey(new Integer(762)));

        orderStoreControl.verify();
    }

    public void testFindByPrimaryKey_NotFound() throws Exception {
        mockOrderStore.exists(new Integer(762));
        orderStoreControl.setReturnValue(false);

        orderStoreControl.replay();

        try {
            logic.ejbFindByPrimaryKey(new Integer(762));
            fail("Found object?");
        }
        catch (ObjectNotFoundException expected) {
        }

        orderStoreControl.verify();
    }

    public void testLoad() throws Exception {
        Integer orderId = new Integer(762);
        OrderRow orderRow = new OrderRow(orderId, "jbrains");

        mockOrderStore.findByOrderId(orderId);
        orderStoreControl.setReturnValue(orderRow);

        orderStoreControl.replay();

        logic.ejbLoad(orderId);
        assertEquals(orderRow, logic.getOrderRow());

        orderStoreControl.verify();
    }

    public void testLoad_DataStoreException() throws Exception {
        Integer orderId = new Integer(762);
        OrderRow orderRow = new OrderRow(orderId, "jbrains");

        mockOrderStore.findByOrderId(orderId);
        DataStoreException exception =
            new DataStoreException(
                "Unable to find order",
                new SQLException());

        orderStoreControl.setThrowable(exception);

        orderStoreControl.replay();

        try {
            logic.ejbLoad(orderId);
            fail("Should have thrown an exception");
```

```
        }
        catch (DataStoreException expected) {
            assertSame(exception, expected);
        }

        orderStoreControl.verify();
    }
}
```

Of course, we need to test the command executers in isolation; fortunately, that is easy to do. First we need to verify that the EJB-based command executer does its job of turning `DataStoreException`s into `EJBException`s.

Listing A.19 `OrderStoreCommandExecuterEjbImplTest`

```
package junit.cookbook.coffee.model.ejb.test;

import javax.ejb.EJBException;

import junit.cookbook.coffee.data.*;
import junit.cookbook.coffee.model.ejb.OrderStoreCommandExecuterEjbImpl;
import junit.framework.TestCase;

import org.easymock.MockControl;

import com.diasparsoftware.store.DataStoreException;

public class OrderStoreCommandExecuterEjbImplTest extends TestCase {
    private MockControl orderStoreControl;
    private OrderStore mockStore;

    public void testStoreThrowsException() throws Exception {
        final DataStoreException cause = new DataStoreException();

        OrderStoreCommand crashTestDummyCommand =
            new OrderStoreCommand() {

            public void execute(OrderStore orderStore) {
                throw cause;
            }
        };

        orderStoreControl =
            MockControl.createNiceControl(OrderStore.class);

        mockStore = (OrderStore) orderStoreControl.getMock();

        String failureMessage = "I expect failure";

        OrderStoreCommandExecuterEjbImpl executer =
            new OrderStoreCommandExecuterEjbImpl(
                new SimpleOrderStoreCommandExecuter());

        try {
```

```
            executer.execute(
                mockStore,
                crashTestDummyCommand,
                failureMessage);

            fail("Executer did not throw EJBException");
        }
        catch (EJBException expected) {
            assertTrue(
                expected.getMessage().startsWith(failureMessage));

            assertSame(cause, expected.getCausedByException());
        }
    }
}
```

This test uses a Crash Test Dummy, `OrderStoreCommand`, hard coded to throw a `DataStoreException`. As we have described elsewhere, it is easier to simulate error conditions than try to recreate them. This test verifies not only that the EJB command executer throws an `EJBException`, but it verifies the exception message and the root cause. This is an example of the technique we describe in recipe 2.8, "Test throwing the right exception." We can test the JDBC command executer similarly: we use a mock object approach and verify that the command executer obtains a connection, invokes the command, and then closes the connection. See Chapter 10, "Testing and JDBC," for examples of using the SQL/JDBC part of the Mock Objects package.

This has been a rather extensive example of refactoring a J2EE component to make it easier to test. It turns out that we spent approximately 12 hours to apply these refactorings, and you might wonder whether the benefits (easier to test) are worth the cost (12 hours of refactoring). From our experience, the trade-off is a no-brainer: the benefits far outweigh the cost. The alternative is to test the BMP entity bean in a live container against a live database. We have already discussed the hidden costs in testing against a live database. It should be clear that maintaining live test data and executing slow tests has an *unbounded* cost, as opposed to the 12 hours we spent applying these refactorings. Moreover, we have uncovered several small, generic components, or at least components that we can easily make more generic (such as the command executers). These components will help us build other entity beans, as well as simplify their tests. Assuming that we use BMP entity beans often in our system, we will recover our costs quickly.

The most compelling return on the investment in these refactorings is yet to come: if we build all future entity beans to be testable, then our progress will be steadier, safer, and ultimately faster.

B Essays on testing

The following is a short collection of essays on testing, ones to which the recipes refer in order to cover some essential ground. Because this is a book about recipes, we wanted to limit the amount of free-range prose. Still, there are a few concepts that are not effectively written as recipes but are nonetheless fundamental to understanding some of our reasoning in the recipes. To keep the spirit of recipes, each essay is divided into two parts: *The point* and *The details.*

As you might hope, we give you the point first, rather than waiting until the end of the essay. Once you have read the point, you can decide whether to keep reading. If we have piqued your interest, great; but if not, come back to it later. You choose.

Also, as these are essays, they include some opinions. We may sometimes fall into the trap of proclaiming our opinion as truth, and if we do that, do not believe it. Take it as literary license, gather some experience, make some observations, and then judge for yourself. If we turn out to be wrong we will not mind your saying so, although food and drink might soften the blow.

Enjoy.

B.1 Too simple to break

◆ The point

Some code is *too simple to break.* We think you should concentrate your effort on testing code that might break, rather than testing code that clearly cannot. The trick, of course, is to decide how simple is "too simple."

◆ The details

Let us begin with one of the classic testing questions: "Should I test getters and setters?" We discuss this in detail in chapter 2, "Elementary Tests," so we will only summarize here. This simple question divides the Programmer Testing community in two: many believe you ought to test these methods like any other and the rest believe that they are *too simple to break.* The first camp cites this common problem as a reason to test these methods:

```
private String lastName;

public void setLastName(String lastName) {
    lastName = lastName;
}
```

Here is an example where an ambiguous statement—which `lastName` variable is being assigned to which?—creates a potential problem for the programmer.[1] This statement simply assigns the value of the formal parameter `lastName` to itself, which is certainly *not* what the programmer wants, and so is certainly a defect. The first of the two camps would say, "If we do not test our setters, then we will not catch these kinds of defects." Well, yes and no. Yes, in that if we write no test for this method then no test will catch this defect; however, this is such an elementary error that there are other safety nets in place to catch it: the compiler, the IDE, or a style-checking package such as PMD. Our toolset has improved to the point where it is almost impossible for a defect such as this to survive long enough to be executed! Long before that time, either the compiler or your IDE will warn you: "this statement has no effect"—and if it does *not* warn you, then spend some time figuring out how to enable the warning. If another tool can detect a problem more simply than a JUnit test can, then the course is clear: use the tool, rather than JUnit.

Now, we are not saying that testing this method is a *bad thing*. No one will shun you if you decide to test it; however, the return on investment for this kind of test is quite low, and it pays to remember the goal of testing. The idea is to spend a certain amount of time and effort on uncovering ways in which the system behaves differently from what you would expect (called "defects"), with the goal of saving money (time, effort, sanity) by catching these problems as soon as possible after you created them. There is, therefore, a trade-off between the effort you expend on testing and the confidence level that you attain in the process. At some point, spending more effort on testing is not worth the corresponding increase in your confidence in the code—or at least, that the code does not fail in a painful way. It is for this reason alone that we have the notion of *too simple to break*. If testing were free, we would test absolutely every line of code absolutely every way we could imagine.

Back to our getters and setters:, there are some kinds of setters that warrant being tested. In particular, a setter that updates more than one variable based on some calculation is a good candidate to be tested. We would test this setter because it does something more complex than merely assign a value to a variable. It is possible for us to write code that the compiler does not criticize, that the IDE does not criticize, and have it do the wrong thing. This is a reasonable definition

[1] The statement is ambiguous to the programmer, but not to the Java compiler, and that is where the trouble begins.

for *complex enough to be tested.* Still, there are some such methods that we would generally not bother testing.

It is common in Object-Oriented Programming to see a large amount of "delegation." That is, an object that wraps another and delegates much of its behavior to the object it wraps. The Decorator design pattern is built on this notion: the Decorator performs some small service, but mostly invokes the object it decorates. In Java, the I/O libraries contain examples of Decorators. If you browse the source for, say, `ObjectOutputStream`, you will notice that some of its methods merely invoke the corresponding method on the `BlockDataOutputStream` it contains. Consider the method `ObjectOutputStream.write(int)`, for example:

```
public void write(int val) throws IOException {
    bout.write(val);
}
```

We believe that this method—indeed any method that merely delegates its job to another object—is *too simple to break.* There is no way for this method to fail a test, assuming that the neighboring classes have been reasonably well tested. Our reasoning goes like this: the only things that could go wrong are either that `bout` is `null` or that `BlockDataOutputStream.write()` is broken. This method cannot possibly be held responsible for either of these unfortunate circumstances; therefore, we ought to focus our attention on ensuring that those two things never happen, rather than worrying about this method. This method is too simple to break *on its own,* and that is what we really mean by this catchphrase: a method that cannot break in any way on its own is a method not worth testing.

There may be no complete way to classify methods as being *too simple to break.* We have provided a couple of reasonable heuristics in this essay, and if you participate in the JUnit mailing lists, you will occasionally see this topic discussed—often in gory detail. We recommend that you test until fear turns to boredom: if you think it might break, then test it until your thinking changes. If you are just starting out with JUnit, then you may find it comforting to test getters and setters, just to get your feet wet with testing. If you have just spent four hours debugging a problem related to a malfunctioning setter, then you might decide to be extra vigilant about testing setters—for a while. We recommend focusing your energy on code that can easily break, rather than code that may be *too simple to break,* but never forget that *they're just rules.*[2]

---

[2] www.xprogramming.com/Practices/justrule.htm

◆ *Postscript*

Not everyone agrees with our assessment of what constitutes *too simple to break.* Among these people the most vocal is Simon Chappell, who errs more on the side of caution when testing objects. He believes that it is important to test getters and setters, and does so. In reviewing this essay for the book, Simon pointed out one additional reason not to be overly cavalier about code being *too simple to break.*

> This (testing behaviors we claim are *too simple to break*) is also a way that I help to future-proof our system. Knowing that it is a strategic system, it'll be around for a while and I may not always be working on it or leading the development effort. And while I might know all there is to know about the value objects and understand all of their consequences, I have no way other than leaving appropriate tests to communicate that effectively to the developers that come after me. (Yes, I could document it, but we know how often such documents get read and how diligently they are updated!) Leaving a full(er) suite of tests that are incorporated into the build process is the best investment that I can make in the future of any system that I write.

We use mean time between failures (MTBF) to measure the likelihood that a given piece of code will fail to do what we expect. Each of us has a slightly different internal MTBF threshold, past which code is *too simple to break.* If we focus entirely on MTBF without considering the lifetime of the system, then we may not make good decisions regarding what is *too simple to break.* As the system's lifetime increases and MTBF remains constant, the likelihood of a defect occurring increases, so perhaps for longer-lived systems we ought to lower our *too simple to break* threshold and err more on the side of caution, as Simon does.

B.2 Strangeness and transitivity

◆ *The point*

The way we typically define `equals()` for Java objects is such that the transitivity property is guaranteed, so there is no need to test explicitly for it: testing for reflexivity and symmetry is enough. There are, however, ways to implement `equals()` that might look reasonable, but do not work, and you need the transitive property to expose the defect. The good news is that once you know which kind of `equals()` implementation is troublesome, essentially *all* troublesome `equals()` implementations fall into this category.

◆ *The details*

You will have to excuse us, as this description is going to be a bit mathematical in nature. If that does not interest you, then here is a shorter version: as long as your objects define `equals()` in terms of fieldwise equality, then you do not have to worry about whether GSBase's `EqualsTester` might steer you wrong, because it would not be able to. By "fieldwise equality" we mean comparing the corresponding fields for equality, such as in this simple case from the Coffee Shop application:

```
public class CoffeeCatalogItem {
    public String productId = "";
    public String coffeeName = "";
    public Money unitPrice = Money.ZERO;

    public boolean equals(Object other) {
        if (other instanceof CoffeeCatalogItem) {
            CoffeeCatalogItem that = (CoffeeCatalogItem) other;

            return this.productId.equals(that.productId)
                && this.coffeeName.equals(that.coffeeName)
                && this.unitPrice.equals(that.unitPrice);
        }
        else {
            return false;
        }
    }
}
```

According to this `equals()` method, two `CoffeeCatalogItem` objects are equal if their corresponding fields are equal. This is an example of defining `equals()` in terms of fieldwise equality. For these kinds of objects, there is no need to test the transitive property, which follows from the reflexive and symmetric properties. We can generalize this a little with some semiformal reasoning.[3]

Suppose your `equals()` method is reflexive (`a.equals(a)`) and symmetric (`a.equals(b)` means that `b.equals(a)` and the other way around). Now suppose further that these objects are equal because there is no difference between them—in other words, aside from being in different regions of memory, there is no way to distinguish one from the other. This means that you can substitute these objects for one another and no collaborating object will notice a difference. Value Objects typically fall into this category. What about transitivity in this case? Well, let us see.

---

[3] Just because it is informal, does not make it incorrect; it just tries to use symbols as little as possible. Do not confuse formality with rigor. (Similarly, do not confuse formal software processes with effective ones.)

Pick three objects a, b, c with the properties that a.equals(b) and b.equals(c). What about a.equals(c)? Is it true or false? Well, if there is no way to tell the difference between a and b, then we ought to be able to substitute a in place of b without changing the behavior of any program that uses them. We are just applying the definition we have given of "no difference between a and b." So we can put a wherever b is. Specifically, take b.equals(c), put a in place of b, and you have a.equals(c). We have proven transitivity. This proof is not very formal, but it is certainly rigorous: we defined equals() a certain way, applied our definition, and reached the conclusion we needed to reach.

But then how can a reasonable implementation of equals() ever be reflexive and symmetric but *not* transitive? It turns out that this is surprisingly easy to do. Consider our Money class again. Someone comes along and implements Money a little differently: in particular, they try to handle the rounding error problem by relaxing the notion of equality, rather than rounding off the amount in the constructor. You may already know that floating-point arithmetic is inherently inaccurate for computers, because it is impossible to represent 0.1 *exactly* using a finite number of bits. You may even have seen this classic infinite loop:

```
public class FloatingPointArithmeticDemo {
    public static void main(String[] args) {
        for (float i = 0.0f; i != 1.0f; i += 0.1f);
        System.out.println("Done.");
    }
}
```

Wait as long as you want—it takes an incredibly long time for this program to print "Done." It takes the massive accumulation of rounding errors and repeated overflow of the variable i. We do not know how long it takes, but we guess it takes years, at least, and the fact that it terminates at all is an accident—without the ability to overflow, it would never happen! The problem is that 0.1f is not quite 1/10, and when you compound that error, it takes only a few operations for the error to be noticeable.

All right—how does our fictional Money-implementing programmer deal with this problem? Well, rather than round off to the nearest cent, our intrepid programmer stores the amount of money as a floating-point value and says, "Hey—half a cent is pretty close. If two Money objects are within half a cent, that's good enough for me." He creates the class TolerantMoney and implements equals() this way:

```
public class TolerantMoney {
    private double amount;
```

```
        // ...

        public boolean equals(Object other) {
            if (other instanceof TolerantMoney) {
                TolerantMoney that = (TolerantMoney) other;
                return Math.abs(this.amount - that.amount) <= 0.005d;
            }
            else {
                return false;
            }
        }

        public int hashCode() {
            return 0;
        }
    }
```

Look! He even uses `double`, rather than `float`, to achieve the greatest precision Java allows.[4] So what could be wrong with this? Here is a test for the `equals()` property, checking the RST properties:

```
import junit.framework.TestCase;

public class TolerantMoneyTransitivityTest extends TestCase {
    public void testRstProperties() throws Exception {
        TolerantMoney a = new TolerantMoney(1.00d);
        TolerantMoney b = new TolerantMoney(1.0033d);
        TolerantMoney c = new TolerantMoney(1.0067d);
        TolerantMoney d = new TolerantMoney(1.01d);

        // Reflexive property OK...
        assertEquals(a, a);
        assertEquals(b, b);
        assertEquals(c, c);
        assertEquals(d, d);

        // Symmetric property OK...
        assertEquals(a, b);
        assertEquals(b, a);

        assertEquals(b, c);
        assertEquals(c, b);

        assertEquals(c, d);
        assertEquals(d, c);

        // Transitive property?
        assertEquals(a, b);
        assertEquals(b, c);
        assertEquals(c, d);
        // therefore...
```

[4] Well, there is `BigDecimal`, but it turns out that that would not help, anyway.

```
            assertEquals(a, d);
        }
    }
```

We have highlighted in bold print the assertion that fails. The transitive property does not hold, so our programmer's `equals()` implementation does not respect the contract of `Object.equals()`. What went wrong?

The problem is that our programmer attempted to define `equals()` as "close enough." He decided that two `Money` amounts are equal if they are just close enough to one another—"Who cares about half a penny?"—as it were. A relation like this can *never* satisfy the transitive property, and so can never be used as a valid implementation of `equals()`.[5]

"Fine," you may say to yourself, "I can't imagine I'd ever want to do that, anyway." That is partly our point: when we first looked at GSBase's `EqualsTester`, we noticed that it is does not explicitly test the transitivity property. When we asked Mike Bowler about it, he merely said that it had never been a problem for him—in other words, excluding those checks from his `EqualsTester` had never resulted in an incorrect `equals()` method passing all his tests. The reason? Most `equals()` implementations define themselves in terms of fieldwise equality, and not in terms of "close enough." Moreover, although we do not know how to prove it, it appears to us that *any* `equals()` method that fails only the transitive property *must* be related to this "close enough" notion somehow. So as long as you say that values are either identical or not identical, you will never have an `equals()` method that satisfies the reflexive and symmetric properties (thereby passing all `EqualsTester`'s tests) but that does not satisfy the transitive property (and is therefore an incorrect implementation).

There...we bet you will sleep a little more soundly tonight.

B.3 Isolate expensive tests

◆ *The point*

We use mock objects to shield ourselves from expensive external resources during testing. It is unwise to just pile on the mock objects in an attempt to work around the problem. Eventually you *do* need to test that part of your system that depends on, say, a database. If you isolate those tests, then you can continue to benefit from

[5] You want proof? Start here: http://planetmath.org/encyclopedia/ArchimedeanProperty.html. The rest is an exercise to the reader. (Sorry, we just could not resist writing that at least once.)

them without having them get in the way of your flow while you work. This involves some refactoring, and is therefore difficult to do in legacy systems that you are not allowed to change.

◆ *The details*

Let's dive right on into an example. We have a `RequestPoller` and a `RequestProcessor`. We do not know what a request processor does, except that it processes files somehow—hence the name. The `RequestPoller`, among other things, retrieves all the files in a directory and then submits them to a `RequestProcessor` for processing. If you find these responsibilities vague, we do not blame you, because so do we. That is the nature of sitting down to code you did not write. We are thankful that we have a test to help us understand what these objects do! Specifically, we have the following test:

```
package junit.cookbook.essays.test;

import java.io.File;
import java.util.*;

import junit.cookbook.essays.*;
import junit.framework.TestCase;
import junitx.framework.ArrayAssert;

public class RequestPollerTest extends TestCase {
    private File[] expectedFiles =
        new File[] {
            new File("c:/unittest/tmp/file1.xml"),
            new File("c:/unittest/tmp/file2.xml"),
            new File("c:/unittest/tmp/file3.xml"),
            new File("c:/unittest/tmp/file4.xml")};

    public void setUp() throws Exception {
        (new File("c:/unittest/tmp")).mkdirs();
        for (int i = 0; i < expectedFiles.length; i++) {
            File newFile = expectedFiles[i];
            newFile.createNewFile();
        }
    }

    public void tearDown() throws Exception {
        for (int i = 0; i < expectedFiles.length; i++) {
            File newFile = expectedFiles[i];
            newFile.delete();
        }
        (new File("c:/unittest/tmp")).delete();
        (new File("c:/unittest")).delete();
    }

    public void testPoll() throws Exception {
```

```
        File directory = new File("c:/unittest/tmp/");
        final List actualFiles = new ArrayList();
        RequestProcessor processor = new RequestProcessor() {
            public void process(File[] files) {
                actualFiles.addAll(Arrays.asList(files));
            }
        };

        RequestPoller poller = new RequestPoller(
            directory, processor);

        poller.poll();

        ArrayAssert.assertEquals(
            "Unexpected poll values",
            expectedFiles,
            actualFiles.toArray());
    }
}
```

We find it helpful to describe what the test does in words, as this helps us focus on the responsibilities under test. When we ask a poller to poll, we want to verify that the poller's processor processes all the files in a given directory. From this we can infer the responsibilities of each object.

- The processor is responsible for processing a given list of files, whatever "processing" means.
- The poller is responsible both for retrieving files from a directory and asking the processor to process those files.

There is a clue in that last sentence: this test attempts to verify two distinct responsibilities for one object. A test that tries to do two things at once is easily distracted. In particular, it is incapable of telling us where the problem is when it fails. Beyond this, however, the glaring problem with this test is the excessive test fixture setup: the test creates a directory, puts files in that directory, then cleans it up. This seems to be an awful lot of work, considering that *we do not care how the request processor processes the files.* We should not need to create actual files on the file system to verify that the request poller does its job properly, because only the processor needs to deal with the content of those files. To test the poller, we should only need the correct list of objects representing files, irrespective of whether those files are really on the file system.

Well, perhaps not. The `RequestPoller` *does* have the responsibility of correctly retrieving all the files in a directory, and something there could go wrong, depending on whether the `RequestPoller` ought to retrieve just the files in the directory or all the files in that subtree of the file system. Should it recursively retrieve all files in each subdirectory or not? There might be enough doubt around this issue to warrant some tests. The important point is this: those tests have nothing whatsoever to do with processing the files or submitting the files for processing. You may ask, "Who cares?"

We care. Let us describe how coupling to external test data makes a programmer's job difficult. First you write one test that depends on a small data set: a few files in a single directory. So far there is not much of a problem. The next test verifies a more complex case, so now we need to create an empty subdirectory. Still not too bad. The next test verifies an even more complex case, so now we need to create another subdirectory, this one not empty. And then we need to create a third subdirectory with a deep subtree inside it. Now we need files named a certain way.... The test data is sprawling out of control. Eventually we have a bunch of files strewn about the file system as part of our test data. We need to manage this data in our version control system; we need to worry about where those files are on the file system (not everyone has an E: drive); we need to worry about timing issues related to creating and destroying those files on the file system—reliance on asynchronous behavior is always tricky business. The whole thing grows complex quickly. You ought not be worrying about so much complexity when all you want to test is whether the `RequestPoller` submits the correct list of files to a `RequestProcessor` for processing. Why worry about managing test data on the file system when the `RequestProcessor` is not even going to look at the files? (What were we trying to test again?)

That last question summarizes the problem. When we couple business logic to implementation details, we lose our focus and spend a majority of our time handling details that are not germane to what we really need to test. Let us restate the responsibility we are testing without referring to implementation details: "When we ask a `RequestPoller` to poll, it should retrieve files from a container and submit them to a `RequestProcessor` for processing." Now that we have a goal, let us refactor the test to take us there. The first step is to remove the reliance on actual files on the file system.

The `RequestPoller` needs to obtain the files in a given directory. To decouple it from the live file system, we introduce an interface `FileLister`[6] with a method to retrieve the list of files in a directory. We create the interface and change

[6] On rereading this essay, we do not like the interface name `FileLister`, as objects should generally be named with noun phrases and not verb phrases. We do not need a "file lister," but rather a container of files, and so if we had it to do over, we would call this interface `FileSet` and the method `getFiles()`. (A design is never really finished.)

RequestPoller to accept a FileLister, rather than a directory, in its constructor. Here is the new test:

```
public void testPoll() throws Exception {
    final List actualFiles = new ArrayList();
    RequestProcessor processor = new RequestProcessor() {
        public void process(File[] files) {
            actualFiles.addAll(Arrays.asList(files));
        }
    };

    FileLister fakeFileLister = new FileLister() {
        public File[] listFiles() {
            return expectedFiles;
        }
    };

    RequestPoller poller = new RequestPoller(fakeFileLister, processor);
    poller.poll();
    ArrayAssert.assertEquals(
        "Unexpected poll values",
        expectedFiles,
        actualFiles.toArray());
}
```

And here is the new interface:

```
package junit.cookbook.essays;

import java.io.File;

public interface FileLister {
    File[] listFiles();
}
```

We have called the file lister object fakeFileLister, because it hard codes the list of files, and so is properly called a "fake."[7] We execute this test and it continues to pass, so the first change was a success. Notice also that we removed the line of code that specified the directory containing the expected files. The FileLister does not care about the origin of the list of files, but we need a production implementation of FileLister that actually scans a directory, so let's do that now. We create a new test for a new implementation of FileLister. This test verifies that we can retrieve files correctly from a directory.

```
package junit.cookbook.essays.test;

import java.io.File;
```

[7] At least, according to Dave Astels' taxonomy of the various kinds of mock objects. See *Test-Driven Development: A Practical Guide* (Prentice Hall PTR, 2003) p. 169.

```
import junit.cookbook.essays.FileLister;
import junit.framework.TestCase;
import junitx.framework.ArrayAssert;

public class ListFilesInDirectoryTest extends TestCase {
    private File[] expectedFiles =
        new File[] {
            new File("c:/unittest/tmp/file1.xml"),
            new File("c:/unittest/tmp/file2.xml"),
            new File("c:/unittest/tmp/file3.xml"),
            new File("c:/unittest/tmp/file4.xml")};

    public void setUp() throws Exception {
        (new File("c:/unittest/tmp")).mkdirs();
        for (int i = 0; i < expectedFiles.length; i++) {
            File newFile = expectedFiles[i];
            newFile.createNewFile();
        }
    }

    public void tearDown() throws Exception {
        for (int i = 0; i < expectedFiles.length; i++) {
            File newFile = expectedFiles[i];
            newFile.delete();
        }
        (new File("c:/unittest/tmp")).delete();
        (new File("c:/unittest")).delete();
    }

    public void testFilesInCurrentDirectory() throws Exception {
        FileLister fileLister =
            new DirectoryFileLister(new File("c:/unittest/tmp"));
        ArrayAssert.assertEquals(expectedFiles, fileLister.listFiles());
    }
}
```

Notice that we have copied the fixture from the `RequestPollerTest` into this new test. We figured that it was the easiest place to start: that other fixture already had four files in a directory, so we reused it. We make a note that we might want to extract the common test fixture (see recipe 3.5, "Factor out a test fixture hierarchy"), but do not do it yet. It turns out that making this test pass is quite simple, so we do that by creating `DirectoryFileLister` and implementing it as follows:

```
package junit.cookbook.essays.test;

import java.io.File;

import junit.cookbook.essays.FileLister;

public class DirectoryFileLister implements FileLister {
    private File directory;

    public DirectoryFileLister(File directory) {
```

```
        this.directory = directory;
    }

    public File[] listFiles() {
        return directory.listFiles();
    }
}
```

We now make a note that the tests for `DirectoryFileLister` are woefully incomplete: in particular they do not address the question of processing subdirectories. We will add those later. The point, however, is what happens to `RequestPoller-Test`. We remove the `setUp()` and `tearDown()` methods *and the test still passes!* We have successfully eliminated all that smelly test setup. Perhaps more correctly, we have moved it away from the business logic and put it with the implementation details, where it belongs. We now have this test for the `RequestPoller`:

```
package junit.cookbook.essays.test;

import java.io.File;
import java.util.*;

import junit.cookbook.essays.*;
import junit.framework.TestCase;
import junitx.framework.ArrayAssert;

public class RequestPollerTest extends TestCase {
    private File[] expectedFiles =
        new File[] {
            new File("c:/unittest/tmp/file1.xml"),
            new File("c:/unittest/tmp/file2.xml"),
            new File("c:/unittest/tmp/file3.xml"),
            new File("c:/unittest/tmp/file4.xml")};

    public void testPoll() throws Exception {
        final List actualFiles = new ArrayList();
        RequestProcessor processor = new RequestProcessor() {
            public void process(File[] files) {
                actualFiles.addAll(Arrays.asList(files));
            }
        };

        FileLister fakeFileLister = new FileLister() {
            public File[] listFiles() {
                return expectedFiles;
            }
        };

        RequestPoller poller = new RequestPoller(
            fakeFileLister, processor);

        poller.poll();

        ArrayAssert.assertEquals(
```

```
                "Unexpected poll values",
                expectedFiles,
                actualFiles.toArray());
        }
    }
```

We can simplify the test a little by moving the assertion into our Spy `Request-Processor`. If you had not noticed that this test used a Spy `RequestProcessor` by now, then read recipe 14.5, "Test an object factory," for a discussion about using Spy objects in tests. We fix up a few names and have a final version of the test:

```
package junit.cookbook.essays.test;

import java.io.File;

import junit.cookbook.essays.*;
import junit.framework.TestCase;
import junitx.framework.ArrayAssert;

public class RequestPollerTest extends TestCase {
    private File[] expectedFiles =
        new File[] {
            new File("c:/unittest/tmp/file1.xml"),
            new File("c:/unittest/tmp/file2.xml"),
            new File("c:/unittest/tmp/file3.xml"),
            new File("c:/unittest/tmp/file4.xml")};

    public void testPoll() throws Exception {
        FileLister fakeFileLister = new FileLister() {
            public File[] listFiles() {
                return expectedFiles;
            }
        };

        RequestProcessor spyRequestProcessor = new RequestProcessor() {
            public void process(File[] files) {
                ArrayAssert.assertEquals(
                    "Unexpected poll values",
                    expectedFiles,
                    files);
            }
        };

        RequestPoller poller =
            new RequestPoller(fakeFileLister, spyRequestProcessor);

        poller.poll();
    }
}
```

Do we need any more tests for `RequestPoller.poll()`? We may want to try invalid parameters to the constructor, such as `null`. We may want to consider what happens if processing a file throws an exception. Otherwise, this appears to be the only test we need. We are now testing business logic *completely independently* of implementation details, such as the content and existence of real files.

Now the point of this essay was to talk about isolating expensive tests, so it behooves us to return to the point. We have moved the expensive part of `RequestPollerTest` into `ListFilesInDirectoryTest`, and you may still be wondering how that helps. The key benefits to this change include the following:

- We can test all the important boundary cases for listing files in a directory without involving irrelevant objects such as request processors and pollers.
- We can use the `DirectoryFileLister` anywhere else in our application that might need it, and we can test *those* components without involving the file system either.
- Once we implement the `DirectoryFileLister` correctly, *we do not need to change it*, because the `File` API in Java is not likely to change any time soon. This means that we can execute the accompanying tests much less frequently, such as in the background using Cruise Control or Anthill.

We believe this last benefit to be the key: We have isolated an implementation detail and made it *closed*—in the sense of the Open/Closed Principle[8]—so that our other tests would be free and not have to depend on them. By isolating the thing that annoyed us and moving it out of the way, we no longer let expensive, tedious-to-maintain tests get in the way of our work. We can get back to writing correct business logic, which is more important than mucking around with the file system. This is a benefit that we can experience now and continue to experience for the rest of the project: the tests execute more quickly and are easier to maintain. Everyone wins.

B.4 The mock objects landscape

◆ The point

We use mock objects to make testing easier, particularly when we need to add tests to existing code. There are a number of ways to use mock objects, so it can be difficult to know where to start. Some of the terms are overloaded and can cause confusion, so it is a good idea to understand a few of the essential mock objects techniques and what distinguishes them from one another. In spite of this complexity,

8 See www.objectmentor.com/resources/articles/ocp.pdf for a discussion of this design principle.

EasyMock (www.easymock.org) provides the majority of what you need to take advantage of the various mocking techniques into your tests.

◆ *The details*

In 2000, Tim Mackinnon, Steve Freeman, and Philip Craig wrote the paper "Endo-Testing: Unit Testing with Mock Objects,"[9] in which they introduced the notion of mocking method invocations to facilitate isolated Object Tests. The term "mock object" refers to an object that stands in place of the object you would use in production: often it is an alternate implementation of a given interface. In particular, a mock object emulates the behavior of the real thing without duplicating it entirely: for example, a method may return the same result every time, ignoring its parameters. The goal is to simulate as little of an object's behavior as you need for the current test. What makes a mock object more than just a *stub* is that it also makes assertions about the way it is used. It expects a particular method invocation, or certain parameters, or a given sequence of method invocations. To use a mock object, you instantiate it, tell it what to expect, supply it to the object under test, then ask it to verify whether the object being tested used it correctly. The term "endo-testing" refers to the fact that one passes a mock object as a parameter to the object under test, dynamically introducing assertions into the production code (testing from the *inside*) without leaving them there to be removed later. The rest of the testing we do can therefore be termed "exo-testing": testing from the outside. As mock objects have become more commonplace in Object Tests, an entire vocabulary has evolved around them, and we think that you ought to know these terms in order to better understand them and communicate your mock objects techniques to others.

First, we need to draw a distinction between mock objects and Mock Objects (www.mockobjects.org). The generic term—or simply "mocking"—refers to the general technique of substituting an alternative implementation of an interface (or individual method) in place of the production-quality collaborator for the purposes of testing an object.[10] When testing JDBC client code, we say that we "mock the database," which may involve using a mock implementation of the `Connection` interface, serving up mock `Statement` objects. There are many ways to mock a method or an interface, as we will describe here. The term Mock Objects,

---

[9] You can find the article online or in *Extreme Programming Examined* (Addison-Wesley, 2001), a collection of papers on Extreme Programming edited by Giancarlo Succi and Michele Marchesi.

[10] We have begun to call these kinds of objects "test objects," especially when speaking, because it is difficult to use a verbal cue to distinguish a "mock object" from a "Mock Object."

with the words capitalized, makes us think of Tim, Steve, and Philip's work: a specific kind of mock implementation: one that knows how to expect to be used, and verifies that it was used that way. Much of what we discuss in this essay concerns the generic mocking technique, although we make heavy use of Mock Objects in our work.

The simplest mocking technique is a "stub." The community is divided on whether stubs really support mocking, because they do nothing: a stub is an empty implementation of an interface. All its methods do nothing and return default values. It is there merely to allow the system to compile and execute. Test-Driven Development practitioners usually build a stub to implement an interface they have just decided they need. Stubs are of limited use in testing: mostly as a means of keeping an object out of the way. You may be testing a method that takes five parameters, but for *this* test you only need three of those parameters. The method under test throws an exception if you try to pass it `null` parameters, so to satisfy the method's demands you pass it the simplest possible implementation of that parameter's type: a stub. Some stubs turn into Null Objects,[11] and others become Java interface adapters. Stubs are of limited use in testing because they return default values, such as `0`, `false`, and `null`.

If you decide that the stub is not *really* a mocking technique, then the next-simplest mocking technique is the "fake." A fake method is one that returns a fixed value every time it is invoked, and so a fake object is an object with fake methods. Faking a method makes it possible to test how the object under test responds to the various kinds of behavior it can expect from its collaborators. For example, an online store has a product catalog. The shopper may ask to display the details on a particular product: she first browses the catalog and finds a link to the product she wants to see, then gets up and leaves her computer for ten minutes. In the meantime, the product manager pulls that product from the shelves, because it has not been selling well.[12] He executes the administrative command to remove the product from the catalog, but the shopper still has that link in her browser. When she clicks that link, which contains a product number of some kind to identify the product to display, there is no product matching that product number. The system needs to be able to handle that, rather than blow up with an exception that the web container finally handles. There are two approaches to test this condition.

---

[11] http://c2.com/cgi/wiki?NullObject

[12] Yes, it would be better to pull the product off the shelves during off-hours, but this is an online store—somewhere in the world one of their customers is awake and using their site.

A direct approach is to write the test using a product number that you *know* is not in the catalog; however, this forces you to deal with implementation details that need not concern you for the current test. It does not matter *which* product you try to display—it just matters what happens when that product is not in the catalog. A more robust testing approach involves using a fake catalog that always answers "no" when you ask it, "Does this product exist?" The idea is to test how the product display logic reacts to a nonexistent product without worrying about using "the magic product number with no associated product." In your test fixture, use a `FakeCatalog` such as this one:

```
public class FakeCatalog implements Catalog {
    ...
    public boolean exists(String productId) {
        return false;
    }
    ...
}
```

Typically, a fake object returns hard-coded values, and so you would need to create a different class for each different way you want to fake a method. If you find yourself in this situation, you may decide to build a fake object whose hard-coded values you can set programmatically. Returning to our example, you may want to build a `FakeCatalog` to which you can add a known list of products, as opposed to the production catalog which retrieves them from a database.

```
public class InMemoryCatalog implements Catalog {
    private Map products = new HashMap();

    public void addProduct(Product product) {
        products.put(product.getId(), product);
    }

    public boolean exists(String productId) {
        return products.containsKey(productId);
    }
    ...
}
```

Now you can prime the catalog with a known list of products for each test without having to put data into database tables. The trouble with this kind of fake object is that it often leads the programmer to duplicate logic from the production-quality object. We already see that here: even though the *code* for the `exists()` method is different between the `InMemoryCatalog` and the production catalog (which checks a database table), the *logic* is duplicated: "a product exists if I can find its product ID." This duplication may well be benign, but it does not take long to reach the point where you are no longer faking methods, but rather providing a production-quality alternate implementation of the interface to which the method belongs. In this case, you might be tempted to build an in-memory repository for all your domain objects. Something that complex needs to be tested itself, and who wants to test the test objects? The key to faking methods and objects effectively is to keep the fakes dead simple: if they want to do something more complex than return one or two hard-coded values, then either the test is not narrowly focused enough or you need to use a more powerful mocking technique. There are two kinds of fake objects that deserve particular attention. They have evolved as common patterns for faking methods: the Spy and the Crash Test Dummy.

A Spy is a fake object that "gathers intelligence" about how it was used, then "reports back" to the test. The test can then make assertions about what the Spy "saw." One common application of the Spy fake object pattern is when you test an event source (see recipe 14.2, "Test an Observable"). The Spy event listener collects the events it receives, then provides the test access to that collection. The test can then compare the events the Spy heard against the list of events that the test expects the event source to generate. As in our recipe on the subject, it is common to use the Self-Shunt pattern in this case, so that the test case class itself becomes the Spy event listener. In general, you can use a Spy to track the order in which its methods are invoked, along with the parameters passed to each method. This focuses your tests on the interactions between objects, without worrying as much about the way they implement those methods—you will test *that* separately. As you will see, the Mock Object is, among other things, the *über*spy.

The Crash Test Dummy is a fake object that throws exceptions, rather than returning hard-coded values. You can use a Crash Test Dummy to verify how the object under test responds when its collaborator fails somehow. As we have written previously in this book (see recipe 2.11, "Test an object that instantiates other objects"), it is generally much easier to *simulate* failure conditions than it is to *recreate* them. Returning to our example, there is another way to signal that a product does not exist in the catalog: throw a `NoSuchProductException`.[13] The production catalog performs a `SELECT` on the database, then throws `NoSuchProductException` if the `ResultSet` is empty. The corresponding `CrashTestDummyCatalog` simply throws the exception every time:

---

[13] We do not recommend using an exception this way, but you will come across it eventually, so you might as well know how to test it effectively.

```
public class CrashTestDummyCatalog implements Catalog {
    ...
    public Product getProduct(String productId) {
        throw new NoSuchProductException(productId);
    }
    ...
}
```

Just as with the previous `FakeCatalog`, this `CrashTestDummyCatalog` eliminates the need for your test to use the "magic product number with no product associated." No matter which product you try to find, the Crash Test Dummy will not find it. This is a simple way to test how your objects react when their collaborators throw exceptions. These special kinds of fake objects are really not so special: they are merely specific ways to use fake objects. Beyond fakes, however, lie Mock Objects, which provide one very powerful additional feature that merits having them in their own category.

A true Mock Object is a self-verifying Spy. The primary advantage of the Mock Object over the Spy is that the former knows how you expect to invoke it—which methods, with which parameters, and in which order—and verifies how it was used when you invoke the `verify()` method. This simple change in approach makes your tests considerably easier to read and to maintain. Although a Spy can gather the same information as a Mock Object, it is still the test's responsibility to interpret what the Spy "saw." The test has less to do when using a Mock Object. It tells the Mock Object what to expect—how many times a method ought to be invoked, or which parameters to expect—and then passes the Mock Object into the object under test. After using the Mock Object, the test merely invokes `verify()` and the Mock Object verifies that each of the test's expectations were met. The resulting design retains more of its natural encapsulation, as the Mock Object implementations do not need to expose the actual values they gathered to the test for verification. More than this, the Mock Object can *fail fast*—that is, because it knows the expectations placed on it, it can make assertions about how it is used *as the test executes.* As soon as one of those assertions fails, the test fails before the faulty code can do further damage, pointing directly to the problem. Not so with a Spy. Because a Mock Object can fail the moment one of its assertions fail, it is much more likely that the resulting error message indicates the cause of the problem, eliminating the need to step through code with a debugger. A Mock Object, then, is a more highly encapsulated, fail-fast version of the already-powerful Spy object. For further information on the benefits of using Mock Objects, we recommend that you read the paper to which we referred at the start of this essay.

Now that you have seen the landscape of *test objects*, which do you use? And when? There is a simple answer: it depends on the role the object plays in your test. Some objects are involved because they need to provide services and some objects are involved because they need to provide data. For the ones that provide data, fake the data; for the ones that provide services, use a Mock Object. In the case of data, you just need an object to return predictable results, and so faking those results ensures predictability. For example, if you want to test how your business logic reacts when your data layer returns an empty list of products from the catalog, then use a fake catalog that always returns an empty list of products. In the case of services, you only need to know that the object under test invokes its collaborator's methods with the correct parameters, so set that expectation on a Mock Object. For example, you want to verify that your data access logic correctly inserts a domain object into the database. In this case, tell a Mock `PreparedStatement` object which parameters to expect to receive on various invocations of `setString()`, `setInt()`, `setTimestamp()` and so on, then pass the Mock `PreparedStatement` to your data access logic for testing. These are the two prime examples of the mock objects approach on which we rely heavily in our work and which we use often in this book's recipes.

Finally when it comes time to implement Mock Objects, we recommend using EasyMock (www.easymock.org), which uses a record-and-playback mechanism to provide dynamic Mock Object implementations of any interface. You can use this package to implement both fakes and Mock Objects proper: the only difference is whether you invoke `verify()` on the EasyMock object at the end of the test. (EasyMock *does* allow for "nice" controls, which do not fail fast, but we tend not to use them.) Using EasyMock drives you towards strong interface/implementation separation, which is an improvement in most designs. There is much more we could write about mock objects (and about Mock Objects), but this is enough to get you on your way. The best way to understand them, as always, is to start using them.

NOTE In the time between writing this essay and sending the book to be printed, a new dynamic proxy-based mock objects package has appeared on the scene, called jMock (www.jmock.org). It picks up where EasyMock left off, as the EasyMock project went through a temporary lull in activity, between October 2003 and May 2004. Being so new, we do not have any experience using it, and so we cannot say much about it, but it does look promising and bears a look. If you have used EasyMock, then it is worth experimenting with jMock to see the difference. You may find you prefer jMock's approach to that of EasyMock.[14]

[14] Note that EasyMock released version 1.1 in May 2004, and so now there is some competition in this space. That is usually good news for those of us using their packages.

C Reading List

Java Testing

Dave Astels, *Test-Driven Development: A Practical Guide* (Prentice Hall PTR, 2003). This is the first TDD-related book we have seen that uses a Swing application as its central example, rather than yet another web application. This is an excellent tour through all the basics of TDD, some JUnit-related tools, Mock Objects, and a fully developed example, test by test.

Johannes Link, *Unit Tests with Java: How the Tests Drive the Code* (Morgan Kaufmann, 2003).This is another fine look at test-driven development using JUnit.

Vincent Massol and Ted Husted, *JUnit in Action* (Manning, 2004). This is a tutorial approach to JUnit with advice on testing a wide range of Java applications and components.

Andrew Hunt and Dave Thomas, *Pragmatic Unit Testing in Java with JUnit* (Pragmatic Programmers, 2003). From the authors of *The Pragmatic Programmer* (see the General Programming section). This is a no-nonsense look at unit testing using JUnit and Java, including a thorough description of testing with Mock Objects. It is an excellent companion to this book. (There is also a C#/NUnit version of this book.)

Richard Dallaway, "Unit Testing Database Code" (www.dallaway.com/acad/dbunit.html). When people ask us how to test a database with JUnit, we point them first to this article, as it covers the basics and the philosophy very well. Our chapter on testing and JDBC is based in part on the ideas in this article.

Stephen Hall and Simon Monk, "Virtual Mock Objects using AspectJ and JUnit" (http://www.xprogramming.com/xpmag/virtualMockObjects.htm). The first article on the subject, as presented in XP Magazine.

Nicholas Lesiecki, "Test flexibly with AspectJ and Mock Objects" (http://www-106.ibm.com/developerworks/java/library/j-aspectj2/). Another article on the topic of Virtual Mock Objects, presented at IBM DeveloperWorks.

Steve Freeman, "Developing JDBC applications test-first" (http://www.mockobjects.com/wiki/DevelopingJdbcApplicationsTestFirst). An example of building JDBC client code using the Mock Object package.

General Testing

Kent Beck, *Test-Driven Development: By Example* (Addison-Wesley, 2002). This provides an introduction to test-driven development using one longer example in Java and one shorter one in Python. It is a must-read for the JUnit practitioner looking to learn more about writing code test first. It includes patterns both for testing and testable designs.

Tim Mackinnon, Steve Freeman and Philip Craig, "Endo-Testing: Unit Testing with Mock Objects" (www.connextra.com/aboutUs/mockobjects.pdf). This is the introductory paper to Mock Objects, a technique on which JUnit practitioners come to rely quite heavily.

Cem Kaner, James Bach, and Bret Pettichord, *Lessons Learned in Software Testing* (John Wiley & Sons, 2001). The book you hold in your hands describes how to write JUnit tests, but *Lessons Learned* discusses which tests to write and why. Knowing the former without the latter can do more harm than good.

Java Programming

Martin Fowler, *Refactoring: Improving the Design of Existing Code* (Addison-Wesley, 1999). Martin's book is an inspiration for this work and one of those books that belongs on every programmer's bookshelf. Martin provides the context for refactoring, a cohesive example throughout his narrative and a large catalog of refactorings. The names he has presented for his refactorings have become a part of the current lexicon of evolutionary design. We refer to it throughout this book with citations that look like this: [Refactoring, 311], meaning page 311 of Martin's book.

Eric Evans, *Domain-Driven Design* (Addison-Wesley, 2003). Test-Driven Development and Domain-Driven Design are mutually beneficial schools of software practice. A TDD practitioner tends to produce domain-oriented designs, whereas domain-driven designs tend to be easy to test. Evans does an excellent job of communicating the purpose and the mechanics of Domain-Driven Design in this book.

J. B. Rainsberger, "Use your singletons wisely" (http://www-106.ibm.com/developerworks/webservices/library/co-single.html). This article challenges whether your singleton truly is a singleton, offering a few extra questions to consider before making a class into a singleton.

Enterprise Software

Martin Fowler, *Patterns of Enterprise Application Architecture* (Addison-Wesley, 2002). This is another of those books that belongs on the shelf of every programmer working on enterprise software. Following the style of *Refactoring*, it provides a collection of articles describing the specific challenges of enterprise software, followed by a catalog of architecture patterns with code samples in both Java and C#.

We refer to it throughout this book with citations that look like this: [PEAA, 480], meaning page 480 of Martin's book.

Agile Software Development and Extreme Programming

Ron Jeffries, Ann Henderson and Chet Hendrickson, *Extreme Programming Installed* (Addison-Wesley, 2000). JUnit grew out of the Extreme Programming community, so it is fitting to include its literature in this list. Although this is not the first of the Extreme Programming books (Kent Beck, *Extreme Programming Explained: Embrace Change*), we believe that reading *Installed* first makes *Explained* sound less crazy than some people think it sounds. (We do not agree with them about that.)

Jim Highsmith, *Agile Software Development Ecosystems* (Addison-Wesley, 2002). To install the practices in this book in your environment, you need to understand when Agile might work and when it definitely will not. If you find yourself in a hostile environment, concentrate on practicing on your own until either your organization changes or you change organizations.

Mary and Tom Poppendieck, *Lean Software Development* (Addison-Wesley, 2003). We have long been looking for a theoretical model to which to associate the principles of Extreme Programming. The Poppendiecks have provided that model in this excellent book.

General Programming

Andrew Hunt and Dave Thomas, *Pragmatic Programmer* (Addison-Wesley, 1999). A no-nonsense catalog of programming techniques, including "learn one text editor well" and, among our favorites, "write unit tests."

Gerald Weinberg, *The Psychology of Computer Programming* (Dorset House, 1998, Silver Anniversary edition). Much of what you read in this book can be challenging to apply in an environment that is not ready for it. Although concepts such as evolutionary design and programmer testing are not new, spreading the word among your colleagues requires that you understand more about what makes a software team work. Anything Weinberg writes is appropriate, but this is especially illuminating, even nearly 30 years later.

Jim Hyslop, "Conversations: Truth or Consequences" (http://www.cuj.com/documents/s=7977/cujcexp2011hyslop/hyslop.htm). This article describes how easy it is to obscure intent using Boolean parameters in a language that matches parameters by position.

references

Print Sources

Astels, David. *Test-Driven Development: A Practical Guide.* Upper Saddle River, New Jersey: Prentice Hall PTR, 2003.

Barish, Greg. *Building Scalable and High-Performance Java Web Applications Using J2EE Technology.* Toronto, Canada: Pearson Education, 2001.

Beck, Kent. *Test-Driven Development: By Example.* Toronto, Canada: Addison-Wesley Pub Co, 2002.

Bloch, Joshua. *Effective Java Programming Language Guide.* Addison-Wesley Pub Co, 2001.

Brown, William J. et al., *AntiPatterns: Refactoring Software, Architectures and Projects in Crisis.* John Wiley & Sons, 1998.

Castro, Elizabeth. *XML for the World Wide Web.* Berkeley, California, USA: Peachpit Press, 2001.

Fowler, Martin. *Refactoring: Improving the Design of Existing Code.* Don Mills, Ontario, Canada: Addison-Wesley Pub Co, 1999.

______. *Patterns of Enterprise Application Architecture.* Toronto, Canada: Pearson Education, 2003.

Gamma, Erich; Richard Helm; Ralph Johnson; and John Vlissides. *Design Patterns.* Addison-Wesley, 1995.

Haggar, Peter. *Practical Java Programming Language Guide.* Addison-Wesley Professional, 2000.

Harold, Elliotte Rusty. *Processing XML with Java.* Pearson Education, 2002.

Hill, Timothy. *Windows NT Shell Scripting.* Sams, 1998.

Hunt, Andrew and David Thomas. *Programming Ruby.* Toronto, Canada: Addison-Wesley Pub Co, 2001.

Jeffries, Ron; Ann Anderson; and Chet Hendrickson. *Extreme Programming Installed.* Addison-Wesley Pub Co, 2000.

Jeffries, Ron. *Extreme Programming Adventures in C#.* Redmond, Washington, USA: Microsoft Press, 2004.

Kerievsky, Joshua. *Refactoring to Patterns.* Addison-Wesley Professional, 2004.

Laddad, Ramnivas. *AspectJ in Action.* Greenwich, Connecticut, USA: Manning Publications, 2003.

Langr, Jeff. *Essential Java Style: Patterns for Implementation.* Prentice Hall PTR, 1999.

Martin, Robert C. *Agile Software Development: Principles, Patterns, and Practices.* Prentice Hall, 2002.

Massol, Vincent and Ted Husted. *JUnit in Action.* Greenwich, Connecticut, USA: Manning Publications, 2004.

McConnell, Steve. *Code Complete.* Microsoft Press, 1993.

Roman, Ed; Scott Ambler; and Tyler Jewell. *Mastering Enterprise JavaBeans, 2nd Edition.* John Wiley & Sons, 2001.

Tansley, David. *Linux & UNIX Shell Programming.* Toronto, Canada: Pearson Education, 2000.

Williams, Laurie and Robert Kessler. *Pair Programming Illuminated.* Boston, Massachusetts, USA: Addison-Wesley Professional, 2003.

Online Sources

Ananiev, Alexander. MockEJB. www.mockejb.org

Ambler, Scott. www.agiledata.org

Ant. http://ant.apache.org

Aspect-Oriented Programming Home Page. www.parc.xerox.com/aop

Bach, James. "What is Exploratory Testing?" www.satisfice.com/articles/what_is_et.htm

Beck, Kent. "Simple Smalltalk Testing with Patterns." www.xprogramming.com/testfram.htm

Beck, Kent and Erich Gamma. "Test Infected: Programmers Love Writing Tests." http://junit.sourceforge.net/doc/testinfected/testing.htm

Bossicard, Vladimir Ritz. JUnit-addons. http://junit-addons.sourceforge.net

______. "The Third State of your Binary JUnit Tests." 2003. www.artima.com/weblogs/viewpost.jsp?thread=4603

Bowler, Mike. GSBase. http://gsbase.sourceforge.net

______. HtmlUnit. http://htmlunit.sourceforge.net

Cactus. http://jakarta.apache.org/cactus

Cactus. "Cactus Security HOWTO." http://jakarta.apache.org/cactus/writing/howto_security.html

CGLib. http://cglib.sourceforge.net

Chen, Doris. "Developing JSP Custom Tag Libraries." 2001. http://developers.sun.com/dev/evangcentral/presentations/customTag.pdf

Clark, Mike. "JUnit Primer." 2000. www.clarkware.com/articles/JUnitPrimer.html

______. JUnitPerf. www.clarkware.com/software/JUnitPerf.html

______, ed. JUnit FAQ. http://junit.sourceforge.net/doc/faq/faq.htm

Cunningham, Ward. Afterword to Kent Beck, *Sorted Collection.* http://c2.com/doc/forewords/beck2.html

CVS (Concurrent Versions System). www.cvshome.org

Dallaway, Richard. "Unit Testing Database Code." 2001. http://dallaway.com/acad/dbunit.html

DbUnit. http://dbunit.sourceforge.net

Diasparsoft Toolkit, 2004. www.diasparsoftware.com/toolkit

EasyMock. www.easymock.org

Eclipse. www.eclipse.org

Feathers, Michael. "The 'Self'-Shunt Unit Testing Pattern." 2001. www.objectmentor.com/resources/articles/SelfShunPtrn.pdf

Fit. http://fit.c2.com

FitNesse. www.fitnesse.org

Fogel, Karl and Moshe Bar. Open Source Development with CVS, 3rd edition. http://cvsbook.red-bean.com

Fowler, Martin. "POJO." www.martinfowler.com/bliki/POJO.html

Francis, Alan. "Agile Scotland." 2003. www.scottishdevelopers.com/modules/news/article.php?storyid=11

Freeman, Steve. "Developing JDBC Applications Test-First." www.mockobjects.com/wiki/DevelopingJdbcApplicationsTestFirst

Goldberg, David. "What Every Computer Scientist Should Know About Floating-Point Arithmetic." 1991. http://docs.sun.com/source/806-3568/ncg_goldberg.html

Holser, Paul. "Concisions, Concisions... or, (De-)Constructing an Idiom." 2003. http://home.comcast.net/~pholser/writings/concisions.html

HttpUnit. http://httpunit.sourceforge.net

Hyslop, Jim. "Conversations: Truth or Consequences." www.cuj.com/documents/s=7977/cujcexp2011hyslop/hyslop.htm

Javassist. www.jboss.org/developers/projects/javassist.html

Jeffries, Ron. XProgramming.com. www.xprogramming.com

______. "Essential XP: Unit Tests at 100." 2001. www.xprogramming.com/xpmag/expUnitTestsAt100.htm

______. "They're just rules!" www.xprogramming.com/Practices/justrule.htm

jMock. www.jmock.org

JUnit. www.junit.org

JUnitPP. http://junitpp.sourceforge.net

JUnitX. www.extreme-java.de/junitx

Kitchen, Jason. "Test email components in your software." 2003. www.javaworld.com/javaworld/jw-08-2003/jw-0829-smtp_p.html

Lamontagne, Yann. "The Archimidean Property." 2002. http://planetmath.org/encyclopedia/ArchimedeanProperty.html

Log4Unit. www.openfuture.de/Log4Unit

Mackinnon, Tim, Steve Freeman and Philip Craig. "Endo-Testing: Unit Testing with Mock Objects," 2000. www.connextra.com/aboutUs/mockobjects.pdf

Martin, Robert C. "The Interface Segregation Principle," 1996. www.objectmentor.com/publications/ isp.pdf

______. "The Open-Closed Principle," 1996. www.objectmentor.com/resources/articles/ocp.pdf

Maven. http://maven.apache.org

Mock Objects. www.mockobjects.com

NekoHTML. www.apache.org/~andyc/neko/doc/html

Pair Programming, an Extreme Programming Practice. www.pairprogramming.com

Penton Technology Media, "Ensuring Good JDBC Connection Pooling Performance." 2003. www.e-promag.com/epnewsletters//index.cfm?fuseaction=ShowNewsletterIssue&ID=584

PMD. http://pmd.sourceforge.net

Prevayler. www.prevayler.org

Rainsberger, J. B. "JUnit: A Starter Guide." 2002. www.diasparsoftware.com/articles/JUnit/jUnitStarterGuide.html

______. "Use Your Singletons Wisely." 2001. http://www-106.ibm.com/developerworks/webservices/library/co-single.html

______. "Refactoring: Replace Subclasses with Collaborators." 2002. www.diasparsoftware.com/articles/refactorings/replaceSubclassWithCollaborator.pdf

ServletUnit. http://httpunit.sourceforge.net

Subversion. http://subversion.tigris.org

Stobie, Keith. "Test Result Checking Patterns." 2001. www.stickyminds.com/se/S3222.asp

Struts. http://jakarta.apache.org/struts

StrutsTestCase. http://strutstestcase.sourceforge.net

Sun Microsystems. The EJB specifications. http://java.sun.com/products/ejb/docs.html

Sun Microsystems. BluePrints: Core J2EE Patterns. http://java.sun.com/blueprints/corej2eepatterns

Sun Microsystems. "Providing Object Serialization for Your Classes." http://java.sun.com/docs/books/tutorial/essential/io/providing.html

Velocity. http://jakarta.apache.org/velocity

Virtual Mock. www.virtualmock.org

Ward Cunningham's Wiki. http://c2.com/cgi/wiki

Wiki. www.wiki.org

XDoclet. http://xdoclet.sourceforge.net

Yahoo! group for Extreme Programming. http://groups.yahoo.com/group/extremeprogramming

Yahoo! group for JUnit. http://groups.yahoo.com/group/junit

Yahoo! group for Test-Driven Development. http://groups.yahoo.com/group/testdrivendevelopment

index

Numerics

3 As
  See arrange, act, assert
404 File Not Found 522

A

abstract class
  enforcing contract 107
abstract test case 49–50, 52, 107, 118, 628
accept(). *See* TestFilter
acceptance test 110
action
  in a web application 514
ActionForward 518
actual value 282
addTest() 109, 113
addTestSuite() 112–113, 237
  ignores suite() method 238
  incorrect usage 238
aggregation 66
Agile 509
aliasing problem 579
AllTests 11, 115–116, 238, 590–591, 596
  alternatives to 116
  maintenance issues 115–116
Ambler, Scott 172
Ananiev, Alexander 413
anonymous inner class 58
Ant 94, 96, 235, 455, 591
  customizing test results 208–209, 213, 224
  for executing tests 174, 181, 183
  initializing test environment 165
  integration with Cactus 396
  JUnit result formatter 209
  reporting test results 198–199, 202, 205
  using an XML catalog 303
  with system properties 139–140
Anthill 174, 335, 407, 689
Apache 191
appearsEqual() 573, 577, 581, 583
  implementation details 583
  motivation behind 583
  problems with 583
application
  general testing strategy 509
application context 496
application logic
  separate from business logic 484
application servers 394–397, 406–410, 415–418
  automatic deployment 162
  performance problems with 259
  security 529
  testing with 302, 510, 512–513
  testing without 297, 386, 510
  See also containers
Armstrong, Eric 52
arrange, act, assert 6, 23, 414
Arrays.asList()
  for comparing arrays 25
aspect patterns
  Wormhole 649
AspectJ 650
Aspect-Oriented Programming 263
aspects 70, 559, 571, 649
assembly descriptor 529
Assert 14, 23, 225
assert methods 225
assertAppearsEqual() 581
assertAppearsNotEqual() 581
assertCollectionsEqual() 62
assertEquals() 13–15, 23, 37, 61–62, 248, 301, 493, 575, 581, 588
  alternatives to 581
  tolerance level 42
  tolerance level for floating-point numbers 14
assertEventsAppearEquals() 577, 582
assertFalse() 14, 31
assertion 13, 21, 23, 59, 74
  complex 604
  counting 224
  duplication in 617
  overly specific 60, 247
  style 294
  the implicit and 30
  XPath-based 282, 287, 294–298, 301–302, 403, 491
assertion failures
  multiple in test 248
assertion methods 14
AssertionFailedError 15
assertNotEquals() 31
assertNotNull() 14

assertNotSame() 14
assertNull() 14
assertSame() 14, 503
assertThrows() 59–60
assertTrue() 14–15
assertXMLEqual() 269, 273–276, 281–282, 285, 288
assertXMLIdentical() 290
assertXpathEvaluatesTo() 269
assertXpathExists() 269
Astels, Dave 697
asynchronous 376, 414, 427, 606
attribute values, XML 266
attributes
  web form 494
authentication 529–530, 532
authorization 529, 532–533
auto-increment 349, 351
Avalon 191

B

Bach, James 7, 20, 698
Bag 63
bar 174
Base Test Case
  defined 90–91
  managing test data with 145, 155
  when to use 179, 190, 193–194, 337, 616, 620
BaseTestCase (GSBase) 62
<batchtest> 181, 199, 201–202, 596
  fork attribute 182
  merge results 206
bean-managed persistence 374, 408, 653
Beck, Kent 6, 83, 106, 108, 259, 567, 649, 697
behavior 17, 19–20, 81
  complex 19
  enforcing common 48
  expected 23
  incorrect 371
  instead of methods 35
  method without 35
  predictable 6, 83, 245, 556
  scattered throughout 510
  special cases 92
  testing indirectly 46
  testing individually 87
  testing separately 359
Bloch, Joshua 26
BMP 408
  complexity of 408
  reducing complexity of 413
  See also bean-managed persistence
Bossicard, Vladimir 119, 185, 586, 618
boundary cases 490, 689
boundary condition 8, 127
Bowler, Mike 28, 117, 123, 476, 573, 576
breakpoint 5, 10
brittleness 75
  assumption about data format 331
  assumption about local environment 280, 513
  dependency on database 312
  dependency on implementation details 359, 565
  duplication 35, 54
  of test fixtures 556
  overly-precise assertions 60, 247, 294, 465
  subclassing the class under test 571
  vague assertions 269
broken links 510, 522, 525
bugbase-test.log 196
build script 142
buildControlDocument() 639
buildfile 97, 181
buildTestDocument() 639
business data 371
  corrupting 371
business logic
  dependency on container 444
  extracting from EJB 392, 395–396
  extracting from web components 456, 484
  in entity beans 374–375
  in message-driven beans 376
  in session beans 371–374, 387
  in stored procedures 366
  moving into POJO 379
  passing external resources into 386
  testing in isolation 384–386, 449, 689
  testing in memory 379
  testing without 427–430, 444–447, 458–459, 483–484, 510
bytecode magic 263
bytecode manipulation 185, 561

C

cache 181, 183
cache hit
  verifying 183
Cactus 441, 510, 533
  and the Parameterized Test Case pattern 132, 634
  begin method 532
  deploying tests 395
  when to use 137, 393–394, 398, 530–535
CallableStatement 367
callbacks 220
cannot break on its own 41
Cannot instantiate test case 118
cascading stylesheets 296
Catalina 479
Celis, Shane 248
CGLib 67
Chappell, Simon 677
checkstyle 616
class
  as a unit to test 4
class loader
  problems 254
class loading 235
  problems 234
class path 251, 394
  See also classpath 11
class reloading
  problems 250
class under test
  subclassing 490, 507
ClassCastException 254
  narrowing EJB reference 253
class-level method 68, 433
  problems faking out 70
ClassNotFoundException 591
CLASSPATH 235
-classpath 235
<classpath> 235
classpath 234
CLEAN INSERT 170

clearParameters() 358
client data 446
client state 381
clone() 573, 579–580
consistent with equals() 579
limitations of 579
when to use it 580
Cloneable 573, 580
pitfalls with 579
Closure 59
CMP. *See* container-managed persistence 400
code and fix 4
code path
as a unit to test 4
cohesion 9, 20, 60, 107, 373
collaboration 328
collecting test case classes 586
collecting tests
specific ones 107
Collection.add(Object) 34
collections 26
comparing 61, 247
duplicate elements 62
unordered 62
Collections.synchronizedList() 24
com.gargoylesoftware.base.testing.TestUtil 581
com.sun.jms.MapMessageImpl 424
command interpreter 45
command line 155, 161, 189, 195
building tests 94
command line options 142
command shells 199
Command/Query Separation Principle 419
comments
appropriate use of 471
common fixture 125, 244
communication
through good names 17
ComparabilityTestCase 586
Comparable 586–587
ComparableAssert 589
compareTo() 586–587
consistent with equals() 588
complexity 319, 368
of EJB 372
test environment 137
composition 66
<concat> 201
confidence 56, 675
ConfigurableTestCase 159–160
configuration 377
configuration document 303
configuration errors 302
configuration files 145, 266, 401
XML 147
configuration management 438
configuration tests 145
connections
cleaning up 335
pooling 170, 335
consistency 31
console 546
construction
polymorphic 40
constructor
testing 37
testing default values 38
container 385, 409
container-managed persistence 374, 397, 401, 403
container-managed relationships 398, 401
effect on test complexity 375
testing meta data 375
containers 409–410, 413, 423, 501, 509, 529
difficulties testing with 259, 422
initializing with ServletRunner 454
minimizing use of 439
security 535
simulating 387, 396
testing EJBs with 372, 374–376, 394–399, 401, 413, 417
testing EJBs without 378, 396, 401, 411, 415
testing JMS components with 438
testing JMS components without 444, 474, 480
testing with 396, 413, 418, 505
testing without 417–418, 420, 526
trusting 484, 536
context root 454
continuous build 407
continuous integration 375
contract 5, 53
Controller 246, 371, 374, 376, 379, 444, 451, 490, 496, 498, 500, 509, 514
Cooley, Curtis 366
copy and paste reuse 433
CountingAssert 225
coupling 9, 20, 60, 70, 107, 145, 193, 301, 309, 312, 321, 334, 374–375, 415, 429, 437, 445, 448, 451, 479, 483, 491, 545, 559, 563, 607, 684
effect of test data 137
excessive 293
tests and environment 143–144
with Singletons 558
coverage 9
Craig, Philip 318, 690, 698
createControlInstance() 65
creation method 40, 49, 562
CredentialProvider 527
credentials 526, 530, 533
CRUD 366
Cruise Control 94, 174, 335, 375, 398, 407, 464, 689
Cunningham, Ward 135, 352
custom assertion 60, 90–91, 267, 269, 290, 589, 604, 617
assertThrows() 58
design tips 619
custom suite method 108, 128, 134, 238
custom test suite 112, 128, 237
building programmatically 117
JUnit ignores 237
Customer Tests 79, 87, 91, 110, 120, 474
custom file format 135
CVS 121, 274

D

Dallaway, Richard 172, 309, 697
data access layer 310, 335
Data Bean 496
data components 309–310
Data Definition Language 328
data hiding 38–39
data repository 142
data source 401, 409, 411, 440, 478
data transfer document 304
database administrators 327, 350

database connection 161
  as test resource 170
database fixture 341
database meta data 334
  alternatives to 331
  making assertions on 329
database schema 327, 329, 366, 406
  dependency on 333
  enabling change 328
database servers 165
DatabaseMetaData.getSchemas() 330
databases 249, 309
  and entity beans 375
  and message-driven beans 421
  and test data 137, 139, 157, 170, 346, 597
  as a test resource 586, 593
  collective ownership 327
  connection parameters 142
  development 352
  exclusive access 406
  four for testing 309
  free alternatives 350
  integration 310
  issues testing against 334
  large data sets 171
  leftover data 332
  legacy 363
  meta data 329
  minimizing tests against 261, 312
  multiple schemas 363
  ownership issues 350
  problems using 157, 401
  reducing dependency on 261
  referential integrity 406
  resetting state between tests 138
  shared 309, 349
  stored procedures 366
  testing entity beans without 389, 409
  testing the schema 328, 352
  testing with 333, 360, 398, 557, 596, 599, 672, 681
  testing without 317, 322, 332, 357–359, 599
DatabaseTestCase 170
data-driven tests 103, 127, 133
  and Cactus 132
dataset 361, 364
DataSource 162, 325, 594
DbUnit 91, 138, 170, 360, 363, 365, 399, 596
  flat XML format 360
  limitations 362
dbunit.qualified.table.names 363
DDL. *See* Data Definition Language
deadlock 177–178, 600
debug mode 5
debug(Object message, Throwable t). *See* Log4Unit
debugger 4–5, 7, 74
debugging 4, 20, 178, 190, 334, 500, 536, 676
declarative security 525, 535
  how not to test 529
declarative transactions 536
default test suite 235, 237, 243
DefaultConsole 601
DefaultDataSet 362
defects 8, 36, 474, 614, 675
  caused by missing test 38, 56, 110
  come back 4, 182
  diagnosing 297, 305
  hiding 351, 478, 616
  impact of 371, 451
  in an external library 186
  in J2EE 1.3 412
  in the platform 394
  isolating 20–21, 378, 399
  low-priority 186
  mean time to find 114, 607
  pattern 352
  recurring 302, 397
delegate 379
delegation 676
DELETE_ALL 170
dependency 259, 282, 310, 312, 333, 371
  avoiding 485
  checking 204
  database tables 334
  eliminated 613
  on file system 604
deployed component
  alternatives to testing 272
deploying 513
  database schema objects 352
  JSP tag library 474
  tests 590
deployment 372, 399, 506
  complexity of 378
  simulating 423
deployment descriptors 266, 415, 529, 536, 538
  and ServletUnit 445, 454–455
  forgetting to write 474
  testing 272, 399, 475, 477
deployment information
  hard coding 513
deployment problems 513
deployment script 591
Deployment Tests 280, 409, 439, 477, 536, 591
design
  indicator of good 460
  testable 452
design improvement 66, 108
  See also refactoring
design pattern 162, 544
  Abstract Factory 544
  Action 45
  Bridge 373, 376
  Command 45, 55, 663
  Composite 544
  Decorator 162, 179, 427, 544, 665, 676
  Event Listener 545, 576
    See also design pattern, Observable
  Event Source 545, 550
    See also design pattern, Observer
  Factory 562
  Front Controller 490
  Model View Controller 371
  Null Object 691
  Observable 544, 550, 555, 574, 621
  Observer 215, 544–545, 548, 621
  Prototype 580
  refactoring towards 544
  Registry 593
  Remote Facade 379, 386
  Singleton 68, 169–170, 181–184, 440, 544, 556–557, 559, 561
  Strategy 509
  suggested by tests 544
  Template Method 566
  Wrapper. *See* design pattern, Decorator

design problem 346
destroy() 480
DetailedDiff 288
Diasparsoft Toolkit
  CollectionUtil 331
  EntityBeanMetaDataTest 403
  ExceptionalClosure 59
  FakeHttpSession 490
  FileSystemWebConnection 491
  FileSystemWebResponse 491
  ForwardingServlet 459
  GoldMasterFile 462
  HttpUtil 516
  JDBC utilities 330, 660
  RequestDispatcherAdapter 490
  ValueObjectEqualsTest 64
DiFalco, Robert 181
Diff
  XMLUnit 275
Diff engine
  XMLUnit 281
Difference 284
DifferenceConstants 283
  ATTR_VALUE 283
  TEXT_VALUE 283
differenceFound() 284–285
DifferenceListener 272, 280, 282, 285, 287
differences
  ignoring in XML documents 272, 281
  in XML documents 274, 289
  multiple in XMLUnit tests 288
DirectorySuiteBuilder 119, 175, 590, 596
  compared to RecursiveTestsuite 119
disable 185
distribution 386
doAfterBody() 470
DocBook 273, 276
Doctor Dobbs Journal 159
Document Object Model 278, 283, 294, 476
  custom 287
Document Type Definition 272, 303, 403, 521
  network connectivity 279
  using locally 280
doEndTag() 470
doFilter() 503
doGet() 456
DOM 220, 291
  See Document Object Model
Domain Model 27, 379, 381, 383–384, 386, 587
domain object 318
  converting to database object 314
DOMParser 295
don't test the platform
  EJB container 375, 397, 399
  Java compiler 40
  JDBC 310
  JMS server 433
  web container 505, 525, 529
doPost() 447, 456, 488–490, 499
doRunTest() 215
doStartTag() 470
downloading JUnit 10
DTD 304, 401, 477
  See also Document Type Definition
DuplicateKeyException 399
duplication 9, 59, 248, 309, 316, 420, 548
  and shared test resources 593
  eliminating 25, 35, 89, 617
  extracting into test fixture 73, 83
  in database tests 310, 337, 362
  in production code 318, 446
  in test names 92, 110
  in tests 92, 113, 127, 432, 637
  of assertions 301, 403, 604, 617
  of production code in tests 563–565
  of production logic in fake objects 692
dynamic content 496
dynamic invocation handler 576

E

Eames, Mark 444
*.ear 395
EAR file 143
EasyMock 67, 318, 409, 437, 560, 690, 695
  alternative to Self-Shunt 555
  examples of use 436, 438, 488, 549, 626–627, 669
Eclipse 99, 140, 180, 251, 596, 610
  Java Build Path 235
ed bar 174
EJB 162, 259, 420
  failure when narrowing 253
  suitability 371
  why we use it 386
  See also Enterprise JavaBeans
EJB container 385, 392, 397, 399, 410, 530
  avoiding 372–373, 392
  live 374, 377, 398, 414, 672
  mocking 392
  simulate 374, 386, 392
  testing without 400
EJB implementation class
  instantiating directly 392, 411
EJB server. *See* EJB container
EJB specification 382, 399
ejbCreate() 385, 427
ejbLoad() 410
EJBQL 398, 401, 406
emacs 200
email 199
encapsulation 37, 45
endo-testing 690
End-to-End Tests 7, 262, 494, 510, 519
  alternatives to 446, 457, 470, 474, 491
  as safety net 335
  CMP entity beans 375, 399, 407
  for legacy code 455
  for security 525
  HtmlUnit 513
  organizing 79, 101, 120, 123
  purpose of 509
  test fixtures 87
Enterprise JavaBeans 253, 371, 496
  as thin as possible 372
  lifecycle methods 393, 408, 659
entity beans 374, 386, 397, 400, 408, 440, 536, 653
  BMP 376, 408
  reducing the cost of testing 406
  testing meta data 401
  trade-off between BMP and CMP 374
EntityContext 409–411
environment setup 164
environment variables 138, 142–144, 147, 235

equality 25–26, 31
approximating with
appears equal 581
of XML documents 269
equals() 25–29, 32, 586–587, 677
and compareTo() 588
and EventCatcher 576
and JavaBeans.
See appearsEqual() 581
and object cloning 573, 579–580
and testSerliaization() 578
and TestUtil.testClone() 573
and XML documents 287
description of contract 27
for collections 62
for Value Objects 27
implementing correctly 26
not implemented correctly 581
testing 26
testing without
EqualsTester 29
when to implement 45
EqualsHashCodeTestCase 32, 63, 65
EqualsTester 28–29, 32–33, 63, 678, 681
example of using 28
parameters 28
special handling of
subclasses 28
equivalence relation 27
error 16, 57, 545
how it occurs 56
notification 216
what it indicates 16
what it means 57
error conditions 490
error handling
for JMS components 427
error-case testing 437
ERwin 328
Evans, Eric 698
event handler 213
event listener 81, 693
universal 576
event source 81, 576, 693
EventCatcher 573–576, 582–583
event-handling logic 548
events
simulating 549
test execution 213
exception 15
expected 56
ignoring expected ones 58
object-oriented test
approach 58
throwing from tests 105
throwing the right one 56
unexpected 57
ExceptionalClosure 59
excluded.properties 250, 252, 254
location on file system 251
multiple copies 251
expectations 8, 392
expected result 25
expected value 24, 34, 282
comparing to actual value 24
expensive tests 681
isolating 689
exploratory testing 7, 20
extending JUnit 189, 586
external data 346
external library
class loading problems 250
handling defects in 186
external resource 249, 593, 613, 681
avoiding 260, 334, 376, 442, 510, 608
effect on test execution
speed 114
extracting into test fixture 86
mitigating the cost of 438
simulating 415
tests dependency on 120

F

factory method 562
fail fast 694
fail() 57, 330
failed assertion. *See* failure
failed test. *See* failure
failing status code 528
failing test
one per incorrect behavior 245
FailingHttpStatusCodeException 528
failure 16, 57, 90, 382, 545
affecting other tests 106
determining the cause 293
how it occurs 56
message 15, 59, 90, 177, 589
multiple in test 244
notification 216
signaling 15
what it indicates 16
failure message 59, 131, 271, 287, 333, 442, 554, 618
customized 620
misleading 333
specialized 290
XMLUnit 288
fake 287, 489, 516, 545, 669, 685, 691–693
fake method 67
fake objects 486
false failures 418, 475, 513, 523, 607, 612
false positive 432
feedback 7–8, 21, 111, 250, 371
file
cleaning up between tests 604
reading data from 608
file system 149, 280, 458, 466, 604–605, 607
cleaning up between tests 605
load web pages from 491
scan for tests 117
testing without 606, 608
file system operations
asynchronous nature 605
FileAssert 620
filename
relative 610
<fileset> 201
filter 283
See also web resource filter
FilterChain 503
finally 336
finder methods 398
finite state machine 514
Fit 135, 509
FitNesse 509–510
fixtures 18, 83, 521, 532, 605, 686
amount of duplication 89
and order-dependent
tests 123–124
and Parameterized Test
Case 129, 132, 181
and Self-Shunt 432

fixtures *(continued)*
as instance-level fields 109
as XML documents 134
changing for each test 128
common services as 90, 304
complex 556
database 340
duplication 84
effect on test readability 86
excessive 683
expensive to set up 161, 164
external data in 346
extracting code into 338, 456
for database tests 346
hierarchy 87
keeping separate 112
large 87
one per entity bean 403
one per method 373
one per Transaction Script 372
one-time setup 158, 161, 170, 249
organizing tests around 20, 73, 92
setup problems 234, 239
shared 106, 164, 249, 332, 346, 557, 559–560, 586, 597, 599
special case tests 18, 92, 372
splitting 73
See also setUp() and tearDown()
foreign key 400
foreign key constraints
effect on test complexity 334
foreign keys 327
<formatter> 199, 202, 224
formatter type
for <batchtest> 199
Fowler, Martin 129, 310, 328, 334, 372, 698
frames 204
framework 234, 259, 501, 519
for unit testing 6
learning process 239
Freeman, Steve 318, 690, 697–698
functional test 110

G

Gamma, Eric 6
Gang of Four 215
garbage collection 336, 417–418
garbage-in, garbage-out 304
getDatabaseConnection() 361
getDataSet() 361
getInitParameter() 479
GetMethodWebRequest 454
getName() 178
getPrimaryKey() 410
getProperties() 139
getResourceAsStream() 150–151
getters 41
when to test 42
whether to test 674–675
global data 46, 66, 70, 235
reset between tests 182
global functions
session bean methods as 373
going dark 242
Gold Master 323–327, 462, 466, 494
externalizing to file 325
for page templates 457–459, 461, 468, 475, 494
other examples of use 280, 354, 578
when not to use 465
See also Guru Checks Output
Golden Master. *See* Gold Master
golden results. *See* Gold Master
GoldMasterFile 462
good practices 17, 114, 123, 137, 144, 148
Grandma's Ham 46
graphical user interface 164
green bar 189, 250
GSBase 573, 590, 619–620
assertCollectionsEqual()
BaseTestCase 62, 91
EqualsTester 63, 678
See also EqualsTester
JDBC resource wrappers 343
OrderedTestSuite 123
RecursiveTestSuite 117, 121, 175
See also RecursiveTestSuite
testing equals() 28
See also Base Test Case
GUI 106, 164, 399
GUI events 574
Guru Checks Output 326
See also Gold Master

H

Haggar, Peter 26
Hall, Stephen 697
happy path 17, 311, 435
hashCode() 322, 576
consistent with equals() 32
heavyweight 558
Henderson, Anne 699
Hendrickson, Chet 699
here document. *See* herefile
herefile 147–148
Hibernate 375–376
HierarchyEvent 575
Highsmith, Jim 699
Hollywood Principle 260
Holser, Paul 284
hot deployment 162
HSQLDB 309, 350
HTML 276, 290
badly-formed 291
form elements 455
ID attribute 301
parsers 291
parsing as XML 290
test results as 189, 202, 205, 215
HTMLConfiguration 295
HtmlPage 494, 522
creating from the file system 491
HTML-tolerant parser 272
HtmlUnit 91, 302, 512–513, 539, 573, 645
broken links 522
defect in version 1.2.3 523
for End-to-End Tests 444, 509
testing EJB security 530
testing static web pages 291
testing web security 526–527
when to use 455
without a web server 491
HTTP 445
HTTP request 455, 496, 498
accessing with ServletUnit 455
parameters 485
processing 483
simulating 486
HTTP response
accessing with ServletUnit 455
HTTP session 374, 446, 448–449, 452, 490, 496, 501
interaction 451
HttpClient
limitations 523
HttpServletRequest 485, 495, 499, 516

HttpServletRequest.getParameterMap() 485
HttpServletResponse 529
HttpSession 452, 455
HttpUnit 91, 444, 454
HttpUtil 516
Hunt, Andrew 42, 697, 699
Husted, Ted 697
Hyslop, Jim 699

I

IDE 115–116, 165
  effect on organizing source code 78
IDEA 180
identical
  XMLUnit 269, 273
identifier
  for expected exceptions 57
IDENTITY 349, 351, 362
ignorance
  celebrating 241
_ignored 186
ignored tests
  false positives 187
ignoring tests 107, 185
implementation pattern
  testing setter methods 44
  throwing the right exception 57
incremental 9, 245
indices 327
infinite loop 177–178
info(Object message). *See* Log4Unit
infrastructure 137, 145, 148, 190
inheritance
  drawbacks to 193
init()
  invoking directly 478
InitialContext.lookup() 253
initialization
  and ServletContext 480
initialization parameters 480
<init-param> 277
insane object 54
INSERT 170
installing JUnit 10
integration 509
Integration Tests 79, 123, 137, 162, 625
integrity constraint violation 332
intercept
  method invocations 486
interface
  faking out 67
  multiple 53
  publishing 48
  testing 48
  tests as semantics specification 52
invocation context 455, 499
isolated tests 106–108, 298, 408, 429, 480
  problems with 544, 557
  See also test isolation
isolation 509, 545
  impediments to testing in 66
  testing business logic in 412, 430
  testing entity beans in 399
  testing in 5, 19, 66
  testing message-driven beans in 426
  testing objects in 387
  testing responsibilities in 434, 484, 495
  testing session beans in 391
  testing web components in 444, 457, 468
  testing web pages in 513, 523
isValid() 38, 54
IterationTag 469, 473

J

J2EE 138, 253, 371, 577
  use of XML 266
J2EE applications 266, 508, 510
J2EE server 162
j2ee.jar 413
Jakarta Commons 59, 523
Jakarta Commons Logging 198
*.jar file
  collect tests from 586, 590
<jar> 591
Jasper 455, 457, 463
<java> 175
Java language specification 40
Java logging API 193
Java system properties 144
Java Virtual Machine 16
java.io.tmpdir 142
java.lang.Cloneable 580
java.lang.System 139
java.logging 190
java.util.Calendar 54
java.util.Properties 148
java.util.ResourceBundle 152
JavaBeans 38, 44, 54, 457, 469, 581, 583
  presentation layer 466
  structure of 54
  testing 54
<javac> 96
Javadoc 204
JavaMail 419, 432
JavaServer Pages 272, 444–445, 491, 514, 520
  alternatives to 267, 298
  and HTTP sessions 455
  forwarding from servlet 455
  rendering 456–457
  tag handler 468
  tag library 474
  testing data passed to 495
  testing in isolation 457
Javassist 185
javax.rmi.Remote 382
jaxen 267
JAXP 223
  test failure using 252
JBoss 185, 386, 401, 403, 413, 434, 441, 530, 534
JDBC
  alternative to 158–159
  common trouble spots 321, 333
  design criticism 322
  duplication in tests 310
  for test data 399
  problems testing 309
  provider 310, 330
  reducing dependency on 261, 312, 314, 317
  testing queries 317
JDBC client code 408–409
JDBC resources 336, 340, 367
  cleaning up 335
  effect on test execution 336
  in production code 343
JdbcResourceRegistry 340, 362
JDO 386
jEdit 180
Jeffries, Ron 135, 259, 699
Jelly 189
Jetty 495

Jini
  alternative to EJB 385
jMock 67, 488, 695
JMS 259, 548
JMS exceptions 437
JMS message consumer 376, 420–421, 426, 430–432
JMS message listeners
  See JMS message consumers
JMS message producer 376, 433–434
JMS server 434, 438
JNDI directory 385, 411–412, 414–415, 427, 439–441, 510, 657
  as common test resource 593
  avoiding 376, 392
  in-memory 440
  mocking. *See* MockEJB
  testing contents of 393, 430, 442
JNDI lookups 253, 373, 431, 440
  effect on test execution speed 396
  testing in isolation 386
JNDI namespace
  nonglobal 412
jndi.properties 413
JSP engine 457
  simulating 468, 470
  standalone 463
JSP. *See* JavaServer Pages
JspWriter 473
JTidy 296
JUnit
  alternatives to 675
  design philosophy 245
  when not to use 322, 366
<junit> 175, 189, 198–199, 201–202, 224
  alternative to 215
  custom formatter 214
  forking the JVM 181
  formatter attribute 209
  printsummary attribute 204
  using system properties 140
  See also <junitreport>
JUnit FAQ 253, 255
JUnit Yahoo! group 52, 164, 181, 185, 215, 234, 236, 618
junit.framework 13, 23
junit.framework.AllTests 113
junit.framework.Assert 14
junit.framework.AssertionFailedError 15
junit.framework.Test 216
junit.framework.TestCase 13, 240, 395
  AllTests pattern 113
junit.framework.TestListener 215
junit.jar 95, 175, 223, 234, 250
junit.log4j.LoggedTestCase 194–195
junit.logswingui.TestRunner 195
junit.runner.TestRunner 215
junit.swingui.TestRunner 174
junit.tests.AllTests 112, 115
junit.textui.TestRunner 11, 174
JUNIT_HOME 175
JUnit-addons 586, 592
  assertNotEquals() 31
  ComparabilityTestCase 589
  ComparableAssert 589
  custom assertions 619–620
  DirectorySuiteBuilder 119, 175, 590
  documentation defect 601
  EqualsHashCodeTestCase 32, 64
  ignoring tests 186
  ResourceManager 593
  test runner 176–177, 179, 600
  TestClassValidator 614
  TestSetup 164, 598
JUnitEE 137
junit-frames.xsl 205
junit-noframes.xsl 205
JUnitPerf 161, 539
JUnitPP 138, 159, 592
  default directory 160
<junitreport> 176, 189, 202, 204–206, 208–209, 214–215, 224, 596
  customizing output 205
  junit-frames.xsl 205
  junit-noframes.xsl 205
  with custom stylesheet 207
JunitResultFormatter 209
JUnitX 248, 480, 604, 620, 622, 626
junitx.extensions.ComparabilityTestCase 587
junitx.framework.TestProxy 621
junitx.runner.Resource 597
junitx.runner.TestRunner 176
junitx.util.ArchiveSuiteBuilder 590
junitx.util.ResourceManager 593
just for testing 81, 384, 624–625
JVM properties.
  See system properties

K

Kaner, Cem 698
Kay, Michael 297
keep the test 21, 43
Kerievsky, Joshua 544
key properties 65

L

Laflamme, Manuel 170
Langr, Jeff 117
Latkiewicz, George 313, 326, 385, 407, 478
leaking resources 335
learning
  by writing tests 61
learning curve 234
Learning Test 40, 312, 329, 332, 335, 353, 397, 648
legacy code 108, 323, 357, 389, 422, 626
  assertEquals() 581
  file system 607, 614
  JDBC 341, 349, 357, 359–360
  message-driven bean 422, 429
  no return value 620
  private methods 604, 625
  session bean 387
legacy J2EE components 262
Lesiecki, Nicholas 697
lifecycle
  of JSP tag handlers 468
lightweight container 445, 454
Link, Johannes 697
LinkageError 252
List 24
List.equals() 25
ListAssert 619–620
location
  in a web application 514

log()
  overriding in servlets 479
Log4J 190–191, 194, 196, 198, 509
  extra logging output 197
Log4Unit 194, 196
  default behavior 194
  limitations 198
  using 194
LoggedTestCase 198
logging 194, 196
  configurability 193
  how not to use 190
LogKit 190–191
look-and-feel 299

M

Mackinnon, Tim 318, 690, 698
Madhwani, Rakesh 164
<mail> 201
mailto 523
maintenance 348
Manaster, Carl 352
manual tests 322, 483
  for EJB security 530
mapping
  for CMP entity beans 398
Massol, Vincent 697
Maven 189
McConnell, Steve 46
memory
  testing entirely in 379
Menard, Jason 36
mental model 17
Message 421
message listener 259
  instantiating directly 427
message-driven beans 376, 417–418, 427, 430, 432
  difficulty testing 420, 426
  legacy code 422
  testing with MockEJB 423
  testing with the container 414
  testing without the container 420
MessageDrivenContext 420
MessageListener 426
message-processing logic 427, 429–430
messaging server 438, 478
  testing without 426, 434, 438
meta data 397, 404
  for CMP entity beans 400
method
  as a unit to test 4
method invocation
  intercepting 488–490, 576
  recording 549
method invocation sequences
  recording and verifying 555
  verifying with EasyMock 411
Method test name not found 236
Mimer 309, 350
mock data source 368
Mock Objects 312, 318, 325, 344, 357, 473, 672, 690, 694–695
  JDBC 357
mock objects 260, 318, 345, 359, 368–369, 386, 392, 409, 426, 430, 432, 518, 568, 649, 681, 689
  effect on complexity 319
  JDBC 358, 368
  JDBC provider 312
  JMS 439
  overuse 439
mock objects approach 260, 351, 409, 420, 442, 484, 510, 613
MockCallableStatement 367
MockConnection2 368
MockContext 411–412, 438
MockDataSource 412
MockEJB 387, 391, 393, 396, 399, 411–412, 420, 423, 425, 438, 440
  supported EJBs 393
MockJspWriter 473
MockMaker 488
MockMultiRowResultSet 318
MockPageContext 471
MockPreparedStatement 313
MockResultSet 321
MockSingleRowResultSet 318
Model 371, 509
Monk, Simon 697
multiple assertions 244
  alternatives to 244
  motivations for 246
multiple failures 245, 247
  for detailed test results 248
multiple test runs 164
multiple tests
  using same data 106
Multiset. *See* Bag
mutable objects 579
MVC. *See* design pattern, Model View Controller
MySQL 350

N

naming conventions 131, 154, 576
  for special case tests 18
  for test case classes 18
  for test packages 80
  for tests 17, 73, 242
naming rules
  for tests 242
narrow() 254
narrowing EJB references 253
navigation 519
navigation engine 511, 514, 518, 520
navigation rules 371, 509–511, 514, 518–520
  modelling 514
  testing in isolation 518–519
NekoHTML 291, 294, 302
  configuration notes 294
  default configuration 295
  HTML DOM configuration 294
  HTMLConfiguration 294
  instantiating parser 295
  Xerces compatibility 296
nekohtml.jar 294
network connection 268, 279, 401
network connectivity 279
No test cases found 236
NoClassDefFoundError
  when executing tests 234
noframes 204
noloading 198
novice programmers 40
null reference 16
nullable 334
nullable columns 327
NullPointerException 479, 499

O

object model
  for HTML 513
Object Tests 5, 10, 335, 414, 470, 474, 556–557, 593
  alternatives to 625

Object Tests *(continued)*
  and mock objects 690
  automated 7–8
  different from Test Object 67
  for data components 310, 321
  for EJBs 414
  for J2EE applications 509–510
  for legacy code 263
  for web components 455, 465, 468, 474, 484, 494
  importance of Value Objects 26
  object-oriented design 66
  organizing code for 79
  positive feedback 9
  programmer confidence 9
  repeatable 7
  rhythm of 6, 12
  self-verifying 8, 15
  test data for 137, 157
Observer 550
one problem at a time 247
one-time setup 165, 249, 521, 597
onMessage() 414
  invoking directly 423
open source 6, 194, 245, 290
Open/Closed Principle 613, 689
operating system 165
optimize
  test suite 162
order of tests 106
  controlling 108
  JUnit default behavior 109
order-dependent tests 123, 126
  example 124
OrderedTestSuite 124–125
  as a refactoring tool 125
ordering of objects 586
org.apache.catalina.core.StandardWrapper. 479
org.custommonkey.xmlunit.Diff 274
org.custommonkey.xmlunit.DifferenceListener 282
org.dbunit.DatabaseTestCase 170, 361
org.dbunit.dataset.IDataSet 170
org.w3c.dom 217, 223
orthogonality 245
owning the plug 349, 352

P

package hierarchy 114
page context 470, 473
page flow 509–510, 513–514
  testing in isolation 511
page templates 267, 514, 520
  testing data passed to 495
Pair Programming 241
parameterize 127, 139
Parameterized Test Case 65, 131–132, 634
  executing a single test 180
  externalizing fixture data 134
  for database tests 327, 345, 356
  for J2EE applications 516, 538
  for JNDI directories 442
  for web components 473, 506
  problem with Cactus 442
  using XML 134–135, 630
Parameterized tests. *See* Parameterized Test Case
parameterizing
  test data 137
<param-name> 277
<param-value> 277
passivation 393
PDF 209
  test results as 205
performance 147, 259, 336, 419, 464, 525
  problem with containers 259
permissions 356
  database objects 352
persistence 376, 386, 388, 408
  pluggable 375
Pettichord, Bret 698
philosophy 107
Plain Old Java Objects 379, 386, 424, 432
  and equals() 287
  and lightweight frameworks 386
  examples 664, 669
  extracting from EJBs 373, 379, 421
  extracting from JMS components 431
  refactoring Singleton into 558, 560
  with web components 490
plain-vanilla JVM 413
PMD 241, 616
POJO. *See* Plain Old Java Objects
Poppendieck, Mary and Tom 699
PostMethodWebRequest 454
Postscript 209
PreparedStatement 311–312, 322, 695
  making assertions on 313
presentation engine 267, 272, 304, 465
presentation layer 297, 299, 301, 304, 374, 499
  testing without 510
presentation object 371
Preuß, Ilja 32, 58
prevalent system. *See* Prevayler
Prevayler 375, 509, 607
primary key 408–409
primitive values
  comparing 23
printf 20, 330
printsummary 201, 204
private data
  gaining access to 622
private methods 480, 604, 625, 627
  testing 81
PrivateTestCase 621
problems
  common 234
procedure 372–373
production code
  shipping tests with 590
productivity 224
Programmer Test suites 111
Programmer Testing 4–5, 41, 66, 309, 396, 607
  goals of 334
  good practices 106
Programmer Tests 110, 120, 464, 509
  relationship to Customer Tests 111
  simplest 23
progress 224
properties 138, 148, 152, 156, 325, 591
  built-in 142
  for test data 138
  Java system 139
  reading from file 149
  setting 139

properties file 147, 164
  location in source tree 151
  managing multiple 592
  test data as 586
PropertyManager 586, 591
  limitations 592
protected methods 76, 604
public interface
  testing entirely through 37
publisher. *See* design pattern, Observable

Q

queries 311
query expressions
  for XML 266
query method
  add for testing 36
quick green 383

R

rathole 365
readability 158
readable properties 24
  testing a class without 38–39
recompiling
  avoiding 139
RecursiveTestSuite 117–118, 120–121, 175, 590
  compared to DirectorySuiteBuilder 119
  parameters to 117
red bar 250
reducing dependency 260
refactor 19, 302, 337
  unable to 389
  when you cannot 377
refactoring 9, 75, 181–182, 444
  and coupling 19, 80
  and legacy code 360, 389
  assertions 302
  away from containers 259
  away from the database 312, 334, 357
  effect on AllTests 115
  EJBs 376, 395, 408, 413, 430
  Extract Class 507
  Extract Method 619
  fixtures 88, 304
  into a Base Test Case 337
  Move Method 379
  Replace Subclass with Collaborator 490
  tests 159, 341, 604
  tests as safety net 70, 259, 334, 349
  tests as safety net. *See* safety net
  to methods instead of constants 325
  towards a Parameterized Test Case 345
  towards a testable design 309–310, 379, 430, 452
  towards design patterns 544
  towards test isolation 123, 125
  without tests 419, 422, 561
referential integrity 406, 597
  arguments for 407
  overuse 400
reflection 105, 131, 243
  to invoke test method 109
registerServlet() 455
regression 7
  test 330
relational data
  converting to objects 317
ReloadedTestCaseDecorator 183, 185
remote connection
  eliminating from tests 280
remote method invocation 577
<report> 202, 205
  defect in 207
  styledir attribute 205
  using frames 204
reporting test results 16, 189
reports
  custom format 189, 205
  customizing 205
  format of 189
request 446
request dispatcher 490, 518
request handler
  behavior of 518
resetFixture() 126
resource references 412
ResourceBundle 138, 151–153, 164
ResourceBundle.getBundle (String baseName) 153
ResourceManager 586, 596
ResourceManagerTestSetup 596
resources
  order of initialization 597
ResourceTestSetup 593
responsibilities
  separating 548, 550
result
  in a web application 514
result sets 330
  cleaning up 335
ResultPrinter 545
ResultSet 311, 318, 322, 345
  creating domain objects from 317
  hardcoded 319
  mapping data from 319
ResultSetMetaData 331
return on investment 38
  testing setter methods 48
return value 23, 26
  legacy method without 620
  method without 414, 484, 545
  testing a method with 23
  testing a method without one 33
  XML document as 266
revealing intent 17, 55, 59, 75, 128, 403
rhythm
  of a test 105
  of an Object Test 6
rich client 374
ripple effect 111, 556
RMI. *See* remote method invocation
Ruby 59
rules 56
runBare() 86, 243
runSuite() 215
runTest() 109, 179, 241
  alternatives to overriding 242
  invoking multiple test methods 242
  overriding 132, 234, 241–242, 570, 634
RuntimeException 16, 59

S

safety net 7, 108, 125, 182, 334, 511, 625–626, 675
  and legacy code 349, 422
  benefits of 259
  changing code without 561
  false sense of security 78
  refactoring without 70, 419
  using Cruise Control 398
  See also refactoring, tests as safety net
sanity check 54
scenario 372
schema-qualified tables 363
scripting 189
  variable 469
ScriptIt 166
security 386, 395, 398, 509–510, 527, 529, 532–533
  EJB 530
  programmatic 409
  web resource 525
security server 478
SecurityException 533–534
SELECT 317
self-documenting 9, 15
sense of completion 114
sequence diagram 421, 427
sequence difference
  in XML documents 281
serial version UID 578
SerializabilityTest 573
Serializable 382
serialization 573, 577
server-side tests 394
service() 455–456
services
  as plug-ins 261
servlet session
  accessing with ServletUnit 453
ServletConfig 479
ServletContext 480–481, 483
ServletRunner 445, 454, 499
servlets 259, 444–445, 451, 484, 494, 507, 513, 518, 613, 637
  and filters 500
  and XSL transformations 304
  design problems 259
  executing server-side tests 396, 442
  extracting business logic from 444
  forwarding to JSP 455
  initialization 454, 477
  initialization parameters 277, 287
  legacy code 263, 452
  multiple 481
  passing data to web pages 496
  processing requests 483, 486
  redeploying 162
  request attributes 277
  session attributes 277
  session data 446, 449, 455–456
  specification 277
  typical behavior 483
ServletTestCase 395, 441
ServletUnit 444–445, 455–456, 460, 488, 495, 499
  and HTTP session 453
  for legacy code 448, 455
  note on InvocationContext 456
  testing filters 505
  testing J2EE applications 518
  testing ServletContext 481
  URL mapping 456
  when to use 456, 498
  with Jasper 457
ServletUnitClient 455
session
  design issues 446
  reducing interaction with 451
session bean 372, 384, 394, 396, 440
  delegating to domain object 379
  relationship to entity beans 399
  stateful 374, 446
  testing implementation directly 385
  testing methods independently 372
  testing outside the container 378
session data 446, 452
set method
  difficulties testing 45
  See also setters
setEntityContext() 411
setExpectedCloseCalls() 345
setters 44
  whether to test 674–675
setUp() 84–86, 148–149, 158, 170, 178, 191, 239, 242, 272, 287, 337, 340, 347, 363, 403, 483, 488, 528, 532, 567, 600, 605, 687
  incorrectly overriding 614
  invoking super.setUp() 88, 239
  log messages 196
  once per test suite 161
  one-time 162
  typo 239
shared fixture
  effect on test isolation 106
shared test fixture
  as a design issue 599
shared test setup 346
side effect 35, 484, 545, 549
  invisible 36, 478, 546
  observable 34–36, 38, 45, 548, 620, 625, 649
similar XMLUnit 269, 273
SimpleCredentialProvider 527
simplifying interface 434
simulate 392, 526, 529, 690
  error conditions 69
simulator
  for web container 454
Single Responsibility Principle 81, 548, 555, 608
Singleton
  wise usage 46, 67
Smalltalk 6, 15, 59, 61, 117, 324, 397
SMTP 415
SMTP server 419
source code
  difficult to navigate 111
source control 155
source trees 77
special case tests 18
Specification by Example 65
specifications 5, 392, 468
  and third-party software 471
spreadsheets
  tests as 509
Spring 386
spy 46, 425
  event listener 82

SQL 158
  parsers for Java 309
  query validator 309
  verifying commands 322
<sql> 157
SQL commands
  manual tests for 322
state diagram 510
stateless session beans
  ease of testing 373
statements
  cleaning up 335
static web page 457
Stobie, Keith 327
stored procedures 158, 355, 366–368
  deployment tests 352
  testing without JUnit 366
StringAssert 620
StringReader 145
Struts 246, 278, 302–303, 495, 510–511, 518–522, 639
  testing without 519
struts-config.xml 302, 518–519, 521
StrutsTestCase 510
stub 690–691
stub method 67
stultifyingly abstract 64
<style> 206
style-checking software 240
stylesheets 204–206
subclassing
  alternatives to 193
  class under test 503
subscriber. *See* design pattern, Observer
Subversion 121
suite of suites 109, 112, 114–115
suite() 104, 108, 113, 115, 123–124, 128–129, 134, 162, 164, 174, 184, 191, 237–238, 442, 596, 634
  default behavior 105
  duplication in 110
  forgetting to update 104
  ignoring 112
  incorrectly coding 614
  invoking explicitly 238
SuiteBuilder 586
SUnit 6, 397
Swing 374, 573–574
Swingler, Neil 183
syntax 604
<sysproperty> 140–141
system properties 138, 141, 148, 153, 155, 160
  managing 591
  omitting from reports 206
  setting test data 140
System.getProperty() 143
System.out 189, 194, 197

T

tablespace 350
tag handler 468, 474
tag interface
  for classifying tests 121
tag library 477
tag library descriptors 475, 477
TDD. *See* Test-Driven Development
team environment 190, 204
tearDown() 85, 158, 170, 191, 239, 242, 337–338, 340, 347–348, 567, 597, 599, 605, 607, 687
  and fixture setup errors 598
  incorrectly overriding 614
  invoking super.tearDown() 89, 239
  log messages 196
  once per test suite 161
  one-time 162
  typo 239
Telnet 199
temporary files 142
temporary test suite
  when fixing a defect 110
<test> 199
test case 8
  performance problems 162
  reloading classes 183
test case classes
  correspondence to production class 373
  each test is an instance 109
  handling multiple 111
  inheriting tests 107
  large 18
  many in one package 111
  naming convention 117
  one per production class 93, 373
  order of tests 123
  syntax of 614
test data 127, 132, 137–138, 155, 157, 349, 362, 389, 396, 398, 409, 591, 612, 630, 634, 657, 684
  alternatives to XML 157
  centralizing 592
  command line arguments 138–139
  database 157, 346
  describing with XML 156
  entity bean commit options 399
  excessive 400
  externalize 103, 148, 152, 158
  externalizing 132
  file-based repository 154
  for database 360
  formats 156
  generating 137
  global 142, 166, 169, 181–182
  hardcoded 139, 148, 157, 460
  hierarchical 138
  in files 145
  in multiple files 152
  in properties files 591
  initialize once per JVM 168
  JUnit-addons test runner 177
  large amounts 154
  locating within tests 155
  naming conventions for files 156
  organizing 156
  organizing in source control 156
  parameterized 148
  properties files 159
  resetting between tests 170
  resetting global state 181
  restoring between tests 171
  restoring to initial state 138, 158
  setup complexity 360
  shared 137
  shared repository 154
  small amounts 139, 141
  static 138
  system properties 138
  tabular 356
  under version control 155
  using JDBC 362

test database 312, 349, 360
  sharing 349
test environment 498
  as a tool 165
  auditing 190
  automating 166
  complex 393, 413, 548, 611
  complexity 396
  one-button 166
  one-time setup 168
test file 142
test fixture 106, 131, 236, 239, 249, 346, 445, 483
  complex 597
  extracting 133
  extracting data into 128
  hierarchy 239
  naming 18
  setup problems 239
test hierarchies
  behavior in JUnit 52
Test Infected 104, 108
test isolation 108–109, 480, 544, 557, 563, 605, 614, 625
  effect of databases 334, 346
  effect of shared fixtures 346, 597, 605, 608
  effect of Singleton 559
  effect of Singletons 556, 560
  refactoring towards 123, 125
test listener
  open architecture 586
  See also TestListener
test management system 205
test methods
  coding errors 235
  execute in its own JVM 181
  mistyped name in suite() method 236
  naming convention 104
  naming guidelines 236
  not found 235
  similar 127
  throwing exceptions 105
Test Object 67
Test Objects 67, 390–391, 412, 426, 488, 559, 695
  crash test dummy 69
  fake 67
  mock 67
  simulating error conditions 69
  stub 67
  substituting 69
test package hierarchy 80
test reports
  customizing 586
test resources
  shared 586, 593
test results 217
  as HTML 202
  auditing 190
  custom format 208
  customized 224
  customizing 190, 215
  in XML 223
  logging 190
  management system 209
  plain text 198
  sending in email 201
test runner 8, 11, 111, 174, 220
  AWT-based 174
  built-in 189
  class path problem 235
  class-loading problems 250
  custom 167, 174, 194, 586
  extending 224
  JUnit-addons 176, 187, 596, 602
  launching 174
  Log4Unit 197
  problems with EJBs 254
  specifying test data files 148
  status bar 177
  Swing-based 167, 174, 178
  terminate() 168
  text-based 11, 141, 166, 174, 178, 195, 215, 599
test suite 8, 103, 398, 586, 607, 630
  arbitrarily complex 103
  arbitrary collection of tests 111
  as XML document 133
  build automatically 103, 105
  build from file system 116
  build manually 104, 108
  builder 117
  building a bigger one 109
  building manually 104
  collecting tests into 103
  create from a package 111
  custom 236, 249
  data-driven 127
  default 105, 107, 236
  define using XML 157
  executing repeatedly 169
  extract automatically 112
  for the entire system 114
  how JUnit executes 109
  maintenance issues 116
  managing 103
  manual 184
  not executed 237
  portable 138
  test order 103
test until fear turns to boredom 38, 56, 406, 676
testability 36
testable design 74, 82, 108, 259, 385, 608, 620, 626
  effect of class-level methods 70
  refactoring towards 309, 378, 422
TestCase 12, 18, 189, 225
  difference between class and instance 242
  executing only one 180
  extending 190
  extension 194
  inheritance rules 52
TestCase class
  one per production class 72
TestCase hierarchy 73
TestCaseClassLoader 254
TestClassValidator 614, 616
testClone() 579–580
Test-Driven Development 9, 87, 137, 185, 245, 250, 406, 573, 691
  and Exploratory Testing 7
  and legacy code 125
  and organizing code 74, 79
  and test isolation 106, 108
  effect on design 70, 82, 91, 378
  example of 547
  fixing defects 110
TestFilter 117–118, 120–121
  ignore abstract tests 118
testing
  effect of referential integrity constraints 400
  manual 7
  only for 36–37, 418, 558
  the goal of 675
testing department 4
testing methods together 35

Testing Patterns
Abstract Test Case 52, 544, 587
AllTests 112, 114
Crash Test Dummy 399, 429, 569, 672, 693
fixture barrier 126
Isolated Test 106
Log String 567, 649
one failure per problem 107
Parameterized Test Case 128, 241, 243, 506, 516, 538, 630
Self-Shunt 184, 389–391, 425–432, 545, 550–555, 623, 693
Spy 422–432, 507, 552, 563, 567, 574, 626, 649, 688, 693
testing, only for 419, 618
TestListener 215, 232, 545, 552, 555, 596, 602
event handlers 216
TestProxy 623
TestResult 249, 552, 554–555
TestRunListener 600
TestRunner
as a listener 215
extending 215, 220
JUnit-addons 600
tests
annotated 509
as specification 36
categorizing 103
cost of executing 464
deploying 590
execution speed 259
general form of 25
JUnit cannot find 104, 235
JUnit not executing 104
long-running 190
manual 7
order of 123
order-dependent 249
problems implementing 234
seemingly too simple 41
too simple to write 38
written by non-programmers 510
testSerialization() 577–578
TestSetup 138, 161–162, 164, 170, 521, 586, 593, 599
effect on fixture implementation 164
JUnit-addons implementation 598
tearDown problems 164
TESTS-TestSuites.xml 207
TestSuite 105, 108, 133, 525
text node
with empty content 271
TextUtil 493
third-party library. *See* external library
Thomas, Dave 42, 697, 699
Thread.sleep() 417
throwing the right exception
how not to test 58
throws Exception
declaring test methods 57
Tidy 291, 296
tolerance level
for floating-point numbers 14
Tomcat 463, 479
too simple to break 39, 41, 43–44, 55, 379, 384, 410, 421, 451, 562, 674
rebuttal 677
Torque 376
Transaction Script 372
transactions 380, 386, 398–399, 427, 509–510, 662
attributes 536, 538
behavior 348
container-managed 536, 538
isolation 539
isolation level 536
rollback trick 347
Transform 300
transitivity property
of equals() 677
triggers 327
trusted libraries 312
<tstamp> 201
typing, too much 24
typo 604

U

unchecked exception 437
unexpected state
after failed test 106
uniqueness constraints 333
unit testing 4, 137
UNIX 274
UnknownHostException
thrown by XMLUnit 279
unpacking JUnit 10
unpredictable state
for future tests 107
UnsupportedOperationException 32
upgrade 252
useless tests 40
user.home 142, 155

V

validation
testing in constructor 39
Value Object 26–27, 32, 311, 321, 575–576, 578, 581, 617, 678
as XML document 268
primitive wrapper classes 27
with many properties 63
ValueObjectEqualsTest 64
Vector 382
Velocity 246, 272, 371, 444–445, 465, 491, 493–494, 499, 514, 520
public fields 467
rendering template 465, 467
standalone mode 467
testing data passed to 495
VelocityContext 466
verify() 411, 694–695
version control 253
View 371, 496
Virtual Mock 70, 561
Virtual Mock Objects 263
visual inspection 299, 461, 494, 496, 498
VisualAge for Java
effect on test packages 82
void. *See* return value

W

Wake, Bill 6, 23
web applications 246, 267, 272, 291, 293, 303, 444, 483–484, 513, 522, 533
deploying tests for 395
designing for testability 376, 500–501
presentation layers 297
testing components in isolation 446, 448, 505, 509–510
testing navigation rules 509–510, 519
web deployment descriptors 278, 481
See also deployment descriptors

web browser 290
simulating 291
web components 444, 474, 495
web container 399, 444–445, 468, 479, 483, 505
avoiding 445, 484
for processing JSPs 464
simulating 445, 455
testing interaction with 456
testing with 445
web deployment descriptor 277–280, 287, 303, 527, 532, 637
generating 280
web forms 494, 523
web page content 491
web page templates 291
web pages 267, 296, 299, 301, 448, 514
comparing 301
dynamic 291, 493
static 290–291, 493
testing in isolation 272
web request 513
web resource 530
web resource filter 500, 507
responsibilities 500
web server 165
testing web page without 491
testing without 491
web services 267–268
Web Services Description Language 266
web.xml. *See* web deployment descriptor
web-authoring tools
compatibility with 294
WebClient 522, 527–528
WebRequest 454, 499
Weinberg, Gerald 699
well-factored 135
well-factored design. *See* refactoring
Wenner, Robert 616
what not to test 55
white space 273
in XML documents 270–271
white space only
elements and XMLUnit 272
Wiki 510
Woolley, Chad 70
wrapper classes
for primitive types 27
wrappers 372, 385, 421, 490
See also design pattern, Decorator

X

Xalan 208, 267, 297
XDoclet 538
Xerces 223, 294, 297, 648
XHTML 266, 272, 290, 296
scarcity of 290
tag name standards 296
XJavaDoc 538
XML 145, 148, 155–156, 215, 217, 220, 266, 401, 403, 475, 535, 587, 630
causes JUnit failures 252
comparing documents 267, 270, 280
defining test suites with 133
object marshalling 267, 273
order of elements 273
storing test data 138
test results as 189
well-formed 291
XML documents 519, 637
as a return value 266
element structure 270
for configuration 303
for data transfer 303
hardcode in tests 298
ignoring differences 287
ignoring the order of elements 277
listing all differences 289
making assertions on 269
problems with line breaks 270
testing without files 268
to describe a database 328
unexpectedly equal 275
validating 272, 477, 519, 537, 645
validating in tests 302
validating incoming data 304
walking the DOM 278
writing assertions for 521
XML parsers 266
XML parsing 147, 279
XML schema 272, 303–304
avoiding overuse 306
XMLJUnitResultFormatter 214
XMLTestCase 267, 401, 619
XMLUnit 269, 401, 464, 477, 495, 519, 530, 537, 619, 639
and DTDs 477
assertXMLEqual() 273, 276
buildXmlDocument() 279
detailed failure message 288
diff 275
Diff engine 281, 288
example test 270
failure message 271
for EJB meta data 375
for J2EE deployment descriptors 401, 505, 535
for JavaServer Pages 464
for JSP custom tags 475
for Struts applications 519
for XSL transformations 298, 301
identical documents 273, 275
ignoring differences 272, 282
ignoring white space 271
limitations of 278
order of sibling elements 276
org.custommoney.xmlunit.Diff 274
parsing 279, 639
with HTML documents 292
See also XMLTestCase
XPath 266, 287, 293, 328, 403, 475, 521, 538, 639
API 267, 278
assertions using 266
XSL 204–206, 209
XSL stylesheet 298, 301, 639, 645
testing in isolation 297
XSL transformation 266–267, 297–298, 304, 645
alternative to JSPs 297
as presentation layer 282
testing in isolation 272
XSLT 272, 304
See also XSL transformation
xUnit 6, 61

Y

YAGNI 91

Z

ZipFile 590